Trade, Ideology and Urbanization

Trade, Ideology and Urbanization

South India 300 BC to AD 1300

R. Champakalakshmi

OXFORD
UNIVERSITY PRESS

OXFORD
UNIVERSITY PRESS

Oxford University Press is a department of the University of Oxford. It furthers the University's objective of excellence in research, scholarship, and education by publishing worldwide. Oxford is a registered trademark of Oxford University Press in the UK and in certain other countries

Published in India by
Oxford University Press
22 Workspace, 2nd Floor, 1/22 Asaf Ali Road, New Delhi 110 002, India

First Edition published in 1996
Oxford India Paperbacks 1999
30th impression 2025

ISBN-13: 978-0-19-564875-1
ISBN-10: 0-19-564875-7

Printed in India by Replika Press Pvt. Ltd.

For
Jayee, Radha and Vanaja

Preface

In the course of my explorations of historical sites in the river valleys of Tamil Nadu, early in my teaching career, I was struck by the size and monumental architecture of Pallava-Cōḷa centres like Kumbhakōṇam (Kaveri Valley), Kāñcīpuram (Palar Valley) and Ambasamudram (Tamraparni Valley). Despite some differences, they attracted attention due to their long historical past, development of enduring institutions like the temple and centuries of evolution into huge temple towns in medieval times. A nagging and compelling thought that such centres need to be studied not only for their striking visibility as towns/cities but more importantly as a part of the processes of urban development in pre-modern India, pursued me especially as urban processes had not received the attention that was due. In the late seventies my interest grew and ideas were refined which instigated a close look at urbanization and the city.

Hence began a most stimulating series of exercises in trying to understand the urban processes and the character of the city in early medieval South India (AD 600–1300), starting from Kumbhakōṇam, to Kāñcīpuram and Tañjāvūr, their hinterlands and role as prime movers in the shaping of the politico-economic and cultural configurations of this region. Better perspectives on early medieval urbanism emerged when a comparative study was made with the early historical period. (300 BC–AD 300). Early historical urbanism was shown to have significant differences in urban form and experience, with maritime trade and external links dominating the urban process and with urban centres developing along South India's long coastline but lacking institutional foci like the temple.

This book is the end result of forays into these two periods of urbanization. Of the present collection of eight essays, six are revised and enlarged versions of published ones (see list on p. viii), while the other two have been written for this volume together with an introduction setting out its aim and formulations.

14 May 1996 R. CHAMPAKALAKSHMI

List of Published Essays

1. 'Growth of Urban Centres in South India: Kuḍamūkku-Paḷaiyāṟai, the Twin-city of the Cōḷas', in *Studies in History*, vol. I, no. 1, January-June 1979. (Chapter 6 in this volume).
2. 'Urbanization in Medieval Tamil Nadu', in *Situating Indian History* for Sarvepalli Gopal, Sabyasachi Bhattacharya and Romila Thapar (eds), OUP, Delhi, 1986. (Chapter 4 in this volume).
3. 'Urbanisation in South India: The Role of Ideology and Polity', Presidential Address, Ancient India Section, *Indian History Congress*, 47th Session, Srinagar, 1986. (Chapter 1 in this volume).
4. 'Tañjāvūr, the Ceremonial City of the Cōḷas', in *Indian Archaeological Heritage*, K.V. Soundararajan Felicitation Volume, II, C. Margabandhu, K.S. Ramachandran, A.P. Sagar and D.K. Sinha (eds), Agam, Delhi, 1991. (Chapter 8 in this volume).
5. 'Urban Configurations of Toṇḍaimaṇḍalam: The Kāñcīpuram Region, *c.* AD 600–1300', in *Urban Form and Meaning in South Asia* (Studies in the History of Art, 31), Howard Spodek and Doris Meth Srinivasan (eds), National Gallery of Art, Washington D.C., 1993. (Chapter 7 in this volume).
6. 'Medieval South Indian Guilds: Their Role in Trade and Urbanisation, in *Society and Ideology in India*, Essays in Honour of Professor R.S. Sharma, D.N. Jha (ed.), Manohar, Delhi, 1996. (Chapter 5 in this volume).

Acknowledgements

It is to Professor Romila Thapar that I owe this book, in which I have put together my essays on urbanization in South India, an endeavour, which I would not have undertaken but for her suggestion and constant assurance that the essays stand together due to their thematic unity and common framework. My thanks are due to Professor Shereen Ratnagar, my friend and colleague, who willingly spared long hours of her time discussing some of my problems in dealing with the concept of urbanism and urban processes. My colleague Dr Neeladri Bhattacharya has in many ways helped in the organization and presentation of the volume.

My special thanks are due to Professors Atiya Habib Kidwai and K.S. Sivasami of the Centre for the study of Regional Development (CSRD), Jawaharlal Nehru University, for making available to me maps of South India for preparing the base maps for the cartographic illustrations in the book. To Mr Akilesh Mathur, the Cartographer in CSRD, I express my sincere thanks for doing the maps in a remarkably short time for the publication. These maps are based on earlier versions prepared by Messrs A.N. Sharma, Deshpande and Dr Sudhir Malakar. Y. Subbarayalu's work on the Political Geography of the Chola country has been of immense value in the location of *nāḍus* and *kōṭṭams* in the maps.

For the illustrations in the chapter on Tañjāvūr, I am indebted to the Indira Gandhi National Centre for the Arts, especially its Academic Adviser Dr Kapila Vatsyayan, for providing me with the relevant photographs and slides on the Tañjāvūr temple. Dr M.C. Joshi, Member secretary, IGNCA and Ms Krishna Dutt, in charge of the project on Tañjāvūr were extremely helpful to me in choosing the best in their collection.

The map on the Tamraparni valley urban core (Map 8) is an adaptation from the map of this region published in R. Tirumalai's book *Rajendra Vinnagar*. To Mr N. Sethuraman of

Kumbhakōṇam, I am grateful for the Map of the town in 1980, which has been suitably modified for the chapter (Map 12) on this centre. The ground plan of the Varadarājasvāmi temple in Kāñcīpuram follows closely the one published in Dr K.V. Raman's book *Sri Varadārajaswāmi Temple Kāñci: A study of its History, Art and Architecture.*

My grateful thanks are also due to Mr Venkatesh Naik, research student in the centre for Historical Studies, J.N.U., who prepared the index to this volume and to Mrs Choodamani Venugopal and Mrs Kameswari Viswanatham for typing the Manuscript.

It is with great pleasure that I express my thanks to the Oxford University Press, New Delhi, for not only publishing the book with remarkable speed but also for doing it well.

Contents

Maps

Illustrations

(Between pages 430 and 431)

Abbreviations

ARE	*Annual Report on (South) Indian Epigraphy*
BRW	Black and Red Ware
IA	*Indian Antiquary*
IAR	*Indian Archaeology A Review*
IATR	International Association of Tamil Research
IESHR	*Indian Economic and Social History Review*
IGNCA	Indira Gandhi National Centre for the Arts
IHC	Indian History Congress
IHR	*Indian Historical Review*
IIRNS	Indian Institute of Research in Numismatic Studies
JAS	*Journal of Asian Studies*
JESHO	*Journal of the Economic and Social History of the Orient*
JIH	*Journal of Indian History*
KRK	Korkai
NBP	Northern Black Polished (Ware)
NS	New Series
OUP	Oxford University Press
PMC	Punch Marked Coins
RC	Radio Carbon
RCP	Russet Coated Painted (Ware)
SII	*South Indian Inscriptions*
SISSW	South India Saiva Siddhanta Works
TASSI	*Transactions of the Archaeological Society of South India*
UHAI	Urban History Association of India

Introduction

Urbanism and the city have been the focus of scholarly attention among social scientists despite the elusive character of urban theory and definition of the city. Attempts have been made to evolve perspectives of urbanism and urbanization from the simplest of explanatory criteria for urban centres to complex theoretical formulations to understand urban processes in their spatial and temporal diversity and in a variety of socio-historical contexts.

One of the major questions, which has been posed by these exercises, is whether it is the form of urbanism or the substance which characterizes it that should be the focus of analysis. The tendency of attributing analytical significance to the form at the expense of the substance seems to have been influenced by the powerful impact that the western industrial city has as a 'social form' in which 'the essential properties of larger systems are grossly concentrated and intensified'.[1]

The impact of the western city has also led to a sharp distinction being made in the studies of western and Asian cities, the western cities as symbols of economic vitality[2] and political autonomy, and the Asian cities or urban forms as predominantly political and cultural rather than economic phenomena.[3] Recent research has pointed out that this dichotomy is as hallowed as the contrast between town and country.[4] The second major question often raised in urban studies is that of the validity of the conceptual separation between the town and the country, i.e. that of a dual economy, the rural and the urban. This duality is now being abandoned except as a 'social division of labour in the larger whole'.[5] The inseparability of the town from the larger social environment is stressed and towns are regarded as sites in which the history of larger social systems—states, societies, modes of production, world economies—is partially but crucially worked out.[6]

Similarly, the validity of treating the town as a distinctive social structure, i.e. a special entity having a structural autonomy or as 'a focus of analysis in its own right', is now largely rejected and instead, urban analysis 'through a broader societal analysis' or as 'a part of the analysis of those broad socio-economic changes with which history is concerned',[7] has gained general acceptance. Hence, in the more recent works on urban history and the city, the central concern has been urbanization, i.e. the processes of urban growth leading to the rise of the city. In other words, urbanism is perceived as the product of societal change, the manifestation of certain economic and social systems at work, as exemplified by the temple cities of South India, which are marked out by their form and role in society as both physical and social objects.

It is the above approach to urban studies that is adopted in the present volume. In addition, other significant and influential concepts relating to the city and urban forms have also been found relevant to the study of urbanization in pre-modern South India.

Typology has been an important though 'orthodox'[8] device in urban analysis both among historians and sociologists. The best known among typologies is the classic distinction made by G. Sjoberg[9] between the industrial and pre-industrial cities, which would seem to coincide with the distinction sociologists make between cities in traditional and modern societies. Sjoberg's is a useful distinction but is only a 'constructed type', no homogeneity or uniformity in structural pattern being implied for the pre-industrial city. There is no 'one basic language' as Fernand Braudel pointed out, 'for all cities of the world within their very depths'.[10]

The orthogenetic and heterogenetic cities, a model introduced by Robert Redfield and Milton Singer,[11] has influenced studies of traditional and colonial/modern cities as seen in Susan Lewandowsky's study of Madurai and Madras.[12] Colonialism has often provided a visible marker for differentiating the cities in Asia as traditional (orthogenetic) and colonial (heterogenetic). The impact of colonialism has been so overrated as to be able to explain a 'drastic' change in the urbanism of India, China and Southeast Asian countries. With colonialism, the western kind of city is believed to have been imported. This would seem to be an incredibly simple explanation of the emergence of new types of cities, where the physical structure and composition of the city change due to the heterogeneity of ethnic and cultural groups. The real question, however, is how far was it a metamorphosis and how far, if at all, did it affect the internal (core) aspects of the local cultures, i.e. the pre-existing forms and structures. That no uniformity can be recognized in the colonial context is pointed out by studies on colonial towns in South India, which stress the importance of understanding pre-existing forms.[13] Some of these pre-existing structures are the main concern of the present volume.

Furthermore, the orthogenetic and heterogenetic cities are not exclusive to traditional and modern cities respectively, as has been shown by the neo-Weberian approach of Eisenstadt and Shachar,[14] who distinguish between forces of centrality and those of concentration operating in different periods and different socio-historical contexts. A similar distinction is made by Howard Spodek in what he calls a nodal vision or perspective for heterogenetic centres and a palimpsest, i.e. stability within indigenous culture for orthogenetic centres of urban activity. Spodek tries to evolve this distinction on the basis of a study made by several scholars of cities in South Asia ranging from early historical Taxila to modern/colonial Madras.[15]

Typologies or distinctions in city-types are also made within specific historical contexts and are often attributed to factors to which a certain primacy is given as causative or innovative, leading to types such as political/administrative centres, military centres, trade or commercial centres, religious centres and so on. While this is common in the conventional economic histories, it persists in more recent works on urbanism,[16] which lay stress on the causative role of certain factors. However, in the long period of social and economic change generating urban forms, an elaborate complex of factors is mingled in a processual change. Agricultural expansion and intensification is often a necessary pre-condition to change in which improved technology, e.g. irrigation, is a major resource. Social division of labour, productive labour and surplus, storage of surplus, institutional mechanism for surplus extraction, large-scale communal and monumental activity, a complex social organization and a well-developed power structure contribute to the formation of cities. Population increase, competition for land, warfare and tribute are recognised as the outward manifestation of urbanism, particularly in early cities.[17] Stable systems of trade, artisans and merchants as permanent community fixtures, specialization of crafts, transport innovations,[18] all of which are often cited as urban forms, would seem to operate in different degrees and at different levels in the evolution of urban centres. Thus, causative factors may occur in different orders of primacy in creating distinctive types. While economic factors are basic to urban growth, often what is required is a focal point for mobilization and redistributive activities, which, in pre-modern societies, was often provided by an ideology, usually religious. As Paul Wheatley[19] points out:

> It is doubtful if any single autonomous causative factor will ever be identified in the nexus of social, economic and political transformations which resulted in the emergence of urban forms, but one activity does seem in a sense to command a sort of priority. Whatever structural changes in social organization were induced by commerce, warfare, or technology, they needed to be validated by some instrument of authority if they were to achieve institutional permanence.

Given the diversity of the phenomena called 'urban' Wheatley's characterization of the concept of urbanism 'as compounded of a series of sets of ideal type social, political, economic and other institutions which have combined in different ways in different cultures and at different times',[20] is significant. In other words, urban studies should be situated in specific socio-historical contexts in terms of their spatial and temporal spread.

Urban sociologists would treat towns as fields of social power as an alternative framework of analysis, i.e. towns as social realization of power, stressing the continuity of social stratification between town and country. Power and the pattern of domination have been the main concerns in the discussion of towns by Weber, Braudel and even Sjoberg, who see the town internally and externally as an institutional expression of power.[21] Following Weber, Philip Abrams uses what he calls the complex of domination[22] for a better understanding of the nature and functions of towns in a larger social context, i.e. a struggle to constitute and elaborate power.[23]

Weber's concept of 'non-legitimate domination' appeared crucial for the medieval European town where the burghers usurped power in pursuit of rational economic action, freed from the dependence on the 'legitimate' (feudal) authorities and in turn established dominance over artisans and peasants. This, it is believed, was conducive to the building of the cultural and economic base for the emergence of capitalism.[24] These 'non feudal islands in the feudal seas' have been characterized as the primary source of change and economic growth towards capitalism.[25]

On the contrary, more recent research looks at the rise of towns as a process internal to the feudal system and medieval towns are considered as integral elements of it.[26] The persistence of feudal patterns of social control within towns, it is argued, acted as a disincentive to economic innovation, pointing out the rural rather than urban origins of capitalism.[27]

In India, the feudalism theory as applied to the study of the land grant system and polity and society in the early medieval period and the continuing debate on the validity of the concept in the context of several regional studies, especially that of South India, have raised several questions, one of which is related to the emergence of a burgher class creating a situation of 'non-legitimate domination'. No burgher class seems to have emerged in India which confronted the existing patterns of rural and urban overlordship, as one may recognize in the nature of the *nagarattār* or merchants of South India, whose market towns were complementary to the agrarian regions, of which they were markets, and not opposed to them.[28]

In the study of urban processes, another useful distinction is that of primary and secondary urbanization. In primary urbanization the rise of cities is solely the result of internal developments, although not in complete isolation, for external influence in varying degrees could induce such development as in Shang China and to some extent in Mesopotamia and Central America.[29] Wheatley would see the character of Chinese cities as a distinct independent development—i.e. *sui generis*—or a process of generation and not imposition of urban forms.[30]

Secondary urbanization is the direct outgrowth of the expansion of empire, wherein forts and regional administrative centres, established for political and economic control, could act as centres of diffusion of metropolitan culture, i.e. technology and other knowledge. The workings of the sophisticated administrative and technological structure of the conquering society provide the skills to the locals, helping them to ultimately to assert their independence. This appears to be directly relevant to colonial history which provides examples of secondary urbanism. Apart from the relevance of secondary urbanization in a colonial context, it would also be interesting and pertinent to see whether the expansion of early empires like that of the Mauryas, characterized as a metropolitan state,[31] induced secondary urbanism in regions like the Deccan and Andhra, where, in the post-Mauryan period, Mauryan influence both in administrative structures and trading networks would seem to have been predominant.[32] It would also appear then that primary and secondary urbanization are representative of the same processes as those of the formation of pristine and secondary states of Morton Fried.[33]

In secondary urbanization there is either a process of generation inspired by the extension of empire, or direct imposition of urban forms, i.e. organizational patterns developed by the conquering state. Wheatley uses this distinction to explain the establishment of early Chinese style settlements in a colonial context in Sine-Viet territories as urban imposition, and the internally induced restructuring of society in the 'Indianized' realms of mainland Southeast Asia as urban generation,[34] although of the secondary form.

The city's role as a locus for change,[35] the city as the focus of power and dominance, and the city as an organizing principle or creator of 'effective space',[36] have been the most influential paradigms in the concept of the ceremonial centre, admirably worked out by Paul Wheatley[37] for early Chinese cities and subsequently applied to Southeast Asia (Angkor) and Sri Lanka (Anurādhapura).[38]

It is in working out the concept of the ceremonial centre that a religious ideology and the institutions that were evolved to create 'effective space' and to constitute and elaborate power, became the main issues in the study of 'pre-industrial' or traditional cities. It is by no means implied here that religion was a primary causative factor. Rather it was one which, as in the Mesopotamian case, 'permeated all activities, all institutional change and afforded a consensual focus for social life which manifested itself in all cult centres'.[39] Religion became the focal point for collection and redistribution of resources and religious centres had their granaries and records of accounts.[40] The control over such institutions was taken into the hands of the priestly-cum-ruling elite as economic administrators and, thus, religious authority and political and social power became inseparable. Massive constructions like palaces (China), tombs (Islamic centres) and temples (India) undertaken at the ceremonial centres were beyond the power of local groups. They are symbols of the concentration of social and political power derived from a sacrally sanctioned authority.[41] It may be pointed out that the power structure developed by the *brāhmaṇa-kṣatriya* elite controlling the ceremonial centre in South India, where political and religious authority is poorly discriminated, is an important illustration.

The ceremonial complex receives central importance in the emergence of urban forms and in the shaping of pre-modern (pre-industrial) cities in studies on urban historical geography. In his study of West Asian cities, Harold Carter[42] makes urban history space and period specific, related to locations where urban spatial history and urban historical geography overlap and merge. The approach to urban historical geography is through the city as artefact and spatial patterning as the central theme. Spatial pattern is the consequence rather than the central focus in urban history. However, the city and its patterning can provide the evidence for interpreting attitudes and ideology. Here, religion is not given primacy as the single cause, but as providing a focus, a validating instrument for urban institutions.

Religion does not mean the mere existence of beliefs in the other world and cult practices, which admittedly precede urban beginnings. It is that point of development in which a formalised system of beliefs and practices, with claims to universalism, plays a significant part in the process of transformation, requiring mediation through worship and sacrifice,[43] i.e. through institutional means, and enables a certain politico-religious elite to command priority and exercise authority. As Eisenstadt[44] points out, in the progression of various technological and other factors, a catalyst led to a metamorphosis of the older kin-structured tribal organization into a class based one—such as the temple, fortress or market place. In South India, such a change may be perceived from the early historical urbanism to the early medieval urbanism, the early medieval temple assuming the institutional focus.

The basic modes of symbolism used in the process of working out the concept of the ceremonial centre are adopted by Wheatley from the work of Mircea Eliade.[45] These are the imitation of celestial archetype, parallelism between macrocosm and microcosm, participation in the symbolism of the centre, technique of orientation to define the sacred territory within the continuum of 'profane' space involving an emphasis on the cardinal compass directions.

Some form of centralization of control over labour and land, as well as all kinds of produce, is taken to be an invariable component in the rise of the ceremonial centres. The main functions of such centres were those of redistribution, the movement of commodities being towards the centre, the appropriative role being implicit in the physical disposition, as well as the organization of the shrine. The crystallization of urban forms also brought into existence at the same time the earliest state institutions.[46] To a considerable extent this is illustrated by the early medieval urban forms and state institutions of the Tamil macro region.

II

Three major periods of urbanization have been identified in pre-medieval (pre-Sultanate) India. The first is represented by the proto-historic cities of the Harappan/Indus Valley culture assignable to a long period from the middle of the third millennium to the middle of the second millennium BC. The urban character of this phase is recognizable in a hierarchy of settlement sites, in the planned cities, in the urban infrastructure provided at Mohenjo-daro, their design, monumental architecture and orientation, apart from other significant archaeological evidence. This culture was, however, confined to the Indus region, spilling over into other geographical regions of the subcontinent and interacting with other cultures. The major part of the subcontinent remained unaffected by this early urbanism, which, in fact, left no legacy beyond the middle of the second millennium BC.

The second period of urbanism, the epicentre of which is located in the Ganges valley, was spread over a long period, from the middle of the first millennium BC to the third century AD, and is often attributed to the maturity of the iron age and the expansion of trade within the Ganges valley, and from the Ganges valley to other parts of India, covering almost the whole of the subcontinent.[47] In the Ganges valley, this phase of urbanism was one of primary generation, i.e. a process of internal development. Its impact in peninsular India may be seen as generating urban forms due to the spread of trade and commercial activities from the Ganges valley. More significant in peninsular India was the impact of maritime trade. In the Deccan and Andhra regions this period is understood to be one of secondary urban generation and secondary state formation, which became two inter-related processes induced by the expansion of the Mauryan empire.[48] While this general assumption appears to be valid in terms of political processes in the Deccan and Andhra in the post-Mauryan times, the generation and nature of secondary urbanism in these regions is yet to be substantiated on the basis of detailed studies of towns from the Mauryan to the Ikṣvāku periods (third century BC to third century AD), both in the Ganges valley and peninsular India. Regional variations in this phase of urbanism are crucial to an understanding of the degree and intensity of secondary urban forms in Tamiḻakam, where the impact of Indo-Roman trade was greater and the influence of Mauryan polity was minimal.

For peninsular India, this phase represents the first urbanization, which is better understood through regional and subregional studies, although commonalties may exist across regions. Only a beginning has been made in this direction, i.e. in the understanding of urban processes in regional contexts.

Much of the Andhra and Deccan areas, studded with various types of settlements, is yet to be researched from the standpoint of urbanization. The study of settlement patterns, i.e. historical geography, is a necessary step towards this understanding and a few works have been undertaken based on such an approach. For Tamiḻakam, in the early historical period, the study of settlement patterns, ecology and forms of production has demonstrated the need for such an approach and provided useful insights into the nature of economy and urban forms.[49]

The Deccan and Tamiḻakam illustrate contrastive urban experiences, particularly in the emergence of trading patterns. Larger networks, guild organization of merchants and craftsmen, which facilitated a more intensive and organized commerce, marked the new economic system of the Deccan, to which were integrated several centres of craft production in a situation where trade was not stimulated by an agricultural surplus but by supply of manufactured items. It was this factor which sustained some of the central Deccan settlements, as a recent study[50] shows on the basis of archaeological data. The segmented nature of political power of the pre-Sātavāhana times changed under the new forces of Ganges valley urbanism and Mauryan polity, enabling interaction between traders and craft production in areas under the control of tribal communities. Attention is drawn to differences in the character of settlements in central, southern and western Deccan and Andhra region (eastern Deccan) in such studies.[51] Thus, the need for studying sub-regional patterns is partially met by these works. The Andhra region still remains largely unexplored from this point of view.

Notwithstanding such basic differences in the nature of settlements, a major thesis by R.S. Sharma[52] on urban decay and de-urbanization in post third century AD in the whole of the subcontinent treats the early historical settlements as homogeneous, i.e. makes no distinction between rural or urban basis of economic activities in them, nor tries to identify the functionally different character of crafts and trade centres. That such a homogeneity did not exist may be illustrated with the help of several sites in the Tamil region (as in other regions of the peninsula), where similarity in artefacts/material culture in different contexts, like Megalithic sites, inland and coastal settlements, cannot be construed as evidence of urbanism or its decline. The problems with this theory of de-urbanization and its consequences in relation to Tamiḻakam are discussed in greater detail in the next section (Section III).

According to this theory of urban decay, the climax of the early historical urbanism is to be located between 300 BC and AD 300, and an overall decline may be recognized in the archaeological evidence of the early historical sites. A long period of de-urbanization is believed to have set in during the Gupta and post-Gupta times (AD 300 to AD 1000), the first stage, third to sixth centuries AD, representing a transition, and the second stage, seventh to tenth centuries AD, a new socio-economic formation. The prime causal factor in urban decay is traced to the decline of long-distance (maritime) trade, i.e. Indo-Roman trade and trade with Southeast Asia, by the third century AD, and the manifestations of the decline are seen in the absence of Roman coins after third century AD, a general paucity of coins as well as the poor nature of archaeological remains of the Gupta period in the northern sites.[53] Literary and epigraphic evidence is also sought in the lack of references in inscriptions to artisans and traders and the latters' participation in administration, of forecast of bad days for the artisans and merchants in literary texts and references in foreign accounts to desertion of towns, especially Buddhist centres, by travellers like Fa Hsien and Hsuan Tsang.[54] Sharma's emphasis on urban decay is significant especially because an attempt is made to establish a causal link between urban decay and the emergence of feudalism, with a ruralization of the economy. A series of changes is related to this decline, such as ecological changes in the Ganges valley, the social upheaval associated with the Kali age of the *Purāṇas* first occurring in the third and fourth centuries and subsequently in the seventh–eighth centuries, land grants or grants of villages and even towns as fiefs in an all pervasive land grant system, which feudalized the economy, including the towns where even merchants and artisans were transferred to the beneficiary of the grant. Other consequences of the decline which are enumerated are the migration of artisans and *brāhmaṇas* from towns, localization of crafts in rural areas, obliteration of distinction between town and country, demonetization of economy, closed economy, the *jajmāni* system and sub-infeudation. The strengthening of the agrarian economy and the regrouping and reorganization of social relationships within the ideological framework of the *varṇa* system, all occupational groups ossifying into castes, are seen as the social aspect of the change.[55]

The decline of early historical urban civilization is envisaged in terms of a collapse of the early historical social order, rending the fabric of that 'normative order', the transition to the early medieval period being located in the social upheaval, i.e. the crisis of the *Kaliyuga*. The crisis and the fall of the early social order is further associated by yet another study by R.N. Nandi,[56] with a change in the nature of brahmanical *dāna* rites, introduction of new ones by the *brāhmaṇas*, change from the urban gift exchange of the *Gṛhya* texts to the agro-based *dāna* oriented *jajmāni* relations of early medieval *Smṛti* and Purāṇic literature. The idea of the *tīrthayātra* linked to expiatory and purificatory rites is said to have helped the *brāhmaṇas* to build up a new clientele and new avenues of support. What is significant in this connection is the attempt to establish that the decay of early historical towns led to migration of *brāhmaṇas* from these towns to rural areas and that as a result of the new *dāna* rites and *tīrthayātra* concept, these early towns turned into *tīrthas* or pilgrimage centres.

The historical phenomenon of the decline of urban centres by the third century AD is generally accepted among historians studying early historical urbanism and the new socio-economic order of the early medieval period.[57] Yet, researches in early medieval urbanism have raised several questions as to the validity of this generalization for the whole subcontinent and the long period of de-urbanization after the third century AD. Examples of the continuity of inland trade and of urbanization associated with it are found in early medieval centres of the ninth century AD in the Doab and Western Ganges valley in the Gūrjara Pratihāra period (ninth to eleventh centuries). Typological differences notwithstanding, these centres, which were not planned townships, appear as central points in local commerce, in which the conglomeration of *haṭṭas* (godowns) and residential areas led to initial urbanization, not precluding the effect of long-distance trade.[58]

In Rajasthan, evidence of the emergence of exchange centres has been found in different pockets as a continuous process in an agrarian context.[59] They appear as nodes among clusters of rural settlements, where commercial levies were collected, some of them also being centres of political power, e.g. Naḍḍula or Nadol, a Chāhamāna centre. Although the intensity of commercial exchange was unequally distributed, a complex pattern of trade involving a wide range of goods, agricultural as well as high value items, use of coined money along with other means of exchange and a hierarchy of exchange centres have been identified. The ascendancy of local merchant lineages, like the Oesvālas and Śrīmālas, their interaction with itinerant traders from distant regions in an expanding network of intra-regional and inter-regional trade are other significant aspects of this urbanism.

No definitive studies on early medieval urbanism in the Deccan and Andhra regions are available. Yet, similar patterns are indicated by current research on early medieval urbanization and some aspects of economy in general,[60] which highlight the economic aspects of urban growth in comparative studies of selected sites.[61] It may be noted that the tendency in all these works is to emphasise the importance of trade, both inland and maritime, as the major factor in urban growth, thus assigning primacy to economic factors and ignoring others, including the political.[62] One of the major concerns in the present collection of essays is to study the mingling of several factors, economic, political and ideological, in varying degrees of importance in early medieval urban processes.

Trade, crafts and commercial activities and their institutional organization seem to dominate studies on urbanization, both in the early historical and early medieval periods. Hence, in the attempt to seek overall perspectives, no difference is perceived in the basic nature of early historical and early medieval urbanization.[63]

Economic criteria are no doubt basic, often dominant and uniformly significant in urban genesis and particularly useful in distinguishing spaces allotted for rural and urban functions. Yet, a predilection for economic criteria, as capable of explaining urban forms and patterns in different periods, often results in a partial understanding of the processes and structures. It has been pointed out that even where direct correlations are found between forms of urbanism, on the one hand, and modes and stages of economic growth, on the other, such relationships cannot be treated as self- explanatory.[64] Cultural and ideological forces could bring about new institutional foci for economic activities and could induce processes different from one phase of urbanism to another, or even play a dominant role in determining the city's ultimate character and morphology by leading to the genesis of its institutions for creating 'effective space', i.e. that organizing and regionalizing principle, which is the essence of urbanism.[65]

It is in the nature of this organizing principle and its institutional forms that the early medieval urbanism differed from that of the early historical period. The distinction lay in the ideology, *viz.* on the one hand Buddhism and its institutions, in the early historical urban phase facilitated the evolution of urban forms in the trade and commercial centres, and the building of communication networks; on the other, the brahmanical ideology created new institutional means to build up cultural and religious networks, which facilitated trade and commerce in the early medieval period.

The differences go beyond institutional forms to the sphere and pattern of patronage and relations of dominance that developed in the two periods. Buddhism, patronised by rulers and merchant communities alike, initiated a process of change in societal organization by providing institutions like the *Sangha* and a more universal ethic, at least in theory, and a social thought cutting across caste and creating a sense of community, a community of monks (renouncers) and lay followers, a contrast to the brahmanical ideal of *varṇāśramadharma*.[66] Urban centres being places where people interact, work and have transactions with others not of their own caste or community, the Buddhist ideal of non-caste organization and association would, no doubt, have enabled institutionalized dealings with strangers (non-kin and other caste groups) and with foreigners.

State patronage to Buddhist institutions was more in the interests of promoting trade and networks of resource movement and accumulation and less an act of legitimation of their power.

The complex of domination in those centres of Buddhism was distinct from the political centres, particularly those of the Sātavāhanas and Ikṣvākus. Indeed, the Buddhist *Sangha* was an alternative source of authority distinct from priestly power and the coercive authority of the state.[67] On the contrary, the early medieval authority structure was created by the state, in which a coercive ruling power and priestly authority combined to bring about a complex of domination, both in the rural and urban centres, and a continuum of social hierarchy, which was more fully enacted in the cities.

The monumental forms like the *stūpa* were not royal projects but were a result of individual gifts brought together through a religious identity and a more loosely defined social identity.[68] The *stūpa* became the symbol of the *Sangha* and its authority. Interestingly, the *vihāra* or the monastic structure, as well as the *stūpa* were located in the outskirts of most urban centres and did not form the nucleus of an expanding settlement. Community patronage declined from the middle of the first millennium AD and it was replaced by royal and priestly patronage as well as elite participation in gift-giving. In fact, the early medieval temple was invariably a royal project, both for legitimation of political authority and as an institution of integration, mobilization and redistribution of resources. The pattern of social dominance is reflected in the architectural components of the temple complex, particularly in cities, as centres of politico-cultural regions within the Tamil macro-region, a conclusion which is inevitable as seen in the studies of centres like Tañjāvūr and Kāñcīpuram.[69]

III

The present collection of essays aims at providing regional perspectives based on empirical studies of specific urban centres within a socio-historical and cultural context highlighting the major incentives and focal points for urban growth. The region chosen for study is Tamiḻakam, which in the early historical period covered a larger geographical* area than the present Tamil

* From the tip of the peninsula in the south to 13° north latitude would roughly indicate this region.

Nadu or even the early medieval Tamil macro region, i.e. it included present Kerala region as well till about the seventh-eighth centuries AD. The periods covered by these essays are the early historical and the early medieval, i.e. third century BC to third century AD and sixth to thirteenth centuries AD.

In the early historical period, urban forms emerged in restricted zones, i.e. urban enclaves in two eco-zones, viz., the *marutam* (plains) and *neital* (coast/littoral) in the form of consumption points and trading ports. Some transit zones like the semi-arid Kongu region, rich in mineral resources, acted not only as route areas but also as craft production enclaves.[70] This early urbanism was not the result of the forces of an inner growth but was of a secondary generation induced by inter-regional trade, mainly coastal, between the Ganges plains, Andhra and Tamil regions and overland between the Deccan and Tamil region. More significantly, it was induced by maritime commerce between South India and the Mediterranean west and subsequently with Southeast Asia. However, unlike in Sātavāhana Deccan, this secondary urban development does not seem to be related to secondary state formation, as Mauryan imperial and cultural influences were less direct than in the Deccan and Andhra regions. In other words, political processes were not functionally related to urban genesis, which was mainly the result of external stimulus and hence were not at the core of the transformation. Early Tamil society did not emerge fully out of its tribal basis to evolve into a full-fledged state-society.

It would seem that 'urban revolution' in this period was an almost 'mystically sudden impulse'[71] to change due to external stimuli, i.e. maritime trade. The withdrawal of the stimuli led to the decline of this phase of urbanism which coincides with the disappearance of the early ruling families of the Cōḷa-Cēra-Pāṇḍya lineages creating a 'political vacuum', i.e. lack of clear political and economic configurations till the rise of the early medieval kingdoms of the Pallavas and Pāṇḍyas by the end of the sixth century AD.

Urban decay, which is believed to be a general historical phenomenon in the subcontinent in the post third century AD, is less clearly attested to in this region both in archaeological records and Tamil literary traditions, the latter being more concerned with the decline of the ruling families than with the decay of urban centres. Nor do they refer to artisans and merchants falling on bad days or to their migration. On the contrary, the post-Sangam literary works such as the epics, *Śilappadikāram* and *Maṇimēkalai*, point to a continuity of trade activities in at least the major centres of the early historical period like Kāñci, Vañci and Madurai apart from Kāvērippūmpaṭṭiṇam, the major port of entry into the region.

In so far as Tamiḻakam is concerned, the theory of urban decay and the consequences of deurbanization pose several problems. First is the nature of the archaeological data and its interpretation. As pointed out in an earlier section (II) all sites with similar archaeological data were not urban.[72] Sites such as Kunnattūr, Nattamēḍu, Aḻagarai, Tirukkāmpuliyūr etc., which have come up with archaeological material similar to others like Arikamēḍu, Kāvērippūmpaṭṭiṇam, Koṟkai, etc., cannot be categorised as urban. There was a general change in the pattern of settlements both with a rural and urban base. No uniformity or homogeneity in the pattern and nature of settlements is attested to by the archaeological data. Monumental remains occur in very few centres, especially those on the coast, while the inland centres hardly equalled them in such remains.

More important, the social upheaval located in the crisis of *Kaliyuga* has no relevance to early historical Tamil society, where the brahmanical social order of the *varṇa* had taken no roots and had no validity as the normative basis for social organization. Nor is there evidence of evil days for *brāhmaṇas*, artisans and others or of *brāhmaṇa* migration from towns to rural areas in the post-Sangam, i.e. post- third century AD period. The *Kaliyuga* crisis is adopted in the early medieval land grants (seventh–ninth centuries AD)[73] mainly as a formula to emphasize the need to establish the brahmanical order, to enhance the importance of monarchy as an institution and the role of the *kṣatriya* or ruling families in the preservation of the 'normative' social order, i.e. *varṇa* order as the theoretical basis of societal organization. The function of the *brahmadeya* of the early medieval period is mainly as an institution integrating pre-existing pastoral and agricultural settlements into a new agrarian order and as the disseminator of brahmanical ideology.

Early medieval urbanization was one of primary (inner) urban growth and not of secondary generation as in the early historical period. The essays in the present collection are aimed at showing this process in which new urban centres emerged with the temple as the nucleus—a rural-urban continuum in institutional and structural forms. More important, it was a period of re-urbanization for some of the early historical urban centres like Kāñcīpuram. Kāñcīpuram's urban character was mainly due to its commercial importance in the early period, while in the period of transition (third to sixth centuries), it continued to hold its position in an external trade network with Southeast Asia, and was brought into an inland commercial network with an expanding agricultural hinterland in the re-urbanization of the early medieval period.[74]

It may also be pointed out that in the early historical period, the religio-political foci for the transformation of the tribal, kinship based communities into stratified, hierarchically organized societies were absent, despite the fact that both the brahmanic and Śramaṇic religions were prevalent, especially in the *marutam* and *neital* eco-zones, none of them enjoying a predominant status. Significantly, Buddhism had a larger following in the coastal towns, Jainism in the inland centres marking trade routes and both these religions in addition to the brahmanic religions had a significant presence in the larger urban centres like Kāñcīpuram, Madurai, Uṟaiyūr and Vañci.

Such religio-political foci are the major factors of the early medieval period in the emergence of urban forms which created the physical and functional spaces for urban economic activities, for social dominance and political authority.

The present state of empirical research on urban history, the elusive character of urban theory, the limited scope of models and the variety of contexts to be dealt with prevent these essays from aiming at a goal too high to reach, viz. an overall perspective and analytical framework for the two periods of Indian history dealt with here. What is proposed in this collection is to examine the sets of relationships that a town/city establishes with its immediate surroundings or hinterland and the wider network of settlements of a similar nature and of different economic functions. Another major concern is with the ideological forces behind the development of such centres and the role they play either in perpetuating certain societal norms and values or introducing changes through 'new ideas and new ways of doing things'.[75] A distinction between economic development and cultural change needs to be made, without overstressing the importance of one over the other. Here, the idea of the town as a locus for change or prime mover in change also becomes useful.

If urban studies are made for a given cultural region, wherein historical geography can provide some useful insights, then a necessary step forward would have been taken in making comparative studies possible and towards achieving overall perspectives for urban history in India. These essays, it is hoped, have taken that step forward.

References

1. Philip Abrams and E.A. Wrigley, *Towns in Societies: Essays in Economic History and Historical Sociology*, Cambridge University Press, 1978, Introduction: Louis Wirth traces the notion of city as an independent variable to the influence of studies on Western Industrial Cities. 'Urbanism As a Way of Life', *American Journal of Sociology*, July 1938, vol. XLIV, no. 1, 1-24.
2. M.M. Postan, *The Medieval Economy and Society*, University of California Press, Berkeley, 1975, 212.
3. Rhoads Murphy, 'Traditionalism and Colonialism: Changing Urban Roles in Asia', *Journal of Asian Studies*, 1969-70, vol. 29, 68.
4. Ravi Arvind Palat, 'Symbiotic Sisters: Bay of Bengal Ports in the Indian Ocean World Economy', in Resat Kasaba (ed.), *Cities in the World System*, Contributions in Economics and Economic History, 1991, no. 126, Greenwood Press.
5. Abrams and Wrigley, *Towns in Societies*, Introduction, 3-4.
6. Ibid.
7. Harold Carter, *An Introduction to Urban Historical Geography*, London, 1983, Foreword, xiv.
8. Abrams, 'Towns and Economic Growth', in *Towns in Societies*, 21.
9. G. Sjoberg, *The Pre-Industrial City, Past and Present*, Glencoe, Illinois, 1960.

10. F. Braudel, *Capitalism and Material Life: 1400-1800*, London, 1973, 373. Pre-industrial cities are not necessarily a homogeneous phenomenon. *See* Robert J. Smith, 'Town and City in Pre-modern Japan: Small Families, Small Households and Residential Instability', in A. Southal (ed.), *Urban Anthropology*, New York, 1973, 104.
11. Robert Redfield and Milton Singer, 'The Cultural Role of Cities', *Economic Development and Cultural Change*, 1954, III, 53-73.
12. Susan Lewandowsky, 'Changing Form and Function of the Ceremonial and Colonial Port City in India: An Historical Analysis of Madurai and Madras', in K.N. Chaudhuri and Dewey (eds), *Economy and Society*, OUP, 1979, 299-329.
13. Narayani Gupta, 'Towers, Tanks and Temples: Some Aspects of Urbanism in South India: Eighteenth and Nineteenth Centuries', Occasional Paper Series-5, Urban History Association of India, 1983.
14. S.N. Eisenstadt and A. Shachar, *Society, Culture and Urbanization*, Beverley Hills, 1987, 357-61.
15. Howard Spodek, 'Beyond Rorschah Tests: Palimpsests and Nodes. Conflicts and Consciousnesses in South Asian Urban Theory', in Howard Spodek and Doris Meth Srinivasan (eds), *Urban Form and Meaning in South Asia: The Shaping of Cities from Pre-historic to Pre-colonial Times*, National Gallery of Art, Washington D.C., 255-68.
16. *See* Renu Thakur, 'Urban Hierarchies, Typologies and Classification in Early Medieval India: *c.* 750-1200', *Urban History*, April 1994, vol. 21, part I, 61-76.
17. *See* Richard Basham, *Urban Anthropology, The Cross Cultural Study of Complex Societies*, Mayfield, Palo Alto, California, 1978, 41.
18. Robert McC. Adams, *Evolution of Urban Society: Early Mesopotamia and Pre-Hispanic Mexico*, Aldine, Chicago, 1965, 126-7.
19. Paul Wheatley, *The Pivot of the Four Quarters, A Preliminary Enquiry into the Origins and Character of the Ancient Chinese City*, Edinburgh, 1971, 319.
20. Wheatley, 'The Concept of Urbanism', in Peter, J. Ucko, Ruth Tringham and G.W. Dimbleby (eds), *Man, Settlement and Urbanism*, London University, London, Duckworth, 1972, 600-37.
21. Abrams, 'Towns and Economic Growth', 25.
22. Ibid., 31-2.
23. Horace Miner defines the city as a centre of dominance. *See* 'The City and Modernization, An Introduction', in H. Miner (ed.), *The City in Modern Africa*, New York, 1967, 3, 5-10.

24. M. Weber, *Economy and Society*, New York, 1250ff.
25. H. Pirenne, *Medieval Cities: Their Origins and Revival of Trade*, Tr. by Frank D. Halsey, Doubleday, Garden City, New York, 1956; M.M. Postan, *The Medieval Economy*, 212.
26. John Merrington, 'Town and Country in the Transition to Capitalism', in R.H. Hilton (ed.), *The Transition from Feudalism to Capitalism*, London, 1978, 170-95.
27. Abrams, 'Towns and Economic Growth', Introduction, 1 and 11; Palat, 'Symbiotic Sisters', 19.
28. *See* Chapter 1 in this volume.
29. Basham, *Urban Anthropology*, 43.
30. Wheatley, *The Pivot of the Four Quarters*, 8.
31. Romila Thapar, 'Towards the Definition of an Empire: The Mauryan State' in *The Mauryas Re-Visited*, Calcutta, 1987.
32. Sudershan Seneviratne, 'Kalinga and Andhra: The Process of Secondary State Formation in Early India', in H.M. Claessen and P. Skalnik (eds), *The Study of the State*, Mouton, The Hague, 1981, 317-38.
33. Morton Fried, 'On the Evolution of Social Stratification and the State', in Stanley Diamond (ed.), *Culture in History: Essays in Honour of Paul Rodin*, Columbia University Press, New York, 1960, 713, 729-30.
34. Wheatley, 'Urban Genesis in Mainland Southeast Asia', in Smith and Watson (eds), *Early South East Asia: Essays in Archaeology, History and Geography*, New York, 1973, 288-303.
35. B.F. Hoselitz, 'Generative and Parasitic Cities', *Economic Development and Cultural Change*, 1954-5, III, 278-94.
36. John Friedmann, 'Cities in Social Transformation', *Comparative Studies in Society and History*, 4, 86-103.
37. Wheatley, *The Pivot of the Four Quarters*.
38. R.A.L.H. Gunawardana, 'Anuradhapura: Ritual, Power and Resistance in a Pre-Colonial South Asian City', in Daniel Miller, Michael Rowlands and Christopher Tilly (eds), *Domination and Resistance*, London, 1989, 155-78.
39. Wheatley, *The Pivot of the Four Quarters*, 319. The primary role of religious belief in the origin of Islamic cities is compared to the case of nationalism put forward by Reissman in relation to modern urbanization. *See* Reissman, *The Urban Process, Cities in Industrial Society*, New York, 1964, 188.
40. Adams, *Evolution of Urban Society*, 50.
41. City morphology in Asian countries is believed to have been influenced by its ceremonial character, the centre being marked

by a monumental building, either religious or political. The seventeenth-century Europeans' description of Asian cities also looks at them as ceremonial and administrative phenomena. (*See* Murphy, 'Traditionalism and Colonialism', 69.)

42. Carter, *Urban Historical Geography*, Foreword, viii.
43. Wheatley, *The Pivot of the Four Quarters*, 319.
44. S.N. Eisenstadt, 'Social Change, Differentiation and Evolution', *American Sociological Review*, 1964, vol. 29, 377 (375–86).
45. Mircea Eliade, *Le Mythe de l'eternal Retour*, Paris, 1949.
46. Wheatley, *The Pivot of the Four Quarters*, 258ff, 308ff, 398ff.
47. B.D. Chattopadhyaya, 'Urban Centres in Early Medieval India: An Overview', in S. Bhattacharya and R. Thapar (eds), *Situating Indian History*, New Delhi, 1986, 11ff.
48. *See* Seneviratne, 'Kalinga and Andhra', for the Impact of Mauryan Polity over the Deccan.
49. *See* Chapter 2 in this volume, and Rajan Gurukkal, 'Forms of Production and Forces of Change in Ancient Tamil Society', *Studies in History*, July–Dec. 1989, vol. 5, no. 2, 159–76.
50. Aloka Parasher, 'Social Structure and Economy of Settlements in the Central Deccan (200 BC–AD 200)', in Indu Banga (ed.), *The City in Indian History: Urban Demography, Society and Politics*, Manohar, (UHAI), 1991, 10–46.
51. Parasher, 'Social Structure', *idem* 'Nature of Society and Civilization in Early Deccan', *Indian Economic and Social History Review*, 29, 4 (1992), 437–77. Also H.P. Ray, *Monastery and Guild: Commerce Under the Satavahanas*, OUP, Delhi, 1986.
52. R.S. Sharma, *Urban Decay in India (c. 300–c. AD 1000)*, Munshiram Manoharlal, New Delhi, 1987.
53. Ibid.
54. Ibid., chapter 6.
55. Ibid., chapter 9.
56. R.N. Nandi, 'Client, Ritual and Conflict in Early Brahmanical Order', *Indian Historical Review*, July–Jan. 1979–80, vol. 6, nos 1 and 2, 64–118.
57. Vijay Kumar Thakur, *Urbanisation in Ancient India*, Abhinav, New Delhi, 1981, chapter VII; B.D. Chattopadhyaya, 'Trade and Urban Centres in Early Medieval North India', *Indian Historical Review*, Sept. 1974, vol. 1, no. 2, 203–19; also 'Urban Centres in Early Medieval India'.
58. Chattopadhyaya, 'Trade and Urban Centres'.
59. Chattopadhyaya, 'Markets and Merchants in Early Medieval Rajasthan', *Social Science Probings*, Dec. 1985, vol. 2, no. 4, 413–40.

60. M. Abraham, *Two Medieval Merchant Guilds of South India*, Manohar, New Delhi, 1988, chapters II and III-H.
61. Chattopadhyaya, 'Urban Centres'.
62. A. Ghosh would, however, assign primacy to both political and economic factors in early historical urbanism, See *The City in Early Historical India*, Simla, 1973.
63. Chattopadhyaya, 'Urban Centres'.
64. Abrams, 'Towns and Economic Growth', 20.
65. Wheatley, *The Pivot of the Four Quarters*, 398.
66. Romila Thapar, *Cultural Transaction and Early India: Tradition and Patronage*, OUP, Delhi, 1987, 28ff; also *idem* 'Patronage and Community', in Barbara Stoler-Miller (ed.), *The Powers of Art*, OUP, Delhi, 1992, 19-34.
67. Thapar, 1987.
68. The donors were merchants, crafts guilds, families of *gahapatis* (householders), monks and nuns: but among them there was only a 'smattering of families from royalty or high political or administrative office' who are associated with monuments like the *stūpa*—*See* Thapar, *Cultural Transaction* and 'Patronage and Community'.
69. *See* Chapters 7 and 8 in this volume.
70. *See* Chapter 2 in this volume for a detailed discussion of early historical urbanism in Tamiḻakam.
71. These terms were introduced by Robert J. Braidwood and Gordon R. Willev (eds), *Courses Towards Urban Life: Archaeological Consideration of Some Cultural Alternates*, Viking Foundation, Anthropology, no. 32, 1962.
72. Sharma, *Urban Decay in India c. AD 300-1000*, New Delhi, 1987, The list of sites in south India.
73. Champakalakshmi, 'Ideology and the State in Medieval South India', Mamidipundi Venkatarangiah Memorial Lecture, *Proceedings of the Andhra Pradesh History Congress, 13th session*, Sri Sailam, 1989.
74. *See* Chapter 7 in this volume.
75. B.F. Hoselitz, 'The Role of Cities in the Economic Growth of Underdeveloped Countries', *Journal of Political Economy*, LXI, 1953, 199.

1

Phases of Urbanization: An Overview

Urban history is an area of comparatively recent interest among historians, particularly historians of India. The central concern in historical research in India has more often been with agrarian systems, peasant history, and the general pattern of socio-economic change, rather than urbanization *per se*. Growth of urban centres is of marginal interest even to the studies on trade patterns, merchant and craft organizations and the role of the state in the promotion of such activities. For the early historical and early medieval periods in India, even the few available works on urban centres suffer from a woeful lack of clear orientation and a meaningful framework. There is a tendency to follow the notion that 'a town is a town, wherever it is', and that, being a visual phenomenon, the town/city should be made an object of study in its own right. As a result, these works are nothing more than compilations of lists of towns under various categories such as market, trade and commercial centres, political and administrative centres, and religious centres.[1] Any attempt to explain the causal factors in the emergence of towns is incidental to this approach. Historians have often succumbed, it would seem, to the tendency of studying the 'form' at the expense of the 'substance' of the urban characteristics of a place.

In the more recent attempts[2] to understand the range of issues involved in the urbanization of early medieval India, the major concern has understandably been with the processes of urban growth. While their emphasis has been on the need for overall perspectives and analytical framework as against typologies, they also highlight the problems in such exercises due to the inadequacy of empirical research.

The concern with processes rather than typologies also brings us to the central issue in urban history, namely, whether the visual presence of towns is a justification for treating what is 'essentially a physical object' as a 'social object' to be 'turned into a focus of analysis in its own right', i.e. a reified concept of the city as a decisive agency or independent variable in the process of social change,[3] or whether urban history should be pursued as 'part of the analysis of those broad socio-economic changes with which history is concerned',[4] i.e. those socio-economic changes which generate urban forms. It has been reiterated that the 'proper concern should not be with cities as such but with complex societies, in which cities and their hinterlands are interwoven into tight political and economic webs'.[5] In studying the evolution of urban forms, there is the additional hazard of taking a single factor as universal and attributing absolute primacy to it, or overstressing one aspect as innovative or catalytic at the expense of others.

The hazards of searching for a general framework notwithstanding, research available on the ancient and early historical periods in India has shown that there were two major periods of urbanization, to which a third may now be added for the early medieval period.[6] It is also generally accepted that the first urbanization, i.e. the Indus Valley urbanization of the proto-historic period, left no legacy beyond the middle of the second millennium BC.[7] The second or the early historical phase represents a long period of urban growth stretching from the sixth century BC to the third century AD. With its epicentre in the Ganges valley, it spread over the whole of North India by the third century BC, and over Central India, Deccan and the Andhra region between the second century BC and third century AD. It must be stressed, however, that it is the latter part of this long chronological span that witnessed the most clearly visible manifestations of this urbanism.

The end of the second urban phase is a time-marker for the early historical period and provides a starting point for the protagonists of the theory of 'Indian feudalism',[8] i.e. a new socio-economic formation, based on a land-grant system.[9]

I

In South India, the second (or, strictly speaking, the earliest) urbanization is represented by its end phases, evidence of its spread appearing at slightly different chronological points in the Deccan, the Andhra region and the Tamil country. By the beginning of the Christian era, it had become an all-India phenomenon. The beginnings of this urbanization are placed in the sixth century BC with its epicentre in the Ganges valley, where expansion of trade in ripples[10] around the early *janapadas* assumed significant proportions by the third century BC, with a network all over the north, Central India and the Deccan and with arterial links with Central Asia and West Asia. The spread of this network into the Deccan and Andhra region was undoubtedly brought about by overland trade links from the third century BC and the expansion of the Mauryan state. However, it would be erroneous to assume that without the impact of maritime trade, the phenomenal increase in the trade activities of the Deccan and Andhra regions from about the second century BC to the third century AD could have taken place.

In the extreme south, i.e. Tamil country (including modern Kerala), the effects of this urbanization were only indirectly felt. Visible clues to the contrastive urban experience of this region are the striking absence of trade networks, lack of organizational coherence (i.e. guilds) and the nature of Tamil polity. No less evident is the absence of a dominant religious ideology. The key to the understanding of these differences lay in the distinctive socio-economic milieu of the eco-system called the *tiṇai*,[11] within which the emergence of towns and the pace of urbanization have to be viewed.

It is not a matter of coincidence that the earliest ruling families or 'crowned kings' (*vēndar*), as they are described in early Sangam Tamil literature, emerged in the *marutam tiṇai*, representing the fertile agricultural tracts of the major river valleys. The earliest towns also arose in these tracts as well as in the *neital* or coastal/littoral. Such centres were consciously developed by the ruling families. These two *tiṇais* were dominated by the Cēras (Periyar valley), Cōḻas (Kaveri valley) and the Pāṇḍyas (Vaigai and Tamraparni valleys). The *marutam* was marked by an inland town of political and commercial importance and the *neital* by a coastal town of commercial importance, e.g. Uṟaiyūr and Kāvērippūmpaṭṭiṇam (Puhār) of the Cōḻas, Madurai and Ko̤rkai of the Pāṇḍyas and Vañci (Karuvūr) and

Muciṟi of the Cēras. These towns in effect represent the development of dual centres of power.[12]

Located in the rice-producing *marutam* tracts, the early chiefdoms or potential monarchies with their *janapada*-like polities[13] evolved out of earlier tribal organizations. The agricultural potential of the major river valleys attracted settlers from very early times and numerous settlements had emerged by the beginning of the Christian era, the Kaveri delta showing a fair concentration of such settlements.[14] It is not clear whether and, if so, to what extent, the ruling families helped in this process, although a late tradition attributes an irrigation work on the Kaveri to one of the Cōḷas. It is possible that the impact of trade, particularly maritime trade, led to intensification of inter-*tiṇai* exchange, which in turn could have provided an incentive for extracting the 'surplus' of the agricultural tracts and channelizing it towards trade. However, no direct and organized control appears to have been acquired by any of the 'crowned kings' over the agricultural tracts, no regular tax structure having been evolved. The institutional forces, which defined the 'excess' requirements, provided for its appropriation and defined its utilization[15] are not known to have existed under the Cōḷas, Cēras and Pāṇḍyas. The hegemony of the *vēndar* was rather loosely held. Performance of Vedic sacrifice and patronage to *brāhmaṇas* were not an intrinsic part of the legitimation process in this period,[16] although evidence of both is available in the Sangam anthologies.[17] Even at such sacrifices wealth would have got distributed rather than accumulated as a resource. The continuance of inter-tribal warfare[18] and war loot was perforce the only recourse to supplementing resources, most of which were redistributed in the form of patronage to poets and bards, and some channelized into trade.

The *kuṟiñci tiṇai* (hilly areas) was particularly rich in resources such as aromatic wood, which were exported outside the Tamil region. A symbiotic relationship developed between these and the *marutam* and *neital* tracts. For, in return for paddy and salt, the people of the *marutam* and *neital* acquired the rich resources of the hilly tracts.[19] Inter-tribal warfare was another means by which the ruling families of *marutam* obtained such resources. In this context, the wars among the *vēndar*[20] or 'crowned kings' themselves become significant, as they represent attempts by each of the three rulers to gain control over the resources of the others. The Cōḷa attempts to gain access to the pearl fisheries of the Pāṇḍya coast and the rich pepper areas of the Cēra Nāḍu, would be significant as showing their interests in establishing an exchange system.

The *mullai tiṇai* on the fringes of settled agricultural tracts represented a transitory ecological zone and could gradually have merged with the latter with the expansion of agriculture and irrigation facilities.[21] Some of the *mullai* tracts were also locations for important routes such as the Kongu region—the Coimbatore and Salem districts—and thus became areas of contention among the *vēndar*. While inter-*tiṇai* exchange would have introduced a symbiotic relationship at one level, there still was a natural element of competition and hostility due to the contrasts in the productivity of the different *tiṇais*. Predatory raids[22] were hence common and references to the razing of the enemies' fields and despoiling of water tanks[23] show that the *kuṟiñci* and *mullai* chiefs were no passive observers of the increasing influence of the *vēndar*, when they fell short of their basic resources.

In the process of establishing inter-*tiṇai* exchange emerged several settlements, probably as foci of inter-*tiṇai* contacts, which from the criterion of modern urban centres, cannot be classified as urban. Yet, in contemporary perception, these settlements were distinct from their hinterlands both in size and antiquity. Such settlements may often be recognized from the terms used to denote them, viz., *mūdūr* (old settlement) and *pērūr* (large settlement),[24] usually found at the junction of inter-*tiṇai* exchange, bordering on *marutam* land or, occasionally, as the centres of the chiefs of the *kuṟṟiñci* and *mullai*.[25]

The more commercially active and organized towns were the *paṭṭiṇams* located on the coast. This accounts for the fewer and sparser urban settlements in the interior and their presence only in the *marutam* and *neital* tracts, i.e. the inland capital and coastal port. Even these were no more than trade enclaves, particularly the *paṭṭiṇam* on the coast like Puhār or Kāvērippūmpaṭṭiṇam. The instance of Puhār is striking, for it was an emporium, an entrepot, acting as a collection centre, perhaps comparable to a gateway city (Puhār means river entrance) to its hinterland, the Cōḷanāḍu.[26] However, evidence of an extensive network connecting this port through subsidiary towns or nodal points does not exist, and the situation was no different in relation to ports like Nīrpeyar̤r̤u (for Kacci or later Kāñcīpuram), Arikamēḍu (Vīrai, a *vēḷir* port), Kor̤kai (of the Pāṇḍyan coast) and Mucir̤i (of the Cēra coast).[27] Local exchange was hardly linked to the type of wholesale or bulk activities of such enclaves, for the local exchange system was subsistence-oriented. The deployment of goods from the ports and into them, was in the hands of individual traders and merchant families, guild activities being least attested to in the Tamil region. The emphasis was on luxury and exotic items of import, some of which were prestige goods, or what are called primitive valuables. They could have been of ideo-technic (or socio-technic) value to the ruling families,[28] and hence it is not clear how significant this trade was as a resource potential to the rulers, who were only little more than tribal chiefs. Yet, their interest in this trade is attested to in several ways as, for example, in levying duties on goods (*ulgu poruḷ*)[29] coming to the port, and in using imported luxuries as an alternative means of supplementing irregular tribute, due to the lack of coercive power to directly tax the people of the rich agricultural tracts, i.e. the farmers. Social distance and a symbolic contrast between the ruler and the ruled may well have been the major advantage.

The inland towns could at best be described as consumption points, although there is some evidence of Ur̤aiyūr, Kacci and Madurai as textile manufacturing centres, forthcoming mainly from literary evidence and, to a limited extent, from archaeological finds.[30] In most cases, archaeological finds have not proved to be particularly illuminating, except for Puhār, where again harbour facilities are attested to,[31] but manufacturing activities are hardly indicated. Even the 'monumental' architecture[32] that has been unearthed in Puhār is chronologically later than the period of intensive commerce. One area of potential archaeological significance is the region of Coimbatore, where a concentration of commercial and artisanal activity is beginning to emerge from the excavations at Koḍumaṇal, the Koḍumaṇam of Sangam works situated on the banks of the Noyyal river.[33] The provenance and distribution of punch-marked and Roman coins in the Coimbatore region lends additional support to its importance. Details of the archaeological evidence regarding other centres, inland and coastal, the artefactual remains of Roman objects, and the Roman factory site at Arikamēḍu, need not detain us here, for these have been highlighted time and again in studies on the Sangam period and on the early Indian trade contracts with the Roman west.[34]

The major concern in discussing the impact of maritime trade on the Tamil society is to assess the nature of urban development and transformation of society through such impact. The Tamil society, especially of the Cōḷa region, i.e. Kaveri valley, had reached the level of a farming society from a former position of tribal organization. Survivals of their tribal origins are still echoed in the early anthologies.[35] Similar to other traditional 'peasant societies', it also retained a high degree of subsistence production which did not find its way to the market place, located at this time only in a few urban centres. The market principle did not govern its exchange and the hinterland people were not dependent for daily requirements on long-distance commerce, which in itself was oriented towards trade in luxury goods. The luxury goods that entered the interiors, circulated through networks of kinship, patronage and clientele, through redistribution and prestation.[36] The foci of long-distance trade were the market centres on the coast, the urban clientele being the rulers, members of the elite–the *cāṉṟōr* and *uyarndōr*–who gained social prestige from which flowed other privileges, predominantly political. Not surprisingly, ruling families like the Cōḷas, consciously encouraged external trade connections, developed ports and planted their agents or officers to supervise and control the flow of goods.[37]

The *kuṟiñci* and *mullai* tracts, as seen earlier, were not directly involved in this commerce, but were brought into the commercial circuit through the *marutam* rulers. They were largely tracts of relative isolation, and were characterized by simpler forms of socio-political organization. Processes leading to the development of socio-economic diversification were limited in these tracts, which could sustain only 'segmentary tribes' in small dispersed settlements.[38] Again, as primitive valuables or prestige goods, the luxury and exotic items could have induced the chieftains of these tracts to encourage the flow of goods, as it gave them the opportunity of enhancing their socio-political status.[39]

It has been argued on the basis of ethnographic data, that trade alone can rarely bring about the evolution of social stratification from a non-stratified society, since such systems have an in-built mechanism to prevent the equilibrium being destabilised.[40] In the *marutam tiṇai* a certain degree of diversity seems to have accompanied the agricultural settlements through the evolution of crafts related to agricultural activities, and smiths, carpenters, jewellers, goldsmiths, weavers and metal workers are constantly referred to in literature. Evidence of a broad dual division of society is provided by the reference to the *cāṉṟōr* or *uyarndōr* and the *iḻicinar*. The position of dominance was occupied by the chiefs or kings and the landed local elite (*vēḷir*, *kiḻavan* or *kiḻān*, *talaivan*, *entai*), collectively referred to as *uyarndōr* and *cāṉṟōr* (the superior ones), while the lower category, generally termed as *iḻicinar*, were engaged in various 'inferior' activities or subsistence production.[41] It is only in the medieval commentaries on Sangam works that references to the superior *vēḷāḷas* (land owning group) and inferior *vēḷāḷas* (cultivators)[42] occur together with the *vēḷir* chiefs as the dominant land owning groups controlling fairly large areas of agricultural land,[43] indicating that stratification based on land distribution and control was believed to have existed even in this early period. The *vēḷir* are described in the Sangam works as lesser chiefs, pastoral-cum-agricultural, but next in importance only to the *vēndar* as a dominant socio-political group and as patrons of the Tamil poets.

The differentiation became more marked in the *marutam* and *neital* regions, where the capitals and ports were located, and where an increase in trade ventures introduced a further element of diversification, such as individual traders, *vaṇikaccāttu* or groups of merchants, king's officers or customs agents, and warehouse guards in the market and port towns,[44] leading to a more complex society. The relatively undifferentiated 'tribal' society was disintegrating and differentiation had set in.

The chief economic activities in the *neital* tracts, apart from trade, were fishing and manufacturing and selling of salt, in which the *Valaiñar* and *paratavar* were involved.[45] The *paratavar* gradually diversified their interests to become pearl fishers and traders, and their increasing participation in coastal trade dealing in expensive items like pearls, gems and horses is indicated in the descriptions of their commerce and life style.[46] Salt manufacture and trade also became a more specialized activity with a group called *umaṇar*. However, the evidence, on the whole, suggests that craft specialization was, with the exception of a few spheres,[47] at a rudimentary level. Nor is there any evidence on craft guilds or artisan guilds. Merchant guilds are also not known to have been a regular part of the commercial organization, although there is a single epigraphic reference to a *nigama* from Tiruveḷḷaṛai[48] and literary reference to a merchant of Kāvērippūmpaṭṭiṉam as a *Māsāttuvāṉ* (*Sārthavāha*).[49] The producer was quite often also the dealer in the commodities manufactured,[50] and manufacturing activities were generally on a low level.

Money as an exchange medium was evidently used only in larger transactions and long-distance trade, and perhaps only by itinerant merchants. Numismatics for this period in the Tamil region is one of the most problematic of sources, despite the fact that a large number of hoards of punch-marked and Roman coins, apart from stray pieces from stratified archaeological levels, are available. With the possible exception of a single hoard of punch-marked coins, assignable to the Pāṇḍyas[51] on the basis of the fish sign on the coins, and another attributed to a lesser chief in the North Arcot region,[52] no regular 'dynastic issues' were known, till the recent discovery, in the nineties, of Cēra and Pāṇḍya coins with legends, and some with portraits.

The *varṇa*-based organization of society is also not clearly attested to, despite the fact that the priestly *brāhmaṇas* are often referred to as a distinct social group enjoying a high status. The *Tolkāppiyam* reference to the four-fold division of society occurs in the *Poruḷ atikāram*[53] of the work, suggesting a later date for the use of this framework of social stratification for the Tamils. The idea of ritual pollution was, however, prevalent, and groups associated with impure activities are said to have lived separately.[54] This may well have been a survival of the tribal system even in the *marutam* region where the *varṇa* differentiation first emerged.

The spread of Buddhism and Jainism, coinciding with the increase in trade and commercial activity, would also seem to have introduced an element of further diversification, especially in the urban centres. Jainism was, more often, predominantly represented in the inland towns, and Buddhism in the coastal towns, especially Puhār. Their patrons came mainly from the commercial community, i.e. merchants and craftsmen,[55] apart from ruling families. The heterogeneity of the urban population of which the *yavanas*[56] (people of West Asian and Mediterranean origin) were also a part, shows that people of different ethnic origins and belonging to various religions aggregated in towns, and brahmanical and folk cults were also well represented in most centres. No single dominant religion is attested to in any of them.

There is little by way of archaeological evidence to establish the social complexity. Some indication of it is seen in the Megalithic burials, many of which are coeval with the period of the Sangam classics.[57] Burials containing a variety of war weapons, apart from other agricultural implements, may be associated with the high status warrior and chiefly groups. The five kinds of burial practices mentioned in the *Maṇimēkalai*,[58] one of the two post-Sangam epics, would also suggest a possible differentiation in the rank and status of the groups involved, which, however, can be assessed only on the basis of a study of all the burial types, their distribution and contents.

Thus, the ultimate manifestation of the impact of trade is seen mainly in the *marutam* and *neital* eco-zones, with a greater diversity of occupations, i.e. 'a new and more complex division of labour'.[59] However, the pace of social differentiation and urban development was not only slower, but hardly reached the level of a system in which tight networks of institutional forms and relationships[60] could emerge similar to that of the Deccan and Andhra region.

Even within the Tamil country, the nature of urban growth in the Pāṇḍya and Cēra countries differed significantly from that of the Cōḷa dominated regions. A major thesis[61] on the effect of the coastal sea traffic on the Pāṇḍya coastal region and of northern Sri Lanka would place the Pāṇḍyas as pioneers in the promotion of coastal and overseas trade, and attributes to them the introduction of the Brāhmī script in the Tamil country, as the earliest Tamil-Brāhmī inscriptions occur in the Pāṇḍya region. Seen together with the possible association of the Pāṇḍyas with the earliest dynastic coinage and their patronage of the Tamil literary academy called the Sangam, it is not a matter of surprise that it was Madurai, the Pāṇḍya capital, which became the Tamil city *par excellence*. In the Pāṇḍyan context, it is suggested, the impact of the western sea trade in the 'urbanization/civilization' of this part of the peninsula and the Sri Lankan coast was minimal, whereas the initial stimulus is attributed to coastal sea traffic from Gujarat in the west to Bengal in the east in the pre-Mauryan and Mauryan times. Overland traffic is assigned lesser importance through the Mauryan times.[62] Equally significant is the fact that the most important transpeninsular route connecting Karnataka and Kerala with Tamil Nadu, passing through the Kongu region, is marked by Brāhmī inscriptions *chronologically later* than those of the Madurai region, once the arid Pudukkottai area is crossed from the south.[63] The commercial importance of the Kongu region has been noted earlier, and the route, which passed through it, was popular down to the medieval times among itinerant merchants.[64]

At this stage, it may be useful to delineate the major differences, and to recapitulate the contrastive urban experiences, of the Deccan and the Tamil country. As we have seen, they are ultimately traceable to ecological and cultural factors as well as political organization. The river system of the Deccan plateau shows certain restraining factors, making the region conducive only to the growth of relatively smaller areas of agriculture. On the contrary, it was less restrictive and more suitable for the growth of communication and transport networks, with the passes in the Western Ghats linking the coast to the interior and the relatively drier zones helping uninterrupted travel and easier movement.[65] The expansion of these routes subsequently to include the Andhra region in a tight commercial network took place when a larger agricultural base in the Krishna Valley was acquired by the Sātavāhanas in the latter part of their period.

The Sātavāhanas adopted brahmanical ideology for legitimating their rule, with their commitment to the *varṇāśrama* ideal probably originating from their earlier priestly affiliations.[66] The advantage of conceding the dominance of Buddhist ideology over merchants, and others involved in commerce and production for trade, both overland and overseas, was also understood by them. In the Deccan the symbiotic relationship which existed between the political structure, the commercial groups and the Buddhist order have been clearly recognised.[67] The power structure which thus evolved, reflects in many ways Mauryan ideological influences or the continuation of Mauryan institutions, in what may be seen as 'secondary state formation',[68] and a monetary system controlled to a large extent by the ruling dynasty. Royal patronage of the expanding trade and a dominant Buddhist ideology, which helped evolve institutions such as the monastery and guild to support it, mark the contrastive processes in urban growth in the Deccan and Tamil country. The only common element was overseas trade, evidence of which is overwhelming.

Reference has been made earlier to the importance of the *tiṇai* in determining the socio-economic development of the Tamil country. Tribute and not tax, warfare for loot and plunder as well as hegemony,[69] use of money in long-distance trade by itinerant traders, and in larger transactions, local exchange remaining out of the circuit of inter-regional commerce, and, more importantly, the absence of institutional forces like the Buddhist monastery and the traders' guild, marked the urban growth of the Tamil region with a remarkably lesser degree of intensity. Added to this were the absence of a clear *varṇa* based social stratification, and the emergence of urban enclaves which left kinship and communal organization relatively untouched over vast agricultural plains and other ecological zones.

Under the *vēndar*, the chiefdoms, which appeared to mark a transitional stage in the evolution of the state, never passed the transitional to the state level.[70] The reasons for their decline may be sought not only in the sudden arrest of urban growth due to the withdrawal of the western trade, but also in the lack of coercive power and institutional control over the agricultural plains themselves. They seem to have been overtaken by a crisis caused by decline in trade and, at the same time, by ambitious chiefs of other eco-zones, whose descent into the plains was not a mere predatory raid but, more, a lasting occupation of rice-yielding tracts, over which the control of the *vēndar* was becoming increasingly tenuous, as their socio-political prestige was at a very low ebb. If urbanization consequent upon long-distance trade could induce the formation of a state society, this did not happen in the Tamil region to the same degree as in other parts of India during the early historical phase. Hence, long-distance trade may be seen both as a cause and an effect of state formation, depending upon factors other than trade itself.[71] In fact, territorial expansion and political unification have been regarded as less indirect consequences of urban genesis than as functionally inter-related processes 'at the very core of the transformation'.[72]

The cultural ethos of Tamil society given to the ideals of love and war (*akam* and *puṟam*, both implying heroism), generosity and patronage, i.e. a kinship-oriented value system, and the predominant folk component in worship and religion, i.e. an 'anthropocentric' worship, would also indicate that social norms had not yet shed their tribal moorings. What was needed was a formalized religious system and its universalization through acculturation, a system which could combine in it many of the folk and popular elements with the Purāṇic Sanskritic tradition that swept the sub-continent by the end of the sixth century AD.

The so-called Sangam period has often been stretched from 300 BC to AD 300 and even beyond. Hence, the use of the Sangam works as a single corpus of sources for the whole period is hazardous, especially in view of the different internal chronologies suggested for these collections, and the fact that they were collected and systematized much later in the eighth to ninth centuries AD. It would, therefore, be more valid to treat them as representing different layers of poetry, and at least two levels of social organization, i.e. the tribal stage persisting in the *mullai* and *kuṟiñci* regions, and an incipient stage of urbanism developing in the *marutam* and *neital*. Such a change was rather suddenly arrested, both due to the decline of trade and lack of an institutional coherence and resource base to fall back upon in a crisis.

II

The early historical phase of urbanism has thus been shown to be the result of external trade, an 'urban revolution'[73] in a restricted locus within which the process was concentrated,[74] leading to the emergence of urban or, more correctly, trade enclaves. The discontinuity caused by the decline of trade[75] around the third century AD, is represented as a period of crisis in Tamil Society of the post-Sangam era, in the later literary and epigraphic records of the seventh to ninth centuries AD. Was it a crisis of urban 'devolution'? Or, was it a breakdown of earlier tribal forms, followed by a transition towards the genesis of a new socio-economic formation in the later period? This period of socio-political subversion is also attributed by later brahmanical records to the onslaught of evil kings (*kali araśar* or *Kaḷabhras*) and the dominance of 'heterodoxy'. If the later socio-religious developments are any indication, this period, for which no contemporary records exist, may be described as one of flux and instability due to the decline of the three traditional *vēndar*, and a possible clash of interests among new aspirants to social and political authority,[76] including the lesser chiefs, and competition among brahmanical, Buddhist and Jain religions for patronage.

The early medieval urbanization may be located within a broad time span of six centuries (seventh to thirteenth centuries), in which one may see the operation of the 'ramp process' applied by Adams for the study of Mesopotamia and Meso-America, two areas of nuclear urbanism, as a metaphor of heuristic value, for it enables one to come to grips with urban revolution as 'an intelligible sequence of change rather than simply accepting it as an almost mystically sudden impulse'.[77] To understand this phase of urbanization, one of the first essential steps would be to study the major shift in agrarian organization and the remarkable degree of agrarian expansion which characterized the centuries of Pallava-Pāṇḍya rule and which continued well into the Cōḷa period, i.e. ninth to eleventh centuries AD.[78]

The first intelligible records pointing to the genesis of a new socio-economic formation are of the seventh to ninth centuries.

Signs of the change were visible much earlier in the *marutam* region with its tendency to extend agricultural activities. The earliest attempt to introduce large-scale agriculture in non-*marutam* areas or drier localities is evidenced by the Pūlānkuṟicci record of early *brahmadeyas* (datable to the fifth century AD).[79] New integrating forces like the *brahmadeya* and the temple under the aegis of the Pallava-Pāṇḍya ruling families, led to the extension of agricultural activities and a more intensive organization of production geared to support large populations in the *brahmadeyas* and temple-centres. Clusters of such settlements emerged as the foci of urban growth by the end of the ninth century AD, showing that an initial search for urban cores among such clusters would result in a better understanding of the processes in this region. Examples of such clusters may be recognised in the Kaveri delta at Kuḍamūkku-Paḻaiyāṟai, the residential seat of the Cōḻas from the ninth century AD, and in the Tamraparani-Ghatana valley in the two *brahmadeyas*, Rājarājacaturvēdimangalam and Ceravanmahādevi-caturvēdimangalam, from the close of the tenth century AD.[80]

The Pallava-Pāṇḍya period would represent a stage of incipient urbanism, when the royal centres or seats of the ruling families show a similar growth around temples, i.e. Kāñcīpuram and Madurai. These cities had a long historical past as the centres of the Tiraiyar and Pāṇḍyas of the Sangam classics. The nature of these cities and their corresponding ports has been discussed earlier. What is important, however, is to perceive the changing character of these cities in the early medieval period as a result of the new institutional forces of integration, which brought them into a much closer relationship with their hinterlands in the northern and southern parts of the Tamil country, as well as with their ports located on the coast, i.e. Māmallapuram and Korkai respectively. In the process emerged a number of *brahmadeyas* in the hinterland with temples as their nuclei, appended to which were the pre-existing agricultural and pastoral settlements with a certain degree of subsistence production.

The *brahmadeya* and the temple were evolved as institutional forces by the *brāhmana-ksatriya* allies in power and, hence, were products of brahmanical ideology expressed through Vedic and Purānic religion, and initially sponsored by the ruling families claiming *kṣatriya* (or the *brahma-kṣatriya*) status and divine descent. That they developed into institutions of substantial political and social power with economic privileges has been demonstrated in most studies relating to them or based on them.[81] However, what has not been made clear in these works is the nature of economic advantage, i.e. as a source of revenue, to the kings who sought to establish their sovereignty through them. This may be explained, to a large extent, as due to the problems of interpretation of the sources, both epigraphic and numismatic. One of the ways in which a recent study on the nature of medieval Indian polity has approached this problem is to underscore the need to look at resource mobilization as logically inseparable from the process of redistribution of resources to integrative elements within the state structure.[82] The failure to understand this interconnection has led to the theory of the 'politics of plunder' as a major mechanism of resource acquisition and redistribution.[83]

Two important spheres in which the *brahmadeya* and temple may be seen as harbingers of advanced farming methods were the technology of irrigation and the seasonal regulation of the cultivation process. For the introduction of both these steps for improving cultivation, there seems to be reliable evidence from the Pallava-Pāṇḍya records, when they are considered in their geographical and ecological setting. With each one of the *brahmadeya* and temple settlements an irrigation system was invariably established, either in the form of tanks, canals or wells in the Pallava-Pāṇḍya regions.[84] Many of them were initiated by the rulers but managed by the local bodies. Elaborate arrangements for their upkeep were made by the *sabhās* or assemblies of the *brahmadeyas*, including maintenance, repair, attention to silting and control of water supply through cesses, and specifying committees (*vāriyams*) for their supervision and administration. Effective management was indeed the key to the difference in the farming societies of the earlier (Sangam) and later (seventh to ninth centuries) periods.[85]

The *brāhmaṇas* were organizers and managers of production in the *brahmadeyas* and the *vēḷāḷas* or land-owning peasants in the non-*brahmadeya* settlements, where the focus of activities was the brahmanical temple. However, it may be surmised that it was the former, who, on the basis of their specialised knowledge of astronomy,[86] would have introduced an element of predictability in yields, on the basis of seasonal sowing and cropping patterns, as well as effective management of water resources. It may be added here that in the records of this period, demarcation of boundaries, establishment of 'ownership' or enjoyment rights, nature and category of land, and the number of crops to be raised become important details.

Brahmadeyas in most cases may have meant the giving away of rights, economic and administrative, to the donees, but instances are not wanting to show that they were not completely exempt from revenue payments to the king.[87] The real advantages lay in integrating older settlements and non-*brahmadeya* villages (*ūr*) into the new agrarian system, and also in bringing virgin land under cultivation, both waste land and forest (*mullai* region). There are also examples of several pre-existing settlements being clubbed together into a new *brahmadeya* or integrated into it. The tax exemptions given to the *brahmadeyas* do not obviously apply to such villages thus brought into the system, unless otherwise specified. That regular dues reached the royal *bhaṇḍāras* is also clear from the 'structured' circulation of resources through the *nāḍu* or *kūṟṟam* and the *brahmadeya* or temple, to the king.[88] The circulation of resources was effected through the temple as the disseminator of the *bhakti* ideal, i.e. through non-economic or extra economic coercion. However, at the local level, the chief beneficiaries of the redistribution process were the locally powerful elite, temples and *brāhmaṇas*, apart from temple functionaries and tenants. The co-ordination of production and distribution processes were in the hands of the *sabhā* and *ūr*, which has been seen as a result of a *brāhmaṇa* and dominant peasantry alliance and the crystallization of a peasant society.[89] The land grant system has also been interpreted as a feudal one, in so far as it provides evidence of the emergence of intermediaries, both religious and secular, between king and cultivator, and suggests exploitative relations between a land controlling class and labouring class of peasants.[90]

Our concern with either the *brāhmaṇa*-peasant alliance and the segmentary state theory that it has evoked, or the feudal polity model for medieval India, is clearly marginal and has particular reference only to the Cōḷa situation, where urban growth and the direct royal involvement in promoting trade and exchange networks by using the *nagaram* as one of the agents of a state synthesis, go against any theory of segmentation of power, as will eventually be shown through a discussion of the character of the Tamil city under the Cōḷas. Nor is the evidence for a feudal polity clear enough to be applied for the South Indian state until the rise of Vijayanagar. In one of the recent attempts to characterize the early medieval polity as feudal, the rigour of analysis and empirical controls needed for understanding the complex nature of inscriptional evidence on agrarian relations are absent.[91] It is also not possible at this stage to see whether the crisis attributed to ranking as the political basis of organization of both local and supra-local structures was a feature of the Cōḷa state, and whether the shifting nature of territorial and political holdings in other parts of medieval India[92] was present in it. For the Cōḷa state was undoubtedly one of the most stable structures known to pre-colonial India, and we believe that it was a powerful ideology which supported the Cōḷa efforts to mobilize a huge resource base.

Before we spell out the ideological underpinnings of the Cōḷa state, which had a distinct influence on the nature of the Cōḷa city, one other major aspect of this agrarian expansion and integration needs to be understood more clearly than has been done hitherto. This was the evolution of agrarian units like the *kōṭṭam*, a pastoral-cum-agricultural region, the *nāḍu* and *kūṟṟam*,[93] which in the main were agricultural regions. By extension, this nomenclature came to be used even for areas of dispersed agricultural settlements, or even those with other resources like salt and pearls (*umbaḷa nāḍu* and *muttūṟṟu kūṟṟam*), where agriculture was a major occupation in addition to salt manufacture and pearl-diving. All the three units pre-date the Pallava-Pāṇḍya period and yet, they emerged as viable units of socio-economic and political importance only in relation to the new ruling elite of the seventh to ninth centuries AD.[94]

This intensive process of agrarian integration is reflected in the numerous *brahmadeyas* and temple centres of the seventh to ninth centuries visibly emerging in the form of religious architecture–rock-cut caves, monolithic temples and structural edifices–of the Pallava and Pāṇḍya regions.[95] Land relations came to be organized around the *brahmadeya* and temple with three categories of landowners–the *brāhmaṇa*, the *vēḷāḷa* and the temple–emerging as the local elite. Societal organization was based on the *varṇa* framework, but expressed through two broad categories–the *brāhmaṇa* and the non-*brāhmaṇa*, within which most of the occupational groups were placed in a ritual hierarchy around the temple, the concept of purity-pollution operating at all levels, thus keeping the untouchables out of the temple precincts. The North Indian evidence shows that untouchables were mainly those who came from 'culturally backward' tribal groups and were condemned to take up menial work and sometimes 'impure' work like carrying dead bodies and sweeping the streets etc.[96] With the growing economic disparity and the large-scale dissemination of brahmanical ideas in the early medieval period, the tribal groups such as the *paṟaiya* became the untouchables in South India.

The absence of a *vaiśya* category[97] in this region has been attributed to 'the growth of the brahmanical *agrahāra* in an agricultural setting, where trade was not a very important factor in the economy of these regions at this stage and the number of communities dependent on trade must have been fairly small to have been practically ignored in the records of this period'.[98] This would appear to be true of the seventh to ninth centuries, but with the gradual expansion in the exchange nexus among the agricultural settlements and the continuation of long-distance trade in coastal areas, the trading community emerged as a distinct class by the eighth to ninth centuries AD. A regional version of the theoretical *varṇa* system developed, with important modifications depending upon the specificities of the politico-economic system that emerged. In the case of the *kṣatriya varṇa*, the indigenous ruling families acquired the *kṣatriya* status and politico-economic dominance. The participation of the ruling families in these processes was as important as that of the *brāhmaṇas*, who composed the genealogies for them, and was mainly intended to establish socio-political dominance with economic privileges, through religious networks, 'the strongest thread in the fabric of the medieval agrarian system'.[99] The Pallavas, who were alien to the Tamil country, and who had imbibed brahmanical ideas in their original home, i.e. the Andhra region, claimed to be *brahma-kṣatriyas* tracing their descent to Brahma, but emphasizing their *kṣatriya*-hood for political dominance.[100] The Pāṇḍyas, on the other hand, were a traditional Tamil power and clung to their older associations with Siva and Agastya, but adopted *kṣatriya* status in their records.[101] All this is, however, relevant only in explaining the imposition of the *varṇa* framework on non-Indo-Aryan societies. The crucial question, however, relates to the diversification of occupation, with the expanding agrarian system, and how it created the need for an ideology to accommodate the newly emerging occupational groups. That such diversification and social differentiation accompanied the growth of *brahmadeya* and temple centres[102] is established by the reference to various categories of temple functionaries, craftsmen in the service of agriculture and agricultural workers, i.e. division of labour. The principle of heredity inherent in the *varṇa* framework would seem to have been stretched so as to bring all these social groups within its vortex under the *jāti* label. Thus, we find the *varṇa-jāti* division coalescing in many cases, with the economic or professional groups. Society had become much more complex, and one more dimension was added to it by the third institution, i.e. *nagaram*, which emerged by the eighth century AD. Thus, social differentiation would seem to be the crux of the problem of urbanization, and it is to those processes which created such differentiation that urban history should address itself.

The relevance of the above survey of societal organization, although repetitive in some of its essential details, lies in the fact that it provides the basis on which answers to several questions which arise in relation to urbanization in pre-industrial societies may be sought. These questions, to which attention has been drawn by historians in general and economic historians in particular, relate to two main issues, namely, agricultural growth and the availability of a surplus as a necessary precondition to urban growth, and the degree of importance commerce and overseas trade have in the development of commodity production, exchange and the growth of towns.

The urban forms generated by the end of the Pallava-Pāṇḍya

period, through centuries of agrarian development, found expression in two categories of centres, the royal centre (capital) and the market or commercial centre. The two royal centres of Kāñcīpuram and Madurai will be taken up for discussion in a later section dealing with royal centres. Our immediate concern here is with the market or commercial centres, i.e. *nagaram*, and as the royal centres were also commercial centres, they were inevitably a part of the expansion of the trade network in the subsequent centuries. In fact, the commerce of this period was organized around these two cities, and the few *nagarams* that are known from the Pallava-Pāṇḍya records were located only in certain key areas linking the capitals with the rich Kaveri basin and with the coast. The nodal points of such commercial links were at the confluence of rivers and in the delta areas, as seen in the case of Viriñcipuram (Seruvālaimangalam), Tirukkōyilūr (Kōvalūr), Tiruvadigai (Adirājamangalyapuram), and Tirukkaḻukkuṉṟam of the Pallava region and Karavandapuram (Ukkirankōṭṭai) and Mānavīrappaṭṭiṇam (Tiruchendūr) of the Pāṇḍya region. The ports of Māmallapuram, a *mānagaram*, and Koṟkai served the Pallava and Pāṇḍya hinterlands respectively. The commercial importance of the Kaveri region upto the ninth century AD was clearly linked to the Pallava- Pāṇḍya regions and hence the *nagarams* of this region are relatively fewer, only two having been attested to by epigraphic evidence so far, i.e. Kumaramārttāṇḍapuram (Tirunāgēśvaram) and Ciṟṟambar oriented to the northern and southern regions respectively. The distribution of the *nagaram* in the seventh to ninth centuries would hence suggest that there existed no direct link between such market centres and their *kōṭṭam* or *nāḍu* in which they were situated, reflective of a town-hinterland relationship, i.e. in the manner in which the *nagaram* came to be linked to the *nāḍu* from the tenth century AD.[103] In other words, the exchange nexus was more oriented towards the commercial needs of the royal centres and less as a regular market for the immediate *nāḍu* or *kōṭṭam*.

The pattern clearly shows that regular marketing facilities became a pressing need from the early Cōḷa period for every *nāḍu*, and led to a spurt in commercial activity which henceforth brought the Tamil region into a larger network of inter-regional and overseas trade and, above all, to the evolution of a full time trading community, looking after the local exchange nexus, as well as participating in wider commerce. The *nagarattār*, i.e. members of the *nagaram*, thus came to be a generic term for all Tamil merchants, a name by which the Ceṭṭiyār community of the Nāṭṭukkōṭṭai region, i.e. Pudukkottai and Ramanathapuram districts, are known to this day.

The *nagaram* members sought validation within the existing institutional means, i.e. the temple, by participating in gift-giving and temple management functions. Their status was hardly different from that of the agricultural groups, for they were agriculturists now taking to trade. Yet, the *nagaram* represents the first 'secular' element in society, in so far as the membership of the *nagaram*, unlike that of the *sabhā* and *ūr*, was determined by a common profession.[104]

The *nagaram* organization assumed the character of a local body maintaining local markets, supervising the flow of goods, providing a regular link between *nāḍus* and itinerant traders, thus breaking the insularity of the *nāḍu* (if it continued to exist under the Cōḷas) and its ties of kinship. Two institutions which thus brought the *nāḍus* closer together in a system of unified political organization and economic exchange were the *brahmadeya* and *nagaram*, both of which were used as interdependent agents of political synthesis under the Cōḷas.

The emergence of market centres for all the agrarian regions, and a commercial network linking the four major *maṇḍalams* or sub-regions known from Cōḷa records, coincided with the rise of the Cōḷas, and the proliferation of the *nagaram* kept pace with the expansion of Cōḷa power. The distribution pattern of *nagaram* in the early, middle and late Cōḷa phases shows a remarkable increase in the middle phase, not only within the Tamil country but also beyond its cultural frontiers, i.e. in the southern Karnataka and the Andhra region, over which Cōḷa power extended in the eleventh century AD. The areas giving access to the powerful neighbouring kingdom in Karnataka, i.e. Kongu region and Gangavāḍi, show a conspicuous increase in *nagaram* centres. In consolidating their conquests the Cōḷas not merely renamed the conquered areas, as for example, Gangavāḍi into Muḍikonda-Cōḷamaṇḍalam, but also founded new *nagaram* centres like Muḍikoṇḍacōḷapuram (Coimbatore district-Kongu region) and Nigarilicōḷapuram (Mālūr-paṭna in Mysore). This was a practice followed by the Cōḷas after every territorial conquest, as seen in case of Rājēndracōḷapuram in the Tirunelveli district after the conquest of the Pāṇḍya region, the eleventh century being a period of the constant movement of Cōḷa troops into the neighbouring kingdoms of the south and of Karnataka and Andhra. The *nagaram* thus established crucial inter-regional links and, as a result, acquired enhanced political influence. This is further corroborated by the reference to Tamils holding ranks of officers, administrators, trustees and managers of temples, apart from merchants, artisans and craftsmen residing in various centres in Karnataka, in addition to settlements of Tiguḷas (Tamils) as far north as Belgaum district in the eleventh to thirteenth centuries AD.[105]

A marginal increase in *nagaram* under the late Cōḷas, and the rise of new ones in the Pāṇḍya region after Cōḷa decline and re-emergence of Pāṇḍya power in the thirteenth century AD, demonstrate the importance of royal or political support to the commercial organizations and their activities. Medieval kingship was certainly not a mere ritual or *dharmic* sovereignty, nor did it preside over a segmentary power structure, when viewed in the context of political and commercial expansion. Resource mobilization, at least under the Cōḷas, whose power structure and territorial authority were more stable than any other medieval South Indian dynasty, was carried out under the aegis of the ruling family and its government.

A second important development in the middle Cōḷa period took place within the *nagaram* organization in the form of a further diversification in trading activities due to specialization in marketing and trade. There now appeared specialists like the *Sāliya nagaram* for trading in textiles, *Sāttum Pariśaṭṭa nagaram* also specializing in textile trade, and *Śankarappāḍi nagaram* as suppliers of oil and ghee, whose activities were, however, confined to specific localities of commercial importance. The *Pāraga nagaram* was another group representing seafaring merchants, who are seen only in areas marking the trans-peninsular routes. In contrast, the *Vāṇiya nagaram* refers to a larger organization of oil-mongers which originated in the Tamil country around the tenth century and became a supra-local trading organization, similar to the *Teliki* of Andhra region, which arose in the eleventh century AD. The *Vāṇiya nagaram* spread out by entering into the inter-regional commercial network, acquiring a viable economic status by the twelfth and thirteenth centuries, so as to be included in important decision making processes involving the merchant community. Horse trading was another specialized occupation of merchants from Malaimaṇḍalam (Kerala) throughout the medieval period. Arab trade in horses was conducted mainly through the western ports, and the *Kudirai ceṭṭis* of Kerala procured and transported them to the Cōḷa country and often acquired residential quarters within the Cōḷa heartland and other areas, like the commercially viable Pudukkottai region, linking the Cōḷa land with Toṇḍi on the eastern coast. The movement of traders individually and collectively over long distances within the Tamil country and between the Tamil country and Kerala, Karnataka and Andhra region, represents the continuation of a long tradition of trading in South India, but the frequency with which references to such traders occur in the Cōḷa records would show that this had become a regular phenomenon due to the demands of external trade, of which spices, aromatics, incense, horses, gems and textiles were the most important items.

The impetus to organized commerce came not only from the revival of peninsular trade but, more importantly, as a part of the revival and expansion of South Asian trade from the tenth century AD, involving the South Asian and Southeast Asian kingdoms and China. Together with the *nagaram* network, the emergence of merchant organizations to look after the long-distance trade proved to be a major factor of urbanization in the eleventh to thirteenth centuries, furthering the process which began in the tenth century AD.[106]

Organized commerce is one of the more important but less understood areas of economic activity in medieval South India, in which corporate trading communities like the *Ayyāvoḷe* and *Nānādeśi* participated. These communities are often described as guilds, although indisputable evidence of their organization into a well-defined, structured and cohesive body is hard to find. The use of the term 'guild' is hence a matter of convenience, rather than for establishing parallels with the medieval European guilds, the Hang of China in Sung and Yuan times, or the Karimi of Egypt. In their own inscriptional records, they are described as a *samaya*, i.e. a convention or organization born out of an agreement or contract, and their code of conduct was the *baṇañju dharma*, a conventional set of rules and regulations.[107]

The organizational aspects of these merchant bodies have been inadequately understood due to the inconsistent descriptions and terminology used to denote them. The occurrence of a number of non-merchant groups like craftsmen, agricultural groups and militant groups jointly in the guild records, especially in the twelfth and thirteenth centuries, have added an element of confusion and complexity to their activities. The presence of local bodies like the *nagarams* and lesser organizations like the *Maṇigrāmam* and *Añjuvaṇṇam*, may also be said to increase the complexity, as it is not easy to determine their individual and collective roles in commercial activities, due to the overlapping spheres of interests.

The obscurity and confusion caused by such overlapping interests implied in their records would disappear, once the context, regional and economic, in which they occur is elucidated. An attempt in this direction has helped, to a great extent, in distinguishing the nature and functioning of these bodies. The inadequacy of all the earlier studies on these guilds is attributable to their failure to recognize the exact relationship of the supralocal to the local bodies and their role in the respective areas. One of the ways in which this may be achieved is to discuss them in the sequential order in which they emerged, and their increasing socio-economic functions and institutional importance *vis-à-vis* other socio-political groups and the state.

As the whole corpus of information on South Indian trade at this time centres round the body, variously called the *Ayyāvoḷe* Five Hundred, the *Aiññūṟṟuvar* (Five Hundred), the *Nānādeśi* and *Valañjīyar*, it would be appropriate to start from the Five Hundred and proceed to enquire into the nature of their organization and relationship with other bodies.

The Five Hundred, which originated in Aihoḷe in the Bijapur district of Karnataka in the eighth century AD, was the largest organization of itinerant merchants of a supra-regional character. They are easily distinguishable from the *Maṇigrāmam* of the Tamil country, a merchant organization operating within specific regions, as the designations 'Uṟaiyūr Maṇigrāmam' and 'Koḍumbāḷūr Maṇigrāmam' and the distribution of their inscriptional references would show. The *Maṇigrāmam* established long-distance trade links early in their history, but subsequently improved them through interaction with the Five Hundred or the moving trade carried on by the Five Hundred in their regions. The *Maṇigrāmam* was apparently a descendent of the group of traders from Vaṇika-grāma in Kāvērippūmpaṭṭiṇam, who, after the decline of external trade in the early period, moved into the interior to places like Uṟaiyūr and Koḍumbāḷūr, where they re-emerged as *Maṇigrāmam*, an organized group of traders, by the ninth century AD. The *Maṇigrāmam*, like the *nagaram*, retained its unified composition and character, as it was also a part of the local agricultural communities which branched out into the trading profession by controlling the local exchange nexus throughout the period. It is an interesting contrast to note that in early medieval Rajasthan, there emerged a number of merchant families who were either resurgent local merchant lineages or new ones, which established wide intra-regional and inter-regional networks. Their names were derived from the places of their origin, such as the *Uesavāla-jñātiya*, the latter day Oswals.[108]

Another body of merchants known as the *Añjuvaṇṇam* represented an organization of foreign merchants, who began their commercial activities on the west coast (Kerala) in the eighth and ninth centuries and spread out to the other coastal areas of South India by the eleventh century AD, interacting both with the local merchants and the Five Hundred, a symbiotic relationship being fostered by trade interests. The earliest known record of the *Añjuvaṇṇam* refers to a group of Jewish traders who acquired settlements on the west coast from the Veṇāḍ (South Travancore) rulers. The term *Añjuvaṇṇam*, wrongly interpreted as a group of five different communities or castes, may well be derived from *Añjuman*, perhaps first used by early Arab Muslim traders of the west coast, a name surviving down to the fourteenth and fifteenth centuries on the Kanara coast among Muslim traders as *Hañjumāna*.

The founding of the *Ayyāvoḷe* (The Five Hundred) in the eighth century AD, may be attributed to a decision of the 500 *mahājanas* of the *mahāgrahāra* of Aihoḷe, to provide an institutional base for the commerce of this region. The organization later expanded its activities to other parts of South India. It would be erroneous, therefore, to assume as Kenneth Hall has done, that this organization originated as groups of expeditionary merchants, who serviced less wealthy or isolated communities of the hinterland and found it profitable to band together for mutual protection, and subsequently became powerful merchant organizations. On the contrary, many of the militant groups which accompanied the Five Hundred as protectors of merchandise, may themselves have been absorbed as part of the organization with a stake in the share of the profit. Its origin in Karnataka may also be seen as a survival of the early historical tradition of merchant guilds, which dominated the commerce of the Deccan, a surmise which is further strengthened by the reference to Aihoḷe as Āryapura and Ahicchatra, thus tracing their origin to Ahicchatra in the Ganges valley, which was a major trading centre in the closing centuries of the first millennium BC and beginning of the Christian era. However, the organization did not remain a single unified body, nor was Aihoḷe its permanent headquarters. The number, Five Hundred, also became conventional, for the name was derived from the parent organization and remained so for the rest of its history, despite the fact that it became a much larger one, drawing its members from various regions and communities. It is in this context that the term *Nānādeśi*, *Ubhaya Nānādeśi* (*svadeśi* and *paradeśi* merchants) have been used almost inter-changeably in their records. The most comprehensive term used for them in Tamil inscriptions is *Nānādeśiya Tiśai Āyirattu Aiññūṟṟuvar*, meaning literally 'The Five Hundred of different countries from thousand directions'. The *Valañjīyar* (*Baṇajigas* = traders) and *Vīra Valañjīyar*, also denote the same organization, but the emphasis in these terms is on their militant character. The *Vēḷaikkāra* group associated with the *Valañjīyar*, especially in Sri Lanka, forms another militant component in this organization. The heterogeneous composition of this organization is attested to clearly in the guild inscriptions, which refer to the different castes of the members, as well as regional and religious associations. Thus, it was a group of people of 'disparate origins associating together for a common purpose', i.e. trade.

With the growth of regional kingdoms, the need to protect regional interests probably led to a bifurcation of guild operations as seen in Karnataka and Tamil Nadu. Yet, the commonality of interests in which it was rooted, generally helped to maintain the larger unity of the guild. The impressive *praśastis* of the guild inscriptions show that it was growing into a powerful organization. Thus arose in South Karnataka, several towns called the southern *Ayyāvoḷe*, in the eleventh and twelfth centuries, especially after the Cōḷa intrusions into these areas. Into the Andhra region, the organization moved evidently in the wake of Cōḷa conquests, and after the unification of Vengi with the Cōḷa kingdom under Kulōttunga I (1070–1120). From its first appearance in the Pudukkottai region in the close of the ninth century, the Five Hundred fanned out into other parts of the Tamil country, covering the Cōḷa and Pāṇḍya heartlands and areas connecting the two, as well as those routes connecting the Tamil region with Karnataka, moving in wherever the Cōḷas stepped in as conquerors, i.e. Kongu and Ganga regions, Andhra and Sri Lanka. They controlled the movement of trade in these areas from important centres of operation like Muḍikoṇḍān, Taḷakkāḍu, Viśākhapaṭṭiṇam and Polonnaruva, respectively. It was in the link area of Pudukkottai and Ramanathapuram that the greatest concentration of guild inscriptions occurs between the tenth and fourteenth centuries. Here, their interaction with the *nagaram* and *Maṇigrāmam* organizations was considerably promoted by the Irukkuvēḷ chiefs of Koḍumbāḷūr, the Cōḷa subordinates of the tenth and eleventh centuries AD.

The close identity of interests between this organization and the Cōḷas is particularly seen in the royal policy of encouragement to overseas trade through trade missions, maritime expeditions and abolition of tolls, opening up new avenues of trade through conscious royal effort, which itinerant trade never failed to make use of. In this context, the presence in Nāgappaṭṭiṇam of Śrī Vijaya agents making gifts to the local temples, and the erection of the Buddhist *vihāra* by a Śrī Vijaya ruler for the *Thēravāda* Buddhists, may be seen as a major example of inter-regional commercial ventures being legitimized by religious grants by the respective ruling families through their political and commercial agents. By far the most significant step in this direction was the institution of royal charters setting up protected mercantile towns called *eṟivīrappaṭṭaṇas* from the eleventh century onwards, on trade routes as well as in areas of settled agriculture. A comparative study of the *baṇañju-paṭṭaṇas* of Karnataka and Andhra regions with *eṟivīrappaṭṭaṇas* shows that the nature of these towns was different from the *baṇañju-paṭṭaṇas*, in which the administration of the town was carried on by a *paṭṭaṇasvāmi*, 'lord of the town', with the help of merchant bodies and other local non-commercial groups. *Eṟivīrappaṭṭaṇas* were more in the nature of protected towns for stocking merchandise, and could well have been distribution points protected collectively by the merchant body. This merchant organization also had temporary or permanent residential quarters in several places falling within the trade network. A significant contrast is, however, seen in the royal centres or *mānagarams* like Tañjāvūr, Kāñcīpuram and Paḻaiyāṟai, where the itinerant merchant body is conspicuously absent, and where the local *nagaram* organizations wielded enormous influence over the exchange nexus. Similarly, the merchant bodies are not seen in Cōḻa ports like Nāgappaṭṭiṇam, which were not only developed by the rulers but also directly controlled by Cōḻa officers and agents. On the contrary, they were active in ports like Viśākhapaṭṭiṇam and Toṇḍi and also Mayilāppūr (part of Madras city), which were not 'royal' ports. In fact, itinerant merchants are seen to be frequenting the coastal route and ports more consistently during the period of Cōḻa decline and after. The emergence of a number of coastal towns, perhaps as halting stations, both on a coastal land route as well as coastal shipping, was a result of this movement.

In the thirteenth and fourteenth centuries, there was a phenomenal increase in guild activities, with a clear tendency on the part of the Five Hundred to expand its sphere of influence and to show less reliance on royal support and patronage, although some of the guild inscriptions were still dated in the reign periods of the late Cōḻa and Pāṇḍya rulers. We have rather impressive evidence that in most centres of distribution and emporia like Pirānmalai, Tirumalai and Toṇḍi, the Five Hundred acted jointly with other organizations like the *Cittiramēḻi Periya Nāḍu* or *Padineṇ Viṣaya*, in the levy of *maganmai* (voluntary contribution) and *paṭṭanappagudi* (tolls or shares of the town) on merchandise. It should be noted, however, that in the elaborate *praśastis* of these inscriptions, the pride of place is given to the *Cittiramēḻi* (meaning the beautiful plough) followed by the Five Hundred. The institutionalization of these two organizations through their joint donations to various temples, and the presence of other bodies like the *Maṇigrāmam*, *Sāmanta Paṇḍasālis* (stockists) and *nagaram* on such occasions, are a conspicuous feature of the thirteenth and fourteenth centuries, marking the decline of the Cōḷa power and the relative weakness of the re-emerging Pāṇḍyas. However, it would appear that the merchant body had on no occasion the authority to levy and grant such tolls, except in conjunction with the *Cittiramēḻi* and *Pandineṇ Viṣaya*, which were organizations of agriculturists controlling production and movement of agricultural goods. Presumably, even in the assignment of brokerage (*taragu*) or monopoly (*valañjiyattil-taniccеṭṭu*) to individuals or groups of traders on certain items, the Five Hundred exercised its authority only jointly with the local *nāḍu*, *nagaram* and the larger *Cittiramēḻi* organizations. This is so even in Karnataka and Andhra regions, where the *okkalu* and *kāmpulu* are constantly present on such occasions, when cesses or tolls were levied or trading rights were assigned. Yet it is undeniable that this organization had become powerful and some of its members were elevated to the status of *samaya cakravarti* (the king/emperor of the trading organization). This, and the increasing influence of individual members who assumed the title of *cakravarti*, as seen in Muṭṭam (Pērūr in Coimbatore district) and in Pirānmalai (Ramanathapuram District), would indicate an impending change caused by the accumulation of wealth and power in the hands of individual merchants, subsequently leading to the emergence of merchant entrepreneurs.

The *Cittiramēḻi Periya Nāḍu* was an organization of agriculturists[109] appearing quite early in Cōḷa history, in the latter half of the eleventh century AD, in Tāmaraippākkam (North Arcot district) known as the Rājēndracōḷa *Cittiramēḻi Perukkāḷar*.[110] The commercial links that they established with the Five Hundred by the twelfth century AD have been referred to earlier. Their association would indicate the growing consumption of food grains and pulses etc. in urban areas, enhancing the importance of the agricultural classes, which alone could mobilize grain and other such products for supply to the itinerant traders at the centres of distribution. Like the Five Hundred, the *Cittiramēḷi* also moved into the South Karnataka and Andhra regions by the twelfth century AD following the Cōḻa conquests. They are referred to as *Mēḷi Sāsiravaru* in Karnataka and *Meḍikūru* in Andhra.[111] The attempt to compare the *kāmpulu* of Andhra and *okkalu* of Karnataka with the *Cittiramēḷi*, does not appear to have any validity, for the *kāmpulu* and *okkalu* were local organizations of cultivators, whereas the *Cittiramēḷi* was of supra-local character.

The Five Hundred and *Cittiramēḷi* were not caste guilds, for they were composed of representatives of all the four castes.[112] Thus we see in both these guilds, an association which was based on occupation, cutting across caste and religious affiliations. The early inscriptions of the Five Hundred in the Pudukkottai region provide clear evidence of the domination of this organization by the Jains,[113] as in Karnataka, while later records indicate that it came to include members from all castes and religions, although the guild deity was called 'Aiyapoḷil Parameśvari'. The *Cittiramēḷi praśasti*[114] is a rather illuminating record, as it refers to the members as *bhūmiputras* (sons of the earth goddess or sons of the soil) whose prosperity is attributed to cow's milk (living by cow's milk) and whose profession, the best in the world, was looking after (feeding) the people of the country. It would appear that here we have the first indication of the pastoral-cum-agricultural origins of the organization which took to trading in agricultural commodities.

As seen earlier, these organizations, originating at different points of time and in different cultural regions, acted only in their independent capacity, enacting roles of patronage due to their economic importance. The *Cittiramēḷi* however, had a greater stake in local relations of dominance, as it acted also in the capacity of dispenser of justice, settling disputes over land rights and cases of criminal offence.[115] The right of fixing cesses and tolls was, however, exercised by them only jointly with the Five Hundred, and only towards the end of the Cōḷa period. Among the other organizations which were also involved in such decision-making processes were the *Sāmanta Paṇḍasālis* and *Añjuvaṇṇam*, who were significantly confined to the ports, and may have participated only in assigning tolls on imports and exports, with which they were directly concerned. Their common eulogy in the guild inscriptions is the first known expression of the ascendancy of trading groups in a predominantly agrarian context. The changing pattern of land ownership in the twelfth and thirteenth centuries also provides an index of the influence wielded by various merchant groups and the weavers, aspiring for a higher social status through acquisition of rights in land and participation in gift giving and temple building activities.

There is one other sphere in which the merchant organization assumed a dominant role, i.e. in relation to craft groups. This is much more directly recorded in the guild inscriptions of Karnataka and Andhra[116] than in Tamil Nadu. The closer interaction between the two interdependent sections of the commercial world in these two regions may be traced back to the early historical phase of urbanism. In the early medieval period they were increasingly brought together when the manufacture of goods and production for market came under merchant control through collective investments. A similar development is perhaps indicated in the Tamil region even as early as the eleventh century AD, when, in a slightly different context, the dependence of the craftsmen on the merchant organization is underlined in the role of the merchants providing an asylum to the craftsmen in Erode[117] in the Kongu region which, from the early historical period, had been an area of craft production. In such areas the merchants also acted as protectors and managers of temples, as for example in Muḍikoṇḍān.

The presence of craft groups with the Five Hundred could also have provided a certain legitimacy to the *Ayyāvoḷe*'s trade in various articles. This is particularly important in the case of weavers, with whom they appear to have established a close link, for the textile trade was handled practically throughout South India and overseas by the Five Hundred. Sometimes *Cīlai ceṭṭis* and *Sāliya nagarattār* (weaver-cum-traders?) themselves took to trading in textiles, especially as this was one of the most important items of trade, having an increasing demand in an ever widening market.

The guild inscriptions refer to a large number of countries traversed by the merchants, including regions outside South India. Their presence in Siam, Sumatra and Burma is attested to by the inscriptions in Takua Pa, Loboe Tiwa and other places. The guild inscriptions also refer to the area of their operation as covering 18 *paṭṭiṇas* (emporia), 32 *vaḷarpurams* (growing markets), and 64 *kaḍigattāvaḷam* (periodic fairs). While the numbers may be treated as conventional, references are available to a number of towns falling in these three categories, although their identification is rendered extremely difficult due to changes in place names or the possibility that many of them declined and, hence, are not recorded in present day reports.[118]

All the economic development outlined above brought about an important innovation in societal organization, which helped to accommodate the craft groups and artisans, as well as lower categories of agricultural workers within the vertical division of the Right and Left Hand castes (*Valangai* and *Iḍangai*). This was a root paradigm[119] for social division of all the non-*brāhmaṇa* and non-*vēḷāḷa* occupational groups and other tribal elements brought in as agricultural workers and menial service men. The improvement in the economic status of some of these castes, especially the weavers, produced rivalry for social mobility and enhanced ritual status. This is expressed in their attempts to be upgraded within this paradigm from the left hand (lower) to the right hand (higher) status groups. It is against this background that frequent occasions of conferring special privileges on the artisan communities (the *anuloma rathakāras* and *kammāḷas*)[120] by the merchant organizations, temple authorities and local chiefs have to be viewed.

The major factors in the urbanization of the eleventh to thirteenth centuries, described as 'temple urbanization',[121] were thus provided by organized commerce through the *nagaram*, the Five Hundred, the *Cittirameḷi* and other merchant bodies, crafts organizations, initially of a local nature (and later of a supra-local nature from the fourteenth century AD), and a tripartite social stratification (*brāhmaṇa*, *vēḷāḷa* and the Right and Left hand castes). The context in which these features are highly visible was provided by multiple-temple centres, single large temple centres, some of which were also pilgrimage centres, and finally, the royal centres. It may also be noted that many of these socio-economic groups were accommodated in the *tirumaḍaiviḷāgam*[122] of the temple centres in acknowledgement of their economic importance. This is especially so in the case of weavers (-cum-traders) who were economically more powerful than the others.

Assessing the impact of money on the commercial organization and the nature of urbanism in this period is one of the most vexing problems confronting numismatic studies. Available numismatic data is perhaps the least capable of providing clues to the degree and effect of monetization, despite the fact that a fair number of Cōḷa coins in gold and copper and a few in silver are known and inscriptional references to coins are fairly numerous. In the centuries before the rise of the Cōḷas, the evidence of money as a medium of exchange is hardly available. The Pāṇḍya region seems to have used Arab money along with a dynastic issue, of which very few specimens have survived. Money was used sporadically and as one medium of exchange based on equivalence with paddy.[123]

Under the Cōḷas, the currency was 'not based on any uniform groups of coins with fixed ratios between different denominations and metals'.[124] The problems in the study of Cōḷa and Pāṇḍya coins have been succinctly stated in several studies on South Indian coins. Paddy seems to have been the overall basis of an exchange system, in which coins were used at various levels with purely local forms of equivalence. Presumably, the *nagaram* and itinerant trade brought money into more frequent use, but despite the references to money gifts to temples, to cesses being paid in cash, and land prices determined in terms of money in the late Cōḷa period, no useful analysis of the monetary system can be made at the present state of numismatic studies. On the whole, monetization in the pre-Vijayanagar period was on a low key, and hence its impact on urbanization is difficult to assess.

The processes outlined above fall into two distinct phases. The end of the Pallava-Pāṇḍya period, i.e. mid-ninth century AD, would represent one level of 'systemic integration', and the end of the Cōḷa period another, the transmutation of these levels involving changes in the structure and patterning of society.[125] The *brahmadeya* and the temple in the first phase, with their *sabhā* and *ūr* and the temple in the second phase, with the *nagaram* in addition to the *sabhā* and *ūr*, are the chief instruments which helped in the restructuring of society. The *nagaram* network and the intersection points of the *nagaram* and itinerant trade conducted the intra-regional and inter-regional commerce, resulting in the emergence of several urban centres of different degrees of importance, with temples as their nuclei. They also brought together the royal/political centres and the ports that were consciously developed by royal policy into a tight economic and political web.

III

The above discussion of the processes of urbanization in early medieval South India has led us to a rather inconclusive state, namely that no single autonomous, causative factor can be identified in the nexus of social, economic and political transformations which resulted in the emergence of urban forms.[126] It has also led us to a final question, namely, what was the one curiously persistent factor which seems to permeate all activities, all institutional change and afford a 'consensual focus for social life', rural or urban, that which commands a sort of priority? The answer would seem to be that it was the act of validation through an ideology in order to achieve institutional permanence and socio-political dominance. Such an ideology, for early medieval South India, was provided by the concept of *bhakti*, or devotion, and the instrument of authority through which it was expressed was the temple. One may see this ideology and the power structure it sustained as the determinants in the ultimate character of the city and in the 'specific complexes of domination', which the cities 'restlessly express'.[127]

Our study of a major urban complex of the Cōḷa period, *viz.*, Kuḍamūkku-Paḻaiyāṟai, has shown that even where trade and commercial activities were major factors, the presence of religious institutions was a necessary concomitant of the urban process.[128] Writing on the economy of Kāñcīpuram in the same period, Kenneth R. Hall and George W. Spencer not only called it a sacred centre, but also reached a similar conclusion that Kāñcīpuram's economy did not function in isolation from *political and religious* institutions (emphasis added), or from the values of the Hindu tradition '. . . the city's eminence as a religious and political centre enhanced its commercial prestige and rendered its continued prosperity a matter of importance to its Pallava and Cōḷa suzerains–for as long as they lasted.'[129] Both these conclusions point to the need for understanding the role of religious ideology in providing an instrument for the creation of 'effective space' for urban forms and in determining the nature of the city and its role as the focus of change.

In the early phase of urbanization, we pointed out the absence of a dominant or formal religion, either in helping to evolve the institution of kingship and a coercive apparatus for taxation, or in producing bases of support to an exchange network, although the stimulus for urban growth was present in the form of maritime trade. In the early period, the person of the Sangam chief/king was the object of adulation–a glorious hero whose authority was based on bravery, success in tribal conflict and generosity to kinsmen. Ideas relating to physical power, energy and stature provided the necessary symbols for super-human power which temporal beings invoked for the exercise of power. Hence the comparisons with tribal deities of super-human valour and stature. In the later period, it was more the office of the king that came to be venerated and hence equated with the divine in medieval monarchy. God became the transcendental reference point, and the *brāhmaṇa* priests the agents of legitimizing temporal sovereignty through divine sanction and fabricated genealogies of divine descent.

It is not just fortuitous that the spread of the Purāṇic religion in the Tamil country coincided with the assumption of sovereignty by the Pallavas and Pāṇḍyas, and the practice of land grants to *brāhmaṇas* and temples started off that long process of agrarian development, followed by social and economic differentiation, generating urban forms. Thus, the control over the temple, the most important 'superordinate redistributive instrument', was in the hands of the *brāhmaṇas*, who through their *sabhā*, assumed the role of economic administrators. The creation of such *brahmadeyas* and temples was an act of validation by some form of divine authority for the *kṣatriyas* to give permanence to their power. This, in fact, led to the forging of a new instrument for the organization of sacred, economic, social and political space.

Purāṇic religion came to be established as the vehicle for propagating a 'cosmological world view'. It is an extremely difficult task to trace the processes through which this happened from the end of the Sangam to the beginning of the Pallava-Pāṇḍya period. Two spheres in which it may be traced are the acculturation of all local and popular folk traditions of worship, some of which were imposed on brāhmaṇism and not merely upgraded due to acculturation, like the *tiṇai* deities, and their absorption into the brahmanical religions of Vaiṣṇavism and Śaivism. Evidence of this process comes from the invocatory verses added to the early Tamil classics, not earlier than the eighth and ninth centuries AD, when the tradition of the Sangam itself and the collection of the verses were systematized.[130] It is only among the later strata of literature like the *Paripāṭal* and the *Tirumurukāṟṟuppaṭai*, composed long after the *akam* and *puṟam* poetry, that the universalization of the two deities Māl (Viṣṇu) and Murukan (Subrahmaṇya) can be recognized, i.e. the first traces of a formalized religion with the temple as its locus. The temple-religion of Viṣṇu was propagated first by the early *āḻvārs* (sixth and seventh centuries AD) through the intensely personal devotional cult of *bhakti*, the central theme of which was the transcendental role of religion and central preoccupation, the attainment of salvation or release (*mokṣa*). The *bhakti* ideology assisted in the process of enhancing the power of both the divine and the human sovereigns through the symbolism of the cosmos/temple/territory.[131]

The concept of *bhakti* acted in two distinct ways in establishing the brahmanical temple as the pivot of the enactment of the various roles of society. One was by countering the increasing influence of the 'heterodox' religions of Buddhism and Jainism, leading to their ultimate decline or subordination.[132] The symbol of royal conversion was central to this conflict. In fact, Jainism, which was more widespread in this region than Buddhism, became as much a part of the Purāṇic religion and temple-based cult as the brahmanical Vaiṣṇavism and Śaivism were. The other was more significant, *viz.*, that it induced messianic expectations among the lower orders of the *varṇa*-based society through the ideal of salvation. In fact, it is possible to show that the *bhakti* ideal emanated in a context of social differentiation, where conflicts centered round such differentiation and social dominance, as, for example, in Kāñcī and Madurai.

The *bhakti* ideology contained in itself the seeds of sectarianism. Although initially *bhakti*, as introduced in its simple form of devotion in the hymns of the *ālvārs*, helped in the propagation of Vaiṣṇavism, it soon changed into a tool of sectarian rivalry as it was perceived in Śaivism. Through the *bhakti* ideal the latter became a more efficacious instrument of acculturation for acquiring a wider popular base in the hands of the Śaiva *nāyanārs* and, subsequently, because of the royal patrons, i.e. the Cōḷas, who developed its propensities systematically. The worship of the *linga*, as the royal cult of the Cōḷas, was of central importance in this acculturation.

The *bhakti* ideology, with its messianic appeal, also became amplified into an ethical (moral) system capable of sanctioning and integrating new values (which the old norms could not provide) into a coherent and viable synthesis. Correspondingly, this led to the expansion of the temple's role as the innovative focus for restructuring society, and facilitating the advance of those branches of knowledge concerned with ritual display, i.e. science of architecture, sculpture, painting and allied arts and crafts–in short, iconography.

A discussion of the measures through which the Cōḷas adopted, elaborated and zealously practised this ideology need not detain us here, because it has been the theme of many studies on the Cōḷas and the religious history of this period. More important for our purposes is the direct relation that such a patronage had to the evolution of their power structure and the royal city. This is seen in their direct sponsorship of the stupendous projects of erecting the two distinctive *drāviḍa* style temples in Tañjāvūr and Gangaikoṇḍacōḷapuram, as an act of deliberate royal policy in creating a royal centre, in imitation of the *bhakti* or sacred centre 'sung' by the hymnists. Through these temples Rājarāja I (985-1014) and Rājēndra I (1012-1044) invoked the temple's superordinate integrative role in order to create, as it were, a ceremonial city, the symbol of a centralizing power.

The focus of political and economic power had shifted conspicuously even under the late Pallavas and early Cōḷas from the *brahmadeya* to the temple. The Pallavas and Pāṇḍyas initiated the art of temple-building for Purāṇic religion. But it was the Cōḷas who gave permanence to all cult centres, replicating the temple's central role in each one of them, through a systematic renovation in stone of old shrines and construction of new ones.[133] The major temple projects were meant, however, only for the royal/ceremonial centres. The paraphernalia of the medieval temple mirrored the royal court. Royal servants and temple servants, the *taḷip-parivāram* and the officials *kōyiṟṟamar* were identically perceived and had identical duties. Above all, the temple idol was taken out in procession for the benefit of the devotees and the king's procession, which followed the same path, was meant for the adulation of his people. The *ulā* literature, eulogising the deity as well as the king, which developed as a *genre* of Tamil poetry under the Cōḷas, was meant to establish this identity.[134] This almost total identity is comparable to the cult of the *dēvarāja*, which was of great importance to the medieval kingdoms of Southeast Asia. In contrast, the medieval ruler of Orissa surrendered his sovereignty to god Jagannatha of Puri, and the late medieval kings of South Travancore ruled as representatives of god Padmanābha of Tiruvanantapuram.

The subtle interplay of the social, economic, religious and political roles of these institutions is elusive and hard to interpret in empirical terms, unless the contextual evidence is brought to the fore constantly. It may, perhaps, be done with a certain degree of efficiency in the case of the Cōḷa royal centre, and there can be no better example of it than Tañjāvūr.

Tañjāvūr, which is located on the southern bank of the Vaḍavāṟu (a distributary of the Veṇṇāṟu, itself branching off from the Kaveri), stands at the south-western extremity of the

Kaveri delta, just as the second royal centre of Gangaikoṇḍa-cōḷapuram stands on the northern edge of the Kaveri delta beyond the Koḷḷiḍam river (Coleroon). It commanded access to the delta region, the perennial resource base of the Cōḷas, thus affording protection to it, as Gangaikoṇḍacōḷapuram did from the north. At the time of its capture by Vijayālaya in the middle of ninth century AD, Tañjai was not more than the centre of a few scattered village settlements under the Muttaraiyar. Its occupation was, therefore, dictated by geographical (location) and strategic considerations. There is no reference to Tañjai as the seat of the Cōḷa royal family in any other source except the Cōḷa copper plates, till it suddenly blossomed into a huge temple town under Rājarāja I, whose monumental project created the most prestigious temple of the *drāviḍa* style of architecture. Henceforth, Tañjāvūr became the royal centre on which Rājarāja and his family bestowed lavish attention.

The city[135] consisted of an internal circuit around the temple (*uḷḷālai*) and an outer circuit of residential quarters (*puṟambaḍi*), the former meant for the residences of the priestly, administrative and other elite groups and the latter for other professional and service groups, including the two *nagaram* organizations. Most of these quarters were named after the king and other royal members whose retinues lived there.

Royal efforts to 'create' this city are recorded on the temple walls. Over 600 employees were requisitioned for the temple from villages and towns all over the Cōḷa kingdom, including the peripheral Pāṇḍya and Toṇḍaimaṇḍalams. Within an estimated span of seven to eight years (though this estimate is questionable) for the construction of the temple, a veritable colonization of this centre took place, suggesting the 'implanting' of a royal centre with all its appendages, including a series of army contingents.[136]

The horizontal stratification of the residential areas is said to be a familiar picture of the 'so-called pre-industrial city'. In such a city 'there was a completely dominant central ceremonial complex carefully engineered to align the city with cosmic structures and forces. The rich and the powerful lived at the centre while the poor lived at the margins. The markets were neither central nor dominant but a product of the demands arising from the nucleation by the ceremonial centre'.[137]

The cosmic symbolism of the Tañjāvūr temple, i.e. the Rājarājeśvara, is revealed by its designation as the Dakṣiṇamēru (the southern *mēru* or mountain–the axis of the universe) and that of the deity Dakṣiṇamēru Viṭankar, a symbolism which also extended to the city as the centre of the territorial authority of the Cōḷas. This is also exemplified by the ritual consecration of the main shrine (*vimāna*) as well as the shrines of the regents of the eight quarters (*aṣta dikpālas*), situated at the cardinal points near the gates.[138] The city would thus seem to be organized in 'the earthly space to replicate and symbolize the order which pertained to the other world structure and this ensured survival and prosperity'.[139]

The economic outreach of the temple is impressive as it covered the whole Cōḷa kingdom, villages from all the *maṇḍalams*, Malaināḍu, Gangapāḍi and Nuḷambapāḍi, and even Īḻam (Sri Lanka) or Mummuḍicōḷamaṇḍalam, being assigned for its upkeep. The number of villages outside the Cōḷa country is relatively smaller. Nonetheless, the fact that revenues were to reach Tañjāvūr, both in paddy and cash, points to the direct control exercised over the peripheral regions, including northern Sri Lanka. So much for the politics of plunder and the segmentation of power. The *sabhās* of several villages were entrusted with the gold deposits of the temple, for payment of interest in the form of provisions, consumable and other articles for rituals and festivals, thus establishing a reciprocal outflow of resources for investment.

The peasantry, artisans and shepherds who supplied the ritual requirements lived in villages in the immediate vicinity of the city. The huge quantity of recorded livestock donated to the temple were entrusted to the shepherds for the supply of milk products. Movement into and out of Tañjāvūr was constant, as some farming activities still continued in the neighbourhood for the temple. The *nagaram* and itinerant traders (*Kongavāḷar angāḍi*) also conducted a brisk commerce, as is evident from the four markets (*angāḍis*) mentioned in the Tañjāvūr inscriptions.

The performance of plays (*Rājarājeśvara Nāṭaka*), festivals on the birth asterisms of the royal family, and similar occasions for which special endowments were made at the behest of the rulers, would also substantiate the inseparable nature of the sacred and secular spheres of interests. Although the Cōḷa palace was perhaps located at a place called Vallam, the ceremonial aspects of the city were centred round the temple. The royal processional path and that of the deity coincided outside the main enclosure.

The temple was made into a veritable treasure-house of arts, through its frescoes representing themes from the stories of the *bhakti* saints, bronze images of various deities and the *bhakti* saints and sculptures of rich iconographic content. Gangaikoṇḍacōḷapuram exhibits all these features to a remarkable degree, although the details of the city's organization are not available from its records.

These two royal centres, however, did not have sanctified *bhakti* shrines as their nuclei like the other Cōḷa cities, where the city grew around *bhakti* shrines, interspersed with which were the new shrines erected by the kings both for worship and as sepulchral monuments of royal members, as in Paḻaiyāṟai. Hence, the royal builders of these two temples had them sanctified by getting hymns composed in their praise by the royal preceptor.[140] This act points much more clearly to the need for a sacred association and nucleus for a new settlement, in this case the royal centre.

Madurai and Kāñcīpuram, two of the oldest cities of this region, also possess the characteristics of a ceremonial centre. However, their antecedents as royal centres may be traced back to the early historical phase. The poetic imagery of these two centres in the Sangam classics is rich and illustrative of the cosmic symbolism attributed to them from early times. Thus, Kacci (Kāñcī) is described as the pericarp of the lotus which issues from the navel of Viṣṇu and Tiraiyan, its ruler, is said to be of the lineage of Viṣṇu. In fact a Viṣṇu shrine (of the reclining form) is alluded to in the early poems as marking the centre of the city. Similarly, in Madurai stood the shrine of Kṛṣṇa in the heart of the town, which in the early poems is called Kūḍal (centre), where, according to conventional description, different quarters with tall buildings met.[141] The shrine is identified with the present Kūḍal Aḻagar temple located in the centre of the city. However, both these cities did not grow into huge complexes until the time of the Pallavas and the later Pāṇḍyas respectively. While Kāñcī developed into a dispersed ceremonial centre, Madurai assumed its present form only in the late medieval period under the *Nāyakas*, when fortifications were added to it and other cities like Tañjāvūr.

A comparative study of the royal/ceremonial centre of the above type with other cities of this period shows that all of them shared the ceremonial aspects to a great degree. However, historical differences provide them with certain traits, on the basis of which typological categories may be distinguished. Among these, Kuḍamūkku-Paḻaiyāṟai and Kāñcīpuram may be classified as multi-temple centres, evolving after centuries of growth from earlier agrarian clusters, each temple which marked their growth representing the locus of the ceremonial complex at different chronological points, thus leading to the emergence of dispersed ceremonial/sacred centres rather than compact ones.[142]

In such centres, the locus of the ceremonial complex shifted from one temple to another, depending upon that temple which was erected or patronized by a particular ruler to legitimate his sovereignty. A third type of urban centre is the sacred centre which originated and evolved around a single cult centre as a *tīrtha* or sacred spot, later assuming the character of pilgrimage centre. To this category may be assigned Chidambaram, Śrīrangam, Tiruvaṇṇāmalai and several other centres, where religion was the major factor in its urban character, which assured its permanence or continuity in a given cultural region. Chidambaram had the added prestige of being the centre of the royal coronation ceremony under the Cōḷas, for it was the most sacred temple (Kōyil) to the Śaivas, just as Śrīrangam was to the Vaiṣṇavas. These two latter types usually have a long history and pass through successive stages of growth.

Cōḷa attempts to develop the agricultural potential of the wet zones of the Tāmraparṇi valley, also brought into existence a fairly extensive urban complex with two new *brahmadeyas* such as Rājarājacaturvēdimangalam (Mannārkōyil) and Ceravanmahādevicaturvēdimangalam (Śērmādēvi) in *Muḷḷi nadu* in the Tirunelveli district. The developmental stages of this complex are attested to by the records of the eleventh and twelfth centuries AD.[143] Particularly important was Cēravanmahādēvi, in which Rājēndra I erected a palace for the Cōḷa-Pāṇḍya prince, who was appointed to govern the Pāṇḍya region conquered by the Cōḷas, and in which arrangements were made for settling 'hundreds' of families by giving them house sites.[144] Together with the *taṉiyūrs* like Madurāntakacaturvēdimangalam,[145] Tirukkaḻukkuṉṟam and others, these centres show a process of agglomeration of a series of settlements around them, similar to the agglomeration designated in tribal societies as sacred territories administrated by the priesthood. Actual physical agglomeration also means that 'citizenship, the crux of belonging, was defined by a specific religious territorial allegiance',[146] also creating a hierarchy based on a sacrally defined order.

None of these early medieval cities or towns were fortified in the sense of being protected by defensive walls, except for the high enclosures of the temple demarcating the sacred precincts.[147] For the role of ensuring safety and security of the people was 'not by walls against physical enemies', but was by religious rites and ritual magic 'against menaces of nature', the mediators between gods and men were the priests, and the communication system was mediated through worship and sacrifice (offering).

Thus, the *nagaram* and the itinerant merchant organizations were also accommodated in the expanding but effective space created by the temple centres. In physical terms, it was the *tirumaḍaiviḷāgam* around the temple, where separate quarters were assigned to the merchant and crafts groups. In south Indian urbanization, the *nagaram* was not a commercial city, i.e. the typology adopted by M.I. Finley for Greek cities.[148] Nor were the trade centres on the routes of itinerant merchants similar to the 'burgher' category of medieval Europe, in the sense of a separation between country and town. Hall and Spencer find many essential similarities in the merchant organizations of long-distance trade in South India and medieval Europe. But the main difference, they point out, lies in the absence of the conflicting burgher interests as against the episcopal or seigneurial authority, i.e. no weakening of relationships with the countryside, despite a separate group consciousness. This is attributed to the superordinate integrative character of the sacred centres like Kāñcīpuram.[149] In the medieval south

Indian context, all the emergent institutions and urban forms were merged into a single systemic relationship, for the commercial guilds were accommodated as a substantial component within the same structure, and had to seek validation 'within the norms of a traditional social order'. In effect, therefore, the network of *nagaram*, commercial centres and ports brought together into a tight economic and political web, the royal/ceremonial/sacred centres.

The question of dominance in all such centres would seem to be closely related to and clearly reflected in the evolution of large temple structures from the nucleus of a single shrine. Stylistically the most remarkable between the seventh and the eleventh centuries are the royal creations, particularly illustrated in the verticality of the *vimāna* (shrine), which reached its culmination under the middle Cōḷas (985–1044), together with the enclosures and the gateway (*gopura*). In a sense they represent the apex of the socio-political hierarchy. The fact that authority relationships changed during the twelfth and thirteenth centuries introduced a significant variation in the emphasis on temple architecture, which now shifted to the additional structures, leading to a horizontal magnification of the temple, i.e. structural expansion through a complex of shrines, pillared halls (*maṇḍapas*) within the enclosures, each marking a further stage in the participation of diverse groups in temple-building and gift-giving activities. The *tirumaḍaiviḷāgam* is also a case in point.

Architecturally, the second imposing structure is the *gopura*[150] which, even in the later period, was mainly the creation of ruling dynasties and their subordinate chieftains, whereas the inner spaces of the enclosures (*prākāra*) covered with smaller edifices were the handiwork of those powerful agricultural and commercial communities seeking validation.

Ceremonial centres are regarded as pre-eminent instruments of orthogenetic transformation.[151] The early medieval city in South India is an example of such transformation, and was evolved in a cultural matrix, of which it became at once the product and the symbol. This culture was itself reared by the state society that emerged under the Cōḷas. The Cōḷa state evolved through a steady process of integrating different sub-cultural zones or pre-existing lineage areas, and became conterminous with the Tamil macro-region, given the fluctuating cultural frontiers between the Tamil plains and the Deccan plateau and the less easily definable frontier separating the Tamil and Andhra plains, which is more a matter of historical than geographical differences. The city, therefore, to the contemporary Tamil world, albeit a limited geographical and cultural entity, was the one which intensely expressed or epitomized this culture and to which people were drawn by the symbols of its sacred and ceremonial functions.

IV

The thirteenth and fourteenth centuries would seem to mark a watershed in the urban history of South India. To understand how important this divide was and what rendered it so, one has to look at the evidence afresh to see what the new features of the urban landscape were, and what were the connections that one might have failed to see between these developments, and the changing pattern of power relationships that evolved under Vijayanagar. These changes may be seen as the next set of disjunctive processes in the urbanization of South India. The process began with the general trend towards militarization and fragmentation of political power. One aspect of major importance to the study of the role of merchant organization in the emergence of towns is the question whether merchants tended to fortify their settlements, both as a measure of safeguard against loss of merchandise, and as a centre of power and domination.[152] The earliest such fortified town attested to in the Tamil region was Karavandapuram (Ukkirankōṭṭai) in the Tirunelveli district, the home of a Vaidya family, which supplied ministers to the Pāṇḍyas of the eighth and ninth centuries AD. The erection of the fort is credited to an eighth century Pāṇḍya king, and the soldiers on guard at the ramparts are referred to in the tenth century inscriptions of Rājasimha (III), who built a big market (*pērangāḍi*) there and left it under the protection of the merchant guild—the *Ayyāvoḷe*. The temples of this settlement were also left in the charge of armed guards.[153] The practice of stationing armies to protect temples was followed in certain areas of importance like newly occupied zones and trade routes such as Tiruvālīśvaram in Tirunelveli district, in the eleventh century under the Cōḷas,[154] and Sangrāmanallūr in Coimbatore district, where the army was required to protect the temple premises.[155]

It is not clear whether the *eṛivīṛappaṭṭaṇas* were protected by defensive walls, for evidence on these settlements would merely indicate the presence of militant groups of the merchant bodies. The stocking of commodities (for sale or distribution) in places known as *cārigaikkōṭṭai* (literally Toll-fort), seems to have been a regular practice under the late Cōḷas and later Pāṇḍyas, as indicated by the Mannārguḍi (Tanjavur district) inscriptions referring to *maḍigais* (is it *maḷigai*?—grocery or provision stores).[156] The emergence of *cakravartis* among the merchants has been mentioned earlier, indicating a tendency on the part of some merchants in the thirteenth century to assume titles of superior status and influence. Interestingly, the increasing importance and power of the merchant bodies in the thirteenth century is also reflected, if not in the type of closed towns of western Europe, in the militarily protected (fortified) towns called *vīradaḷam* and *sūradaḷam*,[157] tending to intrude among the traditional power bases of the agrarian elite and chiefly families. Could this be taken to point to a new trend in the rise of urban power groups in the form of merchant entrepreneurs?

There is evidence of a general parcelling out of various regions under petty chiefs by the Pāṇḍyas, both as a measure of counteracting the increasing intrusion of the Hoysaḷas into the Tamil country, as well as promoting the overseas trade, which at this time continued to be on the increase. Thus were created a series of strongholds under Pāṇḍya subordinates near those centres where the Hoysaḷas had established military stations[158] or garrisons. Mali Fatan, the Pāṇḍya port of Dēvipaṭṭiṇam, was assigned to Abdur Rahman, their Muslim political and commercial agent, who was even permitted the kingly privilege of reading the *Khutba* in his name.[159] Interestingly, many of the Hoysaḷa military stations were centres where the merchant organizations, agricultural guild and their *cāraigaikkōṭṭais* with *maḍigais* were also located, suggesting that the line of Hoysaḷa stations had a definite commercial motive behind their establishment. The Vijayanagar militarization was apparently a continuation of the Pāṇḍya reaction to the Hoysaḷa intrusion, as well as a defensive measure against the new technology of defence and warfare brought in by the Muslim rulers. Another element of change was the rise of the monastic tradition among the Vaiṣṇavas and Śaivas with powerful lineages, which acquired control over temple administration and landed property in various strongholds of these two religions. This is traceable to an attempt on the part of both the sects to expand their social base through reforms, with the result that the northern Sanskritic tradition and the southern Tamil tradition created a schism among the Śrīvaiṣṇavas (Vaḍakalai and Teṇkalai) with their separate monastic lineages. The Śaivas established powerful non-*brāhmaṇa* lineages as custodians of the *Śaiva Siddhānta* canon, on the basis of the support from the *vēḷāḷas*, the merchant and weaver (*kaikkōḷa*) groups.

During the Vijayanagar period the mercantile community seems to have entered into new forms of contractual relationships, especially with the new loci of power, and eventually came to terms with the shift in the major centre of power to the Tungabhadra region in Karnataka under the Vijayanagar rulers. Craft organization strengthened itself by moving out of purely local contexts. The weaver communities, of which the *kaikkōḷas* displaced the *sāliyas* as the most influential group, now organized themselves into a *Mahānāḍu* of supra-local character, with its headquarters at Kāñcīpuram.[160] With the emergence of merchant entrepreneurs and master craftsmen favourable conditions for a new form of economic interdependence were created.[161]

Militarization of the state under Vijayanagar also brought into existence a new set of fortified urban centres of the subordinate *nāyaka* chiefs, generally on hills and in other older political or royal centres, which were now converted into a new kind of militarily viable fortified towns (Madurai and Tañjāvūr). Counterposed to them were the old temple and pilgrimage centres, where power relationships were still established through religious heads and monastic lineages. A new alliance was forged with powerful monastic heads, authority was shared but dominance remained strictly at the political level of the state, exemplified by its kingship. Some of the sacred centres became supra-regional pilgrimage centres (Tirupati, Tiruvaṇṇāmalai, Kāñcīpuram and Śrīrangam) where the question of dominance was resolved by the re-affirmation of the deity's supremacy, as evidenced by the *Sthalapurāṇas*.

The multiple loci of power and militarization, rending the fabric of the unitary culture of the Cōḷa period, left the old ideological apparatuses incapable of preventing the gradual secularization of political power, although the ceremonial/political centre still retained the traditional symbols of validation. Secularization first appears in the physical demarcation of the royal centre through special ramparts from the sacred complex, the sacred aspects of the earlier ideological tradition dominating the religious complex, and the ceremonial and military aspects of the new urban forms dominating the royal residential or administrative complex, as in Hampi.[162] It is also seen in the greater emphasis laid on ceremonies like *Mahānavami* centering round the royal person rather than the tutelary deity. The processes are not easy to discern, but the differentiation of political and religious authority is expressed through the increasing dependence of political power on a balance of forces between the secular and sacral leadership. The dichotomy was not between the rulers and ruled, for it was now replaced by a quadripartite division, in which cultural, religious and politico-military elites were opposed to lower rural (peasant) and urban (predominantly artisan and merchant) groups.[163] Hence the differentiation in sacred and secular domains.

The entry of the European companies with their joint stock formation introduced a further element of change in the seventeenth century AD, followed by colonialism, when the factory replaced the temple as the nucleus of a different type of urban centre in the coastal areas.

References

1. This is seen in the following works: P. Niyogi, *Contributions to the Economic History of Northern India: From the Tenth to the Twelfth Century* AD, Calcutta, 1962, chapter v on 'Towns and Town-planning'; K.C. Jain, *Ancient Cities and Towns of Rajasthan: A Study of Culture and Civilisation*, Delhi, 1972; O.P. Prasad, 'A Study of Towns in Karnataka on the Basis of Epigraphic Sources', *Indian History Congress (IHC) Proceedings of the 38th Session* (1977), 151-60 and 'Two Ancient Port Towns of Karnataka', *Indian History Congress (IHC) Proceedings of the 39th Session* (1978), 55-61. In works on economic history also a similar tendency is seen, e.g. G.R. Kuppuswamy, *Economic Conditions in Karnataka,* AD *973-*AD *1336*, Dharwar, 1975; as also in works on historical geography *see* P.K. Bhattacharya, *Historical Geography of Madhya Pradesh from Early Records*, Delhi, 1977. Some attempt at understanding the causative factors in urban growth in early Tamilakam is made by T.K. Venkatasubramanian *see* 'Growth of Urban Centres in Early Tamilakam', *IHC, 43rd Session*, Kurukshetra, 1982.
2. B.D. Chattopadhyaya, 'Trade and Urban Centres in Early Medieval India', *Indian Historical Review (IHR)*, vol. 1, no. 2, 1974; *idem* 'Urban Centres in Early Medieval India: An Overview', in Sabyasachi Bhattacharya and Romila Thapar (eds), *Situating Indian History*, New Delhi, 1986; Champakalakshmi, 'Growth of Urban Centres in South India: Kuḍamūkku-Paḷaiyāṟai, the Twin-city of the Cōḷas', *Studies in History*, 1979, vol. 1, no. 1, *see* Chapter 6 in this volume; *idem* 'Urban Processes in Early Medieval Tamil Nadu', in *Situating Indian History*; *see* Chapter 4 in this volume; also K.R. Hall, 'Peasant State and Society in Chola Times: A View from the Tiruviḍaimarudūr Urban Complex', *The Indian Economic and Social History Review (IESHR)*, 1981, vol. 18, nos 3-4.
3. Philip Abrams, 'Towns and Economic Growth', in Philip Abrams and E.A. Wrigley (eds), *Towns in Societies: Essays in Economic History and Historical Sociology*, Cambridge, 1978.
4. Harold Carter, *An Introduction to Urban Historical Geography*, London, 1983, Foreword, xiv.
5. Richard Basham, *Urban Anthropology: The Cross-Cultural Study of Complex Societies*, Palo Alto, California, 1978, 51.
6. Chattopadhyaya, 'Urban Centres', 11-13. The use of the term 'third urbanization' for the whole of India may be necessary, if one takes the Indus valley urbanization into account. However, for south India, it should be taken as 'the second urbanization'.

See Champakalakshmi, 'Urban Processes in Early Medieval Tamil Nadu', in Indu Banga (ed.), *The City in Indian History: Urban Demography History and Politics*, 1991, 47–68.

7. Chattopadhyaya, 'Urban Centres', 11. *See also* A. Ghosh, *The City in Early Historical India*, Simla, 1973. S. Ratnagar, *Encounters: The Westerly Trade of the Harappa Civilization*, New Delhi, OUP, 1981, xiii.
8. R.S. Sharma, *Indian Feudalism*, Calcutta, 1965, 65ff. Also his 'Decay of Gangetic Towns in Gupta and Post-Gupta Times', *IHC, 33rd Session*, Muzaffarpur, 1972, 92–104.
9. This phase is discussed in Section II of this Chapter.
10. For the widening orbit of trade and its rippling effects over the Ganges valley in this period, *see* Thapar, 'State Formation in Early India', *International Social Science Journal*, vol. XXXII, 655–69.
11. K. Sivathamby, 'Early South Indian Society and Economy: The Tinai Concept', *Social Scientist*, 1974, 20–37, gives a very useful appraisal of the *tinai* concept for understanding these eco-zones.
12. Champakalakshmi, 'Urban Processes', 48.
13. For the essential features of a *janapada*, *see* Thapar, *From Lineage to State*, OUP, Bombay, 1984, 121ff.
14. Champakalakshmi, 'Archaeology and Tamil Literary Tradition', *Puratattva*, 1975–6, vol. VIII, 113ff.
15. 'Surpluses are always defined and mobilized in a particular institutional setting', R. McC. Adams, *The Evolution of Urban Society: Early Mesopotamia and Pre-hispanic Mexico*, Chicago, 1966, 45–7. In other words, surplus is a social product.
16. R.S. Kennedy, 'King in Early South India as Chieftain and Emperor', *IHR*, 1976, vol. III, 2. Patronage and liberality towards bards and minstrels were the most important means of legitimation of the kingly office, so much so that jewels, gold, elephants, chariots and fine clothes were distributed to the *pāṇar*, *akavunar* and *porunar*, (minstrels) for praising the qualities of leadership and liberality, thus justifying his position.
17. Champakalakshmi, 'Archaeology', 120; Nicholas B. Dirks, 'Political Authority and Structural Change in Early South India', *IESHR*, 1976, vol. XIII, no. 2, 125–57. Also *Puṟanāṉūṟu*, 16, 224, 367, 377, 400.
18. 'Tribal conflicts are endemic to non-urbanised societies at all levels of development and are not necessarily self augmenting'. *See* Paul Wheatley, *The Pivot of the Four Quarters: A Preliminary Enquiry into the Origin and Character of the Ancient Chinese City*, Edinburgh, 1971, 301.

19. For inter-*tiṇai* exchange, *see* J.V. Chelliah, *Pattuppāṭṭu—The Ten Tamil Idylls* (tr. into English with Introduction and Notes), Tirunelveli, *SISSW*, 2nd edn, 1962, 73-5; *Porunarāṟṟuppaṭai*, ll. 214-25.
20. *Akanāṉūṟu*, 36, 57, 125, 246, 253 and 345; *Puṟanāṉūṟu*, 7-9, 23, 25, 31-2, 33, 35-6, 39-40, 227, 371ff. *Kuṟuntokai*, 393. *See* K.A. Nilakanta Sastri, *The Cōḷas*, Madras, 1975, 30. The pearl-rich Pāṇḍya coastal region and the pepper-rich hilly tracts of the Cēras must have been a constant source of conflict among the three 'crowned kings'. The Cōḷa interest in these areas is well known.
21. Sivathamby, 'An Analysis of the Anthropological Significance of the Economic Activities and Conduct Code Ascribed to the *mullai tiṇai*', *Proceedings of the First International Conference Seminar on Tamil Studies*, 1966 (1968), *IATR*, vol. I, 325.
22. G.W. Spencer, *The Politics of Expansion: The Cōḷa Conquest of Sri Lanka and Sri Vijaya*, Madras, 1983, 17-18.
23. *Puṟunāṉūṟu*, 15, 16, 23, 52, 57; *Paṭṭinappālai*, ll. 239-68; *Maduraikkāñcī*, ll. 148-76. Also Rajan Gurukkal, 'Aspects of Early Iron Age Economy, Problems of Agrarian Expansion of Tamilakam', *IHC, 42nd Session*, Bodh Gaya, 1981, 74.
24. *Perumpāṇāṟṟuppaṭai* (on Kacci), ll. 373-412; K. Zvelebil, *The Smile of Murugan*, Leiden, 1973, 100. *See* R. Sumathi, 'Trade and its Impact on the Early Tamils: The Cola Experience', M.Phil. Dissertation (unpublished), Jawaharlal Nehru University, 1984, chapter VI.
25. In contrast to the urban centres of *marutam* and *neital*, the *mūdūr* of the other tracts described in the *Malaipaṭukaṭām*, and *Ciṟupāṇāṟṟuppaṭai* seem to have been merely camps of the chieftains of the hilly-pastoral tracts.
26. The concept of a 'gateway city' has been discussed by Burghardt as an alternative to the central place theory. That such cities are fed by a 'dendritic network' is not indicated in the case of Puhār. *See* Burghardt, 'A Hypothesis About Gateway Cities', *Annals of the Association of American Geographers*, 1971, vol. LXI; also K. Hirth, 'International Trade and the Formation of Pre-historic Gateway Communities', *American Antiquity*, 1978, vol. XLIII, 38. J. Bird mentions another type of gateway city which is an 'exchange gateway', where 'there is mature exchange of products in two or more directions', but does not discuss it in detail. *See* Bird, *Centrality and Cities*, Routledge, London, 1977, 119.
27. Each inland capital undoubtedly had links with its port. The existence of routes connecting the inland towns with the coastal

towns is known from the *Ciṟupāṇāṟṟuppaṭai* (ll. 142–3) and *Perumpāṇāṟṟuppaṭai* (ll. 319, 371–3). *See also* N. Subrahmanian, *Sangam Polity*, 1966, 123. However, a network of routes connecting various other smaller settlements and nodal points with the ports is hardly attested to. *See* K.V. Soundararajan, 'Determinant Factors in the Early History of Tamil Nad', *Journal of Indian History (JIH)*, 1967, part I. Network also means an organized commercial system in which urban institutions develop, which in the Tamil region did not.

28. L.R. Binford, 'Archaeology and Anthropology', in L. Binford (ed.), *An Archaeological Perspective*, New York, 20–32. The stress was on exporting and importing elite and treasure goods, viz., Roman wine, gold, *Yavana* lamps and guards, horses and gems.
29. *Paṭṭinappālai*, ll. 120–36. The description of Puhār in *Paṭṭinappālai* suggests an elaborate and fair-sized town with well-defined quarters for merchants and officials, with their shops and offices and residential quarters.
30. Archaeological finds identifiable as remains of dyeing vats are reported from Uṟaiyūr and Arikamēḍu. Kacci and Madurai, the well known textile centres, have not provided similar finds. For Uṟaiyūr, see *Indian Archaeology: A Review (IAR)*, 1964–5, 25–6; 1965–6, 26; 1967–8, 30–1; and for Arikamēḍu, R.E.M. Wheeler et al. 'Arikamedu–An Indo-Roman Trading Station on the East Coast of India' in *Ancient India*, 1946, no. 2. Madurai is referred to in the *Arthaśāstra*, as one of the centres for the best cotton fabrics and 'Argaritic Muslins' of the Cōḷa country, probably from Uṟaiyūr, are referred to in the *Periplus*: 59, *see also* Champakalakshmi, 'Archaeology'.
31. Kāvērippaṭṭiṉam excavations reported in *IAR*, 1961–2; 1963–4; *see also* Champakalakshmi, 'Archaeology', 113.
32. Clarence Maloney, 'The Beginnings of Civilization in South India', *Journal of Asian Studies (JAS)*, 1970, vol. XXIX, no. 3, 603–16; *idem* 'Archaeology in South India–Accomplishments and Prospects', in B. Stein (ed.), *Essays on South India*, New Delhi, 1976, 1–40.
33. I am thankful to Y. Subbarayalu for the information on Koḍumaṇal, where he has been excavating for several seasons from 1984.
34. R.E.M. Wheeler et al., 'Arikamedu'; Warmington, *Commerce Between the Roman Empire and India*, New Delhi, 1974 reprint; T.V. Mahalingam, *Report on the Excavations in the Lower Kaveri Valley: Tirukkāmpuliyūr and Aḻagarai, 1962-64*, Madras, 1970; J. Filliozat,

'Intercourse of India with the Roman Empire During the Opening Centuries of the Christian Era', *JIH*, part I, vol. XXVIII, 23-44; Hall, 'The Expansion of Maritime Trade in the Indian Ocean; Roman Trade in the Indian Ocean–An Indian Perspective', *The Elmira Review*, vol. I, 36-42; R. Nagaswamy, 'Exploration and Excavation', *Damilica*, 1970, vol. I; *Vasavasamudram*, Madras (Tamil Nadu State Department of Archaeology), 1978; K.S. Ramachandran, *Archaeology of South India*, Delhi, 1980.

35. *Puṟanāṉūṟu*, 29, 123 and 125. *See* Gurukkal, 'Early Iron Age Economy', 75, for continuity of tribal traditions under the *Vēndar*, 'crowned kings'.
36. The generous gifts to poets and bards included elephants, horses, gold, gems etc. Poets and bards sharing the king's feast and the intimacy of patron-client relationship are a part of this redistribution and prestation economy.
37. *Paṭṭinappālai*, ll. 120-36. The sea-faring interests of the Tamil rulers, which must have led to the special care bestowed by them on the ports, are obviously derived from a remote past hinted at in the poems claiming that the Cōḷas were descendants of an ancestor who harnessed the monsoon winds for sea trade. *See* Nilakanta Sastri, *History of South India*, OUP, 1958, 124; Maloney, 'The Effect of Early Coastal Sea Traffic on the Development of Civilization in South India', Ph.D. thesis (unpublished), University of Pennsylvania, Microfilm xeroxography, 1968, 150, and 'The Beginnings of Civilization in South India', *JAS*, 1970, vol. XXIX, no. 3, 615.
38. S. Seneviratne, 'Kalinga and Andhra: The Process of Secondary State Formation in Early India', in Claessen and Skalnik (eds), *The Study of the State*, Mouton, The Hague, 1981, 320.
39. The bards sought the patronage of the 'crowned kings' as well as the tribal chiefs. The main theme around which the *Āṟṟuppaṭai* works were composed relates to patronage and the lament of the poets about the decline of the patron-client relationship, possibly a reference to the decline of the chiefdoms or a reluctance on the part of the *Vēndar* to give generous gifts. *See* G.L. Hart, *Poets of the Tamil Anthologies–Ancient Poems of Love and War*, Princeton, 1979, 176.
40. M. Sahlins, *Tribesman*, Prentice Hall, Engelwood Cliffs, 1968; M. Fried, *The Evolution of Political Society*, New York, 1967.
41. R. Kailasapathy, *Tamil Heroic Poetry*, OUP, 1968, 11-13, 73-4 and 260; Hart, 'Ancient Tamil Literature: Its Scholarly Past and Future', in Stein (ed.), *Essays on South India*, New Delhi, 1976,

56-7, *see also* K. Sivaraja Pillai, *Chronology of the Early Tamils*, Madras, 1932, 192-3 for the nature of social differentiation.

42. This is, in fact, what the medieval commentator on *Tolkāppiyam* makes out from the reference in that work. *See* N. Subrahmanian, 1966, 259.
43. *See* Champakalakshmi, 'Archaeology', for areas over which the *vēḷir* exercised control.
44. Groups designated as *vambalar, umaṇar, paratavar, vaṇikar, vilaiñar* and *pakarnar*, would refer to the itinerant trader or the new comer, salt trader, fisher and trader merchant, seller and hawker respectively. See *Tamil Lexicon*, IV, 2380 and 2496; V, 2380; VI, 3492, 3586 and 3715.
45. Zvelebil, *Murugan*, 100.
46. The fact that the *paratavar* diversified their economic activities and became rich traders (*Akanāṉūṟu*, 340; 16-17; 350: 11) and their prosperity as described in the poems may well be a development due to maritime trade. The coastal *paratavar* who are earlier portrayed as a rustic, happy and simple folk (Maloney, 'Early Coastal Sea Traffic', 231-2) subsequently enhanced their economic status through extensive trade, and acquired a better life-style. Sea trade was particularly important to them. They worshipped Varuna and the chank (conch) was of special cult significance to them.
47. The earliest craft well attested to as a specialised one was weaving. *Tirumurukāṟṟuppaṭai*; 138 and *Porunarāṟṟuppaṭai*; 81-3, of the later strata of Sangam works.
48. I. Mahadevan, 'Corpus of the Tamil Brahmi Inscriptions', in Nagaswamy (ed.), *Seminar on Inscriptions*, Madras, 1966 (1968), nos 3 and 6. The term *Kāviti* is taken to be a guild chief by Sivathamby, 'The Social and Historical Perspective (of the Early Tamil Poems)', in Sivathamby, *Drama in Ancient Tamil Society*, New Century Book House, 1981, 172. However, the references to the *Kāviti*'s position and functions would seem to indicate that he was more a counsellor to the ruling chiefs/kings. This is the meaning attributed to the term by historians like Nilakanta Sastri and N. Subramanian. See *Sangam Polity*, 1966, 86 and 96.
49. *Śilappadikāram*, I: 33. A *Vaṇikaccāttu* (merchant caravan) is mentioned in *Kuṟuntokai*, 390. It had armed escorts. *Akanāṉūṟu*, 89. *See* Subramanian, *Sangam Polity*, 235. Also, the same author's *Pre-Pallavan Tamil Index*, Madras, 1966, 667.
50. K.K. Pillay, *A Social History of the Tamils*, Madras, 1975, reprint, 247.

51. T.G. Aravamuthan, 'A Pandiyan Issue of Punch-marked Coins', *Journal of the Numismatic Society of India*, part I, vol. VI, 1ff.
52. The 'Cengaṃ hoard' from Āṇḍipaṭṭi in the North Arcot district is assigned to the chief Nannan of Cengam, referred to in the *Malaipaṭukaṭām*.
53. *Tolkāppiyam*, *Poruḷ*: 625-6, 632 and 635. That this division hardly applied to the whole of the Tamil society or that it was not a well-understood framework, is seen in references to the four categories, which include people like *tuḍiyar*, *pāṇar*, *paṟaiyar* and *kaḍambar–Puṟanāṉūṟu*, 335.
54. The *paṟaiyar*, *pāṇar*, *tuḍiyar* and others. *See* Hart, *The Poems of the Ancient Tamils–Their Milieu and their Sanskrit Counterparts*, 1975, 119ff; Maloney, 'Archaeology in South India', 17.
55. Most of these donations are of a comparatively simple nature (carving of stone beds and making natural caverns habitable for monks) and do not match the ostentatiousness of the contemporary donations in western Deccan and Andhra Region. *See* Vidya Dehejia, *Early Buddhist Rock Cut Temples: A Chronological Study*, London, 1972; Anjana Chatterjee, 'Socio-economic Conditions in Early Andhra 200 BC–AD 300: A Study of the Transition from Megalithic to Early Historic Culture', Ph.D. thesis (unpublished), Jawaharlal Nehru University, New Delhi, 1976.
56. The present 'veḷḷaiyan iruppu' in Kāvērippūmpaṭṭiṇam is said to be the site of an ancient *yavana* colony. See *Paṭṭinappālai*, ll. 214-18; *Śilappadikāram*, v, 6-12; VI, 130-3; 143.
57. Champakalakshmi, 'Archaeology'. An attempt is made in this essay to correlate archaeological evidence from the Megalithic burials and their distribution with the literary evidence of the anthologies and epics.
58. *Maṇimēkalai*, chapter VI, 67-8. The structural features of the Megalithic burials show that they would have involved considerable expenditure and manpower. *See* K.R. Srinivasan, 'Some Aspects of Religion as Revealed by Early Monuments and Literature of the South', *Journal of the Madras University*, 1960, vol. XXXII, no. 1, 133-4.
59. McC Adams, *The Evolution of Urban Society*, 2.
60. 'It is precisely the growth of the collective symbols and institutions of the primitive states that can explain the conversion of peasant leisure into foodstuffs in urban store-houses', Adams, *Evolution*, 45.
61. Maloney, 'Early Coastal Sea Traffic'.
62. Before Kauṭilya there seems to have been a general preference for

open sea routes, whereas Kauṭilya gives importance to land routes and sea routes that followed the coast. (*Arthaśāstra*, VII, 12).

63. It is doubtful whether at this early stage there were many traversable paths in the intercourse of the Tamil country. *See* Soundararajan, 'Determinant Factors', 667.
64. Champakalakshmi, 'Urban Processes', 51.
65. Himanshu P. Ray, *Monastery and Guild: Commerce Under the Satavahanas*, OUP, 1986, chapter I.
66. Ibid., chapter 5.
67. Thapar, *A History of India*, vol. I, 111–12; Dehejia, 1972 and Chatterjee, 'Early Andhra'. The sponsoring of Buddhist institutions by kings and merchants alike, and the rise of mercantile establishments, served as 'symbolic integrative media for a dominant politico-mercantile elite'. *See* J. Heitzman, 'Early Buddhism, Trade and Empire', *Journal of Southeast Asian Studies*, March 1989, vol. XX, no. 1, 121–37.
68. Seneviratne, 'Kalinga and Andhra: The Process of Secondary State Formation in Early India'.
69. *See* M.G.S. Narayanan, 'The Warrior Settlements of the Sangam Age', *IHC, 43rd Session*, Kurukshetra, 1982, 102-9; Gurukkal, 'Early Iron Age Economy', 70-82. For frequent inter-tribal wars and strifes there is abundant evidence *see* Kailasapathy, *Tamil Heroic Poetry*, 258-60.
70. Webb uses the term 'conditional state' to describe highly developed, sometimes durable chiefdoms which appear to be transitional to the state, and in which the transformation may never take place. 'The lack of a reliable source of force which may be applied in a crisis' makes 'obedience of the separate segments of a society to the leadership' conditional. It is the element of coercion, which is emphasized here as a distinguishing feature of the state from other elementary forms of political organizations. *See* M. Webb, 'The Flag Follows Trade–An Essay on the Necessary Interaction of Military and Commercial Factors in State Formation', in Sabloff and Lamberg Karlovsky (eds), *Ancient Civilization and Trade*, Albuquerque, 1975, 156ff. These early Tamil chiefdoms disappeared into oblivion rather suddenly and dramatically, *see* Champakalakshmi, 'Urban Processes', 51. For lack of coercive power among the *Vēndar*, *see* Gurukkal, 'Early Iron Age Economy', 76.
71. *See* Ratnagar, *Encounters*, 240, R.A.L.H., Gunawardana, 'Social Function and Political Power: A Case Study of the Evolution of the State in Irrigation Society', in Classen and Skalnik (eds), *The*

Study of the State, 1981, 145ff; R. Cohen, 'State Origins: A Reappraisal', in Claessen and Skalnik (eds), *The Early State*, The Hague, 44-5.

72. Adams, *Evolution*, 46-7.
73. V. Gordon Childe, 'The Urban Revolution', *Town Planning Review*, 1950, 29, 3-17. Two of the important criteria listed by Gordon Childe, namely, the freeing of a part of the population from subsistence tasks for full-time craft specialization, and the substitution of a politically organized society based on territorial principles–the state–for one based on kin ties, were absent in this phase.
74. Adams, *Evolution*, 9.
75. *See also* B.N.S. Yadava, 'The Accounts of the Kali Age and the Social Transition from Antiquity to the Middle Ages', *IHR* (July 1978-Jan. 1979), vol. V, nos 1-2, 61; Also Spencer, 'Religious Networks and Royal Influence in 11th Century South India', *Journal of the Economic and Social History of the Orient (JESHO)*, 1969, part I, vol. XII, 47. It has been argued that the decline of trade in the 3rd century AD was followed by the decay of towns in north India, for which archaeological evidence has been cited. (R.S. Sharma, *IHC, 33rd Session*, Muzaffarpur, 1972, 92-104). These decaying towns, it is suggested, were converted into *tīrthas* or places of pilgrimage in early medieval times. *See* R.N. Nandi, 'Client, Ritual and Conflict in Early Brahmanical Order', *IHR*, 1979-80, vol. VI, nos 1 and 2.
76. The *Kuṟaḷ*, which extols the importance of agriculture, seems to provide a clue by referring to the breakdown of political ethics causing strain on the cultivators due to forcible demands.
77. Adams, *Evolution*, 18.
78. *See* Chapters 4 and 6 in this volume.
79. The text of this inscription remains unpublished, but preliminary reports clearly refer to lands 'granted' to *brāhmaṇas*. Pūlānkuricci is in the semi-arid Ramanathapuram district. *See* Nagaswamy, 'An Outstanding Epigraphical Discovery in Tamil Nadu', *Fifth International Conference Seminar on Tamil Studies*, Madurai, 1981.
80. *See* Chapter 4 in this volume.
81. There is no single monograph to date which has failed to recognize this, yet a major methodological and analytical difference exists between the earlier 'conventional' historiography of South India and the recent studies. The difference is also one of static and dynamic, or narrative and analytical frameworks in these two approaches, e.g. C. Minakshi, *Administration and Social*

Life Under the Pallavas, Rev. 2nd edn, Madras, 1977; Mahalingam, *South Indian Polity*, Madras, 1955; Nilakanta Sastri, *The Colas*, Madras, and so on. Contra, Sharma, *Indian Feudalism*, Calcutta, 1975; Stein, *Peasant State and Society in Medieval South India*, OUP, 1980; N. Karashima, *South Indian History and Society: Studies from Inscriptions AD 850-1800*, OUP, 1984, and so on.

82. Chattopadhyaya, 'Political Processes and Structure of Polity in Early Medieval India: Problems of Perspective', *Presidential Address, Ancient India Section, IHC, 44th Session*, Burdwan, 1983, 16. *Idem The Making of Early Medieval India*, OUP, 1994.
83. Stein, *Peasant State*, Chapter on 'The State and the Agrarian Order'; Spencer, 1983.
84. C. Minakshi, *Administration and Social Life*, chapter VII; T.M. Srinivasan, 'Irrigation and Water Supply in South India up to AD 1300', M.Litt. Thesis (unpublished), Madras, 1968, for the Pallava region, where the connections are completely missed. *Idem* 'A Brief Account of the Ancient Irrigation Engineering Systems Prevalent in South India', *The Indian Journal of History of Science*, 1970, vol. 5, no. 2; Gurukkal, 'The Agrarian System and Socio-Political Organisation Under the Early Pandyas *c.* AD 600-1000', Ph.D. Thesis (unpublished), Jawaharlal Nehru University, 1984, chapter III, where the links are clearly understood.
85. It has also been suggested that in this period, there is evidence of inter-societal technology transfer in irrigation between South India and Sri Lanka. Gunawardana, 'Inter Societal Transfer of Hydraulic Technology in Pre-colonial South Asia: Some Reflections Based on a Preliminary Investigation', *Tonan Ajia Kenkyu (South East Asian Studies)*, Sept. 1984, vol. 22, no. 2. In both the Pallava and Pandya regions, perennial and inundation techniques were extensively used in areas suitable for such methods, a practice which was prevalent from the Sangam Period. There are literary traditions associating Karikāla Cōḷa of the Sangam period with a major irrigation work (dam) on the Kaveri near Tiruchirappalli (Uṟaiyūr), and the deforestation of the northern Tamil region in order to settle 48,000 *Vēḷāḷa* families. Although it may refer to such activities even prior to the *brahmadeya* period, there is no clear evidence that this irrigation project, believed to have been carried out with slave labour (prisoners of war), was successfully managed by the Cōḷas of the Sangam period. In fact, a study of the present site of this dam points to a medieval date for the dam. In this context, the views of D. Ludden may be mentioned. 'Developing river irrigation was part of building regional political

order. The sangam period technology was rudimentary, based solely on inundation'; and, 'The dam and channel systems in the up-river tracts, were highly productive, but the Tamraparni region near Ambasamudram was the locus of the most dramatic agricultural and political development under the Medieval dynasties', 'Patronage and Irrigation in Tamil Nadu, A Long Term View', *IESHR*, 1979, vol. XVI, no. 3, 349ff. *See also* D. Ludden, *Peasant History in South India*, Princeton, 1985, chapter I. Under the Pāṇḍyas of the later period, the strengthening of the bunds of existing tanks and construction of several new ones are recorded in the eighth-ninth century inscriptions. The use of stone for the new bunds and the special technique of sluice construction to regulate water supply are also attested to for the first time in these records as well as in those of the Pallavas. *See* Gurukkal, 'Aspects of the Reservoir System of Irrigation in the Early Pandya State', *Studies in History*, n.s., vol. II, no. 2, 155-64; Minakshi, chapter VII; T.M. Srinivasan, 'Irrigation and Water Supply', *see also* D. Ludden, 'Ecological Zones and the Cultural Economy of Irrigation in Southern Tamil Nadu', *JAS*, n.s., 1978, vol. I, no. 1.

86. It may be noted that invariably all the *brahmadeya* records show an intimate knowledge of astronomy, evidently on the part of the *brāhmaṇas*, the grantees, by their references to eclipses and other astronomical phenomena, apart from the methods of dating, which include precise calendraic details, a boon to chronologists, who have been able to date many such records with great exactitude.

87. When new settlements were brought into existence through *brahmadeya* or *agrahāra* grants, the expansion of the revenue base is implied in the phrase that such villages were 'non-taxable for twelve years', after which they would be brought under the taxable category. *See* T.V. Mahalingam, 'Genesis and Nature of Feudalism under the Pallavas of Kāñcī', Paper presented at the Seminar on *Socio-Economic Formation in the Early Middle Ages—AD 600-1200*, Allahabad, 1977. This is also illustrated by the references in Karnataka inscriptions recording the settlement of *agrahāras*. Sometimes, the revenue dues from such *agrahāras* were also fixed in cash. *See* S. Leela Shanthakumari, *History of the Agrahāras, Karnataka 400-1300*, Madras, 1986, 16-17.

88. Gurukkal, 'The Agrarian Society', chapter III, 168ff. Tax terms like *puravu-pon*, *puravu-vari* (land tax) *āyam*, *kāṇam*, *daṇḍam*, *karai*, and *kaḍamai* are commonly found in Pallava-Pāṇḍya records. That revenue demands were on the increase in the early medieval

period shows that agricultural surplus sustained the ruling and non-ruling elites of the period. This is much more clearly attested under the Cōḷas. *See* Chattopadhyaya, 'Political Processes', 16. It has been argued that the devotional cult of *bhakti*, the personal devotion to the deity, symbolizes the tenant-lord or cultivator-landlord relationship of a feudal society, or justifies it, perhaps, by providing 'the delusion of equality among the lower orders which in reality remained beyond their access even in the ritual area'. *See* R.N. Nandi, 'Some Social Aspects of Nālāyira Divya Prabandham', *IHC, 37th Session*, Calicut, 1976, 118–23; Kesavan Veluthat, 'The Temple Base of the Bhakti Movement in South India', *IHC, 40th Session*, Waltair, 1979, 185–94. Here, *bhakti* in effect represents the extra-economic coercion or bond enabling the circulation of resources, i.e. devotion to, and a reciprocal protection from, the deity. See for non-economic considerations in social relations, P. Anderson, *Passage from Antiquity to Feudalism*, London, 1974, 401ff; Maurice Dobb, *Capitalism, Development and Planning*, The Hague, 1971, 208.

89. This is the main theme in all the works of Stein, the culmination of his researches being his monograph, *Peasant State and Society in Medieval South India*. There are many influenced by Stein's theory among American historians of south India, such as Spencer and Hall.

90. The best exposition of this theory is that of *Indian Feudalism* by Sharma. Despite the fact that it has provoked a continuing debate on the prevalence of a feudal society in India on the European model (Harbans Mukhia, 'Was There Feudalism in Indian History', *Presidential Address, IHC*, Section II, Waltair, 1977; *see also* Sharma, 'How Feudal was Indian Feudalism' and Stein 'Politics Peasants and Deconstruction of Feudalism in Medieval India' in *Journal of Peasant Studies*, Jan/April 1985, vol. 12, nos 2 and 3), there are quite a few proponents of this theory. The series of Presidential addresses in the IHC on this subject are sufficient proof of it. *See* D.N. Jha, 'Early Indian Feudalism: A Historiographical Critique', *Presidential Address Ancient India Section, Indian History Congress, 40th Session*, Waltair, 1979; B.N.S. Yadava, 'The Problems of the Emergence of Feudal Relations in Early India', *Presidential Address, Ancient India Section, IHC, 41st Session*, Bombay, 1980; Nandi, 'Growth of Rural Economy in Early Feudal India', *IHC, 45th Session*, Annamalai, 1984.

91. Veluthat, *The Political Structure of Early Medieval South India*, Orient Longman, New Delhi, 1993.

92. Chattopadhyaya, 'Political Processes', 18–19.
93. The most systematic study of the *nāḍu* and *kūṟṟam* for the Cōḷa country is that of Y. Subbarayalu, *Political Geography of the Cola Country*, Madras, 1973. This work, however, restricts its study to the Kaveri valley and adjacent areas in the north and south. This study also confines itself to the middle Cōḷa period, which in fact represents the end of the main phase of agrarian expansion of the Cōḷa region, not the stages of such expansion. The erstwhile Pallava and Pāṇḍya regions need to be taken up for an equally thorough investigation.
94. Studying the political geography of this region may prove to be a very useful method of establishing the chronological sequence of their emergence, which can be done with the help of contemporary inscriptions, providing a remarkable corroboration of the integration of less developed pre-existing settlements, having no irrigation or other facilities, into the newly emerging *brahmadeya* and temple nucleated centres, interesting examples of which may be found in Toṇḍaimaṇḍalam.

    The *kōṭṭam*, of which twenty-four are traditionally assigned to the Pallava region, had in it one or more *nāḍus*, some of which are for the first time attested to only in early Cōḷa or middle Cōḷa inscriptions, indicating, thereby, that the process of development and integration was continuous. The same process is noticeable in the case of *nāḍu* and *kūṟṟam* in the Cōḷa and Pāṇḍya regions even upto the eleventh century AD when the *vaḷanāḍu* was introduced as a revenue division under Rājarāja I, after a major land survey and assessment was initiated by him for revenue assessment. Nearly fifty *nāḍu/kūṟṟam* localities have been listed so far in the Pāṇḍya region between seventh and tenth centuries AD. The expansion of one of these *nāḍus*, viz., *muḷḷi nāḍu* in the wet zone of Tamraparni valley, provides an interesting case of deliberate royal choice of a region for development as a resource base under the Cōḷas.
95. K.R. Srinivasan, 'Pallava Architecture', *Ancient India*, 1958, no. 14; Soundararajan, *Art of South India, Tamil Nadu and Kerala*, Delhi, 1978, 75-105.
96. S. Jaiswal, 'Caste in the Socio-economic Framework of Early India', *Presidential Address, Ancient India Section, IHC, 38th Session*, Bhuvaneswar, 1977, 14.
97. It is only in the medieval *nigaṇḍu* or lexicographic works and commentaries that one comes across references to the Vaiśya and Śūdra categories.
98. Jaiswal, 'Caste in the Socio-economic Framework', 30.

99. Ludden, *Peasant History in South India*, 41.
100. T.N. Subramaniam, *Thirty Pallava Copper Plates*, Tamil̤ Varalāṟṟu Kal̤akam, Madras, 1966.
101. Subramaniam, *Ten Pandya Copper Plates*, Madras, 1967.
102. *See* Minakshi, *Administration and Social Life*, part III, chapter XI; Karashima, *South Indian History and Society*, chapter I.
103. Hall believes that *nagaram* as a market centre for each *nāḍu* evolved even in the Pallava times, i.e. before the 10th century AD. Further, he treats the 400 years of Cōḷa rule as a single undifferentiated unit, failing to see the spatial and chronological increase in the number of *nagarams* as an important indication of the growth of the commercial network. See *Trade and Statecraft*.
104. The medieval *nigaṇḍu* works, refer to the *Vēḷāḷas* as taking up six professions, such as cultivation, smithy, pottery, weaving, cattle rearing and trade. *See* M. Raghava Iyengar, *Vēḷir Varalāṟu* (Tamil̤), Madras, 1964, 3rd edn, 27-8. Also R. Nagaswamy, *Yāvarum Kēḷir* (Tamil), Madras, 1973, 161.
105. *See* Kuppuswamy, *Economic Conditions*, 98.
106. *See* Chapters 4 and 6 in this volume.
107. The discussion on the merchant guilds is based on A. Appadorai, *Economic Conditions in Southern India (AD 1000—AD 1500)*, 2 vols, Madras, 1936; K. Indrapala, 'Some Medieval Mercantile Communities of South India and Ceylon', *Journal of Tamil Studies*, Oct. 1970, vol. II, no. 2; K.R. Venkatarama Ayyar, 'Medieval Trade, Craft and Merchant Guilds in South India', *Journal of Indian History*, 1947, 268-80; Meera Abraham, 'A Medieval Merchant Guild of South India', *Studies in History*, Jan.-June 1982, vol. IV, no. 1. *See* Chapter 5 in this volume.
108. *See* Chattopadhyaya, 'Markets and Merchants in Early Medieval Rajasthan', *Social Science Probings*, Dec. 1985, vol. II, no. 4.
109. K.G. Krishnan, 'Chittiramēḷipperiyanāḍu–An Agricultural Guild of Medieval Tamil Nadu', *Journal of the Madras University*, Jan. 1982, reprint, vol. LIV, no. 1.
110. Nagaswamy, *Studies in Ancient Tamil Law and Society*, Madras, 1978. (Pub. by the Institute of Epigraphy, The State Department of Archaeology, Government of Tamil Nadu), 75-9; Nos 6, 18 and 26 of *Annual Report on Indian Epigraphy (ARE)*, 1953-4.
111. T. Venkateswara Rao, Local Bodies in Pre-Vijayanagar Andhra, Ph.D. Thesis (unpublished), Dharwar, 1975, 76-8.
112. '*Caturvarṇakulodbhava*'. See *South Indian Inscriptions (SII)*, vol. V, no. 496.
113. *Pudukkottai State Inscriptions*, no. 1083.

114. *SII*, VIII, 291, 442 and so on.
115. Nagaṣwamy, *Studies in Ancient Tamil Law*.
116. Venkateswara Rao, 'Local Bodies', chapter VI.
117. 215 of *ARE*, 1976-7.
118. Some of these centres may be recognized from the names of places from where the signatories to guild inscriptions hailed. A careful listing of such place names with their *nāḍu* locations may be helpful in identifying many of them, e.g. *SII*, VIII, no. 442.
119. Vijaya Ramaswamy, *Textiles and Weavers in Medieval South India*, OUP, 1985, 58-9.
120. *See* Chapter 4 in this volume.
121. Stein, *Peasant State and Society in Medieval South India*, OUP, 1980, 241-53.
122. *Tirumaḍaiviḷāgam*—Quarters around temple. *See* T.N. Subramaniam, *South Indian Temple Inscriptions*, Glossary; also *ARE* 1921-2, part II.
123. Gurukkal, 'The Agrarian System', chapter III.
124. Chattopadhyaya, *Coins and Currency Systems in South India, c.* AD *225-1300*, New Delhi, 1976, 137.
125. *See* Wheatley, *The Pivot of the Four Quarters*, 281, for such systemic levels of integration in urbanization.
126. Ibid., 318. The question 'What is urbanism' is 'metaphysical rather than scientific, not easily answered by the empirical methods of social sciences'. *See* Donald Mc Taggart, 'The Reality of Urbanism', *Pacific Viewpoint*, 1965, vol. 6, no. 2, 220-4.
127. On the question of dominance and power relationships, *see* Abrams, 'Towns and Economic Growth: Some Theories and Problems', in Abrams and Wrigley (eds), *Towns in Societies: Essays in Economic History and Historical Sociology*, 9-33, where the author attempts to bring into focus the essence of urban forms and also, in the process, tries to establish that the question of dominance and power relationships is the one important thread that runs through the writings of Max Weber, J. Sjoberg and F. Braudel.
128. *See* Chapter 6 in this volume.
129. 'The Economy of Kāñcīpuram: A Sacred Centre in Early South India', *Journal of Urban History*, February 1980, 148-9.
130. *See* Zvelebil, *The Smile of Murugan: On The Tamil Literature of South India*, Leiden, 1973, 43ff, for an internal chronology of early Tamil works.
131. *See* Friedhelm Hardy, *Viraha-Bhakti: The Early History of Kṛṣṇa*

Devotion in South India, Delhi, 1983, for an excellent analysis of the *āḻvār* poetry and their emotional *bhakti*.

132. Champakalakshmi, 'Religious Conflict in the Tamil Country: A Re-appraisal of Epigraphic Evidence', *Journal of the Epigraphic Society of India*, 5 (1978).
133. S.R. Balasubrahmaniam, *Early Cōḷa Temples*, Orient Longman, 1971, *Middle Cōḷa Temples*, Thomson Press India Ltd, 1975; *Later Cōḷa Temples*, Mudgala Trust, 1979.
134. Champakalakshmi, 'The Sovereignty of the Divine: The Vaiṣṇava Pantheon and Temporal Power in South India', in H.V. Sreenivasa Murthy, B. Surendra Rao, Veluthat and S.A. Bari (eds), *Essays on Indian History and Culture* (Felicitation Volume in Honour of Professor B. Sheik Ali), New Delhi, 1990, 49-66.
135. The description of the city of Tañjāvūr given here is based on the Cōḷa inscriptions of Tañjāvūr, *South Indian Inscriptions*, parts 1, 2, 3 and 4, vol. II.
136. The temple employees included treasurers, accountants, watchmen, musicians, dancers, drummers, carpenters, goldsmiths, braziers, tailors and so on. Many of them received a house site and lands for maintenance.
137. Carter, *An Introduction to Urban Historical Geography*, London, 1983, 14.
138. In the technique of orientation, the emphasis was on the cardinal compass directions. Indian temples invariably face east.
139. Carter, *Urban Historical Geography*, 13.
140. The *Tiruviśaippā* on these two temples is included in the Śaiva Canon.
141. For Kāñcīpuram—*Perumpāṇāṟṟuppaṭai*, ll. 371-3. For Madurai—*Maduraikkāñcī*, l. 429; *Murukāṟṟuppaṭai*, l. 71 and *Paripaṭal*, 20; 25-6. The medieval commentators call the city of Madurai 'Nānmāḍakkūḍal', which means 'the meeting point of the four quarters (streets)'.
142. *See* Wheatley, *The Pivot of the Four Quarters*, 311.
143. *See* Chapter 4.
144. 651 of ARE, 1916.
145. *See* Chapters 4 and 7; *Taniyūr* means independent settlement.
146. Carter, *Urban Historical Geography*, 8.
147. Stein's view is that the temple enclosures with high walls were meant to afford physical protection.
148. M.I. Finley, *The Ancient Economy*, London, 1975 (reprint), chapter v; *idem* 'The Ancient City: From Fustel de Coulanges to

Max Weber and Beyond', *Comparative Studies in Society and History*, 19, 1977.

149. Hall and Spencer, 'The Economy of Kāñcīpuram', 139–40 and 147.

150. *See* James C. Harle, *Temple Gateways in South India: The Architecture and Iconography of the Chidambaram Gopuras*, Oxford, 1963.

151. The orthogenetic and heterogenetic cities have been proposed as models for studying cities in traditional societies and those which developed in modern (colonial and industrial) societies. This is also related to primary urbanization for the city *sui generis* and secondary urbanization (diffusion and imposition of urban forms) and to the values and world views of the ideology of the Little and Great Traditions and that of the modern west. *See* Robert Redfield and Milton Singer, 'The Cultural Role of Cities', *Economic Development and Cultural Change*, 1954–5, III, 53–73. The primary and secondary urbanization follows Morton Fried's distinction of pristine and secondary states in the discussion of Paul Wheatley and, hence, evolution of urbanism and the appearance of the early state institutions are taken to be a simultaneous development.

The concept of the ceremonial centre is admirably worked out by Wheatley, *The Pivot of the Four Quarters*, 311. His study of the Chinese city of the second millennium BC (i.e. Shang, north China) is most interesting from the point of view of 'traditional' societies. Its applicability to the medieval kingdom of Southeast Asia is borne out by the symbolism and structure of the ceremonial centre in the great complex at Angkor in Cambodia. This is also comparable to the process of Synoecism in ancient Greece. However, Wheatley's cross-cultural comparisons with Mesopotamia, Meso-America, Yoruba (Nigeria) and especially the Indus valley, are fraught with great difficulties due to the methodological difficulties in using the kind of archaeological data unearthed in these places.

Following Wheatley, Harold Carter uses the concept of the ceremonial centre to explain the structure of the city in areas of nuclear urbanism as well as secondary urbanism. His methodology, derived as it is from historical geography, is more sound in so far as the structural design and regional variations are capable of being established (Carter, *Urban Historical Geography*, 1983).

In a recent study of Madurai and Madras, Susan Lewandowski tries to analyse the form and function of the ceremonial city and the colonial port as orthogenetic and heterogenetic cities respectively. She tries to establish a distinction between Madurai as representing a unitary urban form and Madras a tripartite urban form, Madurai representing the traditional ideology, the tripartite division of urban Madras being predicated on a western ideology that allowed for horizontal linkages within the city. *See* Susan Lawandowsky, 'Changing Form and Function of the Ceremonial and Colonial Port City in India: An Historical Analysis of Madurai and Madras', in K.N. Chaudhuri and C.J. Dewey (eds), *Economy and Society*, OUP, 1979, 299-329.

152. The implications of such a possibility are relevant to the question whether such towns led to the dissolution of existing social relations between the merchants and the agricultural elite. Emergence of commercial towns (closed towns) and the non-legitimate domination of merchants, it has been argued, led to the dissolution of existing social relations and the decline of feudalism in Europe. It has also been suggested that the merchant groups were alien bodies. Both propositions were found to be difficult to establish and, hence, the question became one of how control over production and towns of productive capacity became an important point of conflict between feudal lords and merchants. *See* Abrams, 'Towns and Economic Growth'.

153. *Epigraphia Indica*, 1935-6, vol. xxiii, 383-5.

154. 120 of *ARE*, 1905.

155. 167 of *ARE*, 1909.

156. *SII*, vol. vi, nos 40 and 41.

157. 264 of *ARE*, 1943-4, 381 of *ARE*, 1939-40; *Inscriptions of the Pudukkotai State*, 1022.

158. These stations have been described as a string of Hoyasaḷa fortresses from Kundāṇi in the Hoyasaḷa region to Rāmeśvaram in the south-eastern coast, to Tiruvaṇṇāmmalai in the north and Mannārguḍi in the Kaveri delta region, holding the core of the Tamil country within a triangular military nexus. *See* K.R. Venkataraman, *The Hoyasaḷas in the Tamil Country*, 47. References to *Paḍaippaṟṟu* as a revenue unit meant for the army, *Paḍaivīḍu* or cantonment, and special levies for the maintenance of forts, cavalry and elephant corps are also frequent in Pāṇḍya records. *SII*, vii, 145, xvii, 141 and 145 and so on.

159. Elliot and Dowson, *The History of India as Told by its Own Historians*, i, 69-70; *see also* Nilakanta Sastri, *The Pandyan Kingdom*, 147; M. Balasubramanyan, 'Administration and Social Life under

the Later Pandyas', Ph.D. Thesis (unpublished), Kamaraj University, Madurai, 1985, chapter VIII.

160. Vijaya Ramaswamy, *Textiles and Weavers*, *IESHR*, 1985, 22, no. 4, 38–40.

161. This may be seen as a step towards *'proto-industrialization'*, a theory recently advanced for the late medieval and pre-colonial period in South Asia. Frank Perlin, 'Proto-Industrialisation and Pre-colonial South Asia', *Past and Present*, 1983, no. 92. Also Vijaya Ramaswamy, 'Artisans in Vijayanagar Society', *IESHR*, 1985, 22, no. 4; *idem* 'The Genesis and Historical Role of Master Weavers in South Indian Textile Production', *JESHO*, vol. XXVIII.

162. For a detailed description of the sacred complex and royal enclosures at Hampi, *see* John M. Fritz, George Michell and M.S. Nagaraja Rao, *The Royal Centre at Vijayanagara, Preliminary Report*, University of Melbourne, Vijayanagara Research Centre, Monograph Series, 1984, no. 4, chapters 2, 3 and 5.

163. For a discussion of these changes as part of the increasing autonomy of each institutional sphere of society making the problem of legitimation even more complex, *see* Wheatley, *The Pivot of the Four Quarters*, 320–1.

2

Stimulus from Outside: Urbanization in the Early Historical Period

c. 300 BC to AD 300

The second urbanization in India, which began in the sixth century BC, with its epicentre in the Ganges valley, became a subcontinental phenomenon by the beginning of the Christian era and registered a general decline by the end of the third century AD. Urban processes were conspicuously intensive between the third century BC and the third century AD, i.e. the early historical period, when they spread to peninsular India in the wake of Mauryan political expansion and economic control over peninsular regions with major resource potential, especially minerals. However, the degree of urbanization and the nature of urban forms varied considerably in the Deccan, Andhra region and Tamiḻakam, the three main geographical and cultural regions of peninsular India.

Tamiḻakam in the early historical period offers an interesting regional version of the second urbanization in the subcontinent. It points to the need for probing into the diversities and regional variations in the processes and forms of early historical urbanism. The early urbanism of Tamiḻakam was not induced by forces of an inner growth but was a secondary development due to inter-regional trade, mainly coastal, between the Ganges valley, Andhra and Tamil regions and also presumably between the Gujarat and Kerala coasts. More significantly, it was stimulated by maritime commerce between South India and the Mediterranean west and subsequently between South India and Southeast Asia, in which Sri Lanka was a major entrepôt. Although maritime trade was the major impulse in the urbanization of peninsular India as a whole, important differences exist in the degree and nature of Mauryan influences over the Deccan and Andhra on the one hand, and Tamiḻakam on the other. Unlike the Sātavāhana Deccan and Andhra regions, where

Mauryan imperial and cultural influences were more direct in the emergence of state societies in the post-Mauryan period,[1] the impact of Mauryan administrative structures was at best only marginal and less direct over the Tamil tribal polities of the Cēra-Cōḷa-Pāṇḍya and the lesser Vēḷir chiefs. With the exception of references in the Aśokan edicts[2] to the Cēras, Cōḷas, Pāṇḍyas and the Satiyaputras, identified with the Atiyamān chiefs of Takaṭūr (present Dharmapuri) as friendly border peoples, there is no evidence of direct interaction. In other words, political processes and territorial expansion were not functionally interrelated to urban genesis, which in Tamiḻakam, was the result mainly of external stimulus, and hence were not at the core of the transformation of a non-state society into a state society.[3] The secondary urbanization of Tamiḻakam, it would seem, was not simultaneous with the emergence of a state society, i.e. state formation.

It may also be pointed out that no religio-political foci for such a transformation had evolved in early Tamiḻakam. The emergence of religio-political foci has been characterized by S.N. Eisenstadt[4] as 'one of the most important breakthroughs of development from the relatively closed kinship based primitive community' and its change into stratified 'class' oriented society. Religio-political foci would also assist in the process of creating 'effective space' in the form of a territory controlled from and oriented to the cult centre. This would also presuppose the emergence of a centralizing power or development of new social institutions cutting across kinship and clan based organization, for which there is no evidence in early Tamiḻakam. It is significant that the impact of the *varṇa* ideology in social stratification is hardly visible in the Tamil region except in its nascent stage and in a restricted zone, viz the eco-zone of *marutam* (plains/river valleys).

The establishment of the early Tamil polities was preceded by centuries of expansion of what is called the Megalithic culture, the earliest extant archaeological evidence of a uniform material culture in South India, the distinguishing traits of which were the use of iron implements (mainly weapons of war and a limited number of agricultural implements) and the Black and Red Ware pottery. The 'Sangam' or the early historical period would seem to represent the end phases of this culture[5] and the emergence of Tamil civilization, which has been attributed to and was simultaneous with urbanization stimulated by coastal and maritime trade.[6]

Emerging in the main rice-producing regions of the Kaveri, Vaigai, Tamraparni and Periyar, the early ruling lineages of the Cōḷas, Pāṇḍyas and Cēras controlled vast tracts of agricultural land in these river valleys. Evidence of irrigation works in these areas, particularly the Kaveri delta, is provided by the Sangam works and later traditions,[7] although archaeological corroboration is at the moment non-existent. Socio-political dominance over early Tamil society was shared by the three major ruling families called the *Mū vēndar* (usually taken to be 'three crowned kings') and the minor chieftains called the *vēḷir*. Strife among the *Mū vēndar* was a common feature, presumably for control over one another's riverine plains as well as other resources and over the minor chiefs, each of them with their administrative or political centre. Maritime trade, the crucial and determinant factor in early urbanization, brought the much needed luxury items as resources for socio-political dominance and patronage, and hence it was more important for these rulers to gain control over the coastal region adjacent to their mainland, through which they could regulate the trade with distant lands. Equally important was their attempt to control areas with rich trade and resource potential belonging to the others. Thus, the pearl-rich Pāṇḍya coast and pepper-rich Cēra coast would have been the major targets of Cōḷa plunder raids.

The Sangam rulers showed a distinct concern with maritime trade and its control, by actively participating in it as major consumers of luxury goods, by consciously developing ports of trade, by levying tolls and customs at the ports and by issuing coins, if the recent discoveries of local coinage is any indication. Hence, we see the emergence of dual centres of power, centres of political and commercial activity in the interior and on the coast respectively—such as Uṟaiyūr and Kāvērippūmpaṭṭiṇam (Puhār) for the Cōḷas, Madurai and Koṟkai for the Pāṇḍyas and Karuvūr (Vañci) and Muciṟi for the Cēras. That other chieftains also emulated these ruling families is indicated by the Tiraiyar of Toṇḍaināḍu (northern Tamiḻakam) with Kacci (later

Kāñcīpuram) and Nīrppeyaṟṟu (Vasavasamudram) in the Palar valley and at its mouth and the lesser chiefs Ōviyar with Māvilankai (Tindivanam) and Vīrai (Arikamēḍu/Vīrāmpaṭṭiṇam-Poduke of Ptolemy) in the contiguous South Arcot district and Pondicherry.

Thus, urban forms are seen to emerge in certain enclaves, restricted to two eco-zones (*tiṇai*), viz. the *marutam* (plains) and the *neital* (coastal/littoral). Craft production was similarly confined to areas rich in mineral resources and raw materials as in the Kongu region, i.e. Coimbatore - Erode (now Periyar) districts, a semi-arid zone as well as a transit zone, which also lay significantly in the Cēra land and on the route linking the western coast to the eastern plains and coast, via the Palghat Pass. Crafts like weaving also seem to have developed in centres commanding access to raw materials like cotton such as Uṟaiyūr, Madurai and also Arikamēḍu.

II

The above brief survey of urbanism in early Tamiḻakam may now be elaborated for explaining the regional variations in urban processes and forms, as also the underlying differences between the early historical and early medieval urbanization in Tamiḻakam.

A useful starting point for the discussion on urbanism would be to provide a general picture of the socio-economic and political configurations of early historical Tamiḻakam.[8] Society in early Tamiḻakam was organized on the basis of kinship ties (*kuḍi* = clan) with clear perceptions of man=environment relationship, as reflected in the distinctive pattern of economic activities in different eco-zones called the *tiṇai*,[9] a dominant theme in Sangam poetry. Five such *tiṇais* are described in the Sangam texts. The *tiṇai* concept, not a mere poetic convention in the Sangam works, is the reflection of a physiographical reality and points to an understanding of human adaptation to environment and, hence, the most relevant from the historian's point of view. Interspersed with one another, the *aintiṇai* or five eco-situations were marked by different forms of production ranging from primitive subsistence level hunting and gathering (*kuriñci tiṇai* = hilly backwoods), pastoralism/ animal husbandry and shifting cultivation (*mullai tiṇai* = pastoral tract/forest), fishing (*neital tiṇai* = coastal/littoral), to agriculture (*marutam* = riverine wetland/plains), while plundering and cattle lifting as an occupation characterized the transitory zone of *pālai* (parched/arid zone). Blending of *tiṇais* also occurred with mixed forms of subsistence. In effect four major forms of production can be identified, viz. animal husbandry, shifting agriculture, petty commodity production and plough agriculture.[10] Forces of change have been recognized only in the *marutam*, where plough agriculture appeared in the later phases and new agrarian units emerged such as *brāhmaṇa* households/settlements and warrior settlements. In the *neital*, apart from fishing, salt manufacturing and eventually trade also became important economic activities. In the *brāhmaṇa* households of *marutam*, the cultivating groups in the service of the *brāhmaṇas* created new relations of production outside the kinship framework, on which all contemporary production activities were based. Such service groups may point to the beginnings of a new stratification by gradually crystallizing into castes, although at a later stage. The change from a tribal to a peasant society would thus become evident in the *marutam*, where vast tracts of agricultural land were controlled by the ruling families, who depended on peasant tribute and who paid attention to irrigation and wet cultivation towards the latter part of this period. Although plough agriculture made its appearance in the *marutam* zone, it was confined to *menpulam* or pockets of cultivable wet rice land in the plains surrounded by *vanpulam* or dry land with other kinds of dry crops. Subsistence agriculture was common to all *tiṇais* and plough agriculture had not yet become dominant.[11]

The *tiṇais*, though uneven in their socio-economic milieux, were basically tribal in organization. Kinship was the basis of production relations in all the *tiṇais*, with no social division of labour even in the *marutam*, where the households increasingly organized and controlled production. Social differentiation, which is the nub of the problem of urbanization, did not develop even in these zones (*marutam* and *neital*), beyond a broad division into two levels the *cāṉṟōr/uyarndōr/mēlōr* (the higher ones) and the *ilicinar/kīḻōr* (the lower ones).[12] Despite the presence of *brāhmaṇa* households there is no evidence of the impact of the *varṇa* ideology, although a late section of the Tamil grammar *Tolkāppiyam*, i.e. the *Poruḷ atikāram*[13] shows that *varṇa* norms were imposed at a later stage as a theoretical framework on what was basically a non-stratified, clan or kinship based organization with evidence of ranking only among the chiefs and ruling lineages.

There is enough evidence to show that specialized craft production also developed such as metal working, weaving and salt manufacturing, evidently in response to local exchange as well as inter-regional and long-distance trade. Such specialists are known both from literature and the early Tamil Brāhmī inscriptions. They have, however, been viewed as mere functionaries in a complex system of co-operation based on the network of kinship relations.[14]

A gift (*koḍai*) was the main means of redistribution, which itself was based on kinship and inter-personal relationship beyond kinship, e.g. the *pulavar* or poets receiving gifts from the chief or patron. The institution of gifts was particularly important as a source of legitimation for the ruling lineages and chiefs. Redistribution through gifts was of two kinds, the one of subsistence level goods and the other of prestigious goods. Three levels of redistribution may be identified. Redistribution of subsistence goods seems to have taken place at all the three levels, the *vēndar*, *vēḷir* and *kiḻār* in a descending order. The *vēndar* provided subsistence goods on various occasions, at the time of war for their henchmen/fighters and also to the lowly bards (*pāṇar*) who sang their praise for their munificence. The *vēndar* were praised by *pāṇar* and *pulavar*, both for their valour and heroism in war and for their generosity. At a higher level the *vēndar* also made gifts to the *pulavar*, such gifts consisting of prestigious items like gold coins and (gold) lotuses, gems and muslin and even horses and elephants. While subsistence goods thus got redistributed at all the three levels, the gift of luxury items became the prestigious form of exchange with an 'ideo-technic' or 'socio-technic' value,[15] but only at the higher levels of *vēndar* and *vēḷir.* Plundered resources got redistributed while luxury items of trade entered the gift exchange.

Thus, more than agriculture, the Cēra-Cōḷa-Pāṇḍya ruling families depended, for socio-political hegemony, on maritime trade which the coastal regions (*neital*) adjacent to their mainland carried on with distant lands. Socio-political dominance was shared by these three ruling families (*Mū vēndar*) and the minor chieftains called *vēḷir.* Strife among the *vēndar* was a common feature for control over each other's riverine tracts and other rich resources like pearls and pepper. Strife as well as matrimonial alliance were common between the *vēndar* and *vēḷir* for hegemony and control over resources of the hilly, forest and other zones. Tribal warfare, endemic to such early societies, is also corroborated by the evidence of archaeology, which shows a predominance of war weapons among the Megalithic burials. More important, however, is the evidence of the ideology of war and heroism that dominates the Sangam poetry, especially the *puṟam* collections (war poems).

The absence of a regular system of tax or tribute is underlined by the idealization of war/plunder and different situations (*tuṟai*) of raids,[16] the glorification of the warrior, the hero and death in battle, the sharing of the great meal by the ruler/chief with his warriors and the reward in the form of land to the warrior, who preferred wet rice cultivating settlement (*ūr*) to dry zones for such gifts.[17] Hence, the lack of evidence on institutional mechanisms for appropriating surplus[18] by the rulers characteristic of a developed state system, points to the tribal character of these chiefdoms, which otherwise had the potential of developing into kingdoms or incipient states. They were more akin to the sixth century BC *janapada* polities of the Ganges valley,[19] with the senior lineages as ruling families with impressive genealogical claims.

It has been pointed out earlier that the impact of Mauryan imperial structures was marginal in Tamiḻakam in contrast to the Deccan and Andhra under the Sātavāhanas. Under such impact the power structure that evolved in the Deccan was derived from Mauryan ideological influences. This has been seen as a 'secondary state formation'[20] which stands in contrast to the absence of such structures in Tamiḻakam. It must also be noted that the Sātavāhanas adopted the brahmanical ideology as a source of legitimation of their rule, committed as they were with their priestly affiliations, to the *varṇāśrama* ideal. The performance of the Vedic sacrifice and the protection of the *varṇāśramadharma* are significant claims made by them in their inscriptional records.[21] No such claims to be protectors of the *varṇa* ideal are made by the early Tamil lineage polities. Although the performance of Vedic sacrifices, especially the *rājasūya*, by the Cōḷas and other major ruling families, i.e. the Cēra and Pāṇḍya, is attested to in the anthologies,[22] *yajña* or sacrifice was not intrinsic to their legitimation process. Another point of difference is in the nature of patronage extended by the Sātavāhanas to Buddhism, the dominant ideology of the early historical period, which brought about a symbiotic relationship among the political structure, the commercial groups and the Buddhist order.[23]

Royal patronage, and more importantly the patronage of a whole community of Buddhist lay followers, representing the trading and artisanal groups, craftsmen as well as economically poorer sections of society, contributed to the building up of institutions like the monastery and the guild in the Deccan and Andhra, with enormous resources. As a result *stūpa* and *vihāra* complexes of huge dimensions, both in the structural and rock-cut styles, came into existence marking the foci urban growth and routes of communication and trade. On the contrary, such networks, which are crucial in establishing links between trade and craft production and a market system, were less developed in Tamiḻakam, and hence the absence of large-scale patronage to Buddhist institutions like monasteries with the impressive architectural output of the Deccan and Andhra type, and the absence of different sectarian groups of Hīnayāna and Mahāyāna Buddhism, which are so prominently visible in the Deccan and Andhra inscriptions.[24]

Institutional forces like the Buddhist monastery, with their impressive monuments and cohesive guild organizations as foci of urban development are not attested to in the archaeological and epigraphic records of early Tamiḻakam, thus marking a major point of difference in the nature and forms of urbanism. The only notable Buddhist structures (of brick) have been unearthed in the port town of Kāvērippūmpaṭṭiṇam, and these are dated to the fourth and fifth centuries AD,[25] while the earlier period has no significant architectural remains.

The references to Buddhism in the earlier poems of the Sangam anthologies indicate that Buddhism and Jainism were among the many religious faiths which had a following in the politico-commercial centres like Puhār, Vañci and Madurai. It is only in the post-Sangam epics *Śilappadikāram* and *Maṇimēkalai* that Buddhism and Jainism appear as influential ideologies among the merchant community and craftsmen. Royal patronage to these two Śramaṇic religions is recorded in the brief donative Tamil Brāhmī inscriptions[26] occurring on the trade route linking the Tamil region with southern Karnataka and with the west coast. These donations hardly reached the level of the stupendous projects of the Deccan and the Andhra regions. They are at best *vassa* or rainy retreats for the wandering Buddhist and Jain mendicants in the form of natural caverns on hills,[27] made suitable for the monks through provision for stone beds and drip ledges to carry rain water away from the caverns. These caverns with stone beds and Tamil Brāhmī inscriptions occur in the hills around the Pāṇḍya capital Madurai, around the Cēra capital Karūr and near the Cōḷa centre of Uṟaiyūr, but more significantly, they are found on the trade routes, with a concentration in transit zones like the Pudukkottai district and Erode (Periyar) district. Here, apart from royal donors of the Pāṇḍya and Cēra families, the Cōḷas do not figure in any of the donative records.[28] Again, the individual donors belong to the trading and artisan communities. No guild organization with the exception of a single reference to a *nigama*, is known from these records. In comparison, the Brāhmī inscriptions of the Deccan and Andhra Buddhist centres, record a number of guilds, traders and craftsmen, apart from whole village communities as donors.[29] Most important is the absence of any direct reference in the Tamil inscriptions to householders comparable to the northern *gahapatis* as donors to any of the Buddhist and Jain teachers. The *gahapati*, who is the most frequently mentioned donor in the Deccan and Andhra and even central Indian Buddhist centres, represents the most important social category, which emerged as an influential landowning (householder) and trading group in the context of early historical Buddhist centres and urban growth.[30]

In the Tamil context, the *kil̤ān* (*kil̤ār* = plural) would seem to be the landowning householder, the equivalence of the *gahapati*, who emerges as the third level in the patron-client gift-exchange system of redistribution. The *kil̤ān*'s position in this redistribution system was mainly that of a village chief/elder and a landed householder but he is hardly visible in the donative records of the Buddhist and Jain centres, unless it is claimed that some of the names in the Tamil Brāhmī inscriptions ending with the suffix *antai*[31] refer to such householders.

The evidence thus points to a situation of multiplicity of religious influences in which neither the Brāhmaṇic nor the Śramaṇic religion had gained dominance over the others. Again the concept of *tiṇai* provides the clue to the nature of Tamil religion, which, in the early historical period was 'anthropocentric' with a predominant folk component, intensively sensual and humanistic.[32] This is evident from the descriptions of the deities of the different *tiṇais* (eco-zones) who are invoked for success in love and war. The tribal basis of these deities is reflected in their verbal imagery and their close association with the ecological/environmental background. Thus, Cēyōn/Murukan was the god of love and war of the *kur̤iñci* tribes (hunters), Māyōn, the pastoral deity of *mullai*, Kor̤r̤avai, the war goddess of the hunters and robbers of *pālai*, Vēndan, the agricultural deity of the *marutam* and Varuṇan, the sea god of the *neital*.[33] None of them had any claims to universality. No formal religious system with an institutional focus is attested to either in literature or in archaeological record.

The spread of Buddhism and Jainism coincided with the increase in trade and commercial activity and introduced an element of heterogeneity in the urban centres. Buddhism registers a significant presence in the coastal towns, while Jainism is confined to the inland centres, both in the political and commercial centres and on trade routes. The heterogeneity of the urban population in the inland and coastal centres shows, however, that people of different ethnic origins, different occupational background and belonging to various religions aggregated in towns, where brahmanical and folk cults were *equally* well represented. There is no evidence of a single dominant religion in any of them. Formal religious systems and dominant traditions developed only in the post-Sangam (i.e. post-third century AD) period, when the concept of *bhakti* and the temple emerged as the innovative focus of socio-cultural organization, transforming a basically tribal folk religion into a formal, universalized brahmanical religious system by the sixth century AD.[34]

III

Different Levels of Exchange

In a society, wherein reciprocity and redistribution were determined by kinship and inter-personal relations, it would be hard to find evidence of a market system, which was linked directly to land, labour and the production base. Regular local exchange in such a society was mainly based on barter, both in day-to-day transactions and in inter-*tiṇai* exchange, i.e. mutual exchange of resources available in the respective *tiṇais*, or a straight exchange of goods of different *tiṇais*—called *noṭuttal*[35]—hill products like wood, honey, bamboo-rice, etc. in exchange for the *marutam* paddy or *mullai* dairy products and the salt of *neital* for the paddy of *marutam*. The centres at which they were exchanged could well have become nodal points on trade routes in the process of the expansion of trading networks.

Another informal exchange is indicated by the term *kuṟi etirppai*,[36] a loan of goods to be paid back (later) in the same kind and quantity. These local exchanges did not involve the concept of profit, as they were governed by the use value of goods. The profit idea does not seem to have operated even in the exchange of craftgoods by specialists at the local exchange centres, where the specialist craftsman was often himself the seller.[37]

The different levels of exchange thus show a barter or person to person exchange of goods of daily consumption like honey, fish, meat, toddy etc. Paddy and salt entered the larger exchange network, while pepper and other spices, pearls, precious stones (beryl, gems, etc.) aromatic woods and cotton textiles may have been produced for the overseas exchange markets. While most items traded in were raw materials, goods like textiles, gems and jewels were among the few manufactured products meant for trade. Such commodities were encountered only in a few market centres, which had inter-regional commercial contacts such as Puhār, Madurai and Vañci. Vast *kuṟinci* and *mullai* tracts and even parts of *marutam* would not have been drawn into such exchange systems.

It is this kind of picture that is depicted in the Sangam texts, with which the correlation of archaeological and numismatic evidence becomes difficult and often questionable. Thus, in the context of the numerous Roman coin finds (gold and silver), mainly in hoards, it has been argued that in a redistributive society of prestation and gifts, where no idea of price or profit prevailed, coins would have seldom functioned as money but only as a category of valuables.[38] A second related problem is whether the forms of internal exchange, which indicate a fairly regular economic interaction within Tamiḻakam, and those of external exchange (with other countries) represent two distinct levels of exchange, or whether there were inter-relationships between them influenced by the expanding trade.

It has been said earlier that the maritime trade of this period had restricted impact in certain zones leading to urbanism and the emergence of trading stations/ports on the coast, which were centres of exchange in long-distance trade, and of consumption points in the inland centres. It is only at such centres that regular buying and selling of goods took place. There were *angāḍis* (markets) and *āvaṇams* (stores?) in places like Puhār, Madurai and Vañci (Karūr), which became major commercial centres due to the expansion of trade on the eastern coast of Tamiḻakam. Significantly, the later works of the *Pattupāṭṭu* collection and the epics *Śilappadikāram* and *Maṇimēkalai* give more detailed descriptions of these centres and their commercial activities.

Two kinds of markets–the *nāḷangāḍi* or the day market, and the *aḻḻangāḍi*[39] or the evening market–are known, and in Puhār these markets were active in the area between the *Maruvūr-pākkam* (coastal area) and the *Paṭṭinappākkam* (residential area).

The volume of trade is indicated by the references to 'the valuable merchandise stored in million bundles',[40] i.e. large quantity, and the items were often rare and prestigious goods sought by the urban elite and rulers.[41] Similar descriptions of the market place at Madurai are also found in the *Maduraikkāñci*.[42]

The market in Puhār was well guarded by the officers of the Cōḷas and the customs men.[43] Puhār, being the foremost among the 'emporia' on the east coast, the Cōḷas would have derived both political and economic advantage by controlling and promoting this port. The merchants of Puhār, we are told, set a fair price on all goods, probably depending on 'supply and demand' for such goods and did not try to get too much in selling their goods nor gave too little when they bought.[44] It is not easy to determine the degree to which the 'market principle', guided these transactions.

There appears to have been in general no market principle which determined the acquisition of subsistence goods or allocation of land and labour resources. Hence, how are these market centres to be characterized? Could they have acted as 'peripheral' markets?[45] If, as pointed out above, intra-regional and local exchange was 'subsistence oriented'[46] and if it was not price but equivalence that determined the exchange of goods, i.e. 'substitutable goods in prescribed proportions',[47] then the internal and external forms of exchange must be treated as representing two different levels. Again, it would also mean that maritime trade, as the crucial factor in the urbanism of this period, could well have been a 'mystically sudden impulse' to change, i.e. 'urban revolution'.[48] In other words, a market system and a definable power structure, two factors which could cause an inner growth of urbanism percolating down to the production base, were absent in early historical Tamiḻakam.

It has been pointed out that 'peripheral markets' are economically important to those engaged in export and import. To foreign traders such markets are not peripheral, however much they may be for the locals.[49] Hence, a more permanent presence of the *yavanas* (a settlement) in such market centres is acknowledged by the texts.[50] Foreigners would have been both buyers and sellers while the local traders (mainly the *paratavar*), purchased merchandise in these markets and carried them for sale to Īḻam (Sri Lanka), Southeast Asia and other distant lands.[51] Here, the market principle may have operated in a limited context. Urban elite was another category of buyers of luxury articles, while at the same time they would have been able to obtain items of daily consumption such as corn, grain, cloth, flowers toddy, scents etc. in these market places. The staple produce of the hinterland, with the exception of paddy and salt, did not find their way to the larger exchange market.

The ports and towns that emerged as a result of this expanding commerce, may be classified under different heads as the Graeco-Roman accounts seem to have done. In the *Periplus Maris Erythrae* (of the *Erythraen* Sea) of the first century AD, centres like Naura (Cannanore? Mangalore?) Tyndis (Toṇḍi, on the west coast) Nelcynda (Kōṭṭayam), Bacare (Porakad) all on the west coast, Camara (Puhār), Poduce (Arikamēḍu) and Sopatma (Marakkāṇam), all on the east coast, have been categorised as 'marts' or market towns'.[52] Subsequently, Ptolemy in his *Geographia* of the second century AD introduced a hierarchy by elevating six of these centres to the status of 'emporia'[53]–Muziris (Muciṟi–west coast), Kolkhoi (Koṟkai), Khaberis (Puhār), Sabouras (Cuddalore?), Podouke (Arikamēḍu) and Melange (Mahabalipuram?) all on the east coast. Elangkon(?), Manarpha (is it Mailarpha = Mayilāppūr in Madras?) and Salour (Sāliyūr near Aḻagankuḷam) were categorised as marts. The inland centres are generally referred to as cities/towns.

The *Paṭṭinappālai* would seem to support the description of Puhār's status as an emporium, which had its own quay, harbour, warehouses and accommodation for foreign merchants. With the Cōḷas officially approving and promoting it as an archoring point, (port), Puhār developed as a place 'where business between people of different nationality may be transacted lawfully, where lawful dues and taxes may be imposed where possibly foreigners reside . . . '.[54]

The textual references are not as direct as one would wish, because the Sangam heroic poetry uses more often a symbolic language which needs to be decoded through semiotics. However, the terms used in the Sangam texts to designate the merchants and the nature of their organization, also indicate the prevalence of two distinct levels of exchange, the day-to-day barter, hawking and peddling on the one hand and the larger transactions by specialized merchants dealing in high value goods for the inter-regional and maritime trade. These terms are *vilaiñar* (seller), *pakarnar* (hawker) as also the *vambalar* (itinerant newcomer? wayfarer?) the *vaṇikar* (trader), *paratavar* (fishermen turned traders) and even the *umaṇar* (salt merchants).[55] The seller and hawkers were also present in cities like Madurai where they sold 'the produce of the hills, the plains and sea' and even items like 'gems, pearls and gold'.[56] The diversification of commerce is reflected in the nature of specialist traders in the markets of Puhār and Madurai, some of whom dealt in high value commodities apart from daily consumption goods. Thus, in the markets of Puhār and Madurai, there were *pūvinar* (flower sellers), *kōdaiyar* (garland sellers), *cuṇṇattār* (aromatic powder sellers), *nīḍu kaḍi ilaiyinar* (betel leaf/arecanut sellers), *kōḍu-cuḍu-nūṟṟinar* (shell lime shell bangle), *kaḍaiñar* (shop keepers), *maṇikkuyinar* (gem or jewel makers), *kalingam pakarnar* (*kalingam*=cloth sellers), *vambu-nirai-mūdinar* (fine garment sellers), *kaḷ-noḍai=āṭṭiyar* (toddy(?) or wine(?) sellers), the *kañca-kārar* (bronze sellers), *cempu-ceyikunar* (copper article sellers) and skilled workers of all sorts.[57] In most cases, the manufacturers or producers of such items were also the sellers.

Occasional caravans (*cāttu*) of itinerant traders such as *umaṇar* and *vambalar*, carrying goods to the interior (hinterland?), such as paddy, salt and sometimes pepper, are also known.[58] The *umaṇaccāttu* (caravan of salt traders) moving their salt to the interior through difficult and inhospitable tracts on their bullock carts is often described in the Sangam texts. *Umaṇar* and others moved with their spare bulls, swords, bows and spears for protection as well as rare and useful things obtained from hills and seas.[59]

The *paratavar* were the most distinctive of such merchants. They were inhabitants of the *neital* tract, involved in such activities as fishing, manufacturing salt and making toddy.[60] From the later poems of the *Pattuppāṭṭu*, it is evident that they had become involved in long-distance trade by diversifying from their traditional fishing to diving for pearls and organizing trade in pearls, chank (conch) bangles, tamarind, fish, gem and horses, which were taken by 'captains of fine ocean vessels' (*peru-nīr-ōccunar*) to distant countries.[61] At Nīrppeyar, the *paratavar* lived in high storeyed buildings on sandy roads, occupying many streets in the port where 'milk white maned horses arrive with riches from the north, in ships standing out in the cool ocean by the sea front'.[62]

The more prosperous among the traders and merchants who moved on highways or major trade routes, made donations of caves and beds to Jain and Buddhist monks. These donations, it must be noted, do not match the ostentatiousness of the contemporary western Deccan and Andhra donations.[63] The early Tamil Brāhmī inscriptions, recording these donations, indeed mark the trade routes, and in many significant ways confirm the literary references to specialist traders, e.g. *uppu vāṇikan* (salt merchant), *panita vāṇikan* (toddy seller), *koḷu-vāṇikan* (ironmonger), *aṟuvai-vāṇikan* (cloth merchant), *pon-vāṇikan* (gold merchant), *maṇiy-vaṇṇakkan* (lapidary)[64] as donors, apart from the Cēra and Pāṇḍya ruling families. Interestingly, some of the poets of the Sangam texts belonged to the merchant community and often carried as a prefix to their names, the names of some major commercial centres to which they belonged and the nature of their trade. Some instances are—Madurai *Aṟuvai* Vāṇikan Iḷavēṭṭanār (Iḷavēṭṭanār, the cloth merchant of Madurai), Madurai *Kūla* Vāṇikan Śīttalai Sāttanār (grain merchant), Madurai *Ōlaikkaḍaiyattār* Nalveḷḷaiyār (palm leaf/jewellery merchant), Uṟaiyūr Iḷampoṉ Vāṇikanār (gold merchant of Uṟaiyūr) Kāvērippūmpaṭṭiṇattu Poṉvāṇikanār Makanār Nappūdanār (Nappūdanār, son of a gold merchant of Kāvērippūmpaṭṭiṇam).[65]

Both literature and epigraphs thus refer to the trader and the nature of his trade. In contemporary Deccan the merchants rarely mention the nature of merchandise they specialised in. Leading Tamil merchants engaged in import-export activities were among the wealthier sections of the urban community. In the later poems of the Sangam collection they are depicted as living in 'fine mansions' and as sporting silk raiments and gold jewellery.[66] The later epics *Śilappadikāram* and *Maṇimēkalai* refer to their affluent life styles. Trade is glorified as one of the two 'esteemed pursuits',[67] the other being agriculture.

The ethical code that the merchants set for themselves is praised in the *Paṭṭinappālai*.[68]

The early Tamil chiefdoms seem to have been directly involved in this commercial exchange, often as the most important consumers of the goods, and as active participants, by making the native goods available for exchange and also, perhaps, by issuing their own coins. It has been argued that in many early societies, the merchant class emerged from among chiefly families, since the redistributional mechanism which operated in most chiefdoms, concentrated economic wealth in the hands of those close to the chief.[69]

Merchants from distant countries settled down in some of these commercial centres. The *yavanas*, it is suggested, had to stay in the Tamil ports for at least a couple of months, due to the pattern of monsoon winds for sailing.[70] Separate quarters of *yavanas* are known in places like Puhār,[71] while Arikamēḍu has been categorised as a Roman trading station. These quarters were, however, not 'autonomous concessions' or 'colonies' similar to latter-day European factories.[72] Similarly, the role of these *yavana* merchants in contemporary trading activities has also been considerably over rated. Filliozat and Maloney[73] would suggest that the Greek traders' activities were generally confined to the major commercial centres, while in the hinterland, the management of production of various commodities and their transportation would have been in the hands of the Tamils. Pliny's statement[74] that pepper was brought for the foreign traders to the port of Bacare in local boats and then loaded on to Greek vessels, and the Vienna papyrus[75] recording an agreement between a Tamil merchant and an Alexandrian Greek (?), regarding a large cargo of goods to be sent to Alexandria, would show that Tamils traded on equal footing (terms) with foreign traders.

It also needs to be stressed that no *yavana* is seen making donations to local religious institutions, whereas a single reference to a person from Īḻam (Sri Lanka), probably a merchant, donating a cave to Jain monks, is made in a Tamil Brāhmī inscription.[76] The Sri Lanka-Tamil interaction is much more explicitly illustrated by a number of such donative records in Sri Lanka where Tamil merchants and people of the *vēḷir* clan are mentioned in the context of gifts to Buddhists.

The *yavanas* of western Deccan bore sanskritized names and were often assigned a lower rank in the *varṇa-jāti* hierarchy in the process of their indigenization in this region.[77] Donations of the Indo-Greeks, Śakas etc. were made to local religious establishments as a part of the process of this indigenization and acceptance in the local society. Thus, it may be seen that Indian perceptions of *yavanas* varied in different regions and among different Indian communities. While the attitude of the *brāhmaṇas* of north India was one of hostility, the Buddhists had a greater curiosity towards *yavana* countries (proselytising missions of Aśoka) and also must have shown a more congenial and friendly attitude to them as traders and patrons of Buddhism.[78]

The Sangam texts represent a somewhat ambivalent attitude to the *yavanas*, for while they have very interesting accounts of the beautiful *yavana* ships bringing cool fragrant wine for the chiefs and elite of Tamil society, there are also expressions of their distancing themselves from the *yavanas* who were aliens, barbarous and spoke a harsh tongue. A hostile tone is used in the account of a Cēra chief who captured the barbarous *yavanas* and divested them of their wine and wealth.[79] They are even called *milecca*. The epics repeat this tone of hostility but at the same time refer to *yavanas* employed as city guards and palace guards. The presence of *yavana* craftsmen (carpenters) in cities is also attested in the epics.[80] The Koḍumaṇal jewel finds as well as the Amaravati river bed finds,[81] in which Graeco-Roman motifs are identified, would also indicate their presence in the craft centre. It has been suggested on the basis of Jewish and Christian legends that Roman craftsmen were shipped to India.[82] A temple of Augustus which is believed to have had two cohorts of Roman soldiers stationed with it, is said to have been located in Muziris.[83] However, there is no conclusive evidence for the identification of the Augustus temple.

Numismatic evidence from Tamiḻakam would also seem to support the conclusion that two levels of exchange were prevalent, one, at the large-scale exchange of goods for goods and goods for coins (money?) at the big emporia of trade, and the other, at the purely local subsistence level exchange. The distribution of punch-marked and Roman coins[84] shows an interesting pattern. They are found along the trade routes, mostly in hoards. They occur in negligible quantity in stratified levels, both in the context of trade centres and in the Megalithic context. Hence, it would appear that coins were used in large transactions, i.e. in long-distance commerce, both overland and maritime.

The circulation of Roman coins and their use as money in South India have been the subject of an inconclusive debate, due to the complexity of the evidence.[85] Yet, it has been suggested that their occurrence in a stratified context, however negligible, would indicate a limited circulation, possibly along the routes of trade and rivers of transport. Use of Roman coins as jewellery, mainly confined to the Tamil region, would also suggest a lesser role for Roman coins as exchange media, except in large transactions.

It has also been argued that there need not be a single explanation for the occurrence of Roman coins mainly in hoards and that these coins may have had more than a single function. A coinciding of various factors may have led to the need to hoard, not necessarily as bullion, for gold was available in India, the Kolar gold fields showing evidence of working from Mauryan times to the early centuries AD. Thus, the coins appearing in hoards could have been protection money to ensure safe passage of goods from one coast to the other, or investments in further trade by visiting traders. Considering the large quantities of merchandise that were traded in, the occurrence of such a large number of Roman coin finds need not be surprising as 'payment for this trade would have required a large monetary outlay'.[86] They were probably required as deposits or sureties. Such a function is supported by the occurrence of countermarks (as identifying marks of the depositor?) on some of the coin finds in hoards, deposited with traders or guilds, particularly the silver *denarii*, which show the majority of countermarks and are confined to Tamil Nadu and Andhra Pradesh. Yet another function of the Roman coins was as an item of gift in the gift exchange system followed by the Tamil chiefs and ruling families and as symbols of status. The Tamil classics have references to gifts of gold to poets (*pulavar*),[87] who were patronized by the rulers. This was one form of redistribution, in which prestige items such as horses, elephants and gold figured.

The distribution and chronology of the occurrence of the Roman coins also show a distinct pattern in South India. The earliest Roman coins, i.e. the Republican issues of the first century BC reported from south India are confined to the Kerala region and sites near the Palghat gap (pass), the first region to be visited by the early Mediterranean traders. Roman coins of the pre-Christian era are unknown not only in coastal Tamil Nadu but also in Andhra Pradesh. In the early centuries of the Christian era, they appear in coastal Tamil Nadu and Andhra. An intensification of the trading activities on the east coast seems to have taken place by the first and second century AD, when the circumnavigation of the cape had become common. Byzantine coins of the fourth and fifth centuries AD are also mostly confined to coastal Tamil Nadu, Madurai, Karūr and Sri Lanka, pointing to a shift in the regions of intensive trade.

The distribution of the Roman Rouletted Ware suggests a more widespread pattern, though in fewer sites, and points to the rouletting technique travelling from the coast up the rivers to the interior sites on trade routes. The amphora, an expensive item, is found only in selected sites, urban in character, with a prosperous 'elite' clientele, i.e. consumers of wine, foodstuffs, olive oil preserved in such jars.[88] Vasavasamudram and Kāñcīpuram are two such sites. In the latter, however, the identification of the conical jars as amphorae is questionable.

The Koḍumaṇal excavations[89] would also confirm the trading pattern and routes, particularly the overland route from the western to the eastern coast in the early phases and a continuous trading activity in the later phases between the Cēra land (Karūr-Koḍumaṇal) and the east coast. The Kongu region (Cēra land), with its beryls and other semi-precious stones, was a rich resource area and included important iron ore sites.

Evidence of 'dynastic' coinage of the Cōḷas, Cēras and Pāṇḍyas is now increasingly available, although not in a stratified context, with the exception of a few Cōḷa coins (copper) in the Kāvērippūmpaṭṭiṇam excavations.[90] They are known from private collections and as surface and stray finds. The most significant is the discovery, in the Amaravati river bed near Karūr, of silver coins with the 'portrait' (bust) of a Cēra king and the legend Mākkōtai.[91] Coins with the legend 'Kuṭṭuvan

Kōtai'[92] and 'Kollippuṟai'[93] along with the Cēra symbols of the bow and arrow (and with the double fish and tiger), assignable to the Cēras, have also been found. The 'portrait' coins, it is claimed, were influenced by the Roman coins, of which a major concentration of hoards is found in the land of the Cēras (Coimbatore region), which was also a transit zone for traders. Coins with the legend 'Vaḻuti' have been assigned to the Pāṇḍyas.[94] If these discoveries are any indication, the Sangam rulers, apart from controlling long-distance trade by levying tolls and customs, could also have been direct participants in the trade. Even some lesser chiefs like the Malaiyamāns and Nannan, (a hill chief mentioned in the *Malaipaṭukaṭām* or Cēntan ?) seem to have issued coins, of which one important hoard was found in Āṇḍippaṭṭi (Cengam) in the North Arcot district.[95]

The Sangam poems refer to *kāśu*, *poṉ* and *kāṇam*, terms, which are used in the early medieval epigraphic records to denote currency units. They have been presumed to be gold coins.[96] However, there is no indication of their metal content or weight, especially in the Sangam texts. No indigenous gold coin has been discovered so far. *Kāṇam* and *kāśu* were often conferred as gifts by patron-rulers on poets and there is some indication that some at least (*kāṇam* and *poṉ*) were gold coins.

Furthermore, the relationship between the local issues, recently discovered, and the Roman coins is not easy to determine, just as the role of the silver punch-marked coins,[97] found in fairly large numbers, *vis-à-vis* other coins, is difficult to assess. It is, however, contended[98] that the punch-marked coins were used as currency, as quite a few of them have been found in worn-out condition and in stratified levels. This is attributed to the general spread and function of punch-marked coins practically all over the subcontinent. Local issues would also include some punch-marked coin varieties and resemble the *janapada* coins of the Ganges valley. The Bōḍināikkanūr hoard (near Madurai) represents one such issue, marked out by the double carp (fish) symbol of the Pāṇḍyas on the reverse with the usual punch marks on the obverse. Under Ganges valley influence, it is suggested, die-struck coins were also issued.[99] The *Periplus*[100] indicates that while at Barygaza the (Roman) specie imported into the port was exchanged partially for 'native currency' (of the Śaka, Kuṣāṇa and Āndhra?), no such reference is made in the context of the Tamil country. This is explained as due to the absence of indigenous coins,[101] an explanation which is no longer valid as local issues have been found in considerable numbers.

IV

Inter-regional Trade
Shifting Patterns

Tamiḻakam was one of several regions in South Asia which traded with Rome. The pattern of trade in each region seems to have varied according to the nature of exchange and local circuits of trade that existed in the period before the Roman trade. The early historical trading patterns within Tamiḻakam and between Tamiḻakam and other regions of South Asia show a gradual expansion from the proto-historic Megalithic circuits* to the regular exchange networks of the early historical period. While the stages through which the networks emerged are not directly and fully visible in the archaeological contexts, the correlation of the early textual data, epigraphic evidence and numismatic record with the Greek sources enhances our understanding of this trading pattern.

Roman trade with South Asia was spread over a long period and covered the regions from Gujarat down to the Tamil coast and up to the Andhra region and the Bengal coast. Initially, it concentrated on the western coast of early Tamiḻakam and the ports of this coast (later Kerala) seem to have been active in the second and first centuries BC, the 'discovery' of the monsoon winds by Hippalus, often figuring as an important factor in enabling direct sailing from the Red Sea coast to the western coast of South India. From here the trade passed overland

* Although this phase is not the main focus of this essay, a study of the grave goods and pottery of the Megalithic sites in peninsular India reveals the existence of exchange circuits within the three main culture zones—Deccan, Andhra and Tamiḻakam, which increasingly come into focus in the early historical period.

through the Palghat gap, the mineral-rich Coimbatore region to the eastern plains and coast. Subsequently, the circumnavigation of the peninsula intensified the trade with the east coast in the first and second centuries AD.

In the early phases, a local circuit of trade appears to have existed between South India and Sri Lanka linking the Megalithic peoples of Tamiḻakam and Sri Lanka.[102] Almost simultaneously, coastal sea traffic linked the Bengal coast (from Tāmralipti) with Sri Lanka, possibly with a looping coastal trade via the Orissan, Andhra and Tamil coasts. Sri Lanka could well have been an early terminal point for this trade from the Mauryan times with contacts resulting in a regular traffic on the east coast.

Early contacts between Tamiḻakam and Sri Lanka are attested by the Megalithic cultural remains of both the regions. Apart from the use of common graffiti (symbols) on the Megalithic pottery and seals,[103] the occurrence of Tamil *vēḷir* names in the third and second century BC Brāhmī inscriptions of northern Sri Lanka as important personages and references to Tamil merchants in Sri Lanka[104] are significant pointers to this contact. Merchants from Sri Lanka are also known in early Tamiḻakam.[105] The presence of Simhala merchants as well as monks and nuns is recorded in the inscriptions also of the Buddhist sites in Andhra, in addition to which the use of Simhalese forms of Brāhmī in the potsherds of the Tamil sites like Arikamēḍu,[106] attests to their movement via the Tamil coast.

With Mauryan expansion and the opening up of trade routes in peninsular India, these contacts became part of a regular exchange, as indicated by some of the earliest Buddhist structures in Sri Lanka, the epigraphic records, sculptures and structural remains of Andhra region and Tamil coast. The effect of this early coastal sea traffic is assigned a major role in the emergence of Tamil civilization and urbanism, with a particular emphasis on the part played by the Sri Lankan contact.[107]

It is into this early circuit that the western (Roman) trade entered directly in the first and second centuries AD, made possible by the circumnavigation of the cape. Earlier the western coast provided the entry point and outlet for the western trade with Muziris (Muciṟi) as the major port of call. The goods passed from and to the west coast overland through the Kongu highway, i.e. the Coimbatore region and Palghat gap. The distribution pattern of Roman coins[108] of the early first century BC (Republican coins) on the west coast and the first to second century AD coins (Augustus, Tiberius, Nero) more predominantly on the Tamil and Andhra coasts, while coins of the third-fourth centuries AD occur mainly in Tamil Nadu and Sri Lanka would provide evidence of this shift, although any conclusion based merely on the chronology of the Roman coins may be questioned. However, there are other significant pointers to the shifting regional pattern. Thus, while the *Periplus* of the first century AD is familiar with the western ports, Ptolemy (second century AD) has more direct knowledge of the eastern coast, i.e. the Tamil and Andhra coasts upto Masalia (Machlipatnam region).[109]

South India (i.e. Tamiḻakam) seems to have been drawn into another circuit, almost simultaneously with the western trade, with the regions across the Bay of Bengal, i.e. Malaya, Southeast Asia and as far as China, through an exchange network which had emerged within the islands of Southeast Asia and China. This latter circuit became more visible in the centuries after the beginning of the Christian era, although it could well have started even by the second century BC.[110] In this circuit, the contacts between Tamiḻakam and Southeast Asia seem to have intensified in the early centuries and continued to be significant down to the fourth-fifth centuries AD. The early medieval trade contacts of the Pallava-Cōḷa periods were undoubtedly a continuation of these contacts, although in a different historical situation.

Evidence of this expansion and intensity of contacts comes from the epics *Śilappadikāram* and *Maṇimēkalai* and the Buddhist remains at Kāvērippūmpaṭṭiṇam dated in the fourth and fifth centuries AD,[111] while Kāñcīpuram comes up with indirect evidence of its continuous interest in the Southeast Asian regions. The *Maṇimēkalai*, in particular, reflects the importance of this circuit, by locating many of the incidents in the story of *Maṇimēkalai*, both in her previous and present births, in the Tamil cities of Puhār, Vañci, Madurai and Kāñcī, and beyond the seas in other regions of South and Southeast Asia (e.g. Sāvakam = Java and Maṇipallavam

= north Sri Lanka?).[112] A Tamil Brāhmī inscription from Klong Thom (Thailand) of the third and fourth centuries referring to a goldsmith, an early Sanskrit inscription from Laos referring to a Pāṇḍya and a copper coin with the tiger emblem are some of the recent discoveries[113] which provide further evidence of these contacts. The Andhra region also comes up with references to people from these distant lands (China) visiting the Buddhist sites,[114] while it is well known that the Buddhist art of Amarāvati influenced the early sculptural art of Champa (Indo China).

These shifts brought the coastal regions into an exchange network of terminal and transit trade and much of the intra-regional exchange in Tamiḻakam was influenced by them. The inter-*tiṇai* exchange and the plunder mechanism of the early Tamil polities for obtaining the resources for exchange (trade) and gift should be seen as an effect of this sea-borne trade, which brought in valuables, i.e. prestigious goods like wine, gold, horses, camphor, aromatic wood, silk, precious stones etc.

The *yavana* ships were the main carriers of this trade as described in the classical sources and the early Tamil texts. There is no evidence of Indian ships going to the ports of the Red Sea, nor is there any indigenous account exhibiting knowledge of the geography of the western regions. However, much of the coastal shipping between the west and east coasts of south India and between the Tamil coast and Bengal may well have been carried on in Indian ships. The references in the *Periplus*[115] to small types of vessels the natives used for coastal traffic and the larger ones called *sangara* (made by logs fastened together) would also refer to the native boats that carried on the coastal traffic. A much larger vessel called the *kolandiaphonta*, meant for high sea voyages, may have been used for transporting spices and woods from the Southeast Asian islands and for journeys to the Ganges delta. The Tamil textual references to *kalam*, *vangam* and *nāvāy*[116] may be to larger boats with masts and sails, while the *pahṟi* (small strong boats) was perhaps used for river transport down to the mouth of rivers. This is attested by the references in *Paṭṭinappālai*[117] to the *pahṟi* at Puhār.

Individual traders from Tamiḻakam also appear to have travelled probably in foreign ships, to the ports of the Red Sea coast. The recently discovered Ostracon inscriptions at Quseir-al-Qadim, written in Brāhmī characters, reading Cātan and Kaṇan,[118] (Tamil names) point to the presence of Tamil traders at the Red Sea ports and perhaps even Alexandria, which was the focus of much of the South Asian trade, from where the goods reached Rome.

Tamil texts allude to the sea-faring instincts of the Tamils and their rulers in the context of voyages and trade. The sea-girt Pāṇḍya chiefdom[119] was subject to deluges affecting the Pāṇḍya coast, resulting in the transfer of their 'capital' from the coast to the interior. The institution of a sea festival by a Pāṇḍya, and the Cōḷa's neglect of the Indra festival causing a deluge submerging the port of Kāvērippūmpaṭṭiṇam, are pointers to the importance of the sea in contemporary beliefs. The Sangam rulers' 'mastery' of the sea is often symbolically described as in the case of the Pāṇḍya who threw a spear to drive back the sea, the sea as the Pāṇḍya's footstool and the Cōḷa claims to have descended from an ancestor who harnessed the monsoon winds for sea trade.[120] The poems often drew their metaphors from the sea. An elephant running amuck is compared to a storm-tossed ship,[121] while ship=wrecks seem to have been common. The Tamils' knowledge of boat/ship building is also attested by the references to artisans skilled in the repair and refitting of ships and by descriptions like 'the timber that swims the great ocean' (*perunkaḍal nūrdiya maram*).[122]

V

Urban Centres in Early Historical Tamilakam

The foregoing discussion on the early Tamil society and economy, with the main focus on the nature of trade, sets the background for situating the urban centres of this period. First, the dual centres of the major chiefdoms, often grandiosely called kingdoms, will be taken up.

The Cera Centres

1. VAÑCI *KARUVŪR* (KARŪR, TIRUCHIRAPALLI DISTRICT)

Vañci/Karuvūr, the ancient political centre of the Sangam Cēras, may be identified with modern Karūr located on the banks of the Amarāvati river, a tributary of the Kāvēri, in the middle reaches of the valley. Karuvūr, known to the Sangam classics, the epics and the later didactic works,[123] was also called Vañci and Vañci Muṟṟam.[124] The river Ān Porunai (Amarāvati) flowed along this place, which was the capital of the Cēra Kōtai.[125]

The earlier identification of Vañci with Tiruvañcaikkaḷam (Kodungallur or Cranganore) on the west coast was based on the similarity of the names Vañci and Tiruvañcaikkaḷam,[126] and the occurrence of a place called Karūr near the latter. The identification with Karūr in the interior subsequently proposed by K.A. Nilakanta Sastri and M. Raghava Iyengar[127] has been confirmed by explorations and excavations in the region inland, i.e. in and around Karūr. Foreign notices by Ptolemy would also show that Korura (Karūr) was an inland town.[128] A number of references from the *Puṟanāṉūṟu*, *Patiṟṟuppattu* and the epics may be cited to show that Karuvūr and Vañci were identical. Later herostone inscriptions from Karūr datable to the eighth century AD refer to the place both as Karūr and Vañci.[129]

Attempts made to locate Vañci in Tiruvañcaikkaḷam near Muciṟi, the Cēra port, have been unsuccessful, as no significant archaeological remains have been found at this site prior to the eighth century AD. That this centre was the capital of the early medieval Cēra kingdom of Mākkōtai (Mahodayapuram) has, however, been established. What is also of interest is that apart from the coastal Muciṟi, a small town called Muciṟi also exists near the inland town of Karūr, on the route to Tiruchirappalli, the ancient Uṟaiyūr of the Cōḷas. Unlike the excavations at Koḍungallūr, the excavations in the inland Karūr by the Tamil Nadu Department of Archaeology have provided positive clues to its location, such as Roman amphora pieces, local Rouletted Ware, a Roman copper coin in one of the lower strata and BRW, some with graffiti marks.[130]

Karūr's importance as a political and commercial centre is

also attested by other archaeological finds in and around the town. Apart from the prized Roman aureus of Claudius (AD 41-54) from Karūr, a large number of Roman coins, especially the hoard from nearby Veḷḷalūr, and the recent discovery of Cēra coins in the Amarāvati river bed provide supportive evidence. The occurrence of several silver coins of Mākkōtai, with the bust, apparently of the Cēra ruler, believed to be influenced by the Roman coins with portraits, suggests that Karūr may have been a mint town. The literary references to Karūr as a centre of jewel making are corroborated by the finds of some of the oldest finger rings with intaglio, one being a *mithuna* of the Amarāvati style, others with Graeco-Roman motifs like cupid, a warrior figure on a prancing lion with Hellenistic attire, with Buddhist symbols like the *triratna/nandipada* and Brāhmī legends with personal names, all assignable to the period between second century BC and first century AD.[131] It is also significant that the Veḷḷalūr hoard of Roman coins contained jewels with Roman intaglios.[132] A gold merchant from Karūr figures as the donor of a stone bed to a Jaina ascetic at Pukaḷūr, not far from Karūr.[133]

Coins, without portraits, but with symbols like the bow and arrow, the Cēra emblem, a mountain, double fish and a tiger and legends reading 'Kollippuṟai' (meaning Poṟaiyar, the rulers of the Kolli hills, have also been found in Karūr.[134] This would further support the presence of a mint in this centre. Different lineages of the Cēras with suffixes like the Kōtai (Mākkōtai), Poṟai (Irumpoṟai) and/or Ātan (Ceralātan) are known from the Sangam texts and the epigraphic and coin finds confirm that they ruled in and around Karūr. Significantly, the Tamil Brāhmī inscriptions from Pukaḷūr and Arachchalūr, not far from Karūr on the Kongu highway, recording gifts to the Buddhist and/or Jaina ascetics, by the Cēra ruling family and by merchants, craftsmen etc., refer to three generations of Cēra rulers[135] and point to the influence of the Śramaṇic religions over the trading community and the rulers. Koḍumaṇal, the Koḍumaṇam of *Patiṟṟuppattu*, situated nearby, with evidence of a large gem and jewel manufacturing centre, adds to Karūr's importance as a commercial centre.

The evidence of the epics, which are chronologically later than the Sangam anthologies, would again point to the development of Karūr into a large urban complex and the inclusion in it of Buddhist and Jain establishments. The *Maṇimēkalai* refers to a *caitya* in Vañci, believed to have been built by a predecessor of Kōvalan (the hero of the *Śilappadikāram*), who became a monk after giving away his wealth, evidently to the Buddhist institution. He, it is said, was a friend of the contemporary Cēra ruler and the *caitya* was built 'in brilliant white stucco with its turrets reaching the sky'.[136] At Vañci, an *Indra vihāra* is also said to have been built resembling the one at Puhār.[137] The reference to *Indra vihāras* suggests that Buddhist establishments came up on the outskirts of big urban centres and it became a common literary tradition to ascribe them to divine authorship or to great kings like Aśoka, by pilgrims and foreign travellers. In some cases, as in Vañci and Puhār, they may have been erected by merchants or trading groups, while later tradition provided them with great antiquity.[138] At the time of a famine in Kāñcīpuram, we are told, the Buddhist mendicants abandoned the city and settled down in the *vihāra* at Vañci.[139] In the excavations at Karūr, however, no such structures or their remains have been unearthed, whereas Puhār has something to offer in the form of remains of *caitya* and *vihāra* structures, albeit of the period from fourth to sixth centuries AD.

2. *MUCIṞI* (KOḌUNGALLŪR/CRANGANORE, TRICHUR DISTRICT, KERALA)

Muciṟi, the first and the earliest major port of call,[140] was the famous Cēra port where the ships of the *yavanas* called in large numbers, and in exchange for gold took back cargoes of pepper and other products.[141] According to the *Periplus*, Muziris abounded in ships sent there with cargoes from Ariake (Arabia) and Greek ships from Egypt.[142] Pliny, however, warns that pirates from Nitrias (Cannanore or Mangalore?) make Muziris not a desirable place of call and ships had to anchor at some distance from the shore and the cargoes had to be landed and shipped by employing boats.[143] It was the land of the Coelobothros (Keralaputra?) and pepper came from Cottanara (Kuṭṭanāḍu).

Muziris and Nelcynda are often spoken of together by the

Periplus while listing the imports and exports from this port. Nelcynda was, however, a Pāṇḍyan port. The imports were 'a great quantity of coin, topaz, thin clothing–not much, figured linens, antimony, coral, crude glass, copper, tin, lead, wine–not much (?) but as much as at Barygaza, realgar, orpiment, wheat, enough for the sailors, for this is not dealt in by the merchants there'. The exports were 'pepper from Cottanara, great quantities of fine pearls, ivory, silk cloth, spikenard from the Ganges, malabathrum from the places in the interior, transparent stones of all kinds (beryls etc.?), diamonds, sapphires and tortoise shell,–that from Chryse island and that taken among the islands along the coast of Damirica'.[144] What is significant is that many of these items as exports and imports are archaeologically attested in South India, while a trade agreement of the second century AD between a Muciṟi merchant and a Greek refers to quite a few of them.

Muciṟi's importance as a major port of trade remained unaffected from second century BC to second century AD even after the circumnavigation of the peninsula took Greek ships directly to the Coromandel coast, where Puhār developed as the chief port. As late as the second century AD, evidence of trade in bulk goods between Muciṟi and Alexandria in Egypt comes from a papyrus in the Vienna Museum[145] recording a trade agreement in Greek between a *vaṇikar* from Muciṟi and a trader (Greek?) from Alexandria. The agreement was apparently written in Alexandria, according to which certain specified quantities of Gangetic nard (700 to 1700 lb.), ivory items (4700 lb.) and a variety of textiles (790 lb.), whose value was equal to the price of 2400 acres of land in Egypt (one shipment–a single merchant's merchandise) were to be exported from Muciṟi, in ships to a Red Sea port, then taken on camel crossing the desert and the Nile, reaching Coptos and then shipped to the Mediterranean town of Alexandria. It was subject to a 25 per cent customs duty on import, the costs covering risks of possible brigandage *en route*. It is estimated that one ship could carry the merchandise of about one hundred and fifty merchants. What the Muziris contract underlines is that the Indian trade was of a substantial scale by the second century AD with Muziris continuing to be the emporium for goods even from the east coast,[146] requiring enormous financial outlay.

The Pāṇḍya Centres

5. *MADURAI* (MADURAI DISTRICT)

Madurai, the political centre of the Pāṇḍyas, was perhaps the most important of the Tamil cities in the early historical period. As the seat of the third Tamil Sangam (literary academy), which the Pāṇḍyas patronized, it was the Tamil city *par excellence*, where the Tamil cultural traditions were fostered. A whole text of the Sangam collection, viz. *Maduraikkāñci*, is devoted to its description, just as *Paṭṭinappālai* to Puhār. It was the scene of many enlightening episodes and stories connected with the Sangam poets, which later became inscribed in the traditions of the city, and also the second major setting for the story of Kōvalan and Kaṇṇaki of the *Śilappadikāram* of the fifth to sixth centuries AD, the first being Puhār.

The *Maduraikkāñci*, the longest poem in the *Pattuppāṭṭu* collection, and datable to the second century AD, gives a graphic description of Madurai as a large and beautiful city, with a palace, a number of temples, two large markets (bazaars?) and well laid out streets with lofty mansions.[147] It had protective ramparts (walls) with huge gates and towers, surrounded by a deep moat, with the Vaigai river skirting the city walls forming a natural defence on one side. People of different social strata and speaking different languages lived in different localities, professionals and craftsmen crowding the streets with their wares. Peddlars and petty traders also plied a brisk trade in the shade of the lofty mansions. Vedic/brahmanic and non-Vedic/non-brahmanic (Śramaṇic) religious houses or places of worship also existed.[148] The *Neṭunalvāṭai* repeats some of these descriptions and adds that the apartments of the palace were lit by *yavana* lamps and drunken *mileccas* (*yavanas*?) roamed about the streets with their dresses hanging loose on the back and front.[149] It is doubtful whether such verbal imagery of the Madurai city and its mansions is a reflection of the reality, for no site of early historical Tamiḻakam has revealed archaeological remains commensurate with the conventionalized descriptions in the texts.

The picture of the market place in Madurai is equally graphic in *Maduraikkāñci* and *Neṭunalvāṭai* and yet need not be set aside as conventional, for, the artisanal and trading activity as described in the text are supported by the nature of vestiges around Madurai and in other early sites. The texts say that it was a big market, a converging point for traders, a centre of crafts like gold jewels, gold statues (?) ivory, inlay work and stucco images. The gold merchants were specialists who could testify to the fineness of gold and goldsmiths, well skilled in drawing thin wires from molten gold. There were traders in pearls and precious gems who had their shops in the markets. Chank cutting and bangle making were also important.[150] That it was the source of the best cotton is mentioned in the *Arthaśāstra*, although whether this text meant the old Madurai on the coast or the one in the interior is not certain.[151]

Meaningful archaeological excavations in the present town of Madurai are virtually impossible due to its continuous occupation. Yet, the region around Madurai has come up with interesting epigraphic evidence in the form of the earliest Tamil Brāhmī inscriptions (second century BC onwards) from Tirupparankuṉṟam, Aḻagarmalai, Māṅkuḷam and other sites. Roman coins have also been found, some in Madurai itself,[152] while a hoard of silver punch-marked coins, from a place called Boḍināikkanūr, with the double carp symbol on the reverse (along with other punch marks on the obverse), has been assigned to the Pāṇḍyas as their issue.[153] Square copper coins (with the elephant and fish symbols) found in the region are also considered as Pāṇḍya dynastic issue. Recent discoveries of coins with the legend 'vaḷutiy' or Peruvaḷutiy,[154] would add support to the view that local coin issues (of Cēras and Pāṇḍyas) were influenced by the large maritime commercial transactions of the period.

4. *KORKAI (TIRUNELVELI DISTRICT)*

Koṟkai was another major port and one of the dual centres of the Sangam Pāṇḍyas. The Pāṇḍyas are often called Koṟkai

Kōmān and Koṟkai Vēndu (Vēndu and Kōmān mean the great chief/king).[155] Located on the south-east coast at the mouth of the Tamraparni river, Koṟkai is now six kilometres to the interior due to the recession of the sea in recent times. The urn burial site of Adichanallur, also on the banks of the Tamraparni, is about fifteen kilometres west of the present village of Koṟkai. Sawyerpuram, the microlithic site (teri site) is only three kilometres away. Altogether the area is rich in archaeological remains, with an important group of proto-historic sites.

An early occupation of Koṟkai by the urn-burial folk, i.e. much earlier than the other dated sites of the Megalithic phase in the Tamil country, is indicated by the Adichanallur urn-burials of a large size, the urn-burials of the Megalithic phase and the Radio Carbon dates of the lowest levels of occupation at Koṟkai, i.e. 785 BC.[156] The occurrence at Koṟkai, of BRW, Roman Ware, Rouletted Ware of local origin, sherds with graffiti, inscribed potsherds with Brāhmī characters of second century BC to second century AD, and brick structures is consistent with the results so far obtained from other excavated sites in the Tamil country. However, a few sherds identified as of Northern Black Polished Ware (or are they a special fine variety of Rouletted Ware?) takes this site back at least to third century BC (Mauryan period), while the charcoal sample and a piece of wood at the lower levels of KRK-I have given an R.C. date of 785 BC, taking it further back in time.[157] This early date for Koṟkai, in many ways, points to the growth of early coastal traffic and trade linking the Bay of Bengal coasts from Bengal to northern Sri Lanka, via Andhra and Tamil coasts.

Koṟkai, according to Sangam literary tradition, was a far-famed port (*Pugaḻ mali śiṟappiṟ Koṟkai munturai*) and reputed for its pearls.[158] Kāyal (meaning salt pans) which is located not far from Koṟkai, was well known for its salt pans.[159] The *Periplus* talks of Colchi (Koṟkai) and its pearl fisheries worked by condemned criminals.[160] To the Greeks the Gulf of Mannar was Colchic gulf.[161]

The occurrence of pearl oysters at various levels in the Koṟkai excavations provides confirmation of the literary evidence that Koṟkai was a centre of pearl fishers and trade in pearls.[162] The *Arthaśāstra*'s reference to the pearls of the Pāṇḍya country and the number of places where they were obtained also suggests that the whole stretch of coasts of the Indian-Ceylon straits was the source of pearls.[163]

The Cōḷa Centres

5. *URAIYUR* (TIRUCHIRAPALLI DISTRICT)

Uṟaiyūr, at present a part of Tiruchirapalli town, represents the site of the ancient 'capital' of the Sangam Cōḷas. It was also known as Kōḻi and Vāraṇam.[164] Descriptions of Uṟaiyūr in the Sangam texts indicate that it was a strongly defended city and its outskirts had burial grounds which were full of stones and hence 'there were many obstacles to easy movement'.[165] This description is strongly suggestive of the existence of Megalithic cairn circles and burials. The earliest levels of the excavated site in Uṟaiyūr have BRW and other early pottery as in other excavated sites and point to the Megalithic antecedents of early Tamil culture.

The Cōḷa Karikāla is said to have enlarged this town, fortified it and enriched it with beautiful buildings.[166] It was as important as Puhār or Kāvērippūmpaṭṭiṇam, the port city of the Cōḷas and both these centres were developed by the same Cōḷa ruler, Karikāla.

Excavations at Uṟaiyūr[167] have established a cultural sequence of three periods. Period I[168] is represented by BRW, the Russet-coated Painted Ware, the Rouletted Ware, Arretine Ware, together with the associated Red and all-Black Wares. Sherds with graffiti and Brāhmī inscriptions assignable to the first and second centuries AD have also been met with. Period II shows a gradual disuse of BRW and the emergence of the Red Slipped Ware. A rectangular cistern, which the excavators describe as a dyeing vat, also belongs to this period. This, if correct, would confirm the literary evidence on the famous Uṟaiyūr textile industry and the reference in the classical sources to Argaritic, a fine fabric form Argaru, i.e. Uṟaiyūr.

Evidence of flood and waterlogging in one of the cuttings would suggest a disturbance due to the destruction of this site by a flood in the Kāvēri. Reference to a flood which occurred in the area in *c.* AD 944 is made in an inscription from Allūr, five kilometres from Uṟaiyūr.[169] The flood may thus be associated with period III, assigned to the eighth-fourteenth centuries, which is represented by a crude ill-fired Red Ware, Celadon Ware, besides terracotta figurines and beads of semi-precious stones. Uṟaiyūr, as is well known, continued to be a political centre of the imperial Cōḻas of ninth to thirteenth centuries AD. The only epigraphic evidence on the antiquity of this site, taking it back to the early historical period, comes from a Brāhmī inscription at Tiruchirapalli.[170]

Thus, it would appear that archaeological remains in Uṟaiyūr are not very illuminating for the early historical period and in no way equal to the literary descriptions of the place. The problems that confront the archaeologist here are of the same nature as in other early historical urban centres, i.e. their continuous occupation and the disturbance caused by it. A large urban complex developed here in the medieval and modern periods and Uṟaiyūr became a part of it.

6. KAVERIPPŪMPAṬṬIṆAM/PUHAR (TAÑJAVŪR DISTRICT)

Kāvērippūmpaṭṭiṇam or Puhār, one of the dual centres of the Cōḻas, was the chief port on the east coast in the early historical period and continued to be so till at least the fifth to sixth centuries AD. It was known to the *Periplus* as Camara and to Ptolemy as Khaberis.[171] Much of our knowledge of this town is derived from the Sangam works and the epics. The *Paṭṭinappālai*, one of the Sangam collections, is devoted wholly to its description, while the post-Sangam epics, *viz* the *Śilappadikāram* and the *Maṇimēkalai* contain numerous references to the town, its various quarters, religious and secular buildings. Its development into a fairly large urban complex is evident from the *Paṭṭinappālai*, while the epics show that it included Buddhist and Jain establishments, apart from a number of shrines of the brahmanical and folk deities.[172]

The city was known by several names such as Puhār, Kākandi and Sampāpati.[173] The last name seems to be preserved to this day in the name of the Sampāpati temple, believed to have been the tutelary deity of the town. The city is described in literature as Pērūr and Mānagar (big town/city).[174] No less than forty odd sites may be located near the present site of Kāvērippūmpaṭṭiṇam which once formed part of the city. Some of them are Vānagiri, Veḷḷaiyaniruppu (the abode of the white men–*yavanas*?). Sāyāvanam, Maṇigrāmam (Vaṇika-grāma) and others, where archaeological digging has brought to light occupational debris belonging to a period ranging from *c.* third century BC to fifth century AD. The diggings at Veḷḷaiyaniruppu have, contrary to expectations, not revealed any early *yavana* settlement, but only show a deposit going back to the ninth century AD.[175]

The city had two main parts, the Paṭṭinappākkam or the residential area and the Maruvūrpākkam or the coastal area with its harbour. The residential area is also called Akanagar (internal city), which was evidently the prosperous section, where the richer classes lived and where there were residential buildings (of brick), feeding houses, gardens, public meeting places, public baths, tanks and religious structures, etc.[176] The coastal area contained the harbour, customs offices with the tiger emblem (of the Cōḷas) on their doors, storehouses, godowns, merchants' quarters and a fishermen's colony. People speaking different tongues, including foreigners, lived there.[177] The *nāḷangāḍi* (day market) and the *aḷḷangādi* (evening market) met in the spacious open area between the two main divisions of the city on the east and the west.[178]

The cemetery and burial ground situated on the outskirts of the city also had their guardian deities such as the deity in the pillar.[179]

Excavations, however, have not revealed relics of early structures of such magnitude and grandeur as described in literature. The only significant finds are of a brick structure in Kīḷaiyūr, identified as a wharf, where boats were anchored with the help of wooden pegs.[180] The wharf is dated to about the fourth to third century BC based on the R.C. date (315 BC) for the wooden sample from this structure, apart from the evidence of the BRW deposits. The size of the wharf would also show that it was probably an anchoring site for boats (*paḥri*) bringing goods from the interior or from large ships halting a little away from the shores, as evidence of a harbour with docking facilities is lacking.[181] The tradition that Kāvērippūmpaṭṭiṇam was submerged in the sea on account of a curse on the city due to the failure of a Cōḷa king to conduct the Indra festival,[182] has led to the belief that part of the ancient city is now under water. Efforts are on to check such a possibility through underwater archaeology. A survey conducted on the beach about six kilometres from the water's edge is reported to have shown indications of buried archaeological remains under the sand (?). As late as 1849, encroachments of the sea are believed to have washed away part of the ancient town.[183]

Remains of a semi-circular brick structure with an internal diametre of eight metres, have been unearthed at Vānagiri, which may represent a water reservoir fed by a wide inlet channel of eighty-three centimetres from the Kaveri. Associated deposits yielded BRW and Rouletted Ware, and, as such, a first century AD date is indicated.[184]

The most striking remains are those of a Buddhist *vihāra* at the site called Pallavaneśvaram consisting of a full wing of cells and a long verandah on the south. A subsidiary structure, probably of an apsidal *caitya*, together with other Buddhist objects found here, has been assigned to the fourth to fifth centuries AD, with constructions of a still later phase.[185] The Buddhist remains generally confirm the evidence of the epics.

The site of Maṇigrāmam yielded deposits of BRW and Rouletted Ware of different fabrics, in addition to terracotta figurines and square copper coins of the Cōḷas, all assignable to the beginning of the Christian era.[186] The coins bear the figure of a standing tiger (?) on the obverse and an elephant on the reverse. One of the symbols on the coins has also been identified as a fish or *kalpavṛkṣa*.[187] The name Maṇigrāmam (or Vaṇika-grāma) indicates the presence of a merchant quarter. Significantly, Maṇigrāmam is also the name borne by a famous merchant guild of early medieval South India.[188] Thus, it would appear that the urban complex of Puhār included in it a merchant colony, which provided the background to the story of the *Śilappadikāram*.

Puhār, the Cōḷa port, seems to have superseded all other ports of South India, when, in the perennial conflict among the *vēndar* for hegemony and control over the resources of one another, the Cōḷas emerged more successful and developed their port as the port of destination and embarkation for the major resources of Tamiḻakam, Sri Lanka and Southeast Asia, and stationed their officers to oversee the import and export of commodities. Thus, the merchandise that came to Puhār shows a great variety.

> War horses that came by sea
> Bags of black pepper brought overland by cart
> gems and gold from the northern mountain
> sandal and *akil* wood from the western mountain
> pearls of the southern and corals of the eastern sea
> The produce of the Ganges basin and Kaveri valley
> Foodstuffs from Ceylon and luxuries from Kaḍāram
>
> (*Paṭṭinappālai* ll. 185-191)

What is perhaps more important is that it retained its pre-eminent position at least till the fifth-sixth centuries AD, providing a major outlet and entry point (Puhār = entry point? or does it refer to the Kāvēri entering the sea?) for the commerce with Southeast Asia. It would, therefore, be tempting to characterize it as a gateway[189] to Tamiḻakam till the early medieval period, when it was superseded by Nāgappaṭṭiṇam as the major Cōḷa port.

The Centres of the Tiraiyar (Toṇḍaimān)

7. KACCI (KAÑCIPURAM, CHINGLEPUT DISTRICT)

Kāñcīpuram, well known in history as the capital of Pallavas as early as mid-fourth century AD,[190] was the Kacci of the Sangam texts. In early Tamil literature Kāñcī is known as Kacci, Kaccimuṟṟam and Kaccippēḍu, the last one probably a suburb, from where a number of Tamil poets hailed. Kāñcī and Kāñcīnallūr also refer to the same town.[191]

The Kāñcīpuram excavations have been spread over several parts of the city and the relevant ones for the early historical period are those conducted in the premises of the Śankara *maṭha* and near the Kāmākṣī temple.[192] The first site has indicated three periods of occupation, of which Period IA (second century BC to third century AD?) has BRW in early levels, Black

Slipped Ware and Rouletted Ware and conical jars in the upper levels, apart from a coin of Rudra Sātakarṇi of the second century AD and terracotta figurines. Period IB is assigned to the fourth–ninth centuries AD, i.e. of the Pallavas, and is represented by Bright and Red Slipped Ware, lead and copper coins and moulds. Period II is of early medieval times (Cōḷa period) and period III is of modern occupation.

In the excavations near the Kāmākṣī temple, a three period stratification has been made, of which the first two are relevant.[193] Period I is represented by fine BRW in its lower levels (IA), and Painted Ware assignable to the period from the third century BC to first century BC, and the upper levels (IB) show BRW, Rouletted, Arretine Wares, beads, terracotta objects and iron objects and remains of a baked brick structure identified as a Buddhist shrine. Period II (fourth to ninth centuries AD) is represented by conical jars (miscalled amphorae) or local imitations of amphorae, fine Bright Red and Orange Slipped Wares, glass and other objects. The small 'circular' structure identified as a votive *stūpa*[194] cannot conclusively be proven to be a *stūpa*, as, apart from a few courses of brick, neither the outline or plan of the structure nor its shape is traceable. The bricks are, however, of considerable size (50/22/6 cm) and comparable to those of Andhra Buddhist sites.

Traditions regarding the Buddhist associations of Kāñcī appear only in the post-Sangam texts, no specific references occurring in the Sangam anthologies to Kāñcī as a Buddhist centre. Buddhist institutions are first mentioned in the *Maṇimēkalai*. Again, it is only in the accounts of Hsuan Tsang that Kāñcī's Buddhist associations are stressed and the Chinese pilgrim suggests great antiquity for Buddhism in Kāñcī by referring to *stūpas* of the Aśokan period.[195] The *Mattavilāsa Prahasana*, a burlesque attributed to the Pallava king Mahendravarman of early seventh century AD, refers to a Buddhist *vihāra* in Kāñcī.[196] Similarly, with the exception of the Tamil Brāhmī inscription from Māmaṇḍūr the earliest datable evidence of the presence of Jainism also belongs to the fourth–sixth century period, as seen in the Tirunātharkuṉṟu epitaph of the fourth century AD, the Jain work called the *Lokavibhāga* of the fifth century AD and the Paḷḷankōyil copper plates of *c.* AD 550.[197]

The *Perumpāṇārruppaṭai*[198] gives a graphic description Kacci as a 'Mūdūr' (old town) formed by a number of settlements. It had tall buildings of brick and was fortified by high walls. The palace of Iḷamtiraiyan, the chief of the Toṇḍaiyar, is described with poetic fancy, marked by occasional glimpses of realism. The river Vēghavatī (Veḥkā), on which the city stood, comes in for elaborate treatment and its associations with Māl (Viṣṇu) are highlighted. Such descriptions hardly find archaeological corroboration. Archaeological work in cities like Kāñcī is confronted with problems arising from continuous occupation and a lack of potential areas for digging. However, through trial digging, insights into the antiquity of such sites can be provided. There is thus little doubt that the archaeological record in Kāñcī goes back to the Megalithic or BRW period.

Kāñcī's contacts with the world outside may be traced back to at least second century BC, if the work of Pan Kou, a Chinese writer of the first century AD, is to be trusted. Pan Kou's *Ts'ien han Chou* points to contacts between Houang-tche (Kāñcī) and China, by referring to the exchange of goods and presents between the Chinese emperor P'ing (Yuan-che period) and the king of Houang-tche. According to Pan Kou, the Chinese emperor sent presents to the king of Houang-tche and asked for a return 'embassy' with a live rhinoceros as tribute. People from Houang-tche sent tributes from the time of emperor Wou (140-86 BC). Other goods like shining pearls, glass and rare stones in exchange for gold and silk are also mentioned. The journey from China took about ten months to one year through Pagan (Burma).[199]

With the Roman world, Kāñcī's contacts seem to have been indirect, perhaps through its port Nīrppeyarru. Although no Roman coins have been found in Kāñcī, the fact that several finds are known from the region around it, i.e. in Toṇḍaināḍu–such as Māmallapuram (port), Madurāntakam (a place called Ālamporai), Saidapet and Mambalam (both in present Madras city) would point to the region's participation in the Roman trade. The Rouletted Ware found in Kāñcī may be of a local variety, with the rouletting technique travelling from the ports (coastal area) to the interior. While the Arretine Ware finds in Kāñcī are negligible, the red conical jars were imitations of the amphora, the true amphora finds being confined to Arikamēḍu and Vasavasamudram,[200] apart from a site called Kāraikkāḍu.

8. VASAVASAMUDRAM (NEAR SADRAS, CHINGLEPUT DISTRICT)

Situated at the mouth of the river Palar, this site is about thirteen kilometres south of Māmallapuram. Excavations at this site have unearthed pieces of amphora, Rouletted Ware, double ring wells and other objects like beads. Remains of brick structures, terracotta ovens and heaps of shell lime, all assignable to a single period of occupation (1.92 metres deposit) from the first to third century AD have also been found. Significantly, there is no BRW deposit at the site, although the general assemblage and antiquities correspond to those at Arikamēḍu.[201] Hence, Vasavasamudram represents the later phase of Roman trade, when the east coast's trade had become intensified. It also seems to have continued to be a part of it when the Roman trade was at its lowest ebb in the Byzantine period.

The real significance of Vasavasamudram lies in its location in relation to Kāñcī. Situated on the banks of the Veghavati, a tributary of the Palar, Kāñcī has access to the sea only through Palar and hence some early port at the mouth of the Palar, may well have served as the ancient port of the Tiraiyar of the Sangam texts. Vāyalūr, where a historic inscription of Rājasimha Pallava datable to early eighth century has been found, is located two miles south of Vasavasamudram. The latter could well have been a part of Vāyalūr, which is known as the 'pilavāyil'—entrance way.[202]

The *Perumpāṇārruppaṭai*,[203] one of the Sangam works, containing descriptions of Kāñcī and other places in Toṇḍaināḍu, refers to a port called Nīrppeyarru. Nīrppeyarru is described as a big port with a lighthouse (in the days of Toṇḍaimān Iḷamtiraiyan, a contemporary of Karikāla Cōḷa), with broad streets, tall houses (of merchants), fishermen's quarters (*paratavar*), godowns guarded by professional men, and with a harbour full of ships bringing white horses and precious stones. The tall lighthouse on the shore guided the ships. This site has been identified with Nīrppēr in the Madurāntakam taluk of Chingleput district and with Māmallapuram.[204] It is said that Nīrpāyaṟṟuṟai (*tuṟai* = ghat = harbour) was later corrupted in to Nīrppeyaṟṟu.

It is, however, more in keeping with the archaeological evidence at Vasavasamudram to identify it with Nīrppeyaṟṟu, with evidence of its connections with the western trade. Although Māmallapuram has some evidence in the form of Roman coins, the location of Vasavasamudram is of greater importance in its identification. It may have been superseded by Māmallapuram even by the fourth and fifth centuries AD, when the Pallavas are known to have occupied Kāñcīpuram. Hence, the occupational deposit at Vasavasamudram indicates a single period.

Other Centres

9. AḺAGANKUḶAM (RAMANATHAPURAM DISTRICT)

Aḻagankuḷam is located at the mouth of the Vaigai river, on its northern bank, now some distance away from the coast, from where the opposite coast of Sri Lanka (north west) can be reached by boat in about twenty-five minutes. It is identified with Sāliyūr of the Sangam works.[205] Here, the occupation levels indicate a period from pre-third century BC to the beginning of the sixth century AD. The earliest levels show NBP ware, followed by BRW, silver punch-marked coins of first and second centuries AD, together with Roman Rouletted Ware (local?), amphorae, and a very interesting and rare Pink Ware, of which thousands of sherds have been found. Finally occur the late Roman coins of Valentine II, Theodesius (388–393) and Arcadius (394–408).[206] The Pink Ware has been alternatively described as an African Red Slipped Ware or an Afghan Ware and compared to some potsherds of similar fabric from Arikamēḍu.[207] Beads, semi-precious stones and terracotta objects have also been reported. Square copper coins of the Pāṇḍyas with the elephant, fish (?) and auspicious symbols such as wheel and vase (*pūrṇaghaṭa*) are other finds from the site. Some of the BRW sherds have graffiti and Brāhmī inscriptions.

The presence of the NBP may point to its importance in early coastal traffic or trade with the Bengal coast and Andhra coast, while the later levels with Roman antiquities suggest a more direct involvement in the Roman trade from the second to fifth centuries AD. This port is considered to be as important as Puhār, Koṟkai and Arikamēḍu in the early historical trade of Tamiḻakam with the Mediterranean region, and needs to be carefully explored and mapped out. For, in its vicinity, are located some sites which are identifiable with settlements mentioned in the Sangam works.

The name Aḻagankuḷam is evidently a later one for this ancient port. The ancient site may be the same as Marungūr paṭṭiṇam mentioned in the *Akanāṉūṟu*. Two parts of this town,[208] *viz.* Ūṇūr (Nellin Ūṇūr), which abounded with paddy, and Marungūr, which was the commercial area on the coast, as described in this work, recall the two divisions of Kāvērippūmpaṭṭiṇam (Puhār), i.e. Paṭṭiṇappākkam and Maruvūrpākkam. The *Maduraikkāñcī* also refers to a Nellin Ūr as a busy port with ships bringing goods from different countries. The waiting ships are compared to a group of mountains about to seize the floods.[209] Nellin Ūr and Nellin Ūṇūr could well have been the same. Between Koṟkai and Toṇḍi (another Pāṇḍya port known from early medieval sources) is a village called Marungūr near the coast.

10. ARIKAMEDU (PODUCA/PODOUKE), PONDICHERY

One of the earliest sites to be excavated on the east coast, confirming the Sangam literary evidence on the Roman trade, Arikamēḍu, south of Pondicherry town, has been described as an Indo-Roman trading station.[210] The Arikamēḍu excavations have often served as a reference point offering 'a firm datum line from which the classification of pre-medieval South Indian cultures can begin'. The site is assigned to the first and second centuries AD by the early excavators. The associated BRW at this site, it is believed, has been dated with greater precision on the basis of the occurrence of the Arretine and Rouletted Ware and the Roman amphorae. However, more recent excavations have attempted to push back the beginnings of the site to the second century BC, again on the basis of the Rouletted and Arretine

Ware and hence, also to date BRW earlier than the first or second century AD.[211]

The earlier excavations have also brought to light brick structures, one in the northern sector, identified as a warehouse, and another in the southern sector, a structure with tanks and courtyards, as one used in the preparation of muslin cloth, a notable export from the Tamil region. Bead and glass manufacture has also been identified. In addition, gems with intaglio designs found in the site have been assigned to Graeco-Roman craftsmen, suggesting their presence in Arikamēḍu.

Arikamēḍu has been identified with Vīrai, the modern Vīrāmpaṭṭiṇam near the site, which was one of the *vēḷir* strongholds known to Sangam literature. In the *Akanāṉūṟu*, it is described as a harbour of the *vēḷir*, while the *Naṟṟiṇai* says that it was the centre of the *vēḷir* chieftain Vīrai Veḷiyan Veṇmān.[212] Evidence in support of the *vēḷir* association of this centre has been recognised in a BRW sherd with a Brāhmī inscription of the first century AD reading Yadu Balabhūti-y or Balabhūti of the Yadu Clan.[213] The *vēḷir* claimed descent from the Yādavas.[214] A Possible derivation of the Poduca/ Podouke of the *Periplus* and Ptolemy is interesting in this connection. Podouke may be derived from Podikai, a meeting place in a clan settlement. Such Podikais were common among the *vēḷir* settlements of early Tamiḻakam.[215]

Arikamēḍu's importance in the Roman trade is generally accepted. That traders from other countries were also regular visitors to this port is suggested by the use of Simhalese characters in the early Brāhmī inscriptions on potsherds, one of which has been read as *bū ta śa*, using the old Simhalese form *śa* for the genitive case ending of the personal name *būta*.[216] This would further strengthen the evidence on early coastal sea traffic along the east coast down to Sri Lanka, from where Buddhist monks and nuns are known to have visited the Andhra Buddhist centres.

11. KOḌUMAṆAL,[217] PERUNDURAI TALUK (PERIYAR / ERODE DISTRICT)

Koḍumaṇal, the ancient Koḍumaṇam of *Patiṟṟuppattu*, a Sangam work, described as a centre of gem and jewel manufacturing, is located on the north bank of the Noyyal river about forty kilometres from Erode. Paḍiyūr, with its beryl mines, is about six kilometres south of it. The site's location in the Kongu region (the Coimbatore, Salem and Periyar districts) with a concentration of Roman coin finds in hoards, must have influenced its role as a nodal point on the overland trade route linking the Kerala coast, through the Palghat gap, with the middle and lower reaches of the Kāvēri down to the ports of the east coast. Archaeological excavations have confirmed its importance as a jewel manufacturing centre, with a large quartz zone providing semi-precious stones. Due to the absence of chalcedony in this quartz zone, with the exception of carnelian, which was brought probably from Gujarat, all other semi-precious stones[218] are available in the region. A factory site for quartz objects has also been identified in the excavations at the centre. Koḍumaṇal must have been a large supplier of crystal objects to the port of Muciṟi, possibly in exchange for Roman gold and silver coins and pottery.

The other major industry was of iron, with evidence of a wide range of iron weapons, and other objects like spindles, a large number of rusted iron stirrups, apart from slags along with a factory site–perhaps the earliest iron foundry for melting iron ore. Possibly iron objects were also meant for export. Hardly twenty kilometres from Koḍumaṇal lay an iron belt from the Sennimalai (at present a weaving centre), with its magnetic iron ore, upto Kanjamalai.

The site seems to have been in occupation from at least the second century BC to the fourth century AD, when it was probably abandoned. Two cultural periods have been marked in the occupational layers. Period I is represented by BRW, which continues throughout in the habitation site, RCP in the burials, iron objects, Red Polished and Black Polished Ware, and evidence of artisanal and craft activities, especially gems. BRW Graffiti is a crucial piece of evidence linking the habitation with the burial site, as in both contexts the same graffiti occurs. Each Megalithic burial has a special symbol on its pottery, probably of a specific clan (?). The graffiti is similar to some of the symbols occurring on punch-marked coins and in early Tamil Brāhmī inscriptions. Similar symbols are reported from other Megalithic sites.[219] Graffiti gives place to more Brāhmī letters in the upper levels. Carnelian predominates in the burials. This period is dated from the second century BC to the second century AD. Period II is assigned to the second and third centuries AD, when BRW and other pottery types continue, but the scratching of letters goes into disuse. Evidence of active iron-working and more agricultural activity is attested to in the second period.

The site would thus seem to have been continuously active in the early trade, both inland and maritime. The whole region of the Amarāvati and Noyyal rivers comes up with evidence of traders constantly moving across. Along with ornaments of gold (24 carat, though gold is limited), silver rings and a copper tiger inlaid with precious stones, are other finds which point to the nature of craft production and trade in jewels. Some of the rings (silver and copper) have symbols, similar to the Megalithic graffiti, and may have been signet rings or seals of traders.[220] The discovery in the river beds of numerous coins of the Cēra rulers, some with portraits and legends giving names like Mākkōtai and Kuṭṭuvan Kōtai would add to the evidence of the Cēra's interest in promoting this trade. Although very few punch-marked coins and only a single Roman silver coin have been found in the habitation site at Koḍumaṇal itself, the region around the site, as noted earlier, has the greatest concentration of Roman coin finds in South India, leaving no room for dispute regarding the commercial significance of this centre. The term *nigama* occurring on a potsherd would also indicate the presence of a merchant guild. However, as guild organization is less conspicuously attested to in the Tamil context, it may be suggested that trading groups from the Deccan and Andhra may have been involved in the commerce of this region. This is further supported by several names of a Prākrit origin like Viśākhi, Varuṇi and Kuvirian (e.g. Varuṇi akal = the vessel of Varuṇi) found on potsherds, in addition to Tamil names.

Koḍumaṇal is one of the few centres where the links between the Megalithic burial and habitation sites are established by archaeological material, with clear evidence of their contemporaneity. The total area is of about fifty hectares, including a habitation located in ten hectares, and a hundred burials. The site has rich potential for studying the transitional stage from proto-history to the early history of the region.

12. TIRUKKŌYILŪR (SOUTH ARCOT DISTRICT)

Tirukkōyilūr was known to early Tamil texts as Kōvalūr (Kōval) and as the centre of the Malaiyamān chiefs of the *vēḷir* clan. Its importance derives from its location on the banks of the South Pennaiyar (Pennar) and on the route from the west coast to the east coast (Arikamēḍu) *via* the Kongu region. Two significant discoveries in recent years have established its nodal importance. One is the early Brāhmī inscription[221] from a place called Jambai, near Tirukkōyilūr, recording the gift of a *pāḷi* (cave) to a Jaina ascetic by Neṭumān Añci, an Atiyamān chieftain (another *vēḷir* chief), who is here called Satiyaputo (=Atiyamān), possibly after he defeated the Malaiyamāns and occupied this region.[222] The reference to Satiyaputo has established that the Satiyaputras of the Aśokan edicts were the Atikaimān (Atiyamān) of Takaṭūr (Dharmapuri near Salem), who are praised in the Sangam works for their generosity and valour.[223] The second discovery is of a very large hoard of Roman aurei in a nearby village (by a local labourer).[224] The hoard contained 193 coins and some pieces of jewellery, including a diamond ring. The coins are of Nero (54-68 AD), Domitian (?) (93 AD) and Antonius Pius (138-161 AD). Copper coins, believed to be the issues of the Malaiyamān chiefs, have also been discovered in Tirukkōyilūr and in private collections,[225] which may suggest a direct interest shown by these chieftains in the early Roman trade.

Coastal Sites/Towns

At this point it would be useful to follow the classical sources and the coastal sites/towns that they are familiar with, apart from those that have been taken up for description under the dual centres of the early Tamil chiefdoms. While some of them are not known from the Tamil sources, there are quite a few, which can be identified with the help of archaeological material and occasionally, also of literary references.

On the west coast, the *Periplus*, after enumerating other ports down the Maharashtra and Konkan coast, starts with the first markets of Damirica (Tamiḻakam). These are Naura, the Nitra of Ptolemy and Nitrias of Pliny, which is identified with Cannanore, and Tyndis, identified with Ponnāni. Both are located in the kingdom of the Cerobothra.[226] Beyond this, there is no further reference to the nature of these centres, except, that they seem to be no more than villages. After these two comes Muziris, the Muciṟi of the Tamil sources.

The next site of some importance is the Neacyndon of Pliny, Nelcynda of the *Periplus* and Melkynda or Nelkunda of Ptolemy,[227] identified with Kōṭṭayam. Nelcynda is given equal status with Muziris as a market of leading importance, but it is stated to be in the Pāṇḍya (Pandion) country. Ptolemy places it in the country of the Aioi, which closely resembles the name of Āy of the *vēḷir* clan, who ruled from Āykkuḍi (Potikai), the Bettigo of Ptolemy. The Āys were lesser chiefs under the Pāṇḍyas. Nelcynda must have been a part of the pepper trade of this coast, as pepper was the major item from this port and Muziris. Pepper was carried from Cottanara in canoes to Bacare[228] another small town (?) mentioned by the *Periplus*, identified with Porakad, also at the mouth of the river (Meenachilār) on which Nelcynda is located. Large ships are said to have come to these market towns on account of pepper and malabathrum.

Beyond Bacare is another district, we are told, called Paralia stretching along the coast towards the south around Cape Comorin and as far as Adam's bridge. On this coast is located Comari (Cape Comorin/Kanyā Kumāri) which had a harbour and a goddess shrine, where people came and offered worship.[229] Balita (Varkkalai) is another village by the shore with a harbour.[230] After Comari is mentioned Colchi or Koṟkai, the Pāṇḍya port.

Evidence on these sites either from literature or from archaeology, is practically non-existent or, at best, meagre. Hence, it would appear that only those harbours which the major chiefdoms promoted came to attain the status of ports or emporia as they are called in the classical accounts.

The descriptions of Argaru that follow in the *Periplus*[231] are somewhat hazy, for it is said to be a region lying inland from a bay after Colchi. It is from this bay, we are told, that the pearls gathered on this coast and from an island called Epiodoros, as well as muslins called *ebargareitides* (*argarik/argaritic*), were exported. While Epiodoros may be identified with the island of Mannar,[232] Argaru is said to be the same as Uṟaiyūr. The location of Argaru, however, seems to be less certain, as it has also been suggested that it lay somewhere near the Palk Bay,[233] perhaps beyond the mouth of the Vaigai, where Aḻagankuḷam, with its Roman vestiges, stands. Ptolemy mentions a promontory called Kory, and beyond it a place called Argeirou, and an emporium called Salour.[234] Kory is believed to be Kōṭi of the Tamil sources and is identified with Dhanuṣkōṭi (in the Ramesvaram promontory).[235] Interestingly, Salour may be the same as Sāliyūr of Tamil sources, which is located near Aḻagankuḷam. This coast is opposite to the northwestern coast of Sri Lanka.

Sri Lanka (Ceylon), which, in the classical sources, is known as Palaesimundu and Taprobane,[236] is mentioned along with the above coast, where Colchi, Kory, Argaru etc. are located. It is described as a land of large elephants, gold and pearls, precious stones and marble resembling tortoise shell.

Argaru is followed by Camara (*Periplus*) or Khaberis (Ptolemy), the Kāvērippūmpaṭṭiṇam of the Tamil sources, Poduca or Podouke (Arikamēḍu) and Sopatma identified with Marakkāṇam in the South Arcot district, north of Pondichery.[237] Then the description passes on to the sites of the Andhra coast, i.e. Masalia.

References

1. Sudershan Seneviratne, 'Kalinga and Andhra: The Process of Secondary State Formation in Early India', in Claessen and Skalnik (eds), *The Study of the State*, The Hague, Mouton, 1981, 317-38.
2. Rock Edict XIII. See *Corpus Inscriptionum Indicarum*, vol. I, E. Hultzsch (ed.), *Inscriptions of Asoka*, Archaeological Survey of India, 1991, reprint, 43ff, 66ff, 81ff.
3. This relationship is pointed out as an essential part of societies in transformation. *See* Robert McC. Adams, *Evolution of Urban Society: Early Mesopotamia and Pre-Hispanic Mexico*, Chicago, 1966, 46-7.

4. *See* Paul Wheatley, *The Pivot of the Four Quarters, A Preliminary Enquiry into the Origins and Character of the Ancient Chinese City*, Edinburgh, 1971, 377.
5. R. Champakalakshmi, 'Archaeology and Tamil Literary Tradition', *Puratattva*, 1975-6, vol. VIII, 110-22.
6. Clarence Maloney, 'The Beginnings of Civilization in South India', *Journal of Asian Studies (JAS)*, 1970, vol. XXIX, no. 3, 603-16; *idem* 'Archaeology in South India—Accomplishments and Prospects', in B. Stein (ed.), *Essays on South India*, New Delhi, 1976, 1-40.
7. Traditions of Cōḷa Karikāla building a dam across the Kāvēri river are late. However the Sangam works refer to his raising the embankment of the Kāvēri. *See* N. Subrahmanian, *Sangam Polity: The Administration and Social Life of the Sangam Tamils*, Bombay, 1966, 208.
8. Conventional histories of this period lack an integrated approach and hence provide a compartmentalized view of society, economy and polity. *See* e.g. Subrahmanian, *Sangam Polity*. The present discussion is based on the recent perspectives of historians who follow not only an integrated approach but also use anthropological and semiotic methods of analysis. *See* K. Sivathamby, 'Early South Indian Society and Economy: The Tiṇai Concept', *Social Scientist*, 1974, 20-37; *idem* 'An Analysis of the Anthropological Significance of the Economic Activities and Conduct Code Ascribed to the *mullai tiṇai*', *Proceedings of the First International Conference Seminar on Tamil Studies*, IATR, 1966 (1968), vol. I; Rajan Gurukkal, 'Forms of Production and Forces of Change in Ancient Tamil Society', *Studies in History*, July-Dec. 1989, vol. V, no. 2, 159-76.
9. *Tolkāppiyam*, *Poruḷatikāram*, 1, 14, 20, 21, 44, 46, 313 and 497.
10. Gurukkal, 'Forms of Production'.
11. Ibid.
12. R. Kailasapathy, *Tamil Heroic Poetry*, OUP, 1968, 11-13, 73-4 and 260; G.L. Hart, 'Ancient Tamil Literature, Its Scholarly Past and Future', in B. Stein (ed.), *Essays on South India*, New Delhi, 1976, 56-7. *See also* K. Sivaraja Pillai, *Chronology of the Early Tamils*, Madras, 1932, 192-3.
13. The intrusion of the *varṇa* order is perhaps echoed in the fourfold division of *antaṇar*, *aracar*, *vaiśiyar* and *vēḷāḷar* referred to in this section and would be the earliest evidence of such a social division. See *Tolkāppiyam*, *Poruḷatikāram*; 625-6, 632 and 635.

14. Gurukkal, 'Forms of Production', 168.
15. For the importance of primitive valuables in tribal societies, *see* S.F. Ratnagar, *Encounters: The Westerly Trade of the Harappa Civilization*, Delhi, 1981, 242.
16. Gurukkal, 'Towards a New Discourse: Discursive Processes in Early South India', in R. Champakalakshmi and S. Gopal (eds), *Tradition, Dissent and Ideology.*
17. M.G.S. Narayanan, 'The Warrior Settlements of the Sangam Age', *Indian History Congress, Proceedings, 43rd Session*, Kurukshetra, 1982, 102–9.
18. The limited surplus potential, it is claimed, was enough to sustain functionaries like preceptors, bards, dancers, magicians, physicians and astrologers. *See* Gurukkal, 'Forms of Production', 168.
19. For the essential features of a *janapada*, *see* Thapar, *From Lineage to State*, OUP, Bombay, 1984, 121ff.
20. Seneviratne, 'Kalinga and Andhra'.
21. Gurty Venkat Rao, 'The Pre-Satavahana and Satavahana Periods', in G. Yazdani (ed.), *The Early History of the Deccan*, New Delhi, 1982, reprint, parts I to VI, 80–2, 119.
22. Subrahmanian, *Sangam Polity*, 52–3, 269.
23. Thapar, *Cultural Transactions and Early India: Tradition and Patronage*, OUP, Delhi, 1987; also 'Patronage and Community', in Barbara Stoler Miller (ed.), *The Powers of Art*, OUP, 1992. *See also* Himanshu Prabha Ray, *Monastery and Guild (Commerce Under the Sātavāhanas)*, OUP, 1986.
24. Amita Ray, *Life and Art in Early Andhradesa*, Delhi, 1983, chapter III. Anjana Chatterjee, 'Socio-Economic Conditions in Early Andhra 200 BC–AD 300–A Study of the Transition from Megalithic to Early Historic Culture', Ph.D. Thesis (unpublished), Jawaharlal Nehru University, New Delhi, 1976.
25. *Indian Archaeology, A Review (IAR)*, 1964–5, para 42; 1965–6, para 35. *See also* Champakalakshmi, 'Archaeology and Tamil Literary Tradition', 114.
26. I. Mahadevan, 'Corpus of Tamil Brāhmī Inscriptions', in R. Nagaswamy (ed.), *Seminar on Inscriptions*, Madras, 1968.
27. Champakalakshmi, 'South India', chapter 9, in A. Ghosh (ed.), *Jaina Art and Architecture*, Bharatiya Jnanpith, New Delhi, 1974, vol. I.
28. *See* Mahadevan, 'Corpus', nos 1, 2 and 57.
29. For *nigama* in Tamil Brāhmī inscriptions *see* Mahadevan, 'Corpus',

nos 3 and 6. For references to *puga, goṣṭhī, nigama* and *Śreṇi* in Andhra, *see* Chatterjee, 'Socio-Economic Conditions'.

30. Uma Chakravarti, *The Social Dimensions of Early Buddhism*, OUP, New Delhi, 1987, chapter III.
31. Mahadevan, 'Corpus', no. 3, 18-25.
32. *See* Friedhelm Hardy, *Viraha Bhakti: The Early History of Kṛṣṇa Devotion in South India*, Delhi, 1983.
33. *Tolkāppiyam, Poruḷatikāram*, 5.
34. Champakalakshmi, 'From Devotion and Dissent to Dominance: The Bhakti of the Tamil Āḻvār and Nāyanār', in Champakalakshmi and Gopal, *Tradition*.
35. Noṭuttal–*See* Gurukkal, 'Forms of Production', 171.
36. *Kuṟittumaretirppai or Kuṟi etirppai–See* Subrahmanian, *Pre-Pallavan Tamil Index*, Madras, 1966, 305.
37. K.K. Pillay, *A Social History of the Tamils*, University of Madras, reprint, 247.
38. Gurukkal, 'Forms', 172; Thapar, 'Black Gold: South Asia and the Roman Maritime Trade', *South Asia (Journal of the South Asian Studies Association)*, Armidale, NSW, Australia, Dec. 1992, n.s., vol. XV, no. 2, 14–15.
39. *Nāḷangāḍi-Akanānūṟu*, 93: 10; *Maduraikkāñci*, l. 430; *Aḻḻangāḍi-Maduraikkāñci*, l. 544.
40. *Śilappadikāram*, VI, 121-2.
41. *Paṭṭinappālai*, ll. 185-91; *Śilappadikāram*, V: 18–20; 24–33; VI: 134-45.
42. *Maduraikkāñci*, ll. 395-401; 511-21; 536-44; *Śilappadikāram*, XIV: 174–211.
43. *Paṭṭinappālai*, ll. 131-6; 120–4.
44. *Paṭṭinappālai*, ll. 209–12; J.V. Chelliah, *Pattuppāṭṭu, The Ten Tamil Idylls* (Translated into English with Introduction and Notes), SISSW, Tirunelveli, 1962, 2nd edn, 41.
45. *See* Bohannan and Dalton (eds), *Markets in Africa*, North Western University Press, Illinois, 1962, 7-8, for the concept of the 'peripheral' market.

    One of the three kinds of societies mentioned by them is the society with peripheral markets, where the institution of the market place is present, but the market principle does not determine the acquisition of subsistence goods or the allocation of land or labour resources. Bohannan and Dalton also prefer to use the term 'market-place-exchange' and not 'market exchange', as land and labour transactions are absent in such peripheral markets.

46. Rowlands, 'Modes of Exchange and the Incentives for Trade with Reference to Late European Pre-history', in Colin Renfrew (ed.), *The Explanation of Culture and Change*, Pittsburgh, 1973, 591.
47. G. Dalton, 'Karl Polanyi's Analysis of Long Distance Trade and His Wider Paradigm', in Jeremy A. Sabloff and Lamberg-Karlovsky (eds), *Ancient Civilization and Trade*, Albuquerque, 1975, 99.
48. Robert J. Braidwood and Gordon R. Willey introduced these terms in the volume edited by them. *Courses Toward Urban Life: Archaeological Consideration of Some Cultural Alternates*, Viking Foundation, Anthropology, 1962, no. 32; also McC Adams, *The Evolution of Urban Society*, London, 1966, 9.
49. Bohannan and Dalton, *Markets in Africa*, 7.
50. People speaking diverse tongues, that come from great and foreign homes mix freely on friendly terms with those who occupy this glorious town, *Paṭṭinappālai*, ll. 214-17; Chelliah, 1962: 41.

    In different places of Puhar, the onlooker's attention was arrested by the abodes of *Yavana*, whose prosperity was never on the wane. On the harbour are to be seen sailors who come from distant lands, but for all appearances, they lived as one community. *Śilappadikāram*, v: 6-12; V.R.R. Dikshitar, The *Cilappatikāram*, SISSW, Tirunelveli, 1978, 120.
51. *Maduraikkāñci*, ll. 315-25; 75-89.
52. *Periplus*: 53-60. The references to the *Periplus* are taken from J.W. McCrindle, *The Commerce and Navigation of the Erythraean Seas and Ancient India as Described by Ktesias the Knidian*, Calcutta, 1973, Reprint.
53. According to Polanyi, 'Emporium', in classical Greek terminology, referred to 'that part or sector of a coastal town which was devoted to foreign commerce'. It came to denote 'a large centre of commerce' only at a later date. It was a self-contained unit with its own food, market, harbour, quay, warehouses, administrative buildings, mariners' houses and so on. *See* Karl Polanyi, 'Ports of Trade in Early Societies', *Journal of Economic History*, 1963, vol. XXIII, 34.
54. Charlesworth, 'Roman Trade with India: A Resurvey', in Coleman and Norton (eds), *Studies in Roman Economic and Social History*, 1951, 140.

55. Meanings of these terms are given as in the *Tamil Lexicon*, vols v and vi, University of Madras, 1982, reprint.
56. *Maduraikkāñci*, ll, 503-6.
57. *Maduraikkāñci*, ll. 397-401; 511-21; *Śilappadikāram*, v: 24-39.
58. *Akanāṉūṟu*, 39: 10; 167: 7; 245: 6; 291: 15; *Naṟṟiṇai*, 182; 1-2, 254-6.
59. *Perumpāṇāṟṟuppaṭai*, ll. 59-80; Chelliah, 109-11.
60. Kamil Zvelebil, *The Smile of Maurugan, On the Tamil Literature of South India*, Leiden, 1973, 100.
61. *Akanāṉūṟu*, 340: 16-17; 350: 11, *Ainkuṟunūṟu*, 195: 1-2; *Maduraikkāñci*, ll. 315-24; also Maloney, The Effect of Early Coastal Sea Traffic on the Development of Civilization in South India, Ph.D. Thesis (unpublished), University of Pennsylvania, 1968, 117.
62. *Perumpāṇāṟṟuppaṭai*, ll. 319-24; Maloney, 'The Effect of Early Coastal Sea Traffic', 118.
63. *See* Vidya Dehejia, *Early Buddhist Rock Temples*, London, 1972; Chatterjee, 'Socio-Economic Conditions'.
64. Mahadevan, 'Corpus', nos 34, 37, 38, 43, 60-8 and 72.
65. *Akanāṉūṟu*, 302; 306; *Naṟṟiṇai*, 250; *Puṟanāṉūṟu*, 264; *Mullaippāṭṭu*; *See* N. Subrahmanian, *Pre-Pallavan Tamil Index*, Madras, 1966, 148, 189, 269 and 637.
66. *Perumpāṇāṟṟuppaṭai*, ll. 322-4; *Maduraikkāñci*, ll. 500-2.
67. *Maduraikkāñci*, l. 122.
68. *Paṭṭinappālai*, ll. 196-213; Chelliah, *Pattuppāṭṭu*, 41.
69. *See* M. Webb, 'The Flag Follows Trade–An Essay on the Interaction of Military and Commercial Factors in State Formation', in Jeremy A. Sabloff and Lamberg-Karlovsky (eds), *Ancient Civilization and Trade*, Albuquerque, 1975, 179.
70. J. Filliozat, 'Intercourse of India with the Roman Empire during the Opening Centuries of the Christian Era', *Journal of Indian History*, 1950, vol. xxviii, part i, 39.
71. *Śilappadikāram*, v: 6-12.
72. *See* R.E.M. Wheeler, *Rome Beyond the Imperial Frontiers*, London, 1955.
73. Filliozat, 'Intercourse of India', 40-1; Maloney, 'Early Coastal Sea Traffic', 184.
74. Pliny, *Natural History*, v: 105; vi: 26-10; also *Periplus*: 55.
75. *See* Thapar, 'Black Gold', 1992, 25.
76. Mahadevan, 'Corpus', no. 51.
77. Thapar, 'Black Gold', 17ff.
78. Ibid.
79. *Patiṟṟuppattu*, ii, *Patikam*, ll. 4-10; *Mullaippāṭṭu*, l. 66.

80. *Śilappadikāram*, xiv: 66-7; xxviii: 142; v: 7ff; *Maṇimēkalai*, xix: 108; *Mullaippāṭṭu*, l. 60 (*Yavana* carpenters).
81. *See* Koḍumaṇal in the section on urban centres.
82. Charlesworth, 'Roman Trade', 135.
83. Warmington, *Commerce Between the Roman Empire and India*, New Delhi, 1974, 58, reprint.
84. *See* the lists in Appendices A and B.
85. This discussion is based on the work of S. Suresh, 'A Study of the Roman Coins and Other Antiquities in India–With Special Reference to South India', Ph.D. Dissertation (unpublished), Jawaharlal Nehru University, New Delhi, 1993, chapter ii.
86. Thapar, 'Black Gold', 13-15.
87. Subrahmanian, *Sangam Polity*, 56, 214; *Patiṟṟuppattu*, iv–Patikam; vi–Patikam and viii–Patikam.
88. Suresh, 'A Study of the Roman Coins', chapter iii.
89. *See* Koḍumaṇal in the section on urban centres.
90. *Indian Archaeology: A Review* (hereafter *IAR*), 1961-2: 26-7; 1964-5: 25; 1963-4: 20.
91. R. Krishnamurthy, 'Sangam Period Silver Coin with a Portrait and a Legend', paper presented at the *First Oriental Numismatic Congress*, Nagpur, 1990b; *idem* 'Makkotai Coins', in *Studies in South Indian Coins*, 1992, vol. 2, 89-93.
92. Reported in IRNS Newsline; Krishnamurthy, 'Sangam Period Coin Found', News item, *The Hindu*, 24 May 1994.
93. Reported in *The Hindu*, 6 Nov. 1987.
94. Krishnamurthy, *Pāṇḍiyar Peruvaḷuti Nāṇayangaḷ*, Madras, 1987.
95. Krishnamurthy, *Sanga Kāla Malaiyamān Nāṇayangaḷ*, Madras, 1990a; R. Nagaswamy, *Tamil Coins, A Study*, Tamil Nadu State Department of Archaeology, Madras, 1981, 140-2.
96. Subrahmanian, *Sangam Polity*, revised edition, Madurai, 1980, 225.
97. P.L. Gupta, 'A Bibliography of the Hoards of Punch-marked Coins of Ancient India', *Journal of the Numismatic Society of India*, vol. xvii, 15-19.
98. Maloney, 'Archaeology in South India', 19-20.
99. T.G. Aravamuthan, 'A Pandyan Issue of Punch-marked Coins', *Journal of the Numismatic Society of India*, 1944, vol. vi, part 1, 2n.
100. *Periplus*: 49.
101. Warmington, *Commerce*, 278.
102. Seneviratne, 'Social Base of Early Buddhism in South East India and Sri Lanka: BC 3rd Century to 3rd Century AD', Ph.D.

Dissertation (unpublished), Jawaharlal Nehru University, New Delhi, 1987.

103. Potsherds and seals discovered at Kantarōḍai and Ānaikkoḍai in Jaffna district and other places. The close similarity of the symbols with those of Koḍumaṇal potsherds, and of the Aḻagarmalai, Kongarpuḷiyanguḷam symbols show that the use of graffiti and Brāhmī script side by side was common in both the regions. Mahadevan, 'Ancient Tamil Contacts Abroad: Recent Epigraphic Evidence' Reverend Fr. X.S. Thani Nayagam Memorial Lecture, Thani Nayagam Foundation Trust, Colombo, 8 Sep. 1994 (to be published).

104. S. Paranavitana, *Inscriptions of Ceylon*, vol. I, *Early Brahmi Inscriptions*, Archaeological Survey of Ceylon, Colombo, 1970; also Seneviratne, 'Social Base'.

105. E.g. Īḻakuṭumbikan in the Tirupparankuṉṟam Brāhmī Inscription: *See* Mahadevan, 'Corpus', 1968.

106. Mahadevan, 'An Old Sinhalese Inscription from Arikamedu', *Seminar on Epigraphy, Kuppuswami Sastri Birth Centenary*, Madras, 1981b.

107. Maloney, 'Early Coastal Sea Traffic'.

108. Suresh, 'Roman Coins'.

109. McCrindle, *Commerce and Navigation*; *idem Ancient India as Described by Ptolemy*, A fascimile reprint ed. by Surendranath Majumdar and Chukkerverthy Chatterjee, Calcutta, 1927.

110. Pan Kou, a Chinese writer of the first century AD in his *Ts'ien han Chou*, refers to the sea voyage from China to Houng-tche (Kāñcī) in the period of emperor Wou (140-86 BC) and the journey being covered in about ten months. It is historically possible that China had relations with Kāñcī, as mention is made of the goods that were brought as presents during the first century AD, and goods that were asked for as 'tribute' by the Chinese. *See* K.A. Nilakanta Sastri, *Foreign Notices of South India*, University of Madras, 1972, reprint, 44-5.

111. See Section on Urban Centres–Kāvērippūmpaṭṭiṉam.

112. *Maṇimēkalai*, XIV, XV, XXI, XXV and XXVIII.

113. Mahadevan, 'Ancient Tamil Contacts'; P. Shanmugam, 'Tamiḻ Nāḍum Thāilandum Toḍarpugaḷ', in *Āvaṇam*, July 1993, no. 3, 81-4.

114. *See* Ray, *Life and Art*; Chatterjee, 'Early Andhra'.

115. *Periplus*: 60.

116. *Akanāṉūṟu*, 110: 18; 152: 7; *Ainkuṟunūṟu*, 192: 2; *Puṟanāṉūṟu*, 13: 5; 26: 2; 30: 12-13 etc.; *Maduraikkāñci*, 1. 83; 321; *Naṟṟiṇai*, 295:

6; *Paṭṭinappālai*, l. 174; *Perumpāṇārruppaṭai*, l. 321. The reference to a *Mahānāvika* (Navigator) as a donor in the Buddhist centre of Amarāvati and the 'ship' type coins of the Sātavāhanas (ship with one or two masts with a double set of rigging on each) (Maloney, 'Early Coastal Sea Traffic', 153) leave no room for doubt regarding the natives embarking on sea voyages.

117. 'Pegs driven to tie strong boats (*pahṛi*) that stand like steeds in a stable tied. They, come fully laden with grain by barter brought of salt refined'. *Paṭṭinappālai*, ll. 28-32; Chelliah, *Pattuppāṭṭu*, 31.
118. *See* Thapar, 'Black Gold', 8-9; Mahadevan, 'Ancient Tamil Contacts'.
119. D. Devakunjari, *Madurai Through the Ages, From the Earliest Times to AD 1801*, Society for Archaeological, Historical and Epigraphical Research, Madras, 1979 (?), chapter III.
120. *Puṟanāṉūṟu*, 66: 1-3.
121. Nagaswamy, *Tamil Coins*, 5.
122. Ibid.
123. *Puṟanāṉūṟu*, 5 Colophon; ll, 32 etc., *Paḻamoḻi Nāṉūṟu*, 62: 1.
124. *Puṟanāṉūṟu*, 372; 24; *Śilappadikāram*, XXV: 9, 34.
125. *Akanāṉūṟu*, 93: 2; *Puṟanāṉūṟu*, 36: 5; *Śilappadikāram*, XXVII: 231; XXVIII: 126; XXIX: *Vāḷttu*: 7.
126. Sesha Aiyar, *Cēre Kings of the Sangam Period*.
127. *See* for different views, P. Ramalingam, *Karuvūrē Vañci*, Madras, 1977.
128. *See* Pillay, *A Social History of the Tamils*, 269.
129. *See* Nagaswamy, '*Karuvūr-Vañji*, the Capital of the Sangam Cēras', *Journal of Kerala Studies*, Dec. 1974, vol. I, part IV, 395-402.
130. Initial Report, *The Hindu*, 26 June 1973. Amphora fragments, Kaolin Ware, Russet coated painted ware have also been reported in the area, especially from Veḷḷalūr.
131. Suresh, 'Early Archaeological Finds in Karur', paper presented at the *Indian History Congress, 52nd Session*, New Delhi, 1992.
132. K.V. Raman, 'Roman Jewellery and Coins from Karur', *The Hindu*, Sunday, 14 March 1993.
133. Mahadevan, 'Corpus', no. 66.
134. Raman, 'Sangam Cera Coin Found', *The Hindu*, fourteenth March 1993.
135. Mahadevan, 'Corpus', nos 56-7.
136. *Maṇimēkalai*, XXVIII, 122-31.
137. Ibid., XXVIII: 69-72; XXVI: 55; *Śilappadikāram*, X: 13-14; XXVII: 92-3.

138. Romila Thapar suggests that Huien Tsang's informants may have tried to impress the Chinese pilgrim with the antiquity and importance of the places he visited by associating them with Aśoka. Huien Tsang does refer to the existence of Asokan *stupas* in Kanci. *See* Thapar, *Asoka and the Decline of the Mauryas*, OUP, 1973, 2nd edn, 133.
139. *Maṇimēkalai*, XXVIII: 156-7; T.N. Vasudeva Rao, *Buddhism in the Tamil Country*, Chidambaram, 1979, 113.
140. Muziris was, according to Pliny, the first emporium of India–*See* Sesha Aiyar, *Cēra Kings*, 91; Nagaswamy, Tamil Coins, 7.
141. ' . . . Cēra's great river Cuḷḷi splashes with white foam where
Yavanas bring their well built ships
arriving with gold and carrying off pepper
from prosperous Muciṟi, reverberating with the Ocean.'
Akanāṉūṟu: 149: 7-11.
142. *Periplus*: 54; McCrindle, *Commerce and Navigation*, 132-3.
143. Sastri, *Foreign Notices*, 1972, reprint, 53.
144. *Periplus*: 56; Sastri, *Foreign Notices*, 57-8.
145. Mahadevan, 'Ancient Tamil Contacts'; K. Rajan, 'Muciṟi-Tuṟaimukam. Cila Putiya Ceitigaḷ', in *Āvaṇam*, Jan. 1994, 107-10.
146. Thapar, 'Black Gold', 25.
147. *See* Devakunjari, *Madurai*, 44ff.
148. *Maduraikkāñci*, ll. 331-669.
149. *Neṭunalvāṭai*, ll. 31-5; 81-97; 101-5.
150. *Maduraikkāñci*, ll. 316; 411; 504-6; 512-13. *Neṭunalvāṭai*, l. 110; also *Ainkuṟunūṟu*, 194: l; *Kuṟuntokai*, 189; 365: 1.
151. Maloney, 'The Beginnings of Civilization', 605-6.
152. Nagaswamy, *Tamil Coins*, 75.
153. Aravamuthan, 'A Pandyan Issue'.
154. Krishnamurthy, Report in *The Hindu*, 1987.
155. Koṟkai is said to be the port of the Pāṇḍya ruler Vaḷuti of beautiful chariots and the 'capital' of Veṟṟivēl Ceḻiyan–*See* R. Nagaswamy, 'Korkai Excavations', *Damilica*, Dec. 1970, I, 50-2.
156. R. Caldwell, 'Sepulchral Urns in Southern India', *Indian Antiquary*, 1887, 81-3 and Nagaswamy, 'Korkai Excavations', 50ff.
157. In *IAR*, 1969-70, the R.C. date is given as 805 BC, while the report of the excavations in *Damilica*, I, gives the date 785 BC. A sequence of three periods has been marked in Koṟkai:
Period I–Urn burials with Megalithic BRW and Red Ware;
Period II–What is called the Pāṇḍya period (?) with Red Ware, Sawed conches, terracotta beads, spouted potsherds;

Period III–Red Ware and Black Ware of a coarse variety–called post-Pāṇḍya period (?).

158. *Akanāṉūṟu*, 27: 9; 350: 13; *Aiṅkuṟunūṟu*, 185: 1; 188: 2; *Maṇimēkalai*, XIII: 84.
159. *Akanāṉūṟu*, 366: 5.
160. *Periplus*: 59; Nilakanta Sastri, *Foreign Notices*, 59.
161. McCrindle, *Commerce and Navigation*, 141; The Peutingarian Tables refer to it as Colchis Indorum. Ibid.
162. *Akanāṉūṟu*, 27; *Maduraikkāñci*, 134, 138; *Naṟṟiṇai*, 25.
163. Maloney, 'The Beginnings of Civilization', 605. Pāṇḍyakavāṭa (Kapāṭapuram of legend), Tāmraparṇi (the river or Sri Lanka), Kōṭi (Dhanushkoti on the Vaigai delta) Cūrṇi (perhaps Manner in northern Ceylon) Pāśika (a port on the Vaigai mouth) etc.
164. *Śilappadikāram*, *Uraiperukaṭṭurai*, 4; X: 248; XI: 11.
165. *Akanāṉūṟu*, 122: 21.
166. *Paṭṭinappālai*, 1. 285; *Ciṟupāṇāṟṟuppaṭai*, 1. 83.
167. *IAR*, 1964-5; 1965-6.
168. The excavators assigned this cultural deposit to a period between third century BC and first to second centuries AD, *IAR*, 1964-5, 25. In a subsequent report, they have given a different time bracket, i.e. first century BC to fourth century AD, *IAR*, 1965-6, para 37. Similarly, period II has been pushed to 4th-7th centuries AD from 2nd-5th centuries AD.
169. There is an earlier literary tradition about floods in the Kāvēri. *Akanāṉūṟu*, 376: 4.
170. Mahadevan, 'Corpus', no. 68; also Appendix I, no. 10. This is a rather damaged Brāhmī inscription found in the cavern on the Tiruchirapalli rock, and is assigned to about 3rd-4th centuries AD. The reading 'Cenkāyipan' is admittedly doubtful.
171. McCrindle, *Commerce and Navigation*, 142.
172. Shrines (Kōṭṭam) of Kāma (Cupid), Sun, Moon, Indra, Balarāma and *Niganṭhas*, the guardian deity of the market place, i.e. the *Catukkattu Būtam*, Sāttan a folk deity, who had a shrine outside the city. (*Śilappadikāram*, V: 128; IX: 23; XXVIII: 147; *Maṇimēkalai*, VII: 78)–Buddhist and Jain shrines and monasteries, of which one was called the Indra vihāra. (*Śilappadikāram*, X: 14; XXVII: 92; XXVIII: 70; *Maṇimēkalai*, XXVI: 55).
173. Puhār–*Akanāṉūṟu*, 110: 4; *Puṟanāṉūṟu*, 30: 12; *Patiṟṟuppattu*, 73: 9; *Paṭṭinappālai*, 173; *Śilappadikāram*, XVII; *Maṇimēkalai*, V: 109; Kākandi–*Maṇimēkalai*, XXII: 37. A Barhut inscription refers to Kākandi, i.e. Puhār. *See* Mahadevan, 'Identification of Kakandi in Bharhut Inscriptions' paper presented at the International

Seminar on *Tamil Buddhism*, Institute of Asian Studies, Madras, May 1992. Sampāpati–*Maṇimēkalai*, Patikam: 8, 13.

174. *Maṇimēkalai*, vi, 26: 37; xxii: 63; 68.
175. *IAR*, 1962-3, 13.
176. *Maṇimēkalai*, i: 72; iii: 45; xix: 54; *Śilappadikāram*, v: 117; 213; vi: 127; x: 31.
177. *Paṭṭinappālai*, 11. 40-50; 59-74; 116-71; 183-212; 213-18.
178. *Akanānūṟu*, 73: 10; *Śilappadikāram*, v: 63; 196.
179. *Maṇimēkalai*, xxii: 2, 91 etc.; *Śilappadikāram*, ix: 12.
180. *IAR*, 1962-3, 13. *Kaḻi*–meaning backwaters (Subrahmanian, *Pre-Pallavan Tamil Index*, Madras, 1966) and *Aṇai*–meaning wooden peg (*Paṭṭinappālai*, ll. 29ff) probably indicate the area where the boats were anchored.
181. The *Paṭṭinappālai* refers to large boats (*pahṟi*) which carried white salt and returned laden with paddy in exchange (ll. 29-32). Great ships are said to have sailed straight into the harbour of Puhār without slacking sail, a description that does not apply to any site of the present day in the mouth of the delta on account of changes in the course of the Kāvēri river and the shape of the sea board.
182. *See* Subrahmanian, *Pre-Pallavan Tamil Index*, 105.
183. Surveys conducted by the Tamil Nadu Department of Archaeology jointly with the National Institute of Oceanography, Goa, are reported to indicate the remains of structures under water about 4.5 kilometres (?) from the shore, apart from evidence of a late eighteenth century shipwreck. No detailed report or results are so far available. *See* Natana Kasinathan, *Under Sea Explorations off the Shore of Poompuhar*, Department of Archaeology, Tamil Nadu, 1991, 1-6.
184. *IAR*, 1963-4, 20.
185. *IAR*, 1964-5, para 42; 1965-6, para 35.
186. *IAR*, 1963-4, 20.
187. Nagaswamy, *Tamil Coins, A Study*, 1981, 134.
188. This Maṇigrāmam is believed to have later moved to the Pāṇḍya country on the invitation of a Pāṇḍya king. Interestingly, the Nāṭṭukkōṭṭai Cheṭṭiārs and the Cheṭṭis of Tiruchirapalli claim that their ancestors originally belonged to Kāvērippūmpaṭṭiṇam.
189. The concept of the 'Gateway City' is discussed by Burghardt in 'A Hypothesis About Gateway Cities', *Annals of the Association of Geographers*, vol. lxi, 1971. Such cities have a 'dendritic network'

which Puhār does not seem to have had. On the other hand, Puhār may be an 'exchange gateway', where 'there is mature exchange of products in one or more directions'. *See* J. Bird, *Centrality and Cities*, Routledge, 1977, 119.

190. T.V. Mahalingam, *Kāñcīpuram in Early South Indian History*, Bombay, 1969, 19.
191. *Perumpāṇāṟṟuppaṭai*, 420; *Maṇimēkalai, Patikam*, 90; XXVIII. Heading and subheading 152; XXI: 148; 154; 174; *Naṟṟiṇai*, 144; 213; 266; *Kuṟuntokai*, 10: 4; 30: 172.
192. *IAR*, 1962-3, 12ff, and relevant plates; 1969-70, 34ff. A later excavation was conducted in the Varadarājasvāmi temple complex.

    The periodization proposed on the basis of the Kāñcīpuram excavations has generally been uncertain and confusing. On the basis of pottery finds a slightly different periodization has been attempted varying from the one given by the excavations.
    Period IA–3rd century BC to 1st century BC.
    Period IB–1st century BC to 3rd century AD.
    Period II–3rd century AD to 7th century AD.
    Period III–8th century AD to 13th century AD.

    See P. Arasu, 'Ancient Ceramic Industry from Kāñcīpuram Excavations', M.Phil Dissertation (unpublished), University of Madras, 1979; also K.V. Raman, 'Archaeological Excavations in Kancipuram', *Tamil Civilization*, V, nos 1 & 2, 61-2.
193. *IAR*, 1969-70, 34f.
194. Curiously the same structure is assigned to 2nd-1st centuries BC in a subsequent report pointing to a confusion. See *IAR*, 1970-1, para 50.
195. T. Walters, *On Yuan Chuang's Travels in India*, 1905, vol. II, 226f.
196. Mahalingam, *Kāñcīpuram*, 74-5.
197. Mahadevan, 'Corpus', no. 71–Māmaṇḍūr and no. 76–Tirunatharkuṉṟu; The *Lokavibhāga* was a translation into Sanskrit of an earlier Prākrit work and is dated in the reign of Pallava Simhavarman of the fifth century AD Paḷḷankōyil Copper Plates–T.N. Subramanian, 'Pallankovil Jaina Copper Plate Grant of the Early Pallavas', *Transactions of the Archaeological Society of South India*, 1958-9, 41-83.
198. *Perumpāṇāṟṟuppaṭai*, ll. 371-6; 405ff.
199. Nilakanta Sastri, *Foreign Notices*, 44-5.
200. Suresh, 'Roman Vestiges in Kancipuram', in Nandita Krishna (ed.), *Kanchi–A Heritage of Art and Religion*, C.P. Ramaswami Aiyar Institute of Indological Research, Madras, 1992, 56-61.

201. *IAR*, 1970-1, 33; Nagaswamy, 'Archaeology and Epigraphy', *Proceedings of the Third International Conference Seminar, Tamil Studies*, Pondichery, 1973, 60; also Nagaswamy and Abdul Majeed, *Vasavasamudram* (Report on the Excavations conducted in the year 1970), Tamil Nadu Department of Archaeology, Madras, 1978.
202. Nagaswamy, and Abdul Majeed, *Vasavasamudram*, 3-4.
203. *Perumpāṇāṟṟuppaṭai*, ll. 319-27; 346-51.
204. U.V. Swaminatha Iyer quoted in Subrahmanian, *Pre-Pallavan Tamil Index*, 501; P.V. Somasundaranar (ed.), *Perumpāṇāṟṟuppaṭai*, SISSW, 1967, ll. 319-27.
205. Selur, Salur or Salour (Delur) in Ptolemy's *Geographia*. *See* Warmington, *The Commerce Between the Roman Empire and India*, Delhi, 1971, 62.
206. A. Abdul Majeed, D. Thulasiraman and S. Vasanthi, *Alagankulam, A Preliminary Report*, Tamil Nadu Department of Archaeology, 1992, chapter IV (General Editor-Natana Kasinathan).
207. Nagaswamy, 'Alagankulam, An Indo-Roman Trading Port', C. Margabandhu et al. (eds), *Indian Archaeological Heritage* (K.V. Soundararajan Felicitation Volume), Delhi, 1991, vol. I, 247-54.
208. *Akanāṉūṟu*, 18-20: 220.
209. *Maduraikkāñci*, ll. 77-88.
210. R.E.M. Wheeler, A. Ghosh and Krishna Deva, 'Arikamedu: An Indo-Roman Trading Station', *Ancient India*, July 1946, no. 2, 17-124.
211. *See* Vimala Begley, 'Arikamedu Reconsidered', *American Journal of Archaeology*, 1983, 87, 461-81; also *idem* 'Ceramic Evidence for Pre-Periplus Trade on the Indian Coasts', in Vimala Begley and Richard Daniel de Puma (eds), *Rome and India. The Ancient Sea Trade*, The University of Wisconsin Press, Madison, 1991, 176-96.
212. *Akanāṉūṟu*, 206: 13-14; *Naṟṟiṇai*, v: 58. *See* Mahadevan, 'The Ancient Name of Arikamedu', Subrahmanian (ed.), Surya Narayana Sastri Centenary Volume, Madurai, 1970, 204ff.
213. Mahadevan, 'Arikamedu Graffiti: A Second Look', *Damilica*, II, Madras, 1973, 62ff.
214. Champakalakshmi, 'Archaeology and Tamil Literary Tradition', 110-22.
215. For Podikai *see* Subrahmanian, *Pre-Pallavan Tamil Index*.
216. Mahadevan, 'An Old Sinhalese Inscription from Arikamedu',

Seminar on Epigraphy, Kuppuswamy Sastri Birth Centenary, Madras, 1981b (Sanskrit College).

217. I am grateful to Prof. Y. Subbarayalu for making available to me an interim report of the excavations in Koḍumaṇal in several seasons–1986 and 1988-90. This report provides an integrated picture of the entire site and its archaeological material.

218. Koḍumaṇam is praised for its ubiquitous jewel stones, particularly rock-crystal (*paḷinku*) in the *Patirruppattu*. Coral, onyx, amethyst, sapphire, agate, garnet, jasper, beryl, moonstone and crystal are found in this site. *See* K. Rajan, 'Iron and Gem Stone Industries as Revealed from Kodumanal Excavations', *Puratattva*, 1989-90, no. 20, 111-12.

219. B.B. Lal, 'From the Megalithic to the Harappa: Tracing Back the Graffiti on Pottery', *Ancient India*, 1962, no. 16, 4-24. Leshnik, *The South Indian Megalithic Burials: The Pandukal Complex*, Wiesbaden, 1974.

220. Arumuga Sitaraman, 'Kuṛiyīṭṭu Mōdiram', *Āvaṇam*, 4, Jan. 1994, 86-7. One of them is probably a rolling seal.

221. Jambai inscription–from a personal visit to the site and the estampage taken of the inscription.

222. *Puṛanāṉūṛu*, 99.

223. *Puṛanāṉūṛu*, 101.

224. Reported in *Dinamalar*, 5 Oct. 1992. The village is Soraiyappaṭṭu Madurakkōṭṭam.

225. R. Krishnamurthy, *Sanga Kāla Malaiyamān Nāṇayangaḷ*, Madras, 1990.

226. *Periplus*: 53; Nilakanta Sastri, *Foreign Notices*, 56-7.

227. *Periplus*: 53 and 54; Nilakanta Sastri, *Foreign Notices*, 57; McCrindle, 134.

228. McCrindle, *Commerce and Navigation*, 111-12 and 131.

229. Nilakanta Sastri, *Foreign Notices*, 58; Cf. *Maṇimēkalai*, XIII: 5-7.

230. Bammala of Ptolemy? (VII: 1: 9); McCrindle, *Ancient India as Prescribed by Ptolemy*, 139.

231. *Periplus*: 59; Nilakanta Sastri, *Foreign Notices*, 59.

232. McCrindle, *Ancient India*, 140-2; The place called Cūrṇi referred to in the *Arthaśāstra* has been identified with Mannar.
See Maloney, 'The Beginnings of Civilization', 605.

233. Maloney, 'Early Coastal Sea Traffic'.

234. McCrindle, *Ancient India*, 142.

235. Maloney, 'Beginnings of Civilisation . . .', 605.

236. *Periplus*: 61; Nilakanta Sastri, *Foreign Notices*, 49-50; McCrindle, *Commerce and Navigation*, 143-4; also Taprobane and Salica—*Periplus of the Outer Sea by Marcian of Heraclea* in W.H. Schoff, Philadelphia, 1977, 17-18; 24-5.
237. *Periplus*: 60; Nilakanta Sastri, *Foreign Notices*, 59.

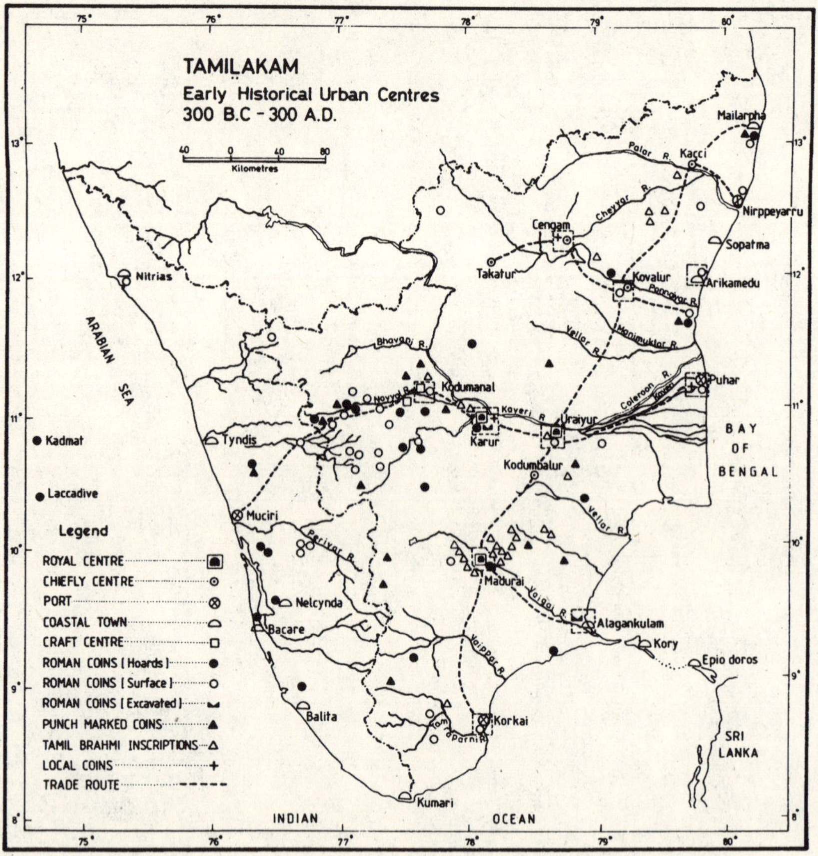

Map 1: Urban Centres - Early Historical Tamilakam

Appendices

A. Punch-Marked Coin Finds in Tamilakam*

Site	*District*	*Metal (Silver) (in numbers)*
Ālampāḷayam	Coimbatore	Silver 63 numbers
Bōḍināikkanūr	Madurai	Silver 1138 numbers
Chāvaḍipāḷayam	Coimbatore	Silver exact number not known
Coimbatore	Coimbatore	Silver 3 numbers
Coimbatore	Coimbatore	Silver large number
Eyyal	Cochin	Silver 12 numbers
Kauniakuṭṭai	Salem	Silver 17 numbers
Koḷattūr	Tiruchirapalli	Silver 346 numbers
Māmbalam	In Madras City	Silver 807 numbers
Neḍumangalam	Ramanathapuram	Silver 212 numbers
Peṇṇār	Coimbatore	Silver a potful
Thayirapāḷayam	Coimbatore	Silver 193 numbers
Toṇḍamanāthan	South Arcot	Silver 27 numbers
Vēmbāvūr	Tiruchirapalli	Silver 991 numbers
Vēmbāvūr	Tiruchirapalli	Silver 1375 numbers
Vīraśikhāmaṇi	Tirunelveli	Silver 287 numbers

* Information supplied by the Director, Government Museum, Madras and also based on P.L. Gupta, 'A Bibliography of Punch-Marked Coins of Ancient India', *Journal of the Numismatic Society of India*, vol. XVII, and R. Vanaja, *The Madras Museum Collection of Punch-Marked Coins, A Study*, M.Litt. Thesis (unpublished), University of Madras, 1955.

B. Roman Coin Finds in Tamiḻakam

I. Hoards

	Site	Taluk	District	No. of Coins & Issuers		Metal	Associated Finds
	Tamil Nadu						
1.	Akhilāṇḍapuram	Pollachi	Coimbatore	30		AR	
				Augustus:	2	(Silver)	
				Tiberius:	3		
				Rest:			
2.	Būdinatham	Udumalaipettai	Coimbatore	1398		AR	
				Augustus:	369		
				Tiberius:	1029		
3.			Coimbatore	73		AR	
				Augustus & Tiberius:	72		
				Gaius:			
4.	Dhārāpuram	Dharapuram	Periyar (Erode)	?	?	?	

5.	Kaliyampattūr	Palani	Dindigul ('Anna)	63		AV (Gold)	
				Tiberius:	6		
				Claudius:	18		
				Nero:	17		
				Gaius:	1		
				Domitian:	5		
				Nerva:	7		
				Rest:	?		
6.	Kaḷḷakiṇar	Palladam	Coimbatore	2		AR	Other Coins (AV, AR ?)
				Republican:	2		
7.	Kāngēyam or Kongēyam	Dharapuram	Periyar	10 +		AR	
				Augustus:	?		
8.	Karivalamvandanallūr	Sankaranainar Koyil	Tirunelveli	6 -		AV	
				Nero:	2		
				Vespasian:	1		
				Domitian:	2		
				Hadrian:	1		
9a.	Karūr	Karur	Tiruchirapalli	Hundreds -		AR	
				Augustus:	?		

B: I. Hoards *Cont'd*

	Site	*Taluk*	*District*	*No. of Coins & Issuers*		*Metal*	*Associated Finds*
9b.	Karūr	Karur	Tiruchirapalli	About 500		AR	
				Augustus:	27		
				Tiberius:	90		
				Rest:	?		
10.	Kāthānganṇi	Dharapuram	Periyar	233		AR	
				Augustus:	49		
				Tiberius:	184		
11.	Kōnēri Paṭṭi	Attur	Salem	35		AR	
				Augustus:	6		
				Tiberius:	29		
12.	Madurai Hills (?)		Madurai	11		AV	
				Claudius:	5		
				Nero:	3		
				Domitian:	1		
				Rest:	?		

13.	Māmbalam		Madras City	1		AR	770
				Augustus:	1		PMC
							AR
14.	Peṇṇār		Coimbatore	1		AR	PMC
				Augustus:	1		(AR)
15.	Poḷḷāchi	Pollachi	Coimbatore	6 +		AR	
				Augustus:	?		
				Tiberius:	?		
16.	Pudukkottai (Karukka-Kuṟichi)	Alangudi	Pudukkottai	501		AV	
				Augustus:	42		
				Tiberius:	168		
				Gaius:	14		
				Claudius:	56		
				Nero:	116		
				Vespasian:	3		
				Rest:	?		
17.	Soriyapaṭṭu	Tirukkoyilur	South Arcot	193 +		AV	
				Nero:	?		
				Antonius Pius:	?		
				Rest:	?		

B: I. Hoards *Cont'd*

	Site	*Taluk*	*District*	*No. of Coins & Issuers*		*Metal*	*Associated Finds*
18.	Toṇḍaimanāthan	Cuddalore	South Arcot	6		AV	27
				Augustus:	1		PMC
				Tiberius:	3		(AR)
				Claudius:	1		
				Nero:	1		
19a.	Veḷḷalūr	Coimbatore	Coimbatore	522		AR	
				Augustus:	135		
				Tiberius:	378		
				Gaius:	3		
				Claudius:	5		
				Nero:	1		
19b.	Veḷḷalūr	Coimbatore	Coimbatore	547		AR	
				Augustus:	189		
				Tiberius:	329		
				Gaius:	8		
				Claudius:	18		
				Nero:	3		

19c.	Veḷḷalūr	Coimbatore	Coimbatore	121 (+ 23 unstruck blanks)		AR
				Augustus:	118	
				Rest:	?	
19d.	Veḷḷalūr	Coimbatore	Coimbatore	Total:	?	AV
				Tiberius:	?	
			Kerala			
20.	Aleppey			Total: (upto Nero)	?	AR
				Tiberius:	1+	
				Others:	?	
21.	Eyyal	Tallapalli	Trichur	83		
				Republican:	5	AR
				Augustus:	47	AR
				Tiberius:	6	AR
				Tiberius:	8	AV
				Claudius:	6	AR
				Claudius:	2	AV
				Nero:	3	AR
				Nero:	1	AV

B: I. Hoards *Cont'd*

	Site	*Taluk*	*District*	*No. of Coins & Issuers*		*Metal*	*Associated Finds*
21. *Cont'd*				Trajan:	1	AV	
				Rest:	?	AR	
22.	Kōṭṭayam	Kottayam	Cannanore	1000s			
				Augustus:	9+	AV	(+ AR?)
				Tiberius:	28+		
				(Majority were of Tiberius)			
				Gaius:	3+		
				Claudius:	17+		
				Nero:	16+		
				Caracallas:	1+		
				Antonius Pius:	?		
23.	Kumbalam	Kanayanoor	Ernakulam	9			
				Hadrian:	1		
				Antonius Pius:	4		AV
				Marcus Aurelius:	4		

24.	Pūthankāvu	Chenganur	Quilon	50 +		AV
				(All issues post-date Theodosius I)		
				Theodosius II:	1+	
				Rest:	?	
25.	Valuvally	North Paravur	Ernakulam	252 +		AV
				Augustus:	?	
				Nero:	6+	
				Vespasian:	6+	
				Titus:	1+	
				Dormitian:	2+	
				Nerva:	1+	
				Trajan:	23+	
				Hadrian:	79+	
				Antonius Pius:	34+	
				Marcus Aurelius:	?	
			Indian Islands			
26.	Kadmat Island			15		AV
				Vespasian:	5	
				Antonius Pius:	9	

B: I. Hoards *Cont'd*

	Site	*Taluk*	*District*	*No. of Coins & Issuers*	*Metal*	*Associated Finds*
	Amindivi Group Lakshadvip			Commodus: 1		
27.	Lakshadvip			712 Republican Period: 266 Augustus: 269 Tiberius: 18 Gaius: 1 (with Agrippina) Hadrian: 1 Rest: ?	AR	

* Information from S. Suresh, 'Roman Coins', Roman Coin Finds in Tamiḻakam.

B. Roman Coin Finds in Tamiḻakam

II. Surface or Stray

	Site	Taluk	District	No. of Coins & Issuers		Metal	Associated Finds
1.	Ālampoṟai or Ālampaṟa	Madurantakam	Chingleput	3	?	AV	
						AR	
2.	Ānamalai	Pollachi	Coimbatore	Total:	?	AR	
				Tiberius:	?		
3.	Arikamēḍu		Pondichery	3		AR	
				Tiberius:	2		
				Imitation:	1		
4.	Bishopadown (Udhagamaṇḍalam)		Nilgiris	Claudius:	1	AV	
5.	Chāvaḍipāḷayam	Palladam	Coimbatore	1		AR	PMC
				Augustus:	1		(AR)
6.			Coimbatore	3		AR	
				Augustus:	1		
				Tiberius:	2		

B: II. Surface or Stray *Cont'd*

	Site	*Taluk*	*District*	*No. of Coins & Issuers*		*Metal*	*Associated Finds*
7.	Cuddalore	Cuddalore	South Arcot	Total:	?	AE	Die-struck
				Valentinian:	?	(Copper	Coins (AE)
				Eudocia:	?	etc.)	Perforated
							Chinese Coins
8.	Kalikanāyakan Pāḷaiyam	Coimbatore	Coimbatore	1		AV	
				Justinianus:	1		
9a.	Karūr	Karur	Tiruchirapalli	9		AV	
				Augustus:	1		
				Tiberius:	1		
				Claudius:	4		
				Marcus Aurelius:	1		
				Antonius Pius:	2		
9b.	Karūr	Karur	Tiruchirapalli	100s genuine and imitation coins unidentified		AE	

10.	Kīḷakkarai		Ramanathapuram	3 +			AE
				Decentius or			BR
				Julianus II (AE):	1		
				Unidentified (AE):	1		
				Unidentified (BR):	1		
11.	Koḍumaṇal	Perundurai	Periyar	2		AR	
				Augustus:	1		
				Tiberius:	1		
12.	Kor̤kai	Srivaikuntaṃ	Tirunelveli (Kattabomman)		?	?	?
13.	Krishnagiri		Dharmapuri	1		AR	
				Republican:	1		
14.	Kuḷattūr Pāḷaiyam or Kuḷattupāḷaiyam	Dharapuram	Periyar	1		AV	
				Theodosius			
15a.	Madurai		Madurai	2		AV	
				Domitian:	1		
				Leo III:	1		

B: II. **Surface or Stray** *Cont'd*

	Site	Taluk	District	No. of Coins & Issuers		Metal	Associated Finds
15b.	Madurai		Madurai	Hundreds		AE	
				Honorius:	?		
				Arcadius:	?		
				Anastasius:	?		
16.	?	Tirumangalam	Madurai	2		AV	
				Theodosius:	1		
				Constantine II:	1		
17.	Madurai	Madurai	Madurai	1		AE	
				Late Roman			
				- Imitation:	?		
18.	Mahabalipuram (Māmallapuram)	Chingleput	Chingleput	Total:	?	AE	
				Theodosius I:	?		
				Valentinian:	?		
				Eudocia:	?		

19.	Malayaḍipudūr or Malayaḍiputtūr	Nanguneri	Tirunelveli (Kattabomman)	4		AV	
				Theodosius II:	1		
				Anastasius I:	1		
				Imitation of Theodosius II:	2		
20.	Pērūr	Coimbatore	Coimbatore	3		AE	
				Constantine I:	1		
				Constantine II:	1		
				Theodosius (I or II):	?		
21.	Saidapet		Madras City	1		AE	
				Unidentified			
22.	Sūlūr	Palladam	Coimbatore	1	?		
23.	Tañjāvūr	Tanjavur	Tanjavur	1		AE	
				Diocletian:	1		
24.	Tiruchirapalli	Tiruchirapalli	Tiruchirapalli	16		AE	
				Issuers		?	
25.	Tirukkōyilūr	Tirukkoyilur	South Arcot	3 +		AE	
				4th cent. AD: Issuers	?		
26.	Tirumangalam	Tirumangalam	Madurai	1		AE	?
				Zeno:	1	or AV	

B: II. Surface or Stray *Cont'd*

	Site	*Taluk*	*District*	*No. of Coins & Issuers*	*Metal*	*Associated Finds*
27.	?	Tirunelveli	Tirunelveli (Kattabomman)	17 Issuers ?	AE	
28.	Tiruppūr		Coimbatore	1 Republican	AR	
29.	Udumalpet	Udumalaipettai	Coimbatore	5 Augustus: 2 Tiberius: 3	AR	
30.	Veḷḷaiyaniruppu Kāvērippūmpaṭṭiṇam	Sirkali	Nagappattinam (Quie-de-Millet)	1 Augustus: ?	AE	
31.	Vallanthavalam		Coimbatore	1 Augustus: 1	AR	
	Kerala					
32.	Idamakuduru		Idukki	1 Claudius: 1	AV or AR ?	
33.	Kīḻalūr (Kizhoor)		Cannanore	?	AV	

34.	Kōṭṭayam	Kottayam	Cannanore	2		AV	
				Theodosius			
				(I & II):	1		
				Nero:	1		
35.	Mankada	Palghat	Palghat	1		AV	
				Nero:	1		
36.	Nirapam (near Tiruvalla)		Idukki	?			
37.	Poonjar	Idukki	Idukki	Augustus:	1;	AV	AV
				Augustus	1	AR	and
				Claudius:	2	AV	AR
				Nero:	1	AV	
				Antonius Pius:	2	AV	

B. Roman Coin Finds in Tamil̤akam

III. Excavations

	Site	*Taluk*	*District*	*No. of Coins & Issuers*		*Metal*	*Associated Finds*
1.	Al̤agankul̤am	Ramanathapuram	Ramanathapuram	4 +		AE	
				Valentinian II:	2+		
				Arcadius:	1		
				Unidentified:	1		
2.	Karūr	Karur	Tiruchirapalli	1		AR	(PMC)
				Augustus:	1		AR ?

AV: Gold
AR: Silver
AE: Copper and other metals
PMC: Punch-Marked Coins

3

External Trade: Evidence from Early Tamil Texts

One of the major categories of sources for the study of early historic Tamil society and economy is the corpus of Tamil literature known as the 'Sangam' literature. It is a remarkable collection of poems containing evidence of early South Indian trade with the West Asian and Mediterranean regions and the Southeast Asian countries.

'Sangam' literature was not the product of a particular social or religious group, nor was it sponsored as a court literature by a ruling elite. It was also not intended to be a record of the activities of any one group. Composed at various points of time over a long span of about six hundred years, and authored by people of various levels–princes, chieftains, peasants, merchants, potters, smiths, carpenters and *brāhmaṇas*, Jains and Buddhists, the poems deal with disparate social groups. Yet, they admittedly provide useful insights into the society and economy of the early Tamils.

To use this corpus as a source of historical evidence, however, clear perspectives on the nature of its poetry need to be evolved, for it represents oral poetry of a heroic age. Being bardic literature in praise of heroes and patrons, its concern with various aspects of society and economy was incidental. Given to conventional, stylized and symbolic language, its preoccupation with stock-phrases and stereotyped expressions makes historical interpretation a hazardous exercise. The need for the use of Semiotics to interpret the signs and symbols of this heroic poetry has also been stressed in recent writings on early Tamil society and economy. This apart, it defies all attempts at an acceptable chronology, only relative chronologies based on internal evidence being possible within the six hundred years–300 BC to AD 300–for which it serves as the source material. Furthermore, the systematic collection of these poems into anthologies, with invocatory verses and colophons, took place several centuries after their composition (i.e. *c.* 7th–8th centuries AD) with the express object of attributing them to a Tamil Sangam of great antiquity and providing them a legitimacy from the world view of the Purāṇic religions.

Pioneering works used the disparate references to trade, both internal and external, centres of exchange, items of trade and trading groups, as direct and collective evidence of a single period and structure, as they did for other aspects of society and economy in this period. To them, trade was an isolated phenomenon, not necessarily to be discussed as a part of the socio-economic processes. Much of their interpretation of the 'Sangam' poems was heavily dependent on the medieval commentaries, themselves the product of a different social milieu.

The new approaches have adopted a more sophisticated methodology derived from anthropological and ethnographic studies for reconstructing what is generally understood to be a 'tribal' society in the process of transformation. Yet, what needs to be emphasised is the fact that the evidence from the 'Sangam' works on trade is often impressionistic and quantitatively less significant than on other aspects of society and economy. Hence, it has been found necessary to situate the references in specific contexts, geographic and ecological, and seek corroborative evidence from other sources like classical accounts, epigraphic records, albeit limited, and archaeological evidence, which, in the Tamil region, is not as illuminating as in the Deccan, to arrive at a more meaningful method of synthesising the data on trade and its impact.

The classical accounts, i.e. Graeco-Roman works, it must be admitted, are significant both because they are datable and because they provide us with valuable data on the Indo-Roman trading network and on the ports, marts, exports and imports of the Tamil country. As Maloney[1] points out, 'the mundane character of the Greek works causes them to be a useful supplement to the Indian literary sources'.

The chronology of the Sangam works, on the other hand, has for long been a keenly debated aspect of Tamil history. Studies in the language and literary forms of these works have made serious attempts to evolve a relative chronology and the most satisfactory exercise is that of Kamil Zvelebil,[2] which has been used in various studies on early historic society and economy.

What the present essay is concerned with is to analyse the data from this literature from the point of view of the developmental processes of trade, its mechanism and organization and the emergence of exchange networks in such early societies, as a result of contact and interaction with the outside world. The epics, *Śilappadikāram* and *Maṇimēkalai*, which belong to the post-Sangam phase of early Tamil literary activities, also have a very important bearing on early trade and hence are used in this essay to understand the nature of this trade.

As mentioned earlier, the 'Sangam' works represent collections of oral poetry of a heroic age whose signs and symbols need to be decoded through semiological methods. A contextual application of this method has resulted in some meaningful appraisals of the ecological basis of the socio-economic differences in the zones called *tiṇai*—a concept which dominates the poems and refers to a 'situation' which explains the different socio-economic milieux. This approach has led to more successful attempts to provide a basic understanding of the forms of production and economic organization in these eco-zones and the processes of change in some of them,[3] pointing to at least two broad phases of development: from a primitive and archaic to a more advanced stage of farming, the latter phase also marking an incipient urbanism, the processes of urbanization showing that the impetus to the growth of urban centres in certain *tiṇais* or eco-zones (like *marutam* and *neital*) was provided by maritime trade activities and interaction with foreign traders.[4]

The concept of the *tiṇai* is in many important ways, a pointer to the nature of early exchange between the subsistence level production systems in these zones. How this inter-*tiṇai* exchange[5] was later brought into a wider system of long distance trade presents an interesting facet of the impact and ramifications of the western trade with South India. The most fruitful exercise would, hence, be an attempt to identify products of different eco-zones which figure in inter-regional and western trade. As a point of illustration, forest and hill products were exchanged for the exotic—luxury items of western trade. To locate their source or regions of origin and the nature of control over them and their movement to the ports of export should be an important concern of any study which seeks to understand the links between inter-*tiṇai* exchange and the wider trading networks in this period.

Before the details of this symbiotic exchange between *tiṇais* and the identification of the articles of trade coming from different zones are taken up, it may be pointed out that the nature of the evidence from the 'Sangam' works shows that the trade contacts between the Roman empire and Tamiḻakam cannot be discussed in isolation from the South Indian contacts with the other parts of the South Asian region and with Southeast Asia, all of which participated in these early commercial activities linking the Mediterranean countries with the South Asia and far eastern countries of Asia. Another point that needs to be stressed is the fact that there are hardly any direct references in the Sangam works to the Romans *per se* and Roman trade. These works make no distinction between Greeks, Romans and West Asians–all of whom were involved in this trade. The term *Yavana*, which occurs in the context of foreigners and their trade activities, refers to them in general. It also occurs in other contexts, as referring to those *Yavana*s who were permanently settled in the region as guards of palaces and royal camps, where the ruling chief was guarded by the 'fierce looking' and brave '*Yavanas*'. Being ignorant of the local tongue and having no local sympathies they made ideal gatekeepers.[6] The *Śilappadikāram*[7] says that, impressed by the stern discipline of the *Yavana* soldiers, the Tamil kings employed them as guards of the fortress gates.

The more significant among the references to *Yavana*s are those on their settlements in important trading and commercial centres like Puhār and Muciṟi.[8] That they were most likely Romans is indirectly attested by the Roman pottery and other associate finds in excavations. That such settlements or *Yavana* suburbs are invariably found on the coast, especially in the big emporia of trade, is no less important in understanding the nature of their contact and interaction. The *Yavana*s would also seem to have moved across important trade routes, as indicated by the distribution of Roman coins and pottery in areas like Pudukkottai and Coimbatore.

The Roman contact was an important factor in the external trade of the Tamil country from about the times of Augustus (27 BC to AD 14), although a considerable antiquity has been assigned to the commerce between the Tamil country and the west.[9] It perhaps started as a mere 'trickle' or sporadic trade or unscheduled exchange, and gradually became a fruitful commerce in which spices, pearls, gems, cotton fabrics and other 'oriental' exotics were traded for Roman gold and wine and other assorted articles for well over two centuries.[10]

The Graeco-Roman 'discovery' of the secret of the monsoon winds (Hippalos), a 'discovery' which was probably made progressively in successive stages, is believed to have introduced a change or spurt in this activity. Traffic based on monsoon winds could have become popular by early first century AD as it is known to both Pliny and the *Periplus*. Thus, when hopping coastal trade was replaced by direct sailing to the western coasts, i.e. from Egypt to the ports of Kerala coast, these ports would have become centres of direct trade with the west. More significantly, this led to the establishment of Roman trading settlements in a few Tamil ports. Hence, the South Indian ports would seem to have become independent centres of trade 'free from Borygaza's economic dominance', i.e. the dominance of the Gujarat coast, and even led to the dominance of the Malabar ports, at least initially 'over the commercial network'.[11]

It would seem that the foreign merchants maintained a force of cohorts at Muziris (Muciṟi) to protect their trade.[12] This is perhaps indirectly confirmed by the *Patiṟṟuppattu*, which refers to a Cēra king, Imayavaramban Neḍuncēralātan punishing the *Yavanas* by binding 'their hands behind them' and 'pouring *ney* (ghee/clarified butter) on their head' and 'walking them along'.[13] The Peutingerian tables mention Tyndis and Muziris and refer to a temple of Augustus on the West coast.[14] There is, however, no reference to it in the Tamil sources.

The importance of the west coast, particularly Muziris (Muciṟi) as the main port of activity, is confirmed by the references in the *Akanānūṟu* and *Puṟanānūru*, which are considered to be the earliest poems. Subsequently, the shift in importance, however gradual, to the Coromandel ports, particularly to Kāvērippūmpaṭṭiṇam or Puhār (Camara or Khaberis), is indicated by

Ptolemy's references of the second century AD and, more significantly, by the *Paṭṭinappālai*, of a date later than the *Akam* and *Puṟam* collections, describing Puhār. The Coromandel ports thence came to be the major links in the transit trade between the Roman west, Southeast Asia and China. It may also be noted that the transcontinental silk route linking China with the west became inoperative due to the disturbances caused by the movements of Parthians in Central Asia around the first century BC. Thus, many of the goods were being deflected to the Coromandel ports through the Southeast Asian ports. For this, either Indian or Malay vessels must have been used to transport the merchandise from the Malacca straits to the Coromandel coast, from where the Greek ships collected them.

It has been suggested that since Greek vessels called at the various Tamil ports to carry back the trade goods, few Tamil merchants and ships ventured west. The basic reason for Tamil merchants not venturing or 'pouring over the seas' to the west lies not so much in the logic of 'western' and 'eastern' minds,[15] as in that of the terminal transit trading patterns, whereby Tamil merchants organized the collection of goods from within the country and from Southeast Asia and Sri Lanka, and Greek shippers came over to collect and transport them. That the Cēra and Pāṇḍya regions were more directly involved in the terminal trade, whereas the Cōḷa region with its ports was concerned with the transit trade linking the rest of the country with Rome, Sri Lanka (Īḻam) and Southeast Asia, is well attested by the Tamil sources with its clues to the nature of goods coming from different eco-zones (*tiṇai*) and from Southeast Asia.

There are some interesting clues to the seafaring instincts of the Tamils in this early period. The *Puṟam* refers to a Pāṇḍya prince who was drowned in the sea (Kaḍaluḷ Māinta Iḷam Peruvaḻudi).[16] A Cōḷa ruler who plied a 'fleet' across the seas and controlled the high winds[17] is an oft-repeated legend in the 'Sangam' age and in later literature. He was a legendary Cōḷa and an ancestor of Karikāla of the second century AD.[18] The Tamils were familiar with the harrowing experience of being caught in a storm in mid-Ocean.[19] However, the 'sails of the ships helped the vessels to pierce the stormy waves of the ocean' and 'on board the ship drums were beaten and tall flags were waving from the mast.[20] While at harbour, the ships were anchored by a thick, long rope to the nether end of which a big stone was attached.[21]

The harbour was called Puhār or 'Kayavōy'. The *Paṭṭinappālai* describes the harbour of Puhār or Kāvērippūmpaṭṭiṇam. The harbour, it is claimed, was generally safe even for bigger vessels. They could enter the harbour without removing cargo or slacking sail and yet be quite stable, steady and safe.[22] Evidence of such a harbour is hardly available in the present Puhār, and the legend of the port's submersion into the sea may well be based on fact. Warehouses were built on the beach near the quarters of the fishermen (*paratavar*?). The two kinds of goods (exports and imports) were found crowded on the quay.[23] Light houses called *kalam karai ilangu cuḍar*—'the light that beckons the ship'—are referred to.[24]

Articles of Trade

Many articles of trade passed through or were directly exported from Tamil ports *en route* to the Roman empire and to other regions of the west. The transit goods, some of which also entered the internal exchange of Tamiḻakam were spikenard from the Ganges region, silk from China, tortoiseshell from Southeast Asia and the islands near the Kerala coast.[25] The Tamil sources refer to silk as *paṭṭu*.[26] However such references do not indicate the direction or region from which it came to Tamiḻakam. Early medieval inscriptional evidence would place the region of origin in China. The *Periplus* points to China as the region from which silk reached the Ganges valley, from where it may have reached Tamiḻakam down the east coast to the Tamil ports, and then was sent to the west. Silk entered the internal circuit of exchange through gifts by rulers to *pāṇar* (bards) and as a luxury item of the ruling and urban elite's attire.

Spices, a major item of export, came predominantly from the western hills of Keraḷa, particularly pepper and cardamom. However, with the increase in the demand for spices by the first and second centuries AD, spices were also procured from Southeast Asia and sent to the Tamil ports to be shipped on to the west.[27] Fragrant woods, although available indigenously, were also a part of the transit trade, for they came from Southeast Asia, in addition to those from the hilly regions of South India.[28]

Wheeler's assessment that with Tamiḻakam the western trade was basically terminal, with a modicum of transit trade,[29] is to be revised in the light of the increase in the movement of spices, pearls, jewel stones and muslins, which came not only from the Tamil region but also from Southeast Asia and Sri Lanka. It is interesting that although 'Argaritic' muslins (from Uṟaiyūr) were in demand in the Roman world, Tamiḻakam imported the *kāḻagam* and *kalingam* (two varieties of fine fabric) from Burma and Kalinga respectively.[30] This would also indicate that the trade in textiles grew in volume and Tamil ports exported both locally produced 'Argaritic' fabrics and those for transit. These fabrics also entered the internal circuit of exchange, mainly through gifts to poets and bards.[31] A variety of thin cloth from Egypt (?) is also known to have been imported in addition to *kāḻagam* and *kalingam.*

Cotton fabric was the only manufactured item of export (apart from jewellery), produced both in the Cōḷa and Pāṇḍya regions. While the *Arthaśāstra*[32] refers to the fabric from Madurai in the Pāṇḍya region, the *Periplus* refers to the 'Argaritic' muslins of Uṟaiyūr in the Cōḷa land.[33] The Tamil sources refer to several varieties of cotton fabrics. *Tuhil* was a fine cotton cloth.[34] It was woven in Tamiḻakam and resembled steam or vapour and had so fine a texture that the threads could not be easily traced. It had floral patterns.[35] It was in great demand among the Romans. The *Śilappadikāram*[36] refers to thirty two varieties of cotton fabrics. Archaeological evidence in this regard is not highly illuminating although the occurrence of terracotta spindle whorls in Kunnattur, Odugattur and Sanur[37] and in Koḍumaṇal,[38] dyeing vats in Arikamēḍu, Uṟaiyūr and Vasavasamudram seem to indicate their manufacture on a considerable scale.

Two other major items of Tamiḻakam's trade with the west were undoubtedly pearls and pepper. Although a variety of gems seem to have been exported from the Tamil ports, the evidence on *muttu* or pearls is direct and indisputable. Of the other gems, beryl is known to be an important item of export, although it is not mentioned in the Tamil literature itself. The beryl mines of Paḍiyūr in the Coimbatore district are well known.[39] It is located not far from Koḍumaṇal, on the Noyyal river, the Koḍumaṇam of 'Sangam' works, famous for its jewel craft and goldsmiths.[40] Surface collections and excavations have yielded a large number of precious and semi-precious stones in Koḍumaṇal, apart from coins, both local and Roman, in the region around Koḍumaṇal, thus providing evidence of its being an important craft centre. Significantly, this centre falls within the region ruled by the Cēras with their capital at Karūr-Vañci, and the reference to Koḍumaṇam occurs in the *Patiṟṟuppattu*, the ten-tens or poems composed on the Cēras. Beryl mines have also been located in Vāṇiyambāḍi in the Salem (North Arcot?)[41] district and additional sources were tapped by the second century AD, perhaps in the days of Ptolemy when Punnata near Melkote in Karnataka and Sri Lanka may also have been exploited.[42]

Excavations in the Coimbatore region have brought to light six-sided beryl prisms, which have been interpreted as evidence of exchange of beryl for Roman coins,[43] for this region abounds in Roman coin finds. It is not clear when and how beryl entered long-distance trade. However, an initial 'trickle' in the pre-Christian era seems to have developed into a sustained commerce in the early centuries AD. The *Arthaśāstra* mentions *vaiḍūrya* (beryl) which, according to the commentators, came from the 'southern mountains'(?).[44] The term *vaiḍūrya* may well have been of Dravidian origin. It is also probable that the Greek word for it—*berullos*—is derived from *vaiḍūrya*.[45]

Diamonds, sapphires, rubies and transparent stones of all kinds were exported. Most of them came from Sri Lanka, famed for the best quality gems[46] and Andhra region (Cuddapah and Kurnool) and Karnataka (the upper Godavari and Kaveri valley) and perhaps even from Gujarat and Kathiawar.[47] The *Paṭṭinappālai*[48] says that to Puhār gems came from the 'northern mountains', which is generally taken to be the Himalayas, but could really have been Cuddapah and Kurnool system of the Deccan and the Vindhyan range. The references in Tamil literature, to sapphire, ruby, crystal, coral and gems (*maṇi*) in general are numerous,[49] but not precise enough to help identify places of their origin. Except for pearls and beryl, the rest would seem to have come from adjacent and other distant regions. The Sangam literary references to varieties of gems, lapidary (*maṇi-vaṇṇakkan*), jeweller (*maṇikuyirrunar*) and goldsmiths (*por-kollar*) etc. would suggest that a direct result of this movement in gem trade was the high degree of skills that the Tamils acquired in jewel-making,[50] and jewels seem to have been an important item of export, especially from the Pāṇḍya country.[51] To the Pāṇḍyan coast came 'horses and other precious things'[52] which were presumably exchanged for gems.

Muttu or pearls, from which the Sanskrit *mukta* is derived, in fact heads the categories of gems exported from the eastern waters. South Indian pearls were rated among the best and highly valued in the ancient world, as borne out by Sanskrit, Greek and Tamil sources.[53] They found their way to Southeast Asia, China and Andhra and Ganges regions in India. They also reached in considerable quantity the Malabar ports of Muziris (Muciri) and Nelcynda (Kōṭṭayam) from where they were exported to Rome.[54] They could have reached the western ports either by the circum-peninsular route or by coastal shipping or even by the transpeninsular route through the Palghat gap. They were used by the ruling elite both in adorning themselves and as gifts to bards.[55] References to their place in the internal trade, however, are few and ambiguous.[56] There are hardly any significant finds in excavations except for Korkai, which has come up with oyster shells.[57] The Cōḷas and Pāṇḍyas, not surprisingly, laid claims to the pearl coast–from the Tamraparni basin to Toṇḍi in the Ramanathapuram district–and it would appear that the Cōḷas were particularly interested in controlling the pearl-rich Pāṇḍya coast as much as the pepper-rich Cēra coast, both pearls and pepper being major items of export. Plunder mechanism was one of the most conspicuous and successful means of acquiring such valuables for exchange and consumption.

Gems (*maṇi*–a generic term) and jewellery made out of them were a part of the decorative paraphernalia associated with the ruling and urban elite and, both as trade items and elite symbols, they are frequently mentioned in Tamil sources. However, excavations, with the exception of Koḍumaṇal, have yielded a rather limited number of crystal, chalcedony, agate, carnelian and other semi-precious stones, while pearls are the least represented in archaeology.[58] It would appear from literary references and archaeological evidence that the main impact of the gem trade was in the area of manufacturing jewels and trading in this finished product, a concentration of archaeological evidence coming from Koḍumaṇal.

It may be suggested that, unlike for pepper and beryl, of which the Tamils had exclusive monopoly, for carnelian, agate and other gems the Tamil merchants would have faced competition from the northern merchants, especially those of Bharukaccha (Barygaza), where these figure as important exports,[59] and also from Sri Lanka, to which the western traders may have turned directly by the second century AD after the 'discovery' of the monsoons, which enabled Greek ships to sail to the island's coasts and the eastern coast of Tamiḻakam. By the third century AD, or immediately after, the ports of the island seem to have become important entrepots, as the evidence of the *Cosmos Indicopleustus* of the sixth century AD[60] indicates, and the focus of trade in the Indian Ocean shifted from the Tamil country to the island.[61]

Thus, at least during the early centuries of the Christian era, the Tamil merchants seem to have acted as middlemen for the Sri Lankan articles exported to the west, and hence faced competition from the indigenous Īḻam (Sri Lanka) merchants. This could well have been the reason behind the several conflicts between the peoples of the island and those of the Tamil mainland.[62] The presence of Tamil merchants in Īḻam making donations to Buddhist shrines[63] and a few Īḻam merchants in the Tamil region,[64] is attested to by inscriptional records of this period. The initiative may have come from the Tamil merchants and later shifted, after competition, to the Sri Lankan merchants.

Spices, not necessarily a luxury item, formed the other major item of export. Among them, in terms of quantity, pepper (*kaṟi*) ranked the highest, especially to the Roman empire. Pepper perhaps made up three-fourths of the total bulk of the average Rome-bound cargo,[65] or more than half.[66] The *Periplus*[67] says that the ships which visited the western (Malabar) ports in the first century AD were of a large size, on account of the pepper that was being carried. Common black pepper was exported from Kuṭṭa nāḍu (Cottanara–the region around Quilon and Kōṭṭayam), where the climate was most conducive to its growth. Thus it is said:

. . . Cēra's great river Cuḷḷi splashes with white foam where Yavanas bring their well built ships, arriving with gold and carrying pepper from the prosperous Muciṟi, reverberating with the Ocean.[68]

The *Paṭṭinappālai*[69] refers to sacks of black pepper reaching the Cōḷa port of Kāvērippūmpaṭṭiṇam by carts, presumably by the circumpeninsular route from the west coast. The references to pepper or other spices going to north India are few, but evidence of its entering the internal exchange system in Tamiḻakam is available. The Cōḷas and Pāṇḍyas would have attempted to control the west coast, the only region where pepper was available, and hence the Cēras having a virtual monopoly over it. The ports of Muziris (Muciṟi) and Nelcynda (Kōṭṭayam) owed much of their prosperity to the pepper trade and became prominent commercial centres. It is possible that Toṇḍi (Tyndis) was also involved in a small way in this trade through the Ponnani river, whose tributaries would have brought down the pepper from the Malabar hills.

About Muciṟi we are told:

Paddy heaped up, traded for fish makes it difficult to distinguish tall ships from the houses.

Sacks of pepper, piled beside the buildings become confusing on the bustling sea front. Articles of gold brought by sea vessels are carried to the shore by boats in the estuary. Products of his (Cēra's) mountains and products of his seas, he brings together to bestow on his visitors, with toddy like a river, the gold mountain Kuṭṭuvan, his noisy Muciṟi throbs as the Ocean.[70]

Cardamom, yet another important spice exported to the west, is found in Travancore, Malabar and the highlands bordering the districts of Madurai, Tirunelveli and Dindigul.[71] However, strangely enough, there is hardly any direct reference to cardamom in the Tamil sources, although it is well known to the classical accounts. Malabathrum 'from the interiors'[72] was another export from the west coast and has been identified as betel leaf or cinnamon bark(?)[73] although it is said to be of inferior quality when compared to that (cinnamon) from China, Sri Lanka, Southeast Asia and the Himalayas.

Nard (Nardus), yet another item of export which figures along with malabathrum, seems to be a grass or leaf (lemon grass?), found in the Cēra region. It was used to extract an oil, a fragrant one, for cosmetic purposes (Cymbopogan Nardus),[74] and the Seleucids are believed to have attempted to naturalize it in their country. It was known to Pliny and the *Periplus* as the sweet-smelling oil of the Nard–the word probably derived from *Narantam* in Tamil.[75]

It has already been noted that, under the impetus of the lucrative spice trade, the early Tamil merchants sought new sources for the spices and turned to the spice rich Southeast Asian islands.[76]

Among the forest products, woods of all sorts–ornamental and aromatic–entered this commercial network. The most notable were sandalwood, teak, ebony and eaglewood, most of which grew in the hilly tracts of Coimbatore–Salem, Malabar and Karnataka.[77] None of them, however, is listed among the exports from the Tamil ports by the *Periplus*.[78] Though the forests of Central India could have been tapped,[79] the forests of Tamiḻakam may also have been a major source. They were also brought, along with spices, from the Southeast Asian islands, presumably in response to increasing demands from the west.

The *Śilappadikāram* says:

> The broad rayed sun ascends from the South. White clouds start to form in the early cool season. Only after this time, across the dark bellowing ocean, the rulers of Toṇḍi dispatch vessels loaded with *akhil* wood (eaglewood), silk, sandal and spices and all sorts of camphor.
> These are wafted with the wind from the east.[80]

The imports to South India, several of which are known from the *Periplus*,[81] consisted of coin, topaz, coral, thin clothing and figured linens, antimony, copper, tin and lead, wine, realgar and orpiment and also wheat, the last mentioned probably for the Graeco-Romans in the Tamil ports. Of these, wine is by far the most conspicuously mentioned item in the Sangam works in a variety of contexts, particularly in connection with the ruling and urban elite. Roman wine was very popular with the Tamils, who were familiar with its quality and fragrance. In the *Puṟanāṉūru*, a poet lauds a Pāṇḍya king:

> O Māṟa, whose sword is ever victorious, spend thou thy days in peace and joy drinking daily out of golden cups presented by the handmaids . . .
>
> the cool and fragrant wine (*tēṟal*) brought by the Yavanas in their good ships . . . [82]

Amphorae sherds have been excavated from Arikamēḍu, Vasavasamudram and Kāraikkāḍu, while those reported from Kāñcīpuram do not appear to be amphorae, but, rather, imitations in the form of conical jars. Some of them show traces of incrustation on the inside caused by wine resin.[83]

The *Yavana* lamp, whose wick was capable of giving out a steady flame without a flicker, was also an item of considerable demand in Tamiḻakam. It was a novelty to the Tamils. Some of them were like statues bearing in their folded palms the *takaḻi* or the container for the lamp.[84] The *pāvai viḷakku*, a female statue holding a lamp in its hands, is a common sight in most temples and households in Tamiḻakam even today. Although there are no references to it in the *Periplus*, the fact that different metals are mentioned as imports, would suggest that some at least would be finished products like lamps. While copper and bronze articles including jewellery are found in Megalithic burials,[85] no evidence of lamps has so far been found in excavations.

Roman coins came in large quantities, in exchange for pepper, beryl and cotton fabrics and a concentration of these coins occurs in major trade routes like the Coimbatore district and the Pudukkottai area. As discussed in a previous chapter, their circulation and use as a medium of exchange have been one of the major points of dispute among scholars. Their value as exchange-medium being indeterminable in the South Indian context, it has often been suggested that they were generally used as bullion, although some, at least, were turned into jewellery, as seen in the pierced coins used as pendants.

The Tamil sources have very little to offer by way of evidence on Roman coins. Even at the level of larger transactions involved in import and export of goods, it is mainly for pepper that Roman gold is said to have been exchanged. There is also no reference to exchange of specie (foreign) at ports with native currency as in the *Periplus*[86] for Barygaza. The term *kāśu*, *poṉ* and *kāṇam* occurring in the Tamil poems and mentioned as currency units in early medieval inscriptions[87] have been presumed to be gold coins.[88] Nothing is known about their metal content or weight. On the other hand, the *kāṇam* and *kāśu* were conferred as gifts by patron rulers on poets. Thus, Ariśil Kiḻār received a gift of 900,000 *kāṇam* (gold) and Kākkaippāḍiniyār Nacceḷḷaiyār 100,000 *kāṇam* (gold).[89] Such references occur in the *padikams* of the *Patiṟṟuppattu*,[90] which are generally believed to be later additions to the main body of the poems.

Tamiḻakam had access to the gold from Karnataka, i.e. Raichur-Bellary plateau which is presumably the region referred to as the northern hills (*vaḍamalai*) in the Tamil texts.[91] The gold mines in Karnataka have provided evidence of ancient workings. Gold articles and jewellery figure prominently among gifts conferred by chieftains on bards[92] and are generally found to be associated with the ruling and urban elite.[93] Goldsmiths and traders in gold (*poṉśey-kollan* and *poṉ-vāṇigar*) are mentioned in *Naṟṟiṇai*[94] and in Tamil Brāhmī inscriptions.[95] However, there are no major finds of gold in the archaeological levels of this period, except for some exquisite pieces of jewellery at Sūttukkeni, three gold beads at Arikamēḍu, what has been reported as a 'goldsmith's mould' from Paiyampaḷḷi,[96] and a few pieces from Koḍumaṇal.

Horses, for the breeding of which the southern climate was not conducive, have always been imported into South India, mainly from the Arab countries. The *Paṭṭinappālai* refers to milk white steeds imported into *Puhār*, while the *Maduraikkāñci* makes a reference to their import to the Pāṇḍyan ports.[97] The Toṇḍaināḍu port of Nīrppeyar received horses in ships.[98] Strangely, horses were also gifted by rulers to bards.[99] References to horses as gifts are fewer than to other items, perhaps due to their military importance to the rulers.[100] Nonetheless, what is interesting is that to the bards or poets, such gifts as those of horses and elephants, appear to be of no immediate use or value.

Horsebits or articles associated with the use of horses are reported in the early levels of excavations at Sāṇūr, Kunnattūr and Ādīchanallūr but the correctness of their identification has been questioned.[101]

The majority of the exports would thus seem to be raw materials, with the exception of cotton fabrics and jewellery made of gold and gems. The impact of such an exchange on the manufacturing activities of Tamiḷakam is hard to assess. The evidence points only to a minimal range of craft production—fabrics and jewels—and their being located at key centres—the consumption points in the interior, the areas where mines were located (beryl—Coimbatore) and the ports where commercial activities were concentrated.

The stress was undoubtedly on the export and import of elite and luxury goods such as horses, gold, gems etc., which were meant for elite consumption and not for local exchange. Chiefly families acquired and used them for enhancing their status and prestige and legitimized it by conferring gifts on poets and bards. The importance of primitive valuables has been stressed for their socio-political significance in early societies.[102] Thus, 'rare and precious things'[103] were gifted away by the Pāṇḍya king. The Cēra ruler is lauded for bringing together products of the seas to bestow on visitors.[104] In return for the valuable gifts, the bards and kinsmen played an important role in legitimizing and sustaining the position of their patron rulers.

The nature of commodities exported (pearls, pepper and textiles) indicates that the Cēra and Pāṇḍya regions, which were in possession of these resources, would have been the chief beneficiaries of this trade, and one could expect a positive impact on the productive system of both these areas. The Cōḷa region (lower Kāvēri valley), which had greater agricultural potential, was not in possession of any of these commodities, with the exception of cotton muslins. They did not directly control any of the hill resources. Their control over the Palk Bay and the beryl mines of the Kongu plateau (which strictly speaking falls within the Cēra region around Karūr-Vañci) and over the routes to the western coast and southern Karnataka, was fluctuating, as it was the result of temporary raids and successes over the Cēras. Yet all the sources, particularly Tamil works like *Paṭṭinappālai*, indicate that most of these commodities produced in the Tamil country and in the neighbouring regions, reached the early Cōḷa port of Kāvērippūmpaṭṭiṇam and were subsequently exported.[105] The Cōḷas seem to have acquired a sort of hegemonic control over Tamiḻakam by constantly exhibiting their superior prowess over the other two of the traditional Tamil trio (chiefly families or kingdoms?) and over the major routes facilitating the internal movement of goods to the ports of embarkation/export, i.e. over the commerce between Tamiḻakam, Roman west, Sri Lanka and Southeast Asian countries.

It is in this context that the *tiṇai* concept of eco-zones of the Tamil works hold a valuable clue to the resources of various regions and to the base that the Cōḷas were able to build up—by way of paddy or agricultural production—and, thereby, possibly promote the acquisition of other resources through paddy and salt. It is significant that the Cēra, Cōḷa and Pāṇḍya ports were located at the mouths of the major rivers of these regions. Of these, which figure prominently in the classical accounts, it is significant that some seem to have been more active in the first centuries BC and AD like Muziris (Muciṟi) and Koṟkai (Colchi), while the Cōḷa port Khaberis (Camara or Kāvērippaṭṭinam) was active in the second century AD. In the time of the *Periplus*, which sets out in detail the ports and commerce of the western coast, the eastern Coromandel coast and the Cōḷa ports seem to have been beyond the bounds of the Greek vessels. Later, by the second century AD, under better incentives, and even to the point of doing away with Tamil intermediaries, the Greeks seem to have surmounted the difficulties of the straits and circumnavigating Sri Lanka and established direct contact with the Cōḷa ports, and even navigated upto the Bengal coast. This is not only reflected in Ptolemy's geography (AD 150), which gives a detailed list of ports and marts along the eastern coast of the sub-continent, but is more directly attested to by the *Paṭṭinappālai*, a work datable to this period, and a work composed with the specific purpose of describing the port city of Kāvērippūmpaṭṭiṇam, which was built and developed by the Cōḷa Karikāla. Similar works describing the other major ports do not exist. In fact, it would appear that the Cōḷas had a clear objective in developing a port, a harbour (Puhār) of this kind, which, in many ways, acted like a 'gateway city' in the early centuries, particularly in the second century AD when the trade in that city was at its peak.[106]

Kāvērippūmpaṭṭiṇam, as portrayed in this work, had well organized markets–*nāḷangāḍi* (day) and *aḷḷangāḍi* (night)–quarters for various social and economic groups in the two major sections called the *Paṭṭinappākkam* (the city or residential area) and the *maruvūrppākkam* (port area) and the major commercial area being located between the two. Excavations conducted here have shown its occupation and use at least from the third century BC to the fourth-fifth centuries AD, and the wharf remains etc. show facilities needed for a harbour. It is located at the mouth of the Kāvēri, where the river itself becomes a rather shallow stream hardly reaching the sea, perhaps as a result of the damming up of the river at Talakaveri and the flow of water controlled so as to channel it towards the Koḷḷiḍam and the distribution of the delta.

While Tamil literature distinctly uses the term *paṭṭiṇam* for a port, all coastal towns are not referred to as such with the exception of Kāvērippūmpaṭṭiṇam (Puhār). To a large extent this port fits in with the description of an emporium. Polanyi[107] points out that in classical Greek terminology, the emporium was that part or sector of a coastal town which was devoted to foreign commerce. However, the emporium was much more than that. It was a self-contained unit with its own food, market, harbour, quay, warehouses, administrative building, mariner's houses and so on. In Puhār the Cōḷa officers with the tiger stamp oversaw all activities, collected tolls/customs etc. As a gateway city, Puhār overshadowed, by its importance, all other entry points to South India.

In another sphere, the impact of maritime trade may be recognized in the changing fortunes of the *Paratavar*, who became the most distinctive merchant group in the latter part of this period of intensive trade. According to the traditional *tiṇai* scheme, they were inhabitants of the *neital* tract, simple rustic folk, following occupations such as fishing, manufacturing salt and making toddy.[108] The later poems of the *Pattuppāṭṭu* collection, however, depict them as being involved in long-distance commerce and also pearl fishing. Under the influence of commercial activities, they diversified from these traditional pursuits and took to organizing trade in pearls, conches, chank bangles, tamarind, fish, gems, horses and other riches.[109] Here trade seems to have been a dynamic intrusive element leading to the development of this tract and its people.[110]

Many other types of merchants were also involved in the buying of goods from the hills and from the sea (coast), and carrying them to various centres within the Tamil region.[111] Specialist merchants operated within the precincts of large commercial cities such as Madurai, Uṟaiyūr and Puhār, where market facilities (*angāḍi*) were available. Their names invariably carried as a prefix the place of their origins, e.g. Madurai Aṟuvai Vāṇikan (the cloth trader from Madurai), Uṟaiyūr Iḷampon Vāṇikan (the young gold trader from Uṟaiyūr) etc.

The occasional caravans (*cāttu*) of itinerant traders carried goods to the hinterlands from ports, and perhaps also returned with goods to be shipped from such ports.[112] Evidence on guild organization is tenuous and not comparable to that of the Deccan.[113] The *Śilappadikāram* is the story of the son of a great caravan leader (*Māsāttuvan*), and hence of considerable value in understanding the nature of trade and trading patterns, both internal and external.

One of the most interesting consequences of the commercial interaction between Tamiḻakam and other regions was the arrival of foreign merchants at the Tamil ports and commercial centres.[114]

In Puhār,

> different kinds of goods (were) brought in ships by foreign merchants (*Pulam-Peyar-mākkaḷ*) who have left their native homes and settled here.[115]

There is very little information about the regions from where these 'foreign merchants hailed, but certainly they included people from Rome, Southeast Asia, Īḻam (Sri Lanka) and even other parts of the subcontinent. Separate quarters existed for the *Yavanas* in the *emporia*, as indicated by the later evidence of the *Śilappadikāram*.[116] However, to conclude that these quarters were 'autonomous concessions' or 'territorial acquisitions' similar to latter day European 'factories', is going beyond the evidence.[117]

Did the Greeks (and Romans) play the most active role in this commerce as is held by various scholars,[118] or did they confine their activities to the major commercial centres, while in the hinterlands, the production and transportation to the waiting ships, were in the hands of local traders and craftsmen?[119] The accounts of Pliny and the *Periplus*[120] would seem to support the latter contention. The Tamil sources, would, much more clearly, indicate the active role of Tamil merchants, a flourishing indigenous mercantile community, while, as Filliozat puts it, the foreigners had probably nothing more to do than load their vessels from the readymade warehouses, and increase the activities of warehouses, without either having to organize or administer them.[121] No foreigners are seen making donations to local religious organizations as in the Deccan, where they were absorbed into the indigenous social organization. Indeed, such large-scale and impressive monumental religious institutions and the ostentatious gifts as found in the Deccan, are absent in the Tamiḻakam of this period. Tamil literature is silent on such gifts, although references are made to some cult centres and shrines, which were not part of an organized and institutionalized religious system.

The life style of the native merchants points to affluence, as the merchants are depicted in later poems as living in 'fine mansions' and sporting silk raiments and gold jewellery,[122] and the later epics *Śilappadikāram* and *Maṇimēkalai* focus on their prosperity and affluent life style. That they followed a self-imposed code of behaviour is known from the general attributes which the *Paṭṭinappālai*[123] speaks of:

> They speak the truth and deem it a shame to lie
> For others' goods they have the same regard as for their own in trade
> Nor do they try to get too much in selling their own goods
> Nor give too little when they buy
> They set a fair price on all things
> Their ancient wealth was thus acquired.

Tamil traders in general seem to have followed different

religious faiths, unlike in the Deccan and Andhra regions, where the trading community's affiliation to the Buddhist (and perhaps also Jain) religion was predominant. While the early Tamil poems reflect the predominance of tribal forms of worship and cult deities specific to different eco-zones as well as the influence of brahmanical religions in the *marutam* zone, the post Sangam epics, *viz.* *Śilappadikāram* and *Maṇimēkalai*, show the increasing influence of Buddhism and Jainism over the trading community and, in an urban context, both in coastal towns and interior politico-commercial centres. The Tamil Brāhmī inscriptions[124] would also support the Buddhist and Jain bias of the merchants, who are seen making gifts to these two sects.

The emergence and crystallization of a merchant community with well organized guilds as in the Deccan and Andhra are not clearly attested to in the literary sources. The Tamil anthologies mention several kinds of traders, including hawkers, peddlers (*vambalar, vilaiñar, pakarnar*) and big traders (*vaṇigar*), as well as those who traded in specific items (*umaṇar*—salt merchants). In the market places (*angāḍis*) of big centres like Puhār and Madurai, several specialist traders selling particular wares are known.[125] Most of them were, however, producers as well as sellers of such articles. They were, in general, different from those involved in trade with distant regions and foreign traders. It would be rather difficult to rank the different traders on the basis of the volume of trade which they conducted. Such evidence is not easy to find in the texts. However, the epics, while referring to the merchants and their influence, would seem to point to wealthy merchants, whose presence in the commercial and port towns was significant. They would most likely be those who conducted large-scale trading and commercial activities and possibly also controlled the movement of goods within the region. Thus, guild organization would have been important in regulating such movement. The references to *Māsāttuvan* (caravan leader) in the *Śilappadikāram*, to *Kāviti* and *nigama* in Tamil Brāhmī inscriptions,[126] interpreted as guild chief (or, more correctly, counsellor) and guild respectively, would indicate the prevalence of such organization. However, organized guilds and trading networks coinciding with the important Buddhist centres with huge monastic establishments of the kind found in Deccan and Andhra regions, are certainly not visible in Tamilakam.

The early Tamil poems are generally silent on the origin of merchants, although in early societies merchants are said to have emerged from among chiefly families, since the redistributional mechanism, which operated in most chiefdoms, led to concentration of economic wealth in the hands of those close to the chief.[127] One may recall in this connection the circulation of wealth through gifts among kinsmen close to the Sangam chiefs, both the *Vēndar* and the *Vēḷir*. Virai was as much a port of the *Vēḷir* chief,[128] as Puhār was of the Cōḷas, Korkai of the Pāṇḍyas and Muciṟi of the Cēras, all of which point to the direct involvement of the ruling elite in the promotion of trade.

In early societies, under the influence of trade and *the* consequent development of a market and its organization, it is believed that an emergent state system resorted to minting coins to facilitate long-distance trade.[129] Yet, in early Tamilakam, long-distance trade does not seem to have had any significant impact over the emergence of a state society, for trade and urban processes were not built into the core of the transformation of a non-state to state society in early Tamilakam. At the same time, recent finds of local coin issues suggest a direct impact of inter-regional and maritime trade.

References

1. C. Maloney, 'The Effect of Early Coastal Sea Traffic on the Development of Civilization in South India', Ph.D. Dissertation (unpublished), University of Pennsylvania, Philadelphia, 1968, xlv.
2. Kamil Zvelebil, *The Smile of Murugan: On the Tamil Literature of South India*, E.J. Brill, Leiden, 1973, 27-43.
3. Rajan Gurukkal, 'Forms of Production and Forces of Changes in Ancient Tamil Society', *Studies in History*, July-Dec. 1989 (n.s.), vol. 5, no. 2, 159-76.
4. *See* Chapter 1 in this volume.
5. *Porunarāṟṟuppaṭai*, ll. 214; J.V. Chelliah, *Pattuppāṭṭu—The Ten Tamil*

Idylls (tr. into English with Introduction and Notes), SISSW, Tirunelveli, 1962, 2nd edn, 73–5.

6. *Mullaippāṭṭu*, ll. 59–66.
7. *Śilappadikāram*, XIV: 67.
8. N. Subrahmanian, *Pre-Pallavan Tamil Index–Index of the Historical Material in Pre-Pallavan Tamil Literature*, Madras, 1966. Also *idem Sangam Polity–The Administration and Social Life of the Sangam Tamils*, Madurai, 1980 (Rev. ed.).
9. R.S. Kennedy, 'King in Early South India: As Chieftain and Emperor', *Indian Historical Review*, 1976, vol. III, 1-15; Maloney, 'Early Coastal Sea Traffic', 228f; K.K. Pillay, *A Social History of the Tamils*, Madras, 1975, reprint, 249f.
10. *Puṟanāṉūṟu*, 343: 1-10; *Akanāṉūṟu*, 149: 7-11; *Periplus*: 56-61. W.H. Schoff, *The Periplus of the Erythraean Sea. Travel and Trade in the Indian Ocean by a Merchant of the 1st Century* (tr. from the Greek and annotated), Longmans, Green & Co., New York, 1912.
11. K.R. Hall, 'The Expansion of Maritime Trade in the Indian Ocean: Roman Trade in the Indian Ocean: An Indian Perspective', *The Elmira Review*, vol. 1, 40.
12. William Logan, *Malabar Manual*, Madras, 1951, I, 199.
13. *Patiṟṟuppattu*, II: 10.
14. Subrahmanian, *Sangam Polity*, 240.
15. Warmington, *Commerce Between the Roman Empire and India*, New Delhi, 1974, reprint, 66. Recently two potsherds have been discovered at Quseir-al-Qadim, a small Egyptian port on the Red Sea, with brief inscriptions in the Tamil Brāhmī script, presumably the names of Tamil traders–Cātan and Kaṇan–reported by Whitcomb and Johnson in the *Oriental Institute (Chicago) Annual Report*, 1977-8, reprint.
16. *Puṟanāṉūṟu*: 182.
17. Ibid.: 66.
18. Subrahmanian, *Sangam Polity*, 241.
19. *Maṇimēkalai*, IV, 29–34.
20. *Maduraikkāñci*: 77-83; *Paṭṭinappālai*: 173–5.
21. *Maduraikkāñci*: 378, smaller boats used in river transport are known as *ambi*, *paḥṟi*, and *Ōḍai* (*Akanāṉūṟu*: 29:18; 101:12; 187:23; *Ainkuṟunūṟu*: 98:2; 168:2; *Naṟṟiṇai*: 74:3; 315:3; 354:7; *Puṟanāṉūṟu*: 261:4; 34; 3:2; 381:24) and larger boats as *Kalam Vangam*, *nāvāy* (and *Timil*?) (*Akam*: 13:5; 26:2; 30:12–13; 56:321; *Naṟṟiṇai*: 295:6; *Paṭṭinappālai*: 174; *Perumpāṇāṟṟuppaṭai*: 321). Were they used for sea voyages? The *Periplus* (60) refers to these types, a small one used by natives for coastal traffic, a larger one called

Sangara made of several logs fastened together (*Kaṭṭumaram*?) and vessels of large bulk called *Kolandiaphonta*, for sea voyages to Ganges delta and Southeast Asia for bringing spices and woods. Whose ships were they?

22. *Puṟanāṉūṟu*: 30; *Maduraikkāñci*: 54.
23. *Paṭṭinappālai*: 130–1.
24. *Perumpāṇāṟṟuppaṭai*: 349–51; Subrahmanian, *Sangam Polity*, 242.
25. *Periplus*: 56–64; McCrindle, *The Commerce and Navigation of the Erythraean Sea and Ancient India as Described by Ktesias, the Knidian*, Amsterdam, 1973, Reprint.
26. *Akanāṉūṟu*: 236: 11; *Paṭṭinappālai*, l. 107; *Porunarāṟṟuppaṭai*, l. 155; *Śilappadikāram*, v. 16; xiv: 86; 205; xxii: 46.
27. *Śilappadikāram*: xiv: 104–12; Maloney, 'Early Coastal Sea Traffic', 162–3.
28. *Śilappadikāram*: xiv: 104–12; Maloney, 'Early Coastal Sea Traffic', 162–3; *Vāsam* is the term used for spices in *Śilappadikāram* (xiv: 108). It denotes five objects, viz. *Takkōlam* or *Ēlam* or cardamom, *Tīmpu* or saffron flower, *Ilavangam* or clove, *Karpūram* or camphor, *Sāti* (*kkāi*) or nutmeg. *See* Subrahmanian, *Pre-Pallavan Tamil Index*, 749.
29. R.E.M. Wheeler, *Rome Beyond the Imperial Frontiers*, Pelican, London, 1955, 164.
30. Subrahmanian, *Pre-Pallavan Tamil Index*, 233, 270; *Puṟanāṉūṟu*, 41: 9; *Paṭṭinappālai*, l. 191; *Śilappadikāram*, xiv, 104–12.
31. *Akanāṉūṟu*, 86: 21; 136: 20; *Puṟanāṉūṟu*, 398: 28; *Kuṟuntokai*, 167: 2; *Maduraikkāñci*, l. 517, 721; *Ciṟupāṇāṟṟuppaṭai*, ll. 85–96.
32. *Arthaśāstra*, ii: 11: 115 (Shama Sastry, *Kauṭilya's Arthaśāstra* (tr. into English, Mysore, 1951, 4th edn)).
33. *Periplus*: 59.
34. *Paṭṭinappālai*, l. 235; *Ciṟupāṇāṟṟuppaṭai*, l. 236.
35. *Puṟanāṉūṟu*, 398: 20; *Porunarāṟṟuppaṭai*, ll. 82–3.
36. *Śilappadikāram*, vi: 88.
37. R. Sumathi, 'Trade and Its Impact on the Early Tamils—The Cola Experience', M.Phil Dissertation (unpublished), New Delhi, Jawaharlal Nehru University, 1984, App.c.
38. Dr Y. Subbarayalu and his team from the Tamil University, Thanjavur, have been excavating at this site for over four seasons now. I am indebted to him for providing me with copies of the interim reports on the site.
39. G. Watt, *The Commercial Products of India*, Today and Tomorrow's Printers and Publishers, New Delhi, 1966, reprint, 556.
40. *Patiṟṟuppattu*, 67: 1; 74: 5.

41. Warmington, *Commerce Between the Roman Empire and India*, 250–1.
42. Ptolemy, vii, 1: 86; vii: 4: 1. (McCrindle, *Ancient India as Described by Ptolemy*, Calcutta, 1927, rev. ed.).
43. Warmington, *Commerce Between the Roman Empire and India*, 251.
44. Shama Sastry, *Kauṭilya's Arthaśāstra*, 71n.
45. Maloney, 'Early Coastal Sea Traffic', 214.
46. Ibid., 24.
47. G. Watt, *Commercial Products*, 556–7.
48. *Paṭṭinappālai*, l. 187.
49. Subrahmanian, *Pre-Pallavan Tamil Index*, 629–30.
50. Champakalakshmi, 'Ornaments in the Sangam Age', *Journal of Indian History*, 1968, vol. XLVII, 281–92.
51. *Maduraikkāñci*, l. 539.
52. Ibid., ll. 322–3.
53. Maloney, 'Early Coastal Sea Traffic', 7f.
54. *Periplus*: 56.
55. *Puṟanāṉūṟu*, 378: 11–17; *Akanāṉūṟu*, 26: 12; *Patiṟṟuppattu*, 23: 7; 67: 4; George L. Hart III, *The Poems of Ancient Tamils: Their Milieu and their Sanskrit Counterparts*, University of California Press, Berkeley, 1975, 60–1; K. Kailasapathy, *Tamil Heroic Poetry*, OUP, 1968, 227.
56. *Akanāṉūṟu*, 13: 1.
57. Maloney, 'Early Coastal Sea Traffic', 9–10.
58. Sumathi, 'Trade and Its Impact', App.c.
59. *Periplus*: 49.
60. *XI*: 445D.
61. Warmington, *Commerce Between the Roman Empire and India*, 117–22; Paranavitana and Nichols, *A Concise History of Ceylon (from the earliest times to Portuguese invasion in 1505)*, Ceylon University Press, Colombo, 1961, 10.
62. *Mahāvamśa*, 21: 10, 13; *Śilappadikāram*, XXX, 160.
63. Paranavitana, *Inscriptions of Ceylon*, vol. I, *Early Brahmi Inscriptions*, Colombo, 1970, nos 356 and 357.
64. Mahadevan, 'Corpus of the Tamil Brahmi Inscriptions', in Nagaswamy (ed.), *Seminar on Inscriptions*, Madras, 1968, no. 51.
65. W.H. Schoff, *The Periplus of the Erythraean Sea*, 214.
66. Warmington, *Commerce Between the Roman Empire and India*, 181.
67. *Periplus*: 56.
68. *Akanāṉūṟu*, 149: 7–11; Maloney, 'Early Coastal Sea Traffic', 182–3.
69. *Paṭṭinappālai*, l. 186.
70. *Puṟanāṉūṟu*, 343: 1–10; Maloney, 'Sea Traffic', 182.

71. Warmington, *Commerce*, 185.
72. *Periplus*: 56.
73. Maloney, 'Sea Traffic', 165; Warmington, *Commerce*, 188-90.
74. *Puṟanāṉūṟu*, 122; 502; *Patiṟṟuppattu*, 2.
75. P.L. Samy, *Sanga Ilakkiyattil Śedikoḍi Viḷakkam* (Tamil), SSPS, Madras, 65-71.
76. *Śilappadikāram*, XIV, 104-12.
77. G. Watt, *Commercial Products*, 976.
78. *Periplus*: 36.
79. G. Watt, *Commercial Products*, 1068.
80. *Śilappadikāram*, XIV, 104-12; Maloney, 'Sea Traffic', 162-3.
81. *Periplus*: 56, 60.
82. *Puṟanāṉūṟu*, 56: 18-21; V. Kanakasabhai Pillai, *The Tamils Eighteen Hundred Years Ago*, SISSW, Tirunelveli, 1966, reprint, 87.
83. Wheeler, *Rome*, 177.
84. *Perumpāṇāṟṟuppaṭai*, 316-18; *Neṭunalvāṭai*, 101-3.
85. B.K. Gururaja Rao, *The Megalithic Culture in South India*, Mysore, 1972, 88; Sumathi, 'Trade and Its Impact', App.c.
86. *Periplus*: 49.
87. B.D. Chattopadhyaya, *Coinage and Currency Systems in South India*, Delhi, 1977, 113.
88. K.K. Pillay, *A Social History of the Tamils*, Madras, 1975, reprint, 245; Subrahmanian, *Sangam Polity*, 225.
89. Subrahmanian, *Sangam Polity*, 225.
90. *Patiṟṟuppattu*, IV, VI, VIII.
91. *Naṟṟiṇai*, 391: 6; *Akanāṉūṟu*, 199: 19; *Paṭṭinappālai*, l. 187.
92. *Puṟanāṉūṟu*, 160:11; *Maduraikkāñci*, ll. 102-4; *Porunarāṟṟuppaṭai*, l. 159; *Perumpāṇāṟṟuppaṭai*, ll. 481-2.
93. *Paṭṭinappālai*, ll. 295-7; *Maduraikkāñci*, 444-6; 775-9.
94. *Naṟṟiṇai*, 313-21; *Maduraikkāñci*, ll. 512-13.
95. Mahadevan, 'Corpus', nos 30 & 66.
96. Sumathi, 'Trade and Its Impact', App.c.
97. *Paṭṭinappālai*, l. 185; *Maduraikkāñci*, l. 323.
98. *Perumpāṇāṟṟuppaṭai*, l. 320.
99. Ibid., ll. 26-8; 481-4; 490-3; *Maduraikkāñci*, l. 224; *Porunarāṟṟuppaṭai*, l. 165.
100. Kailasapathy, *Tamil Heroic Poetry*, 220-1.
101. L.S. Leshnik, *The South Indian Megalithic Burials: The Pandukal Complex*, Wiesbaden, 1974, 47; 51-3; 68.
102. S.F. Ratnagar, *Encounters: The Westerly Trade of Harappa*, OUP, Delhi, 242.
103. *Maduraikkāñci*, 766.

104. *Puṟanāṉūṟu*, 343: 8.
105. *Paṭṭinappālai*, 130-6, 185-95; *Porunarāṟṟuppaṭai*, 238-9; *Śilappadikāram*, XIV, 104-12; *Periplus*: 59, 60 & 63.
106. *See* Chapter 1 in this volume.
107. K. Polanyi, 'Ports of Trade in Early Societies', *Journal of Economic History*, vol. XXIII, 34.
108. Zvelebil, *The Smile of Murugan*, 100.
109. *Akanāṉūṟu*, 340: 16-17; 350: 11; *Maduraikkāñci*, ll. 104-11; 315-24; *Perumpāṇāṟṟuppaṭai*, ll. 319-24; *Aiṅkuṟunūṟu*, 195: 1-2; Maloney, 'Sea Traffic', 117.
110. Maloney, 'The Paratavar: 2000 Years of Culture Dynamics of a Tamil Caste', *Man in India*, 1969, vol. XLVIII, no. 3, 231-2.
111. *Maduraikkāñci*, 379-400; 511-21; *Śilappadikāram*, 24-39.
112. *Akanāṉūṟu*, 39: 10; 167; 245: 6; 291: 15; *Naṟṟiṇai*, 183: 1-2; 254: 6; *Perumpāṇāṟṟuppaṭai*, ll. 59-80; Chelliah, *Pattuppāṭṭu*, 109-11.
113. There are only references to a trading guild, e.g. *Nigama* of Veḷ-aṟai, Māṅkuḷam inscription—Mahadevan, 'Corpus', nos 3 & 6; and the *Nigama* occurring on a potsherd from Koḍumaṇal.
114. *Paṭṭinappālai*, 214-17; *Śilappadikāram*, V: 6-12; *Maduraikkāñci*, 359-60.
115. *Śilappadikāram*, VI: 130-3; V.R.R. Dikshitar, *The Cilappatikāram*, SISSW, Tirunelveli, 1978, 142.
116. *Śilappadikāram*, VI: 6-12.
117. Wheeler, *Rome*, 152.
118. Warmington, *Commerce*; Wheeler, *Rome*, and others.
119. J. Filliozat, 'Intercourse of India with the Roman Empire during the Opening Centuries of the Christian Era', *Journal of Indian History*, 1950, vol. XXVIII, part I, 40-1; Maloney, 'Sea Traffic', 184.
120. Pliny, VI: 105; VI: 2-10; *Periplus*: 55.
121. Filliozat, 'Intercourse of India', 41.
122. *Perumpāṇāṟṟuppaṭai*, ll. 322-4; *Maduraikkāñci*, 500-2.
123. *Paṭṭinappālai*, 196-213; Chelliah, *Pattuppāṭṭu*, 41.
124. Mahadevan, 'Corpus'.
125. Sumathi, 'Trade and Its Impact', chapter IV.
126. Mahadevan, 'Corpus', no. 3.
127. M. Webb, 'The Flag Follows Trade—An Essay on the Necessary Interpretation of Military and Commercial Factors in State Formation', in Jeremy A. Sabloff and C.C. Lamberg Karlovsky (eds), *Ancient Civilization and Trade*, Albuquerque, 1975, 179.
128. Champakalakshmi, 'Archaeology and Tamil Literary Tradition', *Puratattva*, 1975-6, vol. VIII, 110-23.

129. Maloney, 'Archaeology in South India: Accomplishments and Prospects', in B. Stein (ed.), *Essays on South India*, New Delhi, 1976, 17.

4

Developments Within: Urban Processes in the Early Medieval Period AD 600 *c.* to 1300

In recent years much of the historical research on medieval South India has concerned itself with agrarian structures, peasant settlements and the general pattern of socio-economic changes. Problems in the interpretation of epigraphic records, the confused state of numismatic evidence and the inadequacy of statistical data have deterred scholars from reconstructing the history of urban development, despite their interest in trade patterns, merchant and craft organizations, and state participation in such activities.

Conventional historical works[1] abound in references to urban centres and trade organizations, but fail to provide any meaningful framework, conceptual or chronological, for understanding urban processes. One of the major flaws from which such works suffer is purely methodological and lies mainly in their isolated treatment of agrarian and urban institutions–and their development–as entirely unrelated aspects, as also in covering wide spans of time without pausing to recognize and demarcate the phases indicating change or progress.

The study of the Cōḷa state by Burton Stein[2] introduces a new conceptual model for the medieval South Indian state, namely the segmentary state. This work makes serious efforts to provide a framework for the empirical data on South India, rather ambitiously attempting to cover a vast span of time, a 'longitudinal interest' of about seventeen centuries. Notwithstanding the interest that it has aroused and the critiques that it has provoked, the work has little to offer on urban institutions. It takes passing note of the *nagaram* as an organization of merchants and makes oblique references to 'temple urbanization' of the twelfth–thirteenth centuries as an inevitable part of the changing scene at the decline of Cōḷa power. The author's treatment of the *nagaram* is cursory and incidental to his major concern, namely peasant society and the agrarian order.

Some useful investigation in the direction has been made by Kenneth R. Hall, whose works[3] are mainly devoted to the study of the *nagaram* as a marketing centre. The works of both Stein and Hall have undoubtedly been inspired by and draw largely upon the scientific study of the agrarian unit called the *nāḍu* and its assembly, the *Nāḍu*, by Y. Subbarayalu,[4] the *nāḍu* being the segment in Stein's analysis of the Cōḷa state and the *nagaram* its marketing centre in Hall's interpretation. While Hall's works are admittedly more relevant to the study of urban processes, they also exhibit the same tendency as the others in treating the whole of the Cōḷa period (AD 850–1278) as an undifferentiated unit, particularly in using epigraphic data of widely divergent dates for the study of urban institutions like the *nagaram* and merchant guilds. His main work, *Trade and Statecraft in the Age of the Cōḷas*, however, lays emphasis on the role of the *Periya nāḍu* and the increasing role of merchants, the latter in collusion with warlords, as a contributory factor in the decline of the Cōḷa state.

Hall's major concern is the *nagaram* and its interaction with other local institutions like the *brahmadeya* and *ūr* and what he, like Stein, calls the supra-local assembly, i.e. the *Periya nāḍu*. His study of the Tiruviḍaimarudūr urban complex is an attempt to view 'the peasant state and society of Cōḷa times' from the vantage point of an urban centre near the core of the Cōḷa region. This is partly a critique of Stein's theory of a powerful *nāṭṭār* and *nāḍu* autonomy. It posits the idea that Cōḷa policy favouring the *nagaram* as much as the *Brahmadeya*—in opposition to the primacy of *nāḍu* institutions—was aimed at reducing *nāḍu* autonomy and discouraging the mutually supportive interactions among local assemblies through the temple. These, in Hall's view, were the centralizing efforts of the Cōḷas, in response to which the *nāṭṭār* created the *Periya nāḍu* as a supra-local unit of societal integration to protect their self-interest *vis-à-vis* the Cōḷas.

It is not my direct concern here to show the incorrectness of the assessment made by both Stein and Hall of the role of the *Periya nāḍu*. It may however be emphasized that the *Periya nāḍu* was a different kind of organization meant to serve as a guild of agriculturists, or, more correctly, of dealers in agricultural commodities, a development of great significance in the urban activities of medieval Tamil Nadu. Hall's study of the economy of Kāñcīpuram is, on the other hand, of greater interest to urban historians, for it provides some comparisons between urban experiences in medieval South India and medieval northern Europe.

This essay aims to identify some areas of fruitful research and promising lines of investigation in relation to urban processes in medieval Tamil Nadu. Two major periods of urbanization can be recognized in Tamil Nadu, the first coinciding with the early centuries of the Christian era, i.e. the Sangam period, and the second with the period of Cōḷas, i.e. from the ninth to the thirteenth centuries AD. The intervening period provides through fairly large-scale agrarian expansion the basis for the growth of urban centres in the Cōḷa period. These two periods represent different kinds of urban experience, characteristic respectively of a tribal society in the process of development and an agrarian society with well organized institutions.

The predominant factor in the urbanization of the Sangam period would appear to be maritime trade,[5] in which the early chiefdoms actively participated. (There is a need to rethink the nature of the polities of the Sangam Cēras, Cōḷas and Pāṇḍyas, which may at best be described as chiefdoms or potential monarchies—although the term *Vēndar* used in Sangam works for rulers has been interpreted as 'kings'). The decline in overseas trade led to the decline of urban centres, most of which were ports or emporia of trade. It also partially explains the sudden disappearance of the early chiefdoms.

Early medieval South India, Tamil Nadu in particular, provides a conspicuous example of rural-urban continuum without a clearcut demarcation of rural-urban boundaries. In this context it is relevant to raise certain crucial questions relating to pre-industrial societies. For example, what are the links between agricultural production and urban growth and the degree to which agricultural growth and the availability of a surplus is a necessary precondition to urban development? Does an increase in commerce and overseas trade, and the consequent emergence of centres of commodity exchange or an entrepot market, stimulate agricultural production? To what extent do towns develop as centres of commodity production or distribution centres in relation to the internal economy, as opposed to the growth of towns in response to the demands of overseas trade?

In the South Indian context, answers to these questions may be sought first in the agrarian development which preceded and continued through the Cōḷa period. In the pre-Cōḷa period, Pallava dominance over the region north of the Kāvēri and the revival of Pāṇḍya power in Madurai (sixth to ninth centuries AD) marked a major shift in agrarian organization through the introduction of new elements as integrative forces, namely, the *brahmadeya* and the temple. Land grants to *brāhmaṇas* (*brahmadeyas*) and the (*dēvadānas*) by ruling classes (and subsequently by socially important groups like the *vēḷāḷa* landowners) were initiated by the Pallavas and Pāṇḍyas, marking the extension of cultivation, an increase in agricultural activities, and a more intensive agrarian organization. This was followed by the emergence of trade centres, initially in key areas, leading subsequently to the evolution in the Cōḷa period of a network of such centres dependent on a degree of agrarian expansion.

A further step towards this process was the development of organized trade through merchant guilds, specialization in the marketing of specific local commodities through the *nagaram*, and exotic and luxury goods through itinerant guilds. Trade and commercial activity were consciously promoted by royal policy through conquests, the development of ports, and the encouragement of production centres and guild activity. In response to this constant demand and encouragement, specialization of crafts followed and production centres catering to an expanding market–internal and external–through organized commerce, emerged. A conspicuous shift in the emphasis from agricultural to non-agricultural economic activities and commercial agriculture in some centres was also a part of this process.

Urban growth in the Cōḷa period relates mainly to the expansion of existing rural settlements. Clusters of such settlements emerged in the core areas or delta regions, forming the nuclei of medieval kingdoms. They may be described as 'pluralistic' settlements, with several temples as centres of different socio-religious groups pursuing various economic activities.

The temple as the institutional base for socio-economic and political integration assumes great significance from the period of the Bhakti Movement (seventh to ninth centuries AD).[6] Under the Cōḷas some of the *bhakti* centres became leading political, sacred or pilgrimage centres and evolved into huge urban complexes, either around a single large temple or with multiple temples together forming parts of an urban complex. Such temples were built by the major ruling dynasties and their subordinates, either to legitimize their sovereignty or to bring various socio-economic groups within the orbit of *bhakti* centres. Temples became landed magnates, with tenants and temple servants remunerated through land. They also received gold and money endowments from the ninth century and invested such grants again in land, or occasionally in trade.

The growth in the economic activities of such temples led to urban development. There was also a corresponding expansion in the architectural structure of the temple from a small nuclear shrine into huge horizontal temple complexes with several enclosures and towering gateways, encompassing many shrines, halls of educational and cultural activities, hospitals, and monastic establishments with lineages of religious heads controlling temple administration.

The rural-urban continuum is best illustrated by such centres, which had a dependable hinterland where agricultural output was assuredly above subsistence level. The trade in agricultural commodities and local goods as well as luxuries and exotic items from distant lands that such centres attracted must be seen as a complementary factor in this development. The demand generated by the local elite and the temple for locally unavailable goods brought itinerant trade to these markets and encouraged the large-scale settlement of craftsmen and artisans, who were eventually accommodated in the temple centre.

The process was slow and spread over a span of four centuries. Thus, initially one could look for urban growth among core regions where clusters of *brahmadeyas* and *dēvadānas* emerged (Table II, pp. 258-9). One of the leading examples of such urban growth is Kuḍamūkku-Paḻaiyāṟai, the residential capital and twin city of the Cōḻas.[7]

This twin city came up on the banks of the Ariśilāṟu and Muḍikoṇḍān, distributaries in the Kāvēri delta (See Map 10), which was the resource base of the Cōḻas both in the early period (the second century BC to the second century AD) and later, when they re-emerged as the most powerful South Indian dynasty in the ninth century. The resource potential of this region is indicated by the numerous peasant settlements dating from the early historical period and also by the tendency of early *brahmadeyas* to cluster together and proliferate rapidly in this area. Statistical data shows that the *brahmadeyas* were densest around Kumbhakonam (ancient Kuḍamūkku). During the seventh to the ninth centuries the Pallavas and Pāṇḍyas attempted to colonize the Kāvēri delta through *brahmadeyas* and, in the process, were drawn into a series of armed conflicts with each other, before the re-emergence of the Cōḻas with the same region as their nucleus. The river system in the delta was carefully built up into an irrigation network from the ninth century by the Cōḻas, and thus came to represent a rich source of revenue, with a large surplus capable of supporting a major concentration of population. The foundation of Tañjāvūr and Gangaikoṇḍacōḻapuram as the capitals was perhaps determined by Cōḻa anxiety to protect this resource base.

Two early *nagarams* called Tiraimūr and Kumaramārttāṇḍapuram served as market centres for this region after the ninth century, apart from a colony of merchants called Nandipuram in Paḻaiyāṟai. Kuḍamūkku represented the religious or sacred complex and Paḻaiyāṟai the palace complex. In both the complexes, temples came up at different points of time between the ninth and thirteenth centuries, each with a settlement around it, akin to a modern colony in a large city.

The major economic activities centring around these temples are reflected through endowments in the form of land, cows, goats, gold, and money for a variety of purposes such as religious festivals, the feeding of *brāhmaṇas* and other ascetics, the burning of lamps, reconstruction and renovation of temple structures, ornaments to the deities, religious discourses, and educational institutions. The temples had their treasuries, archives and administrative machinery usually controlled by the landed groups, particularly *brāhmaṇas* and high-caste non-*brāhmaṇas* or *vēḷāḷas*.

The social groups involved in these activities were members of the royal family, Cōḷa officials of high rank, palace servants, personal retinues of the royal members, members of elephant corps, leading landowners from other parts of the Cōḷa kingdom, local merchants, horse traders from the distant Kerala region, merchants from other districts of Tamil Nadu and the itinerant merchant guilds. In order to look after the temple's movable property, such as cows and goats, there was a special class of shepherds called *maṉṟāḍis*. The *Kaikkōḷas* (part-time soldiers and weavers) were another important community involved in the gift-making processes.

Gifts of land came mainly from the landowning groups, while gold and monetary gifts came more often from merchants, local and itinerant. Coined money as a medium of exchange became regular from the tenth century onwards. The Cōḷa mint was located in Kuḍamūkku.

With intensive architectural and sculptural activity between the ninth and thirteenth centuries, regular colonies of architects and sculptors must have existed here throughout the Cōḷa period and after. Two of the major industries of the Cōḷa period, metalware and textiles, were located in this complex. Apart from the making of copper and brass vessels, the ritual needs of the temples led to the evolution of a big centre for the art of casting bronze images for the temples, a craft in which Cōḷa artists achieved unparalleled skill and excellence. To this day the Kumbhakonam region remains a major centre of bronze-casting and vessel-making. Weaving was the second major industry and was so renowned that in the sixteenth and seventeenth centuries weavers from Saurashtra (western India) migrated and settled in Kumbhakonam.

With the decline of the Cōḷas, the administrative and political importance of the city as a nerve centre of Cōḷa administration also declined, and Paḻaiyāṟai, or the palace or residential complex, disintegrated into small villages and hamlets which are at present suburbs of modern Kumbhakonam, a *taluk* headquarters. In the post-Cōḷa period, Kumbhakonam survived as an urban centre due largely to its continuance as a sacred centre.

Apart from the core region of the Cōḷas, situations of a similar nature led to urban growth in other areas, although the pace and extent of growth differed in various degrees.

Two major *brahmadeyas* of the Tirunelveli district became the nuclei of a huge urban complex with the occupation of the Pāṇḍya country by the imperial Cōḷas in the eleventh century. Rājarājacaturvēdimangalam, the present Mannārkōyil, which grew around a Viṣṇu temple built early in the eleventh century by the Cēra subordinate of the Cōḷas,[8] developed into an urban centre by the beginning of the twelfth century. The present Tiruvālīśvaram[9] and Ambāsamudram (Iḷangōykkuḍi),[10] north and south of Mannārkōyil respectively, were also parts of this centre. In Brahmadeśam, east of Mannārkōyil, one may recognize its origin as a *brahmadeya.* Rājēndracōḷapuram was the first *nagaram* or marketing centre of this urban complex and dates from the period of Rājēndra I (1018–44), after whom it was named.[11] The Cōḷa-Pāṇḍya viceroys had their residential quarters in Rājēndracōḷapuram.[12] A second *nagaram* called Vindanūr also came up by the twelfth century in the vicinity of Mannārkōyil.[13] Merchants from the Kumbhakonam region, i.e. from the distant town of Kumaramārttāṇḍapuram[14] and the itinerant merchant guild called the Nānādeśi Tiśai Āyirattu Aiññūṟṟuvar[15] participated in the trade and commercial activities of this city from the eleventh century onwards.

The Śiva temple at Tiruvālīśvaram was entrusted to the care of the Cōḷa army called *Mūṉṟukai Mahāsēnai*,[16] a feature of great significance in temple management and protection, when considered along with the fact that Tiruvālīśvaram acquired the status of an Eṟivīrappaṭṭaṇa,[17] a merchant town protected by armed troops.

The part played by the Goḷakī maṭha in the urban development of Tiruvālīśvaram in the thirteenth century was no less important,[18] for such *maṭhas* attracted itinerant trade on account of their organizational network.[19]

Lying between the Tamraparni and Gatana rivers (called Muḍikoṇḍacōḷappērāṟu and Rājarājappērāṟu in Cōḷa inscriptions)[20] the Mannārkōyil urban centre is located in the picturesque amphitheatre that descends from the Podiyil hills commanding entry into the Pāṇḍya country from the Cēra land (Kerala) (See Map 8). The whole area between the two rivers forms a rich agricultural tract, which the Cōḷas selected as their base in the Pāṇḍya region, creating new *brahmadeyas* and *nagarams*. The size of this urban complex was about 6.44 kilometres/4.83 kilometres,[21] comparable to the Kuḍamūkku complex in the core of the Cōḷa heartland.

Further east was Cēravanmādēvicaturvēdimangalam (Śērmadēvi) on the south bank of the Tamraparni, dating back to the period of Rājarāja I (985–1014), with a concentration of small settlements around it, linked to the main *brahmadeya*. Among its more important hamlets are Karisūlndamangalam or Kailāsamangalam or Ten Tiruvēngaḍam[22] and Pattalmaḍai,[23] with huge Viṣṇu temples in addition to the major Viṣṇu and Śiva temples of the main centre. The *nagaram* of Rājēndracōḷapuram with its palace also served as the major market centre of this region from the eleventh century.[24]

The merchant corporation of the Five Hundred patronized the Viṣṇu temple of Nigarilicōḷa Viṇṇagaram in this centre.[25] Kakikkōla and Sāliya weavers and *terinda-kaikkōḷa* army men, sculptors and merchants, both local and from other towns, were among the many socio-economic groups involved in the commercial activities of this centre.[26] Śaiva and Vaiṣṇava *maṭhas*[27] and a Sarasvati bhaṇḍāra or library attached to one of the Viṣṇu temples[28] are the other institutional forces which contributed to the urban growth of this centre in the twelfth–thirteenth centuries.

The location of the Cōḷa palace in this region and the concerted efforts of the Cōḷas towards the development of the region in the eleventh century would seem to have been greatly influenced by their trade policy, as also their interests, which are visibly heightened in this period,[29] in the northern part of Sri Lanka.

Madurāntakam (Madurāntakacaturvedimangalam) in Chingleput district became the nucleus of an urban centre from the time of Parāntaka I (907–55), its various quarters developing around Vaiṣṇava and Śaiva temples built by the imperial Cōḷas in the tenth–eleventh centuries.[30] It acquired several hamlets through endowments[31] and a market called Vīracōḷappērangāḍi.[32] In comparison with the huge urban complexes in the core region of the Cōḷas and Pāṇḍyas of the eleventh-twelfth centuries, this centre appears to be a small town. Nonetheless, urban features were present in varying degrees in several such small towns, many of which attained the status of a *taniyūr* (*tan-kuru*)[33] due to an increase in size, population and economic functions (Table III, pp. 260–3). Madurāntakam was a *taniyūr* in Kaḷattūr Kōṭṭam. Uttiramērūr, an early *brahmadeya*, also acquired the status of a *taniyūr* in Kāḷiyūr-Kōṭṭam by the tenth century.[34] Eṇṇāyiram (also called Brahmadeśam) and Tribhuvani (Tribhuvanamādēvi caturvedimangalam)[35] in South Arcot district also belong to the same category. The former had a huge Vedic college and a hostel attached to the temple, which attracted Valañjīyar merchants, who traded in articles required by the hostel in return for money deposited with them.[36] Tirukkaḻukkuṉṟam, also a *taniyūr* in Kaḷattūr Kōṭṭam with three temples—one of which dates from Pallava times—had its own *nagaram* or marketing centre by the eleventh century.[37]

Bāhūr (Vāgūr or Aḻagiyacōḷa Caturvēdimangalam) in Pondichery, Uḍaiyārkuḍi, Villupuram (Jananātha Caturvēdimangalam) and Chidambaram, all in South Arcot district, and Tiruvaṇṇāmalai in North Arcot district, are some of the other *taniyūrs* of the Cōḷa period.[38] They became fairly numerous from the middle Cōḷa period and had dependable hinterlands to meet the demands of a sizeable town and an occasionally mobile population.

A major consequence of the earlier agrarian expansion of the seventh-ninth centuries was an increase in commercial activity after the ninth century. Large-scale commercial activity was confined to a few areas in the pre-Cōḷa period. Kacci of the Sangam period assumes the role of the premier city in South India from Pallava times, both as a seat of political power and as the largest textile production and commercial centre, apart from its character as a Ghaṭikāsthāna or seat of learning. It became a sacred centre by acquiring, both under the Pallavas and Cōḷas, a large number of Śaiva and Vaiṣṇava temples. Kacci was sanskritized into Kāñcīpura and Kāñcīmānagara, the latter nomenclature being indicative of its commercial growth into a great or more prestigious market.[39]

Such a *mānagaram* more often owed its creation to state sponsorship than did a mere *nagaram* or market centre.[40] The other *mānagaram* of the Pallavas was the port of Māmallapuram on the coast (Table IV, pp. 264–87). Both acted as centres of a large network of maritime commerce which connected Toṇḍaimaṇḍalam with the outside world. While Māmallapuram is on the coast, Kāñcīpuram's location on the banks of the Veghavati (a tributary of the Palar) provided easy access to the port of Māmallapuram, as also to Vāyalūr, another important Pallava centre on the coast at the mouth of the Palar.

Using the networks and centres model in his study of the *nagaram* as a market centre in South India in the Pallava-Cōḷa period, Hall has argued that Kāñcī's economic growth was also linked to the development of inland commerce, in which it played a dominant role.[41] This model, derived from that of Skinner for rural China, suggests the existence of market centres (i.e. *nagaram*) serving networks of villages, i.e. the *nagaram* as a well developed system even in the Pallava period, with Kāñcīpuram as a *mānagaram* at the apex of a pyramid of different levels of exchange. This system, according to Hall, linked the villages with market centres or *nagaram*, and the *nagaram* in turn with *mānagaram*. However, there is no clear evidence of such a link in the Pallava period, for the earliest datable reference to a *nagaram*, which served as the nuclear marketing centre of the agrarian unit called the *nāḍu* (which was its local marketing territory) is of the early Cōḷa period in the tenth century. In Pallava inscriptions very few *nagarams* are met with and their relation to the pastoral-agrarian unit called *kōṭṭam* of the Pallava period cannot be ascertained. In all, there are four *nagarams* (Table IV, pp. 264–87) known from Pallava inscriptions, apart from Kāñcī and Māmallapuram as *mānagarams*, namely Viriñcipuram in North Arcot district on the south bank of the Palar (Seruvālaimangalam in inscriptions) of the eighth century,[42] Tiruvadigai near Cuddalore on the coast in South Arcot district of the late ninth century,[43] Kiḻūr (Tirukkōvalūr) in South Arcot district, an inland market centre on the banks of the Ponnaiyar,[44] and Tirunāgeśvaram (Kumaramārttāṇḍapuram in inscriptions)[45] in Tanjavur district on the banks of the Ariśil, a distributory in the Kāvēri delta. Twenty four *kōṭṭams* are traditionally assigned to the Toṇḍaimaṇḍalam or Pallava region,[46] of which only a few are known from Pallava records. Such a network-centre model is hence not useful in the context of the Pallava period. On the other hand, Hall's study of the *nagaram* of the Cōḷa period is consistent with this marketing system, into which the itinerant merchant guilds were drawn from the eleventh century onwards. Itinerant merchant guilds which traded with Southeast Asia and Sri Lanka are visible in the Pallava records only in the ninth century. The *Maṇigrāmam*[47] is the only such guild known to Pallava inscriptions and from Takua Pa on the Isthmus of Kra in Southeast Asia.[48]

Kāñcīpuram became a secondary political centre under the Cōḷas, but its commercial character continued as before. Even when it lost its importance as a political centre at the end of the Cōḷa period, its sacred character has helped to retain its vitality as a commercial centre down to modern times. Māmallapuram was superseded by Nāgapaṭṭiṇam as the chief port of the Cōḷas. Yet it continued to be a part of the huge commercial network till about the thirteenth century.

The *nagarams* of Tiruvadi, Tirukkōvalūr (Kiḷūr) and Viriñcipuram continued as market centres under the Cōḷas. In addition, their sacred and political associations kept alive their urban character even beyond the Cōḷa period.

The emergence and proliferation of the *nagaram* kept pace with the increase in commercial activity under the Cōḷas (Table IV, pp. 264–87). The pattern of their distribution led Hall to treat them as marketing centres, a maximum of one per *nāḍu*, each *nāḍu* serving as the local marketing territory for the *nagaram*.[49] While this appears to be generally true, there is evidence of more than one *nagaram* in some *nāḍus*,[50] which may perhaps be attributed to a greater density of settlements in those *nāḍus*. Eventually, the *nagarams* became points of intersection for the exchange of local goods with exotic and locally unavailable goods in which the itinerant merchant corporations traded. Thus, the *nagarams* were brought into a wider network of international trade. Hall's model of networks-centres links the villages of the *nāḍu* to the *nagaram*, the *nagaram* in turn to 'the higher marketing centres' or trade centres called eṟivīrappaṭṭiṇam and *mānagaram*, where the guilds, it is suggested, controlled a major part of the trade and commercial activity.[51] The suggestion of a hierarchy of relationships implied in this network model cannot be overlooked and needs to be more closely examined. Further, commerce in the *mānagarams* was organized and controlled by the local *nagaram* members rather than by itinerant merchant groups.

Nagarams undoubtedly represented potential centres of urban growth. It must, however, be emphasized that not all *nagarams* became huge urban centres, nor were they consistently drawn into this network of inter-regional and overseas trade irrespective of their location. Most of them were no more than a common market for the *nāḍu* villages and helped in the exchange only of local goods. Some, like Tañjāvūr, had powerful *nagaram* organizations[52] over which the itinerant traders had no influence. In a few places, where the demand for goods to and from distant regions created a market for the itinerant merchant groups traversing parts of South India irrespective of political boundaries, the urban growth was rapid and at times phenomenal.

The history of the *nagaram* shows that at least three major phases of its activity can be demarcated in the Cōḷa period (see Table IV, pp. 264–87), corresponding to the early (850–985), middle (985–1150) and late Cōḷa periods (1150–1279). The role of the *nagaram* comes into sharp focus in the reign of Parāntaka I (907–55) with a visible change in the medium of religious gifts to metal (gold and silver) and money, in addition to land and cattle (including goats), and in the quantity of such gifts in the early Cōḷa period, compared to the earlier and later periods. Gold and other expensive gifts increase in the middle Cōḷa period, i.e. under Rājarāja I, Rājēndra I and Kulōttunga I (between 985 and 1120), but dwindle considerably in the late Cōḷa period. Invariably, such gifts came from rulers, elite groups and *nagaram* members.

The evidence of Cōḷa numismatics is not beyond dispute regarding the identification and attribution of coin issues, yet the beginnings of regular coinage are assignable to the early Cōḷa period, particularly to Parāntaka I, whose inscriptions abound in reference to gold and silver coins.[53] A partial monetization of the economy from this period contributed to a greater involvement of the *nagaram* in commercial ventures. Contacts with the larger mercantile organizations is as yet minimal in the delta region and more clearly visible only in certain areas like Pudukkottai, Salem, Uraiyūr, the north western parts Tiruchirapalli district, Tirunelveli district and South Arcot —i.e. the peripheral regions and route areas.[54] As yet there is also no clear evidence of a deliberate royal policy directed towards active encouragement of overseas trade or the development of new ports.[55] Kāvērippaṭṭiṇam seems to have continued to be the major outlet for Cōḷa commerce.

The middle Cōḷa period is marked by a conspicuous increase in *nagarams*, which now cover not only the whole of the Cōḷa heartland but also appear in areas giving access to powerful neighbouring kingdoms and in areas newly conquered by the Cōḷas. In consolidating their conquests the Cōḷas not merely renamed the conquered areas, as for example Gangavāḍi into Muḍikoṇḍacōḷamaṇḍalam, but also founded *brahmadeyas* and *nagarams* such as Muḍikoṇḍacōḷapuram (after Rājēndra I),[56] Nigarilicōḷapuram (after Rājarāja I)[57] and Rājēndracōḷapuram (after Rājēndra I),[58] after the conquest of the Ganga and Pāṇḍya regions. This was a practice followed right through the Cōḷa period, particularly in the reigns of Kulōttunga I and Vikrama Cōḷa—a period of constant movement of Cōḷa troops into Karnataka and Andhra. Thus, the *nagarams* were used as much as the *brahmadeya* as interdependent agents of political synthesis under the Cōḷas.

As a result, the *nagarams* became part of a wider network of inter-regional and overseas trade from the eleventh century, with enhanced political influence in areas of crucial links. Erivīrappaṭṭaṇas, or chartered mercantile towns, also begin to appear only from the eleventh century[59] (Table VI, pp. 291-303), pointing to the need for creating protected warehouses for merchant groups on major trade routes.

The pattern of *nagaram* distribution shows only a marginal increase in the late Cōḷa period in the areas controlled by the Cōḷas, whereas with the re-establishment of Pāṇḍya power early in the thirteenth century, new *nagarams* emerged in the Madurai, Ramanathapuram and Tirunelveli districts. This helped to intensify to a large extent commercial ventures and itinerant trade in the southern region.

A second important development in the middle Cōḷa period due to increased commercial activity relates to specialization in marketing and trade. While *nagaram* refers merely to an organization of local merchants, the increasing specialization in marketing led to the rise of special merchant organizations—such as the Sāliya Nagarattār[60] for marketing textiles and Śankarappāḍi Nagarattār[61] for supplying oil and ghee—whose activities seem to have been confined to a specific locality. In both cases, the *nagaram* would appear to be composed of people who had been practising professions like weaving and oil-producing, but who had turned into merchants. Similar groups like the Sāttum Pariśaṭṭa Nagaram[62] and Pāraga Nagaram[63] refer to organized suppliers of cloth and seafaring merchants (Table IV, last column, pp. 264-87).

The Vāṇiya Nagaram,[64] also dealing in oil, was a wider organization of oil-mongers, which, like the larger merchant organizations, seems to have been composed of merchants from various regions, frequently referred to as Vāṇiya Nagarattār of the eighteen *Viṣaya* (regions).[65] They often figure conspicuously, along with other merchant organizations, in inscriptions granting *maganmai* (tolls) to temples, particularly in the thirteenth and fourteenth centuries (Table VI, pp. 291-303).[66] They are comparable to the Teliki of Vijayavada, a huge organization of oil merchants known from the close of the eleventh century in the Andhra region.[67]

Horse trading was yet another specialized occupation and was entirely in the hands of merchants from Malaimaṇḍalam (Kerala)[68] throughout the medieval period. Arab trade in horses was conducted mainly through the western ports and the Cōḷas depended on Kerala merchants to procure and transport them into the Tamil areas. Settlements of people from Malaimaṇḍalam known as Malaiyāḷanguḍi existed in the heart of the Cōḷa country[69] and in the Pudukkottai region (Table V, pp. 288-90).[70] Even Pārasikas (Persians) figure in a Gangaikoṇḍacōḷapuram inscription of Kulōttunga I.[71]

The *nagaram* organizations and specialization in the marketing of specific commodities thus proved to be a major factor in the urbanization of the eleventh-thirteenth centuries, and is often characterized as 'temple urbanization', for the temples, particularly the large ones, were the biggest consumers, apart from the ruling classes, of goods both local and foreign. The simultaneous appearance of a large number of diverse occupational groups, i.e. non-agricultural groups, in such centres resulted in an elaboration of the temple town, with separate quarters for merchants, artisans and weavers in particular, most of whom were accommodated in the *Tirumaḍaiviḷāgam* of the temple.[72] The highly complex social stratification of the twelfth-thirteenth centuries, with the dual division of the Right and Left Hand castes–distinct from the *brāhmaṇa* and high-caste non-*brāhmaṇa* (or *Vēḷāḷa*) groups–would seem to be another notable feature of this urbanization. This division has baffled all attempts at a clear definition of caste groupings, but its connection with the emergence of specialized crafts and artisan groups is undeniable.

Traders, individually and collectively, are mentioned in inscriptions throughout the Cōḷa period. Organized trade, especially long-distance trade, can be dated from the ninth century. The Pudukkottai region (Munisandai) of Tamil Nadu was involved in this trade for the first time through the Ayyāvoḷe guild, known to Tamil inscriptions variously as the Aiññūṟṟuvur or Nānādeśiya Tiśai Āyirattu Aiññūṟṟuvur (the Five Hundred of the thousand directions of several countries).[73] The Maṇigrāmam of Koḍumbāḷūr (also in Pudukkottai) and Uṟaiyūr (Tiruchirapalli) is another group which, like the Five Hundred, conducted organized trade in the early Cōḷa period.[74] The *Valañjīyar* is the third such organization seemingly a militant component of the larger itinerant organization/corporation, seen in the Cōḷa country from at least the tenth country.[75] The area covered by their movement was initially confined to the peripheral districts of Pudukkottai, the western part of Tiruchirappalli and Tirunelveli, and by the middle Cōḷa period their activities extended over the whole of Tamil Nadu (Table VI, pp. 291-303), although a concentration of the Five Hundred and Maṇigrāmam inscriptions is still to be found in the Pudukkottai region, marking a major trade route. It is also at this point, as mentioned earlier, that the Eṟivīrappaṭṭaṇas begin to appear.

Erivīrappaṭṭaṇas (Table II, IV, VI, last columns, pp. 258ff) have been described as 'inland ports' and are believed to have come up only in remote and inhospitable areas.[76] This view is based on the fact that the Ramanathapuram region has been classified as a tribal area, where the martial tribe of Maravars was predominant even from the Sangam age. It would, however, be more correct to look at these as centres on trade routes used as warehouses by itinerant merchants. These merchants often had such centres converted into specially protected warehouses with royal sanction–or sometimes on their own, in the absence of a recognizable political overlord–and defended them with their own troops. 'Erivīra', which Hall interprets as 'heroes of the road', has earlier been translated as 'mercenary soldiers armed with spears',[77] and, hence, is associated with armed protection. The militant character of these merchant guilds, whose caravans moved with armed protection, is well attested to by epigraphic references to their use of force in some centres.[78] Erivīrappaṭṭaṇas on such trade routes were Basinikoṇḍa (Sirāvallī) in Chittoor district,[79] Aiyapolil Kāttūr (Chingleput district),[80] Tirumālagandārkōṭṭai (Ramanathapuram district),[81] and Vikramacōḷapuram (eleventh-century Vēmbaṭṭi, Coimbatore district).[82] The reference to an Erivīrappaṭṭaṇa in Tirunelveli district[83] is particularly significant as it was part of a large urban settlement where the temple, its treasury and temple servants had been placed under the protection of the army called Mūnrukai Mahāsēnai,[84] taken to be the Cōḷa army stationed there after the Pāṇḍya country was conquered and placed under Cōḷa-Pāṇḍya viceroys.

In the period of Kulōttunga I and Vikrama Cōḷa (1070–1133) the guild activities extended to the Andhra region, with new avenues of trade linking Andhra ports like Kulōttunga Cōlan paṭṭiṇam (Viśākhappaṭṭiṇam), Cōḷapāṇḍya paṭṭiṇam (Ghaṇṭasāla) and Dēśi Uyyakkoṇḍa paṭṭaṇa (later Mōṭupaḷḷi).[85] Almost simultaneously, the Citramēli Periyanāḍu, an organization of Tamil agriculturists, also makes its appearance in Andhra and Karnataka.[86]

In the late Cōḷa period and under the later Pāṇḍyas, i.e. in the late twelfth, thirteenth and early fourteenth centuries, not only do we find a phenomenal increase in their activity but also an attempt to acquire greater control over the movement of goods by the different merchant bodies coming together and jointly fixing the rates of *maganmai* (tolls) and *paṭṭaṇappagudi* (the share of the town) (Table VI, last column, pp. 291-303).[87] Invariably, the inscriptions recording such joint decisions are found in coastal towns other than those directly controlled by the royal families, but which later assumed importance due to the absence of any single political authority.

More important, however, is the association of the Citramēḻi Periyanāḍu with other merchant bodies (Table VI, pp. 291-303), where the Citramēḻi organization seems to assume a position of primacy in the decision-making process. The joint *praśasti* (eulogy) evolved by them for such occasions gives the place of importance to this organization by mentioning it at the head of the *praśasti*.[88] The Citramēḻi organization of agriculturists dates from the middle-Cōḷa times[89] but is hardly mentioned together with other groups till the thirteenth century. In fact all these organizations acted only in their independent capacity and also as mere participants in gift-making, temple-building and allied functions associated with donors. The right of fixing the tolls, commission, share of the town, etc. was exercised by them only in a joint capacity, and, more conspicuously, towards the close of the Cōḷa period when royal authority became virtually ineffective in regions beyond the core area. The Vāṇiya Nagarattār, Maṇigrāmam, Añjuvaṇṇam and Sāmanta Paṇḍasālis were also involved in such joint donations out of the income from taxes on import and exports.[90] This in effect represents the institutionalization of the relationship between different bodies which acted independently at first and later in a joint capacity. Their common eulogy is the first known expression of the ascendancy of trading groups in a predominantly agrarian society.

The composition of some of these organizations makes an interesting study. Recent work on the Ayyāvoḷe guild has shown that such guilds were controlled not by any one religious community but various groups, including the *agrahāra brāhmaṇas*, who were either collectively or individually landowners.[91] Similarly the Citramēḻi Periyanāḍu, which originated in Tamil Nadu and later extended its activities to other parts of South India, was evidently an organization of landowners drawn from various social groups and which wielded great economic and political influence from the twelfth century onwards. Consisting of many non-*brāhmaṇa* landlords (*Vēḷāḷas*), this body, as seen above, joined with merchant guilds in controlling trade in certain areas, particularly urban centres. In addition to textiles, fragrant woods, spices, incense, etc., in which the merchant guilds traded, a number of agricultural commodities are also found mentioned in inscriptions referring to both these organizations.[92] There is some indication that the agricultural surplus was mobilized and brought from rural areas to urban settlements through *nagaram* members. Presumably, the Citramēḻi were in control of this movement by virtue of their position as grain dealers at the centres where merchant bodies met. The marked development of such centres from the twelfth century would indicate that mobilization of agricultural surplus made possible the expansion of urban activities.

A significant change in the pattern of land ownership may also be perceived from the twelfth century, when non-agricultural groups figure more prominently in the control of land, exercising, at the same time, commercial influence. The rise in the power of these landowning groups, such as the weavers (*Kaikkōḷas*) and merchants, apart from the *Vēḷāḷas*, also indicates a greater sharing of authority between *brāhmaṇa* and non-*brāhmaṇa* caste groups and increasing social mobility, as opposed to the dominance of *brāhmaṇas* and a small ruling elite in the earlier period.

The revival in South India of long-distance trade in the tenth century as part of the increase in South Asian trade, involved not only the merchant guilds but considerably influenced the external policy of the Cōḷas. The Cōḷa wars in South Karnataka may be described as an attempt to establish trade links and to control the major trade route between Karnataka and Tamil Nadu, facilitating the easy movement of the Ayyāvoḷe or Nānādeśis. Their attacks on northern Sri Lanka and their occupation of it for nearly eight decades in the eleventh century, were not mere pillaging or plundering attacks, as held by Spencer,[93] but a deliberate policy of encouraging new trade ventures by enabling already existing pockets of Tamil culture dominated by merchants to engage in lucrative commercial ventures. Presumably, mutual benefit rather than tight political control over trade and trading communities was the motivating force behind such ventures. The same motive led to the two major maritime expeditions of Rājēndra I and Kulōttunga I in Southeast Asia ending up in Śrīvijaya,[94] obviously to establish trading rights in these regions, and over the much coveted Isthmus of Kra to reach China. Cōḷa missions to China in the eleventh century and Kulōttunga's physical presence in Cambodia, his coins,[95] exchange of gifts—including the 'tribute missions' mentioned in the smaller Leiden Grant, grants of lands and villages to the Buddhist *vihāra* at Nāgappaṭṭiṇam,[96] and the abolition of tolls,[97] are all part of the trade policy of this early medieval dynasty. It is significant that in the wake of these military expeditions the South Indian trade guilds begin to appear in Burma, Malaysia, and Java. The recent excavations in Takua Pa indicate a great deal of Tamil influence between the ninth and twelfth centuries. Recent work on the dynamics of South Asian trade shows that trade overtures or agreements acquired some form of legitimacy through religious donations to temples and *vihāras.* This is clearly illustrated in the elaboration of the port of Nāgapattiṇam, where a Buddhist *vihāra* of considerable size and importance was erected by the Śailēndra king. To this *vihāra* the Cōḷa rulers made liberal endowments in the eleventh century.[98] Earlier, Nāgappaṭṭiṇam is known through literary references as a *bhakti* centre of the Śaiva and Vaiṣṇava creeds. It was drawn into the huge network of overseas trade with the active trade policy of Rājarāja I and Rājēndra, and later Kulōttunga I in the eleventh-twelfth centuries. The persistence of Buddhist influence in Nāgappaṭṭiṇam—particularly the *Theravāda* influence—in the eleventh-twelfth centuries may be attributed to the trade relationships of Southeast Asian countries with the South Coromandel coast. Through Śrīvijaya, first China and later Burma and Śri Lanka were involved in this activity. Reference has been made to the tribute missions from Southeast Asian islands. Chinese gold came into the port in the eleventh century through the agents of the Śrīvijaya kings.[99] At least three hoards of Chinese copper coins ranging in date from 142 BC to AD 1252 have been found in the Pattukkottai taluk of Tanjavur district.[100] Cōḷa missions to China during the period of Rājēndra I and Kulōttunga I are recorded in Chinese annals.[101]

With Kulōttunga's accession to the Cōḷa throne, much of the trade in the Andhra region was also regulated by the Cōḷa kings through the itinerant guilds. Viśākhapaṭṭiṇam, also called Kulōttunga Cōḷan paṭṭiṇam, became a leading port, where the Ayyāvoḷe acted jointly with the Añjuvaṇṇam[102] or Arab merchant organization which is known to have traded even in the ninth century on the Kerala coast.[103] Tamil merchants settled in Andhra ports and visited other interior trade centres.[104]

State patronage of the Ayyāvoḷe and other major guilds is increasingly attested to by several inscriptions of the Cōḷas and Pāṇḍyas, and oral traditions refers to a specific invitation by the Pāṇḍyas to a Vaiśya community, which was part of the guild, to settle in their kingdom.[105]

The location of some regions such as Pudukkottai-Ramanathapuram and Salem-Coimbatore, facilitating trade routes, was a stimulant to urbanization. The Pudukkottai region, which was a buffer between the Cōḷa Pāṇḍya heartlands, assumed great significance from the tenth century, when the Cōḷas entered into a close alliance through matrimonial ties with the Irukkuvēḷ chiefs of Koḍumbāḷūr[106] in order to gain control over the trade that passed through it to Sri Lanka, and also to extend political control over Madurai and the surrounding region. Being a buffer zone between the Cōḷas and Pāṇḍyas, the major battles between these two powers were fought in or on the outskirts of this region. Its commercial importance in the earlier Sangam age is recognized through numismatic and epigraphic evidence, such as the hoard of Roman coins probably deposited there in the late-first or early-second century AD,[107] and the early Tamil Brāhmī inscriptions in Śittaṇṇavāśal in the Pudukkottai district. Śittaṇṇavāśal was a major centre of the Jains,[108] and the pattern of distribution of early Jain centres[109] shows that they tended to be located along old trade routes.

In this region commerce was not directly linked with a concentration of population and the generation of local demand for goods from outside, nor with the development of a regular exchange system as in the rich Kāvēri valley. The major factor in its commercial importance was its access to the coastal towns through which trade between South India and other countries was carried on. The nearby port of Toṇḍi received in the early period products such as aloeswood, silk and sandal, which are known from the same region even as late as in the thirteenth century under the Pāṇḍyas.[110] The Maṇigrāmam of Kāvērippūmpaṭṭiṇam migrated and settled in this region around the tenth to eleventh centuries, perhaps due to the supersession of Kāvērippūmpaṭṭiṇam by other Cōḷa ports. The marked increase in commerce from the tenth to the thirteenth centuries is reflected in their activity as well as that of the Ayyāvoḷe or Aiññūṟṟuvur guild, both of which appeared here around the tenth century and became extremely active in the Pudukkottai and Ramanathapuram areas, the latter being known as Chettinad in modern times.

Koḍumbāḷūr (Table IV, pp. 264-87) was a *nagaram* of considerable size, where the Maṇigrāmam was active,[111] apart from being the political or administrative centre of the Irukkuvēḷs of Kōnāḍu. Nārttāmalai or Nagarattārmalai (Table IV, pp. 264-87) on the way to Koḍumbāḷūr was a major *nagaram* with which the Tiśai Āyirattu Aiññūṟṟuvur, or the merchant corporation of the Five Hundred, had active links in the eleventh century.[112]

South of Pudukkottai in Ramanathapuram district two major centres of merchant activity were Kamudi and Pirānmalai (Table VI, pp. 291-303), where, in the tenth and thirteenth centuries, members of several merchant organizations met and recorded their endowments to the local deities in a joint donation.[113] In both the records reference is made to 18 *paṭṭiṇams*, 32 *vaḷarpurams* (*vēḷārpuram*) and 64 *kaḍigaittāvaḷams* from which members hailed. While a few of these places can be identified with well-known towns, quite a large number of them cannot be located. *Tāvaḷam* would seem to represent a fair, while *paṭṭiṇam* was undoubtedly a town of considerable commercial importance and more often a port. *Vaḷarpuram* would perhaps be a growing trade centre.

In the twelfth-thirteenth centuries the merchant corporation of the Five Hundred and the Valañjīyar of Sri Lanka are seen making endowments at the temples of Śivapuri, Tirunelvēli and Aruppukkōṭṭai, and also in the Ramanathapuram district

(Table VI, pp. 291-303) during the period of the Pāṇḍyas,[114] who gradually recovered this region from the Cōḷas by the end of the twelfth century.

Several *nagarams* (Table IV, pp. 264-87) of this region are known to have interacted with the itinerant guilds. They are Vānavanmādēvipuram (Sāttūr),[115] Kulaśekharapuram (Dēvadānam),[116] Rājanārāyaṇapuram (Piḷḷaiyārpaṭṭi),[117] and Vēlanguḍi (Vāṇiyanagaram).[118] A late thirteenth-century inscription from Tīttāṇḍatānapuram (Toṇḍi)[119] records an agreement made by several merchant groups like the Añjuvaṇṇam, Maṇigrāmam and the Sāmanta Paṇḍaśālis, on the levy of certain taxes on commodities sold and purchased for the rebuilding expenses of the local Śiva temple (Table VI, pp. 291-303). An *Eṟivīrappaṭṭiṇam* was located at Iḍaivaḻi (Tirumālagandārkōṭṭai, Ramanathapuram district Table VI, pp. 291-303).[120]

The Salem-Coimbatore region (ancient Kongunāḍu) lay along an ancient trade route linking Tamil Nadu with Kerala and Karnataka. The route may be traced with the help of early Jain centres,[121] as in the Pudukkottai region. This region also shows a concentration of early Roman coin-finds and punch-marked coins. Along the same route, once again, merchants of medieval South India travelled constantly, bringing horses from the western ports and perhaps taking textiles back. Seafaring merchants, cloth merchants and merchant guilds frequently used this route, leaving a trail of trading centres behind. Bērikai and Kāvanapaḷḷi in Hosur taluk of Dharmapuri district,[122] were two such horse-trading centres mentioned in twelfth-century inscriptions (Table V, pp. 288-90).[123]

The road to Puramale Nāḍ bordering Mysore is referred to in an early-tenth-century Noḷamba inscription from Dharmapuri.[124] The Atiyamān Peruvaḻi (highway) passed through Pāpināyakanhaḷḷi near Dharmapuri or Tagaḍūr, the capital of the Atiyamāns. Nāvartāvaḷam, where trade fairs were held, was at a distance of twenty-nine *kādam* from Pāpināyakanhaḷḷi.[125]

Traders from Mayilārppil, Paḻaiyāṟai and other places in Tamil Nadu constantly figure in the inscriptions of Salem, Erode, and Coimbatore districts.[126] Perhaps the most remarkable of the trading centres of the Cōḷa period was Muḍikoṇḍān in Coimbatore district (Table IV, pp. 264-87). Founded by Rājēndra I after the conquest of Gangavāḍi, it was known variously as Muḍikoṇḍacōḷapuram, alias Dēśi Uyyakkoṇḍapaṭṭaṇa. The merchants of the eighteen towns north of the Kāvēri, including Tāḷaikkāḍu (ancient Ganga capital), alias Rājarājapura, and those of the eighteen towns south of the Kāvēri, including Muḍikoṇḍacōḷapuram, made several grants to the Viṣṇu temple of this place in the period of Hoysaḷa Viṣṇuvardhana.[127] It was also used as a military station by Ballāḷa II after the withdrawal of Cōḷa power from this region.

Vikrama Pallavapuram (modern Vēmbaṭṭi) in Bhavani taluk, Coimbatore district (Table VI, pp. 291-303) was made into an Erivīrappaṭṭaṇa in the reign of Kulōttunga I, and a militant group of *Vīra Valañjīyar* is known to have resided at this centre.[128]

Among the many *nagarams* established in this region during the Kongu-Cōḷa period (twelfth-thirteenth centuries), mention must be made of Pērūr in the Coimbatore district (Table IV, pp. 264-87), where merchants who had the title 'Cakravartin' resided.[129]

The merchant corporations of Nānādeśi Tiśai Āyirattu Aiññūṟṟuvur and Maṇigrāmam of Koḍumbāḷūr were active in the Kongu region from the tenth to the thirteenth centuries.[130]

Areas of economic importance in medieval Tamil Nadu have not been clearly defined. Production and craft centres are equally difficult to locate, as inscriptions present a great many problems of interpretation. It has, however, been possible to identify centres of textile production, the earliest known industry in South India. Traditional weaving centres have more or less continued down to the modern times, as shown by a comparison, in a recent survey, of modern textile centres[131] with the geographical distribution of weaving centres in medieval India. The right type of soil for the cultivation of cotton, the availability of raw material, especially dyes, and the proximity of ports seems to have been the major factors determining their location.

Of the modern districts of Chingleput, Coimbatore, Madurai, Salem, Tanjavur, Tiruchirapalli and Tirunelveli, with the exception of Coimbatore and Madurai, the other districts have fairly numerous records relating to weaving centres of the Cōḷa period.

It is only after the migration of Dēvānga weavers from Karnataka and weavers from Saurāṣṭra in the Vijayanagar and post-Vijayanagar periods, that Coimbatore and Madurai became major textile producing regions.

Weaving as an industry was systematically promoted by the rulers of South India from pre-Cōḷa times. The Cōḷas bestowed special care on old centres of textile production and also encouraged the settlement of weavers in new areas. Kāñcī was the centre of one of the major cotton-producing regions of Tamil Nadu, the other being Madurai. However, it is only for Kāñcīpuram that evidence of Cōḷa patronage is clear, particularly from the time of Uttama Cōḷa. The demand, both internal and foreign, for the cotton textiles of South India encouraged production, and Kāñcī developed into a premier weaving centre even in pre-Cōḷa times. Although Pallava inscriptions hardly provide detailed evidence of this process of growth, the early Cōḷa records, particularly of Uttama Cōḷa,[132] make special provisions for the weaver communities, indicating that by the tenth century, this city had become the most prestigious textile production centre, with its weavers specially chosen for producing royal garments. By the end of the Cōḷa period, several centres came up around Kāñcīpuram, and eventually, the city came to represent the venue of the Mahānāḍu or corporate organization[133] of weavers, which controlled production and marketing of cloth and its trade.

Regular settlements of weavers were encouraged in other centres as well, in the Tirumaḍaiviḷāgam of the temple, from the late eleventh century, through special privileges or tax concessions. Sirkali, Arantangi, Kumbhakonam and Nannilam taluks in Tanjavur district and Chidambaram taluk in South Arcot district had several weaving centres under the Cōḷas from the eleventh century,[134] to which many more were added under the Pāṇḍyas in the thirteenth to fourteenth centuries.

Under the Pāṇḍyas, weaver settlements appeared in Olagāpuram, Śrīmuṣṇam, Chidambaram and Neṟkuṉṟam, all in South Arcot district, Tillaiyāḍi in Tanjavur district, Pūśankuḍi (Rādhāpuram) and Śērmādēvi in Tirunelveli district, indicating the growing importance of this industry.[135] Weavers-cum-traders formed themselves into Sāliya Nagarattār, as at Chidambaram and Tirukkoyilur,[136] and enjoyed the rights and privileges usually extended to other *nagarams* like the Sankarappāḍi and Vāṇiya Nagarattār.

In the Kongu region (i.e. Dharmapuri, Salem, Erode and Coimbatore districts) several such weaver settlements were established in the twelfth to fourteenth centuries under the Kongu-Cōḷas and Kongu-Pāṇḍyas. Some of them were Kaḍagattūr (Dharmapuri district), Vijayamangalam and Tirumurugan-pūṇḍi (Coimbatore district) and Āragaḷūr (Salem district).[137] Through this region the rich trade in textiles passed into Karnataka and Kerala, as Cīlai Ceṭṭiyārs and merchants from Mayilappūr,[138] an old weaving centre in Madras, are seen moving across the area into Karnataka and other parts of South India.

Fairly detailed references to varieties of silk and cotton textiles, techniques of weaving, printing and dyeing are found in literature and occasionally in inscriptions, indicating the high degree of specialization attained by this craft. Commercial taxes levied on cotton, yarn and woven fabrics, as well as professional taxes on weavers and dyers, progressively increased in the Cōḷa period, showing that the industry was developed to such a degree that the revenue from these taxes was considerable.[139] Not surprisingly, the most frequently mentioned articles of merchandise in the inscriptions of the merchant guilds are cotton and textiles. Comments of foreign travellers like Abdul Feda and Chau-Ju-Kua (thirteenth century) provide a very clear idea of the variety of Coromandel textiles and their popularity abroad.[140]

The development of this highly productive craft led to the enhancement of the economic and social status of the weavers, some of whom rose to the rank of merchants and, perhaps, also master weavers. This is also reflected in the increasing participation of weavers in gift-making, temple rituals and acquisition of land control in the twelfth to thirteenth centuries.[141]

Craft production was perhaps more intensive in the Kongu region, where twelfth to fourteenth century inscriptions indicate large-scale artisan activity, and participation in important civic duties, which conferred special privileges upon them. Privileges were collectively granted to the Kanmāḷar (artisan) communities in Kāñcikkūvalnāḍu (Pariyūr inscriptions of the thirteenth century),[142] of Vēngala Nāḍu (Karuvūr and Moḍakkūr inscriptions of the thirteenth century),[143] of Kāngēya nāḍu and Pūnduṟai nāḍu (Veḷḷōḍu inscription of the fourteenth century)[144] under the Kongu-Cōḷas and Kongu-Pāṇḍyas. Agreements among artisan communities for various purposes also became common during this period. Some kind of craft organization, at least among the artisans of a specific region, was perhaps emerging by the thirteenth century (Table VIII, pp. 309-10). However, their dependence on the merchant organizations is underlined in an inscription of the late eleventh century from Erode, where the Nānādēśi organization set up a 'refugee' centre for the artisans (Table VI, pp. 291-303).[145] Erode and Muḍikoṇḍān were specially noted for merchant domination over local temples, particularly in the latter.[146]

It is also important to note that the Right and Left Hand divisions are more prominently mentioned in the records from areas iṇ which the merchants assumed control and management of temples and even acted as protectors of the craftsmen and artisans, obviously due to the interdependence of these two sections of the commercial world. Rules regarding the Valangai and Iḍangai sects were sometimes framed by the Ayyāvoḷe guild as seen in the thirteenth-century inscription of Teṉkarai, Madurai district (Table VI, pp. 291-303).[147] The artisan community, as participants in gift-making processes, is seen to be coming to its own only after the twelfth century, i.e. in the late Cōḷa and Pāṇḍya periods. In a predominantly agrarian set up, the artisans were attached to the locality, i.e. to the temple and to landed *brāhmaṇas* and *Vēḷāḷas* through interdependent land tenures. However, the demand for their services both by local landed groups and itinerant merchant organizations, particularly in temple-building and allied activities, resulted in their receiving concessions and privileges, conferred sometimes by the temple authorities and local chiefs, and sometimes by the merchant organizations. Thus, in Puñjai (Kiḍārankoṇḍacōḷapuram, Tanjavur district) the temple authorities granted privileges to certain members of the *anuloma* Rathakāra castes–blacksmiths, goldsmiths, carpenters and stone masons–in the late Cōḷa period (late twelfth century).[148] Under the Pāṇḍyas, such instances were more frequent, as seen in the thirteenth-century inscription of Noḍiyūr (Tanjavur district) where the Kanmāḷas of several places met and agreed to assign a tithe collected from among themselves to the local temple, and to get differences settled conjointly with the temple trustees and local chief.[149] The Right and Left Hand divisions are thus more visible in the thirteenth-fourteenth-century inscriptions, claiming privileges which were directed towards the improvement of their social position.

The revival of South India's active participation in Asian trade from the ninth century, once again saw the emergence of coastal towns (Table VII, pp. 304-8), with a shift in the location of major ports now oriented to serve new hinterlands, as, for example, Nāgappaṭṭiṇam at the mouth of the Kaveri serving the core region of the Cōḷas. Special importance was attached to ports developed by ruling families, such as Māmallapuram under the Pallavas and Nāgappaṭṭiṇam under the Cōḷas.

Nāgappaṭṭiṇam superseded Māmallapuram, the latter still the outlet for the Kāñcīpuram hinterland but subordinate to the Cōḷa port. Kāvēripaṭṭiṇam continued to be used under the early Cōḷas, but it gave place to Nāgappaṭṭiṇam in the eleventh century. Of the Sangam (early historical) ports, Marakkāṇam (Sopatma) north of Pondicherry, and Toṇḍi and Koṟkai on the Pāṇḍya coast were still in use. However, a series of secondary towns once more dot the coast-line, starting from Tiruppālaivanam (Chingleput district), the northernmost on the Tamil coast, down south to the coast of the Tirunelveli district where Koṟkai and Kāyal are located.

Tiruppālaivanam and Mayilārppil (now a part of Madras) served the region north of Kāñcīpuram between the eleventh and thirteenth centuries.[150] Kōvaḷam (Vīracōḷapaṭṭiṇam) in the twelfth century,[151] Tiruvaḍandai (and Taiyūr) in the thirteenth century,[152]—all located north of Māmallapuram—Sadras (Sadurangapaṭṭiṇam)[153] and Puduppaṭṭiṇam[154] south of Māmallapuram (both in the thirteenth-fourteenth centuries), Pallava Paṭṭiṇam (Kūḍalūr),[155] Cuddalore (Nissankamallan Paṭṭiṇam) and Tiruvēndipuram[156] in the thirteenth century, show the increase, towards the end of the thirteenth century, in coastal towns where the constant presence of the merchant groups suggests that most of them served as halting places for the itinerant traders on a coastal road, or perhaps for coastal shipping right through. It is also significant that the merchant bodies exercised the right of fixing tolls and duties on articles of merchandise in their joint capacity in these towns,[157] apart from some interior markets. Maṇṇaikoṇḍacōḷapaṭṭiṇam (Tirukkarugāvūr) and Saḍanganpāḍi (Tranquebar) north of Nāgappaṭṭiṇam, were new towns added in the twelfth and thirteenth centuries respectively.[158] Several such towns came up also to the south of Nāgappaṭṭiṇam in the late Cōḷa period.

The salt manufacturing centres (*pēraḷam*) of the Cōḷa period are located near these coastal towns. From Marakkāṇam in South Arcot district down south to Vēdāraṇyam near the salt swamps of Umbaḷa Nāḍu, were a series of salt manufacturing centres established by the Cōḷas from the eleventh century. Named after their royal founders, these were invariably under the care of royal officials who, on the basis of the income from salt, organized the scale of expenses in the local temples.[159] Salt was a major item of exchange in local and inter-regional trade, as indicated by the reference to assignments of salt in Mahipāla-Kulakālapēraḷam (Āchchāpuram in Sirkali taluk) to the Śiva temple at Nallūr Tirupperumaṇam for requirements of sandal paste, incense etc.[160] Salt was carefully excluded from the jurisdiction of the *nagaram*, which had the right of fixing and assigning taxes on all commodities except salt.[161]

It would seem superfluous to speak of the religious factors in the development and sustenance of urban centres, for most certainly religion provides the most constant denominator of all, i.e. the legitimization of all ventures, political, economic and social. However, sacred associations have been the most active determinant of the urban character and survival of centres like Śrīrangam, Tirupati, Chidambaram, Tiruvaṇṇāmalai and many more such temple towns, whose umland extended not merely to the immediate neighbourhood or cultural region, but sometimes over long distances which pilgrims traversed at periodic intervals.

Discussing the pattern of urbanization in South India, particularly in relation to Kāñcīpuram, Hall and Spencer highlight the contrasting urban experiences of medieval northern Europe with those of South India.[162] As against the conflicting episcopal and burgher interests of medieval Europe, they emphasize the integrative aspects of Kāñcīpuram's political, religious and cultural institutions, which helped to preserve its urban character and vitality, although primacy must be assigned to economic factors. The latter, discussed by them at length, stress the importance of Kāñcīpuram as a weaving and commercial centre, a true *mānagaram* whose economic outreach, as indicated by Cōḷa epigraphic evidence, conveys the impression that Kāñcīpuram was a logical meeting place for the merchants of its hinterland.[163]

Kāñcīpuram's role of 'superordinate' integration among political, religious and economic activities was not unique, for similar roles may also be recognized in other multiple temple centres like Kumbhakonam, single temple centres like Tañjāvūr, Chidambaram and others. The difference, however, lay in the accent on and ascendancy of either the political, commercial or religious factor in its urbanization and survival.

Terminology, as seen in place names, is an indicator of the prevalence of urban features, as, for example, when a *puram*, *nagaram* or *paṭṭiṇam* suffix, or a new name with such suffixes, is given to an expanding centre or to new quarters within an expanding centre, as in Kuḍamūkku-Paḻaiyāṟai. Paḻaiyāṟai was also known by names ending with the *puram* suffix, such as Nandipuram and Muḍikoṇḍacōḻapuram. *Paṭṭiṇam* usually refers to a coastal town or port, but interior towns with names ending in *paṭṭiṇam* are also known.[164]

It would perhaps be more useful to look for a hierarchy among urban centres and the nature of inter-relationships, for urban activity invariably tended to move towards core regions where capitals and administrative centres (Table I, pp. 256-7) were located, and all important traffic converged on them, as indicated by medieval highways.[165]

References

1. A. Appadorai, *Economic Conditions in Southern India*, Madras, 1936, vols I and II; T.V. Mahalingam, *South Indian Polity*, Madras, 1955; S. Gururajachar, *Some Aspects of Economic and Social Life in Karnataka* (AD 1000–1300), Mysore, 1974; K. Sundaram, *Studies in Economic and Social Conditions in Medieval Andhra*, Machilipatnam,

1968; G.R. Kuppuswamy, *Economic Conditions in Karnataka* (AD 973–AD 1336), Dharwar, 1975.

2. B. Stein, *Peasant State and Society in Medieval South India*, Delhi, 1980.
3. *Trade and Statecraft in the Age of the Colas*, New Delhi, 1980. Kenneth R. Hall, 'Peasant State and Society in Chola Times: A View from the Tiruvidaimarudur Urban Complex', *Indian Economic and Social History Review*, July-Dec. 1981, vol. XVIII, nos 3 and 4; Kenneth R. Hall and G.W. Spencer, 'The Economy of Kancipuram: A Sacred Centre in Early South India', *Journal of Urban History*, Feb. 1980, vol. 6, no. 2.
4. *Political Geography of the Chola Country*, Madras, 1973.
5. Clarence Maloney has investigated the impact of maritime trade and coastal traffic on the development of civilization in early Tamil Nadu. *See* his 'The Effect of the Early Coastal Sea Traffic on the Development of Civilization in South India', Ph.D. Thesis (unpublished), University of Pennsylvania, 1968; 'The Beginnings of Civilization in South India', *Journal of Asian Studies*, 1970, XXIX, no. 3; 'Archaeology in South India: Accomplishments and Prospects', in B. Stein (ed.), *Essays on South India*, New Delhi, 1976.
6. The exponents of the *bhakti* ideology, namely the Vaiṣṇava *ālvārs* and Śaiva *nāyanārs*, are dated in this period, although evidence of the systematic choice of *bhakti* centres for temple-building is available only from the ninth century AD.
7. *See* Chapter 6 in this volume.
8. R. Tirumalai, *Rajendra Vinnagar*, Madras, 1980, 3.
9. 116 and 119 of 1905. The number refers to the inscription and the year of the *Annual Report on (South) Indian Epigraphy*.
10. *South Indian Inscriptions* (hereafter *SII*), XIV, Inscriptions nos 36 and 155.
11. *SII*, XIV, 145.
12. Ibid.
13. 106 of 1905; 402 of 1916; *SII*, XIV, 145.
14. *SII*, XIII, 241.
15. *SII*, XIV, 36.
16. 120 of 1905.
17. 335 and 348 of 1916.
18. 359 and 361 of 1916.
19. *See* Chapter 6 in this volume; M. Rajamanikkanar, *Saiva Samaya Valarcci* (in Tamil), Madras, 1972, 2nd edn, 206–34.

20. 109 of 1901; *Epigraphia Indica*, XI, 292ff.
21. Tirumalai, *Rajendra Vinnagar*, Introduction, 1.
22. 571 of 1916.
23. 534 of 1916.
24. 614 and 619 of 1916.
25. *SII*, XIV, 153.
26. 544, 633, 635, 653 and 676 of 1916.
27. 544 of 1911; 658 of 1916.
28. 695 of 1916.
29. *See* K.A. Nilakanta Sastri, *The Colas*, reprint of second edition, Madras, 1975, 172-3, 199-200.
30. *SII*, III, 84; V. 991.
31. *SII*, VII, 449, 452, 454, 460, 462, 465, 466, 467, 471 and 472.
32. 395 of 1922.
33. *See* Y. Subbarayalu, 45-6. *Taniyūr* means independent settlement.
34. *SII*, III, 158.
35. Subbarayalu, index to maps, 193; 10, 10a and 213; 5.
36. 343 of 1917.
37. *SII*, V. 465.
38. Subbarayalu, index to maps, 211-16, 38; 1 and 209; 1.
39. Hall, *Trade and Statecraft*, 95-7.
40. Ibid., 188.
41. Ibid., 87ff.
42. 54 of 1888; *SII*, V. 54; 206 of 1939-40.
43. 360 of 1921; *SII*, XII, 71.
44. *SII*, VII, 926.
45. 222 of 1911; *SII*, XIII, 13.
46. Mahalingam, *Kāñcīpuram in Early South Indian History*, Madras, 1969, 3.
47. C. Minakshi, *Administration and Social Life Under the Pallavas*, rev. ed., Madras, 1977, 29, 187.
48. K.R. Venkatarama Ayyar, 'Medieval Trade, Craft and Merchant Guilds in South India', *Journal of Indian History*, 1947 (1948), vol. XXV, parts 1-3, 272.
49. Hall, 130.
50. Tiraimūr Nāḍu had two *nagarams*, namely, Tiraimūr nagaram and Kumaramārttāṇḍapuram; Umbaḷa Nāḍu had two *nagarams*—Irumuḍicōḷapuram and Rājēndraśingapuram (26A of 1961-2); T.N. Subramaniam, 'Pallankovil Fragmentary Copper Plate Grant of Early Chola Period', *Transactions of the Archaeological Society of South India*, 1958-9, 84ff; Subbarayalu, map 12. 119; 3. *See* Table IV for *nagaram* location.

51. Hall, chapter 5.
52. Tañjāvūr was a royal creation, particularly the Rājarājeśvara temple around which the merchant quarters were located. It had two *nagarams* which organized the trade of the city and administered the markets. The personal involvement of the king and members of the royal family in Tañjāvūr's commerce was also a major factor in the city's special status.
53. Terms like *kaḻanju*, *māḍai*, *tuḷaippon* and *Iḻakkāśu* mentioned in inscriptions suggest the use of coins. Regular gold currency seems to have emerged by the middle of the tenth century. This is attributed to contact with Ceylon. A large number of coins known as the Ceylon (man) coins has survived. *See* B.D. Chattopadhyaya, *Coins and Currency Systems in South India*, New Delhi, 1977, 52ff, 122ff, 136ff.
54. 52 of 1928-9; *SII*, IV, 147; 288 of 1964-5; 304 of 1964-5; 439 of 1917.
55. Parāntaka's alliance with the Irukkuvēḷs of Koḍumbāḷūr, his conquest of the Pāṇḍya country and the not very successful Ceylon war, may indicate an attempt in this direction, but the Cōḷa hold over regions beyond Pudukkottai was quite clearly tenuous.
56. Muḍikoṇḍacōḷapuram (Muḍikoṇḍan in the Coimbatore district) and Tāḷaikkāḍu (Talakkad), south and north of the Kāvēri respectively, were located in the Kongu country and Gangavāḍi. Tāḷaikkāḍu came to be called Rājarājapura, evidently after Rājarāja I's conquest of this region. The Kongu country gave access both to the Kanara districts and Mysore area. *See* Nilakanta Sastri, *The Colas*, 174ff. The appointment of Viceroys with Cōḷa-Ganga and Cōḷa-Pāṇḍya titles in these regions is additional evidence of direct control.
57. Mālūrpaṭṇa in Mysore–508 and 509 of 1911. *See also* K.G. Krishnan, 'Tamil Inscriptions in Karnataka', in A.V. Narasimhamurty (ed.), *Archaeology of Karnataka*, University of Mysore, 1978, 175-6.
58. *SII*, XIV, 145.
59. The earliest attested mercantile towns are those of Śirāvalli (Basinikoṇḍa in the Chittoor district) and Kāṭṭūr (in the Chingleput district), both dated to the eleventh century, 256 and 342 of 1912.
60. *SII*, VII, 901.
61. The Śankarappāḍi nagarattār were not merely suppliers of oil and ghee, but were also administrators of endowments of lamps in several temples, e.g. Vālikaṇḍapuram (Tiruchirapalli district), 299, 300 and 310 of 1964-5; 241, 247, 251, 252 and 288 of 1943-4.

300 and 310 of 1964-5; 241, 247, 251, 252 and 288 of 1943-4. Most donations to the temple at Vālikaṇḍapuram were managed by the Śankarappāḍi nagarattār. They seem to have enjoyed a fairly high status as merchants. *See* Hall, 54-5.

62. Śēngālipuram (Jayasimhakulakāḷapuram), Nannilam taluk, Tanjavur district 23 and 30 of 1917 of the reign of Rājēndra I (1018-44).
63. Puḷḷūr (Namakkal taluk, Salem district), tenth century inscription, 325 and 372 of 1939-40.
64. 432 of 1913; 141 of 1974-5; 507 of 1958-9.
65. 263 of 1943-4 and 227 of 1916.
66. 507 of 1958-9.
67. K. Sundaram, 37ff.
68. 161 of 1907; 182 of 1926; 322 of 1958-9.
69. Champakalakshmi, *See* Chapter 6 in this volume.
70. 163 of 1907; *IPS*, no. 218. (*IPS* = *Inscriptions of the Pudukkottai State*).
71. 709 of 1962-3.
72. Tirumaḍaiviḷāgam–a temple square, *ARE*, 1921-2, part II. It is also defined as quarters around the temple. T.N. Subramaniam, *South Indian Temple Inscriptions*, glossary.
73. Several variants of the name occur in Tamil inscriptions. *See* K. Indrapala, 'Some Medieval Mercantile Communities of South India and Ceylon', *Journal of Tamil Studies*, Oct. 1970, vol. II, no. 2, 27.
74. 288 of 1964-5; 519 of 1905; *SII*, XIII, 28; 305 of 1964-5.
75. The Valañjīyar are often mentioned just as Valañjīyar, but sometimes as Valañjīyar of Tennilangai (Sri Lanka), indicating that such bodies existed both in South India and Sri Lanka. *See* Indrapala.
76. Hall, *Trade and Statecraft*, 151.
77. Eṟivīra and Muṉaivīra–armed heroes. *See* K.R. Venkatarama Ayyar, 277.
78. 213 of 1976-7.
79. 342 of 1912.
80. 256 of 1912.
81. 38 of 1931-2.
82. 213 of 1976-7.
83. 358 of 1916.
84. 129 of 1905.
85. *See* Sundaram, 92-6.
86. *See* K.G. Krishnan, 'Chittiramēḻi-p-periyanāḍu–An Agricultural

Guild of Medieval Tamil Nadu', *Journal of the Madras University*, Jan. 1982, vol. LVI, no. 1.

87. 286 of 1964-5; 10 of 1924; 193 of 1939-40.
88. 96 of 1974-5; *SII*, VIII, 442.
89. 179, 183 and 188 of 1973-4.
90. 598 of 1926.
91. M.M. Abraham, 'The Ayyāvoḷe Guild of Early Medieval South India', M.Phil Dissertation (unpublished), Jawaharlal Nehru University, New Delhi, 1978, chapter V; idem *Two Medieval Merchants Guilds of South India*, Delhi, 1988.
92. Abraham, 'The Ayyāvoḷe Guild', 78ff; *SII*, VIII, 442.
93. G.W. Spencer, 'The Politics of Plunder: The Cholas in Eleventh Century Ceylon', *Journal of Asian Studies*, May 1976, vol. 35, 403-19.
94. For a detailed account of these expeditions *see* Nilakanta Sastri, 211-20, 271, 316-18.
95. T. Balakrishnan Nayar, *The Dowlaishwaram Hoard of Eastern Chalukyan and Chola Coins*, Bulletin of the Madras Government Museum, 1966, vol. 9, no. 2. *See also* Chattopadhyaya, 58-61.
96. Smaller Leiden Grant, *Epigraphia Indica*, vol. XXII.
97. Kulōttunga I acquired the epithet of 'Śungam tavirtta Cōḷa' (The Cōḷa Who Abolished Tolls), repeatedly mentioned in his inscriptions: e.g. 124 of 1927. This epithet is also recognized in the legend 'Sung' on some of his coins issued from Nellūr and Kāñcīpuram which were mint towns in his period. *See* Chattopadhyaya, 60.
98. Larger Leiden Grant of Rajaraja I, *Epigraphia India*, vol. XXII.
99. 161 and 166 of 1956-7.
100. Chattopadhyaya, 145.
101. Nilakanta Sastri, 316-18.
102. *SII*, X, 651.
103. M.G.S. Narayanan, *Cultural Symbiosis in Kerala*, Trivandrum, 1972, chapter IV, 35-6.
104. Sundaram, 92-6.
105. Abraham, 103.
106. M.S. Govindswamy, *The Role of Feudatories in Later Chola History*, Annamalai University, 1979, 19-22.
107. R.E.M. Wheeler, 'Arikamedu: An Indo-Roman Trading Station on the East Coast of India', *Ancient India*, July 1946, no. 2, 116-18.
108. *See* I. Mahadevan, 'Corpus of Tamil Brahmi Inscriptions', in

Nagaswamy (ed.), *Seminar on Inscriptions*, Madras, 1968; also *SII*, XIV, no. 45.

109. Champakalakshmi, 'South India', chapter 9 in A. Ghosh (ed.), *Jain Art and Architecture*, Bharatiya Jnanpith, New Delhi, 1974.
110. Abraham, 82-3.
111. 52 of 1928-9.
112. 359 of 1904; *SII*, XVII, 389.
113. 96 of 1974-5; 154 of 1903; *SII*, VIII, 442.
114. 31 of 1928-9; 10 of 1924; 406 of 1914.
115. 332 of 1929-30.
116. 248 of 1940-1.
117. 147 of 1935-6.
118. 507 of 1958-9.
119. 598 of 1926-7.
120. 38 of 1931-2.
121. *See* Mahadevan.
122. Annūr, Coimbatore district, 581 to 636 of 1922; Hosur, Dharmapuri district, 307 of 1969-70; 296 of 1969-70; 259, 272 and 279 of 1969-70.
123. 296 of 1969-70; 477 of 1970-1.
124. 199 of 1910.
125. 169 of 1968-9.
126. 581-636 of 1922; 259, 272 and 279 of 1969-70; *SII*, IV, 147.
127. 2 of 1910.
128. 213 of 1976-7.
129. Ikkarai Boḻuvāmpaṭṭi, Coimbatore district, 415 and 418 of 1958-9. Merchants with the title Cakravarti of a place Called Muṭṭam or Amarabhujanaganallūr in Pērūr Nāḍu identified as a part of Pērūr. See *SII*, v, 228 and 233.
130. *SII*, IV, 147; 97 of 1915; 215 of 1976-7; 17 of 1910.
131. *Economic Atlas of the Madras State*, National Council of Applied Economic Research, New Delhi, 1962, 103.
132. The Madras Museum Plates, *SII*, III, part 4. Also Hall and G.W. Spencer, 'The Economy of Kancipuram–A Sacred Centre in Early South India', *Journal of Urban History*, Feb. 1980, vol. 6, no. 2, 141-3.
133. Vijaya Ramaswamy, 'The Weaver Communities of the Kancipuram Region, *c.* AD 700-1700', M.Phil Dissertation (unpublished), Jawaharlal Nehru University, 48ff.
134. *SII*, XIII, 16; *SII*, VIII, 21 and 22; 508 of 1922; 308 of 1913; *SII*, XII, 154.

135. 132 of 1919; 248 of 1916; 269 of 1913; *SII*, XII, 163; VII, 859; 217 of 1934-5; 238 of 1925; 544 of 1916; 633, 635 and 653 of 1916.
136. 308 of 1913; *SII*, XII, 154; *SII*, VII, 901.
137. 194 of 1910; 204 of 1967-8; 98 of 1915; 438 of 1913.
138. 165 of 1968-9; 259, 272 and 279 of 1969-70.
139. Vijaya Ramaswamy, *Textiles and Weavers in Medieval South India*, Delhi, 1985, chapter II.
140. Nilakanta Sastri, *Foreign Notices of South India*, Madras, 1972, reprint, 148 and 214.
141. 613 of 1920; 248 of 1916; 117, 223-5 of 1973-4.
142. 186 of 1910.
143. *SII*, III, 25.
144. 227 of 1967-8.
145. 215 of 1976-7.
146. 2 of 1910.
147. 138 of 1910; *SII*, XIV, 251.
148. 198 of 1925.
149. 201 of 1932-3.
150. 325 of 1928-9; 372 of 1928-9; 256 of 1912; 261 of 1910.
151. 259 of 1910; 10 and 11 of 1934-5.
152. 261 of 1910.
153. 102 of 1932-3.
154. Ibid.
155. 274 of 1915.
156. 93 of 1943-4.
157. 119 of 1943-4 (Rishivandyam, South Arcot district); 103 of 1932-3 (Sadras); 227 of 1916 (Taiyūr-Śengamal); 372 of 1928-9 (Tiruppālaivanam); 296 of 1964-5 (Tuvarankuṟichchi-Trichy district); *SII*, VIII, 442 (Pirānmali-Ramnad district); *SII*, XVII, 142 (Tirthanagari, South Arcot district).
158. 424 of 1918; 75 of 1890; *SII*, IV, 399; 262 of 1925.
159. 23, 24 and 28 of 1919 (Rājarājappēraḷam–modern Marakkāṇam).
160. 522 of 1918.
161. 309 of 1968-9. (Veḷḷūr, Musiri taluk, Tiruchirappalli district).
162. Hall and Spencer, 145ff.
163. Ibid., 137.
164. E.g. Dēśi Uyyakkoṇḍa Paṭṭiṇam or Muḍikoṇḍacōḷapuram (Muḍikoṇḍān, Coimbatore district)–2 of 1910; Aruviyūr or Dēśi Uyyavanda paṭṭiṇam (Tirupputūr, Madurai district)–97 of 1908.
165. *SII*, XIII, 16; *See also* Chapter 6 in this volume.

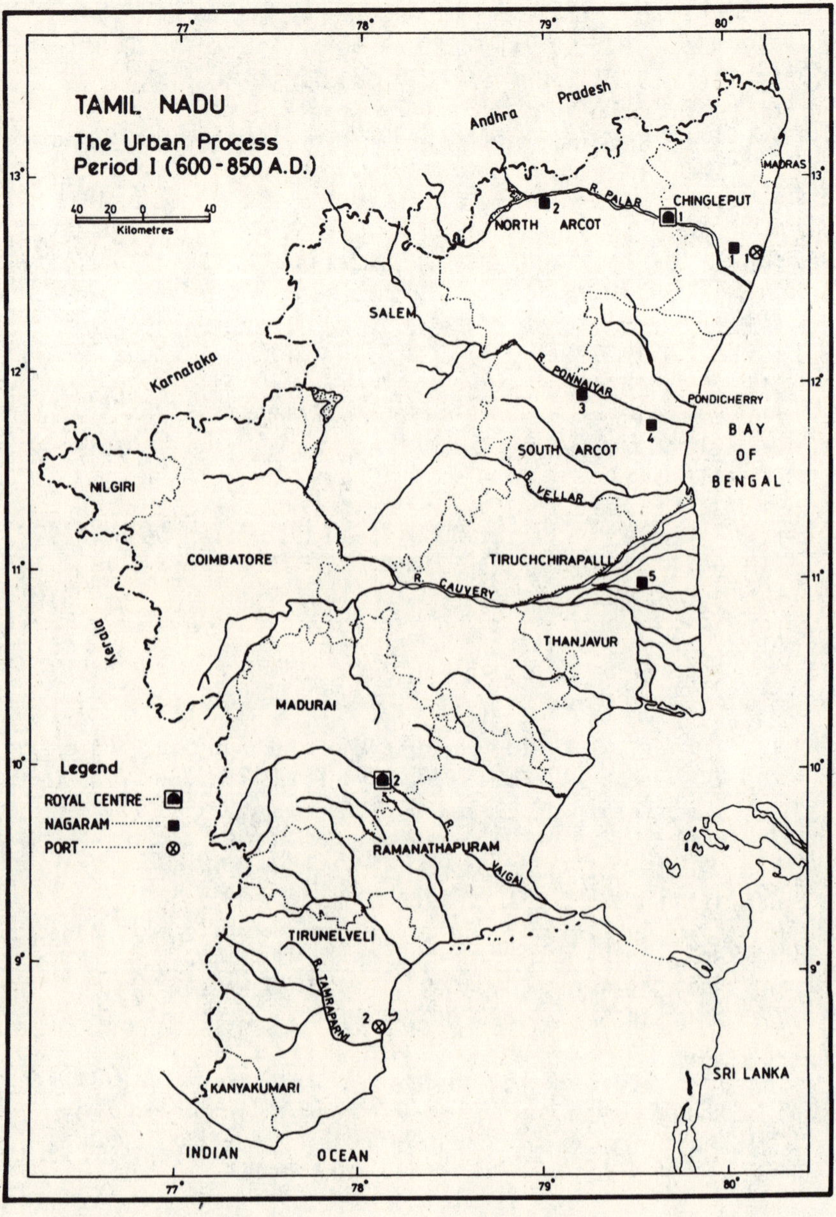

Map 2: Tamil Nadu - The Urban Process: Period I (AD 600 - 850)

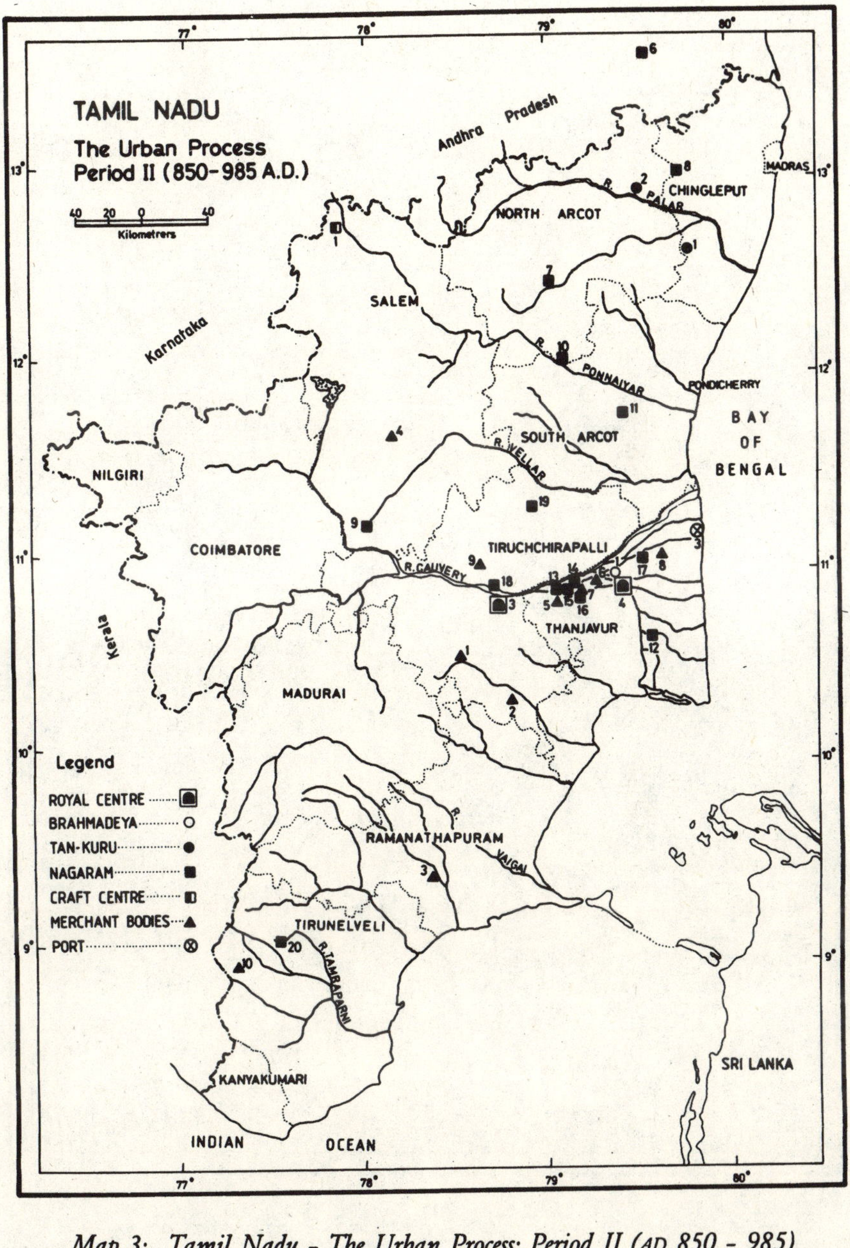

Map 3: Tamil Nadu - The Urban Process: Period II (AD 850 - 985)

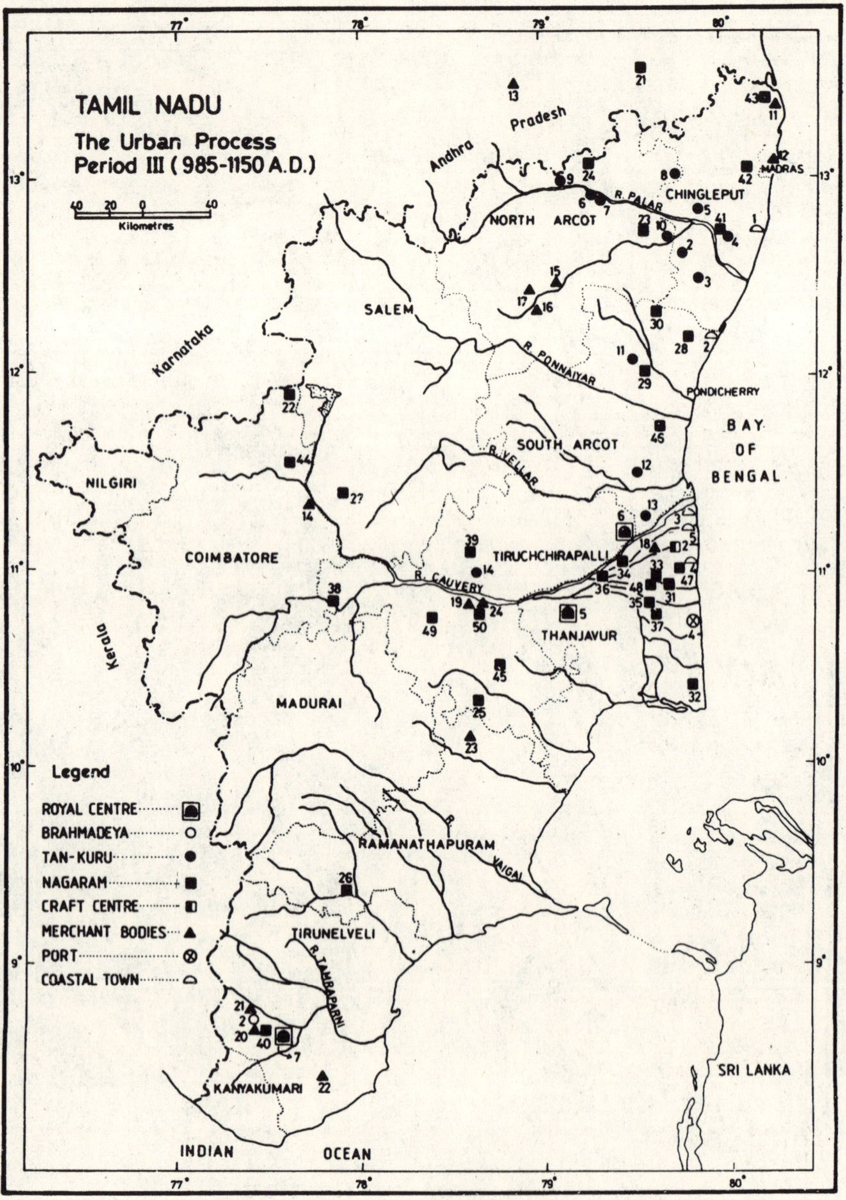

Map 4: Tamil Nadu - The Urban Process: Period III (AD 985 - 1150)

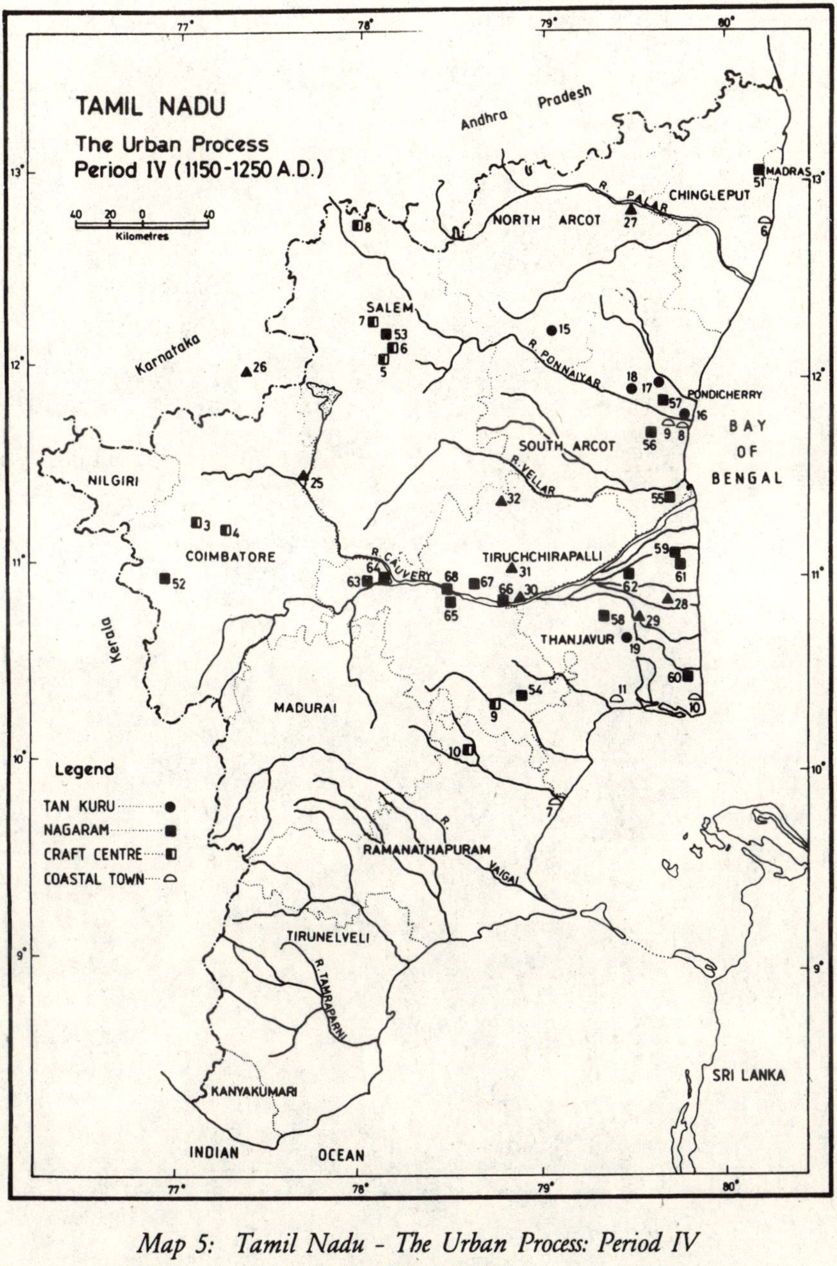

Map 5: Tamil Nadu - The Urban Process: Period IV (AD 1150 - 1250)

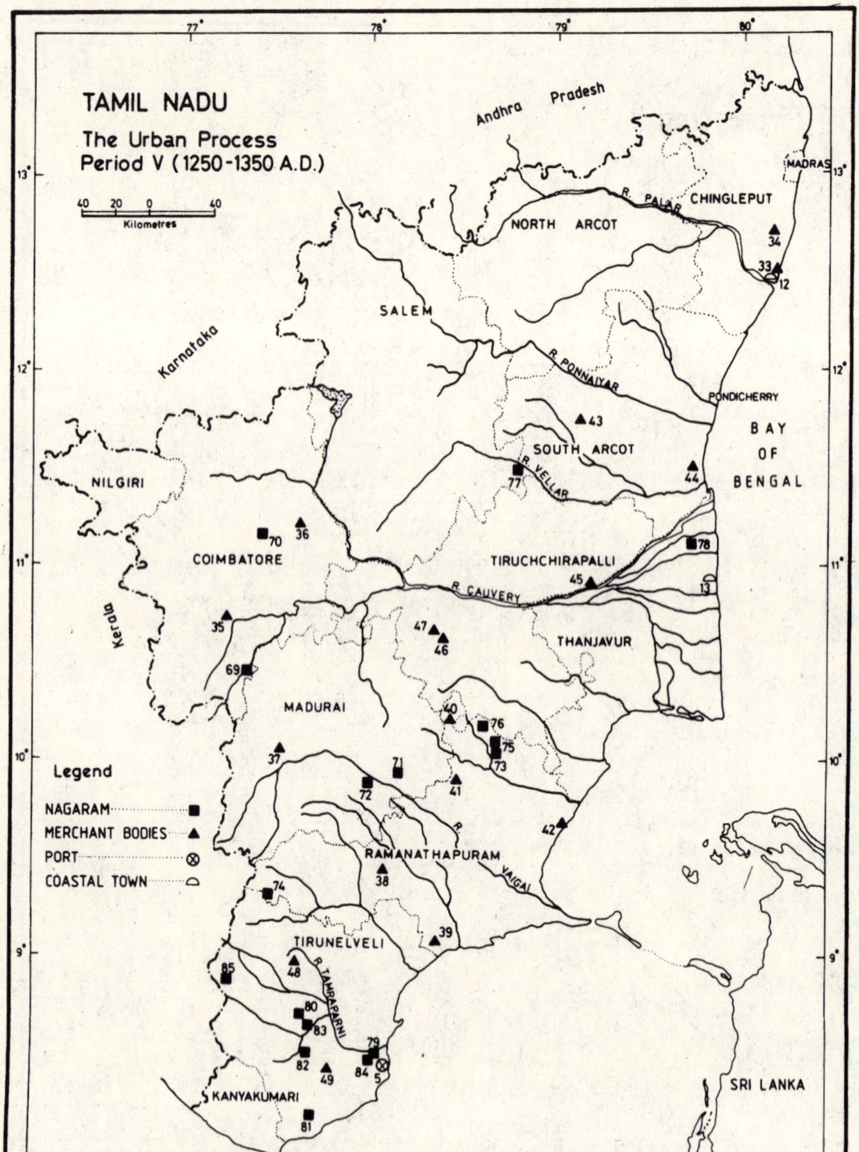

Map 6: Tamil Nadu - The Urban Process: Period V (AD 1250 - 1350)

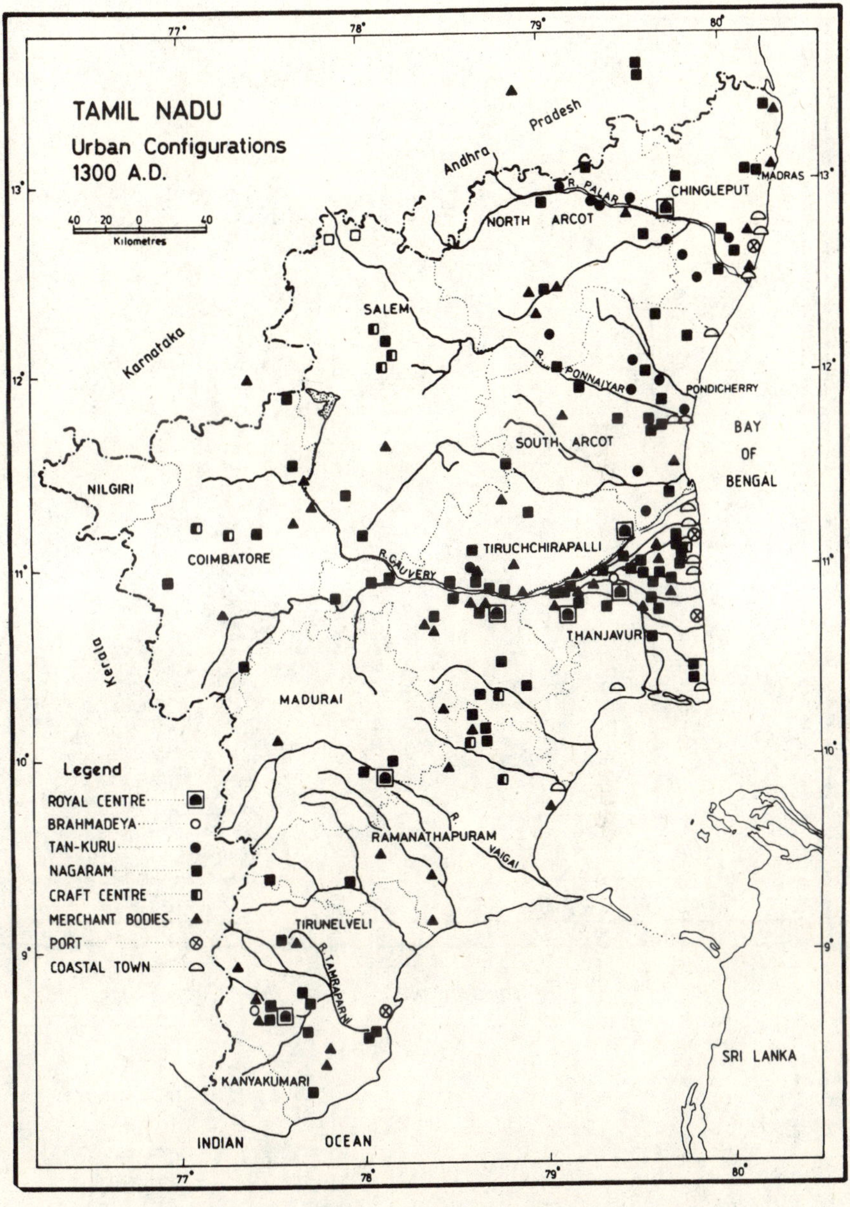

Map 7: Tamil Nadu - Urban Configurations AD 1300

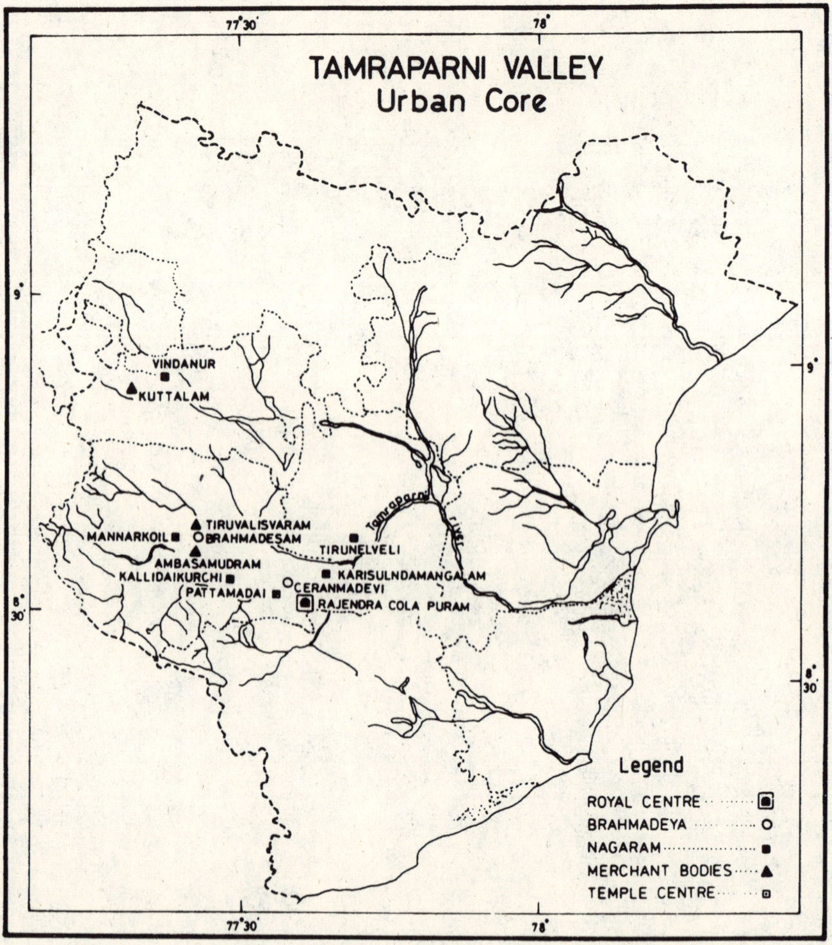

Map 8: The Tamraparni Valley: Urban Core

Index to Maps 2 – 6 (The Urban Process)

Category	*Place Name*	*District*	*Location Code No.*
Map 2, Period I (600-850)			
Royal Centres	Kāñcīpuram	Chingleput	1
	Madurai	Madurai	2
Nagaram	Tirukkaḷukkuṉṟam	Chingleput	1
	Viriñcipuram	North Arcot	2
	Tirukkōyilūr	South Arcot	3
	Tiruvadi	South Arcot	4
	Tirunāgeśvaram	Tanjavur	5
Ports	Māmallapuram	Chingleput	1
	Koṟkai	Tirunelveli	2
Map 3, Period II (850-985)			
Royal Centres	Uṟaiyūr	Tiruchirapalli	3
	Paḻaiyāṟai	Tanjavur	4
Brahmadeyas as Taniyūrs	Uttiramērūr	Chingleput	1
	Kāvērippākkam	North Arcot	2
Brahmadeyas as Urban Centres	Kuḍamūkku	Tanjavur	1
Nagaram	Toṇḍamānād	Chittoor	6
	Cōḷapuram	North Arcot	7
	Takkōlam	North Arcot	8
	Pi(u)llūr	Salem	9
	Jambai	South Arcot	10
	Tirunāmanallūr	South Arcot	11
	Kōṭṭūr	Tanjavur	12
	Tillaisthānam	Tanjavur	13

Category	Place Name	District	Location Code No.
	Tiruppaḷanam	Tanjavur	14
	Tiruvaiyāṟu	Tanjavur	15
	Tiruvēdikuḍi	Tanjavur	16
	Tiruviḍaimarudūr	Tanjavur	17
	Mēlappaḻuvūr	Tiruchirapalli	18
	Vālikaṇḍapuram	Tiruchirapalli	19
	Ukkirankōṭṭai	Tirunelveli	20
Centres of Merchant Bodies	Koḍumbāḷūr	Pudukkottai (Tiruchirapalli)	1
	Muniśandai	Pudukkottai	2
	Kamudi	Ramanathapuram	3
	Salem	Salem	4
	Kōnērirājapuram	Tanjavur	5
	Kōyil Tēvarāyanpēṭṭai	Tanjavur	6
	Tiruchchatturai	Tanjavur	7
	Tiruviḷakkuḍi	Tanjavur	8
	Tiruveḷḷaṟai	Tiruchirapalli	9
	Kuttālam	Tirunelveli	10
Trade Centres	Hosur	Dharmapuri	1
Ports	Kāvērippūm-paṭṭiṇam	Tanjavur	2

Map 4, Period III (985-1150)

Category	Place Name	District	Location Code No.
Brahmadeyas as Taniyūrs	Madurāntakam	Chingleput	3
	Mānāmadi	Chingleput	4
	Brahmadeśam	North Arcot	5
	Sakkaramallūr	North Arcot	6
	Takkōlam	North Arcot	7

Category	*Place Name*	*District*	*Location Code No.*
	Tiruvallam	North Arcot	8
	Ukkal	North Arcot	9
	Brahmadeśam/ Eṇṇāyiram	South Arcot	10
	Vaḷaiyamādēvi/ Eṟumbūr	South Arcot	11
	Vīranārāyaṇa/ Caturvedimangalam	South Arcot	12
	Tiruveḷḷaṟai	Tiruchirapalli	13
Brahmadeyas as Urban Centres	Mannārkōyil	Tirunelveli	2
Nạgaram Phase 1	Kāḷahasti	Chittoor	21
	Muḍikoṇḍān	Coimbatore	22
	Karandai	North Arcot	23
	Mēlpāḍi	North Arcot	24
	Sundaram	Ramanathapuram	25
	Sāttūr	Ramanathapuram	26
	Tirucchengōḍu	Salem	27
	Olagāpuram	South Arcot	28
	Panayavaram	South Arcot	29
	Vayirāpuram	South Arcot	30
	Kōyil Tirumāḷam (Ambar)	Tanjavur	31
	Paḷḷankōyil	Tanjavur	32
	Kūhūr	Tanjavur	33
	Mānāmbadi	Tanjavur	34
	Sēngālipuram	Tanjavur	35
	Tiruppuṟambiyam	Tanjavur	36
	Tiruvārūr	Tanjavur	37

Category	*Place Name*	*District*	*Location Code No.*
	Chinna Dārāpuram	Tiruchirapalli	38
	Singaḷāntakapuram	Tiruchirapalli	39
	Kallaḍaikkuṟicchi	Tirunelveli	40
Nagaram Phase 2	Pālūr	Chingleput	41
	Tirumaḻiśai	Chingleput	42
	Tiruppālaivanam	Chingleput	43
	Vēmbaṭṭi	Coimbatore	44
	Nārttāmalai	Pudukkottai (Tiruchirapalli)	45
	Tirumāṇikuḻi	Tanjavur	46
	Nallāḍai	Tanjavur	47
	Tirunaṟaiyūr	Tanjavur	48
	Śivāyam (Ratnagiri)	Tiruchirapalli	49
	Uyyakkoṇḍān Tirumalai	Tiruchirapalli	50
Centres of Merchant Bodies Phase 1	Kāṭṭūr	Chingleput	11
	Mayilāppūr	Chingleput	12
	Baśinikoṇḍa	Chittoor	13
	Erode	Coimbatore (Periyar)	14
	Kalaśapākkam	North Arcot	15
	Tāmaraippākkam	North Arcot	16
	Viralūr	North Arcot	17
	Tirukkoḷambiyūr	Tanjavur	18
	Kumāravayalūr	Tiruchirapalli	19

Category	*Place Name*	*District*	*Locdtion Code No.*
	Vikravāṇḍi	South Arcot	57
	Ambāsamudram	Tirunelveli	20
	Tiruvālīśvaram	Tirunelveli	21
	Vijayanārāyaṇam	Tirunelveli	22
Centres of Merchant Bodies Phase 2	Śivapuri	Ramanathapuram	23
	Śrīrangam	Tiruchirapalli	24
Trade Centres	Talaichchangāḍu	Tanjavur	2
Ports	Nāgappaṭṭiṇam	Tanjavur	4
Coastal Towns	Tiruvaḍandai	Chingleput	1
	Marakkāṇam	South Arcot	2
	Āchchāpuram	Tanjavur	3
	Tillaiyāḍi	Tanjavur	4
	Tirukkarugāvūr	Tanjavur	5
Map 5, Period IV (1150-1250)			
Brahmadeyas as Taniyūrs	Tiruvaṇṇāmalai	North Arcot	14
	Bāhūr	Pondicherry	15
	Tribhuvane	Pondicherry	16
	Villupuram	South Arcot	17
	Mannāguḍi	Tanjavur	18
Nagaram	Pūndamalli	Chingleput	51
	Pērūr	Coimbatore	52
	Kaḍagattūr	Salem	53
	Tiruvaranguḷam	Salem	54
	Chidambaram	South Arcot	55
	Vānvanmahādēvi-puram (Mañjakuppam)	South Arcot	56

Category	*Place Name*	*District*	*Location Code No.*
	Vikravāṇḍi	South Arcot	57
	Kōvil Veṇṇi	Tanjavur	58
	Pallavarāyan Pēṭṭai	Tanjavur	59
	Tiruttengūr	Tanjavur	60
	Tiruviḍaikkaḷi	Tanjavur	61
	Tribhuvanam	Tanjavur	62
	Karūr	Tiruchirapalli	63
	Tirumukkūḍal	Tiruchirapalli	64
	Sāttanūr	Tiruchirapalli	65
	Tirumaṇamēḍu	Tiruchirapalli	66
	Tiruppangili	Tiruchirapalli	67
	Vellūr	Tiruchirapalli	68
Centres of Merchant Bodies	Kāvēripuram	Coimbatore	25
	Koḷḷēgāl	(Karnataka)	26
	Sakkramallūr	North Arcot	27
	Tirukkaṇṇapuram	Tanjavur	28
	Tiruviḍaivāyil	Tanjavur	29
	Anbil	Tiruchirapalli	30
	Ūṭṭattūr	Tiruchirapalli	31
	Vēngaḷam	Tiruchirapalli	32
Trade Centres	Annūr (Manniyūr)	Coimbatore	3
	Avināśi	Coimbatore	4
	Adiyamānkōṭṭai	Dharmapuri	5
	Dharmapuri	Dharmapuri	6
	Pāpināyakanahaḷḷi	Dharmapuri	7
	Bērikai	Dharmapuri	8
	Pēraiyūr	Tiruchirapalli (Pudukkottai)	9

Category	*Place Name*	*District*	*Location Code No.*
	Tirupputūr	Ramanathapuram	10
Coastal Towns	Kōvaḷam	Chingleput	6
	Pāśi Paṭṭiṇam	Ramanathapuram	7
	Cuddalore	South Arcot	8
	Tiruvēndipuram	South Arcot	9
	Vēdāraṇya	Tanjavur	10
	Adirāmpaṭṭiṇam	Tanjavur	11
Nagaram Period V (1250-1350)	Koḷumam	Coimbatore	69
	Kunnattūr (Tāḷūṇṛi)	Coimbatore	70
	Cēranārāyaṇa-puram	Madurai	71
	Vikkiramangalam	Madurai	72
	Alakāpuri	Ramanathapuram	73
	Dēvadānam	Ramanathapuram	74
	Piḷḷaiyārpaṭṭi	Ramanathapuram	75
	Vēḷānguḍi	Ramanathapuram	76
	Āragaḷūr	Salem	77
	Kīramangalam	Tanjavur	78
	Angamangalam	Tirunelveli	79
	Mārandai	Tirunelveli	80
	Rādhāpuram	Tirunelveli	81
	Śingikuḷam	Tirunelveli	82
	Tirunelveli	Tirunelveli	83
	Vēlūr Kasba	Tirunelveli	84
	Vindanūr	Tirunelveli	85
Centres of Merchant Bodies	Sadras	Chingleput	33

Category	*Place Name*	*District*	*Location Code No.*
	Sengamal	Chingleput	34
	Daḷavāy Paṭṭiṇam	Coimbatore	35
	Vijayamangalam	Coimbatore (Periyar)	36
	Tenkarai	Madurai	37
	Aruppukkōṭṭai	Ramanathapuram	38
	Iḍaivaḻi (Tiru-mālagandārkōṭṭai)	Ramanathapuram	39
	Pirānmalai	Ramanathapuram	40
	Tirumalai	Ramanathapuram	41
	Toṇḍi	Ramanathapuram	42
	Rishivāndyam	South Arcot	43
	Tīrthanagari	South Arcot	44
	Kāmaraśavalli	Tiruchirapalli	45
	Kōvilpaṭṭi	Tiruchirapalli	46
	Tuvarankuṟichchi	Tiruchirapalli	47
	Mānūr	Tirunelveli	48
	Munañjupaṭṭi	Tirunelveli	49
Coastal Towns	Puduppaṭṭiṇam	Chingleput	12
	Tranquebar	Tanjavur	13

A Note on the Tables

1. The geographical location of the centres is given only in Tables I and II.
2. The centres are listed alphabetically under their present names and district-wise, both the present names and modern district names appearing in brackets.
3. The centres are listed under different periods to show the chronological increase or variation in their number.
4. The mark * indicates either that the concerned centre had already come into existence in a previous period but assumed the relevant or specific character only in the period under which it is listed, or that it continued to retain its character in the subsequent periods.
5. Period I, i.e. AD 600–850, represents the pre-Cōḷa period when the Pallavas of Kāñcīpuram and the Pāṇḍyas of Madurai were the ruling powers.

   Period II, i.e. AD 850–985, represents the Early Cōḷa period.

   Period III, i.e. AD 985–1150, represents the Middle Cōḷa period with two phases (Phase 1 = AD 985–1070 and Phase 2 = AD 1070–1150), as shown in Tables IV and VI.

   Period IV, i.e. AD 1150–1250, represents the Late Cōḷa period.

   Period V, i.e. AD 1250–1350, represents the post-Cōḷa period, when the Pāṇḍyas re-emerged as a major power, before Vijayanagar became the dominating factor in South India.

Table I
Royal Centres (Capitals)

No.	*Geographical Location*	*Old Historical Unit (Modern District)*	*Period I 600-850*	*Period II 850-985*	*Period III 985-1150*	*Period IV 1150-1250*	*Period V 1250-1350*	*Other Relevant Information*
1.	Palar Valley	Eyil-Kōṭṭam (Chingleput)	Kāñcīpuram (Kāñcīpuram)	*	*	*	*	Pallava capital (Period I). Multi-temple complex (see also under *nagaram*—Table IV, no. 1)
2.	Vaigai Valley	Māḍakkuḷakkīḻ nāḍu (Madurai)	Matirai (Madurai)	*	*	*	*	Pāṇḍya capital from pre-Christian era
3.	Lower Kaveri Valley	Uṟaiyūr Kūṟṟam (Tiruchirapalli)	Uṟaiyūr (part of Tiruchirapalli)	*	*	*	*	Cōḻa royal centre from pre-Christian era (see also Table VI, no. 10 from *Manigrāmam*)

4.	Kaveri Delta	Pāmbūr nāḍu and Tirunaṟaiyūr nāḍu	Kuḍamūkku-Paḷaiyāṟai (Kumbhakonam)	*	*	*	*	Cōḷa residential capital from 9th century (see Table I, no. 1)
5.	Kaveri Valley	Tañjāvūr Kūṟṟam (Tanjavur)		*	Tañjāvūr (Tanjavur)	*	*	Cōḷa capital (see also under *nagaram*, Table IV, no. 38)
6.	Kaveri Valley	Maṇṇaikoṇḍa Cōḷa Vaḷanāḍu (Tiruchirapalli)			Gangaikoṇḍa-Cōḷapuram (Gangaikoṇḍa-Cōḷapuram)	*	*	Cōḷa royal city founded by Rajēndra I (1014–44)
7.	Tamraparni-Ghatana Valley	Muḷḷi nāḍu (Tirunelveli)			Rājēndrapuram (Śermādēvi)	*	*	Cōḷa-Pāṇḍya viceregal centre (see Table I, no. 2 and Table IV, no. 44)

Table II

Brahmadeyas–Devadānas as Urban Centres

No.	*Geographical Location*	*Old Historical Unit (Modern District)*	*Period I 600-850*	*Period II 850-985*	*Period III 985-1150*	*Period IV 1150-1250*	*Period V 1250-1350*	*Other Relevant Information*
1.	Kaveri delta	Pāmbūr nāḍu and Tirunaraiyūr nāḍu (Tanjavur)		Kuḍamūkkil (or mūkku)-Paḷaiyāṟai (Kumbhakonam)	*	*	*	Known by several other names. Three *brahmadeya-dēvadānas* developing into an urban complex. Two *nagarams* (see Table IV, nos 7 and 19). Nandipuram, a part of Paḷaiyāṟai from 8th century. Residential capital of Cōḷas from 9th century. Royal centre, multi-temple complex. Decline as administrative centre in the 13th century. Continuance as religious centre. Weaving and metal industries.

2.	Tamraparni-Ghatana Valley	Mu<u></u>ḻḻi nāḍu (Tirunelveli)	Rājārājācatur-vēdimangalam. Ceravanmahādēvi-caturvēdi-mangalam. (Mannārkōyil Ambāsamudram and Sērmādēvi)	*	*	Two *brahmadeyas* into urban complex. Two *nagarams* and Cōḷa-Pāṇḍya vicereal centre. Multi-temple complex (see Table IV, nos 43, 44 and 91). Merchant body of Five Hundred. An Eṟivīrappaṭṭaṇa (warehouse of the merchant body) founded in this urban complex (see Table VI, no. 23).

Table III

Brahmadeyas - Devadanas as Taniyurs *

No.	*Old Historical Unit (Modern District)*	*Period I 600-850*	*Period II 850-985*	*Period III 985-1150*	*Period IV 1150-1250*	*Period V 1250-1350*	*Other Relevant Information*
1.	Kāḻiyūr Kōṭṭam (Chingleput)		Uttiramērūr (Uttiramērūr)				*Brahmadeya* made into *Taniyūr*
2.	Paḍuvūr Kōṭṭam (North Arcot)		Avaninārāyaṇa c.m./ Kāvidīppākkam (Kāvērippākam)				*Brahmadeya* into *Taniyūr*
3.	Ūṟṟukkāṭṭukkōṭṭam (Chingleput)			Tiraiyan Ēri/Uttama Cōḻa Caturvedimangalam (Tennēri)			*Brahmadeya* into *Taniyūr*
4.	Āmūr Kōṭṭam and Kaḷattur Kōṭṭam (Chingleput)			Vānavanmahādevi Caturvedimangalam and Tirukkaḻukkuṉṟam			*Brahmadeya* & *Devadana* into *Taniyūr*. Also had a *Nagaram*

5. Kaḷattūr Kōṭṭam (Chingleput)	Madurāntaka Caturvedimangalam (Madurantakam)	*Brahmadeya* into *Taniyūr*
6. Dāmar Kōṭṭam (North Arcot)	Rājamalla Caturvedimangalam (Brahmadeśam)	*Brahmadeya* into *Taniyūr*
7. Dāmar Kōṭṭam (North Arcot)	Cakkaramūdūr (Sakkaramallūr)	*Taniyūr*
8. Kāḻiyūr Kōṭṭam (North Arcot)	Sivacūḷāmaṇi Caturvedimangalam/Aparājita Caturvedimangalam Vikramābharaṇa-Caturvedimangalam	*Brahmadeyas* into *Taniyūr*
9. Maṇayiṟ-Kōṭṭam (Panmā-nāḍu) (North Arcot)	Aparājita Caturvedimangalam/Tiruvūṟal-puram/Rājamārttāṇḍa-Caturvedimangalam Kṣatriyaśikhāmaṇipuram/Kulōttunga-Cōḻapuram (Takkolam)	*Brahmadeya* & *Devadana* into *Taniyūr*. Also a *Nagaram*

Table III *Cont'd*

No.	*Old Historical Unit (Modern District)*	*Period I 600-850*	*Period II 850-985*	*Period III 985-1150*	*Period IV 1150-1250*	*Period V 1250-1350*	*Other Relevant Information*
10.	Paḍuvūr-Kōṭṭam Mīyāṟu Nāḍu (North Arcot)			Tiruvallam/Tikkālivallam/Vānapurattūr (Tiruvallam)			*Taniyūr*
11.	Aṇṇā Nāḍu (North Arcot)			Tiruvaṇṇāmalai (Tiruvaṇṇāmalai)			Śaiva sacred centre into *Taniyūr*
12.	Panaiyūr Nāḍu (South Arcot)			Brahmadeśam and Eṇṇāyiram			*Brahmadeya* into *Taniyūr. Valañjīyar*
13.	Rājēndrasimha Vaḷanāḍu (South Arcot)			Vīranārāyaṇa c.m./ Uḍaiyārguḍi (Kāṭṭumannārkōyil)			*Brahmadeya* into *Taniyūr*
14.	Irungōḷappāḍi (South Arcot)			Vaḷavanmahādevi c.m. (Vaḷaiyamādevi/ Eṟumbūr)			*Brahmadeya* into *Taniyūr*
15.	Nāngūr Nāḍu (Tanjavur)			Perumbaṟṟappuliyūr (?)			*Taniyūr*

16. Rājāśraya Vaḷanāḍu (Tiruchirapalli)	Tiruveḷḷaṟai (Tiruveḷḷaṟai)		*Brahmadeya* into *Taniyūr*
17. Vāgūr Nāḍu (Pondicherry)		Aḻagiyacōḷa c.m./Vāgūr (Bāhūr)	*Brahmadeya* into *Taniyūr*
18. Viḻupparaiya nāḍu (Pondicherry)		Tribhuvana (mahādevi) Caturvedi-mangalam (Tribhuvani)	*Brahmadeya* into *Taniyūr*
19. Vāvalūr nāḍu (South Arcot)		Jananātha c.m. (Villupuram)	*Brahmadeya* into *Taniyūr*
20. Suttamalli vaḷanāḍu (Tanjavur)		Rājādhirāja Caturvedi-mangalam (Mannārguḍi)	*Brahmadeya* into *Taniyūr*

* For Other *Taniyūrs* See Table IV, nos 30, 31 and 60.

Table IV
Distribution of Nagaram

No.	*Old Historical Unit (Modern District)*	*Period I 600-850*	*Period II 850-985*	*Period III 985-1150*	*Period IV 1150-1250*	*Period V 1250-1350*	*Other Relevant Information*
1.	Eyil-Kōṭṭam (Chingleput)	Kāñcīpuram (Kāñcīpuram)					*Mānagaram*, administrative centre (Pallava capital), weaving and commercial centre.
2.	Āmūr nāḍu in Āmūr Kōṭṭam (Chingleput)	Māmallapuram (Māmallapuram)	*	*	*	*	*Mānagaram* and Pallava port (subsequently *nagaram* and subsidiary port)
3.	Kaḷattūr nāḍu in Kaḷattūr Kōṭṭam (Chingleput)	Tirukkaḷukkuṉṟam (Tirukkaḷukkuṉṟam)	*	*	*	*	Also *Taniyūr* from Period III
4.	– (North Arcot)	Seruvālai-mangalam (Virinchipuram)				*	

5.	Kuṟukkai kūṟṟam (South Arcot)	Kīḻūr (Tirukkōyilūr)		*	*	*	Śankarappāḍinagaram in Period III; Sālika nagaram and *Cittiramēli Periyanāḍu* in Periods IV and V
6.	Mēṟkā nāḍu and Kīḻ Ānmūr nāḍu (South Arcot)	Tiruvadigai alias Adhirājamangalyapuram (Tiruvadigai)	*	*	*	*	Salt manufacturing centre from Period III
7.	Tiraimūr nāḍu (Tanjavur)	Kumaramārttāṇḍapuram (Tirunāgēśvaram)	*	*	*	*	*Nagaram* for urban complex of Kuḍamūkku-Paḻaiyāṟai (?) (See Table I, no. 1)
8.	Āṟṟūr nāḍu in Tiruvēngaḍa Kōṭṭam (Chittoor)		Toṇḍamānāṟṟūr (Toṇḍamānāḍ)	*	*		
9.	Pangaḷa nāḍu (North Arcot)		Ulagaḷandacōḷapuram (Cholapuram)	*	*		

Table IV *Cont'd*

No.	*Old Historical Unit (Modern District)*	*Period I 600-850*	*Period II 850-985*	*Period III 985-1150*	*Period IV 1150-1250*	*Period V 1250-1350*	*Other Relevant Information*
10.	Panmā nāḍu (North Arcot)		Tiruvūṟal alias Kṣatriyaśikhāmaṇipuram (Takkolam)	*	*		
11.	– (Salem)		– (Pullur)	*	*		Pāraga nagaram (seafaring merchants)
12.	Vānagappāḍi alias Madurāntaka vaḷanāḍu, Śenkuṉṟa nāḍu (South Arcot)		Vālaiyūr nagaram; Caṇpai alias Virarājendrapuram, Nittavinoda Cōḷapuram (Jambai)	*	*		Śankarappādi nagaram and *Valañjīyar* from Period II

13. Mēlūr nāḍu; Munaippāḍi (South Arcot)	Tirunāvalūr; Rājādittapuram (Tirunāmanallūr)	*	*	
14. Nenmali nāḍu? (Tanjavur)	Kānapuram (near Koṭṭūr)	*		
15. Poygai nāḍu (Tanjavur)	Ādittapuram (Tillaisthānam)	*	*	*Maṇigrāmam* in Period II
16. V(M)irai Kūṟṟam (Tanjavur)	(Tiruppayanam) (Tiruppaḻanam)	*	*	
17. Poygai nāḍu (Tanjavur)	Śivapuri (Tiruvaiyāṟu)	*	*	
18. Ārkkāṭṭu-k-kūṟṟam kiḻār kūṟṟam (Tanjavur)	Parakēsaripuram alias Tiruvēdikuḍi (Tiruvēdikuḍi)	*	*	
19. Tiraimūr nāḍu (Tanjavur)	Tiraimūr (Tiruviḍaimarudūr)	*	*	Did it also serve as one of the *nagarams* for Kuḍamūkku-Paḻaiyārai? (See Table I, no. 1)

Table IV *Cont'd*

No.	*Old Historical Unit (Modern District)*	*Period I 600-850*	*Period II 850-985*	*Period III 985-1150*	*Period IV 1150-1250*	*Period V 1250-1350*	*Other Relevant Information*
20.	Kuṉṟa-k-kūṟṟam alias Uttunga vaḷanāḍu (Tiruchirapalli)		Perumpaḻuvūr, Avanikandarpapuram (Mēlappaḻuvūr)	*			
21.	Van nāḍu (Tiruchirapalli)		Vālikaṇḍapuram (Vālikaṇḍapuram)	*	*		Śankarappāḍi nagaram, *Maṇigrāmam*, *Valañjīyar*, *Tiśai Āyirattu Aiṅṅūṟṟuvar* and Kanmāḷar artisans; Sūradaḷam in Period IV; Left Hand 98 castes in Period IV
22.	Kaḷakkuḍi nāḍu (Tirunelveli)	*	Karavandapuram (Ukkirankoṭṭai)	*	*	*	*Aiyapoḻil*

	Phase I			
23. Āṟṟūr nāḍu in Tiruvengaḍa kōṭṭam in Perumbaṇappōḍi (Chittoor)	Tirukkāḷatti alias Mummuḍi Cōḷapuram (Kāḷahasti)	*	*	Śankarappāḍi nagaram
24. Padināḍu in Gangaikoṇḍacōḷavaḷanāḍu in Muḍikoṇḍacōḷamaṇḍalam (Coimbatore)	Muḍikoṇḍacōḷapuram alias Deśi-Uyyakkoṇḍacōḷapaṭṭaṇa (Muḍikoṇḍān)	*	*	Joint donations by merchants of the Ganga and Kongu regions in Period III; Hoysaḷa military station in Period IV
25. Panaiyūr nāḍu in Rājarāja vaḷanāḍu (North Arcot)	Arumoḻidevapuram near Karandai alias Tiruppaṟambūr (Karandai)	*	*	

Table IV *Cont'd*

No.	*Old Historical Unit (Modern District)*	*Period I 600-850*	*Period II 850-985*	*Period III 985-1150*	*Period IV 1150-1250*	*Period V 1250-1350*	*Other Relevant Information*
26.	Perumbāṇappāḍi in Tū nāḍu in Jayangoṇḍacōḷa-maṇḍalam (North Arcot)			Rājāśrayapuram (Mēlpāḍi)	*	*	
27.	Ollaiyūr Kūṟṟam in Pāṇḍimaṇḍa-lam; Ten Kōnāḍu (Pudukkottai)			Sundaracōḷapu-ram alias Dēśi Uyyavandapaṭṭa-ṇam (Sunda-ram)	*	*	Pearl merchants
28.	Iruñjō nāḍu in Madurāntaka vaḷanāḍu (Rama-nathapuram)			Vānavan mādevipuram (Sāttūr)	*		
29.	– (Salem)			Tūśiyūr (near Tiruccengōḍu)	*		

30. Irāyūr nāḍu or Pērāyūr nāḍu in Ōymā nāḍu (South Arcot)		Olōkamādēvipuram (Olagāpuram)	*	*	Also *Taniyūr*. Weaving centre from the 13th century
31. Puraiyūr nāḍu (South Arcot)		Paravaipuram (Panayavaram)	*		Also *Taniyūr*
32. Tirunallūr nāḍu in Ōymā nāḍu in Jayangoṇḍa-cōḷamaṇḍalam (South Arcot)		Vayirameghapuram; Jananāthapuram (Vayirāpuram)	*		
33. Ambar nāḍu in Uyyakkoṇḍavaḷa-nāḍu (Tanjavur)		Ambar; Koyil Tirumākāḷam; Vikramacōḷa-puram (Ambar) (Kōyil Tirumāḷam)	*	*	
34. Umbaḷa nāḍu (Tanjavur)	*	Irumuḍi cōḷapuram (?)	*		Reference in Paḷḷan-kōyil copper plate of Sundara cōḷa

Table IV *Cont'd*

No.	*Old Historical Unit (Modern District)*	*Period I 600-850*	*Period II 850-985*	*Period III 985-1150*	*Period IV 1150-1250*	*Period V 1250-1350*	*Other Relevant Information*
35.	Tirunraṟaiyūr nāḍu in Kṣatriya śikhāmaṇi vaḷa-nāḍu (Tanjavur)			Kūhūr alias Virudarājabha-yankarapuram Kūhūr	*		
36.	Miḻalai nāḍu (Tanjavur)			Nāganpāḍi; Vīraṇārāyaṇapu-ram, Ilāiccikuḍi (Mānambāḍi)	*		Another *nagaram* called Vikramādit-tan Tirumu-dukuṉṟam is mentioned in local inscriptions
37.	Śēṟṟūr Kūṟṟam in Kulōttunga-cōḷa vaḷa nāḍu (Tanjavur)			Jayasimhakula-kālapuram (Śēngālipuram)	*		Sāttum Pariśaṭṭa *nagaram* (cloth mer-chants) and Sāliya (weavers)

38. Tañjāvūr Kūṟṟam (Tanjavur)	*	Tañcai alias Tañjāvūr (Tanjavur)	*	*	*Mānagaram*, Cōḷa capital; three *nagarams* in the 11th century
39. Aṇḍāṭṭū-k-kūṟṟam (Tanjavur)	*	Tiruppuṟam-biyam (Tirup-puṟambiyam)	*		Battlefield between Pallavas and Cōḷas (9th century). Śan-karappāḍi *nagaram* and Valañjīyar (11th century)
40. Tiruvārūr Kūṟṟam in Gēyamāṇikka vaḷa nāḍu (Tanjavur)		Tiruvārūr (Tiruvārūr)	*	*	Vīrarājendra man-galac-cāttu (horse dealers)
41. Ādanūr nāḍu (Tiruchirapalli)		Rājarājapuram; Ādanūr (Chin-na Dārāpuram)	*	*	(Under Kongu-Cōḷas from the late 12th century)
42. (Mēl) (Vaḷḷuva-ppāḍi nāḍu (Tiruchirapalli)		Śingaḷāntakapu-ram (Śingaḷānta-kapuram)	*	*	*Aiyampoḻil* (The Five Hundred) in the Late Cōḷa period (IV)

Table IV *Cont'd*

No.	*Old Historical Unit (Modern District)*	*Period I 600-850*	*Period II 850-985*	*Period III 985-1150*	*Period IV 1150-1250*	*Period V 1250-1350*	*Other Relevant Information*
43.	Muḷḷi nāḍu (Tirunelveli)			Kṣatriyaśikhāmaṇ ipuram (Kalla-ḍaikkuricci)	*	*	Kaṇmāḷar (artisans) in the post-Cōḷa period. *Nagaram* for urban complex of Mannarkoyil etc. (See Table I, no. 2)
44.	Muḷḷi nāḍu (Tirunelveli)			Rājēndrapuram (a part of Cēra-van mahādevi caturvēdi mangalam) (Sērmādēvi)	*	*	Royal centre–resid-ence of the Cōḷa Pāṇḍya viceroys. Part of the urban complex of Mannār-koyil, Ambāsamud-ram and Sērmādēvi (See Table I, no. 2)

PHASE II

45.	Maiyūr nāḍu in Kaḷattūr Kōṭṭam (Chingleput)		Rājēndracōḷapuram (Pālūr)			
46.	Māngāḍu nāḍu (Chingleput)		Uyyakkoṇḍacōḷapuram (Tirumaḻiśai)	*	*	
47.	Kōḷūr nilai (Chingleput)		Tiruppālaivanam (near Pulicat?)	*	*	*Dhanmadāvaḷar* (merchant body), Paradēśis (foreigners or outsiders) – a coastal town
48.	Śaiyamuri-Nāḍāḻvār nāḍu (Coimbatore)		Vikramapallavapuram (Vēmbaṭṭi)	*	*	*Valañjīyar* (merchant body) Eṟivīrappaṭṭaṉa

Table IV *Cont'd*

No.	*Old Historical Unit (Modern District)*	*Period I 600-850*	*Period II 850-985*	*Period III 985-1150*	*Period IV 1150-1250*	*Period V 1250-1350*	*Other Relevant Information*
49.	Aṇṇalvāyil kūṟṟam in Iraṭṭapāḍikoṇḍacōḷa vaḷanāḍu (Pudukkottai)			Telungukulakālapuram; Kulōttunga cōḷa paṭṭaṇam: Nagarattārmalai (Nārttāmalai)	*	*	*Aiññūṟṟuvar* (The Five Hundred) and the *Padineṇbhūmi* (i.e. 18 regions) organizations
50.	Paṭṭānpākkai nāḍu? Mēṟkā nāḍu in Virudarājabhayankaravaḷanāḍu (South Arcot)			Utavattirumāṇikuḷi; Vānavan mādēvipuram (Tirumāṇikuḷi)	*	*	
51.	Tirunaṟaiyūr nāḍu (Tanjavur)			Nallāḍaimangalam; Kulōttunga cōḷapuram (Nallāḍai)	*		

52.	Tirunaṟaiyūr nāḍu (Tanjavur)		Tirunaṟaiyūr Avaninārāyaṇapuram (Tirunaṟaiyūr)			Is it a pre-Cōḷa centre? Avaninārāyaṇa was a title of Nandivarman III (Pallava)
53.	Kurunāgan(i) nāḍu (Tiruchirapalli)		Tiruvāṭpōkki; Śivapādaśēkharapuram (Ratnagiri and Śivāyam)	*	*	Merchants with the title 'Cakravarti' (merchant princes?) are known from the early 13th century
54.	Uṟaiyūr Kūṟṟam (Tiruchirapalli)		Nandivarmamangalam; Rājāśraya caturvēdi mangalam; Kongukoṇḍacōḷapuram; Kaṟkuḍimalai (Uyyakkoṇḍān-Tirumalai)	*	*	Śankarappāḍi *nagaram* (11th century) and merchant colony (13th century)

Table IV *Cont'd*

No.	*Old Historical Unit (Modern District)*	*Period I 600-850*	*Period II 850-985*	*Period III 985-1150*	*Period IV 1150-1250*	*Period V 1250-1350*	*Other Relevant Information*
55.	Puliyūr Kōṭṭam alias Kulōttunga-cōḷa vaḷanāḍu in Jayangoṇḍacōḷa-maṇḍalam (Chingleput)				Pūvirundava Pūntamalli (Poonam-alle or Pūntam-alli)	*	
56.	Kāngaya nāḍu (Coimbatore)				Abhimāna-cōḷapuram (Kaṇṇa-puram)	*	The *nagaram* of Vik-ramacōḷapuram (alias Villavan mādēvi) (Tāḷūṉṟi?) is also mentioned (Kongu Cōḷa centre)

57.	Pērūr nāḍu (Coimbatore)	Pērūr (Pērūr)	*	Mention is made of Muṭṭam (a part of Pērūr?) where merchants with the title of Cakravarti lived, in the inscription of Ikkarai Boḷuvāmpaṭṭi (see no. 53)
58.	– (Dharmapuri)	Kaḍagattūr (Kaḍagattūr)	*	*Nagarattār* of other centres are also mentioned. A weaving centre
59.	Virudarājabhayankara-vaḷanāḍu (Pudukkottai)	Arumoḷidēvapuram (Tiruvarangulam)	*	Reference to a Kulaśēkhara paṭṭaṇam
60.	Gangaikoṇḍacōḷa Pēriḷamai nāḍu (South Arcot)	Perumparrappuliyūr (Chidambaram)	*	*Taniyūr*, Sālika *nagaram*, Sōḷiya Sāliyas (weavers). Weaving centre

Table IV *Cont'd*

No.	*Old Historical Unit (Modern District)*	*Period I 600-850*	*Period II 850-985*	*Period III 985-1150*	*Period IV 1150-1250*	*Period V 1250-1350*	*Other Relevant Information*
61.	Mēṟkā nāḍu (South Arcot)				Vanavan mahādēvipuram (Manjakuppam)		
62.	Puraiyūr nāḍu (South Arcot)				Bhuvanamāṇikkapuram (Vikravāṇḍi)		
63.	Veṇṇikkūṟṟam in Suttamalli vaḷanāḍu (Tanjavur)				Tiruveṇṇi Tiruveṇṇi (Kōvil Veṇṇi)		
64.	Arumoḷidēva vaḷanāḍu (Tanjavur)				Ottaikkuḍi alias Edirilicōḷapuram (Kuḻikkarai)		

65.	Vindaḷūr nāḍu (Tanjavur)	Rājaśikhāmaṇi-Caturvēdimangalam; Rājēndrapuram alias Vānavan-Kuḷattūr		Reference is from a Pallavarāyanpēṭṭai inscription
66.	Ārvala Kūṟṟam in Rājēndracōḷa Vaḷanāḍu (Tanjavur)	Veḷḷiyīḍu nagaram (Tiruttengūr)	*	
67.	Mangala nāḍu (Tanjavur)	Viḍaiyapuram alias Virudarājabhayankarapuram (Tiruviḍaivāyil)	*	
68.	Tiraimūr nāḍu (Tanjavur)	Tribhuvanavīrapuram (Tribhuvanam)	*	

Table IV *Cont'd*

No.	*Old Historical Unit (Modern District)*	*Period I 600-850*	*Period II 850-985*	*Period III 985-1150*	*Period IV 1150-1250*	*Period V 1250-1350*	*Other Relevant Information*
69.	Umbaḷa nāḍu (Tanjavur)				Rājēndraśingapuram (?)	*	Mentioned in an inscription of Vēdāraṇyam
70.	Vēngala nāḍu (Tiruchirapalli)				Vañjimānagaram; Muḍikoṇḍacōḷapuram (Karuvūr or Karūr)	*	Vañji or Karuvūr dates from the pre-Christian era. An early Cēra capital
71.	Ādanūr nāḍu Taṭṭaikkaḷanāḍu in Kēraḷa nāḍu (Tiruchirapalli)				Madurāntakapuram (Tirumukkūḍal)	*	Mentioned in inscriptions from Tirumukkūḍal

72. Ollaiyūr Kūṟṟam or Taṭṭaikkaḷa-nāḍu in Kēraḷā-nataka vaḷanāḍu (Tiruchirapalli)	Cāttanūr) (Sāttanūr)		*	Mentioned in in-scriptions from Tirumukkūḍal
73. Iḍaiyāṟṟu nāḍu (Tiruchirapalli)	Tirumaṇamēḍu (Tirumaṇa-mēḍu)		*	Vāṇiya *nagaram*
74. Vaḍavaḻi nāḍu (Tiruchirapalli)	Tiruppaiññili (Tiruppangili)		*	Vāṇiya *nagaram*
75. Miḻalai Kūṟṟam—Kīḻ Kūṟu (Tiruchirapalli)	Kōdaṇḍarāma-puram (Veḷḷūr)		*	Weaving centre
76. Karai vaḻi nāḍu (Coimbatore)		Sangrāmana-llūr (Koḻumam)		
77. Vaḍaparappu nāḍu (Madurai)		Cēranārāyaṇa-puram (Cēranārāyaṇa puram)		

Table IV *Cont'd*

No.	*Old Historical Unit (Modern District)*	*Period I 600-850*	*Period II 850-985*	*Period III 985-1150*	*Period IV 1150-1250*	*Period V 1250-1350*	*Other Relevant Information*
78.	Ten Kallāga nāḍu (Madurai)					Vikrama cōḷapuram; Dēśipaṭṭaṇam (Vikramangalam)	Nagaram and *Aiyampoḻil*. Was this centre founded by Vikrama Cōḷa, i.e. Period III?
79.	Kīḻ-kundāṟu nāḍu? (Ramanathapuram)					Śembiya nārāyaṇapuram; Śeḻiya nārāyaṇapuram (Alakāpuri)	
80.	Ānmā nāḍu (Ramanathapuram)					Semmaram alias Kulaśēkharapuram (Devadānam)	

81. Kīḻ-kundāṟu nāḍu? (Ramanathapuram)	Rājānārāyaṇa-puram alias Marudanguḍi (Piḷḷaiyār-paṭṭi?)	Another *nagaram* of Eṇkārikkuḍi in Kāna nāḍu and *Aiññūṟṟuvar* mentioned in the Piḷḷ-ayārpaṭṭi inscription
82. Pūnguṉṟa nāḍu (Ramanathapuram)	Vēlanguḍi (Vēlanguḍi)	Vāṇiya *nagaram* levying tolls
83. Āṟṟūr Kūṟṟam (Salem)	— (Āragaḷūr)	Vāṇiya *nagaram*, Ceṭṭis and weavers
84. Dānava nāḍu (Tanjavur)	Kīramangalam, hamlet of Kiḍārangoṇḍa cōḻapuram (Kīramangalam)	*Nagaram* and the 18 Viṣaya levying tolls

Table IV *Cont'd*

No.	*Old Historical Unit (Modern District)*	*Period I 600-850*	*Period II 850-985*	*Period III 985-1150*	*Period IV 1150-1250*	*Period V 1250-1350*	*Other Relevant Information*
85.	Kuḍa nāḍu (Tirunelveli)					Maḍigai mānagaram alias Vaṇṭai-mānagaram (Angamanga-lam)	*Nagaram*? Levying tolls on merchandise
86.	Muḷḷi nāḍu (Tirunelveli)					Vikrama Pāṇḍyapuram (Mārandai)	
87.	Puṟattāya nāḍu (Tirunelveli)					Pūśankuḍi alias Vara-guṇappāṇḍi-nagaram (Rādhāpuram)	*Nagaram* and Sāliya (weavers)

88.	Teṉkarai nāḍu (Tirunelveli)	Pūḷam alias Rājarājapuram (Śingikuḷam)	
89.	Kīḻ Vēmba nāḍu (Tirunelveli)	— (Śrīvallavapuram)	
90.	Kīḻ Vēmba nāḍu (Tirunelveli)	Kulaśēkharapuram in Tirunelvēli (Tirunelvēli)	
91.	Tiruvaḻudi Vaḷanāḍu (Tirunelveli)	Madurōdayapuram (Veḷḷūr)	
92.	Kuṟumaṟai nāḍu (Tirunelveli)	Vindanūr alias Avanimārttāṇḍapuram (Vindanūr)	*Nagaram* for the urban complex of Mannārkōyil, Ambasamudram, etc. (see Table I, no. 2)

Table V

Trading Centres, Fairs, etc. (Other than Nagaram)

No.	*Old Historical Unit (Modern District)*	*Period I 600-850*	*Period II 850-985*	*Period III 985-1150*	*Period IV 1150-1250*	*Period V 1250-1350*	*Other Relevant Information*
1.	Muraśa nāḍu (Dharmapuri)		– (Hosur)	*	*		Kudirai Sārigai (horse trading). Śungam or tolls in Period IV. Merchants from Cōḷa region in Period IV
2.	Ākkūr nāḍu (Tanjavur)			Talaiccangāḍu (Talaichchangāḍū)	*		Trade centre, merchants from Cōḷa region and Kerala
3.	Vaḍaparisāra nāḍu (Coimbatore)				Annūr (Manniyūr)	*	Trade and commercial centre

4.	Cevvūr nāḍu (Coimbatore)		Tiruppuṭkoḷiyūr (Avināśi)		Trade and commercial centre
5.	Tagaḍūr nāḍu (Dharmapuri)		Atiyamānkōṭṭai (Adhamankōṭṭai)	*	Trade centre. Cīlai ceṭṭi (cloth merchants)
6.	– (Dharmapuri)		Nāvaṟ Tāvaḷam (?)	*	Fair. (Inscription from Pāpināyakanahaḷḷi mentioning the distance to Nāvaṟ Tāvaḷam)
7.	– (Dharmapuri)		Śrīkaraṇapaḷḷi (?)	*	Horse trading (reference in Bērikai inscription)
8.	Kāna nāḍu (Pudukkottai)		Pēraiyūr (Pēraiyūr)	*	Horse trading. Malaiyāḷankuḍi (settlement of Malaiyāḷis from Kerala) in Kāna nāḍu, alias Virudarājabhayankara vaḷanāḍu

Table V *Cont'd*

No.	*Old Historical Unit (Modern District)*	*Period I 600-850*	*Period II 850-985*	*Period III 985-1150*	*Period IV 1150-1250*	*Period V 1250-1350*	*Other Relevant Information*
9.	Keraḷaśinga vaḷanāḍu (Ramanathapuram)	*	*		Aruviyūr alias Dēśi Uyyavanda paṭṭanam (Tirupputtūr)	*	Seems to have been a trade centre even from the early Cōḷa (Period II) times

Table VI

Centres Associated with Merchant Bodies and Other Organizations

No.	*Old Historical Unit (Modern District)*	*Period I 600-850*	*Period II 850-985*	*Period III 985-1150*	*Period IV 1150-1250*	*Period V 1250-1350*	*Other Relevant Information*
1.	Uṟattūr Kūṟṟam (Pudukkottai)		Koḍumbāḷūr (Koḍumbāḷūr),	*	*	*	Maṇigrāmam
2.	Kāna nāḍu (Pudukkottai)		Muniyandai (Muniśandai)				The Five Hundred (Aiññūṟṟuvar)
3.	– (Ramanathapuram)		– (Kamudi)				Cittiramēḻi Periya Nāḍu and merchant bodies
4.	Kīḻkarai Pūnduṟai nāḍu (Salem)		Tiruccengōḍu (Tiruchengoḍu)				Padineṇ Viṣaya (the 18 Viṣaya or regions)
5.	Sēla nāḍu (Salem)		Sēlam (Salem)				Maṇigrāmam of Koḍumbāḷūr

Table VI *Cont'd*

No.	*Old Historical Unit (Modern District)*	*Period I 600-850*	*Period II 850-985*	*Period III 985-1150*	*Period IV 1150-1250*	*Period V 1250-1350*	*Other Relevant Information*
6.	Veṇ nāḍu (Tanjavur)		Tirunallam (Kōnērirājapuram)				Tiśai Āyirattu Aiññūṟṟuvar (The Five Hundred of the Thousand Directions)
7.	Nallūr nāḍu (Tanjavur)		Tiruccellūr in Rajakēsaricaturvēdimangalam (Kōyil Tēvarāyanpēttai)				The Five Hundred
8.	Kiḻār Kūṟṟam (Tanjavur)		Tiruccōṟṟutturai (Tiruchchātturai)				The Five Hundred

9. Kuṟukkai nāḍu Nallāṟṟūr nāḍu (Tanjavur)	Tiruvēḷvikkuḍi of Viḍēl viḍugu caturvēdi mangalam (Tiruviḷakkuḍi)		Nanādēśī, Tiśai Āyirattu Aiññūṟṟuvar Valañjīyar
10. – (Tiruchirapalli)	Tiruveḷḷaṟai (Tiruveḷḷaṟai)		
11. Uṟaiyūr Kūṟṟam (Tiruchirapalli)	Uṟaiyūr (in Tiruchirapalli)		Maṇigrāmam
12. Kuṟumaṟai nāḍu (Tirunelveli)	Kuttālam; Sundara Pāṇḍyanagaraṁ (Kuttālam)		Maṇigrāmam
		PHASE I	
13. – (Chingleput)		Aiyapoḷil-Kāṭṭūr (Kāṭṭūr)	Eṟivīrappaṭṭaṇa; Nanādēśī of Mayilārppil and Valañjīyar
14. Puliyūr Kōṭṭam (Madras City)		Mayilārppil (Mylapore in Madras)	Nanādēśī and Valañjīyar

Table VI *Cont'd*

No.	*Old Historical Unit (Modern District)*	*Period I 600-850*	*Period II 850-985*	*Period III 985-1150*	*Period IV 1150-1250*	*Period V 1250-1350*	*Other Relevant Information*
15.	Mūgai nāḍu in Pūraṇi Mārāya-pāḍi in Jayan-koṇḍa cōḷamaṇḍalam (Chittoor)			Śirāvalli (Basinikoṇḍa)			Nanādēśīya Daśamaḍi Eṟivīrappaṭṭaṇa
16.	Pūnduṟai nāḍu (Coimbatore—now Periyar)			Īrōḍu (Erode)			Aiññūṟṟuvar; Pugaliḍam (refuge) for artisans
17.	– (North Arcot)			– (Kalaśappākkam)			Nanādēśī, Aiññūṟṟuvar
18.	– (North Arcot)			– (Tāmaraippākkam)			Cittiramēḻi Periya nāḍu and Aiññūṟṟuvar
19.	– (North Arcot)			– (Viralūr)			Aiññūṟṟuvar

20.	Tiraimūr nāḍu (Tanjavur)	Tirukkōḷambam (Tirukkoḷambiyūr)	Nanādēśī
21.	Uṟaiyūr Kūṟṟam (Tiruchirapalli)	Kumāravayalūr (Kumāravayalūr)	Aiññūṟṟuvar
22.	Muḷḷi nāḍu (Tirunelveli)	Iḷangōykkuḍi—hamlet of Rājarājacaturvēdi mangalam (Ambāsamudram)	Aiññūṟṟuvar (See Table I, no. 2)
23.	Muḷḷi nāḍu (Tirunelveli)	Cēravan mahādēvi caturvēdimangalam (Śērmādēvi)	Aiññūṟṟuvar (See Table I, no. 2)
24.	Muḷḷi nāḍu (Tirunelveli)	Tiruvālīśvaram; Rājarāja Eṟivīrappaṭṭaṇam (Tiruvālīśvaram)	Mūṉṟukai Mahāsēnai[1] as protectors of the local temple

Table VI *Cont'd*

No.	*Old Historical Unit (Modern District)*	*Period I 600-850*	*Period II 850-985*	*Period III 985-1150*	*Period IV 1150-1250*	*Period V 1250-1350*	*Other Relevant Information*
25.	Nāttāṟṟuppōkku (Tirunelveli)			Vijayanārāyaṇa caturvēdimangalam (Vijayanārāyaṇam)			Aiññūṟṟuvar. Valañjīyakkuricci, a hamlet, mentioned even in Pāṇḍya inscriptions of the 10th century
				PHASE II			
26.	Kēraḷaśinga vaḷanāḍu (Ramanathapuram)			Nṛpaśekhara caturvēdi mangalam; Aruviyūr (Śivapuri)			Aiññūṟṟuvar Dharmapoḻil
27.	Viḷā nāḍu (Tiruchirapalli)			Tiruvarangam (Śrīrangam)	*		Aiyapoḻil; Reference to a Rājēndracōḻapuram

28.	Vañji nāḍu (Coimbatore)	— (Kaveripuram)		Valañjīyar of Tuvaḷai
29.	Padi nāḍu (Coimbatore)	Kollagar, Tribhuvana-mādēvi caturvēdi mangalam (Koḷḷēgāl)		Aiyapoḻil (also weaving centre)
30.	Vaḍa parisāra nāḍu (Coimbatore)	Tirumurugan-pūṇḍi		Aiyapoḻil, Kaikkoḷas (weavers)
31.	Nāḍuvilmalai Perumūr nāḍu (North Arcot)	Cakkaramū-dūr; Vijayapa-ṭṭaṇam (Cakkara-mallūr)	*	Cittiramēḻi Periya nāḍu; Padineṇ-bhūmi Paṭṭaṇam
32.	Marugal nāḍu in Gēyamāṇikkavaḷa-nāḍu (Tanjavur)	Tirukkaṇṇa-puram (Tiru-kkaṇṇapuram)		Valañjīyar of Ten-nilangai (Sri Lanka) Āyōgavas (weavers)

Table VI *Cont'd*

No.	*Old Historical Unit (Modern District)*	*Period I 600-850*	*Period II 850-985*	*Period III 985-1150*	*Period IV 1150-1250*	*Period V 1250-1350*	*Other Relevant Information*
33.	Kuṟumbūr nāḍu (Tanjavur)				Tiruviḍaikkaḻi (Tiruviḍaik-kaḻi)		Aiññūṟṟuvar
34.	Kiḻār Kūṟṟam (Tiruchirapalli)				Kīḻ-Ambil (Anbil)		Cittiramēḻi Periya nāḍu and Aiññūṟṟuvar
35.	Kiḻār Kūṟṟam in Vaḍakarai Rājarājavaḷanāḍu (Tiruchirapalli)				Koṟṟamanga-lam (Koṟṟa-mangalam)		Eluppattonpadu nāṭṭu Padineṇ-bhūmi[2] and Aiññūṟṟuvar[3]
36.	Ūṟṟattūr nāḍu (Tiruchirapalli)				Ūṟṟattūr alias Tāvilunallapu-ram (Ūṭṭattūr)	*	Eṟivīrappaṭṭaṇa; iḍangai 98
36A.	Vengala nāḍu (Tiruchirapalli)				Veṇkuḷam (Vengalam)		

37.	– (Chingleput)	Caturangappaṭṭaṇam; Rājanārāyaṇapaṭṭaṇam (Sadras)	Padineṇ Viṣaya levying tolls (Maganmai); coastal town
38.	Kuml̤i nāḍu in Āmūr Kōṭṭam in Jayankoṇḍacōḷa maṇḍalam (Chingleput)	Taiyūr alias Rājakēsarinallūr (Taiyūr)	Vaiśya and Vāṇiya merchants of the 18 countries levying tolls (Maganmai)
39.	– (Coimbatore)	– (Dalavay Pattanam)	Nanādēśī
40.	Kur̤uppu nāḍu (Coimbatore)	Vijayamangalam (Vijayamangalam)	Cittiramēl̤i Periya nāḍu
41.	Pāganūr Kūr̤r̤am (Madurai)	Ten̤karai (Ten̤karai)	Aiyapol̤il—framing rules for the Valangai and Iḍangai

Table VI *Cont'd*

No.	*Old Historical Unit (Modern District)*	*Period I 600-850*	*Period II 850-985*	*Period III 985-1150*	*Period IV 1150-1250*	*Period V 1250-1350*	*Other Relevant Information*
42.	Kēraḷaśinga vaḷa nāḍu (Ramanatha-puram)					Dēśiya Śiṟiya Paṭṭaṇa (Aru-ppukkōṭṭai)	Valañjīyar of Tenni-langai (Sri Lanka)
43.	Aḷaṟṟu nāḍu (Ramanathapuram)					Iḍaivaḻi (Tiru-mālagandār kōṭṭai)	Eṟivīrappaṭṭaṇa (Iḍaivaḻi–passage or route?)
44.	Kēraḷaśinga vaḷa nāḍu? (Ramanathapuram)					Tirukkoḍun-kuṉṟam (Pirānmalai)	Cittiramēḻi Periya nāḍu and Merchant bodies. Reference to Aruvi-mānagaram alias Kulaśēkhara Paṭṭaṇam in Kēraḷaśinga vaḷanāḍu

No.	Old Historical Unit (Modern District)	Period I 600-850	Period II 850-985	Period III 985-1150	Period IV 1150-1250	Period V 1250-1350	Other Relevant Information
45.	Vaḍa kaḷavaḷi nāḍu (Ramanathapuram)					– (Tirumalai)	Aiññūṟṟuvar. Tolls (Maganmai) by Danmadāvaḷar and other bodies
46.	Muttūṟṟu Kūṟṟam (Ramanathapuram)					Toṇḍi (Tittāṇḍatānapuram)	Añjuvaṇṇam, Maṇigrāmam and Sāmanta Paṇḍasālis levying taxes on commodities jointly.[4]
47.	– (South Arcot)					Iruviñjam alias Rajanārāyaṇa paṭṭaṇam (Rishivandyam)	Paṭṭaṇappagudi (share of the paṭṭaṇa) levied by the 18 Viṣaya, nagaram and nāḍu

Table VI *Cont'd*

48.	Mēṟkā nāḍu (South Arcot)	Tiruttiṇai nagar (Tīrthanagari)	Maganmai (tolls) reassigned by merchant bodies
49.	M(V)irai Kūṟṟam (Tiruchirapalli)	Kāmaravalli caturvēdi mangalam alias Tirunallūr (Kāmarasavalli)	Maganmai (tolls) by people of 18 regions and 79 nāḍus
50.	Uṟattūr Kūṟṟam (Tiruchirapalli)	— (Kōvilpaṭṭi)	Paṭṭaṇappagudi levied by Cittiramēḻi Periyanāṭṭār, Nagarattār of Sundaracōḷapuram (Sundaram), Nārttāmalai, Uttamacōḷapuram and Koḍumbāḷūr Maṇigrāmam

51. Marungūr nāḍu (Tiruchirapalli)	— (Tuvaranku-ricci)	Paṭṭaṇappagudi by Cittiramēḻi and Merchant bodies
52. Kaḷakkuḍi nāḍu (Tirunelveli)	Mānanilai nallūr (Mānūr)	Trading communities of several places
53. Amitaguṇa vaḷa-nāḍu (Tirunelveli)	— (Munañju-paṭṭi)	Aiyapoḻil

1 The term 'Mūṉṟukai Mahāsēnai' seems to indicate that apart from the Valangai and Iḍangai Mahāsēnai (i.e. the Right and Left Hand Armies), there was a third wing of the Cōḷa army. Was it made up of mercenaries? (Mūṉṟu = Three; Kai = Hand.)

2 The organization of the 18 regions of 79 *nāḍus*.

3 The Five Hundred.

4 Añjuvaṇṇam–a merchant organization known from the eighth-ninth centuries, 'Sāmanta Paṇḍasālis' may refer to stockists of commodities.

For urban complexes where merchant bodies were active, see Table I, no. 2 and Table III, no. 3.

For *nagarams* where merchant bodies and other organizations were active, see Table IV, nos 5, 12, 21, 22, 24, 39, 42, 47, 48, 49, 77, 80, 81, 82 and 83.

Table VII
Ports and Coastal Towns

No.	*Old Historical Unit (Modern District)*	*Period I 600-850*	*Period II 850-985*	*Period III 985-1150*	*Period IV 1150-1250*	*Period V 1250-1350*	*Other Relevant Information*
1.	Āmūr nāḍu in Āmūr Kōṭṭam (Chingleput)	Māmallapuram	*	*	*		Mānagaram and port in Period I. Subsequently Nagaram and subsidiary port (see Table IV, no. 2)
2.	Kuḍa nāḍu in Uttama Cōḷa Vaḷanāḍu (Tirunelveli)	Koṟkai; Akkasālai alias Madurōdayanallūr	*	*	*		Pāṇḍya port upto 9th century. Later a Cōḷa port. Was it a mint also (Akkasālai) from late Cōḷa period (Period IV)?

3.	Ākkūr nāḍu (Tanjavur)	*	Puhār nagar Kāvērippūm-paṭṭiṇam (Kāvērippūm-paṭṭiṇam)	*	*		Cōḷa port from pre-Christian era. Superseded by Nāgappaṭṭiṇam in the 11th century (Period III). Subsidiary port from Period III
4.	Paḍuvūr nāḍu (Chingleput)			Tiruviḍavandai (Tiruvaḍandai)	*		Halting station, on coastal route? Merchants from Sōnāḍu (Cōḷa country) and Malai nāḍu (Kerala)
5.	Paṭṭaṇa nāḍu (South Arcot)			Pallavan Paṭṭaṇam Paḻam Paṭṭaṇam (Kūḍalūr)	*	*	Coastal town
6.	Paṭṭaṇa nāḍu in Ōymā nāḍu (South Arcot)	*	*	Eyiṟ paṭṭaṇam (Marakkāṇam)	*	*	Coastal town and salt manufacturing centre

Table VII *Cont'd*

No.	*Old Historical Unit (Modern District)*	*Period I 600-850*	*Period II 850-985*	*Period III 985-1150*	*Period IV 1150-1250*	*Period V 1250-1350*	*Other Relevant Information*
7.	Veṇṇaiyūr nāḍu in Rājādhirāja vaḷa nāḍu (Tanjavur)			Mahipālakulakāla pēraḷam (Āchchāpuram near Nallūr Perumaṇam)	*	*	Coastal town and salt manufacturing centre
8.	Paṭṭaṇa Kūṟṟam in Gēyamāṇikka vaḷa nāḍu (Tanjavur)			Cōḷakulavalli paṭṭaṇam (Nāgappaṭṭiṇam)	*	*	Main Cōḷa port
9.	Kuṟumbūr nāḍu (Tanjavur)			Āḻituṟai; Rājēndracōḷappēraḷam (Tillaiyāḍi)	*	*	Coastal town and salt manufacturing centre
10.	Tiruvāḻi nāḍu in Rājādhirāja vaḷa nāḍu (Tanjavur)			Maṇṇaikoṇḍa cōḷa paṭṭiṇam (Tirukkarugāvūr)	*	*	Coastal town

11. Paḍuvūr nāḍu in Āmūr Kōṭṭam (Chingleput)	Kōvaḷam Paṭṭaṇam; Kōmaḷam; Vīracōḷa Paṭṭaṇam (Kōvaḷam)	*	Coastal town
12. Muttūṟṟu Kūṟṟam (Ramanathapuram)	Pāśi Paṭṭaṇam (Pāśi)	*	Coastal town
13. Mēṟkā nāḍu (South Arcot)	Niśśankamal-lan Paṭṭaṇam (Cuddalore)	*	Coastal town (Also *Taniyūr*?)
14. Mēṟkā nāḍu (South Arcot)	Tiruvayīndra-puram (Tiru-vēndipuram)	*	Coastal town (Paṭṭaṇam)
15. Umbaḷa nāḍu (Tanjavur)	Kulōttunga cōḷan Paṭṭaṇam (?)	*	Mentioned in Vēdā-raṇyam inscriptions. Also reference to Kalyāṇapurankoṇḍa cōḷa Paṭṭaṇam in Kānattūr nāḍu in Umbaḷa nāḍu (Is it Kāriāpaṭṇam?)

Table VII *Cont'd*

No.	*Old Historical Unit (Modern District)*	*Period I 600-850*	*Period II 850-985*	*Period III 985-1150*	*Period IV 1150-1250*	*Period V 1250-1350*	*Other Relevant Information*
16.	– (Tanjavur)				Vīra cōḷa Paṭṭaṇam (Adirām paṭṭaṇam)	*	Coastal town
17.	Mondūr nāḍu in Āmūr Kōṭṭam in Jayankoṇḍa cōḷa maṇḍalam (Chingleput)					Cōḷamārttāṇḍā nallūr (Pudup-paṭṭaṇam)	Coastal town
18.	Kuṟumbūr nāḍu (Tanjavur)					Ṣaḍankanpāḍi alias Kulaśēkhara paṭṭaṇam (Tarangampāḍi or Tranquebar)	Coastal town
19.	Kuḍa nāḍu (Tirunelveli)	*	*	*	*	Kāyal (Kāyal Paṭṭaṇam)	Coastal town

See Table IV, no. 6 for a coastal town and salt manufacturing centre with a *nagaram*.

Table VIII
Centres Associated with Artisan Communities

No.	*Old Historical Unit (Modern District)*	*Period I 600-850*	*Period II 850-985*	*Period III 985-1150*	*Period IV 1150-1250*	*Period V 1250-1350*	*Other Relevant Information*
1.	Ākkūr nāḍu (Tanjavur)		*	*	Kiḍārankoṇḍān; Tirunanippaḷḷi (Puñjai)	*	Anuloma Rathakāras
2.	Pūnḍuṛai nāḍu (Coimbatore)					– (Veḷḷōḍu)	Kaṇmāḷa (artisan) communities given privileges. Reference in inscriptions from Karuvūr, Pariyūr and Moḍakkūr to Kaṇmāḷa association or privileges (all in the Kongu region)

Table VIII *Cont'd*

No.	*Old Historical Unit (Modern District)*	*Period I 600-850*	*Period II 850-985*	*Period III 985-1150*	*Period IV 1150-1250*	*Period V 1250-1350*	*Other Relevant Information*
3.	Nāḍāḻva nāḍu (Salem)					Eḻūr (nāḍu) (?)	Nāmakkal inscriptions. Agreement among 17 Kambaḷ-attār of the Kollar (artisans) caste of Eḻūr nāḍu (*nagaram*?)
4.	Kīḻ Cengili nāḍu (Tanjavur)					– (Noḍiyūr)	Reference to Artisans

See Table IV, nos 21 and 43 for *nagaram* with artisan communities.
See Table VI, no. 15 for refugee centre for artisans.

5

The South Indian Guilds: Their Role in Early Medieval Trade and Urbanization

One of the more important but less understood areas of economic activity in medieval South India is that of the corporate trading communities often called 'guilds'. The term 'guild' immediately conjures up the image of an association of professionals with a well defined structure, a carefully framed code of conduct of rules and membership governed by certain regulations and qualifications. It is hard to get indisputable evidence of such an organization from the South Indian records, although the term *Baṇanju dharma* is the nearest to a code of rules that existed and was adhered to by the itinerant merchant bodies. Hence, it is rather a matter of convenience that the term 'guild' has been used to denote these merchant bodies, and hardly any parallel to the European merchant guilds, or the *Hang* of China in Sung and Yuan times, or the *Karimi* of Egypt, is meant.[1] It would perhaps be more appropriate to use the term organization/association which is the nearest equivalent to the term *Samaya(m)* used in their inscriptions.

A second important aspect of the problem is the nature of the organization and its membership. Names of several groups occur in the epigraphic records all over South India and it is not always easy to identify them and determine their relationship to one another. To illustrate the point, one notices conspicuous references to the *Ayyāvoḷe* or *Aiññūṟṟuvar*, *Valañjīyar*, *Nānādeśi* and *Nagarattār*, apart from various other groups like the *Maṇigrāmam* and *Añjuvaṇṇam*, in the records ranging from the eighth to the seventeenth centuries AD—more specifically between the eighth and fourteenth centuries, both in South India and Sri Lanka. With the exception of *Nagarattār*, all these terms refer to itinerant merchant bodies. While the *Aiññūṟṟuvar*, or the Five Hundred, figure prominently in most of them, some 46 different groups are noticed in association with them at various centres and in different contexts. Listing all these groups, K. Indrapala expresses the difficulties in determining the nature of their relationship with the Five Hundred, and dismisses as untenable the views that the Five Hundred was a federation of all these bodies, or that the latter were sub-divisions of the Five Hundred.[2] Some of these groups were non-mercantile in character, as they refer to occupational groups like the *Pañcālas*, *Kumbhalikas* etc.,[3] and to groups of fighters taken to be mercenaries accompanying the Five Hundred.[4]

From the late twelfth to the fourteenth centuries, there is yet another major organization called *Cittiramēḷi Periya Nāḍu*,[5] or the *Padineṇbhūmi* or *Viṣaya* of the Seventy Nine *Nāḍus*, appearing jointly with the Five Hundred in a position of prime importance in the *praśastis* of the inscriptions recording joint donations of tolls and cesses on merchandise. The pride of place is here given to the *Cittiramēḷi*, and the Five Hundred a secondary position, with their respective emblems, viz. the *Śengōl* and *mēḷi* (the staff and the plough) of the first, and the *paśumpai* (money bag) of the second.[6] There can hardly be any doubt as to the commercial and urban context in which these joint donations occur. This is to be seen as a result of the revival of long-distance trade in South India in the tenth century AD, which was itself a part of the increase in South Asian trade involving such distant regions as Egypt and West Asia, and Southeast Asia and China.

The whole corpus of information of South Indian trade at this time centres mainly round the Five Hundred, and to a lesser extent, on the *Maṇigrāmam* and *Añjuvaṇṇam* and other such organizations. It would, therefore, be appropriate to start from the Five Hundred and proceed to enquire into the nature of their organization and relationship with other bodies. Only then can the complexity of inscriptional data be converted into useful categories of evidence. For reasons which would become apparent in the course of this essay, it would also be useful to distinguish between the Five Hundred on the one hand, and the *Maṇigrāmam*, *Añjuvaṇṇam* and the *Nagaram* on the other. The Five Hundred was a large organization of itinerant merchants, of a supra-regional character,[7] the *Maṇigrāmam* a localized merchant body operating within specific regions, as their designations like *Uṟaiyūr Maṇigrāmam* and

Koḍumbāḷūr Maṇigrāmam[8] would show, although they had inter-regional and long-distance trade links, and interacted with the Five Hundred or the moving trade carried on by the Five Hundred in their regions. The *Añjuvaṇṇam* refers to an organization of foreigners who seem to have begun their commercial activities on the west coast, particularly Kerala, in the eighth and ninth centuries[9] and spread out to the other coastal areas of South India from the eleventh century AD, interacting with both local merchants and the Five Hundred.[10] Initially, *Añjuvaṇṇam* seems to have referred to Jewish traders who came to the west coast and acquired settlements. Later, however, it was also used for Arab Muslim traders.[11]

The *Nagaram* is a much more specific organization of merchants found in every market centre, collection and distribution centre, where local trade and itinerant trade met and exchanged items of trade.[12] The designations of these bodies remain the same throughout the period of their activity. *Nagaram* being a mercantile organization evolving from local groups organizing and controlling local trade, *Nagarattār* became a generic term for all the traders and the trading community, particularly in Tamil Nadu, and hence is used even today by the Nāṭṭukkōṭṭai Cheṭṭiārs.[13]

The Five Hundred, as an organization of merchants, originated in the eighth century AD in Aihoḷe in the Hungund Taluk of the Bijapur district of Karnataka.[14] The founding of the Ayyāvoḷe Five Hundred may be seen as the result of a decision of a group of *Mahājanas* or *brāhmaṇas* (*caturvēdis*), also called the Five Hundred *Svāmis* of the *Mahāgrahāra* of Aihoḷe, to institutionalize control of the existing commerce of that region, thus providing an institutional base for organized commerce.[15] Hence, it would be erroneous to trace the origin of the itinerant merchant organization, as Kenneth R. Hall has done, to small groups of expeditionary merchants who serviced less wealthy or isolated communities of the hinterland, and found it profitable to band together for mutual protection, and to assume that the itinerant merchant organizations of the Cōḷa age developed from such bands of expeditionary traders into quite powerful commercial associations.[16]

Aihoḷe, also known as Āryapura and Ahicchatra in their inscriptions, was, thus, both the progenitor and birth place of the corporation. However, the organization did not remain a single unified body throughout its history, nor was Aihoḷe its permanent headquarters. The number Five Hundred was a conventional one and remained so for the rest of the history of the itinerant traders, who derived their name from the parent organization, despite the fact that the organization became a much larger one, drawing its members from various regions and communities. Other terms like *Nānādeśi*, *Ubhaya-nānādeśi*, *Valañjīyar* or *Vīra Valañjīyar*, *Baṇajiga* etc., were of a descriptive or adjectival nature, used to denote the itinerant merchants following the trading profession or the *Baṇanju dharma*. Hence, these terms are found sometimes used interchangeably in many of their records. Among the other groups who are mentioned along with the Five Hundred, were mercenary fighters who protected their merchandise, probably in lieu of a share in the profit. The militant character of their mercantiḷe organization derives mainly from these groups, whose personal valour and ferocity are indicated by such epithets as Iḷancingam, Cittiravāḷi, Eṟivīrar, Munaivīrar, Kongavāḷar, Vīrakkoṭiyar etc. The militant component of the itinerant trading organization is visible in many of the South Indian epigraphs, but most conspicuously in the Kongu *nāḍu* inscriptions, where the sculptural representations of weapons, horses and elephants accompany some of the records mentioning *attikōśattār* (elephant corps) and *Vīrakośattār* (cavalry).[17] Some of them became traders through long association with the organization. Crafts groups are also sometimes mentioned with the Five Hundred,[18] probably due to the links established between the two for the marketing of commodities, particularly textiles, metalware and pottery. Being the largest itinerant merchant organization covering distant regions and divergent commercial areas, the Five Hundred was the only organization to have mercenaries to protect their goods and to set up protected mercantile towns (with warehouses) called Eṟivīrappaṭṭaṇas.[19]

The name *Ayyāvoḷe*,[20] became, in Tamil, *Āiyapoḻil* and *Danmapoḻil*, and was often used as a descriptive epithet of their towns and the deities they worshipped, e.g. Aiyapoḻil Parameśvari. But the term Five Hundred is more commonly used to denote the group, and is sometimes stretched into *Nanadesiya Tiśai Āyirattu Aiññūṟṟuvar*.*

* Meaning–The Five Hundred of a thousand directions and several countries/ regions.

It has been pointed out earlier that the Five Hundred cannot be treated as a single unified body of merchants throughout its history, nor did it function as one cohesive whole. In the very early days of the organization, there seems to have been some unity and common purpose in the manner in which they functioned, both in Karnataka and in Tamil Nadu. But with the growing development of regional kingdoms and regional interests, there appears a bifurcation between the guild as it operated in the Kannada speaking areas, and as it functioned in the Tamil region.[21] Within these broad divisions the association appears to have functioned at times in large units.

In Karnataka, from the eleventh century onwards, the Ayyāvoḷe acquired new bases and established several towns as 'Southern Ayyāvoḷe', both under the patronage of the Western Cāḷukyas of Kalyāṇi and the Hoysaḷas of Dvārasamudra. Interestingly, in an inscription of AD 1267 from Dodballapur, the Ayyāvoḷe merchants claim descent from the Cōḷas and Cāḷukyas.[22] The 'Southern Ayyāvoḷe' towns are believed to be named after the Ayyāvoḷe in northern Karnataka.[23] However, most of these towns came up in South Karnataka only after regular interaction between Karnataka and Tamil Nadu was established following Cōḷa inroads and a possible movement of the Tamil merchant organization into the link areas and Karnataka. It would, hence, be tempting to see a connection and argue that these towns represent an expansion of the Tamil Five Hundred into Karnataka.

In Tamil Nadu the Aiññūṟṟuvar (Five Hundred) acquired the character of a composite body of itinerant traders who came from different parts of the Tamil speaking areas. One of the most remarkable inscriptions, from the point of view of its composition, comes from Tirumalai in the Sivaganga taluk of Ramanathapuram district. After the usual *praśasti*, it provides a list of the people who belonged the organization and who met at Tirumalai in the Aiññūṟṟuvar Tirukkāvaṇam of the local Śiva temple. The members hailed from different places and are called by their respective regions, like the Tiśai Āyirattu Aiññūṟṟuvar of Vaḍakaḷavaḷi nāḍu, of Tirukōṭṭiyūr Maṇiyambalam, of Vēmbaṟṟūr, of Malaimaṇḍalam, of Aḷagaimānagaram, and many other places.[24] Terms like Aiññūṟṟuva Bhaṭṭan and names like Aiññūṟṟuvan Inban Devan Ceṭṭi would also indicate the heterogeneous caste composition of this body. The Five Hundred was, thus, a group of people of 'disparate origins associating together for a common purpose' (trade), i.e. of several castes, religions and regions.[25]

The first appearance of the Five Hundred in Tamil Nadu is in the Pudukkottai region towards the close of the ninth century, and their presence here and in the Ramanathapuram district is almost continuously attested to down to the fourteenth century AD. Their sudden appearance in the distant Tamil region of Pudukkottai, after Aihoḷe, may be attributed to the established commercial importance of this region from the beginning of the Christian era, and also to the link that this region provided between the trading emporium of Toṇḍi with the Kaveri Valley and the Vaigai region, the Cōḷa and Pāṇḍya heartlands respectively.[26] There is, indeed, a concentration of the 'Five Hundred' inscriptions in the Pudukkottai and Ramanathapuram districts throughout the period under consideration. In this region, the Five Hundred appears to have interacted with the Koḍumbāḷūr *Maṇigrāmam* and the local *Nagarattār*, some of whom may well have become local representatives of the itinerant merchant organization.

The route that the Five Hundred used to reach Tamil Nadu so early (ninth century–Munisandai) after its foundation in Aihoḷe in Karnataka, is not clearly attested to. It has, however, been suggested[27] that they moved into Tamil Nadu through the Chittoor region and Palar valley southwards, a route that was probably used by the Kuṟumbar tribes, who are still to be seen in the Pudukkottai area. This was the route followed by the invading Rāṣṭrakūṭa armies under Kṛṣṇa III in the tenth century AD. Equal claims to have been the regular route of migration or movement between Karnataka and Tamil Nadu may be made for the Kongu region, i.e. from the Ganga country north of the Kaveri through Kongu into the Kaveri valley and further south. This route is better attested to from very early times through the line of Tamil Brāhmī inscriptions (Pugaḷiyūr, Arachalūr,

Tiruchirapalli and Śittaṇṇavāśal) and the discovery of hoards of Roman coins also marking the same route, apart from the tradition of the Digambara Jaina Migration.[28] However, in both these areas, i.e. Palar Valley and Kongu, the inscriptions of the Aiññūṟṟuvar appear only from the eleventh century AD. A second wave of Jaina influence in the eighth and ninth centuries, under Rāṣṭrakūṭa patronage, is also indicated by a series of Jaina epigraphs, marking a line of sites in the North Arcot, South Arcot, Tiruchirapalli, Pudukkottai, Ramanathapuram, Madurai and Tirunelveli, leading on to South Kerala.[29] These migrations may well have followed ancient and early medieval trade routes linking the different cultural regions of South India.

The spatial and chronological distribution of the Aiññūṟṟuvar inscriptions also makes an interesting study. In the Pudukkottai region, their activities in the ninth to eleventh centuries AD[30] were encouraged by the early and middle Cōḷas and their feudatories, the Irukkuvēḷs of Koḍumbāḷūr. The close matrimonial ties between the Cōḷas and Irukkuvēḷs may well have been inspired by the strategic location of the region, linking areas of commercial importance. A rather close identity of interests between this commercial organization and the Cōḷas may be recognised, not only in the fostering of trade in this region, but also in other regions conquered by the Cōḷas in the eleventh and twelfth centuries AD.

The Five Hundred moved in wherever the Cōḷas stepped in as conquerors. Into the region south and north of the upper Kaveri valley, i.e. the Kongu and Ganga countries respectively, the Aiññūṟṟuvar moved in the wake of the Cōḷa conquests under Rājarāja I and Rājendra I (AD 985–1044). Taḷakkāḍu, north of the Kaveri, and Muḍikoṇḍan (Muḍikoṇḍa-cōḷapuram), south of the Kaveri, marked the two major centres of merchant activity.[31] In Muḍikoṇḍan, the merchants of the 18 *paṭṭaṇas* north of the Kaveri and of the 18 *paṭṭaṇas* south of the Kaveri made huge endowments to the local Viṣṇu temple and exercised control over the temple management.[32] In the eleventh century, Aiyapoḷil Kāṭṭūr and Basinikoṇḍa (Śirāvalli) in the Chingleput and Chittoor districts, respectively became *Eṛivīrappaṭṭaṇas* or protected mercantile towns under special charters from the Cōḷa rulers for the Toṇḍaimaṇḍalam region, also called

Jayankoṇḍacōḷamaṇḍalam.[33] In Sri Lanka, following the Cōḷa conquests of the eleventh century AD, the Five Hundred became active in the organized commerce and movement of trade in the northern parts, i.e. Rājaraṭṭha, with Polonnaruwa as an important centre.[34] After the political unification of Vengi with the Cōḷa kingdom under Kulōttunga I (accession AD 1070) the Five Hundred are seen as far north as Visakhapattinam (Kulōttungacōḷan paṭṭiṇam) and other coastal towns upto Draksharama in the Ganjam district of Orissa.[35] Under the Cōḷa royal patronage, Tamil traders moved more frequently into the Andhra region and *Cōḷa maṇḍalamuna Vyāpāri* are referred to in a few interior trade centres, while Ghantasala or Cōḷapāṇḍiyan paṭṭiṇam on the coast became an important emporium of trade.[36] Trade, in fact, was much more directly regulated under the middle Cōḷas, Rājarāja I to Kulōttunga I (AD 985-1118), whose interest in developing the Cōḷa port of Nāgapaṭṭiṇam is well known. Their trade missions to China, maritime expeditions to Śrīvijaya (1025) and abolition of tolls by Kulōttunga I,[37] undoubtedly encouraged the movement of itinerant traders, and helped in establishing trade links with China. Their continuing interest in foreign trade is indicated by the Canton inscription of Kulōttunga I's reign, detailing attempts made to establish a trading presence at that port.[38]

In the heart of the Cōḷa kingdom, i.e. the Kaveri delta, the Five Hundred began its activity in the tenth century in Tiruppuṛambiyam, Tiruviḍaimarudūr and various other centres such as Tiruvēḷvikkuḍi, Tirunaḷḷāṛu, Tiruccengōḍu, Kōyil Tēvarāyanpēṭṭai and Tiruccoṛṛutturai. They are seen as far south as Ukkirankōṭṭai (Karavandapuram), a fortified town in the Tirunelveli district in the same period. In the middle Cōḷa period, they fanned out into Toṇḍaimaṇḍalam, Kongu Nāḍu and Pāṇḍināḍu, the most notable example in the Pāṇḍya region being the *Eṛivīrappaṭṭaṇa* at Tiruvālīśvaram in the Ambasamudram taluk (the newly developed Muḷḷi nāḍu) of the Tirunelveli district, with direct access to South Kerala through the Aramboli pass, and also control over the southern Pāṇḍya region of the Tamraparni.[39]

The *Eṛivīrappaṭṭaṇas* of this period are seen coming up mainly in the trade routes, and even in the region of settled agriculture, like the wet zone of Tamraparni.[40] The participation of local traders and *nagaram* members in itinerant trade reached an unprecedented degree and, hence, a series of settlements named after the Aiññūṟṟuvar or Valañjīyar were established as semi-permanent or permanent residential quarters in various centres.[41] It must, however, be pointed out that in the capitals of Tañjāvūr and Gangaikoṇḍa Cōḷapuram and the imperial port city of Nāgappaṭṭiṇam, and even in Kāñcīpuram and Māmallapuram, the *mānagarams* or local *nagarams* wielded greater influence, while the Five Hundred and other merchant groups were more or less confined to the routes linking all other outlying regions (peripheral areas) with the Cōḷa heartland, and to the commercially important areas like Pudukkottai and Ramanathapuram districts, and Kongu nāḍu, i.e. Salem, Erode (Periyar) and Coimbatore districts.

In the period of the later Cōḷas (twelfth and thirteenth centuries) and the Pāṇḍyas of the thirteenth and fourteenth centuries, we notice a phenomenal increase in the activities of the Five Hundred, with a clear tendency to expand its sphere of influence and to show less reliance on royal support and patronage, although many of the guild inscriptions are still dated in the reign periods of the late Cōḷa and Pāṇḍya rulers. We have rather impressive evidence that in most centres of distribution and emporia the Five Hundred acted jointly with other organized groups like the *Cittiramēḷi* or *Padineṇ Viṣaya* organization in the levy of *maganmai* and *paṭṭaṇappagudi* (tolls and shares or cesses of towns). In the elaborate *praśastis* of these inscriptions mentioning the two organizations, the *Cittiramēḷi* is given the pride of place, followed by the Five Hundred. Notable among these are the records from Tirumalai and Pirānmalai in Ramanathapuram district and Anbil, Koṟṟamangalam, Tuvarankuṟicci and Kōvilpaṭṭi in Tiruchirapalli district.[42] Here they exercised their joint authority to levy and grant cesses and tolls to the local temples on merchandise passing through the region. The institutionalization of the coming together of several organizations and their exercising joint authority is a conspicuous feature of the thirteenth and early fourteenth centuries AD. However, it would appear that merchant bodies, particularly the Five Hundred, had on no occasion the authority to levy and grant such tolls, except in conjunction with the *Cittira-meḷi* or the *Padineṇ Viṣaya*,[43] which refer to organizations of agriculturists and local elite groups controlling production of agricultural and other goods. Presumably, in the assignment of brokerage and monopoly to individuals or groups of traders on certain items of trade, the Five Hundred exercised its authority jointly with the local *nāḍu*, *nagaram* members and the larger agricultural organization of the 18 *Viṣaya* or *Cittiramēḷi*.[44]

The *Cittiramēḷi Periya nāḍu* was an organization of agriculturists, whose inscriptions appear in important trade and urban centres. It has been described as an agricultural guild by K.G. Krishnan, who has analysed the evidence of inscriptions, not only from Tamil Nadu, but also from Karnataka and Andhra,[45] where the *Cittiramēḷi* appears from about twelfth century AD. The *Okkalu* of Karnataka, it is suggested, was a similar organization.[46] The evidence on the *Okkalu*, however, does not point to an organization of the *Cittiramēḷi* type, but more to a group of agriculturists in specific localities.

Dominant agricultural organizations jointly mentioned in the 'guild' inscriptions, probably had commercial transactions with the Five Hundred, exchanging agricultural products for exotic and nonagricultural items. The growth in the power of landowning classes is a marked development of the twelfth century AD, both in South India and Sri Lanka. The links that developed between the merchant guild and associations of agriculturists were mainly due to the increase in the importance of agricultural commodities in trade from the twelfth century onwards. The urban development of this period, and the growing food needs of urban settlements, enhanced the influence of the agricultural classes, for such needs could be satisfied only by powerful peasant groups, who could mobilise grain and other products for supply to itinerant traders through the local markets.

In the late thirteenth and early fourteenth centuries, particularly under the Pāṇḍyas, the joint presence of the weavers with trading communities like the Five Hundred also suggests a closer link between textile production and trade, and a certain legitimacy derived from the presence of the crafts groups. It would appear that weavers gradually took to trading in textiles, or worked for the itinerant merchant body by organizing production for a wider market. At this point, references to *Cīlai* Ceṭṭis in the northern Tamil region (Kāñcīpuram) and in Kongu (Dharmapuri) may be noticed in the thirteenth and fourteenth century inscriptions.[47] The largest craft organization which came to be set up by the fourteenth century AD was that of the weavers, whose *Mahānāḍu* organization had its headquarters in Kāñcīpuram, the most ancient textile centre of South India.[48] The *Sāliyas* and *Kaikkōḷas*, two weaver communities of South India, came to be classified among the Right and Left Hand caste division,[49] which arose in Tamil Nadu in the twelfth century AD as a paradigmatic division, to determine the social and caste status of the artisans and craftsmen apart from new ethnic and economic groups. Craft groups other than the weavers also came to be organized largely under this division. With the urbanization of the twelfth and thirteenth centuries, urban social stratification invariably tended to use the three categories of *brāhmaṇa*, *Vēḷāḷa* and the Right and Left Hand castes. With the increase in organized commerce and itinerant trade and the demand for textiles and other products, the artisan communities also obtained special privileges, either from local chiefs or temple authorities, and sometimes also through the good offices of the merchant organizations.

In a slightly different context, the dependence of the craftsmen on the merchant organizations is underlined, as seen in the role of the merchants providing asylum to the craftsmen in Erode as early as the eleventh century AD.[50] The merchant body sometimes framed rules for the *Valangai* (Right Hand) and *Iḍangai* (Left Hand), or granted them privileges, emphasising the interdependence of these two sections of the commercial world, especially in areas where the merchants assumed control and management of temples and acted as protectors and patrons of artisanal groups, as in the Kongu region. The artisan community is seen to be coming into its own after the twelfth century AD, i.e. in the late Cōḷa and Pāṇḍya periods. In the predominantly agrarian set-up of Tamil Nadu, the artisans were more often attached to the locality, i.e. to the temple, the land-owning *brāhmaṇas* and *Vēḷāḷas* through inter-dependent land tenures. However, changes in the agrarian organization, in the pattern of land ownership and the introduction of an economy based on inter-regional trade, the demand for their services both by local landed groups and by the itinerant merchant organizations, acquired for them certain concessions and privileges meant to improve their social position. In the late twelfth century, the *anuloma rathakāras* in Puñjai had special privileges conferred on them.[51] The artisan community became participants in the gift-making processes, as seen in the thirteenth century inscriptions from Noḍiyūr (Tanjavur district) where the *Kanmāḷas* of several places met and agreed to assign the tithe collected from among themselves to the local temple, and to get differences settled jointly with the temple trustees and local chief.[52]

Craft production was perhaps more intensive in the Kongu region, where the twelfth to sixteenth century inscriptions refer to large-scale artisan activity and their participation in important civic duties, for which special privileges were conferred on them. Privileges were collectively granted to the *Kanmāḷar* communities in Kāñcikkūval nāḍu (thirteenth century), Vengāla nāḍu (thirteenth century), Kāngēya nāḍu and Pūnduṛai nāḍu (fourteenth century), under the Kongu Cōḷas and Kongu Pāṇḍyas.[53] Agreements among artisan communities for various purposes also became common during this period.

Thus, organized commerce by *Nagarams*, *maṇigrāmam* and long-distance trade through itinerant merchant bodies, accelerated the process of urban development, crafts organization, a tripartite social stratification in an urban context in multi-temple centres and single large temple centres, some of which became pilgrimage centres, and also in administrative centres. Many of these newly emerging socio-economic groups were accommodated in the *tirumaḍai viḷāgam* of the temple centres.[54]

The dominant role of the Five Hundred in inter-regional trade and commerce in South India is established beyond doubt by the continuous occurrence of guild records in the three major regions, i.e. Tamil Nadu, Karnataka and Andhra Pradesh. Furthermore, their participation in overseas trade is also attested to by the presence of guild inscriptions in northern Sri Lanka, Siam (South Ṭhailand), Sumatra and Burma.[55] One of these inscriptions, which is found in Barus (Loboe Toewa), Sumatra, is particularly significant, as it refers to Barus as Varōca in Tamil, and describes it as Mātangari Vallava Deśi Uyyakkoṇḍa Paṭṭiṇam and Vēḷāpuram as a part of that *paṭṭiṇam*, in which the Five Hundred made arrangements in AD 1088–89, for a regular income or gift in gold to the local chiefs of merchants, to be paid by the *Marakkala nāyakan* and others from South India who came to that port.[56] This inscription points to the importance of the Southeastern trade in the eleventh century, in which the Five Hundred not only played a dominant role, but even had control of port towns.

The overseas trade links and the itinerant traders' role in establishing these links are attested to by the long lists of expensive imported commodities given in their inscriptions. Notable among them are the Shikarpur inscription in the Shimoga district of Karnataka,[57] and the Pirānmalai inscriptions in the Ramanathapuram district of Tamil Nadu.[58] The Shikarpur inscription talks of the merchants as travelling by land routes, water routes, covering six continents, with superior elephants, well-bred horses, large sapphires, moonstones, pearls, rubies, diamonds, lapis lazuli, onyx, topaz, carbuncles, bdellium, sandal, camphor, musk, saffron . . . selling wholesale or hawking about on their shoulders etc. Through this trade the royal treasury was filled with gold and the royal family encouraged this trade by being the greatest consumers of luxury items. The imported items mentioned in the famous Pirānmalai inscription are of a different kind, like aloeswood (*akhil*), sandalwood, silk, rosewater, camphor oil and perfume, apart from elephants and horses, which are common in most inscriptions of South India. Aloeswood, camphor, sandalwood, horses (and perhaps even camels?) are mentioned in the Kōvilpaṭṭi inscription of about AD 1305.[59] Most of these items came from Southeast Asia, except horses which came from Arabia. Significantly, the Barus inscription referring to the Five Hundred and dated in AD 1088–89 comes from the heart of the camphor growing area of Sumatra.[60]

Silk may have come from China, although whether it reached the Cōḷa-Pāṇḍya coast is not clear. Elephants from Burma and horses from Arabia came both into the ports of the Western coast and into Kāyal paṭṭiṇam on the Pāṇḍya coast, and rosewater from West Asia. South India was both on the transit trade and terminal trade from West Asia to China, through Sri Lanka and Southeast Asia. Toṇḍi and Kulaśekharappaṭṭiṇam were the ports at which many of the items were unloaded and distributed. An interesting record from Toṇḍi dated in AD 1269, registers an agreement by the *Añjuvaṇṇam*, *Maṇigrāmam*, *Sāmanta-Paṇḍasālis* (probably stockists of commodities at the port) and others residing there, to levy certain taxes on commodities sold and purchased at the port, in order to meet the rebuilding expenses of the *maṇḍapa* of the local Śiva temple.[61] Spices, pepper in particular, and incense, were some of the other important items meant both for local consumption and onward trade. The temples and *maṭhas* or monasteries of the Tamil region were, next to the royal family, the greatest consumers of most of the articles mentioned above.

Many other commodities mentioned in the Pirānmalai and other Tamil inscriptions, as well as the Chintapalle inscription of about AD 1240 from Andhra,[62] refer to agricultural products like paddy, sesame, pulses, betel-nuts and leaves, salt and raw materials like cotton. Metals like copper, zinc, lead and iron also figure among the items of trade. In fact, the only manufactured good requiring technological skill and organized production was textile (local cloth), and it is for South Indian textiles that there was an ever-growing demand. Hence, the weaver community gradually acquired a position of great social and economic importance. This is attested to by the references to *Kaikkōḷas* and *Sāliya Nagarattār*, who not only controlled production and marketing of cloth, but participated in temple services, donations, conduct of festivals, administration and management.[63] There is also a noticeable change in the pattern of land ownership, both weavers and merchants becoming important land-owning communities and wielding considerable influence in the localities where they hailed from.

If the presence of the guild inscriptions with their *praśastis* and lists of items of trade may be taken as a direct indication of distribution centres, most of them may be located in the Pudukkottai, Ramanathapuram districts and along the trade routes where *Eṛivīrappaṭṭaṇas* were established. The guild inscriptions often refer to the 18 *paṭṭaṇas*, 32 *Vēḷā* (or *Vēḷār*) *purams*, 64 *Kaḍigai-t-tāvaḷams* from where the traders came.[64] Though it would be difficult to identify and locate all of them, it is quite likely that some of the major centres with guild inscriptions and the ports constantly used by traders are included among them, such as Vañcimānagaram (Karūr), Koḍumbāḷūr, Kulaśekharappaṭṭiṇam, Aḷagaimāngaram, Nārttāmalai, Toṇḍi and Pirānmalai. There also emerged a series of coastal towns starting from Tiruppālaivanam (Pulicat), the northernmost point in Tamil Nadu, down to Koṟkai and Kāyal in the mouth of the Tamraparni, marking a coastal route with halting stations and distribution points used by the itinerant traders. Kovalam, Sadras and Tranquebar were some of these towns which emerged into prominence in the thirteenth and fourteenth centuries AD.[65]

Organized commerce in this period followed exchange by barter and also the use of money, although monetization in medieval South India, at least down to the fourteenth century AD, was mostly on a low key, particularly in Tamil Nadu. The Vijayanagar period saw many important changes, including greater monetization and emergence of individual traders and master craftsmen, which indirectly affected itinerant trading communities and their *Samayam* or organization.

The towns of Tamil Nadu, including the ones with guild activities, differed in their administrative organization from those of Karnataka. The latter had their *paṭṭaṇasvāmis*, who were heads of towns and who presided over or participated in the meetings of the merchant bodies and other local groups[66] (Shikarpur). No such 'lords' of towns are known to have presided over the *nagarams* or market centres or towns with guild inscriptions in Tamil Nadu. There are, however, references to *paṭṭaṇasvāmi*, who along with members of the *Padineṇ Viṣaya*, levied cesses on merchandise as in Pirānmalai.[67] The *nagarams* of Tamil Nadu were administered by the *nagaram* members with the help of accountants (*nagarakkaṇakku*) and other employees, the market governed by a specific set of rules and regulations and maintained through cesses and levies like *angāḍippāṭṭam*.[68] The merchant bodies were subject to the common rules framed by the *nāḍu*, *nagaram*, *padineṇbhūmi* and *cittiramēḷi* organizations, acting jointly in the form of an institutionalized forum, exercising authority through levying cesses and tolls and controlling the distribution of goods.

Localized groups like *Maṇigrāmam* and *Nagaram* were powerful bodies, which diversified their activities by marketing special items, as for example by forming sub-*nagarams* like the *vāṇiya nagaram*, *Śankarappāḍi nagaram*, *sāliya nagaram* and *śāttum pariśaṭṭa nagaram* dealing in oil and cloth respectively at various centres like Vālikaṇḍapuram, Śēngālipuram, Tirukkōyilūr and other places.[69] The *Pāraganagaram* or sea-faring merchants were active in the region of Salem (Puḷḷūr) even as early as the early Cōḷa period.[70] Kudirai Ceṭṭis from Malaimaṇḍalam or Kerala were horse dealers, who catered to the needs of the Cōḷa kingdom from the ninth to the thirteenth centuries.[71]

The *Vāṇiya nagaram* organized itself into a supra-local body called the *Vāṇiya nagaram* of several regions or *Padineṇ Viṣaya*,[72] somewhat like the *Telikis* of Andhra. Individual traders sometimes used the title of Cakravarti, indicating the emergence of merchant princes, as seen in the thirteenth and fourteenth century inscriptions of Muṭṭam (in Pērūr, Coimbatore) and Śivāyam or Ratnagiri (ancient Tiruvāṭpōkki) in the Tiruchirapalli district. Among the signatories to the Pirānmalai guild inscription, mention is made of a *Samaya Cakravarti*.[73] Political stability disappeared with the decline of Cōḷa power in the beginning of the thirteenth century AD. References to *Vīradaḷam* and *Sūradaḷam* in the guild inscriptions of this period[74] probably indicate the usurpation of authority by powerful merchants and local chiefs, taking advantage of the declining Cōḷa power and the relatively weaker Pāṇḍya power of the thirteenth and fourteenth centuries, in order to protect themselves and their newly gained wealth and status from other rivals for power and position. At any rate, the fourteenth century would seem to mark the end of the powerful merchant organizations in Tamil Nadu, although a temporary revival was brought about under Vijayanagar in Karnataka and Andhra regions.

References

1. M. Abraham, 'A Medieval Merchant Guild of South India', *Studies in History*, 1982, vol. IV, no. 1, 1. For the Karimi *see also* M. Abraham, *Two Medieval Merchant Guilds of South India*, Delhi,

1988, 152, 176. A curious and untenable derivation has been made of the term Karimi from *Kāryam*, on the wrong assumption that *Kāryam* (affairs or work) is a Tamil word, whereas, in fact, it is of Sanskrit origin and adopted in all the regional languages of India, including Tamil. *See* Philip D. Curtin, *Cross-Cultural Trade in World History*, Cambridge University Press, 1984, 115.

2. K. Indrapala, 'Some Medieval Mercantile Communities of South India and Ceylon', *Journal of Tamil Studies*, Oct. 1970, vol. II, no. 2, 31.
3. Ibid., 32.
4. Ibid., 37–8.
5. *Cittiramēḷi* means the beautiful plough, which was the emblem of this organization.
6. South Indian Inscriptions (hereafter *SII*) vol. VIII, no. 442 (Pirānmalai).
7. Tirumalai Inscriptions No. 10 of 1924 in *Annual Report on South Indian Epigraphy*, 1923–4 (hereafter *ARE*).
8. *SII*, XIII, no. 28 (Tiruveḷḷaṛai); 283 of *ARE*, 1964–5 (Kōvilpaṭṭi); *SII*, IV, no. 147 (Salem).
9. M.G.S. Narayanan, *Cultural Symbiosis in Kerala*, 4 and 29. Here the *Añjuvaṇṇam* is taken to be an organization of Jewish traders.
10. Visakhappattinam inscription–*SII*, X, no. 651. *See also* K. Sundaram, *Studies in Economic and Social Conditions in Medieval Andhra*, Madras, 1968, 94; Tīttāṇḍatānapuram (Toṇḍi) inscription–598 of 1926, *ARE*, 1926-7.
11. In the Kanara districts, a merchant body called the *Hanjamāna* or *Hanjumanna* was active from about the fourteenth century AD. Was it the same as *Añjuvaṇṇam*? Could *Añjuvaṇṇam* and *Hanjumanna* be derived from *Anjuman*?–Kaikini inscription (South Kanara), *Annual Report on Kannada Research in Bombay Province*, 1939–40, no. 38. *See also* K.V. Ramesh, *History of South Kanara*, Dharwar, 1970, 253, where the author suggests that *Hanjamāna* represented Arab-Persian merchants.
12. *See* Kenneth R. Hall, *Trade and Statecraft in the Age of the Colas*, New Delhi, 1980, chapter 5.
13. *Nagarattār* is the designation of the Tamil trading community, now also known as the Nāṭṭukkōṭṭai Cheṭṭiārs, in the Ramanathapuram and Pudukkottai districts.
14. Aihoḷe Inscriptions–*Indian Antiquary* (*IA*), VIII, LIX; *IA*, VI, 138 f.n. B.K. 289 of *ARE*, 1927–8.
15. Abraham, 'A Medieval Merchant Guild', 6; *Two Medieval Merchant Guilds*, chapter II.

16. Hall, *Trade and Statecraft*, 151.
17. V. Manickam, 'Some Trade Guild Epigraphs and Sculpture', *Journal of the Institute of Asian Studies*, 145-50. In the guild inscriptions of Sri Lanka, the guild members are closely associated with the *Vēḷaikkārar*, and the *Valañjīyar* are often referred to as the ancestors/elders (*mūtātaiyar*) of the *Vēḷaikkārar*, who must have moved into Sri Lanka along with the mercantile community. *See* Indrapala, 'Mercantile Communities', 33.
18. K.R. Venkatarama Aiyar, 'Medieval Trade, Craft and Merchant Guilds in South India', *Journal of Indian History*, 1947, xxv, part 1, 268-80; Indrapala, 'Mercantile Communities', 31-2.
19. *See* Chapter 4, Table VI, in this volume.
20. Abraham, *Two Medieval Merchant Guilds*, chapter II, 41ff.
21. Abraham, 'A Medieval Merchant Guild', 4.
22. 'Cōḷa Kulānvitaram Cāḷukyānvayarum', see *Epigraphia Carnatica*, IX, Dodballapur, 31.
23. *See* Indrapala, 'Mercantile Communities', 26.
24. No. 10 of 1924. Tirumalai inscription dated AD 1233. The other groups mentioned are Pāṇḍimaṇḍala Perunīrāvi Tiśai Āyirattu Aiññūṟruvar, Kōḷikkuṟicci Kaḍittavuia Tiśai Āyirattu Aiññūṟruvar, etc.
25. That the members came from different castes, religions and regions is indicated not only by the Tamil inscriptions, but also by the Kannada and Telugu inscriptions of Karnataka and Andhra–*See* Abraham, *Two Medieval Merchant Guilds*, chapter III.
26. The early Brāhmī inscriptions in Śittaṉṉavāśal and the hoards of Roman coins datable to the early centuries before and after the beginning of the Christian era, indicate an early trade route through this region. *See* Champakalakshmi, 'South India', in A. Ghosh (ed.), *Jaina Art and Architecture*, vol. I, Bharatiya Jnanpith, 1974, chapter 9; Mortimer Wheeler, 'Arikamedu: An Indo-Roman Trading Station on the East Coast of India', *Ancient India*, July 1946, no. 2, 118-21.
27. Abraham, 'A Medieval Merchant Guild', 7-9.
28. P.B. Desai, *Jainism in South India*, Sholapur, 1957, 25-7.
29. Champakalakshmi, 'Kuṟaṇḍi Tirukkāṭṭāmpaḷḷi, An Ancient Jaina Monastery of Tamil Nadu', in *Studies in Indian Epigraphy*, 1975, vol. 2, 89.
30. Munisandai inscription, Pudukkottai State Inscriptions (*PSI*), no. 61; Ceṭṭippaṭṭi inscription, *PSI*, no. 1083.
31. *See* Chapter 4 in this volume, 203.
32. Muḍikoṇḍān Inscription, 2 of 1910, *ARE*, 1909-10.

33. Kāṭṭūr Inscription, 256 of 1912, *ARE*, 1912-13 and Basinikoṇḍa, 342 of 1912, *ARE*, 1912-13.
34. Indrapala, 'Mercantile Communities', 32-3; Abraham, 'A Medieval Merchant Guild', 12-14.
35. Sundaram, *Economic and Social Conditions*, 93-6.
36. Ibid., 92-5.
37. K.A. Nilakanta Sastri, *The Cōḻas*, Madras, 1975, reprint, 331.
38. Abraham, 'A Medieval Merchant Guild', 14; also *Two Medieval Merchant Guilds*, 143.
39. *See* Chapter 4, Table IV, 22 and Table VI.
40. Ibid., 000.
41. Ibid., Table V, no. 25; 150 of *ARE*, 1935-6.
42. Tirumalai–10 of 1924; Pirānmalai–*SII*, VIII, 442; Korramangalam–650 of 1962-3; Tuvarankuṟicci–296 of 1964-5; Kōvilpaṭṭi–286 of 1964-5.
43. *See* Chapter 4, Table VI.
44. *PSI*. no. 125; 103 of *ARE*–1932-3.
45. K.G. Krishnan, 'Chittiramēḻip-periyanāḍu–An Agricultural Guild of Medieval Tamil Nadu', *Journal of the Madras University*, Jan. 1982, reprint, vol. LIV, no. 1.
46. Abraham, 'A Medieval Merchant Guild', 21.
47. 165 of *ARE*, 1968-9; *SII*, VII, 583.
48. Vijaya Ramaswamy, *Textiles and Weavers in Medieval South India*, New Delhi, 1985, 38-9.
49. Ibid., 55, 58-9 and 107-8.
50. Erode Inscription–215 of *ARE*, 1976-7.
51. Puñjai Inscription–198 of 1925 (*ARE*, 1925-6).
52. Noḍiyūr Inscription–201 of *ARE*, 1932-3.
53. 186 of 1911 (*ARE*, 1911-12); *SII*, III, 25; 227 of *ARE*, 1967-8.
54. *SII*, VI, 258 (Maṇimangalam); *SII*, XII, 154 (Chidambaram).
55. *See* Indrapala, 'South Indian Mercantile Communities in Ceylon, 950-1250', *The Ceylon Journal of Historical and Social Studies*, July-Dec. 1971, n.s., vol. I, no. 2; K.A. Nilakanta Sastri, 'Takua Pa and its Tamil Inscriptions', *Journal of the Malaya Branch of the Royal Asiatic Society*, 1949, XXII, part 1, 25-30; Nilakanta Sastri, 'A Tamil Merchant Guild in Sumatra', *TBG* deel. LXXII, 1932, 314-27. (Both these articles are reprinted in Nilakanta Sastri, *South India and Southeast Asia*, Mysore, 1978, 172-7 and 236-47); *Epigraphia Indica*, VIII, 197ff.
56. Y. Subbarayalu, 'Sumatrāvil Tamiḻ-k-kalveṭṭugaḷ', in *Āvaṇam* (Journal of the Tamil Nadu Archaeological Society), Jan. 1994, 116-24.

57. Shikarpur Inscription, *Epigraphia Carnatica*, vol. VII, no. 118.
58. *SII*, VIII, no. 442.
59. 286 of *ARE*, 1964-5.
60. M. Abraham, 'A Medieval Merchant Guild', 4 and 6; also *Two Medieval Merchant Guilds*, 160.
61. Tīttāṇḍatānapuram (Toṇḍi) Inscription–598 of 1926, *ARE*, 1926-7.
62. 277 of *ARE*, 1934-5.
63. 196 of *ARE*, 1912, *SII*, VI, 252 and 257; *see also* Ramaswamy, *Textiles and Weavers*, 41-6 and 54-5.
64. E.g. 154 of 1903; *SII*, vol. VIII, no. 442.
65. *See* Chapter 4, Table VII.
66. Indrapala, 'Mercantile Communities', 29-30; G.R. Kuppuswami, *Economic Conditions in Karnataka* (AD 973-1336), Dharwar, 1975, 101, 113; *Epigraphia Carnatica*, VII, no. 94.
67. *SII*, VII, 442.
68. Hall, *Trade and Statecraft*, 58-60.
69. Vālikaṇḍapuram–309 of *ARE*, 1964-5 (Śankarappāḍi); Tiruppangili–163 of *ARE*, 1938-9 (*Vāṇiya Nagaram*); Sēngālipuram, 23 and 30 of 1917 (*ARE*, 1916-17); (*Śāttum Pariśaṭṭa Nagaram*); Tirukkōyilūr–*SII*, VII, 901 (*Sālika Nagaram*).
70. Puḷḷūr Inscriptions–325 and 372 of 1939-40.
71. *See* Chapter 6, 331.
72. Vālikaṇḍapuram Inscription–264 of *ARE*, 1943-4; Vengālam Inscription–141 of *ARE*, 1974-5.
73. Pirānmalai Inscription–*SII*, VIII, 442. Also in Ikkarai–Boḷuvāmpaṭṭi Inscription–415 and 418 of 1958-9; Śivāyam Inscription–48 of 1913, *ARE*, 1912-13.
74. For *Sūradaḷam see* Vālikaṇḍapuram Inscription, 264 of *ARE*, 1943-4. For *Vīradaḷam see* Vaḷaramānikkam Inscription–Inscriptions of the Pudukkottai State (*IPS*), 1022.

6

Imperial Power and Urban Growth Kuḍamūkku-Paḻaiyāṟai, the Twin Cities of the Cōḻas

Problems of interpretation of epigraphic records, the main source for the study of ancient and medieval South Indian history, and the inadequacy of statistical data, have generally deterred scholars from reconstructing the history of urban development, despite their interest in the evolution of temple complexes, peasant settlements and changes in the socio-economic structure. However, epigraphic sources, when supplemented with traditional and legendary accounts and archaeological data, provide fairly useful, though not exhaustive, information about the nature and evolution of urban centres and the various factors contributing to the urbanization process in the period from the seventh to the thirteenth centuries AD, especially for the areas under the administration of the Cōḻas. This essay is an attempt to study the twin-city of Kuḍamūkku-Paḻaiyāṟai, which developed as an urban centre, mainly during the Cōḻa period in the Cōḻa heartland.

Kuḍamūkku (Map 10-1), alternately known as Kuḍandai, is first mentioned as Kuḍandai in the Sangam works of the first three centuries of the Christian era, and represents one of the earliest Cōḻa settlements in the delta region of the Kaveri valley. It came to be known as Kumbhakonam from the fourteenth century AD,[1] when a general tendency to Sanskritize all ancient Tamil place-names evidently led to the change from Kuḍamūkku into Kumbhakonam.

Paḻaiyāṟai (Map 10-13), the second part of this urban complex, dates from the period of the Śaiva-Vaiṣṇava religious development of the seventh to ninth centuries AD.[2] The name Paḻaiyāṟai has two components—Paḻaiya + āṟai (= āṟṟūr), meaning 'an old settlement on the banks of a river.' It was also known as

Nandipuram, Āyirattḷi, Muḍikoṇḍacōḷapuram and Āhavamallakulakālapuram at various points of time.

The geographical location of both Kuḍamūkku and Paḷaiyāṟai contributed in a large measure to their early development into a rich source of revenue for the Cōḷas. Situated between the Kaveri and the Ariśilāṟu (now called Araśalāṟu), Kuḍamūkku occupies a central position in the most fertile part of the delta region, where the distributaries are close to one another. South of Kuḍamūkku, on either banks of the Tirumalarājan and Muḍikoṇḍān rivers, the city of Paḷaiyāṟai grew around the palace of the imperial Cōḷas.

The Ariśilāṟu, one of the major distributaries of this river system, is perhaps also the oldest. Among the others, the Vīracōḷanāṟu, running north of Kuḍamūkku, apparently owes its origin to Parāntaka I (*c.* AD 907–55), one of whose titles was Vīracōḷa. The Muḍikoṇḍān may be dated from the period of Rājēndra I, who was also known as Muḍikoṇḍacōḷa, a title which provided Paḷaiyāṟai with the alternate name of Muḍikoṇḍacōḷapuram. The Tirumalarājan also seems to have come into existence in the imperial Cōḷa period, for it flows through Nandanmēḍu, an ancient urn-burial and Black-and-Red Ware site near Paḷaiyāṟai. The Veṭṭāṟu and Vaḍavāṟu, running south of this urban complex, may also be dated back to the same period, although no clear evidence of their origins can be found. The existence of a series of canals (*vāykkāl*)[3] in this region would further point to the efforts of the Cōḷas to build and maintain a fairly good irrigation network in this area as well as in other parts of Cōḷamaṇḍalam. At the same time, it may be noted that the maintenance of small canals was often the concern of the local assemblies like the *Sabhā* and *Ūr* and also the *Mūlapariṣad* looking after temple administration.

Kuḍamūkku in the Pre-Imperial Cōḷa Period

The antiquity of Kuḍamūkku is indicated by the early Sangam references to Kuḍandai (and also Kuḍandaivāyil or Kuḍavāyil),[4] where the Koṟṟa Cōḷas kept their treasure strongly guarded. The Cōḷa king Ceṅgaṇān kept his Cēra rival Kaṇakkāl Irumpoṟai imprisoned in Kuḍavāyiṟ-Kōṭṭam,[5] pointing to Kuḍandai as a

Cōḷa stronghold from the Sangam period. Besides Kuḍandai, several other settlements must have emerged before the beginning of the Christian era, for the Sangam literary descriptions of the Cōḷa country clearly attest to the early colonization of the Kaveri valley, 'marked by rows of settlements of numerous clans, who lived amicably with one another'.[6] This is further substantiated by archaeological evidence coming from the Megalithic urn-burial site of Nandanmēḍu,[7] where the urn-burials and Black-and-Red Ware occur in the exposed sections of the Tirumalarājan river. Black-and-Red Ware is also found in the lower levels of Sōḻamāḷigai (Map 3-16), the site of the old Cōḷa palace. The Sangam settlements would seem to represent the end phases of the Megalithic culture in Tamil Nadu and the beginnings of the earliest well-attested pastoral-cum-peasant habitations, as shown by the uniformity with which Black-and-Red pottery occurs in the lowermost levels of every site so far excavated in Tamil Nadu.[8]

Very little is known about Kuḍandai and its environs in the post-Sangam period (the fourth to seventh centuries AD). A general political vacuum set in after the Sangam Cōḷas were defeated by a 'tribe' or 'clan' called the Kaḷabhras who were, from various literary and epigraphic descriptions, a non-orthodox people with strong predilections towards the Buddhist and Jain religions.[9] The Cōḷas remained in obscurity till their re-emergence to power in the middle of the ninth century AD. The importance of the Kuḍamūkku region as a resource base, was, however, so great that the Pallavas of Kāñcīpuram and the Pāṇḍyas of Madurai, the leading powers of the period between the seventh and ninth centuries, were drawn into a series of major struggles for its dominance. Some of the important battles between the two powers were fought on the banks of the Ariśilāṟu (or Aricit)[10] and near Kuḍamūkku itself.[11] The Pallava Nandivarman II was besieged by his Cōḷa-Pāṇḍya opponents at Nandipuram (Map 10-18—a part of Paḻaiyāṟai city), from where he was released after a serious struggle by his general Udayacandra.[12] Nandivarman III (*c.* AD 846–69) is described as the conqueror of Paḻaiyāṟai, where the 'six armies' fell in a mighty onslaught.[13] Tiruppuṟambiyam, north of Kuḍamūkku (Map 10-7), was the battlefield which signalled the decline of the Pallavas and Pāṇḍyas and the rise of the Cōḷas under Aditya I (*c.* AD 871-907).[14]

It has often been suggested that the Cōḷas of this period were the subordinates of the Pallavas and Pāṇḍyas alternately,[15] consequent upon the nature and results of the Pallava-Pāṇḍya conflicts for a hold over this region. It may be further suggested that the Kuḍamūkku region formed the nucleus of the rising power of the Vijayālaya line of Cōḷas. There can be little doubt that the descendants of the Sangam Cōḷas acquired their main resources from this area, which continued to be their stronghold even after the decline of Uṟaiyūr and Kāvērippūmpaṭṭiṉam. The choice of the imperial Cōḷas fell on Tañjāvūr (Tanjore, Map 10) as their new capital, and the capture of Tañjāvūr by Vijayālaya from the Muttaraiyar chieftains[16] was certainly not without significance, considering the geographical situation of the new capital. Located on the south bank of the Vaḍavāṟu, Tañjāvūr commanded access to the delta region, thus affording protection to the perennial resource base of the Cōḷas, represented by the Kuḍamūkku-Paḻaiyāṟai region.

The resource potential of this region is indicated not merely by the numerous peasant settlements dating from the Sangam period, but also by the tendency of all early *brahmadeyas* to be clustered together and to proliferate rapidly in this area in the period between the seventh and ninth centuries. Two of these early *brahmadeyas* known as Simhaviṣṇu-caturvēdimangalam (Kañcanūr) and Mahendramangalam,[17] may be dated back to the period of the early Pallavas, i.e. Simhaviṣṇu (*c.* AD 550-90) and Mahendravarman I (*c.* AD 590-630). One more *brahmadeya* was created in the period of Nandivarman II Pallavamalla (*c.* AD 731-96), viz., Dayāmukhamangalam near Taṇḍantōṭṭam (Map 10-8)[18] located immediately south-east of Kuḍamūkku. A few towns also came into existence by the ninth century AD. Kumaramārttāṇḍapuram near Tirunāgēśvaram (Map 10-2) was a *nagaram* (town), which probably owed its existence to Nandivarman III, one of whose titles was Kumaramārttāṇḍa.[19] Tiraimūr, after which the Tiraimūr nāḍu was evidently named, was a *nagaram* of considerable importance,[20] and seems to have been a part of a larger settlement, including Tiruviḍaimarudūr (Map 10-6), located about five miles east-north-east of Kuḍamūkku.

The Kumbhakonam taluk had twenty-five out of a total of ninety-three *brahmadeyas* in the Tanjavur district, the highest number for a single taluk in the whole of Tamil Nadu, as seen from an estimate made from the inscriptions of this region collected up to the year 1915.[21] Further work in this direction has already yielded evidence of many more *brahmadeyas* in the same taluk, particularly in the environs of Kuḍamūkku, emerging at different stages between the tenth and thirteenth centuries AD.[22]

II

The successive stages in the evolution of the Kuḍamūkku-Paḻaiyāṟai urban complex from the seventh to the thirteenth centuries may be discussed in two parts, the first relating to Kuḍamūkku proper and its dependent settlements like Tirunāgēśvaram, Tiruvalamcuḻi (Map 10-3) and Tirukkarugāvūr (Map 10-4), and the second dealing with the palace complex of Paḻaiyāṟai and its environs. In each part, an attempt will be made to show the expansion of the city during two broad periods, the first representing the period between the seventh and ninth centuries AD, and the second covering the imperial Cōḻa period (ninth to thirteenth centuries). The latter has been further subdivided into three phases: the early Cōḻa (AD 850–985), the middle Cōḻa (AD 985–1120) and the late Cōḻa (AD 1120–1279), for each temple-centred settlement, in order to maintain, as far as possible, a chronological sequence.

The Kuḍamūkku Complex

The evolution of the Kuḍamūkku complex between the seventh and ninth centuries AD is marked by the rise of temple settlements, both Śaiva and Vaiṣṇava, celebrated in religious tradition as the centres visited by the exponents of the *bhakti* cult—the Śaiva *nāyanārs* and Vaiṣṇava *āḻvārs*. The modern town of Kumbhakonam has eight Śiva temples and twelve Viṣṇu temples, of which two Śiva temples and one major Viṣṇu temple date from this period, viz., the Kuḍandai Kīḻkkōṭṭam (the Nāgēśvara temple) and the Kāyāvarohaṇa (the Kāśi Viśvanātha temple) representing the Śaiva settlements and the Sārangapāṇi temple representing the Vaiṣṇava settlement. The *Tēvāram*[23] and *Divyaprabandham*[24] references to these temples are mainly devoted to their religious importance and to the glorification of the respective deities enshrined in them.

Architecturally, these shrines were unpretentious brick structures later converted into stone *vimānas* (central shrines with towers),[25] forming the nuclei of huge temple complexes, which grew steadily in size, from the early Cōḷa period, gaining additions of subsidiary shrines and enclosures and ending with the tall towers (*gopuras*) of the Vijayanagar-Nāyak period.

To the same period may be assigned the emergence of three other temple centres in Tirunāgēśvaram, Tiruvalamcuḷi and Tirukkarugāvūr, although their inclusion in the Kuḍamūkku complex is known only from the early Cōḷa inscriptions. Their architectural development is similar to the temples of Kuḍamūkku proper and points to a progressive growth in size and importance throughout the Cōḷa period. Thus, it would appear that by the time of the rise of the Cōḷas, Kuḍamūkku and its environs came into prominence with five temple-centred settlements, the majority of which were populated by the followers of Śaivism.

Kuḍamūkku, under the imperial Cōḷas, covered a much larger area than the present town of Kumbhakonam. It extended over the whole of Pāmbūr nāḍu[26] (Map 9), which contained a cluster of three *brahmadeya-dēvadānas*, viz., the main Kuḍamūkku (or Kuḍamūkkil), Tirunāgēśvaram, a *pāl* (=literally 'in the vicinity of') of Kuḍamūkku, and Tiruvalamcuḷi. To this group of settlements a fourth one called Tirukkarugāvūr may be added, as it is described as a part of Kuḍamūkkil, although it was not situated within Pāmbūr nāḍu. The *nāḍu* was evidently not an administrative division created by the Cōḷas, but was distinctly an agrarian unit which pre-dates the imperial Cōḷas.[27] This may be seen from the fact that Kuḍamūkku and Paḻaiyāṟai were located in different *nāḍus*, the former in Pāmbūr nāḍu between the Kāvēri and the Ariśilāṟu and the latter in Tirunaṟaiyūr nāḍu, covering the regions watered by the Muḍikoṇḍān and Tirumalarājan (Map 9). The immediate hinterland commanded by this twin-city covered the whole area from the Koḷḷiḍam (Coleroon) river in the north to the Vaḍavāṟu in the south.

During the early Cōḷa period, the expansion of Kuḍamūkku reveals a steady growth, not only in the initial reconstruction in stone of the traditionally important temples and their architectural elaboration, but also in the increasing role they played in the socio-economic and political activities of the centre. The Nāgeśvara temple may be described as the main institutional force through which the early Cōḷas, starting from Parāntaka I, projected their growing power. The royal family was directly involved in its reconstruction and elaboration, and its maintenance through land grants and other gifts.[28] The major economic activity of Kuḍamūkku was centred round this temple, as seen in the nature of the endowments made to it, in the form of land, cows, sheep, gold and money for a variety of purposes like festivals, feeding of *brāhmaṇas* and other ascetics (*Śivayogins*), daily rituals and burning of perpetual lamps. Apart from the royal family, the other social groups involved in these activities were Cōḷa officials of high rank,[29] servants of the palace, personal retinues of the royal members (*Vēḷams*),[30] local merchants[31] and traders from distant lands like Malai nāḍu (Kerala).[32] While land endowments were common, money and gold gifts are found to be equally numerous, the donors in the latter case being usually merchants, and, occasionally, leading landowners[33] (*Vēḷāḷas*) from various parts of the Cōḷa kingdom. The *manṟāḍis* (shepherds) represented another class of people who were closely associated with the administration of endowments, particularly of sheep,[34] while the *Mūlapariṣad* of the temple, consisting mostly of *brāhmaṇas*, had control over the entire range of the temple's activity, including sale and purchase of landed property.[35] Members of the Kaikkōḷa or weaver community, many of whom served as members of the army, as *teriñja kaikkōḷas* (chosen *Kaikkōḷas*) offered gifts of sheep and also, occasionally, land, gold and money.[36]

The monetary gifts and transactions of the temple would show that, apart from lumps of gold, weighed by the *kaḻañju* standard, gold was also used in the form of money for purchase of land,[37] or as gifts for feeding *brāhmaṇas* and ascetics.[38] In fact, it would appear from various such instances that, in the early Cōḷa period, the use of *kaḻañju* as coined money was coming into vogue and was perhaps gradually replacing the use of metal by weight. This is implied in the reference to a gift of one hundred and five pieces of *tuḷaippon* in the reign of Parāntaka I, by a native of Āyirattaḷi (Kaṇḍiyūr) in Kiḻār Kūṟṟam for festivals.[39] The fact that the earliest known Cōḷa gold coin belongs to Uttama Cōḷa[40] (*c.* AD 965–85), would lend additional support to the supposition that use of coined money was known in this period, although the practice of donating lumps of gold continued. In another transaction, the assembly of Kuḍamūkku raised 500 *kaḻañju* of gold by sale of land, in order to pay an impost of 3,000 *kaḻañju* levied on it by Parāntaka I,[41] perhaps in an attempt to raise funds for his Pāṇḍya wars, which plagued the early Cōḷas constantly till the virtual annexation of the Pāṇḍya region by Rājarāja I and Rājēndra I (*c.* AD 985–1044).[42]

The Nāgēśvara temple continued to be the centre of all major activities in Kuḍamūkku till the Kumbheśvara temple assumed precedence in the post-Cōḷa period on account of its religious importance. References to the *Āvaṇakkaḷam* (archives?) and *Śrī Bhaṇḍāram* (treasury and storehouse)[43] of the Nāgēśvara temple would attest to its extensive functions of collection and redistribution.

The second *dēvadāna* settlement in Kuḍamūkku grew up around the Somēśvara temple, which dates from the middle Cōḷa period, for the earliest recorded land grant to this temple is dated in the fifth regnal year of Rājarāja I (*c.* AD 970).[44] It played a relatively less important role in the major activities of this centre, as practically nothing is known about it after the period of Rājarāja I till the late Cōḷa period, when it acquired independent status under the name Somanāthamangalam and came to be separated from Pāmbūr nāḍu.[45] At the same time, lands in distant regions were either gifted or sold to this temple and the number of such transactions far exceeded the land endowments to any other temple in Kuḍamūkku during this period. These lands were situated in the northern parts of Tamil Nadu (Jayankoṇḍacōḷamaṇḍalam), and also in other parts of the Cōḷa country, such as Tiraimūr nāḍu, Mirai Kūṟṟam and Kilar Kūṟṟam. Two major structural additions were also made to it in the form of shrines dedicated to Śiva as Nataraja and Vināyaka.[46]

In the post-Cōḷa period this temple suffered neglect due to the shift in importance to the Vaiṣṇava sections of the Kuḍamūkku complex under Vijayanagar patronage. Hence its present nickname, 'ēḷai Sōmanātha' ('poor Somanātha').[47]

The Sārangapāṇi temple formed the nucleus of a large Vaiṣṇava settlement in Kuḍamūkku. Traditional accounts and the *Divyaprabandham* references would assign its origins to the pre-Cōḷa period, although no corresponding evidence comes forth from other sources. Perhaps an indirect reference to it is made in one of the early Cōḷa inscriptions of the Nāgēśvara temple, mentioning the temple of Jalaśayana,[48] an assumption which is strengthened by the fact that the Sārangapāṇi temple enshrines the reclining form of Viṣṇu-Nārāyaṇa, to which seven of the *āḻvārs* have referred in their verses.[49] However, in the thirteenth century it was certainly an important part of Kuḍamūkku, as seen from the reference to the deity Ārāvamudu (i.e. the name of the deity as given in traditional literature) in a fragmentary inscription, palaeographically assignable to the thirteenth century.[50] Of the original shrine of the earlier period, there is no trace, for the temple seems to have undergone major structural elaboration twice, first under the late Cōḷas, and later under the Vijayanagar rulers. The architectural style and sculptural decorations of the main *vimāna* and the inner enclosures show distinct characteristics of the late Cōḷa style. An additional evidence of this date is provided by the sculptures representing *Bharatanātya Karaṇas* (poses) with label inscriptions datable to the twelfth century on palaeographic grounds.[51]

The second major centre, i.e. Tirunāgēśvaram, forming a part of the Kuḍamūkku complex, is about three miles east of modern Kumbhakonam, situated outside the limits of the present town. Its origins are assignable to the period of the Śaiva *nāyanārs*, but it developed as an important Śaiva centre under the early Cōḷas. It appears to have replaced an earlier Jain settlement around a *paḻḻi* (Jain temple or monastery), which was patronized by the *perunagarattār* (merchants of a big township) of Kumaramārttāṇḍapuram in Tiraimūr nāḍu, who made provisions for renovating parts of it in the close of the ninth century AD.[52]

The *nagaram* of Kumaramārttāṇḍapuram was closely associated with the economic activities of Tiruviḍaimarudūr, and also of the Jain settlement at Tirunāgēśvaram.

Under the early Cōḷas, the Nāganātha temple which replaced the Jain *paḷḷi* at Tirunāgēśvaram was the recipient of land and money endowments from members of the royal family.[53] The direct involvement of the *Mūlaparuḍai* (executive committee) of Kuḍamūkku in the temple administration of Tirunāgēśvaram, is seen in its supervisory role in utilizing a money endowment on behalf of the Nāganātha temple for repairing damages caused by floods to an irrigation channel.[54] The interest of this money endowment was paid in the form of paddy for the exposition of Śivadharma at Tirunāgēśvaram.

The royal family continued to be personally associated with the grants to this temple under Rājēndra I. Senior officials and members of the *vēḷams* also participated in such activities.[55] Members of the elephant corps of Rājēndra's army (*iḷaiya Kuñjira mallar* = junior elephant mahouts) also figure as donors.[56] The accumulated wealth of the temple in terms of jewels, gold, silver vessels etc., were carefully registered by a temple servant, probably under the royal orders of Rājēndra I.[57] The use of gold, both in the form of money and by the weight standard of *kaḷañju*, was a regular feature at this centre in the early and middle Cōḷa periods.[58]

This temple settlement receded into the background due to the withdrawal of active royal patronage after Rājēndra I, although it remained an important part of this urban complex down to the end of the Cōḷa period, and continued to acquire more lands in the twelfth century in the reign of Rājēndra II (*c.* AD 1146–73).[59]

Tiruvalamcuḷi,[60] now located outside the Kumbhakonam town, at a distance of about two miles west, was perhaps the largest of the temple settlements in this urban complex. Its history is traceable, almost continuously, from the pre-Cōḷa to the Vijayanagar periods. The Śiva temple of Kapardīśvara, around which this centre grew up, shares with other temples of this region the 'honour' of being visited by the Śaiva *nāyanārs*, and hence acquired great religious importance under the Cōḷas. The temple passed through successive stages of enlargement under the Cōḷas, and provides a remarkable example of horizontal magnification, a late Cōḷa phenomenon in the architectural history of Tamil Nadu.

In the early Cōḷa period, this temple acquired lands in Innambar nāḍu.[61] It is, however, in the middle Cōḷa period, especially under Rājarāja I and Rājēndra I, that it became the centre of major activities. While numerous tax-free land grants were made by the royal family in Tiraimūr nāḍu, Innambar nāḍu and Veṇṇāḍu,[62] a rich variety of gold ornaments was also presented to it by the Cōḷa princesses in the reign of Rājarāja I.[63] An institution of higher learning called the Māḷigai Mēlaikkallūri in Tukkālivallam (not identifiable) was established under Rājarāja I[64] as a part of this temple centre and provisions were made by the king for its maintenance, evidently through the temple.

Two new *agrahāras* were added to this settlement in the late Cōḷa period. The first was the Veḷḷaivināyaka-caturvēdimangalam (Map 10-12),[65] which was established for the maintenance of the Veḷḷaivināyaka shrine, constructed in the late Cōḷa period in the outer enclosure of the temple. The second *agaram*, known as the Akhilanāyaka-caturvēdimangalam, is described as an *agaram* of Tiruvalamcuḻi.[66]

The majority of the land grants of the late Cōḷa period were intended for the Veḷḷaivināyaka shrine and were located in distant regions. Some of these grants were also made to the main deity of the temple during the troubled period of the Cōḷa-Pāṇḍya wars of the early thirteenth century, both 'for the welfare of the inhabitants of this centre and for the success of Rājarāja III'. The lands and house sites donated to both the shrines were located in Innambar nāḍu, Nallūr nāḍu, and Tirunaṟaiyūr nāḍu.[67] The increase in the land grants to this temple in the late Cōḷa period may be attributed to an attempt to restore its original status to this centre, which became depopulated due to constant wars and great political disturbance.[68] Land and house sites in Koṟṟangudi, a hamlet of Akhilanayaka-caturvēdimangalam, were made over to the temple even under Kōpperuñjinga,[69] the Kāḍava feudatory, who temporarily gained control over the Cōḷas early in the thirteenth century.

Horse dealers (*Kudirai ceṭṭis*) from Malaimaṇḍalam (Kerala) still frequented this region in the thirteenth century and made gifts of land to the temple.[70] The existence in Tiruvalamcuḷi of a group of Malaiyāḷar from Malaimaṇḍalam is also evidenced by the reference to some defaulters of land revenue raising loans from them and from the temple treasury.[71]

Apart from land and gold, gifts of goats for lamp endowments were the most frequent at this temple, and the *maṉṟāḏis* figure prominently, as in other temples, in the maintenance of such grants.[72]

Tirukkarugāvūr (also called Tirukkaḷāvūr), situated about thirteen miles south-west of modern Kumbhakonam, represents the third major settlement outside the present town, which is described as a part of Tirukkuḍamūkku in Pāmbūr nāḍu.[73] It contained three temples dedicated to Śiva, Viṣṇu and Piḍāri, a local deity accepted in the brahmanical fold as an aspect of Śakti. The Śiva temple assumed the dominant role in the evolution of this settlement, and may be dated from the period of Śaiva *nāyanārs*. Originating as a small structure, without great architectural merit, this temple rose to prominence under the early Cōḷas The endowments made in this period consisted mostly of land grants from a variety of people, i.e. members of the royal *vēḷams* at Tañjāvūr,[74] women servants attached to temples,[75] royal officers,[76] elephant mahouts,[77] and also merchants from Nandipuram.[78] Under a royal order from Parāntaka I, the land owned by this temple, together with those of the Viṣṇu and Kāla Piḍāri temples, were listed and carefully recorded.[79]

This centre ceased to be an important part of this urban complex after the tenth century AD, although its religious character persisted, due to its association with the *Tēvāram* hymnists. The withdrawal of royal patronage perhaps led to its neglect by the other social groups in the urban milieu of Kuḍamūkku-Paḻaiyāṟai.

Post-Cōḷa Developments in Kuḍamūkku

In the post-Cōḷa, i.e. Vijayanagar-Nāyak, periods Kuḍamūkku proper underwent a series of changes, resulting in a general decline of the temples of the Cōḷa period and the emergence of new centres of religious importance. There was a clear shift in royal patronage from Śaiva to Vaiṣṇava religious institutions, although the Śaiva temples continued to be centres of worship as they did not lose their hold entirely over the religious sentiments of the people. The Ādi Kumbheśvara gained precedence over the rest of the Śaiva shrines and two new Viṣṇu temples, viz., the Rāmasvāmi and Cakrapāṇi temples, arose and vied with the older Sārangapāṇi temple for royal favour and religious importance.

The Kumbheśvara temple may be dated from the Vijayanagar period, both on the basis of its architectural style and the Vijayanagar inscriptions recording the earliest land grants to the temple.[80] The *Mahāmakam* tank, considered to be the most sacred tank and of great ritual significance, also came to be associated with the festival of *Māśi Magha* (in February) celebrated in the Kumbheśvara temple, thus enhancing the sanctity of the latter. A ritual bath in this tank is believed to be equivalent to a holy dip in all the sacred rivers of India. This event takes place once in twelve years on the *Mahāmakam* day, representing the South Indian counterpart of the Kumbhamela of Prayāga. A series of sculptures representing all the river goddesses of India is found near this tank, in the precincts of the Kāśi Viśvanātha temple. On stylistic grounds, they may be assigned to the early Cōḷa period,[81] thereby indicating the probable sacred associations of Kuḍamūkku with the river goddesses as early as the tenth century AD. The tank and the festival are referred to by the twelfth century Śaiva hagiological work, viz. the *Periya Purāṇam*,[82] while narrating the story of the Śaiva saint Sambandar and his visit to the Śiva temples at Kuḍamūkku. Presumably, the festival is much older than its specific connections with the Kumbheśvara temple in the Vijayanagar period.

The Sārangapāṇi temple owes its renovation and architectural elaboration, including five tall towers (*gopuras*), to the Vijayanagar rulers. Beginning from Virūpaṇṇa Uḍaiyār in AD 1385, when the name Kumbhakonam appears for the first time in the temple inscriptions,[83] many members of this ruling family extended their patronage to it. Kṛṣṇadevarāya chose to make provisions for special worship after setting up a record of his achievements in the temple.[84] Merchants from the Telugu region also began to visit this sacred centre and make land and money endowments.[85]

A Vaiṣṇava maṭha came to be attached to this temple in the period of Raghunātha Nāyaka (seventeenth century),[86] and it has served ever since as an important pontifical seat of the South Indian Vaiṣṇavas. It was, perhaps, also in the same period that a separate *agaram* was formed west of the Sāranga-pāṇi temple, after a gift of house-sites in the main street was made by Kacciyarāyar, a high official residing at Gangai-koṇḍacōḷapuram.[87]

The Rāmasvāmi temple was one of the new Vaiṣṇava centres which came up in this period, and its construction is assigned to Raghunātha Nāyaka of Tañjāvūr.[88] It represents a unique instance of a Rāma temple enshrining in its *sanctum sanctorum* the brothers of Rāma, apart from the usual Rāma group consisting of Rāma, Sītā and Lakṣmaṇa. The huge *maṇḍapas* of this temple carry on their composite pillars interesting iconographic forms of Viṣṇu, apart from secular figures representing members of the Nāyak family.

A large part of west Kumbhakonam, not far from the Sārangapāṇi temple, is occupied by the Cakrapāṇi temple and its residential area, which seem to have come into existence in the Vijayanagar-Nāyak period. The present Viṣṇu temple has evidently replaced an earlier Śiva shrine, as suggested by a thirteenth century inscription built into the *maḍappaḷḷi* (kitchen) of this temple, recording a gift to the shrine of Tirukkōḷīśvaram Uḍaiyār.[89] A Śrī Vaiṣṇava religious head, known as Kōyil Kandāḍai Nāyan Āḷvār Jīyar, made provisions in Ś. 1427 (AD 1505) for offerings to the deity and their redistribution among Śrī Vaiṣṇava pilgrims,[90] thus controlling the redistributive functions of the temple in the sixteenth century AD.

Apart from the Śrī Vaiṣṇava religious organizations mentioned above, Kumbhakonam also became the centre of two other monastic establishments, viz. the Śankarācārya *maṭha* and the Vīra Śaiva *maṭha* (*Hiriya maṭha*). The former seems to have been established as early as the thirteenth century.[91] Endowments were made to it under the late Vijayanagar ruler Vēnkaṭa V in Ś. 1632 (AD 1710).[92] The latter came into existence during the reign of king Vīra Narasimha in early sixteenth century AD.[93] All these monastic establishments exercised considerable influence over the religious life of Kumbhakonam in the Vijayanagar and Nāyak periods, and some of them, like the Śankarācārya *maṭha* and the Vaiṣṇava *maṭha* attached to the Sārangapāṇi temple, continue to play a significant role in the religious activities of South India even today.

The general trend towards Vaiṣṇava dominance may perhaps be attributed not merely to royal patronage, but also to a gradual intensification of the Vaiṣṇava movement after Rāmānuja, i.e. after the twelfth-thirteenth centuries AD. The sectarian split into the Vaḍakalai and Teṉkalai among the Vaiṣṇavas due to the liberalization of Vaiṣṇava ideology initiated by Rāmānuja, led to an increase in Vaiṣṇava *maṭhas*.[94]

The Paḻaiyāṟai Complex: Seventh–Ninth Centuries AD

The Paḻaiyāṟai complex, situated in Tirunaṟaiyūr nāḍu, extended over the banks of the Tirumalarājan and Muḍikoṇḍān. During the course of the seventh-ninth centuries AD it developed as a large city with 'wide streets and tall structures'[95] consisting of a palace of the Cōḷas[96] and the residence of administrative officers. This complex grew around a large number of religious settlements and the administrative and military establishments of the Cōḷas.

The earliest settlement of this region was located at Vaḍaṭali or Vaḷḷalārkōyil near Muḷaiyūr (Map 10-17), which was the scene of a major religious conflict between the Śaivas and Jains,[97] which led to the decline of the Jain settlement which originally existed here. The Jains appear to have settled at various parts of the Kuḍamūkku-Paḻaiyāṟai region in this period. Quite a few Jain settlements are known from references in the inscription of this region. The Tirunāgēśvaram inscriptions, mentioned earlier, and an inscription of the ninth-tenth century AD built into a doorjamb of the Kumbhēśvara temple,[98] which points to the existence of a Jain *paḷḷi* at Dīpankuḍi in the Nannilam taluk, and also the reference to the visit of Jain nuns from Paḻaiyāṟai to the sacred Jain hill at Kalugumalai in the Tirunelveli district,[99] are sufficient proof of the influence that the Jains wielded here before the Śaiva revival.

The second important settlement of this region was Nandipuram (present Nāthankōyil, Map 10-18) which grew around a

Viṣṇu temple referred to in the hymns of Tirumangai Āḻvār as Nandipura Viṇṇagaram.[100] The construction of this temple is attributed to Nandivarman II, the Pallava ruler of the eighth century AD. Amar Nīti Nāyanār, one of the sixty three Śaiva saints of *Periya Purāṇam*, who has been assigned to this period, was a rich merchant who traded in cloth, gold and gems.[101] It may be presumed that he lived in Nandipuram, which was a regular colony of merchants.[102]

A third settlement, which emerged in the same period, was Tiruccattimuṟṟam in Paṭṭīśvaram (Map 10-14). It was the scene of a miraculous episode connected with Tirujñānasambandar, who received a 'pearl canopy' by 'divine grace' when he visited the temple.[103] Evidently, the temple was originally a small shrine, later renovated and enlarged under the Cōḷas.[104]

Paḻaiyāṟai in the Cōḷa Period

The earliest settlement assignable to the Cōḷa period is the Arumoḻidevīśvaram (the present Sōmanātha temple at Kīḻpaḻaiyāṟai) erected by Rājarāja I, whose personal name was Arumoḻideva. It is located at a distance of about half a mile from Nandipuram. The present structure hardly contains any evidence of its date, due to large-scale renovations in the Vijayanagar period, but its existence in the middle Cōḷa period is established by a reference to a *dēvadāna* village belonging to this temple in an inscription of Rājarāja I from Tirunaṟaiyūr (Map 10-9).[105]

Next in the chronological sequence of the emergence of settlements in Paḻaiyāṟai may be placed a *paḷḷippaḍai*, a sepulchral monument (present Rāmanāthan Kōyil in Paṭṭīśvaram), built by Rājēndra I for one of the queens by the name of Pañcavanmahādēvī.[106] This temple seems to have been a centre of the Pāśupata sect of Śaivism, as indicated by a reference to Lakulīśa Paṇḍita, a Pāśupata teacher, in its foundation inscription. The considerable influence that the Pāśupatas wielded in Paḻaiyāṟai is further attested to by the presence of 108 sculptured figures of Śaivācāryas belonging to this sect, with label inscriptions, in the Dārāsuram temple,[107] built in another part of Paḻaiyāṟai in the twelfth century AD.

Two more temple settlements, which came up in Paḻaiyāṟai

in the twelfth century AD, were centred round the Śiva temple called Virudarajabhayankarēśvaram Uḍaiyār, and the remarkable late Cōḷa edifice known as Rājarājeśvaram, now called Dārāsuram (Map 10-19). The former temple is located between the sites of Sōḷamāḷigai and Nandanmēḍu, and is in a highly dilapidated state. The inscriptions of this temple date from about the twelfth century AD and record various grants made by the late Cōḷa rulers. It was replaced by a Viṣṇu temple called Gōpinātha Perumāḷkōyil under the Vijayanagar rulers.[108]

The Rājarājēśvara temple at Dārāsuram was built in the reign of Rājarāja II (*c.* AD 1146–73).[109] Architecturally the most remarkable of the temples of Paḷaiyāṟai, it represents a rare example of Cāḷukya influence over the temple architecture of Tamil Nadu, and may perhaps point to the existence of Cāḷukya architects and sculptors in this centre, especially after Rājādhirāja I's victory over Kalyāṇapura, the Cāḷukya capital, from where he brought back as war trophy a *dvārapāla* image[110] found at the entrance to the main enclosure of this temple. The pillared *maṇḍapas* of this temple, it may be added, carry *madanikā* figures typical of the Cāḷukya style.[111]

Land and other endowments to this temple was fairly numerous and included a fruit garden.[112] Even in the thirteenth century AD the Pāṇḍyas of the 'second empire' are seen making grants of land to this temple for repairs and renovation and for the celebration of festivals.[113]

The major factor in the urban development of Paḷaiyāṟai was obviously its choice by the Cōḷas as their residential capital. The political disturbances of the post-Sangam period kept the Cōḷas in obscurity till they reappear in the same region in the seventh–ninth centuries AD, still in a state of subordination to the Pallavas and Pāṇḍyas. Their re-emergence to political power under Vijayālaya in the ninth century AD was evidently facilitated by their hold over the delta region. All the early inscriptions of Āditya I and Parāntaka I show that their activities were mainly centred round this area. The preference of the imperial Cōḷas for Paḷaiyāṟai is seen in the way every Cōḷa ruler, starting from Āditya I, not only used it as his residential stronghold, but also personally contributed to its development by erecting temples, either in the Kuḍamūkku or

Paḻaiyāṟai section and their environs, and making rich endowments of land and gold.

A series of army cantonments also seems to have surrounded the palace area, as is revealed by the names of several small villages and hamlets at present bearing names ending in *paḍaiyūr* or *paḍaivīḍu* (Map 10-20 to 23).[114] Frequent references to the members of the army (*teriñja Kaikkōḷas*) and elephant mahouts participating in the gift-making processes of various temples have already been noted. A section of the army called the Pāṇḍippaḍai is mentioned in an inscription of Parāntaka I in the Nāgēśvara temple. A whole group of army men (*sēnaiyār*) was entrusted with the protection of temple endowments at Tiruviḍaimarudūr.[115] One of the *paḍaivīḍus* at Āyirattaḷi (Paḻaiyāṟai) is mentioned in the Pallavarāyanpēṭṭai inscription of the eighth year of Rājādhirāja II (*c.* AD 1171), which refers to the removal of the two infant sons of Rājarāja II from the *paḍaivīḍu* to a place of safety,[116] probably on account of the threat to their lives from rival claimants to the Cōḷa throne.

In spite of the fact that the more successful Cōḷas, viz., Rājarāja I and Rājēndra I, either chose Tañjāvūr for their monumental edifices and rich benefactions, or founded an entirely new administrative centre like Gangaikoṇḍacōḷapuram, Paḻaiyāṟai never ceased to function as an administrative centre. The Cōḷa family continued to live in Paḻaiyāṟai. Sundara Cōḷa's preference for Paḻaiyāṟai is implied in a statement found in the commentary on *Vīraśōliyam*, a Buddhist work on grammar, that he was the king of Nandipuram or Paḻaiyāṟai.[117] Rājarāja I himself drew a large number of his employees to the Tañjāvūr temple from various parts of his kingdom, and many of them were originally employed as dancers and musicians at Paḻaiyāṟai and other early Cōḷa centres near Kuḍamūkku.[118] Members of the *vēḷams* at Tañjāvūr are frequently seen at Kuḍamūkku and its environs making endowments to and worshipping at the various temples of this area, evidently due to their personal associations with it. Rājēndra I issued his Tiruvālangāḍu grant from a secret apartment (*maṟaiviḍam*) in Muḍikoṇḍacōḷapuram, i.e. Paḻaiyāṟai.[119] In the reign of Kulōttunga I (*c.* AD 1070–1118), envoys from Kaḍāram (the Śrī Vijaya kingdom of Sumatra and Malaysia) submitted their petition to the king seated in his coronation hall at Āyirattaḷi (Paḻaiyāṟai), for the issue of a grant to the Cūḍāmaṇivarma Vihāra at Nāgappaṭṭiṇam.[120] Tribute bearers from the 'island kingdoms of the wide ocean' waited at the gates of Kulōttunga's palace at Āyirattaḷi.[121]

Thus, the position of Paḻaiyāṟai as the nerve-centre of the Cōḷa administration remained unchanged throughout the Cōḷa period. The Pāṇḍyas of early thirteenth century AD clearly recognized the importance of Paḻaiyāṟai when they celebrated their victory over the Cōḷas by performing *vīra* and *vijaya abhiṣekas* in Paḻaiyāṟai.[122] Following this, the rapid decline of the Cōḷas by the second half of the thirteenth century and their disappearance from the political scene, led to the disintegration of Paḻaiyāṟai into small villages and hamlets representing the sites of the old settlements.

Post-Cōḷa Developments in Paḻaiyāṟai

One of the major developments of the Vijayanagar period was the revival and enhancement of the religious importance of this centre through the renovation and architectural elaboration of the older temples and the erection of new ones. Two of them, in particular, received special attention due to their association with the *Tēvāram* hymnists. Tiruccattimuṟṟam was the recipient of land grants during the reigns of Prauḍhadēva Mahārāya (*c.* AD 1447)[123] and Dēvāraya Mahārāya (*c.* 1450).[124] A towering *gopura* was erected for the temple by a *mahāmaṇḍalēśvara* of this period by the name of Goppayadēva Mahārāya.[125]

A colony of Saurāṣṭra weavers called the Paṭṭunūlkāras came up around the Paṭṭīśvaram temple during the Nāyak period. This community was, perhaps, the dominant social group in this centre, since an agreement made between them and the *ceṭṭis* (merchants?) provided for their ritual precedence in the matter of receiving betel and nut on marriage occasions and offering of cloth, betel leaves and nuts to the goddess of the temple.[126] Subsequently, this temple came to be classified as one of the most sacred Śaiva *tīrthas*, along with Vriddhācala (South Arcot district), Tiruvārūr, Tiruveṇkāḍu and Chāyāvana (Tañjāvūr district).[127]

Paṭṭīśvaram also became the centre of three Śaiva *maṭhas*

named after the Śaiva saints Tirumūlar, Nāvukkaraśar and Sambandar. Existence of these *maṭhas* is known only from a late inscription, perhaps of the Nāyak period,[128] although their origins may be traced back to the late Cōḷa and Pāṇḍya periods, i.e. thirteenth century.[129]

Tiruviḍaimarudūr

Tiruviḍaimarudūr, located about five miles east-north-east of Kumbhakonam, was an outlying town, the development of which had close links with the urban complex of Kuḍamūkku-Paḻaiyāṟai and also with Tañjāvūr and Gangaikoṇḍacōḷapuram. The nucleus of this large temple complex was a Śiva shrine which belongs to the period of the *Tēvāram*. The earliest datable structure, i.e. the main shrine, however, seems to have been constructed in brick by the late Pallava ruler Nandivarman III and rebuilt in stone in the early Cōḷa period.[130]

The *Sabhā* or the *brāhmaṇa* assembly of Tiruviḍaimarudūr and the *nagarattār* of Tiraimūr jointly administered the temple endowments,[131] and evidently also managed the affairs of the two major parts of this settlement, the *brahmadeya* of Tiruviḍaimarudūr and the *nagaram* (town) of Tiraimūr. A large contingent of the Cōḷa army (*sēnaiyār*) was stationed in this centre and was entrusted with the protection of all major endowments to the temple.[132]

Throughout the Cōḷa period, members of the royal family visited the temple and personally offered worship.[133] However, the most significant period of its activity was under the early Cōḷas, when, apart from the royal family, officers of high rank, the *Kaikkōḷa* army and other leading landowners were associated with the temple and its religious functions.[134]

Local merchants, merchants from Kumaramārttāṇḍapuram, Nandipuram, Tiruviśalūr (in the Kumbhakonam taluk) and Mayilārppil (Mayilappūr—one of the oldest parts of Madras city) visited the temple and made various gifts in kind and money.[135] The gold and money endowments in the form of *kaḻanju*, *kāśu* and *īḻakkāśu* (silver coins?)[136] would indicate frequent monetary exchanges in the early and middle Cōḷa periods by local traders and itinerant merchants. The itinerant merchants' guild called the Tigai (Tiśai) Āyirattaiññūṟṟuvūr, seems to have erected a *maṇḍapa* in the temple which was named after the guild.[137]

A *Śālai* of *brāhmaṇas* (educational institution) was attached to the temple, to which several grants were made in the reign of a Parakēsari, one of the early Cōḷa rulers.[138] The *Kāvaṇam* of the temple provided the venue of the meetings of the *nagarattār*.[139] A *nāṭakaśālai* (theatre) also came to be established, with its own troupe of musicians, dancers and a dance master. Special grants of land were made for the maintenance of the theatre and its artists.[140] A separate residential area was set up for the *Uvaccas* (drummers?) of the temple and permission was granted to them to construct houses with tiled roofs,[141] a rare privilege given to such low-caste groups.

The *Tai Pūśam* (*Pusya* day in the month of January–February) was the biggest festival at the centre and attracted a large crowd of pilgrims, who offered various gifts, especially of pots made of copper and silver,[142] which is believed to bestow great religious merit on the donor. The festival drew pilgrims from Tañjāvūr, Gangaikoṇḍacōḷapuram (G.K. Cōḷapuram-Map 10), Kuḍamūkku, Tiruveḷḷaṟai (Tiruchirapalli district), Ānaimangalam, near Nāgappaṭṭiṇam, and other parts of the Cōḷa country, and also from Kāñcīpuram in the northern part of Tamil Nadu.[143]

The urban development of this centre was mainly the result of religious and commercial activities throughout the Cōḷa period. Its proximity to the residential capital of the Cōḷas considerably enhanced its importance, apart from its geographical location on the routes connecting the delta region to the coast and to the northern parts of Tamil Nadu. In the post-Cōḷa period, its religious importance remained as the sole factor in maintaining its urban activities, though on a much smaller scale than before.

III

The most important factor in this process of urbanization would be the geographical situation of Kuḍamūkku in the fertile delta region of the Kāvēri. Numerous peasant settlements arose in this region from the Sangam period down to the thirteenth century, forming the main resource base of the Cōḷas. The crucial stage in its development into an urban centre would be the period of the proliferation of the *brahmadeya-dēvadānas*, the seventh to ninth centuries AD, henceforth a continuous phenomenon, showing the availability of sufficient resources for supporting a large population. For every *brahmadeya* settlement there were about ten to twenty non-*brahmadeya* or peasant settlements, which is seen in the number of places mentioned in the grants recorded in the temples. The non-*brahmadeya* villages pre-dated the emergence of *brahmadeyas*, and would represent the later *veḷḷān-vagai* villages, a classification brought in by the Cōḷas. Burton Stein's description of such *brahmadeyas* as large pluralistic centres with sacred and economic functions[144] would be relevant to Kuḍamūkku also.

The importance of the geographical factor is enhanced by the links that Kuḍamūkku established between the interior and the coastal regions. Under the Cōḷas, a large communication network came to be established in Tamil Nadu, and Kuḍamūkku served as the point of convergence of all major routes which passed through the core region of the Cōḷa kingdom. Of ancient highways, there is a single but nonetheless important reference to the Tañjāvūr Peruvaḻi (the great road to Tañjāvūr) which passed through Muniyūr (Munniyūr in inscriptions), south-west of Kumbhakonam. If modern roads are any indication, Kuḍamūkku may be seen to connect the roads from Tañjāvūr and Uṟaiyūr to Nāgappaṭṭiṇam, the Cōḷa port, and from Gangaikoṇḍacōḷapuram to the coast. The road to Chidambaram in the South Arcot district, which was a major *brāhmaṇa* settlement and religious centre, dating from pre-Cōḷa times, and where many of the imperial Cōḷas preferred to celebrate their anointment ceremony, evidently started from Tañjāvūr and passed through Kuḍamūkku and Śīrkāḻi. From Śīrkāḻi, a road branched off to the earliest Cōḷa port of the Kāvērippūmpaṭṭiṇam, a route which the Sangam Cōḷas may well have used.

It would be difficult to ascertain the importance of rivers in the transport system of the Cōḷa period, for on the navigability of the rivers of this region, there is no contemporary evidence. Yet, it may be surmised that for shorter distances the Kāvēri and its distributaries provided safe transport facilities for goods and people. The Ariśilāṟu, it may be pointed out, reaches the sea near Kāraikkāl, north of Nāgappaṭṭiṇam, and could have, at various points, served in a relay transport between the delta and the coast.

The second dominant factor in the urban development of this region was the choice of Kuḍandai by the Sangam Cōḷas as their stronghold for 'guarding their treasure', and of Paḻaiyāṟai as the residential capital by the imperial Cōḷas. This becomes fairly clear also from the fact that the decline of the Cōḷas, and their total disappearance as a political force in the thirteenth century, resulted in the disintegration of Paḻaiyāṟai into a number of small villages and hamlets, which became suburbs of the modern Kumbhakonam town (Map 12).[145] Similarly, Tiruvalamcuḻi and Tirunāgēśvaram also fell out of Kuḍamūkku, and became separate villages centring round their respective temples. The main centre of Kuḍamūkku alone survived as the remnant of this large urban complex, its modern status as the headquarters of a taluk being largely due to its position as the focal point of a large urban centre.

The changing complexion of this region is already seen in the large-scale renovations and structural additions to the temples and the erection of new ones in the post-Cōḷa period, in an attempt to restore the sacred character of Kuḍamūkku. Thus, under the Vijayanagar-Nāyak rulers (fifteenth to eighteenth centuries) the religious factor persisted as the underlying force retaining the urban character of Kumbhakonam.

Trade was, to begin with, incidental in this process of urbanization. However, it soon acquired a dominant role, as the presence of the royal family, its *vēḷams*, military cantonments and administrative officers, together with its intensive religious activity, inevitably attracted trade, sufficiently lucrative, to draw traders from distant parts of Tamil Nadu like Mayilappūr and from Kerala. Money exchange was becoming a regular feature from the early Cōḷa period, although the use of lumps of metal by a certain weight appears to have continued. The Cōḷa mint is believed to have been located in Kuḍamūkku,[146] and the site of the mint is represented by the Kambaṭṭa-Viśvanātha temple in Rājēndranpēṭṭai. In the same area are also located two streets known as the Nāṇayakkāra Cheṭṭi street (the street of moneyers?) and the grain dealers' street.

Much of the trade and commercial activity was controlled by local merchants of Kuḍamūkku and Nandipuram, who must have been in close contact with the itinerant merchant guilds and traders from outside the Cōḷa country. Although no direct evidence is available of the presence of the larger merchant corporations within the city, there are enough indications of their constant movement in this area. References to the *Valañjīyar* of Tiruppuṟambiyam,[147] the Tiśai Āyirattaiññūṟṟuvar at Tiruviḍaimarudūr, the *nagarattār* of Kumaramārttāṇḍapuram and Tiraimūr are too numerous to be devoid of any significance. The last two were local merchant organizations, while the first two were the larger merchant guilds known to have been active in medieval South India, Ceylon and Southeast Asia.

Articles of trade must have included cloth (silk and cotton), gems, and other luxury items, coconuts, fruits, flowers, arecanuts and betel, incense, oil and ghee. Kuḍamūkku itself was a major centre of betel and areca cultivation, as it still continues to be renowned for both the products throughout South India. The temples were the biggest consumers of such goods, representing the religious counterparts of the royal establishment in Paḻaiyāṟai. Horses and elephants were obviously in great demand in the palace and cantonment area.

Textile and metal-ware were evidently the two major industries which developed in this urban centre. The *Kaikkōḷas*, who were temporarily engaged in military activities in the Cōḷa period, were a weaver community who carried on their profession as weavers simultaneously. They ceased to serve as members of the army in the post-Cōḷa period and confined themselves to weaving, and have, to this day, remained the major weaver community of Tamil Nadu. The evolution of a Paṭṭunūlkārar settlement in Paṭṭīśvaram, and the probable emergence of a Saurāṣṭra colony around the Cakrapāṇi temple in Kumbhakonam in the Nāyak period, would also show that a fairly large weaver population was attracted to this region in the seventeenth century AD, evidently due to its reputation as an important weaving centre. Kumbhakonam continues to manufacture cotton and silk textiles to this day.[148]

Vessel-making was apparently the second major craft of this urban centre, both in the Cōḷa and post-Cōḷa periods. The survival of this traditional craft, which remains unsurpassed in Tamil Nadu, is attested by the rows of vessel-shops in modern Kumbhakonam and 'Kumbhakonam vessel-shops' located all over Tamil Nadu, providing a rich variety of copper and brass vessels. Kumbhakonam vessels are a household feature in Tamil Nadu, particularly in the Tanjavur district.

Bronze-casting by the *cire perdue* process was yet another flourishing craft of this urban centre. The demand for the craft was continuous, as bronze images were set up constantly for processional and ritual purposes and for religious merit,[149] requiring the services of *sthapatis* skilled in this art. The *sthapatis* involved in this activity seem to have had a major centre at Svāmimalai near Tiruvalamcuḻi, where generations of artisans executed bronze images of exceptional beauty, in a technique in which they attained a remarkable degree of perfection. Svāmimalai is even today the major centre of this craft in the Tanjavur district.

This huge urban complex consisted of various social and occupational groups,[150] among whom a fairly large group of architects and stone-sculptors must be included. The continuous presence of architects, stone masons and sculptors is clearly indicated by the incessant temple-building activity from about the ninth century AD to the Vijayanagar-Nāyak periods. Temples began as small 'nuclear' shrines (*garbha-gṛha*), and expanded in size, both vertically and horizontally, in successive stages, thereby requiring constant designing, sculpting and supervising agencies. Such agencies are hardly known from contemporary epigraphic sources, as artists and craftsmen of ancient and medieval India have generally remained anonymous. Their work may be described as more of a collective art than one of individual artistic expression.

IV

The present study brings forth certain interesting possibilities in the directions of enquiry for an understanding of the processes of urbanization and location of urban centres in medieval South India. Four major criteria emerge as determinant factors in urban development, leading to the evolution of four main categories of urban centres. Initially, areas of urban activity may be looked for among the clusters of *brahmadeyas* and *dēvadānas* forming the nuclei of the core regions of early kingdoms.[151] Conscious attempts to establish new political and administrative centres such as Tañjāvūr and Gangaikoṇḍacōḷapuram, perhaps due to their strategic location, would provide a second criterion for identifying them. Kāñcīpuram and Madurai served as political and administrative centres throughout South Indian history, although their religious importance continued to be an underlying factor in keeping alive their urban character.

Sacred associations from very early times, providing special sanctity to religious centres like Śrīrangam (Tiruchirapalli district), Chidambaram (South Arcot district) and Tirupati (now in Andhra Pradesh), would form a third factor towards the development of urban centres. An interesting sub-variety of such sacred centres may also be recognized among the *taniyūrs*,[152] where urban activity was confined to the religious and economic functions of the temples around which centres developed. A number of smaller villages and rural settlements came to be attached to them.

Trade and commercial activities, which were not the dominant factor in the development of Kuḍamūkku-Paḷaiyāṟai, would represent the fourth criterion in locating urban centres like ports and market towns, where their role in urban development would be the dominant one. In such centres religious institutions were established mainly to cater to the needs of the various communities involved in such activity. An obvious example of this group of urban centres would be the port of Nāgappaṭṭiṇam, where, apart from a Śiva temple of some antiquity, a large Buddhist *vihāra* came to be established in the eleventh century AD, evidently to provide for the large population of Buddhist traders, both indigenous and foreign. To this category of urban centres one must add the *vīrappaṭṭaṇas* and *eṟivīrappaṭṭaṇas*, which were market towns protected by mercenary troops attached to big trading guilds like the Nānādēśis or Tiśai Āyirattaiññūṟṟuvar or the Ayyavoḷe Five Hundred. Such centres came up along major trade routes connecting different parts of South India, and their emergence in Tamil Nadu may be dated back to the tenth century AD, or not later than the reign of Rājēndra I (*c.* AD 1014–44).[153]

The above categorization of urban centres would show that in most cases, while trade was a secondary factor, religious activity was a dominant and persistent, though not necessarily the sole, factor. For the sacred functions of a temple or a *brahmadeya* should also be accompanied by major economic activity, in situations where dense peasant settlements and intensive agriculture permitted the mobilization of a large surplus.

It would seem that political factors hastened the processes of urban development. Whereas their withdrawal inevitably led to a diminution in the size and complexity of an urban centre, the continuation and increase of religious activities helped to retain its urban character. Trade and commercial activities could be the main factor in the development of some urban centres; yet even here the presence of religious institutions was a necessary concomitant of the urban process.

References

1. The name Kumbhakonam appears for the first time in a record of the Vijayanagar ruler Virūpaṇṇa Uḍaiyār from the Sārangapāṇi temple dated in Ś. 1307 (AD 1385). *See* 415 of 1954–5 (i.e. inscription number 415 of the *Annual Report* on (*South*) *Indian Epigraphy* for the year 1954–5). *Kuḍam* means pot and *mūkku* is spout or nose (also corner?) and hence Kumbha + Konam. But *kuḍam* also denotes *nagaram* or town, according to an early Tamil *nigaṇṭu* or lexicographic work called the *Pingaḷandai* of about the eighth–ninth centuries AD (verse 3381). It is not clear whether this work mentions *kuḍam* as a town in general or as a particular town. *Kuḍa* in Tamil means a hollow or cavity. *See Tamil Lexicon*.
2. Tirunāvukkaraśar's *Tēvāram*, *Tirumuṟai* V and VI; Sambandar's *Tēvāram*, *Tirumuṟai* II and III; Sundaramūrti's *Tēvāram*, *Tirumuṟai* VII. The *Nandikkalambakam*, a ninth century literary work, praises the Pallava King Nandivarman III on his victory over Paḻaiyāṟai—*Paḍaiyāṟu śāya Paḻaiyāṟai veṉṟāṉ*, i.e., he conquered Paḻaiyāṟai after defeating six armies.

3. Tiruvalamcuḻi inscriptions–618 of 1902; *SII*, VIII, 215; 626 of 1902; *SII*, VIII, 228; Muniyūr inscription–610 of 1902; *SII*, VIII, 207; Tirunāgēśvaram inscription–214 of 1911 in 1911-12 (*SII* = *South Indian Inscriptions*).
4. *Akanāṉūṟu* 60: 13; *Naṟṟiṇai* 379: 7; Kuḍavāyil may also be taken literally as 'western gate'. *Akanāṉūṟu* 44 would, however, suggest that it was a town. *See* N. Subrahmanian, *Pre-Pallavan Tamil Index*, Madras, 1966, 282, 284.
5. *Puṟanāṉūṟu* 74, colophon. Also Subrahmanian, *Tamil Index*, 284. Kuḍavāśal is a village south-east of Kumbhakonam, on the way to Tiruvārūr and Nāgappaṭṭiṇam.
6. *Paṭṭinappālai*, vv. 27-8.
7. B.K. Gururaja Rao, *The Megalithic Culture in South India*, Mysore, 1972, 89. The present writer has also explored this region and collected some urn-burial remains with Black-and-Red Ware, now lying in the museum of the Department of Ancient History and Archaeology, University of Madras.
8. *See* the author's 'Archaeology and Tamil Literary Tradition'. *Purātattva*, 1975-6, no. 8, 110ff.
9. 'The Vēḷvikkuḍi Copper Plates of Pāṇḍya Neḍunjaḍaiyan', in T.N. Subrahmaniam (ed.), *Ten Pandya Copper Plates*, Madras, 1967, 1-18.
10. T.V. Mahalingam, *Kāñcīpuram in Early South Indian History*, Madras, 1969, 214.
11. K.A. Nilakanta Sastri, *The Cōḷas*, Madras, 1975 (reprint), 105.
12. Mahalingam, *Kāñcīpuram*, 171-2.
13. *Nandikkalambakam* quoted in *Paḻaiyāṟait-talavaralāṟu*, Paḻaiyāṟai Devasthāna Publications, 1957, 4.
14. Nilakanta Sastri, *The Cōḷas*, 110.
15. Ibid., 105.
16. Ibid., 110.
17. 265 of 1907; *SII*, III, 138; 189 of 1895; *SII*, V, 723; 20 of 1931; *SII*, XIX, 115.
18. *SII*, II, 99; T.N. Subramaniam (ed.), *Thirty Pallava Copper Plates*, Madras, 1966, 205-36.
19. *SII*, III, part III, 91; XIII, 13. The inscription referring to Kumaramārttāṇḍapuram is dated in the reign of a Rājakēsari identified with Āditya I.
20. *SII*, III, 72; V, 716, 721.
21. B. Stein, 'The Segmentary State in South Indian History', in R. Fox (ed.), *Realm and Region in Traditional India*, New Delhi, 1977, Table I.

22. The author has located several other *brahmadeya-dēvadānas* mentioned in the inscriptions of the Kumbhakonam region. For instance at least 30 *brahmadeya-dēvadānas* are mentioned in the inscriptions from Tiruviḍaimarudūr, Tiruvalamcuḻi, Tirunāgēśvaram and Kumbhakonam apart from the earlier *brahmadeyas* of the Pallava period.
23. *Tēvāram* of Sambandar, *Tirumuṟai* I: verse 72; Tirunāvukkaraśar, *Tirumuṟai* VI, verse 289.
24. *Divyaprabandham*: The seven *āḻvārs* who refer to Kuḍandai are Pūdam (70-97), Pēy (30, 62), Tirumaḻiśai (*Nānmugan Tiruvandādi*, 36; *Tiruccandaviruttam* 56-67), *Tirumangai* (*Tirumoḻi*, I-1-2; 7; I-I-4; II-4-1 etc.), *Nammāḻvār* (*Tiruvāy noḻi*, 5-8), *Periyāḻvār* (*Tirumoḻi*, I-6-2; 6-6) and Andal (*Nācciyār Tirumoḻi*, 13-2).
25. For example, the Nāgēśvara temple at Kuḍamūkku, the Śiva temples at Tirunāgēśvaram, Tiruvalamcuḻi, Tirukkaruugāvūr and Tiruviḍaimarudūr were rebuilt in stone in the early Cōḻa period.
26. *See* Y. Subbarayalu, *Political Geography of the Chola Country*, Madras, 1973, Map 7, which is followed for *nāḍu* divisions in this essay. For the *nadus* and *kūṟṟams* between Coleroon and Vaḍavāṟu, i.e. around Kumbhakonam, mentioned in the present paper, *see* Map 9 of this essay.
27. The *nāḍu* seems to be basically an agrarian region, representing a grouping of agricultural settlements whose formation was influenced by natural factors conducive to agriculture. Each group of such settlements probably consisted mostly of kinfolk, i.e. a cohesive group of agricultural people and tied together by marriage and blood relationships. *See* Y. Subbarayalu, *Political Geography*, 33, 36.
28. Mahalingam 'The Nāgēśvarasvāmi Temple, Kumbhakonam', *Journal of Indian History*, April 1967, vol. XLV, part I, no. 133, 20ff. For a description of the architectural features of the *vimāna*, assignable to the early-Cōḻa style. Some of the royal patrons are portrayed in the sculptures on the *vimāna* walls, and such portrait sculptures belong to a rare series found mostly in early-Cōḻa temples. Ibid., Figures 8-17. Apart from the Cōḻa royal family (*SII*, III, 137; XIX, 323), a gift of 138 cows and 100 *kāśu* for two lamps was made by the Pāṇḍya king Māṟanjaḍaiyan (Varaguṇa II—accession AD 862)—13 of 1908; *SII*, XIV, no. 8.
29. 230, 231 and 233 of 1911: *SII*, III, 200.
30. 226 of 1911: *SII*, III, 201; 225 of 1911: *SII*, III, 204; 245 of 1911: *SII*, XIX, 95; 234 A of 1911: *SII*, XIX, 131.
31. 237 of 1911: *SII*, XIX, 184; 247 of 1911: *SII*, XIX, 96.

32. 248 of 1911: *SII*, XIX, 50.
33. 246 of 1911: *SII*, XIX, 431; 254 of 1911.
34. 243 of 1911: *SII*, XIX, 132; 244 of 1911: *SII*, XIX, 133; 234 of 1911: *SII*, XIX, 205.
35. 255 of 1911 (1911-12), part II, para 15.
36. 228 of 1911: *SII*, 45; 236 of 1911: *SII*, XIII, 108; 251 of 1911: *SII*, XIX, 8; 229 of 1911: *SII*, III, 131; XIX, 204.
37. 247 of 1911: *SII*, XIX, 96.
38. 237 of 1911: *SII*, XIX, 184; 247 of 1911: *SII*, XIX, 96.
39. 254 of 1911 (1911-12). The term *kaḷañju* may be taken to refer usually to a weight and, occasionally, to a coin. *Tuḷaippon*, meaning 'punched gold', has been described as a piece of gold, 'burnt, melted, cooled and found current, i.e. neither wanting in purity nor in weight' (1911-12, part II, para 21). This term occurs in the Nāgēśvara temple, Tirunāgēśvaram and Tirukkarugāvūr inscriptions in addition to *kaḷañju*. *Kāśu* is obviously a piece of metal (gold or copper) of a particular weight and fabric. The term *īḻakkāśu*, which is also common in the inscriptions of this area, may well be a silver coin (*īḻam* = silver), although it has been interpreted as 'Ceylon coin' (*īḻam* = Ceylon). Hence the term *īḻakkarun-kāśu* (242 of 1907: *SII*, XIX, 38) may also be taken as a 'base silver' coin.
40. W. Eliot, *Coins of Southern India*, Delhi, 1970, 152, G. No. 151. R. Nagaswamy, 'Madurantakan Māḍai', *Damilica* I, 1970, 101ff. Also C.H. Biddulph, *Coins of the Cholas*, Varanasi, 1968, part I, Fig. 1, 40.
41. 255 of 1911.
42. Nilakanta Sastri, *The Cōḷas*, 153ff.
43. 245 of 1911.
44. 3 of 1915. The origin of this temple may, however, go back to the early Cōḷa times, for a much damaged inscription in ninth-tenth century characters seems to record some grant for food offerings to the same deity–299 of 1965-6.
45. 295 of 1927 of the 19th year of Kulōttunga III.
46. 296 of 1927; 301 of 1927; 299 of 1927; 294 of 1927.
47. 1926-7, II, para 84. As a result of an enlargement of the Viṣṇu temple of Sārangapāṇi, the additions made to the Viṣṇu temple took away a large portion of the precincts of the Sōmēśvara temple.
48. 255 of 1911 (1911-12), part II, para 15.
49. *Divyaprabandham*. See note 4.
50. 278 of 1964-5.

51. 279 of 1964-5; P.R. Srinivasan, 'Rare Sculptures from Kumbhakonam', *Transactions of the Archaeological Society of South India*, 1958-9, 35-6.
52. 222 of 1911: *SII*, XIII, 13. The *nagarattār* made provisions for the renovation of the *tiruccuṟṟālai* (veranda) and *gopura* (gateway) of the Milāḍuḍaiyārpaḷḷi.
53. 215 of 1911: *SII*, XIII, 197; 218 of 1911.
54. 214 of 1911.
55. 217 of 1911: 212 of 1911.
56. 211 of 1911.
57. 213 of 1911.
58. 218 of 1911: 214 of 1911; The coin kncwn as Rājēndra-sōḷan *kāśu* is also mentioned in an inscription of Rājēndra I–217 of 1911.
59. 220 and 221 of 1911.
60. Tiruvalamcuḷi is described as a part of Tirukkuḍamūkku in Pāmbūr nāḍu in Uyyakkoṇḍār vaḷanāḍu–633 of 1902; *SII*, VIII, 234.
61. Lands in Tattanguḍi and Odiyankuḍi in Innambar nāḍu in Rājēndrasimhavaḷanāḍu–624 of 1902: *SII*, VIII, 222.
62. 624 A of 1902: *SII*, VIII, 223; 620 of 1902: *SII*, VIII, 217.
63. 633 of 1902: *SII*, VIII, 234.
64. *SII*, VIII, 222.
65. 631 of 1902; *SII*, VIII, 229.
66. 629 of 1902; *SII*, VIII, 229.
67. 626 of 1902; *SII*, VIII, 226; 628 of 1902; *SII*, VIII, 228; 193 of 1927-8; 202, 203 and 205 of 1927-8.
68. 211 of 1927-8.
69. 192 of 1927-8: *SII*, XII, 223.
70. 196 of 1927-8.
71. 194 of 1927-8: *SII*, XII, 224.
72. 627 of 1902: *SII*, VIII, 227.
73. 36 of 1910: *SII*, III, 100.
74. 37 of 1910: *SII*, III, 110.
75. 38 of 1910: *SII*, III, 102. The Jayabhīmataḷi mentioned here, of which Nakkan Candiradēvi was a servant or dancing girl, is also referred to in a Tañjāvūr inscription–*SII*, II, 292.
76. 46 of 1910.
77. 44 of 1910.
78. 36 of 1910: *SII*, III, 100.
79. 42 of 1910.
80. 291 of 1927; 298 of 1965-6.

81. Srinivasan, 'Rare Sculptures', 37-8.
82. K. Nambi Arooran, *Glimpses of Tamil Culture Based on the Periya-puranam*, Madurai, 1977, 115.
83. 415 of 1954-5.
84. 420 of 1954-5.
85. 293 of 1927 (1926-7).
86. The *maṭha* is described as *mahā maṭha* in which Govinda Dīkṣita, the *pradhāni* of the king, built the *ācāravāśal* (gateway) and *anantakalyāṇamaṇḍapa*—290 of 1927 (1926-7); also 320 of 1955-6.
87. 416 of 1954-5.
88. *Mahāmaham/Souvenir*, Kumbhakonam, 1968. Article on the temples in and around Kumbhakonam.
89. 306 of 1965-6.
90. 301 of 1965-6. Kandāḍai is even today the name of an important Śrī Vaiṣṇava family whose ritual status is equal to that of religious heads of the Śrī Vaiṣṇava sect.
91. A Telugu Cōḍa Copper plate grant of the period of Vijaya-gaṇḍagopāla (thirteenth century AD) records provisions made for its maintenance, A-62 of 1956-7; *Epigraphia Indica*, XIII, 194ff.
92. A-61 of 1956-7: *Epigraphia Indica*, XVI, 88ff.
93. 318 and 319 of 1955-6.
94. The emergence of the two major divisions, the *Vaḍakalai* (northern) and *Teṉkalai* (southern), among the Vaiṣṇavas with their different lineages of heads and ritual practices, was, in the main, a result of the incorporation of a large *śūdra* element into the Vaiṣṇava fold, leading to the formation of the *Teṉkalai*. The *Teṉkalais* insisted on the importance of the Tamil canonical literature over the Sanskrit tradition, and the *Vaḍakalai* continued to preserve the northern element in the Vaiṣṇava organization. Both the organizations vied with each other for religious supremacy and royal patronage. The Vijayanagar rulers, most of whom were followers of Vaiṣṇavism, extended their largesses in equal measure to both the sects. Kumbhakonam is still one of important centres of the *Vaḍakalai* tradition. The precedence of the non-*brāhmaṇa* element in religious organization can be seen among the Śaivas much earlier, for their *maṭhas* were headed by non-*brāhmaṇa* teachers, and the Tiruccattimuṟṟam (in Paṭṭīśvaram) lineage of Śaiva teachers, the 'Mudaliyārs' as they are called, established branches at various other centres in the thirteenth century AD (*see* note 128).

   The Śankarācārya *maṭhas*, which also began to proliferate in the post-Cōḷa period, represent another major preserve of the

Sanskrit tradition. Thus, the *Vaḍakalais* and the followers of the Śankara tradition stood for continuous 'sanskritization', while the non-*brāhmaṇa* Śaiva *maṭhas* and the *Teṉkalais* cham- pioned the Tamil tradition.

95. The *Tēvāram* references and the *Periya Purāṇam* descriptions of both Paḻaiyāṟai and Kuḍandai are clearly those of a big city. *See* T.V. Mahalingam, 'The Nāgēśvarasvāmi Temple, Kumbhakonam', 19 and *Paḻaiyāṟaittala-varalāṟu*, 1.
96. The site of Sōḻamāḷigai, where trial excavations were conducted both by the Archaeological Survey of India and the University of Madras, has brought to light remains of early structures built of well-sized brick measuring 16″ × 11″ × 3″.
97. The story of this conflict, as narrated by the *Periya Purāṇam*, accuses the Jains of having hidden the *linga* and appropriated the Vaḍataḷi, from where the local Cōḻa ruler retrieved the *linga* at the instance of the saint Tirunāvukkaraśar and forced the Jains to leave the centre. Tirunāvukkaraśar himself describes Vaḍataḷi as full of Jains who practised false doctrines. K. Vellaivaranan, *Panniru Tirumuṟai Varalāṟu*, part I, Annamalainagar, 1972, 235ff.
98. This inscription mentions Ārambhanandi, a Jain teacher of the Tīyankuḍi (Dīpankuḍi) *paḷḷi* in Inga(ḷ) nāḍu–297 of 1965-6.
99. *SII*, V: 320; also K.V. Ramesh, *Jaina Literature in Tamil*, New Delhi, 1974, 181.
100. *Divyaprabandham, Periya Tirumoḻi*, V. 10.
101. Aru Ramanathan (ed.), *Aṟupattu Mūvar Kataikal*, 1973, 2nd edn, Madras, 73, 157ff.
102. A number of merchants from Nandipuram are known from the early Cōḻa inscriptions of Kuḍamūkku, Tirukkarugāvūr, Tiruviḍaimarudūr, Tiruviśalur and Tirukkōḍikkāval (31 of 1931; *SII*, XIII, 259).
103. K. Vellaivaranan, *Panniru*, 98.
104. The earliest inscriptions of the temple belong to the late Cōḻa period and date from about the middle of the twelfth century AD. 265, 266, 267 and 270 of 1927 (1926-7). They record land and money endowments.
105. 157 of 1908 (1908-9).
106. 271 of 1927 (1926-7).
107. 2 of 1915 (1914-15).
108. 524 to 528 of 1921 (1920-1).
109. 17 of 1908 (1907-8); 256 of 1927 (1926-7).

110. 24 of 1908 (1907-8). The image is now kept in the Tanjavur Art Gallery.
111. The sculptures of this temple are a veritable treasurehouse of Śaiva iconography and include, among others, representations of the stories of the Śaiva *nāyanārs* as narrated in the twelfth century Śaiva hagiological work, the *Periya Purāṇam*. *See* 1919-20, part II, for illustrations and descriptions. The Tribhuvanavīreśvara temple in Tribhuvanam (Map 10-5), built by Kulōttunga III, is similar in architectural design and sculptural style.
112. 24 of 1908 (1907-8).
113. 21 and 23 of 1908 (1907-8).
114. Āriyappapaḍaiyūr (also paḍaivīḍu), Maṇappapaḍaiyūr, Puduppapaḍaiyūr and Pampappapaḍaiyūr are four villages around Paḻaiyāṟai representing the sites of the old cantonments, all located within a radius of about two miles. Paḍaivīḍu or paḍaiyūr means a place where an army is stationed.
115. 239 of 1907: *SII*, XIII, 7.
116. Nilakanta Sastri, *The Cōḷas*, 354ff.
117. Ibid., 157.
118. *SII*, II, 66, 69 and 70.
119. Tiruvālangāḍu copper plates, *SII*, III, part III, 205, Tamil text, ll. 6-8.
120. Smaller Leiden Grant, *Epigraphia Indica*, vol. XXII, 268.
121. Nilakanta Sastri, *The Cōḷas*, 318.
122. Ibid., 394.
123. 262 of 1927 (1926-7).
124. 264 of 1927 (1926-7).
125. 263 of 1927 (1926-7).
126. 257 of 1927 (1926-7).
127. 260 of 1927.
128. 261 of 1927.
129. The non-*brāhmaṇa* Śaiva religious heads of these *maṭhas* and their lineage are mentioned in the thirteenth-fourteenth century inscriptions. 218, 392 and 586 of 1908; 1908, part II, 104-5; 108 and 109 of 1911, part II, 75; 1915, part II, 113.
130. 199 of 1907: *SII*, XIX, 91: III, 124. The inscriptions of Nandivarman III, believed to be kept in an underground cellar, were re-engraved at the time of the reconstruction in stone by the early Cōḷas.
131. *SII*, III, 202; V, 716; XIII, 270; XIX, 91 etc.
132. *SII*, XIII, 7.
133. 208 of 1907: *SII*, XIX, 390; 261 of 1907 (1907-8) etc.

134. 132 of 1895: *SII*, III, 72; 228 and 257 of 1907; 148 of 1895: *SII*, V, 772; *SII*, V, 719; 216 of 1907: *SII*, XIII, 270: 244, 253 of 1907.
135. 262 of 1907: *SII*, V, 717; 198 of 1907: *SII*, XIX, 90; 193 of 1907: *SII*, XIX, 248; 147 of 1895: *SII*, V, 711.
136. 147 of 1895: *SII*, V, 711; 219 of 1907: *SII*, XIX, 162: 239 of 1907: *SII*, XIII, 7.
137. 253 of 1907 (1907-8).
138. 150 of 1895: *SII*, V, 714.
139. 208 of 1907: *SII*, XIX, 300.
140. 154 of 1895: *SII*, V, 718; 214 of 1907: *SII*, III, 202, 203; 233 and 306 of 1907.
141. 221 of 1907: *SII*, XIX, 344.
142. 246-8 of 1907 (1907-8).
143. 219 of 1907: *SII*, XIX, 224; 279, 281 and 294 of 1907; 133 of 1895: *SII*, V, 697 and 698; 270 of 1907; 259 of 1907: *SII*, V, 701.
144. B. Stein, 'The State and the Agrarian Order', in B. Stein (ed.), *Essays on South India*, New Delhi, 1976, 80-8.
145. I am thankful to N. Sethuraman of Kumbhakonam for providing me with this map.
146. This belief is strengthened by the fact that till recently copper coins of the Cōḷas could be purchased by the weight in the vessel shops of Kumbhakonam.
147. 71 of 1897: Nilakanta Sastri, *The Cōḷas*, 595.
148. A large co-operative association of weavers is located at Dārāsuram.
149. The bronzes under worship in the temples of Kumbhakonam and other centres of this urban complex are mainly of the Cōḷa period, and occasionally their consecration is referred to in the temple inscriptions.
150. The major groups are the royal family and the *elite*, represented by the officers, *vēḷams*, leading *vēḷāḷas*, and caste groups like *brāhmaṇas* attached to various temples, religious groups like Jains, Śaivas and Vaiṣṇavass, occupational groups like the *Kaikkōḷas* and *maṉṟāḍis*, and a host of other groups attached to the temple in the capacity of tenants, temple servants, dancers, musicians, drummers, etc. Even the Malaiyāḷar and Simhaḷas are known to have been in residence in Tiruvalamcuḻi and Tirunāgēśvaram respectively (215 of 1911: *SII*, XIII, 197).
151. Nuclear areas as relatively autonomous economic units, where human and material resources were mobilized to satisfy not only the basic requirements of subsistence, but also of sophisticated

and complex political, religious and social institutions, particularly in the Cōḷa period, are highlighted by B. Stein in 'Integration of the Agrarian System of South India', in R.E. Frykenberg (ed.), *Land Control and Social Structure in India*, Wisconsin, 1969, 186ff.

152. *Taniyūr* (*taṉ-kūṟu*) means a separate settlement or village. Several such *taniyūrs* are known to have been created mainly due to their expanding economic activities. Quite a few of them, like Tribhuvani (Pondicherry), Mannārguḍi (Tanjavur district) and Chidambaram (South Arcot district), were centres of considerable importance, where urban development centred round the local temples or an original *brahmadeya*. To such centres, many smaller villages came to be attached as *piḍāgais*. *See* Y. Subbarayalu, *Political Geography*, 92–4.

153. M. Abraham, 'The Ayyavole Guild of Early Medieval South India', M.Phil. Dissertation, Jawaharlal Nehru University, 1978, App. A.

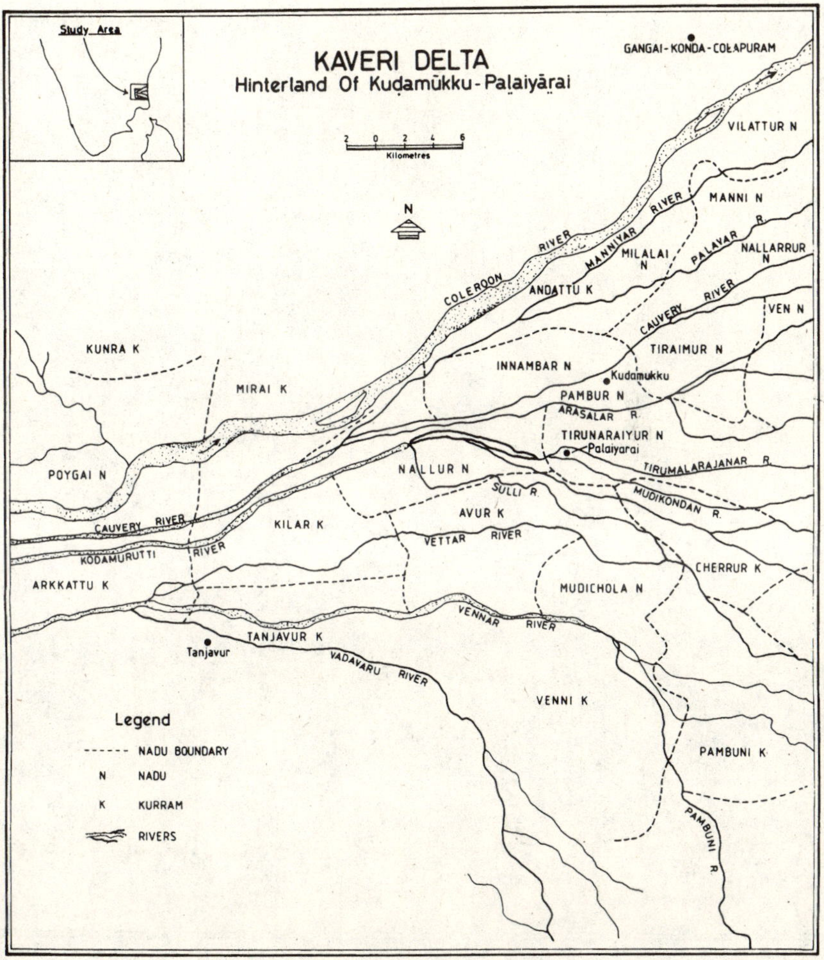

Map 9: The Kaveri Delta - The Hinterland of Kuḍamūkku-Paḷaiyāṟai

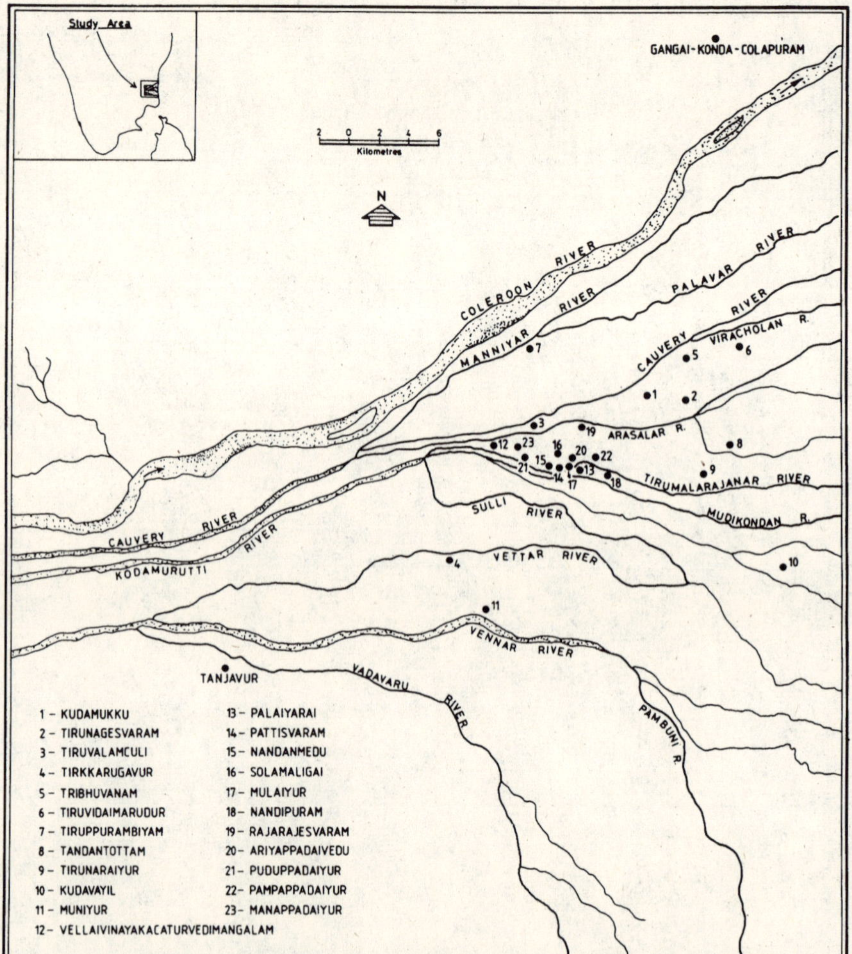

Map 10: Kuḍamūkku-Paḷaiyāṟai - The Urban Core

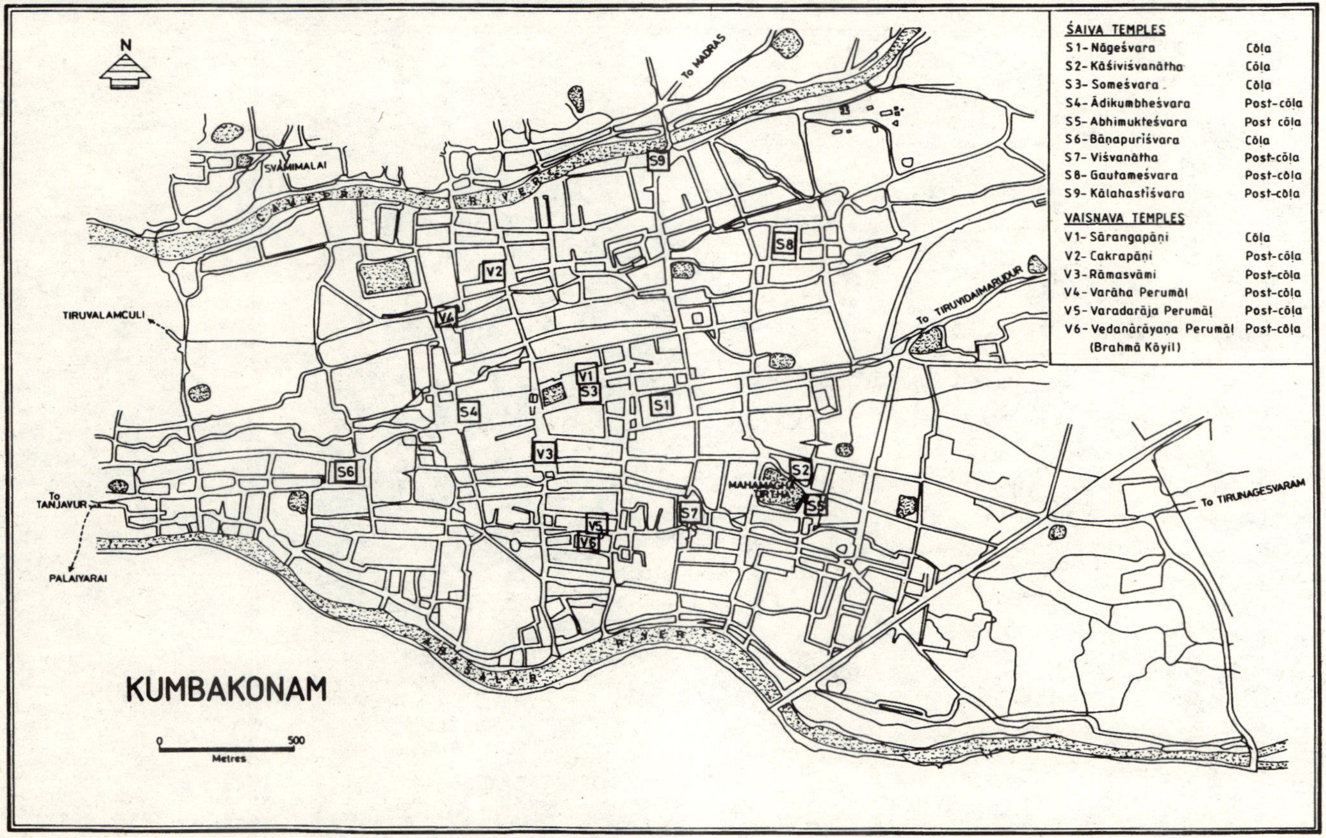

Map 11: Kumbhakonam

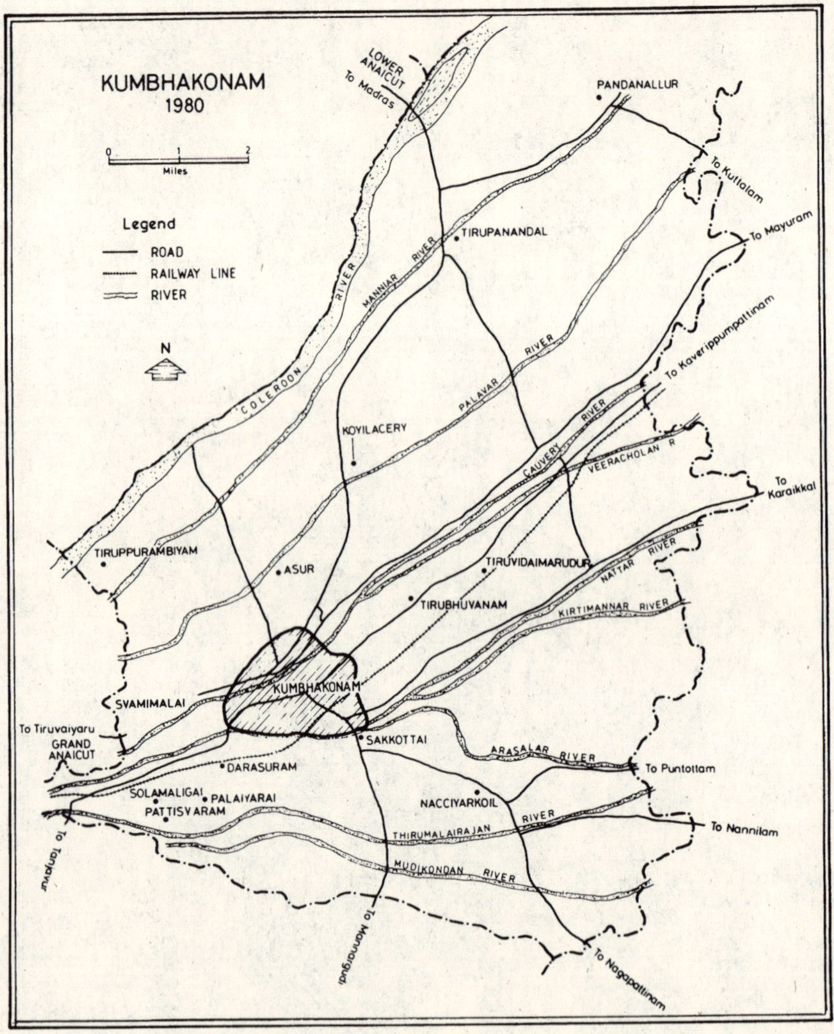

Map 12: Kumbhakonam in 1980

7

The City and the Hinterland: Kāñcīpuram and Toṇḍaimaṇḍalam

Pre-modern Kāñcīpuram and Madras represent two variants of an urban process, a regional manifestation of the larger processes of early medieval urbanization in the whole of the subcontinent.[1] Their urbanism—form and meaning—needs to be situated within a well-defined regional, historical and cultural context, and can be best understood through the pursuit of urban history as a processual change or development, i.e., economic diversification and social stratification, representing different levels of systemic integration through coherent institutional means. Such a regional context for Kāñcīpuram and Madras is provided by Toṇḍaimaṇḍalam, which was a politico-geographic and cultural sub-region of the Tamil macro-region in the early medieval period.

Cities like Kāñcīpuram in Toṇḍaimaṇḍalam, Tañjāvūr in Cōḷamaṇḍalam and Madurai in Pāṇḍimaṇḍalam, were at once products and symbols of a distinctive socio-political culture which evolved through the centuries of Pallava-Pāṇḍya (sixth to ninth centuries) and Cōḷa (ninth to thirteenth centuries) rule, representing two levels of systemic integration through forces, which led to the emergence of institutions, i.e. organized institutional space, and established hierarchical relations of social dominance. To the people of this cultural milieu, the city was where these institutional developments were most conspicuous, most clearly ordered and articulated.[2] Evidence of these developments, as also of the emergence of urban hierarchies, together with typological categories of urban centres, is found in the rich inscriptional records and the powerful *bhakti* (devotional) literature of the Pallava-Cōḷa periods.

Peninsular India passed through two phases of urbanization in the pre-Vijayanagar period, the early historic and the early medieval, each distinct from the other.

It is the second urbanization, i.e. of the early medieval phase (AD 600–1300) with which we are concerned here, the processes being well and clearly reflected in the region of our study. Being significantly different from the early historic urbanization, it marks a processual change, i.e. an intelligible sequence of change, rather than a result of an almost mystically 'sudden impulse'[3] like that of the earlier phase.

The historian's interest in processes and the sociologist's preoccupation with models supplement each other in studying 'traditional' and 'modern' (pre-industrial and 'colonial and/or industrial') societies and the urban forms generated by them. The model of the 'orthogenetic' and 'heterogenetic' cities proposed by Robert Redfield and Milton Singer, and the closely allied concept of the ceremonial centre, an orthogenetic form, which has been admirably worked out by Paul Wheatley in his study of the Chinese city of the second millennium BC, are most interesting and useful from the point of view of 'traditional' societies.[4]

A variant of this model, with a neo-Weberian, comparative civilizational approach, offers the alternative concept of the processes of centrality and concentration,[5] to analyze various aspects of the urban phenomena, and to understand the character of the pre-modern city, by bringing together sociological, anthropological and geographical perspectives.

Centrality has been defined as the process whereby the symbolic and political centres of a society, through which it transcends its daily routine of existence, are constructed and crystallized. It implies the crystallization and symbolization in a specially defined space and ecological setting, of the cultural, political and moral order of a society and the domination of a society by such a centre. The two most important characteristics of the forces of centrality were the religious and politico-administrative manifestations, that appeared sometimes simultaneously. Concentration is the concentration of population, usually as a result of demographic and economic processes that lead to such concentration in a specific area, generating processes of social differentiation and division of labour and growing interaction between various groups, and the emergence of crafts and services. In both processes, there are a *number* of variations within the internal structure, in the extent and intensity of socio-economic manifestations. A combination of both processes may also occur.[6] The strong emphasis, in the above concept, on cultural dimensions and the possibilities of the transformation of forces of concentration into those of centrality, are of special interest to our understanding of medieval South Indian urbanization, and its applicability to the cultural and regional context of Toṇḍaimaṇḍalam, without, however, going into its merits in cross-cultural comparisons of urban phenomena, particularly the city.

Toṇḍaimaṇḍalam: The Region

The concept of the *maṇḍalam* was evolved by the Cōḷas under Rājarāja I (AD 985–1014) and was applied to the different politico-cultural sub-regions of the Tamil country,[7] unified under Cōḷa hegemony through common politico-cultural formulae. Each of them, however, had a long historical past, and retained, to a large extent, its distinctive character as a sub-cultural zone. Hence, the urbanism of Kāñcīpuram to which the Madras region was linked both politically and culturally, needs to be discussed within the context of the urban configurations of Toṇḍaimaṇḍalam[+], which forms a backdrop, as it were, to the central role that Kāñcīpuram played. It is to the processes of the urbanization of this region that one should turn in order to explicate this role.

The name Toṇḍaimaṇḍalam is used here to denote the older region called Toṇḍaināḍu, which was renamed Jayankoṇḍa-cōḷamaṇḍalam under Rājarāja I (AD 1001), when an officer called Toṇḍai nāḍu vagai śeida uḍaiyār surveyed and resettled Toṇḍai-nāḍu, making several additions to it to form Jayankoṇḍacōḷa-maṇḍalam.[8] The latter region is important as a larger territorial unit created by the will of a political authority for administrative convenience. However, the heart of the pre-Cōḷa cultural region, dominated by the Pallavas, lay in Toṇḍai nāḍu, i.e. the northern parts, wherein Kāñcīpuram and Madras are located.

+ *See* Map 13, Toṇḍaimaṇḍalam AD 1300—Urban Configurations

In geographic terms, Toṇḍaināḍu is the region drained from north to south by the Arni and Kortallaiyar rivers and the Palar-Cheyyar-Veghavati rivers.[9] In historical-geographic terms, it covers the area of the traditional twenty-four *kōṭṭams*, now represented by the Chingleput district, a major part of the North Arcot district, the northernmost part of the South Arcot district, and even parts of the Chittoor and Nellur districts, now in Andhra Pradesh. Thus, the north-western portions of Toṇḍaimaṇḍalam are represented by the ancient Bāṇa chieftaincy of Perumbāṇappāḍi and parts of Pangaḷa-nāḍu located between Perumbāṇappāḍi and another chieftaincy called Vāṇakōppāḍi in the North Arcot district.

Toṇḍai nāḍu, in the early historic phase, was marked largely by tracts of relative isolation–*kuriñci* (hilly) and *mullai* (forest/pastoral)–while the *marudam* (plains) and *neital* (coastal/littoral) eco-zones were confined to the Palar-Cheyyar valley, the extent of which was in no way as significant as the Kaveri plains. They could sustain only small communities or segmentary tribes[10] in small dispersed settlements. The descriptions of the region in one of the Sangam works[11] also points to large tracts of unsettled land, forest and hilly regions, with few settlements and fewer still of big ones (*pērūr*) like Kāñcīpuram and its port, Nīrppeyaṟṟu.

The tradition recorded in the *Toṇḍaimaṇḍala-Śatakam* of the twenty-four *kōṭṭams* and of the Kuṟumbar, a pastoral tribe, which occupied them,[12] is also indicative of an agriculturally less developed region. The Megalithic remains, associated in popular tradition and belief with this tribe,[13] further points to the pastoral-cum-agricultural organization of the proto-historic and early historic cultures of the region. The *kōṭṭam* as reflected in the Pallava-Cōḷa inscriptions, in fact, holds a clue to the relatively small subsistence-oriented and dispersed nature of agricultural settlements, pastoralism being the dominant occupation, a feature which is also confirmed by the large number of cattle raids recorded in the hero-stones of the North Arcot district between the sixth and tenth centuries AD,[14] and the predominantly numerous gifts of cattle to the temples of the Pallava and early-Cōḷa periods, i.e. sixth to tenth centuries AD.

The integration of the *kōṭṭams* of Toṇḍaimaṇḍalam under the Pallavas marks the beginnings of early medieval urbanization in the region, the chief instruments of integration being the *brahmadeya* or brahman settlement and the temple, which turned the subsistence-level agricultural settlements into surplus-oriented ones (*ūr*), grouped into *nāḍus* within the *kōṭṭams*. Thus, the *kōṭṭam* and the *nāḍu* emerged as viable socio-economic and political units only in relation to the new ruling families (Pallavas) and the landed elite, i.e. the *brāhmaṇas* and superior *vēḷāḷas* (agricultural community) of the seventh to ninth centuries.[15]

The *brahmadeya* and the temple were products of brahmanical ideology. Sponsored and promoted by the ruling families claiming *kṣatriya* status and divine descent, they developed into institutions of substantial political power and social dominance with economic privileges, as demonstrated by most studies.[16] While it is hard to spell out in precise empirical terms the nature of the economic advantages to the rulers who sought to establish their sovereignty through them,[17] there is little doubt, however, that they led to a more intensive organization of production, geared to support large populations in *brahmadeya* and temple centres. The real advantage lay in integrating older settlements and non-*brahmadeya* villages (*ūr*) into the new agrarian system and bringing virgin land under cultivation (both waste and forest). Examples of several pre-existing settlements being clubbed together into a new *brahmadeya* are also known.[18]

The process was spread over three phases, continuing well into the Cōḷa period. The initial phase is marked by the *brahmadeya* as the chief integrative force, and in the second phase, i.e. ninth to tenth centuries, the temple assumed a major role. The third phase represents the culmination of the process in the eleventh century, the revenue assessment and reorganization of revenue units under Rājarāja I (AD 1003)[19] marking the height of political and ideological levels of integration and the emergence of a distinctive socio-political culture.

Under the Pallavas, i.e. seventh to eighth centuries, agrarian expansion through *brahmadeyas* took place in certain key areas in the Palar-Cheyyar valleys, invariably accompanied by irrigation works (*taṭāka* = reservoir or *ēri* = lake), the region around Kāñcīpuram receiving greater attention. By mid-ninth century, Pallava *brahmadeyas* had come into existence in six *kōṭṭams*. Most of them remained predominantly rural/agrarian centres, while some, at a later stage, developed into nuclei of urban activities. In the second half of the ninth century, Pallava rulers like Nṛpatunga and Kampavarman, whose period coincided with the rise of Cōḷa power under Vijayālaya and Āditya I, initiated several irrigation works, which were later elaborated or improved under the early Cōḷa king Parāntaka I (907–55), when new irrigation works appeared in almost every *kōṭṭam*, and existing ones were augmented with a simultaneous increase in *nāḍus* within the *kōṭṭams*. Elaborate arrangements for their upkeep by *sabhās* or *brāhmaṇa* assemblies, provision for maintenance and management by *vāriyams* (committees) construction of *tūmbu* (sluice), waste weir and channels, desilting and repair, become important details in the Pallava-Cōḷa inscriptions. Demarcation of boundaries of land, ownership or enjoyment rights, nature and category of land, and the number of crops to be raised, are invariably and increasingly recorded.[20] Thus, it was not a case of mere demographic growth and extension of cultivated area, but a restructuring of the agrarian economy through large-scale irrigation works and effective management of resources, which was indeed the very key to the difference in the farming societies of the early (Sangam) and the later (Pallava-Cōḷa) periods. For, viewed in their geographical and ecological setting, the *brahmadeya* and the temple may be seen as harbingers of advance farming methods such as irrigation technology and seasonal regulation of the cultivation process through proper management of resources.

In this process, construction of large-scale reservoirs begun by the Pallavas and continued under the Cōḷas would hence appear to be a major factor in agrarian expansion. Interestingly, there is a general correspondence between the steady increase in irrigation works mentioned in the inscriptions of the seventh to eleventh centuries and the increase in the *nāḍus* during the same period.

At least a minimum of seventy-two *nāḍus* are known to have had at least one important irrigation source each.

The correlation is particularly striking in the period of Parāntaka I (907–55), with new *nāḍu* units appearing for the first time in inscriptions, a phenomenon common to all the Cōḷa dominated regions.[21] This was the foundation on which the restructuring of the economy reached its culmination under the middle Cōḷa ruler Rājarāja I and Rājēndra I, creating an extensive resource base in the river valleys and a widening agricultural hinterland for Kāñcīpuram. As a major centre of urban concentration, Kāñcīpuram's economic reach in the twelfth century AD covered all the *nāḍus* of the Palar-Cheyyar valleys and even beyond.

Distribution of Irrigation Works and Nadus (AD)

7th Century	*8th Century*	*9th Century*	*10th Century*	*11th Century*	*12th Century*
3 *nāḍus* one in each	2 *nāḍus* one in each	17 *nāḍus* +	30 *nāḍus* +	12 *nāḍus* +	8 *nāḍus* +
3 *kōṭṭams*	2 *kōṭṭams*	in 6 *kōṭṭams*	in 11 *kōṭṭams*	in 8 *kōṭṭams*	in 3 *kōṭṭams*
2+ irrigation works	2+ irrigation works	16+ irrigation works	30+ irrigation works	9+ irrigation works	8(?) irrigation works

The organization of agrarian relations around the *brahmadeya* and the temple led to the emergence of the *brāhmaṇa* (priestly caste), *vēḷāḷa* (non-*brāhmaṇa*) landowners and the temple, administered by *brāhmaṇas* and *vēḷāḷas* as landed elite and to a re-structuring of society within the *varṇa* or caste framework, the regional specificities of the Tamil country producing a variant of the caste system, which was expressed through two broad categories, the *brāhmaṇa* and non-*brāhmaṇa* or *śūdra*. Within the second category, most of the occupational and service groups (*jātis*) were placed. Social differentiation through diversification of economic activities and occupational differences in the form of different categories of temple functionaries, craftsmen in the service of agriculture and agricultural labourers, i.e. division of labour, was interwoven in this process.

With the gradual expansion of the exchange nexus among the agricultural settlements within the *nāḍus* and the revival of long-distance trade by the ninth century AD, another important dimension to the complexity of societal organization was added, viz., the *nagarattār* or a full-fledged trading community. The *nagaram*[22] came to be the third major institutional force, the *nagarattār* controlling local and intra-regional trade.

Purāṇic religion and the *bhakti* cult provided the ideological premises and the institutional means, i.e. the temple, to create effective space–rural and urban–for the emerging complexity of social organization.[23] In the medieval South Indian context all the emergent groups–rural and urban–were merged into a single systemic relationship, as substantial components within the same structure, 'seeking validation within the norms of a traditional social order'. The acts of validation mainly centered round the temple, its construction, participation in gift-giving and ritual activities in a ranked hierarchy.

Urban nuclei: 1. Taṉ-Kūṟu

By the tenth to eleventh centuries, urban nuclei emerged in the major *brahmadeyas* and temple centres, which were mainly royal creations, located near large irrigation projects. Such *brahmadeyas* came to be organized as separate revenue units and designated as *taṉ-kūṟu*[24] and later as *taṉi-ūr* (independent unit). In terms of revenue administration, the *taṉ-kūṟu* is comparable to the *vaḷa-nāḍu*, a larger revenue unit, comprising of several *nāḍus* created in the eleventh century by Rājarāja I. While the *vaḷanāḍu* organization dominated the Cōḷa heartland and newly conquered chieftaincies in Naḍuvil nāḍu and Pāṇḍi nāḍu,[25] *taṉ-kūṟus* were more numerous and more systematically introduced in Toṇḍai-nāḍu and a few areas south of it, but rarely in Cōḷa nāḍu proper.[26] The *vaḷa-nāḍu* nomenclature was used occasionally for the *kōṭṭams* in Toṇḍai nāḍu.[27]

The *taṉ-kūṟu* increased in size and population with the addition of several *piḍāgai* (hamlets) and *puṟam* (full fledged revenue village) as *dēvadānas* or grants to temples between the tenth and twelfth centuries.[28] This is also suggestive of a defining and redefining of economic and socio-political units within the *kōṭṭam*, for when older *brahmadeyas* became *taṉiyūrs* under the Cōḷas, their *nāḍu* affiliation ceased to operate and their *kōṭṭam* location alone is mentioned, as also in the case of newly-created *taṉiyūrs*. Such restructuring would also seem to be an act of deliberate royal policy for creating agencies of a state synthesis under the Cōḷas. In effect, it introduced a virtual hierarchy among *brahmadeyas* and different levels of urbanization, the *taṉiyūrs* being capable of widening the orbit of their economic functions, with markets developing within and attracting traders from outside, a *nagaram* sometimes being attached to them or created for them, taxes assessed independently and direct links established with the king's government.

The *taṉiyūrs* show a distinct pattern of socio-political dominance, economic and administrative functions with a higher status than other *brahmadeyas* and temple centres. Members of the royal family bestowed special attention on them, extending their direct patronage to temples, closely interacting with the local elite and priestly groups in the socio-religious sphere, with a direct politico-economic control. Temples in the *taṉiyūr* were invariably royal foundations. The *taṉiyūrs* were named and renamed after the founder kings and their successors.[29] More importantly, they were internally so structured as to have several *cēris* or quarters demarcated for elite groups in the centre of the inner square (main streets around the temple), for professional groups in the immediate neighbourhood (i.e. outer square), and for those at the fringes of society in the outskirts. The *cēris* were also named either after royal members (Madurāntakam) or after the patron deity (Uttaramērūr).[30] The main roads and markets (*pērangāḍi* and *angāḍi*–big and small markets) were also similarly named.[31] The markets, which were located at central points, where commerce was a regular activity, attracted traders from *mānagarams* like Kāñcīpuram and royal ports like Māmallapuram, as well as from the distant Cōḷa and Pāṇḍya regions. Highways linked them to other *nagarams*, *mānagarams* and to royal centres.[32] The standard weights and measures used in the *taṉiyūr* were often those prevalent in royal centres, e.g. Kāñcīpuram.[33] Monetary transactions are also found to be more frequent in these centres. Land owning elite from other regions also figure as donors in the *taṉiyūrs*.

Social dominance in these centres was expressed through the construction of the temple and its precincts with subsidiary shrines, as well as by the nature and volume of endowments. The main shrine (*vimāna*) was invariably a royal foundation or, occasionally, the work of chiefly families[34] like the Bāṇas in Toṇḍai nāḍu. Additional shrines and structures were built by officers and dignitaries like the *Mūvēnda vēḷār*.[35]

The *Taṉiyūr* acted as an information channel, especially for royal orders. Rules regarding the organization of the *sabhā* and its functioning through elected *vāriyams* (committees) are recorded in such centres.[36] More importantly, royal orders relating to defaulters of land revenue affecting the whole region or several regions, were invariably recorded and publicized through these centres.[37] The high visibility of royal officers, civil and military, both as donors and officials discharging executive functions, convening the *sabhā* and executing royal orders, is another notable feature indicating the central place functions of the *taṉiyūr*. A similar role is also recognizable in the late-Cōḷa and post-Cōḷa periods, i.e. thirteenth-fourteenth centuries, when the Telugu Cōḷas, Pāṇḍyas and Śambhuvāryas chose to record their orders relating to refixing, remission or revision of taxes on traders, weavers, oil-mongers and other professional groups in the same *taṉiyūrs* as well as *nagarams*.[38]

Major craft production centres like weaving centres, centres of oil production and salt manufacture, were often attached as *dēvadānas* to the *taṉiyūrs*, and it is of great significance that such centres were sometimes located in other *kōṭṭams* or at considerable distances.[39] A combination of the *taṉiyūr* and *nagaram* is illustrated by Tirukkaḻukkuṉṟam, a *nagaram* in Kaḷattūr Kōṭṭam, which was linked to Vānavanmahādēvicaturvēdimangalam, a *taṉ-kūṟu* in Āmūr Kōṭṭam in the eleventh century AD.[40] *Taṉiyūrs* inevitably became multi-temple centres of more than one or two religious affiliations. Each of these components was structured on the same pattern, showing a general concentration of population, sometimes covering an area of five or six square kilometres and more.

The evolution of the *tirumaḍai viḷāgam*, i.e. the temple square with house sites and streets aligned at right angles, is conspicuously illustrated in the *taṉiyūr*.[41] Temple priests (*Śivabrāhmaṇas* and *Vaikhānasas*), *uvaccar* or musicians and *tapasvins* (ascetics), resided in the inner square as also the landed elite, while professional communities like weavers, oil-mongers and *dēvaraḍiyār* (temple servants) were permitted to settle down in the outer premises, and areas were set aside for mixed castes known as the *Śankarappāḍi*, showing the careful demarcation of effective space in these centres. *Maṭhas* (monasteries) of various lineages, Śaiva and Vaiṣṇava, which were attached to the temples, were accommodated as a major component in the temple precincts[42] even from the twelfth century, contributing to the increase in urban activities of these centres.

The horizontal stratification of residential areas in the 'pre-industrial' city characterized as a ceremonial centre has been referred to earlier.[43] Here the ceremonial centre is so planned as to align the city with cosmic structures and forces, where the elite lived at the centre and the others at the margins. Markets were neither central nor dominant, but a product of the demands arising from the nucleation by the ceremonial centre. The *taṉi-yūr* would seem to represent a smaller and less compact version of such a centre, and cities like Kāñcīpuram, the enlarged version. The *taṉiyūr* is also a supreme example of rural-urban continuum.

It is hard to find evidence of a *taṉiyūr* in each *kōṭṭam*, but its emergence in key areas, and the distribution of *taṉiyūrs* in ten *kōṭṭams* (so far identified) would perhaps indicate the possibility of their occurrence in the ratio of at least one to a *kōṭṭam*. This, together with the fact that some chiefly centres like Tiruvallam[44] also became a *taṉiyūr* under Rājarāja I, is a feature of considerable importance in revenue administration and political linkages.

Urban nuclei: 2. Nagaram or Market Centre

The urban forms generated by the end of Pallava rule, i.e. ninth century AD, found expression only in two categories of centres, the royal or administrative centre, and the market or commercial centre. As Kāñcīpuram, apart from being a royal centre, was also a major commercial centre in the expanding trade network under the Cōḷas, it is the *nagaram* or market centre, which is of immediate concern here. Commerce in the Pallava period was organized around Kāñcīpuram, the capital and Māmallapuram, the royal port. The other Pallava *nagarams* (four) were located at nodal points linking the capital with other regions, particularly the Kaveri Valley. The distribution of *nagarams* in the seventh to ninth centuries does not show any direct correlation with the *kōṭṭams* or *nāḍus* reflective of a town-hinterland relationship or that of a market to its marketing areas.[45] The exchange nexus, in other words, was oriented more towards the commercial needs of the royal centre and less as a regular market for each agrarian unit.

The proliferation of the *nagaram* from the tenth century shows that the need for marketing facilities increased with the agrarian expansion of the seventh to ninth centuries. Its distribution pattern shows a steady increase in the early Cōḷa period, a remarkable increase in the middle Cōḷa period, and a marginal increase in the late Cōḷa period, keeping pace with the rise, expansion and decline of Cōḷa power.[46] As a local body, the *nagaram* maintained local markets (*angāḍi*), supervising the flow of goods, providing a regular link among the *nāḍus* and with itinerant traders.[47] There is some indication that each of the twenty-four *kōṭṭams* of Toṇḍai nāḍu ultimately acquired at least one *nagaram*, for a late Cōḷa inscription from Tirukkaccūr[48] refers, among other things, to the twenty-four *nagarams* of the region and the Vāṇiyar or oil-mongers, who met in Kāñcīpuram to make decisions regarding certain levies on oil mills to be endowed to the Tirukkaccūr Śiva temple.

In the tenth and eleventh centuries, a further diversification in markets and trading pattern is attested to by the emergence of specialized trading groups like the *Sāliya nagaram* (weaver-traders). *Śankarappāḍi nagaram* (supplies of oil and ghee) and the *Vāṇiya nagaram* (oil mongers).[49]

The role of the *nagarams* in the commerce of Toṇḍai nāḍu and inter-regional trade was significant, reflecting to a great degree the level of monetization in the Cōḷa period. The volume of gold deposits and gifts to the temple was considerably larger in the early Cōḷa period (the reign of Parāntaka I and Uttama Cōḷa, i.e. the tenth century), when compared to the Pallava period, while gold and money gifts show an increase in the period of Rājarāja I and Rājēndra I (985–1044).[50] In Kulōttunga's reign (1070–1118), due to the royal policy of encouraging trade through abolition of tolls and the extension of trade ventures into all conceivable areas in South India, Southeast Asia and China, a more regular use of money is attested to by the constant inscriptional references to coins, as well as by the issue of a new currency by Kulōttunga I, modelled on the gold issues of the Eastern Cāḷukyas.[51] These would show not only a quantitative increase, but also a higher level of monetization, as interest rates were now calculated in terms of money and differentiation was made between old currency in use and new ones as legal tender. After a temporary lull under the successors of Kulōttunga I, new currencies came into use in Toṇḍai nāḍu with the coin issues of the Telugu Cōḷas (Nellūr Pudu Māḍai, Gaṇḍagōpālan-māḍai) and the Pāṇḍyas in the thirteenth century AD.[52] Land prices show an upward trend[53] in the late Cōḷa period (1150-1279) and commodity production went up, considerably enhancing the economic status of traders. However, the level of monetization under the Cōḷas was, on the whole, considerably low when compared to the Vijayanagar period, and its impact on rural exchange was minimal.

The outward flow of the gold and money deposits from the *nagarams* to the hinterland is attested to by the fact that they were entrusted to the *sabhās* and *ūrs* of the hinterland, bringing in a reciprocal flow of interest in paddy, ghee and other ritual requirements to the *nagaram* and *mānagaram* temples. While initially the rates of interest were in kind,[54] money interests became regular from the period of Kulōttunga I.[55]

Individual merchants show a great deal of mobility between different regions (*maṇḍalams*) from the early Cōḷa period, as seen from the references to Māyilaṭṭis and Ceṭṭis travelling from Cōḷa and Pāṇḍya regions to the Toṇḍai nāḍu *nagarams* and making individual donations to temples.[56] However, it was through collective action and patronage, as well as supportive political roles, as in Kāñcīpuram, that the merchant class established its social prestige and economic status in the early and middle Cōḷa periods.

Itinerant trade and its organization

With the increase in peninsular trade and the revival and expansion of South Asian trade, commercial ventures came to be organized and conducted by larger trading groups (*samaya*), usually described as guilds or corporations, like *Ayyāvoḷe* or *Tiśai Āyiraṭṭu Aiññūṟṟuvar*, *Nānādeśi* and *Valañjīyar*, the *Maṇigrāmam* (local traders) and *Añjuvaṇṇam* (foreign traders). The last mentioned was active only in the coastal areas of Toṇḍaimaṇḍalam,[57] whereas in the Cōḷa, Kongu and Pāṇḍya regions, the *Maṇigrāmam* controlled prestigious markets in Kāvērippūmpaṭṭiṇam, Uṟaiyūr and Koḍumbāḷūr, showing greater mobility in the commercially important link areas like the Pudukkottai region.[58]

The interaction of these merchant bodies with the *nagarams*, some of which were intersection points in itinerant trade, was a factor of great importance in early medieval urbanization, especially due to the Cōḷa policy of encouragement to overseas trade, through trade missions, maritime expeditions and abolition of tolls, which facilitated their movement both inland and overseas. Protected merchant towns called *eṟivīrappaṭṭaṇas* were established under royal charters from the eleventh century AD, such towns appearing on trade routes, commercially important areas and distribution points. Kāṭṭūr in the Chingleput district (near Madras) and Basinikoṇḍa (Śirāvalli) in the Chittoor district were two such centres of the eleventh century in Toṇḍaināḍu.[59] The *Nānādeśis* of Mayilappūr formulated rules of conduct for the traders and controlled Kāṭṭūr, which they were instrumental in converting into a protected merchant town.

The itinerant merchant body is less conspicuous in the capitals (royal centres) and ports, which were *mānagarams*, where it is visible only in the capacity of a trader or donor extending patronage to temples or setting up *maṭhas* as in Kāñcīpuram,[60] but hardly exercised any political or social influence. Here, the local *mānagaram* or *nagaram* organization wielded enormous socio-political influence as administrators of commercial ventures, patrons and managers of local temples,[61] i.e. as high prestige groups, in the hierarchy of local relations of dominance. In Toṇḍaimaṇḍalam, this merchant body does not appear to have had temporary or permanent residential quarters in major centres as in Cōḷamaṇḍalam and Pāṇḍimaṇḍalam,[62] except presumably in the *eṟivīrappaṭṭaṇas* or in coastal towns like Mayilappūr, which was not a royal port.

By the end of the eleventh century, i.e. the reign of Kulōttunga I, whose interests in promoting trade are well known, the whole coastal region (later called Coromandel) from the Pāṇḍya coast in the south to Viśākhapaṭṭiṇam[63] in the north (Andhra region), came to be linked through itinerant trade and, perhaps, also by coastal shipping and coastal land routes. The Toṇḍaimaṇḍalam coast, henceforth, assumed great importance, as seen in the series of coastal trading centres appearing between the twelfth and fourteenth centuries, from Tiruppālaivanam (Pulicat) in the north to Marakkāṇam in the south.[64]

Trade, Craft Production and Maṭha

Nagaram and craft-production centres provide interesting contextual evidence, which would indicate a close relationship between the increase in trade activities, craft-production—especially oil and textiles—and the institution of Śaiva *maṭhas* (monasteries) of various sects and lineages, starting from the Kālāmukha (Pāśupata) *maṭhas* of the ninth and tenth centuries in centres like Mayilāppūr and Tiruvoṟṟiyūr[65] (the Madras region), the *bhakti maṭhas* named after Śaiva saints in the eleventh and twelfth centuries,[66] and the well organized *maṭhas* of the Gollā/Gōlakī or Lakṣādhyāyi lineages of the twelfth to fourteenth centuries AD, tracing descent from the Gollā maṭha of Vārāṇāsi (Banaras).[67] They are invariably located in trade and craft centres. Itinerant traders are also often found to be patrons of *maṭhas*, some of which are named after them as *Nānādeśi*, *Valañjīya* and *Danmadāvaḷa maṭha*.[68] The monastic network seems to have provided a great impetus to trade and craft production in Toṇḍaimaṇḍalam, as in other parts of Tamil Nadu.

South Indian textiles had a growing demand and widening market in the medieval period, and, hence, the weaver communities of Toṇḍaimaṇḍalam (especially of the Kāñcīpuram region) acquired a special importance in the commerce of this region. The *sāliyas* (*paṭṭasālin*) and the *kaikkōḷas* were two weaver communities producing varieties of silk and cotton cloth for inland and overseas markets. The *sāliyas* gained considerable influence in Kāñcīpuram, as the chosen weavers of royal garments and temple administrators from the tenth century AD,[69] while the *kaikkōḷas*, the larger community, are not visible as an influential group till the twelfth century AD. Early records refer to them more often as warriors, some of them with high ranks as commanders (*sēnāpatis*) and chiefs (*mudalis*), participating in gift-giving activities.[70] The *kaikkōḷas* without such status titles were apparently weavers who had no economic influence, being dependent on traders for organizing the marketing of textiles. However, by the twelfth century AD, the *kaikkōḷas* are seen making expensive gifts like jewels, land, etc., the volume of gifts indicating an enhanced economic status, which ultimately gave them avenues of upward social mobility through temple management as trustees of endowments and members of the temple executive.[71] Their aspirations to higher status took different forms of seeking validation—through setting up images and dedicating members of their family as *dēvaraḍiyār* (temple servants and perhaps also dancing girls), to whom house sites were allotted or sold in the thirteenth century in the *tirumaḍaiviḷāgam* of the temple.[72] Their status, both ritually and socially, was lesser than the merchants or *Sāliya nagaram*, though they were also entitled to temple honours in the later period.

The change in their economic status, however, was also accompanied by increase in taxes on weavers and their looms,[73] a feature noticeable even from the period of Kulōttunga I, which led to severe tax burdens, forcing the weavers to abandon various centres. They were induced to stay on or return by remission or revision of taxes under the Śambhuvarāyas and Pāṇḍyas in the thirteenth and fourteenth centuries.[74] This became one of the major issues in the Vijayanagar period, when the demand for South Indian textiles was on the increase.

The interdependence of trade and craft is further emphasised in the records of the same period, when collective gifts through voluntary levies were made by merchants and weavers. Merchants, weavers, oil-mongers and other professional groups are increasingly mentioned together in the thirteenth and fourteenth centuries, in *nagaram* and craft centres, where such remissions or revisions of taxes were recorded.

The twelfth century innovation in societal organization, which helped to accommodate the craft groups, artisans, as well as lower categories of agricultural workers, within the vertical division of the Right and Left Hand (*Valangai* and *Iḍangai*) castes,[75] is not recorded in the Toṇḍaimaṇḍalam inscriptions till the fourteenth and fifteenth centuries AD. Presumably, this division was known, as seen in the assignment of Right Hand status to *sāliyas* and Left Hand status to the *kaikkōḷas*,[76] which points to the fact that criteria other than occupation played an important part in such classification, traceable to their economic and political influence even in the early Cōḷa period.[77] Status enhancement was achieved only through upward ritual mobility. Even the Right and Left Hand division introduced only a new basis, 'a root paradigm' for caste grouping, but still functioned within the traditional norms of validation, i.e. temple ritual and social privileges through such ranking.

Kaikkōḷa aspirations to enhanced ritual status were thus confined, in the later period, to attempts to be upgraded within this 'root paradigm' from the Left to the Right Hand. Right and Left Hand caste rivalries, however, became a regular feature only in the Vijayanagar and post-Vijayanagar periods.

Supra-local Organizations

An organization of agriculturists known as the *Cittiramēḻi Periyanāḍu* appears in inscriptional records of Toṇḍaimaṇḍalam from the middle of the eleventh century AD in the reign of Rājēndra Cōḷa II (1052-1064).[78] It has often been described as a *Periya nāḍu* (larger *nāḍu*) assembly formed by the *nāṭṭār* (*vēḷāḷas*) to resist the centralizing efforts of the Cōḷas.[79] It would appear, however, that the need for such an organization was created more by the growing consumption of food grains and pulses in urban areas and the efforts of agriculturists to control the movement of grains and other agricultural products, which they alone could have mobilized for exchange with itinerant traders. A more logical assumption would be that it was an agricultural guild,[80] which established commercial links with the Five Hundred by the twelfth century AD. A close interaction between these organizations is indicated by the presence of the *Tiśai Āyirattu Aiññūṟṟuvar* or *Nānādeśi* in centres where the *Cittiramēḻi* inscriptions are found, either mentioned separately as in Tāmaraippākkam (North Arcot district),[81] or as jointly making donations in other parts of Tamil Nadu, particularly in the commercially important Pudukkottai-Ramanathapuram region, and in the Cōḷa heartland.[82]

On the basis of the earliest occurrence and the spatial and chronological distribution of the *Cittiramēḷi* inscriptions, it would be tempting to assign the origins of this organization to the conscious efforts of the Toṇḍaināḍu agriculturists, later spreading to other parts of the Tamil country, and even into South Karnataka and Andhra. In Tāmaraippākkam, the *nāṭṭār* of several *kōṭṭams* and other areas included in Jayakoṇḍa-cōḷamaṇḍalam, assembled to discuss common problems of the *vēḷāḷa* community. Yet, the *praśasti* of this organization, which is an illuminating record, shows that its members, who claimed to be *Bhūmiputras*, were drawn from all the four *varṇas* and that it was not a caste organization. It also appears to have had greater stakes in local relations of dominance than other supra-local bodies, for it acted as a dispenser of justice, settling land disputes and cases of criminal offence.[83] Later, in the twelfth and thirteenth centuries, the *Cittiramēḷi* exercised the right of fixing cesses and tolls on merchandise passing through distribution points and coastal towns of Toṇḍaimaṇḍalam, jointly with the Five Hundred and other bodies like the *Vāṇiya nagaram*,[84] at the time of the decline of Cōḷa power, and in the post-Cōḷa period.

The pre-fix *Padineṇbhūmi* and/or *Eḻupattoṇpadu nāḍu* (eighteen countries and/or seventy-nine *nāḍus*) is also used to designate this organization, as well as the *Vāṇiya* and *Vaiśya* organizations in the thirteenth and fourteenth centuries.[85] It is not easy to define the geographical region covered by this description, and presumably, the 'eighteen countries' had become a traditional nomenclature for the whole of South India, although the 'seventy-nine *nāḍus*' could originally have referred only to Toṇḍaimaṇ-ḍalam.[86]

The *Cittiramēḷi*'s importance is further confirmed by the fact that it founded *brahmadeyas*, *paṭṭaṇams* and built temples, apart from consecrating images and even dedicating temple servants, including dancing girls.[87]

The common eulogy of the *Cittiramēḷi* and merchant bodies represents the first institutional expression of the ascendancy of traders in the predominantly agrarian set up. This is reiterated by the coming together of *nagaram* or *Vaiśya* organizations and *Cittiramēḷi* for various purposes, including fixing tolls and cesses (*maganmai*), commission or share of the town (*pattaṇappagudi*), conspicuously towards the close of the Cōḷa period, when royal authority became virtually ineffective in the peripheral regions like Toṇḍaimaṇḍalam, and receded to the core area, and also in the post-Cōḷa period, when new chieftaincies like the Telugu Cōḷas and Śambhuvarāyas emerged in Toṇḍaimaṇḍalam, and found it profitable to encourage their autonomy and movement. These chieftaincies extended special concessions[88] and support to merchant organizations and also migrant traders from the Cōḷa heartland, residing in the coastal towns of Toṇḍaimaṇḍalam.[89] Kerala merchants trading in Kāñcīpuram and other *nagarams*, and the Nellūr traders who constantly moved into Toṇḍaimaṇḍalam with the ascendancy of Telugu Cōḷas over Kāñcīpuram in the thirteenth century, conducted active commerce in this region, and even identified themselves with the larger trading community of Toṇḍaimaṇḍalam by making joint endowments to temples and participating in temple construction.[90]

In the thirteenth century, yet another supra-local forum emerged in Toṇḍaimaṇḍalam, when the *Tiruvāyppāḍi Nāṭṭavar* (cattle keepers/shepherds) of the 'eighteen countries', assembled at Tiruvattiyūr near Kāñcīpuram and assigned a voluntary levy of cattle and sheep to the local temple for favours received by their 'caste' and 'clan'(?).[91] In their eulogy, they called themselves, significantly, Nandaputras of the Yādava lineage, descendants of the lord of Dvāraka, i.e. Kṛṣṇa, settled in Toṇḍaimaṇḍalam. This appears to be a unique organization of the pastoral families of Toṇḍaimaṇḍalam.

Kāñcīpuram in the Early Historic Phase

Kāñci, the Kāñcīpuram/Kāñcīmānagaram of the early medieval period, was one of the restricted loci of major urban concentration in the early centuries of the Christian era, with access to maritime trade through its port Nīrppeyaṟṟu, which, on the basis of archaeological evidence, may be identified with

Vasavasamudram near Vāyalūr, at the mouth of the Palar.[92] Tiraiyar (people of the waves), the name of the early rulers of Kacci, would suggest a possible association with the sea and sea-faring, and indicate their interest in trading ventures overseas and in establishing socio-political dominance through control over external trade. Like the other Tamil powers such as the Cōḷas, Cēras and Pāṇḍyas, the Tiraiyar encouraged the flow of luxury goods, and founded dual centres of power—Kāñcīpuram (Kacci) and its port—as a consumption point in the interior and a port on the coast. Kāñcī was, however, more than a mere consumption point, for it was the major weaving centre in Toṇḍaimaṇḍalam, being located in one of the cotton producing regions, like Uṟaiyūr in Cōḷanāḍu and Madurai in Pāṇḍināḍu.

The antiquity of Kāñcīpuram's commerce and external trade is also established by archaeological evidence in the form of remains of Roman pottery and the 'ship' type coins of the Sātavāhanas (first and second centuries AD),[93] and on the basis of early Chinese references to Houang-tche and its trade.[94] Evidence of its urban character is also provided by the *Maṇimēkalai*,[95] a Buddhist work of the post-Sangam period, whose locale was Kāñcīpuram, and by its description as a *mānagaram* (big city) in all subsequent literary works and inscriptions. Its status as a *mānagaram* was enhanced by the multiple roles that it acquired by the time of the rise of the Simhaviṣṇu line of Pallavas in the sixth century AD, as a royal centre, as well as a commercial and craft centre, with a heterogeneous population composed of Buddhists, Jains and followers of the brahmanical religions of Vaiṣṇavism and Śaivism. Its continuous importance in inter-regional trade was sustained even in the period of crisis following the decline of Roman and West Asian trade, when Kāñcī revitalized its commerce by turning to Southeast Asia, where Indianized kingdoms and colonies had emerged by the fourth and fifth centuries AD. By the sixth century Māmallapuram had also developed as the major outlet for Kāñcīpuram's trade.

Kāñcī's early Buddhist connections[96] are attested to not only by the *Maṇimēkalai*, but also by the seventh century accounts of Hsuan Tsang[97] and the *Mattavilāsa Prahasana*,[98] the Sanskrit farce of Mahendravarman I, the Pallava ruler (575–630). The Jain associations of Kāñcī are at least as old as AD 550, the date of the Paḷḷankōyil copper plates of Simhavarman,[99] referring to Jina-Kāñcī or Tirupparuttikkuṉṟam and its Jain temple. Above all, Kāñcī's associations with Vedic brāhmaṇism and Purāṇic religion are of greater antiquity, and date back to the second century AD, the probable date of *Perumpāṇāṟṟuppaṭai*, a Sangam work, referring to Kāñcī. The *Ghaṭikā* of Kāñcī, a brahmanical institution of higher learning referred to in the copper plates and inscriptions of the Pallavas and Kadambas,[100] also proclaimed the dominance of *brāhmaṇas* and *kṣatriyas*, even from the fourth and fifth centuries AD. Thus, Kāñcī was truly heterogeneous in its socio-religious affiliations even before the rise of the Pallavas, and tended to evolve four major sectors in its internal structure by the seventh century AD, viz., Buddhist, Jain, Vaiṣṇava and Śaiva.

The Early Medieval Phase

Kāñcīpuram's urban character underwent significant changes when it was drawn into the reurbanization process of the early medieval period, which began with the agrarian integration of Toṇḍaināḍu. The agricultural hinterland, which sustained the city's population, was initially confined to Eyil Kōṭṭam in which Kāñcīpuram was located. Its expansion beyond Eyil Kōṭṭam began with the Pallava land grants of the seventh to ninth centuries,[101] but more significantly from the ninth century, when a higher level of agrarian integration began under the Cōḷas. Correspondingly, the Śaiva, Vaiṣṇava and Jain sectors of the city came to expand, so as to cover almost the whole area of modern Kāñcīpuram. From the tenth to thirteenth centuries, under the Cōḷas, the city's growth was continuous, the expansion of its hinterland* corresponding to the city's expansion** in the form of new temples, or rebuilding and elaboration of existing ones, to all of which grants of land and *dēvadāna* villages were made in various *Kōṭṭams*. By the mid-thirteenth century, over sixty

* *See* map on Kancipuram, the Hinterland, Map 14.

** *See* map of Kancipuram City, Map 15.

dēvadāna villages, two *paḷḷicandam* (Jain) villages for Jina-Kāñcī and lands in several other *brahmadeya* and non-*brahmadeya* centres, were made over to the Kāñcīpuram temples, covering fourteen *kōṭṭams* and over eighteen *nāḍus* in Toṇḍaimaṇḍalam, from which agricultural and other products reached Kāñcīpuram. Over fifty per cent of these grants were made by the end of the eleventh century, and the rest by mid-thirteenth century, a major share being assigned to the largest Viṣṇu temple, that of Varadarājasvāmi+ in Attiyūr, which had become an integral part of the city by the end of the eleventh century AD.

Under the Pallavas, Kāñcīpuram's commercial hinterland was confined to three major points, i.e. Kāñcīpuram, Mallai (Māmallapuram) and Mayilai (Mayilāppūr), representing an exchange nexus limited to the needs of the royal centre of Kāñcīpuram, which had external links of greater importance till the eighth century AD than internal links with a trade network. The few market centres of the period known from Pallava records do not provide evidence of such a regional network.

Kāñcīpuram's commerce came to be linked to the *nagaram* network only with the emergence of the inland exchange nexus through the centuries of Cōḷa rule, i.e. ninth to thirteenth centuries. This was achieved through the reciprocal flow of funds (gold and money deposits) from Kāñcīpuram to different *brahmadeyas* and *nagarams* of Toṇḍaināḍu,[102] where the local *sabhā* and *nagaram* were entrusted with the deposits on payment of interests, in the form of paddy, service and other commodities as ritual requirements which reached Kāñcī. Temple funds were thus invested in both urban and rural enterprises and perhaps also in cotton production, as Kāñcī was the biggest weaving centre. Kāñcīpuram's umland extended even into Poysaḷa (Hoysaḷa) rājya in South Karnataka, where several *gāvuṇḍas*, *pradhāna mudalis* of Iḍai nāḍu gifted land for the supply of cardamom to the Varadarāja temple in the thirteenth century.[103]

Kāñcīpuram's commercial importance is also reflected in the enormous influence and prestige wielded by the *mahānagarattār*, even from the period of Dantivarman Pallava (796–846),[104] as executors of royal orders and managers of temples.

+ See ground plan of Varadarajasvami temple, Map 17.

Kāñcī's relegation to the position of a secondary political centre under the Cōḷas, however, did not affect its commercial supremacy. The Cōḷas, were, in fact, more directly interested in promoting its weaving industry and textile trade. This is illustrated by the detailed financial arrangements made for the Ūragam temple by Uttama Cōḷa in late tenth century AD,[105] in which the *mahānagarattār*, *sāliyar* or *paṭṭasālins* (weavers) and other groups were involved, the *nagarattār*, in a managerial and supervisory role and the *sāliyar*, the weavers of royal garments, as temple accountants and administrators. The *kaikkōḷas* looked after the cultivation and reclamation of lands of the Ūragam temple during the reign of Uttama Cōḷa, and subsequently, under Kulōttunga I.[106]

The city's commercial area was marked by several big streets where merchants lived, two big streets, where the weavers resided,[107] apart from the four weavers' quarters and another site called Sōḻaniyamam, which are mentioned in the copper plate grant of Uttama Cōḷa. These weavers' quarters were associated with the Ūragam temple and its management. All these streets and quarters seem to fall within the ancient Kacci, the nucleus around which Kāñcīpuram grew into a big city. They would also indicate a well defined commercial and craft production area within the city.

In the hierarchy of social dominance, the *nagarattār*, in general, occupied a position next to the landed elite, and contributed in a large measure to the establishment of economic links. The Kāñcīpuram *mānagarattār*, however, enjoyed a more prestigious status than other *nagarams*, and greater autonomy *vis-à-vis* other professional groups, as politically powerful elite. More importantly, they were also involved in large-scale land transactions and gifts to the Kāñcīpuram temples,[108] especially during the early and middle Cōḷa periods, with a conspicuous increase in the volume of gifts under Rājarāja I, Rājādhirāja I and Kulōttunga I, in terms of land, gold and money.

The presence of itinerant trading organizations like the *Nānādeśi* or *Tiśai Āyirattu Aiññūṟṟuvar* in the same period (eleventh to twelfth centuries),[109] further confirms the increase in Kāñcīpuram participation in South Indian trade. The period of Kulōttunga I (1070-1118) witnessed not only a spurt in commercial ventures, but also the movement of itinerant traders into other parts of South India. Special attention was paid to the textile trade and weaver's craft by the introduction of a series of regulatory measures in the form of cesses on looms and weavers, for controlling the production and distribution of cotton and textiles. The Kāñcīpuram region received a major share of the attention bestowed upon textile trade and promotion of the weaving industry.

The volume of trade further increased in the thirteenth century under the late Cōḷas and Telugu Cōḷas, with the movement of Nellūr (Andhra) traders and Kerala merchants, who became major participants in Kāñcīpuram's commerce in the thirteenth and fourteenth centuries. A general weakening of the *nagarattār*'s hold over Kāñcī is seen in the changing pattern of patronage and the nature and volume of gifts made by traders from Andhra and Kerala.[110] It may also be attributed to the tendency for increased monetization, which inevitably broke the *nagaram*'s autonomy and enviable status in the commercial hierarchy. Another factor which led to the breaking of the *nagaram*'s independence was the use of the several currencies introduced by the Telugu Cōḷas and Pāṇḍyas, which the traders from outside Toṇḍaināḍu used in commercial transactions, as well as land endowments to temples by purchase.[111]

Kāñcīpuram became the major destination in South India, a point of convergence for South Indian trade in the thirteenth and fourteenth centuries, i.e. before the rise of Vijayanagar. Chinese and Arab trade increasingly concentrated on the Kerala coast (Kollam = Quilon) and the Pāṇḍya coast (Toṇḍi). The merchants of Malaimaṇḍalam (Kerala) brought horses, spices and other commodities to Toṇḍaināḍu and presumably returned with textiles. Cīlai Ceṭṭis (cloth merchants) also moved out of Kāñcīpuram and Mayilāppūr to the west through the Kongu highway, i.e. Salem-Coimbatore region.[112]

Kāñcīpuram had also become the headquarters of the supralocal organization of the *Vāṇiya nagaram* by the end of the twelfth century AD.[113] Although the *mahānāḍu* (supralocal) organization of the *kaikkōḷas*, with Kāñcīpuram as its logical meeting place, is not known from inscriptions prior to the Vijayanagar period, i.e. fifteenth century,[114] there are strong indications of the existence of such a forum for the weavers even by the thirteenth century AD.

Kāñcīpuram's urbanism also derives from its role as the political centre of Toṇḍaimaṇḍalam from the commencement of the Christian era. However, direct political control over Toṇḍaimaṇḍalam was established only under the Pallavas of the Simhaviṣṇu line in the sixth century AD. Kāñcīpuram's role as an administrative centre continued with equal vigour under the Cōḷas, although it had been relegated to the position of a secondary capital. Kāñcī served as the base of military operations under the early and middle Cōḷas,[115] particularly during the Cōḷa-Rāṣṭrakūṭa (tenth century) and Cōḷa-Cāḷukya (eleventh and twelfth centuries) conflicts. Later, under Kulōttunga I and his successors, Cōḷa commanders from Kāñcīpuram led expeditions as far as Kalinga (Orissa).[116] Cōḷa royal officers, both civil and military, are highly visible in Kāñcīpuram's inscriptions, as donors, administrators and military leaders.[117] The auditing of temple accounts in various centres of Toṇḍaimaṇḍalam was carried out from Kāñcīpuram, and occasionally from Tiruvoṟṟiyūr,[118] another centre of direct control exercised by the Cōḷa government over the city and its hinterland. The royal palace of the Cōḷas in Kāñcīpuram is referred to in a number of inscriptions from the period of Sundara Cōḷa (*c.* AD 956–73).

Cultural Role of Kāñcīpuram

Kāñcīpuram's role in socio-religious changes and cultural creativity in Toṇḍaimaṇḍalam, in fact the whole of South India, was more significant than that of any other medieval city. Kāñcī's autonomy, as well as its very heterogeneity, as a centre of different religious affiliations and urban concentration, led to serious socio-religious conflict in the early medieval period. Under the Pallavas, it was the major centre for the propagation of the Purāṇic religions of Śaivism and Vaiṣṇavism, and the scene of the religious conflict between the brahmanical sects on the one hand and the Buddhist and Jain sects on the other, leading to the decline of Buddhism and the subordination of Jainism. The symbol of royal conversion was central to this conflict,[119] and the *bhakti* (devotion) cult was the chief instrument through which the dominance of the Purāṇic religion was achieved. Often characterized as a protest against caste hierarchy, the *bhakti* movement was, in reality, pitched against the 'heterodox' Buddhist and Jain sects. It is significant that the early Vaiṣṇava (Poygai āḻvār) and Śaiva Saints (Appar) of the *bhakti* cult are associated with Kāñcīpuram region. The *bhakti* hymns derived their content from the epic, Purāṇic, and Āgamic tradition fostered by the Pallavas.

The *bhakti* ideal emanated in a context of social differentiation, where conflicts centred round social dominance, influence and patronage, as in Kāñcīpuram under the Pallavas and in Madurai under the Pāṇḍyas.[120] Initially, the Pallavas succeeded in projecting the Purāṇic world view, and expressed their Purāṇic (brahmanical) ideology through their exquisite rock-cut and structural temples in *dravida* style in Kāñcīpuram, Māmallapuram and other parts of Toṇḍaimaṇḍalam.

Under the Cōḻas, i.e. the second phase, the *bhakti* ideology was more systematically used by the ruling family, with a conspicuous shift in the focus of political and economic power from the *brahmadeya* to the temple. Stories of the religious conflict were narrated in the hagiographic works like the *Periya Purāṇam* of the eleventh and twelfth centuries, when the Cōḻas encouraged the collection of hymns and composition of hagiographic works, in order to revitalize the *bhakti* ideology. The Cōḻas, indeed, gave permanence to all cult centres sanctified by *bhakti* hymns, replicating the temple's role as the superordinate instrument of integration in each of them and in the newly emerging agrarian centres and urban nuclei. This was achieved through renovation in stone of old shrines and construction of new ones. Architecturally, the major temple projects were meant, however, only for the royal/ceremonial centres like Kāñcīpuram.

The above process is reflected, to a remarkable degree, in the expansion of the city of Kāñcīpuram, where all the major shrines, Vaiṣṇava and Śaiva, glorified by the *bhakti* hymns, with the exception of the Parameśvaravinnagaram,[121] evolved as temple centres under the Cōḻas. The process is repeated in the whole of Toṇḍaimaṇḍalam, where not a single temple of the *bhakti* cult was constructed earlier than the early Cōḻa period (AD 850–985).[122]

Sectarianism and conflict were inherent in the *bhakti* cult, and even within the Purāṇic religions, it led to a serious rivalry between Śaivism and Vaiṣṇavism and a societal crisis in the twelfth century, the former having consolidated itself under the Cōḷas and the latter seeking a wider popular base. Rāmānuja, the Vaiṣṇava teacher-reformer, spent his formative years in Kāñcīpuram,[123] where he imbibed the ideals of *Viśiṣṭa-advaita* (qualified monism) and founded the Śrī-Vaiṣṇava religion. The most eventful phase of his activities was more fully enacted in Śrīrangam, the greatest of the Vaiṣṇava centres, and subsequently, in Tirupati and Melkote (Mysore region). Rāmānuja's liberal measures to widen the social base of Vaiṣṇavism involved a reorganization of rituals in Śrīrangam and the incorporation of non-*brāhmaṇa* (*śūdra*) elements into Vaiṣṇava worship, thus creating avenues of status enhancement for the artisanal and other lower caste groups, the weavers (*kaikkōḷas*) being one of the chief beneficiaries. The Śrī Vaiṣṇava community later split on this issue into the *Vaḍakalai* (northern and Sanskritic) and the *Teṉkalai* (Southern and Tamil Prabandhic) sects.[124] Although Viṣṇu worship in Kāñcīpuram was as old as the 'Sangam age', the period after Rāmānuja saw the most remarkable shift in Kāñcīpuram's ceremonial centre to the Viṣṇu temple at Attiyūr, the Vaiṣṇava section of Kāñcīpuram. The shift had its reverberations in the hinterland, where in most Cōḷa centres Viṣṇu temples were either newly constructed or older ones revived. Many of them linked themselves with Kāñcīpuram by following the ritual traditions of the Varadarāja temple.[125] The reformist zeal of Rāmānuja seems to have precipitated the Śaiva-Vaiṣṇava rivalry for patronage, when looked at from the evidence of the Vaiṣṇava texts referring to Rāmānuja's persecution by a Cōḷa ruler, possibly Kulōttunga II.[126] The Śaiva protagonists not only resorted to a harking back to the *bhakti* tradition by composing hagiologies, but also organized Śaiva *maṭhas* as custodians of the hymnal literature, the *Śaiva Siddhānta* canon evolving from this period.[127] The Śaiva propagatory measures are well articulated through the proliferation of monastic lineages all over the Tamil country, a number of *maṭhas* coming up in the weaving and trading centres of Toṇḍaimaṇḍalam, particularly around Kāñcīpuram.[128]

Two important connections may be made in retrospect, which

are relevant to the Kāñcīpuram region. In the earlier conflict, the Jains and Buddhists suffered a general decline, and, judging by later history and traditions, many of the Jain centres[129] around Kāñcīpuram, which appear to have been weaving centres, were converted into Śaiva ones dominated by the Kālāmukhas (-Pāśupatas). The second is the near total decline of Buddhism, although a later thirteenth century reference to the Bauddhapaḷḷi (Buddhist monastery) in Kāñcīpuram[130] along with the streets of merchants, would indicate its survival despite the traditional belief that Śankara, the *Advaita* philosopher, rooted out Buddhism from Kāñcīpuram when he established the Śākta Pīṭha (the present Kāmākṣi temple) in this centre.[131] The Buddhist sector in Kāñcī thus merged with the Śaiva one. Jainism, however, survived in Jina-Kāñcī and other centres in Toṇḍaimaṇḍalam, and this should be attributed to the adoption of the Purāṇic tradition and the temple-based worship by the Jains.

Kāñcīpuram's multiple roles as a dynastic, commercial and cultural centre, would show that it is its urban context, i.e. as a city of heterogeneous population of different socio-religious affiliations, that generated conflict and tension. However, constant shifts in the ideological base by politically powerful elite, and new societal alliances, helped to resolve such conflicts in medieval South India, as reflected in the growth of Kāñcīpuram into a multi-temple complex. In its role as a centre of cultural creativity, especially art, religion and literature, Kāñcīpuram surpassed all other medieval cities of South India. Its continuous importance as a prime mover in the ideological shifts, cultural changes and the reorganization or restructuring of Tamil Society and patterns of patronage, was not shared even by Madurai, which was the Tamil city *par excellence* in the early historical period. Tañjāvūr, on the other hand, was a ceremonial centre created entirely by the political will of the Cōḷas.

The Madras Region*

The modern city of Madras did not develop, like Kāñcīpuram, as a unified, compact centre of urban concentration in the

* *See* Map 16.

pre-modern period. It developed out of several clusters of settlements, the inter-relationships of which are not easy to trace, due to large-scale renovations and changes in modern times. These clusters are distributed mainly in two *kōṭṭams*, the Puliyūr and Puḻal *kōṭṭams*.

Mayilāppūr (Mayilarppil) on the Madras coast was the major centre of trade in Puliyūr Kōṭṭam. The antiquity of its commerce is attested by Ptolemy's reference to Mailarphan, identified with Mayilāppūr,[132] and the Mambalam hoard of punch-marked coins,[133] datable to the second century AD. Along with Mallai and Kāñcī, it formed part of an early exchange nexus dominated by external trade. During the early medieval urbanization, it came to be linked with the network of *nagarams* and inland commerce from the ninth century AD. The presence of two major *bhakti* temples, the Śiva temple in Mayilāppūr and the Viṣṇu temple in Tiruvallikkēṇi, which was a part of Mayilāppūr, and a Jain section of the same centre, which was apparently located in the Santhome area,[134] suggest an early urban concentration in this centre. All traces of Pallava-Cōḻa constructions have been obliterated in the large-scale renovations of the temples of this area. From the ninth and tenth centuries, the commerce of Mayilāppūr was handled by the *Nānādeśi* or *Valañjīyar*, with their mercantile town at Kāṭṭūr, and later by the *Maṇigrāmam* and *Añjuvaṇṇam*.[135] Traders from Mayilāppūr travelled to Cōḻa centres in the distant Kāvēri delta and Tamraparni valley, where fairly large urban complexes had developed under the Cōḻas.[136] Mayilāppūr, as a weaving centre, was linked to the larger Kāñcīpuram region,[137] which had a concentration of weaving communities.

In the eleventh century, a cluster of settlements emerged with Tiruvānmiyūr, a *bhakti* centre on the coast, south of Aḍayāṟu (i.e. south of Mayilāppūr), and Veḷiccēri or Dīnacintāmaṇi Caturvēdimangalam, as the two Śaiva dominated centres in Kōṭṭūr nāḍu in Puliyūr Kōṭṭam.[138] A second cluster of settlements grew up around modern Pallavaram (ancient Pallavapuram) with Tiruccuram (Triśūlam) Vānavanmahādevi Caturvēdimangalam (Pallavaram) in Surattūr nāḍu, Tirunīrmalai and Ādampākkam,[139] the last mentioned becoming a *puṟam* or revenue village assigned to Tiruvoṟṟiyūr in Puḻal Kōṭṭam. Māngāḍu, Pūndamalli and

Tirumaḻiśai, located on the highway to Kāñcīpuram, represent the third cluster of settlements.[140] Pūndamalli, a *nagaram*, was a centre of oil trade with the *Vāṇiya* traders participating in the meetings of the larger body of oil-mongers in Kāñcīpuram.

Puḻal Kōṭṭam, now represented by the northern and north-western parts of Madras city, also had several settlements, of which Pāḍi (Tiruvalidāyam), Tirumullaivāyil and Tiruvēṟkāḍu were the most important, as their interaction with the other centres in the two *kōṭṭams* is attested to by their inscriptional records.[141]

The major centre in Puḻal Kōṭṭam, however, was Tiruvoṟṟiyūr which served as the nucleus of the second urbanization of this region, achieving a high level of integration among Puḻal, Puliyūr and Paiyūr Kōṭṭams, between the tenth and thirteenth centuries AD, linking the northernmost point of the Tamil coast, i.e. Tiruppalaivanam, an important trading centre, with the interior and with other *nagaram* centres.

Tiruvoṟṟiyūr was itself linked to the *brahmadeya* of Maṇali or Simhaviṣṇu Caturvēdimangalam, which was a *puṟam* of Tiruvoṟṟiyūr.[142] The latter's *sabhā* was instrumental in founding the Śiva temple of Tiruvoṟṟiyūr in the ninth century AD. Tiruvoṟṟiyūr's importance arises from its association with an ancestor of the Cōḷas called Oṟṟiyūran, the father of Vijayālaya,[143] the founder of Cōḷa power, and from its sectarian affiliations with Kālāmukha-Kāpālika Śaivism.[144] As an ancestral trust, every Cōḷa ruler bestowed his attention on this centre, beginning from the reign of Parāntaka I. It developed all the characteristics of a *taniyūr*, without being designated as such, and assumed multiple roles, politico-economic, commercial and religious. Next to Kāñcīpuram, it was the chief centre from which royal officials supervised and audited the income and expenditure of other temples in the region, as also that of the Tiruvoṟṟiyūr temple.[145]

Tiruvoṟṟiyūr acquired over ten *dēvadāna* villages and lands in twenty other centres, all located in the three *kōṭṭams* mentioned above. The *nagarattār* of this centre were a powerful body entrusted with the huge gold and money endowments of royal members, and managing temple lands.[146] It was, in addition, a weaving centre with a *Sāliya nagaram*[147] looking after its trade in textiles.

In medieval South India and in the region of our study in particular, the processes of centrality would seem to have been predominantly at work in the emergence of urban hierarchies and the shaping of the contours of the city. However, a subtle but important distinction exists between Kāñcīpuram and other areas in Toṇḍaimaṇḍalam, including Tiruvoṟṟiyūr and Mayilāppūr. The latter would seem to be more directly shaped by the processes of centrality. Kāñcīpuram offers a significant variation, in that it evolved its urban contours and hierarchies through a combination of both these processes of centrality and concentration. Kāñcīpuram's individuality or distinctive character lies in its relative autonomy as a city, a politico-cultural and commercial centre, in which the forces of centrality furthered the processes of concentration and vice-versa.

References

1. A legitimate concern with processes rather than typologies of urban centres and emphasis on the need for overall perspectives and analytical frameworks are found in all recent works on urban history, urban anthropology and urban geography. *See* Philip Abrams and E.A. Wrigley (eds), *Towns in Societies: Essays in Economic History and Historical Sociology*, Cambridge, 1978; Richard Basham, *Urban Anthropology*, 1978; Harold Carter, *An Introduction to Urban Historical Geography*, London, 1983. For India, the more recent works are B.D. Chattopadhyaya, 'Urban Centres in Early Medieval India: An Overview', and R. Champakalakshmi, 'Urban Processes in Early Medieval Tamil Nadu', in S. Bhattacharya and R. Thapar (eds), *Situating Indian History*, New Delhi, 1986. (Chapter 4 in this volume).
2. Champakalakshmi, 'Urbanisation in South India: The Role of Ideology and Polity', Presidential Address, Ancient India Section, *Indian History Congress (IHC)*, 47th Session, Srinagar, 31–41. (Chapter 1 in this volume).
3. *See* R. McC Adams, *The Evolution of Urban Society, Early Mesopotamia and Pre-Hispanic Mexico*, Chicago, 1966, 18.
4. *See* Introduction.
5. S.N. Eisenstadt and A. Schachar, *Society, Culture and Urbanization*, Sage, 1987, 357-61.

6. Ibid.
7. Y. Subbarayalu, *Political Geography of the Chola Country*, 1973, chapter IV on *Maṇḍalam*.
8. Ibid. Chapter VII on *Chieftaincies and Political Units*. The other areas included in Jayankoṇḍacōḷamaṇḍalam were politico-geographic regions dominated by traditional chiefly families positioned between Toṇḍai nāḍu and Cōḷanāḍu.
9. The southern boundary of Toṇḍaināḍu was not the river Pennai, as is often wrongly assumed, for it extended from 13°50′ (Pulicat Lake) North Latitude to 12°15′ North Latitude, which is 64 kilometres north of the Pennai river. To the south lay Naḍuvilnāḍu, later called Naḍuvilmaṇḍalam, and beyond it lay Cōḷa nāḍu.
10. Sudershan Senivaratne, 'Kalinga and Andhra, The Processes of Secondary State Formation in Early India', in Claessen and Skalnik (eds), *The Study of the State*, The Hague, Mouton, 320; K.A. Nilakanta Sastri, 1958, 121; T.V. Mahalingam, *Kāñcīpuram in Early South Indian History*, Madras, 1969, 15.
11. *Perumpāṇārruppaṭai.* The whole work is intended as a 'guide' to the route to Kacci (Kāñcīpuram) for those who were exhorted to seek the patronage of Iḷamtiraiyan, the ruler of Kacci.
12. Mahalingam, *Kāñcīpuram*, 9; also idem (ed.), *Mackenzie Manuscripts*, Madras, 1972, vol. I, Ms no. 13, Section 7.
13. *See* K.S. Ramachandran, *A Bibliography of Indian Megaliths*, Madras, 1971, no. 34, 14–15. The Kuṟumbar are believed to be of Karnataka origin and to have had Puḻal as their centre in Toṇḍaimaṇḍalam.
14. *Chengam Nadukaṟkaḷ* (in Tamil), R. Nagaswamy (ed.), Natana Kasinathan, *Hero-Stones in Tamil Nadu*, Madras, 1978, 1–15.
15. *See* Chapter 1 in this volume, 17 and note 94.
16. *See* C. Minakshi, *Administration and Social Life under the Pallavas*, 2nd edn, Madras, 1977; Mahalingam, *South Indian Polity*, Madras, 1955; K.A. Nilakanta Sastri, *The Cōḷas*, Madras, 1975. For a more analytical approach *see* Burton Stein, *Peasant State and Society in South India*, New Delhi, 1980; N. Karashima, *South Indian History and Society, Studies from Inscriptions, AD 850–1800*, New Delhi, 1984.
17. *See* Chapter 1 in this volume.
18. For example, Udayacandramangalam. *See* Udayendiram Copper Plates of the 21st year of Nandivarman II–*South Indian Inscriptions* (hereafter *SII*), vol. II, 74.
19. Y. Subbarayalu, *Political Geography*, chapter VI on *Vaḷanāḍu*.
20. *See* Chapter 1 in this volume, 15; Minakshi, *Administration*; Rajan Gurukkal, 'The Agrarian System and Socio-Political

Organisation under the Early Pandyas *c.* AD 600–1000', Ph.D. Thesis (unpublished), Jawaharlal Nehru University, 1984.

21. Evidence of the increase in irrigation works or their elaboration under the middle Cōḷa rulers Rājarāja I, Rājēndra I (985–1044) and even under Kulōttunga I (1070–1118), together with new *nāḍu*s, indicates that the process was continuous. Interpretations of the epigraphic data on the *nāḍu*s differ considerably. Subbarayalu's view that the data indicates the evolutionary character of the *nāḍu* under the Cōḷas (Subbarayalu, *Political Geography*, chapter v) is contradicted by Stein, who takes the position that the first mention of a *nāḍu* in inscriptions does not mean a new appearance but a new recognition of the *nāḍu* by the Cōḷas. (Stein, *Peasant State*, 97–9). A careful examination of the contextual evidence of irrigation works and *nāḍu* names derived from them, especially in Toṇḍaimaṇḍalam (e.g. Ambattūr ēri kīḻ nāḍu) would strengthen Subbarayalu's assumption. *See also* R.A.L.H. Gunawardana, 'Inter-Societal Transfer of Hydraulic Technology in Pre-Colonial South Asia: Some Reflections based on a Preliminary Investigation', *Tonan Ajia Kenkyu (South East Asian Studies)*, September 1984, vol. 22, no. 2.
22. *See* Kenneth R. Hall, *Trade and Statecraft in the Age of the Cōḷas*, New Delhi, 1980. *See* Chapter 4 in this volume.
23. *See* Chapter 1 in this volume, 31–41.
24. Uttaramērūr (A Pallava *brahmadeya*) in Kāḷiyūr Kōṭṭam is designated a *taṉ-kūṟu* in the tenth century under Parāntaka I (AD 907–55); Kāvērippākkam (a late Pallava *brahmadeya* of the ninth century) as a *taṉ-kūṟu* in Paḍuvūr kōṭṭam in the tenth century; Madurāntakam in Kaḷattūr-kōṭṭam in the tenth–eleventh century; Ukkal in Kāḷiyūr Kōṭṭam in the eleventh century, and so on. The *taṉ-kūṟu* would seem to be a creation of Parāntaka I.
25. Subbarayalu, *Political Geography*, chapter VI.
26. Mannārguḍi was the only *taṉiyūr* in Cōḷa nāḍu. A variation of the *taṉ-kūṟu* or *taṉi-ūr* occurs in Naḍuvilnāḍu, where Chidambaram in the South Arcot district, designated as a *taṉiyūr*, became the centre of a fairly large urban complex, with an immediate hinterland marked by several *pēriḷamai nāḍu*s, representing an agglomeration of existing and newly created agricultural settlements. In all these cases, the *taṉ-kūṟu* represents the agglomeration of such settlements around an urban nucleus, a process similar to the agglomeration designated in tribal societies as sacred territories administered by priesthood and also creating a hierarchy based on a sacrally defined order.

27. Puḻal Kōṭṭam was also called Vikramasōḻa Vaḷanāḍu and Puliyūr kōṭṭam, Kulōttunga sōḻa Vaḷanāḍu.
28. Madurāntakacaturvēdimangalam in Kaḻattūr Kōṭṭam had fourteen hamlets or villages attached to it, two of which were weaving centres and one salt manufacturing centre located in Sembūr Kōṭṭam.
29. Uttamacōḻacaturvēdimangalam (Tennēri–AD 1005), *SII*, VII, 412; Śivacūḷāmaṇicaturvēdimangalam (Ukkal–AD 998), *SII*, III, 2; Uttaramērūr was renamed Rājēndracōḻacaturvēdimangalam (eleventh century) and later as Gaṇḍagopālacaturvēdimangalam (thirteenth century).
30. Madurāntakam–*Cēris*, *SII*, VII, 457, 465, 466; *SII*, V, 1003; Uttaramērūr–*Cēris*, *SII*, III, 165, 166, 178, 186, 187; Tennēri–*Cēris*, *SII*, VII, 412.
31. Vīracōḻappērangāḍi in Madurāntakam–395 of *Annual Report on (South) Indian Epigraphy* (hereafter *ARE*), 1922 in 1922-3.
32. Kāñcipperuvaḻi–from Uttaramērūr. Uttaramērūr Vadi–from Kāñcī–*SII*, III, 68; *see also SII*, IV, 133. Mēlapperuvaḻi–from Ukkal–*SII*, III, 4.
33. Tennēri–*SII*, VII, 411.
34. The Śiva temple at Kaḍappēri, a part of Madurāntaka Caturvēdimangalam, was constructed by a chief called Śengēṇi Sāttan Cōḻan–*SII*, V, 1003.
35. An officer called Kumāra Kālan Vāsudēvan, alias Atiśayacōḻa Mūvēnda Vēḷān, built the Śiva temple at Ukkal–158 of *ARE*, 1939-40.
36. Tennēri–240 and 241 of 1922, *ARE*, 1921-2; Kāvērippākkam–*SII*, XIII, 307.
37. *SII*, III, 9; *SII*, V, 473.
38. 139 of 1924; 195 of 1923, *ARE*, 1922-3; 156 and 157, 177, 178 and 189 of 1939-40; 40 of 1940-1; *SII*, XII, 202.
39. Śeyyūr in Śembūr Kōṭṭam was a salt manufacturing centre attached to Madurāntakam. Tiruppulivanam, a weaving centre, was attached to Uttaramērūr.
40. 216 of 1930-1 for Vānavanamahādevi Caturvēdimangalam and Tirukkaḻukkuṉṟam (*Taṉiyūr* and *Nagaram*).
41. Madurāntakam (Kaḍappēri)–397 of 1922, *ARE*, 1922-3. Sakkaramallūr–29 and 35 of 1940-1.
42. E.g. Maṭha in Brahmadeśam–247 of 1915, *ARE*, 1915-16; and several other *taṉiyūrs* like Madurāntakam and Tiruvallam.
43. Carter, *Urban Historical Geography*, 14. *See* Chapter 1.
44. Tiruvallam or Vāṇapurattūr of the Bāṇa chiefs became a *taṉiyūr* in Rājarāja I's reign–*SII*, III, 51.

45. *See* Chapter 4, Table IV, Period I.
46. Ibid., Table IV, Periods II to IV.
47. Hall, *Trade and Statecraft*, chapters 3 to 5.
48. Tirukkaccūr inscription of AD 1224–261 of 1909, *ARE*, 1909-10.
49. *See* Chapters 4 and 1 in this volume.
50. Early Cōḷa Period–*SII*, III, 103, 104, 105; *SII*, V, 1357; *SII*, XIX, 185; 176 and 181 of 1912, *ARE*, 1912-13. Middle Cōḷa Period–*SII*, V, 1354; 130, 133, 137, 140, 141, 235 of 1912, *ARE*, 1912-13; 171, 176 of 1915, *ARE*, 1915-16; 226 to 232 of 1961-2.
51. *See* T. Balakrishnan Nayar, *The Dowlaishwaram Hoard of Eastern Chalukyan and Chola Coins*, Bulletin of the Madras Government Museum, 1966, vol. 9, no. 2.
52. Different *Māḍais* (coins), *SII*, IV, 854, 861; 360, 385, 386, 428, 441 and 453 of 1919; 2 and 40 of 1921.
53. *SII*, V, 483, *Cennaimānagarakkalveṭṭugaḷ*, R. Nagaswamy (ed.), Madras, 1970, 81b (1967); 477 of 1919, *ARE*, 1919-20.
54. E.g. *SII*, I, 146, 147.
55. E.g. *SII*, IV, 813; V, 849.
56. 247 of 1938-9; 284 of 1959-60.
57. *Cennaimāngarakkalveṭṭugaḷ*, 120 (1967).
58. *See* Chapter 4 in this volume.
59. Kāṭṭūr–256 of 1912, *ARE*, 1912-13; Basinikoṇḍa–342 of 1912, *ARE*, 1912-13.
60. 264 and 273 of 1955-6.
61. *Infra*, Kāñcīpuram.
62. *See* Chapter 4, Table VI.
63. K. Sundaram, *Studies in Economic and Social Conditions of Medieval Andhra*, Machilipatnam, 1968, Appendix. Canton inscription of Kulōttunga I for trading interests of Cōḷa merchants in China (Tan Yeok Seng, 'The Srivijayan Inscription of Canton–AD 1079', *Journal of South-East Asian History*, 5, 2, 1964, 17-24).
64. *See* Chapter 4, Table VI.
65. Mayilāppūr–*Cennaimāngarakkalveṭṭugaḷ*, 95 and 125 (1967), 454 of 1962-3. Tiruvoṟṟiyūr–371 of 1911, *ARE*, 1911-12; 127 of 1912, *ARE*, 1912-13, Tirukkaḻukkuṉṟam–145 of 1932-3; Mēlpāḍi–*SII*, III, 18.
66. Tiruppāccūr - Tirunāvukkaraśan Maṭha–127 of 1929-30, Tiruvoṟṟiyūr - Tirujñānasambandan maṭha–238 of 1912, *ARE*, 1912-13.
67. Golakī maṭha–111 of 1929-30. Lakṣādhyāyi maṭhas (Mudaliyār lineages)–352, 360 of 1911, *ARE*, 1911-12; 207, 215 and 239 of 1912, *ARE*, 1912-13; 247 of 1915; *ARE*, 1915-16; 106, 115 and 196 of 1939-40.

68. *See* note 60. 264 and 273 of 1955-6.
69. *Infra*, Kāñcīpuram.
70. *SII*, v, 999; vii, 451; 208 of 1923, *ARE*, 1923-4.
71. Vijaya Ramaswamy, *Textiles and Weavers in Medieval South India*, New Delhi, 1985, 53-6; 108 of 1929-30.
72. 284 of 2910; 361 of 1911; *ARE*, 1911-12; 250 of 1919, *ARE* 1918-19; 346, 352 of 1923, *ARE*, 1923-4; 137 of 1924; 47 and 57 of 1932-3.
73. Loom tax–300 of 1910; 195 of 1923, *ARE*, 1922-3; 138 of 1924; 35 of 1940-1; 198 of 1961-2. House tax–228 of 1910; 276 of 1912, *ARE*, 1912-13.
74. 228 of 1916, *ARE*, 1915-16; 149 of 1929-30; 156 of 1939-40.
75. *See* Arjun Appadurai, 'Right and Left Hand Castes in South India', *Indian Economic and Social History Review*, June-Sept. 1974, xi, nos 2-3, 216-39.
76. Ramaswamy, *Textiles and Weavers*, 58-9.
77. It would appear that the *Kaikkōḷas* had also come to be graded as superior and subordinate strata, based on the acquisition of economic status and influence.
78. Tāmaraippākkam–6, 18 and 26 of 1953-4; *See* R. Nagaswamy, *Studies in Ancient Tamil Law and Society*, Madras, 1978, 75-9.
79. Hall, *Trade and Statecraft*, 203-4.
80. K.G. Krishnan, 'Chittaramēḻip-Periyanāḍu–An Agricultural Guild of Medieval Tamil Nadu', *Journal of the Madras University*, January 1982, reprint, vol. liv, no. 1.
81. 183 and 188 of 1973-4; Merchant Guild–173 of 1973-4.
82. Piranmalai–*SII*, viii, 442. Anbil etc. *See* Chapter 4 in this volume, Table VI.
83. Nagaswamy, *Ancient Tamil Nadu*, 75-9. *See* Chapter 1 in this volume.
84. Sengamal–227 of 1916, *ARE*, 1915-16; Sadras–103 of 1932-3; Viriñcipuram, 193 of 1939-40.
85. *See* Chapter 4, Table VI.
86. *See* Subbarayalu, *Political Geography*, 30 for the traditional account of the division of Toṇḍaimaṇḍalam into 24 *Kōṭṭams* and 79 *nāḍus*.
87. Cittiramēḻicaturvēdimangalam (Eḻuvāmpadi)–91 of 1941-2; Cittiramēḻipadinenbhūmi Paṭṭaṇam (Sakkaramallūr)–40 of 1940-1; Cittiramēḻi Nangai (Kuṉṟattūr).
88. Kāñcīpuram–607 and 609 of 1919, *ARE*, 1919-20.
89. Uṟaiyūr merchants in Puduppaṭṭiṇam–102 of 1932-3.
90. Tiruppāccūr inscription–120 of 1929-30.
91. Tiruvattiyūr–92 of 1939-40, part ii, para 57.

92. Nagaswamy, *Vasavasamudram*, Madras, 1978; Champakalakshmi, 'Archaeology and Tamil Literary Tradition', *Puratattva*, vol. VIII, 1975-6. Also *see* Chapter 2 in this volume.
93. *Indian Archaeology*, A Review, 1961-2; 1963-4.
94. Nilakanta Sastri, *Foreign Notices of South India from Megasthenes to Ma Huan*, Madras, 1939, 45. Also Stein, 'Medieval Coromandel Trade in India', in John Parker (ed.), *Merchants and Scholars: Essays in the History of Exploration and Trade*, Minnesota, 1965, 49.
95. *Maṇimēkalai*, Canto XXVIII. *See also* T.N. Vasudeva Rao, *Buddhism in the Tamil Country*, Annamalainagar, 1979, chapter 2. This author, however, favours an early date, i.e. second century AD for the *Maṇimēkalai*, which is better assigned to the post-Sangam period.
96. Buddhism, which was more or less confined to the coastal regions of Tamil Nadu from the 'Sangam' period, is well represented in the coastal towns, in which the impact of the Andhra coastal trade links was considerable and art impulses of the Amarāvati-Nāgārjunakoṇḍa schools of Buddhist art were strong. Kāñcīpuram was likewise influenced by 'Andhra' Buddhism and may well have been oriented outward due to its importance as a weaving centre.
97. T. Watters, *Yuan Chuang's Travels in India*, vol. II, 1905, 227. Hsuan Tsang refers to Buddhism, which was on the decline, to the Nirgrantha (Jain) sect, which was still influential, and to the brahmanical (*deva*) temples, which had become dominant.
98. The heterogeneity of Kāñcī in terms of religious groups and sectarian affiliations is also attested to by the *Mattavilāsa*, wherein the Kāpālikas and Buddhist *bhikṣus* (monks) are ridiculed. The Rājavihāra, probably the Buddhist monastery referred to by Hsuan Tsang, is also mentioned. *See* Mahalingam, *Kāñcīpuram*, 74-5.
99. The Paḷḷankōyil, Jaina Copper Plate Grant, ed. by T.N. Subramaniam, *Transactions of the Archaeological Society of South India*, 1958-9.
100. The *Ghaṭikā's* capture is attributed to the early Pallavas of the fourth-fifth centuries AD by the Copper plate records of the later Pallavas. *See* Vēḷūrpāḷaiyam Copper plates of Nandivarman III—ninth century AD. T.N. Subramanian, *Thirty Pallava Copper Plates* (The Tamil History Academy, Madras); *see* T.G. Aravamuthan, 'The Early Pallavas of Kāñcī', *Silver Jubilee Volume of the Archaeological Society of South India* (1962), 63. Also, Tālaguṇḍa Pillar Inscription of the Kadamba Kākutsthavarman, *Epigraphia Indica*,

VIII, 24-36, for the importance of the *Ghaṭikā* as a brahmanical institution.

101. Not a single *brahmadeya* of the Pallava period is so far known from Eyil Kōṭṭam, wherein Kāñcī was located, the only exception being Pulvēḷūr, referred to in a late ninth century inscription from Tiruvālangāḍu. Kāñcī itself does not seem to have originated as a *brahmadeya*, although it is called so in a later inscription (AD 1030, *SII*, VIII, 5). Pallava records refer mainly to gifts of gold and sheep for various services in the temples, their land grants to the Kāñcī temples being negligible, the only *dēvadāna* village (Nāyivaṭṭi Kuḷattūr) was the one granted to the Vaikuṇṭha Perumāḷ temple by Nandivarman II (*SII*, IV, 827).
102. *SII*, I, 146, 147, 149; *SII*, III, 128 (Madras Museum Copper Plates); *SII*, IV, 828, 867; 428 of 1919; 17, 18 and 19 of 1921. *ARE*, 1920-1; Śivapuram–227 to 232 of 1961-2; Vēppanguḷam–*SII*, VIII, 3 and 5.
103. 562 of 1919, *ARE*, 1919-20.
104. For Dantivarman, *see SII*, IV, 132. For Nandivarman II's accession, *see* Mahalingam, *Kāñcīpuram*, 142. For the role of the *Mahānagarattār* of Kāñcīpuram, *see also* Hall and George W. Spencer, 'The Economy of Kāñcīpuram: A Sacred Centre in Early South India', *Journal of Urban History*, February 1980, vol. 6, no. 2, 127-51.
105. The Madras Museum Copper Plates of Uttama Cōḷa, *SII*, III, part III, no. 128.
106. 39 and 46 of 1921, *ARE*, 1920-1.
107. Kūraivāṇigapperunteru and Ravikulamāṇikkapperunteru were the streets where weavers lived. Arumoḷidēvapperunteru, Rājarājpperunteru, Nigarilisōḷapperunteru and Gaṇḍagopālapperunteru were the four streets where merchants lived.
108. Sale of lands by *Nagarattār* to the Muttavāḷ Perṟa Kaikkōḷar, who gifted it to the Sokkīśvara temple in the period of Uttama Cōḷa–*SII*, XIX, 365 and 377; sale of lands to the Kaccapeśvara temple in the reigns of Rājarāja I and Rājēndra I. Donations of land to the Karukkinil Amarndavaḷ temple in the early Cōḷa period–210 of 1975-6.
109. They made provisions for a feeding service in the Nānādeśi or Aiññūṟṟuvan Maṭha in the Sīteśvara temple–264 and 273 of 1955-6.
110. A large number of Kerala traders, some of them with impressive titles of high social rank (e.g. Nāyakar), made huge donations

in the Telugu Cōḷa period. They hailed from several centres, including Kollāṇam (Quilon) in Kerala.

111. Large sums of money, e.g. 1750 Nellūr Pudu Māḍai, were paid for repurchasing land for gift by merchants from outside. *See* 447 of 1919, *ARE*, 1919-20.
112. 165 of *ARE* 1968-9; 259; 272 and 279 of 1969-70.
113. *See* note 48.
114. Ramaswamy, *Textiles and Weavers*, 40.
115. Nilakanta Sastri, *The Cōḷas*, chapters VII, VIII, IX and X.
116. Ibid., chapters XIII and XIV.
117. *SII*, IV, 816, 817; XIX, 365, 377; 229 of 1910; 36, 68 and 79 of 1921; 240 of 1930-1.
118. Kāñcīpuram–226 to 229 of 1921, *ARE*, 1921-2; 240 of 1930-1; 387 of 1958-9. Tiruvoṟṟiyūr–386 of 1958-9.
119. Champakalakshmi, 'Religious Conflict and Persecution in the Tamil Country', *Proceedings of the Indian History Congress*, 37th Session, Calicut, 1976 and idem, 'Religious Conflict in the Tamil Country: A Reappraisal of Epigraphic Evidence', *Journal of the Epigraphic Society of India*, 5, Madras, 1978.
120. K. Vellaivaranan, *Panniru Tirumuṟai Varalāṟu*, part I, Annamalai University, 1972, 60-171; 172-253.
121. This temple was built during the reign of Nandivarman II (731-96) and glorified by the hymns of Tirumangai Āḻvār.
122. This is true of all the *bhakti* centres in the whole of Toṇḍaimaṇḍalam. A rather curious exception is Kuranganilmuṭṭam, also a *bhakti* centre, where a cave temple assignable to Mahēndravarman I (575-630) exists. Similarly, the Rājasimheśvara at Kāñcī also came to be linked with the story of Kaḻarśingan, a *bhakti* saint, identified with Rājasimha Pallava.
123. *See* K.V. Raman, *Sri Varadarajaswami Temple–Kanci: A Study of its History, Art and Architecture*, New Delhi, 1975, 62-5; B.V. Ramanujam, *History of Sri Vaishnavism in South India upto Ramanuja*, Annamalai University, 1973, 268-71.
124. N. Jagadeesan, *History of Srivaishnavism in the Tamil Country* (Post-Ramanuja), Madurai, 1977, 39 and 169; Appadurai, *Worship and Conflict under Colonial Rule, A South Indian Case*, Cambridge University Press, 1981, chapter 2.
125. In most of the Vaiṣṇava *bhakti* centres like Tirunīrmalai, Tiruvallikkēṇi, Tirumaḻiśai, etc.
126. Nilakanta Sastri, *The Cōḷas*, 644-5.
127. M. Rajamanickanar, *Śaiva Samaya Vaḷarcci*, Madras, 1972, chapter 9.

128. Tiruvōttūr (Tiruvattiyūr)–115 of 1939-40; Tiruvānakkōyil–352, 360 of 1911, *ARE*, 1911-12.
129. Tiruvōttūr, Māgaṟal, Perunagar around Kāñcīpuram, and perhaps even Mayilāppūr.
130. 607 of 1919, *ARE*, 1919-20.
131. V.A. Devasenapati, *Kāmakkōṭṭam, Nāyanmārs and Ādi Śankara*, Institute of Traditional Cultures, Madras, 29.
132. K.V. Raman, *The Early History of the Madras Region*, Madras, 1959, 23-4.
133. R. Vanaja, 'The Madras Museum Collection of Punchmarked Coins–A Study, M.Litt. Thesis (unpublished), University of Madras, 1955, 7.
134. Raman, *Early History*, 190; also Mahalingam, *Mackenzie Manuscripts*, Introduction XLVII-XLVIII; *Cennaimānagarakkalveṭṭugaḷ*, 245, 1967.
135. *Cennaimānagarakkalveṭṭugaḷ*, 120, 1967.
136. *See* Chapter 4 in this volume.
137. E.g. 460 of 1919, *ARE*, 1919-20.
138. Tiruvānmiyūr–77 to 83 of 1909, *ARE*, 1908-9; Veḷiccēri–*SII*, III, 114, 116, 119; XII, 205; XIX, 97; 302 to 317 of 1911; *ARE*, 1911-12.
139. Tirunīrmalai–532-60 of 1912, *ARE*, 1912-13. Tiruśūlam & Pallavaram–*SII*, VII, 538-49.
140. Pūndamalli–31 to 34 of 1910, *ARE*, 1910-11; 560 of 1912, *ARE*, 1912-13; 292 to 302 of *ARE*, 1938-9; *SII*, VII, 537. Tirumaḻiśai–18 and 19 of 1911, *ARE*, 1910-11.
141. Pāḍi–*SII*, III, 181. Tirumullaivāyil–*SII*, III, 114, 141, 174, 196; XVII, 719, 723, 724, 727, 730, 731, 735, 738; 282 of 1960-1. Tiruvēṟkāḍu–386 to 396 of 1958-9.
142. *SII*, XII, 99, 100, 105.
143. Nagaswamy, *Tiruttaṇi and Vēlancēri Copper Plates*, Madras, 1979, 26-7.
144. David Lorenzen, *The Kāpālikas and Kālāmukhas. Two Lost Saivite Sects*, New Delhi, 1972, 83 and 166-7.
145. *SII*, III, 145; 103, 130, 146 of 1912, *ARE*, 1912-13; 386 of 1958-9.
146. 132 of 1912; *ARE*, 1912-13.
147. 136 of 1912, *ARE*, 1912-13.

Appendix

Kāncīpuram's Expansion Through Temples

From Kacci of the Sangam period, which had a single Viṣṇu shrine of central importance, Kāncīpuram grew into a huge multi-temple centre, comparable to Kuḍamūkku-Paḷaiyāṟai (Kumbhakonam) in the Kāvēri delta. The successive stages of its growth are marked by the appearance of several temples dedicated to Viṣṇu, Śiva and Śakti and their elaboration under the Pallavas and Cōḷas. This multi-temple complex evolved through centuries of growth from earlier agrarian clusters, the temples which marked its growth representing the loci of the ceremonial complex at different chronological points, leading to the emergence of a dispersed ceremonial centre. The locus of the ceremonial complex shifted from one temple of major importance to another, depending upon the changing pattern of patronage of the ruling families and the new temple projects, which were royal creations for legitimation. Such multi-temple centres differed from the sacred/pilgrimage centres, where the locus of the ceremonial complex remained unchanged, as in Chidambaram of Śrīrangam.

The following table attempts to show the growth of Kāncīpuram through a tentative chronological sequence of the origin and elaboration of its temples based on epigraphic, architectural and literary data. Although tradition, as recorded in the *Kāncīmahātmya**, assigns seventy-two temples (including small shrines within larger temples) to Kāncīpuram by the seventeenth and eighteenth centuries, evidence of only about thirty odd temples is available for the period ending AD 1300.

* See Marie-Claude Porcher, '*La Representation de l'espace Sacré dans le Kancimahatmya*', *Puruṣārtha*, 8 (1985), 23–51.

Visṇu Temples (Bhakti Centres)

	I		II	III				IV Cōla Period		
No. in Map of Kāñcī-puram city	*Name of the temple*	*Sangam Period, 1st–3rd Centuries*	*Early Āḻvārs (bhakti) 5th–6th centuries*	*Later Āḻvārs (bhakti) 7th–9th centuries,*	*Pallava Period 7th–9th centuries*	*Early Phase 850–985*	*Middle Phase 1 985–1070*	*Middle Phase 2 1070–1150*	*Late Phase 1150–1250*	*Late Phase 2 1250–1300*
1.	Yathokta-kāri	Veḥkā	Tiruveḥkā	Tiruveḥkā		Parāntaka I 907–55		Structural Elaboration		-
2.	Ulagaḷanda Perumāḷ		Ūragam	Ūragam	9th century Nandivar-man III	Uttamacōḷa 965–85	-	Structural Elaboration	-	-
3.	Pāṇḍava Perumāḷ		Pāḍagam	Pāḍagam		-	-	Structural Elaboration	-	-
4.	Vaikuṇṭha Perumāḷ			Parameśvara Viṇṇagaram	8th century Nandivar-man II	-	-	Structural Elaboration	-	-

5.	Varadarāja Svāmi	Attiyūr or Attigiri		Rājādhirāja I 1018–54	-	Structural Elaboration	-	Elaboration
6.	Aṣṭabhuja Perumāl	Aṭṭabuya karam		Rājendra I 1014–44				
7.	Dipaprakāśa	Tiruttaṇkā Viḷakkoḷi	-	-	-	Structural Elaboration	-	-
8.	Narasimha	Tiruveḷiruk-kai	-	-	-	Structural Elaboration	-	-
9.	Pavalavaṇṇa Perumāḷ	Pavaḷa-vaṇṇam	-	-	-	-	-	-

Three more Viṣṇu shrines mentioned in *Bhakti* literature, viz, Nīragam, Kāragam and Nilāttingaḷ Tuṇḍam are small shrines within larger temples in Kāncīpuram.

Siva Temples (Bhakti Centres)

		III	IV The Cōla Period					
No. in Map	*Name of the temple*	*Period of Śaiva Nāyanārs 7 to 9th centuries*	*Pallava 7th-9th centuries*	*Early Phase 850-985*	*Middle Phase 1 985-1070*	*Middle Phase 2 1070-1150*	*Late Phase 1 1150-1250*	*Late Phase 2 1250-1300*
10.	Tirukkālīśvaram	Kacciner̤ik Kāraikkāḍu	-	-	Rājendra I 1014-44		Elaboration	Elaboration
11.	Ēkāmreśvara	Ēkambam-Mayānam	-	-	Rājādhirāja I 1018-54		Elaboration	Elaboration
12.	Anēkatangāvatam	Anēkatangāvatam				Kulōttunga I 1070-1120	Elaboration	Elaboration
13.	Tirumērraḷi	Tirumērrali,						Śambhuva-rāya chiefs
14.	Tiru Ōṇakānteśvara	Tiru Ōṇakāntan Taḷi	-	-	-	-	-	-

Other Temples (Saiva and Sākta)

Inscriptional and Structural Evidence

		III		*IV The Cōḷa Period*				
No. in the Map of Kanci-puram	*Name of the temple*	*Pallava Period 1*	*Pallava Period 2*	*Early Phase 850-985*	*Middle Phase 1 950-1070*	*Middle Phase 2 1070-1150*	*Late Phase 1 1150-1250*	*Late Phase 2 1250-1300*
15.	Kailāsanātha (Rājasimheśvara)	Rājasimha 7th century						
16.	Airavātēśvara		9th century					
17.	Iravatēśvara		9th century					
18.	Matangēśvara		9th century					
19.	Muktēśvara		9th century					
20.	Piṟavātēśvara		9th century					

Other Temples *Cont'd*

		III		*IV The Cōḷa Period*				
No. in the Map of Kanci-puram	*Name of the temple*	*Pallava Period 1*	*Pallava Period 2*	*Early Phase 850-985*	*Middle Phase 1 950-1070*	*Middle Phase 2 1070-1150*	*Late Phase 1 1150-1250*	*Late Phase 2 1250-1300*
21.	Phanmaṇīśvara			Pārthivendra 956-69				
22.	Sokkīśvara			Uttama-Cōḷa 969-85				
23.	Kaccapeśvara (Kaccālai Uḍaiya Mahādeva)				Rājarāja I 985-1014	Structural Elaboration Kulōttunga I - 1070-1120	Elaboration	
24.	Karukkinil Amarndavḷ				Rājendra I 1012-44			

25.	Sītēśvara (Sarvatīrtham)		Rājādhirāja 1018-54		
26.	Kāraṇīśvara			Kulōttunga I 1070-1120	
27.	Jvaraharēśvara			Vikrama Cōḷa 1118-33	
28.	Agaranagarīśvara			Kulōttunga II 1133-50	Rājādhirāja II 1052-64
29.	Tiruvīraṭṭānēśvara				Rājādhirāja II 1052-64
30.	Puṇyakoṭīśvara				Rājarāja III 1216-53
31.	Nagarīśvara				13th century
32.	Kāmākshī (Kāmakkōṭṭam)	Śankarācārya and Pal-lava(?)	Rājendra I 1014-44		Structural Elaboration
33.				Kulōttunga I (?)	

Other Temples *Cont'd*

		III				*IV*		
No. in the Map of Kanci-puram	*Name of the temple*	*Pallava Period 1*	*Pallava Period 2*	*Early Cola 875-985*	*Middle Cola 1 985-1070*	*Middle Cola 2 1070-1150*	*Late Cola 1150-1250*	*Late Cola 1250-1300*
33.	Kumarakkōṭṭam					Kulōttunga I (?)		
34.	Kāli Kōṭṭam					Kulōttunga I (?)		
				Jain Temples *Tirupparuttikkuṉṟam (Jina-Kānci)*				
35.	Vardhamāna (Trikūṭa basti)	AD 550 (Simhavarman)	-	-	-	Renovation Kulōttunga I 1070-1120	Elaboration	-
36.	Candra-Prabha	Rājasimha 7th century	-	-	-	-	-	-

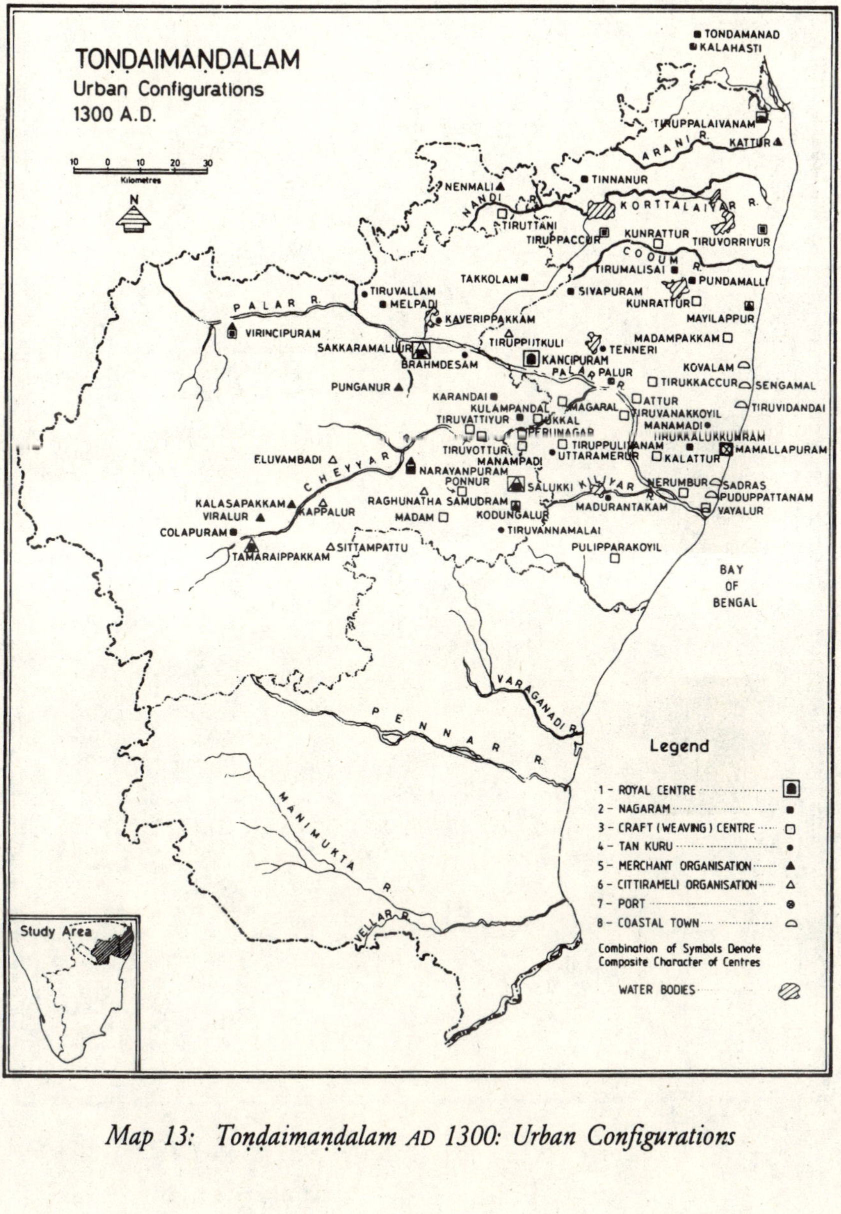

Map 13: Toṇḍaimaṇḍalam AD *1300: Urban Configurations*

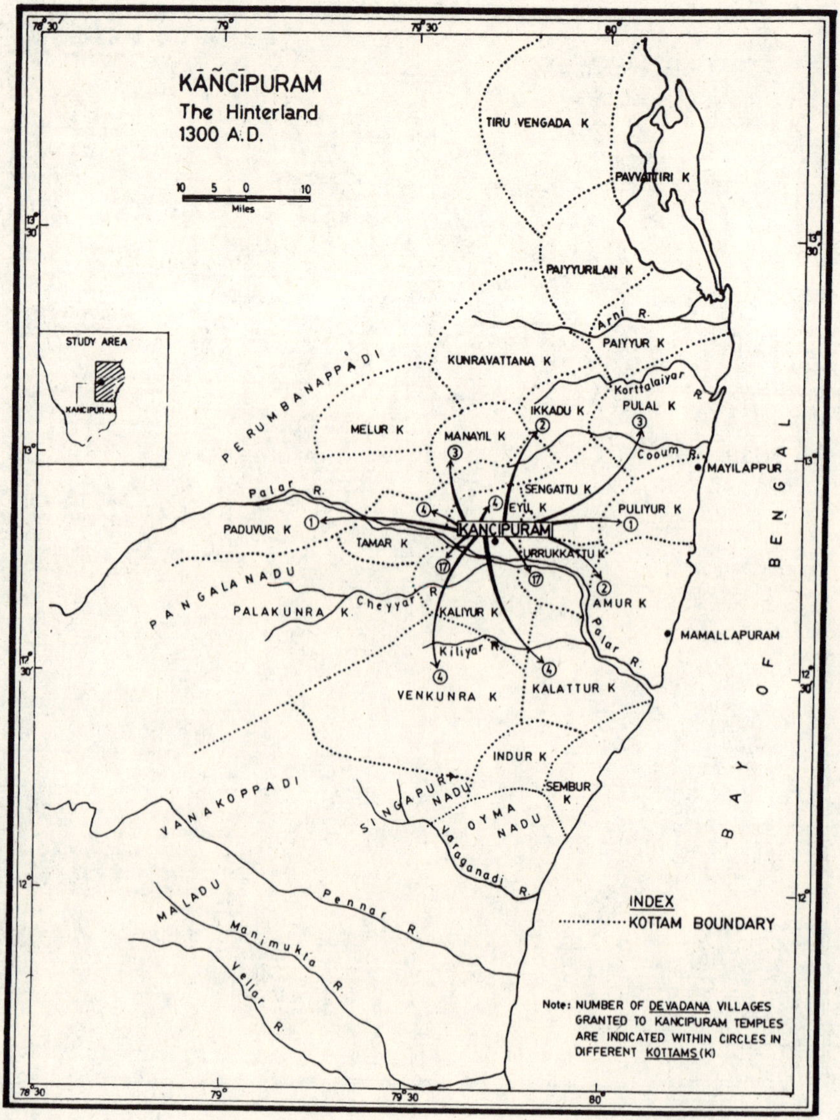

Map 14: *Kañcīpuram: The Hinterland* AD 1300

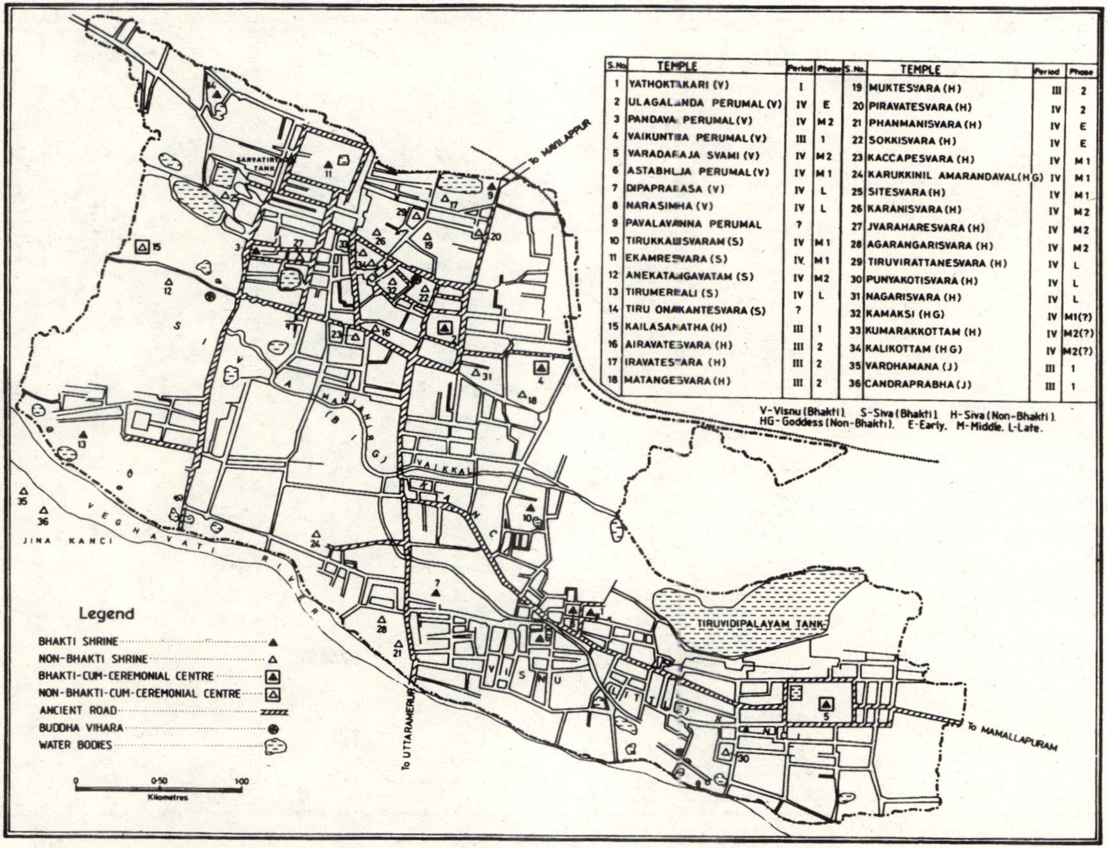

S.No.	TEMPLE	Period	Phase	S.No.	TEMPLE	Period	Phase
1	YATHOKTAKARI (V)	I		19	MUKTESVARA (H)	III	2
2	ULAGALANDA PERUMAL (V)	IV	E	20	PIRAVATESVARA (H)	IV	2
3	PANDAVA PERUMAL (V)	IV	M 2	21	PHANMANISVARA (H)	IV	E
4	VAIKUNTHA PERUMAL (V)	III	1	22	SOKKISVARA (H)	IV	E
5	VARADARAJA SVAMI (V)	IV	M 2	23	KACCAPESVARA (H)	IV	M 1
6	ASTABHUJA PERUMAL (V)	IV	M 1	24	KARUKKINIL AMARANDAVAL (HG)	IV	M 1
7	DIPAPRAKASA (V)	IV	L	25	SITESVARA (H)	IV	M 1
8	NARASIMHA (V)	IV	L	26	KARANISVARA (H)	IV	M 2
9	PAVALAVANNA PERUMAL	?		27	JVARAHARESVARA (H)	IV	M 2
10	TIRUKKALISVARAM (S)	IV	M 1	28	AGARANGARISVARA (H)	IV	M 2
11	EKAMRESVARA (S)	IV	M 1	29	TIRUVIRATTANESVARA (H)	IV	L
12	ANEKATANGAVATAM (S)	IV	M2	30	PUNYAKOTISVARA (H)	IV	L
13	TIRUMERRALI (S)	IV	L	31	NAGARISVARA (H)	IV	L
14	TIRU ONAKANTESVARA (S)	?		32	KAMAKSI (HG)	IV	M1(?)
15	KAILASANATHA (H)	III	1	33	KUMARAKKOTTAM (H)	IV	M2(?)
16	AIRAVATESVARA (H)	III	2	34	KALIKOTTAM (HG)	IV	M2(?)
17	IRAVATESVARA (H)	III	2	35	VARDHAMANA (J)	III	1
18	MATANGESVARA (H)	III	2	36	CANDRAPRABHA (J)	III	1

V-Visnu (Bhakti). S-Siva (Bhakti). H-Siva (Non-Bhakti).
HG-Goddess (Non-Bhakti). E-Early. M-Middle. L-Late.

Map 15: Kañcīpuram: The City

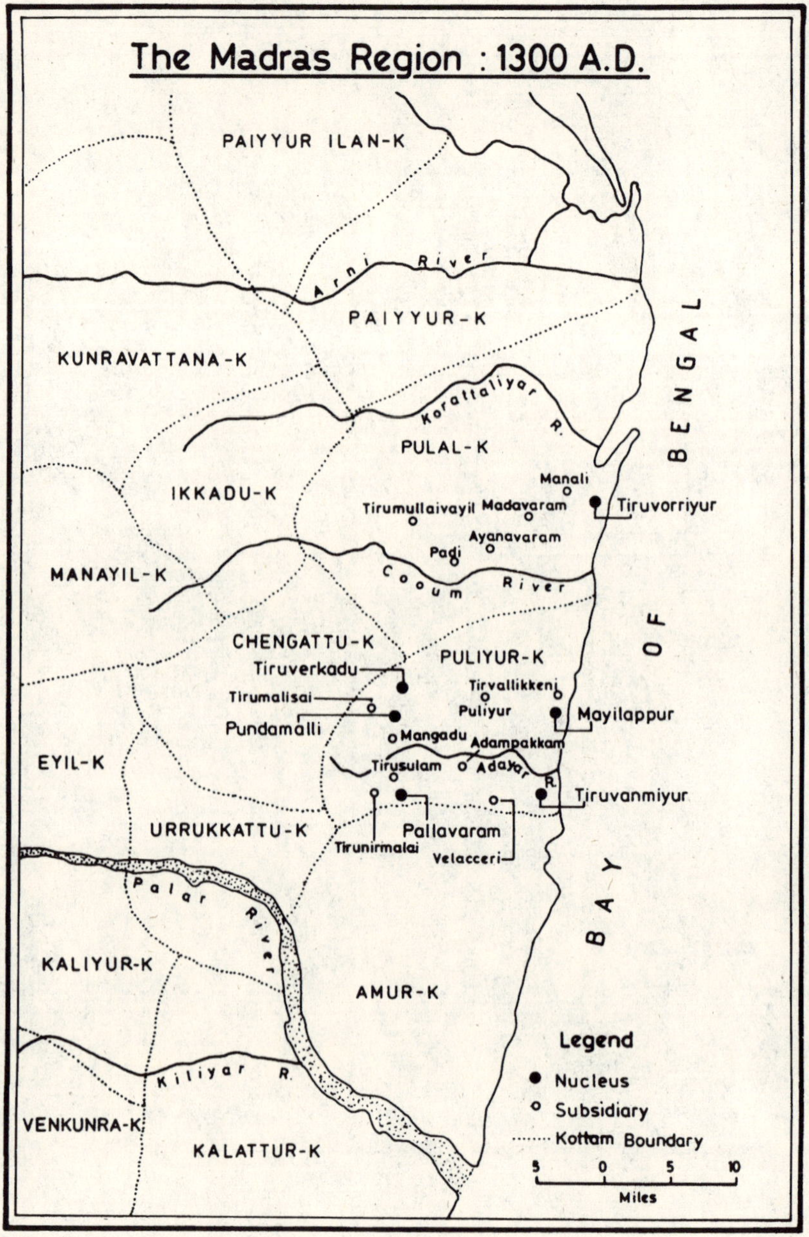

Map 16: The Madras Region AD *1300*

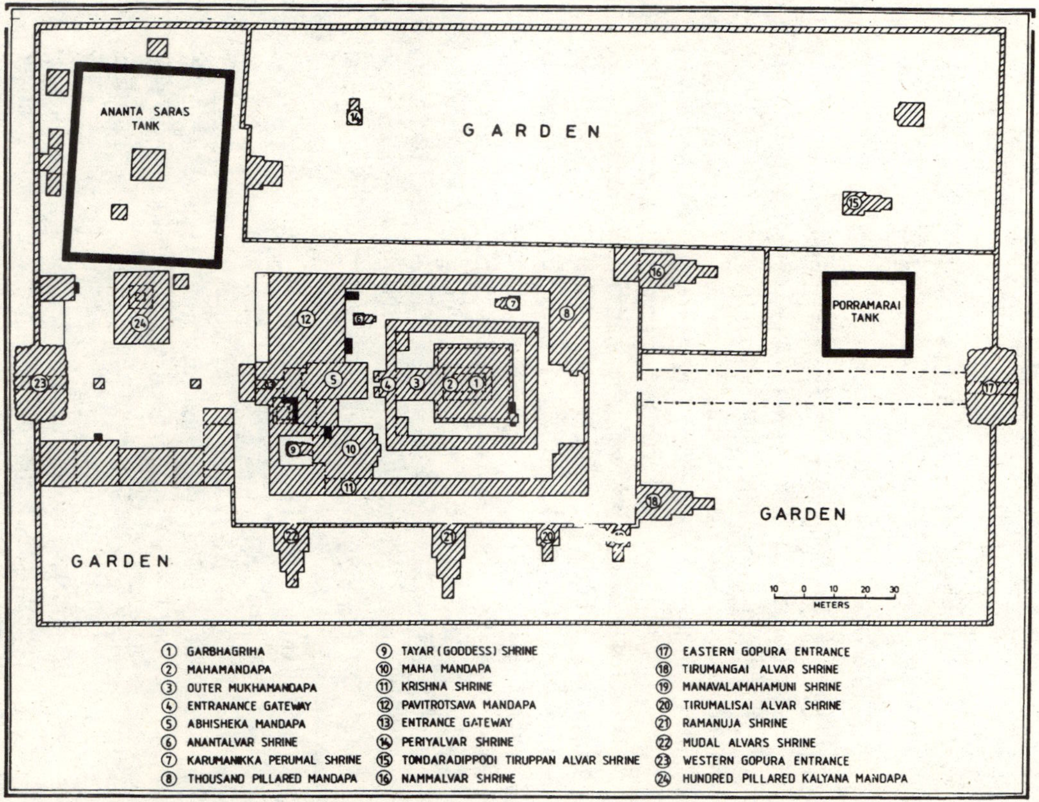

Map 17: Ground Plan of the Varadarājasvāmi Temple, Kañcipuram

8

Urbanization from Above: Tañjāvūr, The Ceremonial City of the Cōḷas

The Cōḷa city of Tañjāvūr, like many other cities of early medieval South India, was a temple city. It was, however, different in many significant ways from others, both as a ceremonial and political centre. The distinctive character of Tañjāvūr lies in the fact that it was not only a royal/ceremonial centre, but was created by a deliberate act of royal policy, in imitation of a sacred *bhakti* centre with the temple as its nucleus and, hence, was at once a product and symbol of the socio-cultural milieu of the Cōḷa period. As a political centre, it represented a state which evolved through a steady process of integrating different pre-existing politico-cultural zones such as the Pallava, Pāṇḍya and Kongu (Cēra) regions, each given a new nomenclature such as Jayankoṇḍacōḷamaṇḍalam, Rājarāja Pāṇḍimaṇḍalam and Muḍikoṇḍacōḷamaṇḍalam respectively, the *maṇḍalam* zone being a new creation of the Cōḷas to demonstrate their territorial expansion.[1]

As the authors of one of the most stable state-structures of pre-colonial South India, the Cōḷas established a powerful monarchy, which was exemplified in their royal/ceremonial centres like Tañjāvūr and Gangaikoṇḍacōḷapuram. The role of the *bhakti* ideology and its chief institutional force, *viz.* the temple, was crucial in the emergence of such centres, and to the political visibility of Cōḷa monarchy.

From the ninth century AD, under the Cōḷas, there is substantial evidence of the systematic pursuit of the *bhakti* ideology by the rulers through temple building,[2] institution of grants for ritual singing of *bhakti* hymns,[3] apotheosis of the *bhakti* saints, especially the Śaiva *nāyanār*, and the development of the sciences of architecture, sculpture, painting, as well as the allied arts of music and dance. Another sphere in which there was involvement of royalty in the propagation of the *bhakti* cult was in the collection of hymns under Rājarāja I (AD 985–1014) and the composition of the twelfth century hagiographical works like the *Periya Purāṇam*, narrating the stories of the *bhakti* saints, at the behest of Kulōttunga II, and the inclusion of members of the royal family among the sixty-three *nāyanār* such as Kōccengaṇṇān, the ancestor of Vijayālaya, the founder of the Cōḷa power, and Gaṇḍarāditya, one of the early Cōḷa kings.[4] It is also reflected in the sacred and secular spheres of royal functions, which became almost indistinguishable in those centres which were founded by an act of deliberate royal policy, i.e. a project in imitation of the *bhakti* or sacred centre 'sung' by the hymnists. Notable illustrations are the temples at Tañjāvūr and Gangaikoṇḍacōḷapuram,[5] founded by Rājarāja I and Rājendra I (AD 985–1044), where they had to invoke the temple's integrative role to create a royal/ceremonial city.

Tañjāvūr, known as Tañjai in the Cōḷa inscriptions of late tenth century and early eleventh century, was the centre of a *kūṟṟam*, i.e. a collection of village/rural settlements,[6] which the Muttaraiyars of this region controlled before it was captured by Cōḷa Vijayālaya in the middle of the ninth century AD. There is no reference to Tañjai, except in the Cōḷa copper plates[7] as the prize capture of Vijayālaya, who built a temple for the goddess Nisumbasūdhani, till it suddenly blossomed into a huge temple town under Rājarāja I, whose stupendous project, i.e. the Rājarājeśvaram (the Bṛhadīśvara temple) created the most prestigious temple of the *drāviḍa* style of architecture.

It was the strategic location of Tañjāvūr on a relatively higher ground at the south-western extremity, i.e. at the start of the distributary system of the Kāvēri delta, that dictated its choice as a royal centre by the Cōḷas, just as Gangaikoṇḍacōḷapuram, north of the Koḷḷiḍam river (Coleroon), subsequently became one such chosen site for a new 'capital'. Together they protected the delta, or the core resource base of the Cōḷas. Capitals are elusive in medieval South India, for the Cōḷas themselves had their residential centre at Paḻaiyāṟai, while Uṟaiyūr, the Sangam Cōḷa 'capital', continued to be another headquarters. Thus, it would seem that Cōḷa political needs, ideological forces and the protection of the core resource base, *viz.* the delta, brought into existence the Tañjāvūr temple and the city.

As the nucleus of a city created by the Cōḷas, the Tañjāvūr temple represents a ceremonial complex around which urban forms grew. The concept of the ceremonial centre applied to cities in pre-modern/traditional societies, is best exemplified in the studies on imperial cities of China, of Southeast Asia and Sri Lanka.[8] Such a city was organized on earthly space to replicate or symbolize the order which pertained to the other world structure, and this ensured survival and prosperity.[9] The cosmic symbolism of the Tañjāvūr temple, as revealed by its designation 'Dakṣiṇamēru' (the southern Mēru as the axis of the universe) and that of its lord as 'Dakṣiṇamēruviṭankar', also extended to the city as the centre of the territorial authority of the Cōḷas. This is further supported by the ritual consecration, along with that of the main shrine, also of the shrines of the regents of the eight quarters (*aṣṭadikpālas*), *viz.*, Indra, Agni, Yama, Nirṛti, Varuṇa, Vāyu, Soma and Īśāna, situated at the cardinal points.[10] Thus, the Rājarājēśvara temple was the central ceremonial complex dominating the city, and was carefully engineered to align the city with cosmic structures and forces. One may see here the impact of the *bhakti* ideology, which assisted in the process of enhancing the power of both the divine and human sovereigns through the symbolism of the cosmos/temple/territory. The performance of a play called *Rājarājēśvara Nāṭaka*[11] in the Tañjāvūr temple, festivals and offerings on the birth asterisms of the royal family[12] etc., for which special endowments were made by royalty, would also substantiate the inseparable nature of the sacred and secular spheres of interests. Although a palace site has been located at Vallam,[13] seven miles on the road to Tiruchirapalli, the main activities, ceremonial and political, were centred round the temple.

Architecture, sculpture and other arts served as metaphors to convey the different levels of meaning[14] behind the obvious religious function of the temple, signifying changing world views and interrelationships between religious and political functions. The main features of these art forms, i.e. architecture, sculpture and painting, in Tañjāvūr may be presented here to provide an integrated view of the form and meaning of the temple and its synthesizing role.

The architecture of the Rājarājēśvaram was planned and designed to represent cosmic structures, in keeping with the Cōḷa ideology of equating temple/cosmos/territory (Map 18). Conceived as a *māḍakkōyil* of the *uttama* variety, the temple is a *sāndhāra-prāsāda* (double walled *vimāna*) standing on a high terrace (*māḍam*), unequalled by any other Cōḷa monument, including the one at Gangaikoṇḍacōḷapuram. The total height of the *vimāna* is 63.41 metres from the floor of the courtyard. The temple complex covers an area (rectangle) of 240.79 metres east to west and 121.92 metres north to south.[15] According to one estimate, the built-up stone of the *vimāna* and *ardhamaṇḍapa* alone covers 5144 sq. metres,[16] not taking into account the *tiruccuṟṟālai* (corridor around the court), *parivāra* (attendant deities) shrines, the two *gopuras* and the shrines in the courtyard. The whole temple complex is compact, laid out and designed simultaneously. A perfect balance between architecture and sculpture is achieved.

The main shrine, i.e. Dakṣiṇamēru, stands in the centre of a huge courtyard, conveying its symbolic position as the axis of the universe. The *dikpāla* shrines at the three cardinal points and four corners of the *cuṟṟālai* (corridor around the court), with Indra's shrine merged into the northern flank of the Rājarājan tiruvāśal (entrance), emphasize this symbolism. Each of these shrines is a *dvitala vimāna* (two storeyed shrine) with an *ardhamaṇḍapa* in front, forming a continuous line with the cloistered *cuṟṟālai*, itself a double-storeyed construction.[17] Thus, ritual consecration was performed not only of the main shrine but also of the shrines of these regents of the eight quarters. The Caṇḍēśvara shrine, a *dvitala vimāna*, north of the *ardhamaṇḍapa*, is coeval with the main shrine, and the Amman (goddess) shrine, is a late Cōḷa addition. The Caṇḍēśvara shrine, with its position north of the *ardhamaṇḍapa*, was an invariable feature of a Śiva temple. The shrines of Subrahmaṇya, Gaṇapati and even Karuvūr Dēvar are later structures.

The consecration of Caṇḍēśvara as the *mūlabhṛtya* (the chief servant/officer) of Śiva,[18] is an important aspect of Rājarāja's innovations in the temple's iconography, which acquired greater prominence in the Gangaikoṇḍacōḷapuram temple built by Rājēndra I, where, apart from a shrine for Caṇḍēśa, the theme is executed in a sculptured panel of great beauty at the northern entrance to the *ardhamaṇḍapa*.

Structural experiments in the Tañjāvūr temple are significant from the point of view of architectural stability, balance and aesthetic impact. Some of these are a new type of *potikai* (T. *potikai*)* a new *upāna* (*upa-pīṭha*), an innovative *kāl* and the *kumbhapañjara* in the *vimāna* recesses.[19] The *antarāla*, which was initially a false one in the early Cōḷa phase, and which turned into a true one at Śrīnivāsanallūr, assumes great architectural and aesthetic value in Tañjāvūr, as it now acquires a new structural element, i.e. the staircase on the north and south, leading to the *ardhamaṇḍapa* (*antarāla*) and additions like the most imposing *dvārapāla* figures, whose size and volume are a metaphor in stone for power. They seem to underline the fact that the Cōḷa *Śilpācārya* (architect) Rājarāja *perumtaccan* (great mason) had a more imposing size, design and form in mind for the temple.[20]

The designers of the temple sought and achieved solutions to several problems such as instability inherent in the principle of corbelling, the solution being the *vimāna* tower's height (Fig. 1) being in a ratio of 2 : 1 to its width, and the ingenious system of inward corbelling to reduce space starting at the transition from the basal square *talas* (storeys) to the pyramidal superstructural *talas*–a cellular mode of construction. The oversized cupola is also the result of experiments carried out to find a permanent solution to the stability of the roof.[21]

Cōḷa architectural style derived its forms and features from Pallava, Pāṇḍya and even Cāḷukya temples, but made significant innovations, as pointed out above, the designing of the *devakoṣṭhas* (niches) being the greatest contribution. It evolved into its mature phase under Rājarāja I and Rājēndra I. The most skilled craftsmen and *sthapatis* were brought to Tañjāvūr and the major inspiration was perhaps provided by the atelier of the Śembiyanmahādevi temples.

* *Potikai*–base moulding; *upāna*–subsidiary base; *kāl*–pillar/pilaster; *kumbhapañjara*–motif of a pilaster with a pot base; *vimāna*–shrine with a tower; *antarāla*–inner passage between shrine and pillared hall; *dvārapāla*–doorkeeper.

The spires of the two royal temples at Tañjāvūr and Gangaikoṇḍacōḷapuram represent striking features. The pyramid profile at Tañjāvūr is steep, the relation between height and width being 2 : 1. The Gangaikoṇḍacōḷapuram superstructure is lower by six metres but shows a remarkably concave curvature. The *sthapatis* (architects) seem to have applied the square and circle as fundamental concepts underlying the Tañjāvūr and Gangaikoṇḍacōḷapuram spires respectively.[22] This mature phase is clearly marked by the vertical ascent of the *śikhara* (tower), the innovations and solutions to architectural problems and decorative aspects showing a high technical advance. Well conceived, balanced and majestic, the temple's architecture is the product of an imperial vision.

The iconographic programme of the Tañjāvūr temple marks the most creative period in Cōḷa art and in South Indian iconography. In addition to the traditionally inherited iconographic forms of Śiva, the Tañjāvūr sculptors introduced other forms for which they invented a new layout in the double-tiered *vimāna* wall with a double row of niches and the *ardhamaṇḍapa*. These forms include Bhikṣāṭana, Vīrabhadra, Dakṣiṇāmūrti, Kālāntaka, Naṭarāja, Harihara, Lingodbhava, Candraśekhara, Ardhanārīśvara and Bhairava,[23] apart from other deities such as Sarasvati, Gajalakṣmī, Viṣṇu, Gaṇēśa and Durgā, and, above all, the Tripurāntaka form of Śiva, relatively less known in the earlier temple *vimānas*. It is this icon which is of considerable significance in Tañjāvūr.

The Tripurāntaka form is repeated in two postures in all the *niches* of the upper portion of the *vimāna* wall (Fig. 2). So far no satisfactory explanation of such a repetition has been provided. K.R. Srinivasan initially dismissed it as due to the upper level not being visible, while the lower level niches carry different forms. Subsequently he related it to the analogy of the Buddha and Viṣṇu as representing the concept of Cakravartin and, hence, used by earlier dynasts and suggested that the Cōḷa, Rājarāja, adopted Tripurāntaka as his favourite choice as the Śaiva counterpart of the Cakravartin ideal.[24] Other explanations emphasize the warrior aspect of Tripurāntaka and the Cōḷa Rājarāja's choice of this form, as indicating his prowess as a warrior.[25]

Garry J. Schwindler,[26] in an attempt to interpret this repetitive use of the Tripurāntaka form (there are, in addition to the images on the *vimāna* walls, two sculptured panels of this theme and a huge fresco panel of Tripurāntaka in the inner ambulatory), counts thirty such representations, and includes the metal image of Tañjai Aḷagar, identified by Nagaswamy as Tripurāntaka, (FIG. 3) and now housed in the Tañjāvūr Art Gallery, carrying the same characteristics as the others. He further argues that the Tripurantaka motif has an additional and certainly more profound significance than being a 'portrait' of the king as warrior. Strangely, he ends up by saying that this form of Śiva was Rājarāja's personal deity, a model and patron, *iṣṭadevata*, and that he used its unique iconographic symbology to restore to his lineage the honour and dignity damaged by their defeat by the Rāṣṭrakūṭas at Takkōlam. It is, he says, evidence of the king's conscious assimilation of the divine and royal roles.

Schwindler does not accept the explanation of the warrior and military aspects of the Cōḷa king, as he follows the theory of the American scholars B. Stein and G.W. Spencer in characterizing the Cōḷa state as 'a weakly organised polity', and the temple as not indicating the glorification of a powerful despotic ruler's patronage, but as 'a method adopted by an ambitious ruler to enhance his very uncertain power'.[27]

The real significance of the Tripurāntaka motif and its dominant presence in the Tañjāvūr temple, cannot be understood, unless one looks at the temple's programme of iconography as a whole. The temple being a symbol of royal power, the Tripurāntaka form needs to be related to the ideology of the Cōḷa state under Rājarāja I, who was instrumental in shaping the ideological apparatuses for establishing the superiority of Śaivism and Śaivism as the state religion. To start with the *Tēvāram* hymns, which Rājarāja 'rediscovered', and the *bhakti* ideology which was derived from these hymns, the Tripurāntaka episode is one of the dominant myths constantly referred to by the hymnists, the number of hymns being six hundred and four. Other forms of Śiva deliberately chosen for description by the hymnists[28] are the Lingodbhava and Dakṣiṇāmūrti, which had become a part of the iconographic layout even before Rājarāja. However, Tripurāntaka, equally significant for Śaivism

1

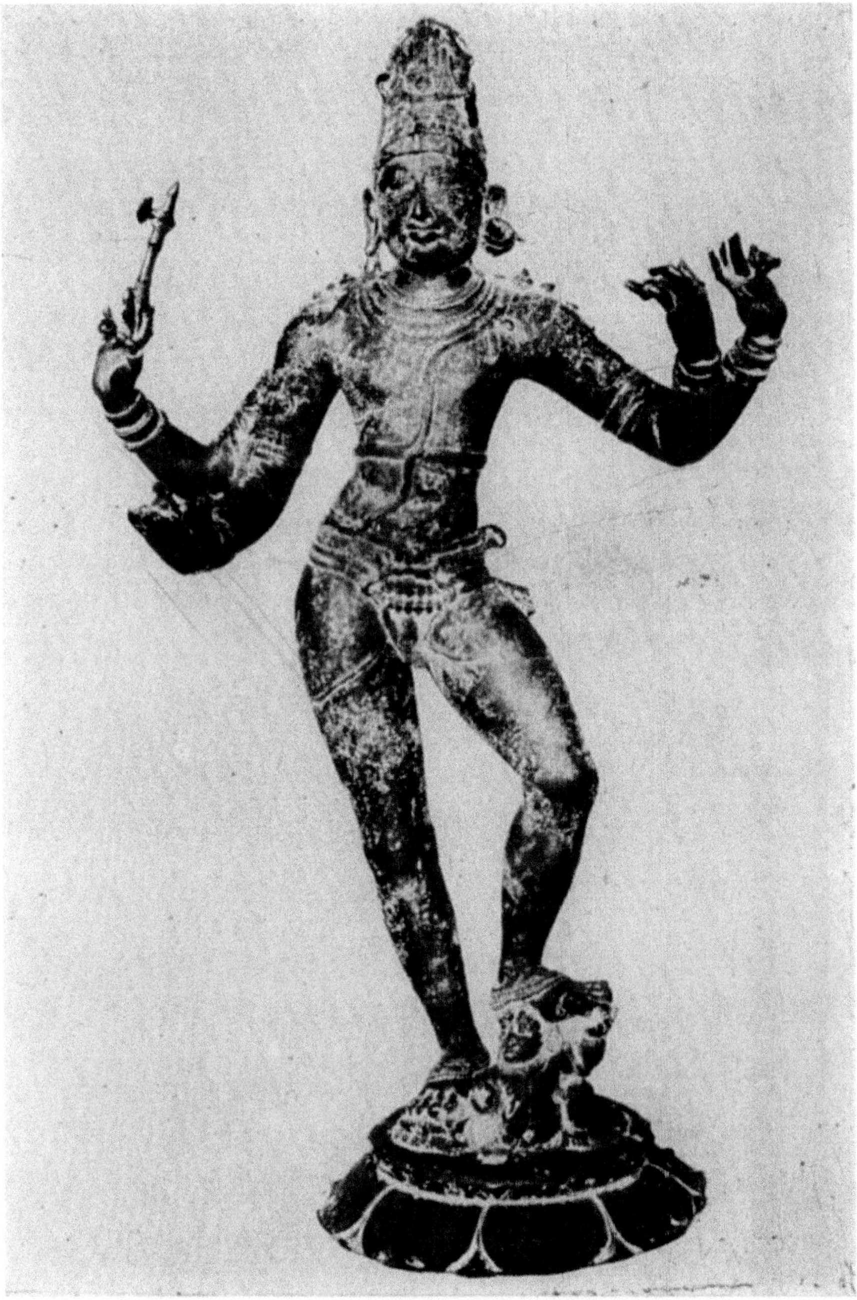

3

in establishing its superiority over other religions like Buddhism and Jainism, was hitherto not chosen for prominent representation. Hence, its repetition in the upper niches would appear to be a conscious act to emphasize its importance. Tripurāntaka also symbolized the warrior aspect in which he was served by Brahma as charioteer, Agni as the arrow and other deities in a supportive but subsidiary role in the battle against the three *asuras* (fresco in chamber 11–Fig. 4). The *Vedas* became the four wheels of Śiva's chariot and the Mandara mountain his bow. Viṣṇu as Māyāmoha deluded the *asuras* into following a 'heterodox' faith, but the *asuras* remained staunch devotees of Śiva. Hence, after destroying their three *puras*, Śiva accepted two of them as his doorkeepers and the third as the drummer playing the *kuḍamuḷā*. This whole episode represents not only a comprehensive attempt to make every other faith subordinate to Śaivism, as there is a veiled attempt to subordinate Viṣṇu as Māyāmoha, but also is known in all its details to the *Tēvāram* hymnists and the *Kallāḍam*[29] in a southern version. By using this myth and the iconographic form in the temple's art in a dominant position and in the narrative paintings, Rājarāja achieved his aim of consolidating Śaivism and subordinating other faiths. He may have been inspired by Gaṇḍarāditya and Śembiyanmahādevi and, hence, the grand plan could well have begun even at the time of his accession in AD 985.

If the Tañjai Aḻagar of the Tañjāvūr inscriptions[30] represents the metal image of Tripurāntaka, as suggested by Nagaswamy, it would be an additional supportive evidence to show that Tripurāntaka was only next in importance to Dakṣiṇamēru-viṭankar, the chief idol, and with Āḍavallān (Naṭarāja), who is prominently represented in the frescoes (chamber 9) and metal images of the temple, Tripurāntaka would be one of the three dominant forms of the Tañjāvūr temple.

As for the *bhakti* hymnists, the most significant fact is their apotheosis and representation in metal images in Tañjāvūr, where the *mūvar* or *Tēvāram* trio,[31] Śiruttoṇḍar and Meipporuḷnāyanār (Milāḍuḍaiyār) and, above all, Caṇḍēśvara, the *mūlabhṛtya*, are depicted. Interestingly, the stories of Śiruttoṇḍar, Caṇḍēśvara, and Meipporuḷ Nāyanār are alluded to in the groups of copper images set up by various royal officers in the temple.[32] The importance given to the *Tēvāram* hymns and the *nāyanār* is also indicated by the reference to the metal image of Candraśekhara as Dēvāradēvar,[33] and the special arrangements for *patikam* (hymn) singing in the temple.

The iconographic programme of Tañjāvūr was indeed the political iconography of Rājarāja, whose reign saw the most significant efforts at centralization of power through various measures like revenue surveys, assessment, redefining *nāḍus*, introducing *vaḷanāḍus* and a revenue department, and conscious efforts to promote trade and *nagaram* organization, for which the institutional means were the temple and its art and ritual, i.e. the ideological apparatuses. The Tañjāvūr temple itself was the recipient of revenues from several villages located, not only in Cōḷamaṇḍalam, but also in Jayankoṇḍacōḷamaṇḍalam, Gangapāḍi, Nuḷambapāḍi, Malaināḍu, Pāṇḍināḍu and Īḻamaṇḍalam. The economic outreach of the temple was impressive, as it covered the whole kingdom.[34] The *sabhā*, *ūr*, *nagaram* of several centres, where lands or whole villages were granted to the temple, and which were entrusted with the gold deposits of the temple for payment of interest in the form of provisions, i.e. consumable and other articles for rituals and festivals, hastened to fulfil these requirements, establishing a reciprocal flow of resources. From northern Sri Lanka came paddy, money, as well as oil seeds from a tree, the *bania longifolia*, the last item for burning lamps.

The gifts of a wide variety of ornaments to the various images by the royal family were made out of the enormous booty from the wars against the Cēras, Pāṇḍyas and Cāḷukyas, apart from out of the temple treasury.

Contrary to a weakly centralized polity of a segmentary state, as suggested in the works of B. Stein and G.W. Spencer, and even Kenneth R. Hall,[35] a theory which has influenced many recent studies on the Cōḷa state, it is possible to show through an integrated study of the Tañjāvūr temple, that political elements cannot be distinguished from ritual elements in Cōḷa polity, political and ritual sovereignty coincided, and the divine and temporal realms were conterminous.

One may also add here that Kundavai set up images of her father Poṉmāḷigaittuñjinadēvar (Sundara Cōḷa) and his queen, and the images are referred to as *tirumeni* (sacred body),[36] as in the case of the images of deities. This may indicate the practice of setting up ancestors' images as a part of temple worship, recalling to mind the *Devakula* set up in Mathurā by the Kuṣāṇas of the early centuries of the Christian era.

Turning to the frescoes, the themes of these murals, from the point of view of the royal author's intentions in sponsoring this huge temple project, are also well suited to the context in which they occur.

The narrative panels in chambers 5, 7, 9 and 11 hold the key to the symbolism of these frescoes. The themes have been taken from Śaiva mythology and the stories of the Śaiva saints, which were popular even before their final redaction in the hagiographical *Periya Purāṇam* of the twelfth century AD. They are meant to glorify the royal centre through its association with Śiva as the cosmic dancer, the lord of the famous Tillai (chamber 9), the most sacred of the Śaiva centres, i.e. the *Kōyil*, apart from Dakṣiṇāmūrti (chamber 5) and Tripurāntaka (chamber 11). An earlier study of the frescoes made by me has led to interestingly fresh identifications of the murals.[37]

Starting from chamber 5, the panel on the north wall represents Dakṣiṇāmūrti as the central figure, preaching the 'highest knowledge' to the sages, dispelling their ignorance. The figure of Dakṣiṇāmūrti is highly mutilated. Yet, the identification is made possible with the help of two seated figures, a *ṛṣi* and his royal disciple (?), to the right of Dakṣiṇāmūrti. These figures are crucial, as they are very much akin to the painted figures of Rājarāja and Karuvūr Dēvar in chamber 10, and also resemble the two sculpted figures often represented to the right of Dakṣiṇāmūrti on the south wall of the *vimāna*. Hence, it represents an attempt to show that the royal author was an ardent devotee of Śiva and had himself portrayed in the sculptures (on the south wall) and the murals.

As a background to the central figure, is a huge forest with an eight armed Bhairava on the left, accompanied by a dog and a seated devotee, and the sages of the forest and their wives in their cave dwellings. The presence of Bhairava and the forest background with sages cannot be explained, unless we see an attempt here to introduce the Dārukāvana myth associated with

Bhairava, who after cutting off one of Brahma's heads, atoned for *brahmahatya* as Bhikṣāṭana.

The whole scene recalls Sundarar's hymn on Tiruniṉṟiyur, which describes in detail, how Sundarar, one of the *nāyanār*, himself heard the great truth revealed by Śiva to the *kinnaras*, tigers, venomous serpents, ferocious lions, blameless *tapasyas* (sages), while the god was seated under the beautiful banyan tree. The saint attained eternal happiness and Śiva's gracious feet. What is of great interest is a group of metal images set up in the temple by Rājarāja, which consisted of Dakṣiṇāmūrti, a mountain and tree with branches, animals etc. of the forest, as recorded in an inscription of the temple.[38]

In chamber 7 is the remarkable panel of Sundara ascending to Kailāsa on the elephant, after his wedding is stopped by the intervention of Śiva as Taḍuttāṭkoṇḍadeva, and Cēramān Perumāḷ, his friend, preceding him on horseback. This narrative is important, as it contains a depiction of Cēramān Perumāḷ worshipping Naṭarāja in a shrine, probably in Tiruvañcaikkaḷam or Tillai. The top portion of this panel represents Śiva and Pārvati in Kailāsa with the two saints seated in front.

The friendship of Sundarar and Cēramān Perumāḷ, Sundarar's visit to the Cēra capital Tiruvañcaikkaḷam and Cēramān's visit to Tillai, and their ascent to Kailāsa are known, not only from the later *Periya Purāṇam*, but even from their own hymns and Nambi Āṇḍār Nambi's *Tiruttoṇḍar Tiruvandādi* of the period of Rājarāja I. The choice of this theme by Rājarāja was again meant to extol Śiva's greatness, particularly as the cosmic dancer, destroyer of *apasmāra* and protector of devotees. Interestingly, the king did not show a preference for the stories of Appar and Sambandar, evidently because they were more of crusaders against 'heterodoxy', whereas the stories of Sundarar and Cēramān had the unique character of revealing Śiva's greatness as Āḍavallān, who was being invoked by Rājarāja as Śivapādaśekhara. At the same time, the tradition attributing to Rājarāja the 'rediscovery' of the *bhakti* hymns from a secret chamber at Tillai, for which he brought the images of the *Tēvāram* trio, is also attested by the metal images (*pratimā*) of the trio set up in the Tañjāvūr temple.

Chamber 9 has the most interesting panel of Cēramān

Perumāḷ's visit to Tillai and worship of Naṭarāja, whose dance he longed to witness in person while he was still in his capital Tiruvañcaikkaḷam. His wish was fulfilled during his sojourn to the Tamil region and visit to Tillai. That the earlier identification of the royal worshipper as that of Rājarāja I with his queens is incorrect, is clearly indicated by the fact that the figure of the royal worshipper is exactly similar to the figure of Cēramān in chamber 7, and, further, the 'portraits' of Rājarāja with his preceptor in chamber 10 hardly bear any resemblance to the royal figure in the Naṭarāja panel of chamber 9. Cēramān also sang the *Poṉvaṇṇattandādi* in Tillai during this visit, in praise of Naṭarāja. The whole scene contains details which, in every respect, follow the description of the episode in the *Periya Purāṇam*. Tillai is the central stage of this panel, for the sage had journeyed all the way from his kingly abode in Kerala to witness Śiva's cosmic dance. In chamber 11, the two themes depicted in the frescoes are Rāvaṇānugrahamūrti and Tripurāntaka. While the latter has been discussed in detail earlier, the Rāvaṇānugraha can also be traced to the descriptions in the *Tēvāram* hymns.[39]

It may be added here that Tillai (Chidambaram) was also the most sacred Śaiva centre, where the Cōḷa rulers chose to crown themselves, the coronation being performed by the *brāhmaṇas* of Tillai, a supreme act of legitimation of Cōḷa sovereignty. Here one may also recall the story of Kūṟṟuva Nāyanār,[40] who sought the legitimacy of being crowned by the Tillai *brāhmaṇas*, but was denied the privilege as he was not a Cōḷa.

Turning to the administrative and ritual arrangements of the temple, a comparison with the royal court would be useful. The paraphernalia of the Cōḷa temple mirrored the royal court. Royal and temple servants–the *taḷipparivāram* and *kōyiṟṟamar*–were identically perceived and had similar duties. The *Śrīkāryam* (the chief manager) of the temple and of the royal court had comparable functions to discharge. It is interesting that, like the king, the temple images also had army groups separately assigned to them.[41] The role of Caṇḍēśvara as the *mūlabhṛtya* looking after the accounts of the temple, assigning revenues, investing through deposits, receiving paddy and other forms of interest and ritual requirements, would also indicate an imitation of the royal court. It would even appear that here the king himself acts through Caṇḍēśvara.

The Cōḷa king would thus seem to have acquired a near total identity with divinity, comparable to the cult of *devarāja* in Kambuja, the medieval kingdom of Southeast Asia. In medieval India the king of Orissa surrendered his sovereignty to god Jagannāth of Puri, and the king of Travancore ruled as the representative of god Padmanābha.

The interplay of the temple's role in religious, political, economic and social aspects of the Cōḷa period is extremely difficult to grasp without the contextual evidence being highlighted and correlated. For Tañjāvūr this has been found possible only with an integrated approach to various aspects such as architecture, sculpture and painting, which act as metaphors and symbols of great significance.

With the temple as its centre, the city of Tañjāvūr emerged in the following pattern. It consisted of an *uḷḷālai* (inner quadrangle around the temple) and a *puṟambaḍi* (an outer circuit), demarcated respectively (1) for the residences of the priestly, administrative and other elite groups, and (2) for the living quarters (streets) of other professional groups, including the *nagarams* and their *angāḍis*, for the palace servants (*vēḷams*), retinues of the royal family (*parivāra*), all of which were named after the king and members of the royal family.

Royalty requisitioned employees from various parts of the kingdom (Cōḷamaṇḍalam and other *maṇḍalams*) to serve the temple and thereby colonize the city. Musicians numbering forty-eight to recite/sing the hymns (*patikam*), dancing girls (*taḷippeṇḍu*) numbering four hundred, dance masters, drummers, parasol bearers, lamp lighters, and craftsmen like tailors, braziers, goldsmiths and even astrologers, were brought to Tañjāvūr. *Brāhmaṇas* as temple servants and accountants also came from various centres. By the time the temple construction reached its final stages, a veritable colonization had taken place, indicating the implanting of a royal city, including a series of army contingents. Many were given house sites and lands for their maintenance.[42]

The peasantry and artisans who supplied the city with ritual furniture and services in general lived in the villages in the surrounding countryside. Many shepherd families of Tañjāvūr and other centres were entrusted with the huge livestock donated to the temple. The brisk commerce of Tañjāvūr was conducted by the four markets (*angāḍis*) and *nagarattār*, while itinerant traders like the *Kongavāḷar* interacted with them.[43]

The distinctive character of Tañjāvūr as a city derives from the fact that it was a planted city–that it was created by a deliberate act of royal polity in imitation of a sacred *bhakti* centre with the temple as its nucleus, to sanctify which the royal author got hymns composed by the royal preceptor, and, finally, that it was at once the product and symbol of the socio-cultural milieu of the Cōḷa period.

A comparison of the royal/ceremonial centre of the type of Tañjāvūr with the other cities shows that all of them shared the ceremonial aspects. Gangaikoṇḍacōḷapuram also possessed similar features of a city implanted by an act of royalty, beautified by its temple arts, in this case to commemorate the expedition of Rājēndra I to the Ganges region. While these cities had a single dominant ceremonial complex, others such as Kuḍamūkku-Paḷaiyāṟai and Kāñcīpuram may be classified as multi-temple centres evolving after centuries of growth from earlier agrarian clusters, each temple, which marked their growth, representing the locus of the ceremonial complex at different chronological points, thus leading to the emergence of dispersed ceremonial/sacred centres, rather than compact ones like Tañjāvūr.

A third type of city was the sacred centre, which, in its origin and survival down the centuries, is centered round a single cult centre or a *tīrtha*, later assuming the character of a pilgrimage centre. To this category may be assigned Chidambaram,[44] Śrīrangam, Tiruvaṇṇāmalai and others, which usually have a long history passing through successive stages of growth, reflected in the horizontal magnification of the temple structure.

References

1. Y. Subbarayalu, *Political Geography of the Chola Country*, Madras, 1973, 14-16.

2. S.R. Balasubrahmanian, *Early Cōḷa Temples*, 1971; *Middle Cōḷa Temples*, 1975; *Later Cōḷa Temples*, 1979.
3. Champakalakshmi, 'Patikam Pāṭuvār: Ritual Singing as a Means of Communication in Early Medieval South India', *Studies in History*, n.s., July-Dec. 1994, vol. x, no. 2, 199-216. (Special issue on Literacy and Communication in Indian Tradition).
4. Champakalakshmi, 'From Devotion and Dissent to Dominance: The Bhakti of the Tamil Āḻvār and Nāyanār'; Champakalakshmi and Gopal (eds), *Tradition, Dissent and Ideology*.
5. The Rājarājeśvara Temple at Tañjāvūr is not a *bhakti* shrine 'sung' by the *Nāyanār*. However, the Tañjai Taḷikkuḷam is probably the site of an early shrine on which *bhakti* hymns were composed. The royal authors of the Tañjāvūr and Gangaikoṇḍacōḷapuram temples got hymns composed on their temples in imitation of the *bhakti* centres 'sung' by the hymnists.
6. Subbarayalu, *Political Geography*, Map 7, and list of villages in Cōḷamaṇḍalam.
7. E.g. Tiruvālangāḍu Plates of Rajendra I. *South Indian Inscriptions (SII)*, vol. III, no. 205, 45-6.
8. Paul Wheatley, *The Pivot of the Four Quarters: A Preliminary Enquiry into the Origins and Character of the Ancient Chinese City*, Edinburgh, 1971; *idem* 'Urban Genesis in Mainland Southeast Asia', in R. Smith and W. Watson (eds), *Early South East Asia: Essays in Archaeology, History and Historical Geography*, New York, 1979. R.A.L.H. Gunawardhana, 'Anuradhapura: Ritual, Power and Resistance in a Pre-Colonial South Asian City', in Daniel Miller, Michael Rowlands and Christopher Tilly (eds), *Domination and Resistance*, London, 1989.
9. Harold Carter, *An Introduction to Urban Historical Geography*, 1983, 13.
10. In the technique of orientation, the emphasis was on the cardinal compass directions.
11. *SII*, II, no. 67.
12. *SII*, II, no. 28 (On Śadayam, the natal star of Rājarāja I, there were several).
13. This has been reported by Y. Subbarayalu, Professor of Archaeology, Tamil University, Thanjavur.
14. E. Panofsky, who talks about 'disguised Symbolism' in *Early Netherlandish Paintings; Its Origin and Character*, Cambridge, Massachusetts, 1953, 2 vols, and 'levels of meaning' in *Studies in Iconology*, New York, 1939. Also E.H. Gombrich, Introduction, *Symbolic Image*, Oxford, 1980, for a different view regarding 'levels

of meaning', wherein he emphasizes the need for setting the art object in its context.

15. These descriptions are taken from S.R. Balasubrahmanyam, *Middle Chola Temples* (AD 985–1070), Thomson Press, Faridabad, 1975, chapter 2; K.R. Srinivasan, 'The Peruvudaiyar (Brihadisvara) Temple, Tanjavur: A Study', in *Indian Archaeological Heritage* (Shri K.V. Soundararajan, Festschrift), Delhi, 1991, vol. II, 525–38.
16. G. Hoekveld-Meijer, *Koyils in the Cōḷamaṇḍalam, Typology and Development of Early Cōḷa Temples,* University of Amsterdam, 1980, note 58, 191.
17. The Shrines and *Cuṟṟālai* were constructed by Kṛṣṇan-Rāman, a military officer (commander) of Rājarāja I. See *South Indian Inscriptions (SII)*, vol. II, Ins nos 31, 33, 39. This essay follows the texts as given in R. Nagaswamy, *Tañjai-p-peruvuḍaiyār Kōyil Kalveṭṭugaḷ*, Pub. by Tamil Nadu Dept. of Archaeology, 1969, vol. I.
18. *SII*, vol. II, nos 24 and 29; *see also* Srinivasan, 'The Peruvudaigar', 534.
19. Hoekveld-Meijer, *Koyils*, chapter 7, 317–18.
20. Srinivasan, 'The Peruvudaiyar'.
21. Hoekveld-Meijer, *Koyils*, 4; Srinivasan, 'The Peruvudaiyar', 537.
22. Hoekveld-Meijer, *Koyils*, 321.
23. Commenting on the iconographic accent in the Tañjāvūr temple, K.V. Soundararajan would suggest an affiliation with Māhēśvara Śaivism and the design of the Pañcārāma temples of Andhradesa and as characterised by the Aghora, Sadyojāta and Vāmadeva manifestations of the niche sculptures. He would also see here a clash as well as co-existence of the *Tēvāram* (Śaiva *bhakti* hymns) and the Māhēśvara brand of Śaivism. The clash, according to him, led to the decrepitude of an earlier Śiva temple, 'sung' by Sambandar of the *Tēvāram* trio. Contrary to this assessment of the iconographic thrust of the Tañjāvūr temple, one can see a closer link with the *Tēvāram*, and in fact its dominance over other canonical injunctions. *See* K.V. Soundararajan, 'Iconographic Accent and Inflexion in the Rājarājēśvaram, Tañjāvūr', paper presented at the seminar on *Bṛhadīśvara. The Monument and the Living Tradition*, IGNCA, Madras, 1993.
24. K.R. Srinivasan, 'An Interesting Sculpture in Tañjāvūr', quoted by Gary J. Schwindler—*see* note 26 below.
25. C. Sivaramamurti, *Royal Conquests and Cultural Migration in South India*, Calcutta, 1955, 29.
26. Gary J. Schwindler, 'Speculations on the Theme of Śiva as Tripurāntaka as it appears during the Reign of Rājarāja I in the

Tañjāvūr Area, *c.* AD 1000', *Ars Orientalis*, 1987 (pub. 1989), vol. 17, 163-78.

27. George W. Spencer, 'Religious Networks and Royal Influence in Eleventh Century South India', *Journal of the Economic and Social History of the Orient*, 1969, vol. 12, part I, 42, 45.
28. Indira Viswanathan Peterson, *Poems to Śiva, The Hymns of the Tamil Saints*, Delhi, 1991, chapter 5 and Appendix D.
29. D. Dayalan, 'Hymns of Nāyanmārs and the Tripurāntaka Episode in the Big Temple, Tañjāvūr', *Indian Archaeological Heritage*, Delhi, 1991, vol. 1, 445-8.
30. *SII*, vol. II, no. 51.
31. *SII*, vol. II, no. 38.
32. *SII*, II, nos 29, 40, 43. The groups of images are 1. Śiruttoṇḍar, his wife Tiruveṇkāṭṭu nangai and his son Sīrāḷan; 2. Caṇḍeśvara, his father and the Śiva *Linga* worshipped by him.
33. *SII*, II, no. 38. Here Rājarāja is said to be referred to as Periya Perumāḷ, for whom the Candraśekhara image is set up as Dēvāra-dēvar.
34. *SII*, II, nos 4, 5 and 92.
35. Burton Stein, *Peasant State and Society in Medieval South India*, OUP, Delhi, 1980; Spencer, *The Politics of Expansion: The Chola Conquest of Sri Lanka and Srivijaya*, New Era, Madras, 1983; Kenneth R. Hall, *Trade and Statecraft in the Age of the Cōḷas*, Abhinav, Delhi, 1980.
36. *SII*, II, no. 6, Kundavai was the elder sister of Rajaraja I.
37. Champakalakshmi, 'New Light on the Tanjore Frescoes', *Journal of Indian History*, Golden Jubilee Volume, 1973, 349-60.
38. *SII*, II, no. 50.
39. Peterson, *Poems to Śiva*, Appendix D.
40. Vellaivaranan, *Panniru Tirumuṛai Varalāṛu*, vol. II, Annamalai University Publication, 1980, 1220-1.
41. *SII*, II, no. 4, 12.
42. *See* Inscriptions Published in *SII*, vol. II.
43. Carter, A., An Introduction to Urban Historical Geography, 1983, 13, 14. *See* Chapter 1.
44. B. Natarajan, *The City of the Cosmic Dance*, 1974.

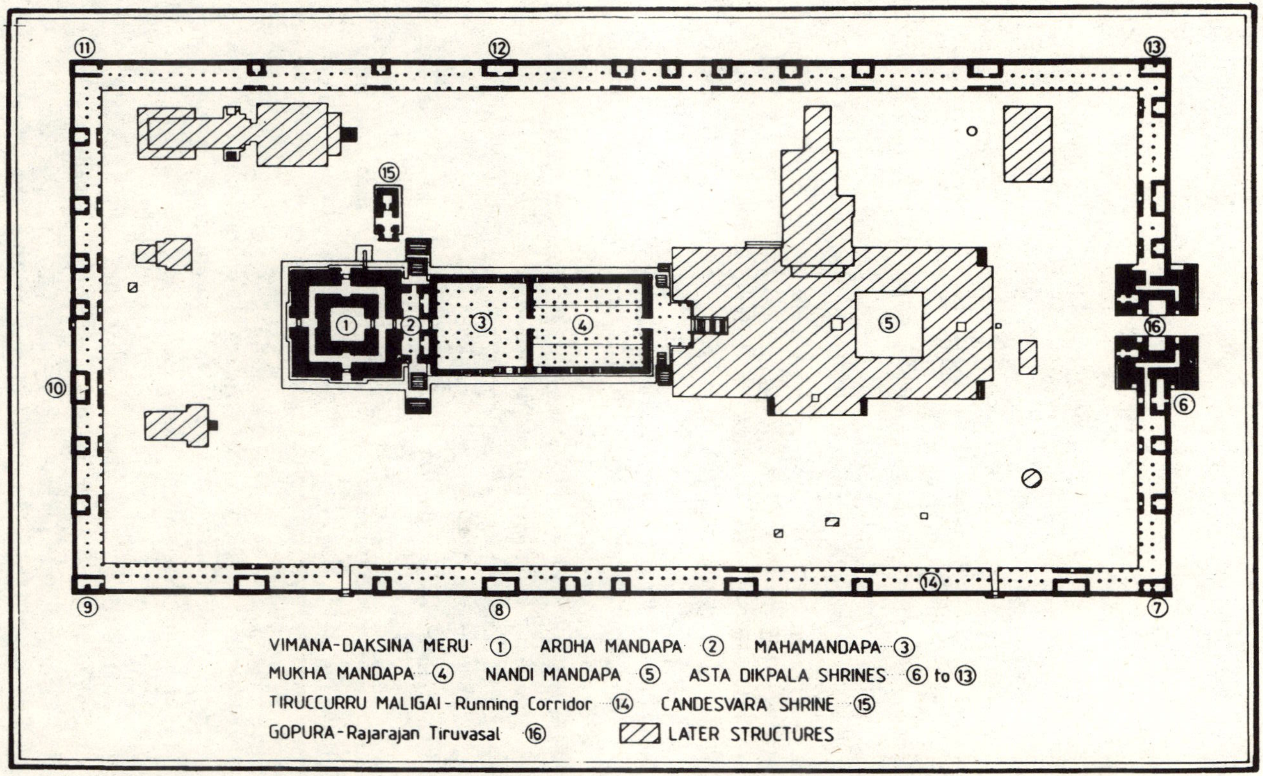

Map 18: Ground Plan of Rājarājeśvaram, Tañjāvūr

Bibliography

Original Sources

Corpus Inscriptionum Indicarum, vol. I, *Inscriptions of Asoka*, E. Hultzsch (ed.), Archaeological Survey.

Epigraphia Indica, Relevant Volumes, New Delhi: The Director-General, Archaeological Survey of India.

Indian Archaeology: A Review (IAR), 1961-2, 1962-3, 1963-4, 1964-5, 1965-6, 1970-1, New Delhi: The Archaeological Survey of India.

Inscriptions of the Pudukkottai State (IPS), 1941 & 1946, pts 1 & 2. Tr. into English by K.R. Srinivasa Aiyar, Pudukkottai State Press.

South Indian Inscriptions (SII), vols I to XXIV, New Delhi: The Director General, Archaeological Survey of India.

South Indian Temple Inscriptions, 3 Volumes, 1953-7, T.N. Subramanian (ed.) (Madras Government Oriental Series), Madras Government Oriental Manuscripts Library.

Nagaswamy, R., 1969, *Tañjai-p-peruvuḍaiyār Kōyil Kalveṭṭugaḷ*, vol. I, Tamil Nadu Department of Archaeology.

— 1970, *Cennaimānagar–k–kalveṭṭugaḷ*, Madras: Tamil Nadu State Department of Archaeology.

Subramanian, T.N., 1966, *Thirty Pallava Copper Plates*, Madras: The Tamil History Academy (Tamil Varalāṟṟu Kaḻagam).

— 1967, *Ten Pandya Copper Plates*, Madras: The Tamil History Academy.

Arthaśāstra, 1951, Kautilya's *Arthaśāstra* translated into English by Shama Sastry, Mysore, 4th edition.

Eṭṭuttokai

Ainkuṟunūṟu, 1980, U.V. Saminathier (ed.) with Tamil commentary, Madras: U.V. Saminathier Publication, 6th edition.

Akanāṉūṟu, 1951-4, Venkatacaminattar and Venkatachalam Pillai (eds), vols I-3rd edition, II-3rd edition and III-2nd edition, Tirunelveli: South Indian Saiva Siddhanta Works (SISSW).

Kuṟuntokai, 1978, P.V. Comacuntaranar (with commentary), Tirunelveli: SISSW, 4th edition.

Naṟṟiṇai, 1976, A. Narayanacami Aiyar (with commentary) and P.V. Comacuntaranar (with supplementary commentary), Tirunelveli: SISSW.

Patiṟṟuppattu, 1955, Auvai Duraicami Pillai (ed.) (with commentary), Tirunelveli: SISSW, 2nd edition.

Puṟanāṉūṟu, 1971, U.V. Saminathier (ed.), Madras, Tiruvanmiyur: Dr. U.V. Saminathier Library.

Pattuppattu, 1974, U.V. Saminathier (ed.) (with Naccinarkkiniyar's commentary), Madras: U.V. Saminathier Library.

1. *Cirupāṇāṟṟuppaṭai*
2. *Maduraikkāñci*
3. *Mullaippāṭṭu*
4. *Neṭunalvāṭai*
5. *Paṭṭinappālai*
6. *Perumpāṇāṟṟuppaṭai*
7. *Porunarāṟṟuppaṭai*

Maṇimēkalai, 1992, Venkatacami Nattar (ed.) (with commentary), Tirunelveli: SISSW (reprint).

Nālāyira Divya Prabandham (Text only) 1971, Madras: Published by V.N. Devanathan.

Palamoḻi Nāṉūṟu, 1991 (ed.), Madras: Puliyur Kesikan, Pari Nilaiyam.

Śilappadikāram, 1992, Venkatacami Nattar (ed.) (with commentary), Tirunelveli: SISSW.

Tēvāram Tirumuṟais, II, III, V, VI and VII. (Tevaram of Tirujnanacampantar, Tirunavukkaracar and Cuntarar).

Tolkāppiyam, Poruḷatikāram, 1982, With Iḷam Pūraṇar's commentary, Madras: SISSW.

Pattuppāṭṭu, The Ten Tamil Idylls, 1962 (Tr. into English by J.V. Chelliah with Introduction and Notes), Tirunelveli: SISSW, 2nd edition.

Secondary Works

Abdul Majeed, A., Thulasiraman, D. and Vasanthi, S., 1992, *Alagankulam, A Preliminary Report,* Madras: Tamil Nadu, Department of Archaeology.

Abraham, M., 1978, 'The Ayyāvoḷe Guild of Early Medieval South India', M.Phil Dissertation (unpublished), New Delhi: Jawaharlal Nehru University.

—— 1982, 'A Medieval Merchant Guild of South India', *Studies in History,* vol. IV, no. 1, Jan–June.

—— 1988, *Two Medieval Merchant Guilds of South India,* New Delhi: Manohar.

Abrams, Philip and Wrigley, E.A., 1978, *Towns in Societies, Essays in*

Economic History and Historical Sociology, Cambridge University Press.

Adams, R. McC, 1965 (1966), *The Evolution of Urban Society: Early Mesopotamia and Pre-historic Mexico*, Chicago: Aldine.

Anderson, P., 1974, *Passages from Antiquity to Feudalism*, London.

Appadorai, A., 1936, *Economic Conditions in Southern India*, 2 Volumes, Madras.

Appadurai, Arjun, 1974, 'Right and Left Hand Castes in South India', *The Indian Economic and Social History Review (IESHR)*, II, June-September 1974.

— 1981, *Worship and Conflict under Colonial Rule: A South Indian Case*, Cambridge University Press.

Arasu, P., 1979, 'Ancient Ceramic Industry from Kāñcīpuram Excavations', M.Phil Dissertation (unpublished), University of Madras.

Aravamuthan, T.G., 1944, 'A Pandyan Issue of Punchmarked Coins', *Journal of the Numismatic Society of India (JNSI)*, VI, pt. 1.

— 1962, 'The Early Pallavas of Kanci', *Transactions of the Archaeological Society of South India (TASSI)*, Silver Jubilee Volume, 1962 (63).

Aru Ramanathan, 1973, *Aṛupattu Mūvar Kataikal*, Madras, 2nd edition.

Balakrishnan Nayar, T., 1966, *The Dowlaishwaram Hoard of Eastern Chalukyan and Chola Coins*, Bulletin of the Madras Government Museum, volume 9, no. 2.

Balasubrahmanian, S.R., 1971, *Early Cōḷa Temples*, Orient Longman.

— 1975, *Middle Cōḷa Temples*, Thomson Press India Ltd.

— 1979, *Later Cōḷa Temples*, Mudgala Trust.

Balasubramanyam, M., 1985, 'Administration and Social Life Under the Later Pandyas', Ph.D. Thesis (unpublished), Madurai: Madurai Kamaraj University.

Basham, Richard, 1978, *Urban Anthropology of Complex Societies*, California, Mayfield: Palo Alto.

Begley, Vimala, 1983, 'Arikamedu Reconsidered', *American Journal of Archaeology*, 87, 461-81.

— 1992, 'Ceramic Evidence for Pre-Periplus Trade on the Indian Coasts', in Vimala Begley and Richard Daniel De Puma (eds), *Rome and India: The Ancient Sea Trade*, Madison: The University of Wisconsin Press.

Bhattacharya, P.K., 1977, *Historical Geography of Madhya Pradesh from Early Records*, Delhi.

Biddulph, C.H., 1968, *Coins of the Cholas*, Varanasi.

Binford, L.R., 'Archaeology and Anthropology', in L. Binford (ed.), *An Archaeological Perspective*, New York: Seminar Press.

Bird, J., 1977, *Centrality and Cities*, London: Routledge, 6 Kegan Paul.

Braidwood, Robert J. and Gordon R. Willey (eds), 1962, *Courses Towards Urban Life: Archaeological Consideration of Some Cultural Alternates*, Viking Foundation, Anthropology, no. 32.

Braudel, Fernand, 1973, *Capitalism and Material Life: 1400-1800*, London.

Bohannan and Dalton, G., 1962, *Markets in Africa*, Illinois: North Western University Press.

Burghardt, A.T., 1971, 'A Hypothesis About Gateway Cities', *Annals of the Association of American Geographers*, LXI, 269-85.

Caldwell, R., 1887, 'Sepulchral Urns in Southern India', *Indian Antiquary*.

Carter, Harold, 1983, *An Introduction to Urban Historical Geography*.

Chakravarti, Uma, *The Social Dimensions of Early Buddhism*, New Delhi: OUP.

Champakalakshmi, R., 1968, 'Ornaments in the Sangam Age', *Journal of Indian History*, XLVII.

— 1973, 'New Light on the Tanjore Frescoes', *Journal of Indian History*, Golden Jubilee Volume.

— 1974, 'South India', in A. Ghosh (ed.), *Jaina Art and Architecture*, vol. I, New Delhi: Bharatiya Jnanpith.

— 1975, 'Kurandi Tirukkāṭṭāmpaḷḷi: An Ancient Jaina Monastery of Tamil Nadu', *Studies in Indian Epigraphy*, vol. 2.

— 1975-6, 'Archaeology and Tamil Literary Tradition', *Purātattva* (Archaeological Society of India), VIII, 110-22.

— 1978, 'Religious Conflict in the Tamil Country: A Reappraisal of Epigraphic Evidence', *Journal of the Epigraphic Society of India*, no. 5.

— 1979, 'Growth of Urban Centres in South India: Kuḍamūkku-Paḻaiyāṟai, the Twin-City of the Cōḻas', *Studies in History*, vol. I, no. 1 (Jan.-June), 1-30.

— 1986a, 'Urbanization in Medieval Tamil Nadu', in Sabyasachi Bhattacharya and Romila Thapar (eds), *Situating Indian History*, New Delhi: OUP.

— 1986b, 'Urbanisation in South India: The Role of Ideology and Polity', Presidential Address, Ancient India Section, *IHC*, 47th Session, Srinagar.

— 1989, 'Ideology and the State in Medieval South India', Mamidipudi Venkatarangaiah Memorial Lecture, *Proceedings of the Andhra Pradesh History Congress*, 13th Session, Srisailam.

— 1990, 'The Sovereignty of the Divine: The Vaiṣṇava Pantheon and Temporal Power in South India', in H.V. Sreenivasa Murthy, B. Surendra Rao, Kesavan Veluthat and S.A. Bari (eds), *Essays on Indian History and Culture* (Professor B. Sheik Ali, Felicitation Volume), New Delhi.

— 1990, 'Sangam Literature as a Source of Evidence on India's Trade with the Western World–Problems of Methodology and Interpretation'. Paper presented at the International Seminar on *India and the Roman World between the 1st and 4th Centuries AD*, Madras: INTACH.

— 1991a, 'Urban Processes in Early Medieval Tamil Nadu', in Indu Banga (ed.), *The City in Indian History and Politics*, New Delhi: (UHAI) Manohar.

— 1991b, 'Tañjāvūr, the Ceremonial City of the Cōḷas', in C. Margabandhu et al (eds), *Indian Archaeological Heritage* (K.V. Soundararajan Felicitation Volume), Delhi.

— 1992a, 'Buddhism in Tamilakam: Patterns of Patronage', Paper presented at the International Seminar on *Tamil Buddhism*, Madras: Institute of Asian Studies.

— 1992b, 'The City in Medieval South India: Its Form and Meaning', in Narayani Gupta (ed.), *Craftsmen and Merchants: Essays in South Indian Urbanism*, Chandigarh: UHAI.

— 1993, 'Urban Configurations in Toṇḍaimaṇḍalam: The Kāñcīpuram Region *c.* AD 600-1300', in Howard Spodek and Doris Meth Srinivasan (eds), *Urban Form and Meaning in South Asia: The Shaping of Cities from Pre-historic to Pre-colonial Times*, Washington D.C.: National Gallery of Art.

— 1994, 'Patikam Pāṭuvār: Ritual Singing as a Means of Communication in Early Medieval South India', *Studies in History*, n.s., vol. X, no. 2, July-December 1994.

— 'From Devotion and Dissent to Dominance: The *Bhakti* of the Tamil Āḻvār and Nāyanār', in R. Champakalakshmi and S. Gopal (eds), *Tradition, Dissent and Ideology*, Essays in Honour of Romila Thapar, OUP, 1996.

Charlesworth, M.P., 1951, 'Roman Trade with India: A Resurvey', in Coleman and Norton (eds), *Studies in Roman Economic and Social History*, in Honour of Alan Chester Johnson.

Chatterjee, Anjana, 1976, 'Socio-Economic Conditions in Early Andhra 200 BC 300 AD—A Study of the Transition from Megalithic to Early Historic Culture', Ph.D. Thesis (unpublished), New Delhi: Jawaharlal Nehru University.

Chattopadhyaya, B.D., 1974, 'Trade and Urban Centres in Early Medieval North India', *Indian Historical Review*, vol. 1, no. 2, September, 203-19.

— 1977, *Coins and Currency Systems in South India*, New Delhi: Munshiram Manoharlal.

— 1983, 'Political Processes and Structure of Policy in Early Medieval India: Problems of Perspective', Presidential Address, Ancient India Section, *Indian History Congress (IHC)*, 44th Session, Burdwan.

— 1985, 'Markets and Merchants in Early Medieval Rajasthan', *Social Science Probings*, vol. 2, no. 4, December, 413-40.

— 1986, 'Urban Centres in Early Medieval India', in Sabyasachi Bhattacharya and Romila Thapar (eds), *Situating Indian History*, New Delhi: OUP.

Childe, V. Gordon, 1950, 'The Urban Revolution', *Town Planning Review*, 29.

Cohen, R., 'State Origins: A Reappraisal', in J.M. Claessen and Peter Skalnik (eds), *The Early State*, Mouton, The Hague.

Curtin, Philip, D., 1984, *Cross-Cultural Trade in World History*, Cambridge University Press.

Dalton, G., 1975, 'Karl Polanyi's Analysis of Long Distance Trade and his Wider Paradigm', in J. Sabloff and C.C. Lamberg Karlovsky (eds), *Ancient Civilization and Trade*, Albuquerque.

Dayalan, D., 1991, 'Hymns of Nāyanmārs and the Tripurāntaka Episode in the Big Temple, Tañjāvūr', in C. Margabandhu, K.S. Ramachandran, A.P. Sagar and D.K. Sinha (eds), *Indian Archaeological Heritage* (K.V. Soundararajan Festschrift), vol. 1.

Dehejia, Vidya, 1972, *Early Buddhist Rock Temples*, London.

Desai, P.B., 1957, *Jainism in South India and Some Jaina Epigraphs*, Sholapur.

Devakunjari, D., 1979, *Madurai Through the Ages from the Earliest Times to 1801 AD*, Madras: Society for Archaeological, Historical and Epigraphical Research.

Devasanapati, V.A., *Kāmakkōṭṭam, Nāyanmārs and Ādi Śankara*, Madras: Institute of Traditional Cultures.

Dirks, Nicholas, B., 1976, 'Political Authority and Structural Change in Early South India', *IESHR*, XIII, no. 2, 125-57.

Dobb, Maurice, 1971, *Capitalism, Development and Planning*, The Hague.

Economic Atlas of the Madras State, 1962, New Delhi: National Council of Applied Economic Research.

Eisenstadt, S.N., 1964, 'Social Change, Differentiation and Evolution', *American Sociological Review*, 29, 375-86.

Eisenstadt, S.N. and A. Shachar, 1987, *Society, Culture and Urbanization*, Beverley Hills: Sage.

Eliade, Mircea, 1949, *Le Mythe de L'eternal Retour*, Paris.

Elliot, W., 1970, *Coins of Southern India*, Delhi.

Elliot and Dowson, *The History of India as told by its Historians*, I.

Filliozat, J., 1950, 'Intercourse of India with the Roman Empire during the Opening Centuries of the Christian era', *Journal of Indian History*, XXVIII, pt. 1.

Finley, M.I., 1975, *The Ancient Economy*, London (reprint).

— 1977, 'The Ancient City: From Fustel de Coulanges to Max Weber and Beyond', *Comparative Studies in Society and History*, 19.

Fried, Morton, 1960, 'On the Evolution of Social Stratification and the State', in Stanley Diamond (ed.), *Culture in History: Essays in Honour of Paul Rodin*, New York: Columbia University Press.

— 1967, *The Evolution of Political Society*, Random House, New York.

Friedmann, John, 'Cities in Social Transformation', *Comparative Studies in Society and History*, 4, 86-103.

Fritz, John M., Michell George and Nagaraja Rao, M.S., 1984, *The Royal Centre at Vijayanagara, Preliminary Report*, University of Melbourne, Vijayanagara Research Centre, Monograph Series, no. 4.

Ghosh, A., 1973, *The City in Early Historical India*, Simla: Indian Institute of Advanced Studies, 1.

Gombrich, E.H., 1980, *Symbolic Image*, Oxford.

Govindaswamy, M.S., 1979, *The Role of Feudatories in Later Chola History*, Annamalai University.

Gunawardhana, R.A.L.H., 1981, 'Social Function and Political Power: A Case Study of the Evolution of the State in Irrigation Society', in J.M. Claessen and Peter Skalnik (eds), *The Study of the State*, The Hague: Mouton.

— 1984, 'Inter Societal Transfer of Hydraulic Technology in Pre-Colonial South Asia: Some Reflections Based on a Preliminary Investigation', *Tonan Ajia Kenkyu (South East Asian Studies)*, vol. 22, no. 2 (September).

— 1989, 'Anuradhapura: Ritual, Power and Resistance in a Pre-Colonial South Asian City', in Daniel Miller, Michael Rowlands and Christopher Tilly (eds), *Domination and Resistance*, London, 155-78.

Gupta, Narayani, 'Towers Tanks and Temples: Some Aspects of Urbanism in South India: Eighteenth and Nineteenth Centuries', Occasional Paper Series–5, Urban History Association of India.

Gupta, P.L., 'A Bibliography of the Hoards of Punch-marked Coins of Ancient India', *Journal of the Numismatic Society of India*, XVII, 15-19.

Gurukkal, Rajan, 1981, 'Aspects of Early Iron Age Economy: Problems of Agrarian Expansion of Tamilakam', *IHC*, 42nd Session, Bodhgaya.

— 1984, 'The Agrarian System and Socio-Political Organisation under the Early Pandyas', Ph.D. Thesis (unpublished), New Delhi: Jawaharlal Nehru University.

— 1986, 'Aspects of the Reservoir System of Irrigation in the Early Pandya State', *Studies in History*, n.s., vol. II, no. 2 (July-December).

— 1989, 'Forms of Production and Forces of Change in Ancient Tamil Society', *Studies in History*, n.s., vol. V, no. 2, July-December, 159-76.

— 'Towards a New Discourse: Discursive Processes in Early South India', in Romila Thapar Felicitation Volume.

Gururaja Rao, B.K., 1972, *The Megalithic Culture in South India*, Mysore: Prasaranga, University of Mysore.

Gururajachar, S., 1974, *Some Aspects of Economic and Social Life in Karnataka* (AD 1000-1300), Mysore.

Hall, Kenneth, R., 'The Expansion of Maritime Trade in the Indian Ocean: Roman Trade in the Indian Ocean: An Indian Perspective', *The Elmira Review*, vol. I.

— 1980, *Trade and Statecraft in the Age of the Cōḷas*, New Delhi: Abhinav Publications.

Hall, Kenneth, R. and Spencer, G.W., 1980, 'The Economy of Kāñcīpuram: A Sacred Centre in Early South India', *Journal of Urban History*, vol. VI, no. 2 (February).

Hardy, Friedhelm, 1983, *Viraha Bhakti: The Early History of Kṛṣṇa Devotion in South India*, Delhi: OUP.

Harle, James, C., 1963, *Temple Gateways in South India: The Architecture and Iconography of the Chidambaram Gopuras*, Oxford.

Hart, George, L., 1975, *The Poems of the Ancient Tamils: Their Milieu and their Sanskrit Counterparts*, Berkeley: University of California Press.

— 1976, 'Ancient Tamil Literature, its Scholarly Past and Future', in B. Stein (ed.), *Essays on South India*, New Delhi.

— 1979, *Poets of the Tamil Anthologies–Ancient Poems of Love and War*, Princeton.

Heitzman, James, 1987, 'Temple Urbanism in Medieval South India', *The Journal of Asian Studies*, vol. 46, no. 4.

— 1989, 'Early Buddhism, Trade and Empire', *Journal of South-east Asian Studies*, XX, no. 1, March.

Hirth, K., 'International Trade and the Formation of Pre-Historic Gateway Communities', *American Antiquity*, XLIII.

Hoekveld-Meijer, G., 1980, *Koyils in Cōḷamaṇḍalam, Typology and Development of Early Cōḷa Temples*, University of Amsterdam.

Hoselitz, B.F., 1953, 'The Role of Cities in the Economic Growth of Under-developed Countries', *Journal of Political Economy*, LXI.

— 1954-5, 'Generative and Parasitic Cities', *Economic Development and Cultural Change*, III, 278-94.

Huntington, G., 1980, *The Periplus of the Erythraean Sea*, London.

Indrapala, K., 1970, 'Some Medieval Mercantile Communities of South India and Ceylon', *Journal of Tamil Studies*, vol. II, no. 2 (October).

— 1971, 'South Indian Mercantile Communities in Ceylon–950-1250', *The Ceylon Journal of Historical and Social Studies*, vol. I, no. 2 (July-December).

Jagadeesan, N., 1977, *History of Srivaishnavism in the Tamil Country (Post-Ramanuja)*, Madurai: Koodal Publishers.

Jaiswal, S., 1977, 'Caste in the Socio-Economic Framework of Early India', Presidential Address, Ancient India Section, *IHC*, 38th Session, Bhuvaneswar.

Jha, D.N., 1979, 'Early Indian Feudalism: A Historiographical Critique, Presidential Address, *IHC*, 40th Session, Section 1, Waltair.

Kailasapathy, R., 1968, *Tamil Heroic Poetry*, OUP.

Kanakasabhai Pillai, V., 1966, *The Tamils Eighteen Hundred Years Ago*, Tirunelveli: SISSW (reprint).

Karashima, N., 1984, *South Indian History and Society, Studies from Inscriptions*, AD *850-1800*, New Delhi: OUP.

Kennedy, R.S., 1976, 'King in Early South India: As Chieftain and Emperor', Indian Historical Review, III.

Krishnamurthy, R., 1987, *Pāṇḍiyar Peruvaḷuti Nāṇayangaḷ*, Madras.

— 1990a, *Sanga Kāla Malaiyamān Nāṇayangaḷ*, Madras.

— 1990b, 'Sangam Period Silver Coin with a Portrait and a Legend', *First Oriental Numismatic Congress*, Nagpur.

— 1992, 'Mākkōtai Coins', *Studies in South Indian Coins*, vol. 2.

Krishnan, K.G., 1978, 'Tamil Inscriptions in Karnataka', in A.V. Narasimhamurthy (ed.), *Archaeology of Karnataka*, University of Mysore.

— 1982, 'Chittiramēḻi-p-periyanāḍu–An Agricultural Guild of Medieval Tamil Nadu', *Journal of the Madras University*, vol. LVI, no. 1 (January).

Kuppuswamy, G.R., 1975, *Economic Conditions in Karnataka (AD 973-1336)*, Dharwar: Karnatak University.

Lal, B.B., 1962, 'From the Megalithic to the Harappa: Tracing back the Graffiti on the Pottery', *Ancient India*, no. 16.

Leela Shantha Kumari, 1986, *History of the Agraharas, Karnataka, 400-1300*, Madras: New Era.

Leshnik, L.S., 1974, *The South Indian Megalithic Burials: The Pandukal Complex*, Wiesbaden: Franz Steiner Verlag Gmbh.

Lewandowski, Susan, 1979, 'Changing Form and Function of the Ceremonial and Colonial Port City in India: An Historical Analysis of Madurai and Madras', in K.N. Chaudhury and Clive Dewey (eds), *Society and Economy in India*, OUP.

Logan, William, 1951, *The Malabar Manual*, I, Madras (reprint).

Lorenzen, David, 1972, *The Kapalikas and Kalamukhas: Two Lost Saivite Sects*, New Delhi.

Ludden, David, 1978a, 'Ecological Zones and the Cultural Economy of Irrigation in Southern Tamil Nadu', *Journal of Asian Studies*, n.s., I, no. 1.

— 1978b, 'Patronage and Irrigation in Tamil Nadu, A Long Term View', *IESHR*, XVI, no. 3.

— 1985, *Peasant History in South India*, Princeton: Princeton University Press.

Mahadevan, I., 1968, 'Corpus of Tamil Brahmi Inscriptions', in R. Nagaswamy (ed.), *Seminar on Inscriptions*, Madras.

— 1970, 'The Ancient Name of Arikamedu', N. Subrahmanian (ed.), *Surya Narayana Sastri Centenary Volume*, Madurai.

— 1981a, 'Arikamedu Graffiti: A Second Look', *Damilica*, II, Madras.

— 1981b, 'An Old Sinhalese Inscription from Arikamedu', *Seminar on Epigraphy*, Kuppuswami Sastri Birth Centenary: Madras.

— 1992, 'Identification of Kākandi in Bharhut Inscriptions', Paper Presented at the International Seminar on *Tamil Buddhism*, Madras: Institute of Asian Studies.

— 1994, 'Ancient Tamil Contacts Abroad: Recent Epigraphic Evidence', Reverend Fr. X.S. Thani Nayagam Memorial Lecture, Thani Nayagam Foundation Trust, Colombo, *Journal of the Institute of Asian Studies*, vol. XII, no. 1, 136-55.

— 1995, 'Old Sinhalese Inscriptions from Indian Ports, New Evidence for Ancient India Sri Lanka Contacts', Paper Presented at the Postgraduate Institute of Archaeology, Colombo (forthcoming).

Mahalingam, T.V., 1955, *South Indian Polity*, Madras.

— 1969, *Kāñcīpuram in Early South Indian History*, Bombay: Asia Publishing House.

— 1970, *Report on the Excavations in the Lower Kaveri Valley (Tirukkāmpuliyūr and Alagarai, 1962-4)*, Madras: University of Madras.

— 1967a, 'The Nagesvarasvami Temple, Kumbhakonam', *Journal of Indian History*, vol. XLV, pt. 1 (April).

— 1967b, *The Mackenzie Manuscripts: Summaries of the Historical Manuscripts in the Mackenzie Collection* (Tamil and Malayalam), vol. I, Madras: University of Madras.

— 1977, 'Genesis and Nature of Feudalism under the Pallavas of Kanci', Paper Presented at the Seminar on *Socio-Economic Formation in the Early Middle Ages 600-1200 AD*, Allahabad.

Mahamaham Souvenir Kumbhakonam, 1968.

Maloney, Clarence, 1968, 'The Effect of Early Coastal Sea Traffic on the Development of Civilization in South India', Ph.D. Thesis (unpublished), Pennsylvania.

— 1969, 'The Paratavar: 2000 Years of Culture Dynamics of a Tamil Caste', *Man in India*, vol. XLVIII, no. 3 (September), 224-40.

— 1970, 'The Beginnings of Civilization in South India', *Journal of Asian Studies (JAS)*, XXIX, no. 3, 603-16.

— 1976, 'Archaeology in South India: Accomplishments and Prospects', in B. Stein (ed.), *Essays on South India*, New Delhi: Vikas.

Manickam, V., 1987, 'Some Trade Guild Epigraphs and Sculpture', *Journal of the Institute of Asian Studies*, vol. I, September.

Mc Crindle, 1927, *Ancient India as described by Ptolemy*, A Fascimile Reprint by Surendranath Majumdar, Chukkerverthy, Chatterjee, Calcutta.

— 1973, *The Commerce and Navigation of the Erythraean Sea and Ancient India as described by Ktesias, the Knidian*, Amsterdam, Calcutta (reprint).

Mc Taggart, Donald, 1965, 'The Reality of Urbanism', *Pacific Viewpoint*, vol. VI, no. 2.

Merrington, John, 1978, 'Town and Country in the Transition to Capitalism', in R.H. Hilton (ed.), *The Transition from Feudalism to Capitalism*, London.

Minakshi, C., 1977, *Administration and Social Life under the Pallavas*, University of Madras, Revised edition.

Miner, Horace, 1967, 'The City and Modernization: An Introduction', in H. Miner (ed.), *The City in Modern Africa*, New York.

Murphy, Rhoads, 1969–70, 'Traditionalism and Colonialism: Changing Urban Roles in Asia', *Journal of Asian Studies*, 29.

Mukhia, Harbans, 1977, 'Was there Feudalism in Indian History!', Presidential Address, *IHC*, Section II, Waltair.

Nagaswamy, R., 1970, 'Korkai Excavations', *Damilica*, I (December).

— 1973a, 'Archaeology and Epigraphy', Pondichery: *Proceeding of the Third International Conference Seminar, Tamil Studies.*

— 1973b, *Kāverippaṭṭiṇam--A Guide*, Madras: Tamil Nadu State Department of Archaeology.

— 1973c, *Yāvarum Kēḷir*, Vacakar Vattam.

— 1974a (ed.), *Seminar on Hero Stones*, Tamil Nadu: State Department of Archaeology.

— 1974b, 'Karuvūr-Vañji, the Capital of the Sangam Cēras', *Journal of Kerala Studies*, I, pt. IV.

— 1978a (ed.), *Chengam Naḍukaṛkaḷ* (Tamil), Madras: State Department of Archaeology, Tamil Nadu.

— 1978b, *Studies in Ancient Tamil Law and Society*, Madras: The Institute of Epigraphy, The State Department of Archaeology, Tamil Nadu.

Nagaswamy, R. and Abdul Majeed, 1978, *Vasavasamudram* (Report on the excavations conducted in the year 1970), Madras: Tamil Nadu, Department of Archaeology.

— 1979, *Tiruttaṇi and Vēlañcēri Copper Plates*, Madras: State Department of Archaeology, Tamil Nadu.

— 1981, 'An Outstanding Epigraphical Discovery in Tamil Nadu', *Fifth International Conference Seminar on Tamil Studies*, Madurai.

— 1991a, *Tamil Coins: A Study*, Madras: Tamil Nadu State Department of Archaeology.

— 1991b, 'Alagankulam: An Indo-Roman Trading Port', in C. Margabandhu et al. (eds), *Indian Archaeological Heritage* (K.V. Soundararajan, Felicitation Volume), Delhi.

Nambi, Arooran K., 1977, *Glimpses of Tamil Culture Based on the Periya Puranam*, Madurai: Koodal Publishers.

Nandi, R.N., 1976, 'Some Social Aspects of Nalayira Divya Prabandham', *IHC*, 37th Session, Calicut.

— 1979-80, 'Client, Ritual and Conflict in Early Brahmanical Order', *Indian Historical Review*, vol. VI, nos 1 and 2 (July-January), 64-118.

— 1984, 'Growth of Rural Economy in Early Feudal India', *IHC*, 45th Session, Annamalainagar.

Narayanan, M.G.S., 1972, *Cultural Symbiosis in Kerala*, Trivandrum: Kerala Historical Society.

— 1982, 'The Warrior Settlements of the Sangam Age', *Indian History Congress, Proceedings*, 43rd Session, Kurukshetra.

Natana Kasinathan, 1978, *Hero-Stones in Tamil Nadu*, Madras: State Department of Archaeology, Tamil Nadu.

— 1991, *Under Sea Explorations off the Shore of Poompuhar*, Madras: Department of Archaeology, Tamil Nadu.

Natarajan, B., 1974, *The City of the Cosmic Dance*, New Delhi: Orient Longman.

Nilakanta Sastri, K.A., 1932, 'A Tamil Merchant Guild in Sumatra', TBG, Deel, LXXII, Reprinted in K.A. Nilakanta Sastri, *South India and South East Asia: Studies in their History and Culture*, Mysore.

— 1949, 'Takua Pa and its Tamil Inscriptions', *Journal of the Malaya Branch of the Royal Asiatic Society*, XXII, pt. 1.

— 1958, *A History of South India: From the Earliest Times to Vijayanagar*, Madras: OUP.

— 1972, *Foreign Notices of South India from Megasthenes to Ma Huan*, University of Madras (reprint).

— 1975, *The Cōḷas*, Madras: University of Madras (reprint).

— 1982, *The Pandyan Kingdom*, Madras: Swathi Publications (reprint).

Niyogi, P., 1962, *Contributions to the Economic History of Northern India (From the Tenth to the Twelfth Centuries AD)*, Calcutta.

Paḻayāṟai–t–talavaralāṟu, 1957, Paḻaiyāṟai Devasthanam Publication.

Palat, Ravi Arvind, 1991, 'Symbiotic Sisters: Bay of Bengal Ports in the Indian Ocean World Economy', in Resat Kasaba (ed.), *Cities in World System*, Contributions in Economics and Economic History, no. 126, Greenwood Press.

Panofsky, E., 1939, *Studies in Iconology*, New York.

— 1953, *Early Netherlandish Paintings: Its Origin and Character*, 2 vols, Cambridge: Massachussets.

Paranavitana, S. and Nichols, 1961, *A Concise History of Ceylon (From the Earliest Times to Portuguese Invasion in 1505)*, Colombo: Ceylon University Press.

Paranavitana, S., 1970, *Inscriptions of Ceylon, Early Brahmi Inscriptions*, vol. I, Colombo: Archaeological Survey of Ceylon.

Parasher, Aloka, 1991, 'Social Structure and Economy of Settlements in the Central Deccan (200 BC–AD 200)', in Indu Banga (ed.), *The City in Indian History: Urban Demography, Society and Politics*, Manohar (UHAI), 19-46.

— 1992, 'Nature of Society and Civilisation in Early Deccan', *The Indian Economic and Social History Review*, 29, 4, 437-77.

Perlin, Frank, 1983, 'Proto-industrialisation and Pre-colonial South Asia', *Past and Present*, no. 92.

Peterson, Indira Viswanathan, 1991, *Poems to Siva: The Hymns of the Tamil Saints*, Delhi: Motilal Banarasidas.

Pillay, K.K., 1969, *A Social History of the Tamils*, Madras: University of Madras (reprint).

Pirenne, Henri, 1956, *Medieval Cities: Their Origins and Revival of Trade*. Tr. by Frank D. Halsey, Garden City, New York.

Polanyi, Karl, 1963, 'Ports of Trade in Early Societies', *Journal of Economic History*, XXIII.

Postan, M.M., 1975, *The Medieval Economy and Society*, Berkeley: University of California Press.

Porcher, Marie-Claude, 1975, 'La Representation de l'espace Sacre' dans le Kancimahatmya', *Purasartha*, 8 (1985).

Prasad, O.P., 1977, 'A Study of Towns in Karnataka on the Basis of Epigraphic Sources', *IHC Proceedings*, 38th Session.

— 1978, 'Two Ancient Port Towns of Karnataka', *IHC*, 39th Session.

Raghava Iyengar, M., 1964, *Vēḷir Varalāṟu* (Tamil), Madras.

Rajamanikkam, M., 1964, *Saiva Samaya Valarcci* (Tamil), Madras, 2nd edition.

— 1972, *The Development of Saivism in South India, AD 300-1300*, Dharmapuram.

Rajan, K., 1989-90, 'Iron and Gem Stone Industries as Revealed from Kodumanal Excavations', *Purātattva*, no. 20.

— 1994, 'Muciṟi-Tuṟaimukam: Cila Putiya Ceitigaḷ', *Āvaṇam (Journal of the Tamil Nadu Archaeological Society)*, 4, January 1994.

Ramachandra Dikshitar, V.R., *The Cilappatikāram*, Tirunelveli: SISSW (reprint).

Ramachandran, K.S., 1971, *A Bibliography of Indian Megaliths*, Madras: State Department of Archaeology, Tamil Nadu.

— 1980, *Archaeology of South India*, Delhi.

— 1993, 'Roman Jewellery and Coins from Karur', *The Hindu*, 14 March.

Ramalingam, P., 1977, *Karuvure Vanci*, Madras.

Raman, K.V., 1959, *The Early History of the Madras Region*, Amudha Nilayam Private Ltd.

— 1975a, *Sri Varadarajasvami Temple–Kāñcī: A Study of its History, Art and Architecture*, New Delhi.

— 1975b (ed.), *Excavations at Uraiyur (Tiruchirappalli), 1965-9*, Madras: University of Madras.

— 1987, 'Archaeological Excavations in Kāñcīpuram', *Tamil Civilisation*, V, nos 1 and 2.

Ramanujam, B.V., 1973, *History of Sri Vaishnavism in South India upto Ramanuja*, Annamalai University.

Ramaswamy, Vijaya, 1976, 'The Weaver Communities of the Kancipuram Region. Circa AD 700–1700', M.Phil Dissertation (unpublished), New Delhi: Jawaharlal Nehru University.

— 1985a, *Textiles and Weavers in Medieval South India*, New Delhi: OUP.

— 1985b, 'Artisans in Vijayanagar Society', *IESHR*, 22, no. 4.

— 1985c, 'The Genesis and Historical Role of Master Weavers in South Indian Textile Production', *Journal of the Economic and Social History of the Orient, JESHO*, XXVIII.

Ramesh, K.V., 1970, *History of South Kanara*, Dharwar.

— 1974, *Jaina Literature in Tamil*, New Delhi: Bharatiya Jnanpith.

Ratnagar, S.F., 1981, *Encounters: The Westerly Trade of the Harappa Civilization*, Delhi: OUP.

Ray, Amita, 1983, *Life and Art in Early Andhradesa*, Delhi.

Ray, H.P., 1986, *Monastery and Guild: Commerce Under the Satavahanas*, Delhi: OUP.

Redfield, Robert and Singer, Milton, 1954, 'The Cultural Role of Cities', *Economic Development and Cultural Change*, III.

Reissman, 1964, *The Urban Process: Cities in Industrial Society*, New York.

Rowlands, M.J., 1973, 'Modes of Exchange and the Incentives for Trade with Reference to Late European Pre-History', in Colin Renfrew (ed.), *The Explanation of Culture and Change*, Pittsburgh.

Sahlins, Marshall, 1968, *Tribesman*, Englewood Cliffs: Prentice Hall.

Samy, P.L., 1982, *Sanga Ilakkiyattil Śeḍikoḍi Viḷakkam* (Tamil), Tirunelveli: Saiva Siddhanta Publishing Society.

Schoff, W.H., 1912, *The Periplus of the Erythraean Sea: Travel and Trade in the Indian Ocean by a Merchant of the First Century* (Tr. from the Greek and annotated), New York: Longmans, Green and Co.

Schwindler, Gary, J., 1989, 'Speculations on the Theme of Siva as Tripurantaka as it Appears during the Reign of Rajaraja I in the Tanjavur Area, *c.* AD 1000', *Arts Orientalis*, vol. 17.

Seneviratne, Sudershan, 1981, 'Kalinga and Andhra: The Process of Secondary State Formation in Early India', in J. Claessen and P. Skalnik (eds), *The Study of the State*, The Hague: Moutcn, 317-38.

— 1987, 'Social Base of Early Buddhism in South East India and Sri Lanka: BC 3rd Century to 3rd Century AD', Ph.D. Thesis (unpublished), New Delhi: Jawaharlal Nehru University.

Seng, Tan Yeok, 1964, 'The Srivijayan Inscription of Canton AD 1079', *Journal of South East Asian History*, vol. 5, no. 2.

Sesha Aiyar, K.G., 1937, *Chera Kings of the Sangam Period*, LUZAC.

Shanmugam, P., 1993, 'Tamiḻ Nāḍum Thāilanḍum. Toḍarpugaḷ', *Āvaṇam*, no. 3 (July).

Sharma, R.S., 1965, *Indian Feudalism*, Calcutta.

— 1972, 'Decay of Gangetic Towns in Gupta and Post-Gupta Times', *IHC*, 33rd Session, Muzaffarpur.

— 1985, 'How Feudal was Indian Feudalism?', *Journal of Peasant Studies*, vol. 12, nos 2 and 3 (Jan.-April).

— 1987, *Urban Decay in India (c. 300–c. 1000 AD)*, New Delhi: Munshiram Manoharlal.

Sitaraman, Arumuga, 1994, 'Kuṟiyīṭṭu Mōdiram', *Āvaṇam*, 4 (January).

Sivaraja Pillai, 1932, *Chronology of the Early Tamils*, Madras.

Sivaramamurthi, C., 1955, *Royal Conquests and Cultural Migrations in South India and the Deccan*, Calcutta: Indian Museum.

Sivathamby, K., 1966 (1968), 'An Analysis of the Anthropological Significance of the Economic Activities and Conduct Code Ascribed to the Mullai Tiṇai', *Proceedings of the First International Conference Seminar on Tamil Studies (IATR)*, I.

— 1974, 'Early South Indian Society and Economy: The *Tiṇai* Concept', *Social Scientist*, vol. 29, 20-37.

— 1981, 'The Social and Historical Perspective of the Early Tamil Poem', in K. Sivathamby (ed.), *Drama in Ancient Tamil Society*, Madras: New Century Book House.

Sjoberg, Gideon, 1960, *The Pre-Industrial City, Past and Present*, Illinois: Glencoe.

Smith, Robert, J., 1973, 'Town and City in Pre-modern Japan: Small

Families, Small Households and Residential Instability', in A. Southal (ed.), *Urban Anthropology*, New York.

Soundararajan, K.V., 1967, 'Determinant Factors in the Early History of Tamil Nadu', *Journal of Indian History (JIH)*, pt. 1.

— 1978, *Art of South India, Tamil Nadu and Kerala*, Delhi.

— 1993, 'Iconographic Accent and Inflexion in the Rājarājeśvaram, Tañjāvūr', Paper presented at the Seminar on *Bṛhadīśvara: The Monument and the Living Tradition*, Madras: IGNCA.

Spencer, G.W., 1969, 'Religious Networks and Royal Influence in 11th Century South India', *Journal of the Economic and Social History of the Orient (JESHO)*, XII, pt. 1.

— 1976, 'The Politics of Plunder: The Cholas in Eleventh Century Ceylon', *Journal of Asian Studies*, vol. 35, May.

— 1983, *The Politics of Expansions: The Chola Conquest of Sri Lanka and Sri Vijaya*, Madras: New Era.

Spodek, Howard, 'Beyond Rorschah Tests: Palimpsests and Nodes, Conflicts and Consciousnesses in South Asian Urban Theory', in Howard Spodek and Doris Meth Srinivasan (eds), *Urban Form and Meaning in South Asia: The Shaping of Cities from Pre-Historic to Pre-Colonial Times*, Washington D.C.: National Gallery of Art, 255–68.

Srinivasan, K.R., 1958, 'Pallava Architecture', *Ancient India*, no. 14.

— 1960, 'Some Aspects of Religion as Revealed by Early Monuments and Literature of the South', *Journal of the Madras University*, XXXII, no. 1.

— 1991, 'The Peruvuḍaiyār (Brihadīśvara) Temple, Tañjāvūr: A Study', in *Indian Archaeological Heritage* (Shri K.V. Soundararajan Festschrift), vol. II, Delhi.

Srinivasan, P.R., 1958–9, 'Rare Sculptures from Kumbhakonam', *Transactions of the Archaeological Society of South India*, 1958–9.

Srinivasan, T.M., 1968, 'Irrigation and Water Supply in South India upto 1300 AD', M.Litt. Thesis (unpublished), University of Madras.

— 1970, 'A Brief Account of the Ancient Irrigation Engineering Systems Prevalent in South India', *The Indian Journal of History of Science*, vol. 5, no. 2.

Stein, B., 1965, 'Medieval Coromandal Trade', in John Parker (ed.), *Merchants and Scholars Essays in the History of Exploration and Trade*, Minnesota Press.

— 1969, 'Integration of the Agrarian System of South India', in R.E. Frykenberg (ed.), *Land Control and Social Structure in India*, Madison: University of Wisconsin.

— 1976, 'The State and the Agrarian Order', in B. Stein (ed.), *Essays on South India*, New Delhi.

— 1977, 'The Segmentary State in South Indian History', in Richard Fox (ed.), *Realm and Region in Traditional India*, New Delhi.

— 1980, *Peasant State and Society in Medieval South India*, Delhi: OUP.

— 1985, 'Politics, Peasants and De-Construction of Feudalism in Medieval India', *Journal of Peasant Studies*, vol. 12, nos 2 and 3 (January-April).

Subbarayalu, Y., 1973, *Political Geography of the Chola Country*, Madras.

— 1994, 'Sumatrāvil Tamil̤-k-kalveṭṭugal', *Āvaṇam* (January).

Subrahmanian, N., 1966, *Sangam Polity: The Administration and Social Life of the Sangam Tamils*, Bombay: Asia Publishing House (reprint 1980).

— 1966, *Pre-Pallavan Tamil Index* (Index of the Historical Material in Pre-Pallavan Tamil Literature), Madras: University of Madras.

Subrahmaniam, T.N., 1958-9, 'Pallankovil Jaina Copper Plate Grant of Early Pallavas', *Transactions of the Archaeological Society of South India*, 41-83.

Sumathi, R., 1984, Trade and its Impact on the Early Tamils–The Cola Experience, M.Phil Dissertation (unpublished), New Delhi: Jawaharlal Nehru University.

Sundaram, K., 1968, *Studies in Economic and Social Conditions in Medieval Andhra*, Machilipatnam: Triveni Publishers.

Suresh, S., 1991, 'Roman Vestiges in Kancipuran–An Investigation into the Early Mediterranean Contacts with the Chingleput Region', in Nandita Krishna (ed.), *Kanchi–A Heritage of Art and Religion*, Madras: C.P. Ramaswami Aiyar Institute of Indology.

— 1992, 'Early Archaeological Finds in Karur', *IHC, Proceedings*, 52nd Session, New Delhi.

— 1993, 'A Study of the Roman Coins and Other Antiquities in India with Special Reference to South India', Ph.D. Dissertation (unpublished), New Delhi: Jawaharlal Nehru University.

Tamil Lexicon, 1982, 6 Volumes and Supplement, University of Madras.

Thakur, Renu, 1994, 'Urban Hierarchies, Typologies and Classification in Early Medieval India: *c.* 750-1200', *Urban History*, 21, pt. 1 (April), Cambridge University Press, 61-76.

Thakur, Vijay Kumar, 1981, *Urbanisation in Ancient India*, New Delhi: Abhinav.

Thapar, R., 1973, *Asoka and the Decline of the Mauryas*, OUP, 2nd edition.

— 1982, *A History of India*, vol. 1, Penguin (reprint).
— 'State Formation in Early India', *International Social Science Journal*, xxxii.
— 1984, From Lineage to State, Bombay: OUP.
— 1987, 'Towards the Definition of an Empire: The Mauryan State', in *The Mauryas Revisited*, Calcutta.
— 1987, *Cultural Transaction and Early India: Tradition and Patronage*, Delhi: OUP.
— 1992a, 'Patronage and Community', in Barbara, Stoler Miller (ed.), *The Powers of Art*, Delhi: OUP.
— 1992b, 'Black Gold: South Asia and the Roman Maritime Trade', *South Asia* (Journal of the South Asian Studies Association), Armidale NSW, Australia, n.s., vol. xv, no. 2 (December).
Tirumalai, R., 1980, *Rajendra Vinnagar*, Madras: The Institute of Epigraphy, Tamil Nadu State Department of Archaeology.
Vanaja, R., 1955, 'The Madras Museum Collection of Punch-marked Coins: A Study', M.Litt Thesis (unpublished), University of Madras.
Vasudeva Rao, T.N., 1979, *Buddhism in the Tamil Country*, Chidambaram: Annamalainagar.
Vellaivaranan, K., 1972, *Panniru Tirumurai Varalaru*, pt. 1, Annamalainagar.
Veluthat Kesavan, 1979, 'The Temple Base of the Bhakti Movement in South India', *IHC*, 40th Session, Waltair, 185-94.
Veluthat, Kesavan, 1993, *The Political Structure of Early Medieval South India*, New Delhi: Orient Longman.
Venkat Rao, Gurty, 1982, 'The Pre-Satavahana and Satavahana Periods', in G. Yazdani (ed.), *The Early History of the Deccan*, pts i to vi, New Delhi (reprint).
Venkatarama Ayyar, K.R., 1947 (1948), 'Medieval Trade, Craft and Merchant Guilds in South India', *Journal of Indian History*, xxv, pts 1-3.
Venkataraman, K.R., 1950, *The Hoysalas in the Tamil Country*, Annamalai University, Historical Series, no. 7, Annamalai Nagar.
Venkatasubramanian, T.K., 1982, 'Growth of Urban Centres in Early Tamilakam', *IHC*, 43rd Session, Kurukshetra.
Venkateswara Rao, T., 1975, Local Bodies in Pre-Vijayanagar Andhra, Ph.D. Thesis (unpublished), Dharwar: Karnataka University.
Warmington, E.H., 1974, *The Commerce Between the Roman Empire and India*, Delhi, 2nd edition (Revised and enlarged).

Watt, G., 1966, *The Commercial Products of India*, New Delhi: Today and Tomorrow's Printers and Publishers (reprint).

Watters, T., 1905, *On Yuan Chuang's Travels in India*, vol. II.

Webb, M., 1975, 'The Flag follows Trade–An Essay on the Necessary Interaction of Military and Commercial Factors in State Formation', in Jeremy A. Sabloff and C.C. Lamberg-Karlovsky (eds), *Ancient Civilization and Trade*, Albuquerque.

Weber, M., *Economy and Society*, New York.

Wheatley, Paul, 1971, *The Pivot of the Four Quarters: A Preliminary Enquiry into the Origins and Character of the Ancient Chinese City*, Edinburgh.

— 1972, 'The Concept of Urbanism', in Peter J. Ucko, Ruth Tringham and G.W. Dimbleby (eds), *Man, Settlement and Urbanism*, Duckworth: London, London University.

— 1973, 'Urban Genesis in Mainland South East Asia', in R.B. Smith and W. Watson (eds), *Early South East Asia: Essays in Archaeology, History and Geography*, New York, 288-303.

Wheeler, R.E.M., Ghosh A. and Krishna Deva, 1946, 'Arikamedu: An Indo-Roman Trading Station on the East Coast of India', *Ancient India*, no. 2 (July).

Wheeler, R.E.M., 1955, *Rome Beyond the Imperial Frontiers*, London: Pelican.

Wirth, Louis, 1938, 'Urbanism as a Way of Life', *American Journal of Sociology*, XLIV, no. 1 (July), 1-24.

Yadava, B.N.S., 1978, 'The Accounts of the Kali Age and the Social Transition from Antiquity to the Middle Ages', *Indian Historical Review*, nos 1-2 (July 1978-January 1979).

— 1980, 'The Problems of the Emergence of Feudal Relations in Early India', Presidential Address, Ancient India Section, *IHC*, 41st Session, Bombay.

Zvelebil, Kamil, 1973, *The Smile of Murugan. On the Tamil Literature of South India*, Leiden: E.J. Brill.

Index